PAGE 52 ON THE ROAD

PAGE 253 SURVIVAL GUIDE

VITAL PRACTICAL INFORMATION TO HELP YOU HAVE A SMOOTH TRIP

THIS EDITION WRITTEN AND RESEARCHED BY

Oliver Berry
Brendan Sainsbury

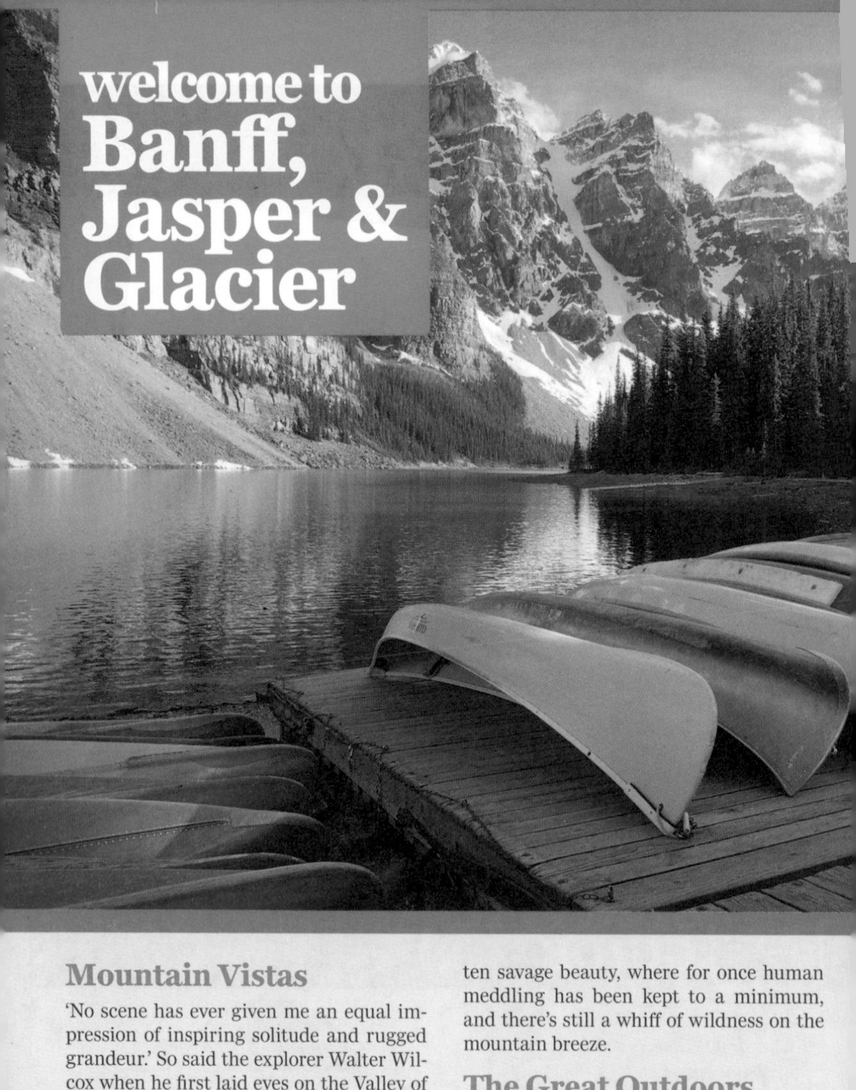

welcome to Banff, Jasper & Glacier

Mountain Vistas

'No scene has ever given me an equal impression of inspiring solitude and rugged grandeur.' So said the explorer Walter Wilcox when he first laid eyes on the Valley of the Ten Peaks, near Lake Louise, in 1899, and it's a maxim that could happily apply to any of these three national parks. They might not be quite the same untouched landscape experienced by pioneers such as David Thompson, Tom Wilson and Mary Schäffer at the end of the 19th century, but these mountain parks are still among the best places to see the raw machinery of Mother Nature in action. These precious regions harbor some of the world's grandest landscapes: vistas of stunning and often savage beauty, where for once human meddling has been kept to a minimum, and there's still a whiff of wildness on the mountain breeze.

The Great Outdoors

Whether it's hiking along a snow-dusted ridgeline or trekking through the spray of a thundering waterfall, Banff, Jasper and Glacier collectively boast some of the finest outdoor activities that North America has to offer. Getting out and about in the great outdoors is an essential part of experiencing the national parks, and there are activities to suit all ages and abilities – even if that just means a gentle stroll along a lakeshore or a soak in one of the region's

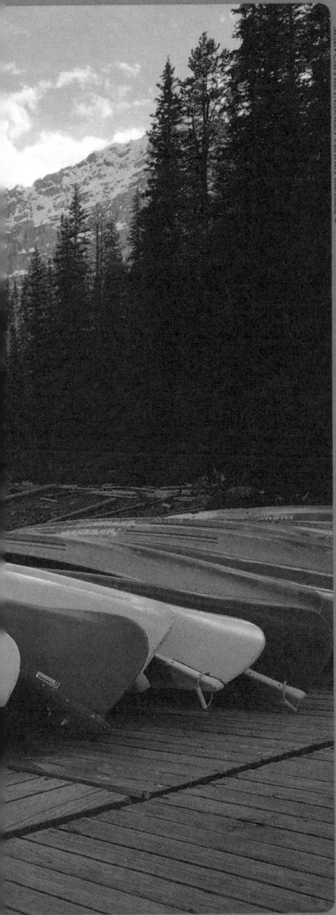
SEAN CAFFREY/LONELY PLANET IMAGES ©

From snowcapped mountains and pristine valleys to shimmering lakes and glittering glaciers, few places on Earth can match Banff, Jasper and Glacier when it comes to sky-topping scenery.

(left) Moraine Lake (p68), Banff National Park
(below) Mountain goat at Glacier National Park (p176)

MARK NEWMAN/LONELY PLANET IMAGES ©

natural hot springs. For more active types, there's no end of ways to get your adrenaline racing – from exploring the endless network of backcountry trails to kayaking the restless white-water rapids of the Kicking Horse River.

Wonderful Wildlife

There's nothing quite like glimpsing animals in their natural habitat, and the Rocky Mountains has some of the best wildlife watching in North America. Shaggy mountain goats, curly-horned mountain sheep, hooting marmots and majestic moose are just some of the inhabitants you're likely to encounter, and if you're really fortunate, you might glimpse a wild black or grizzly bear moseying down the avalanche slopes, perhaps with a couple of fuzzy cubs in tow. Seeing a bear in the wild is the holy grail for wildlife watchers, and as long as you remember to keep your distance, it'll be an experience that will remain with you long after the Rockies have faded from view.

Banff, Jasper & Glacier National Parks

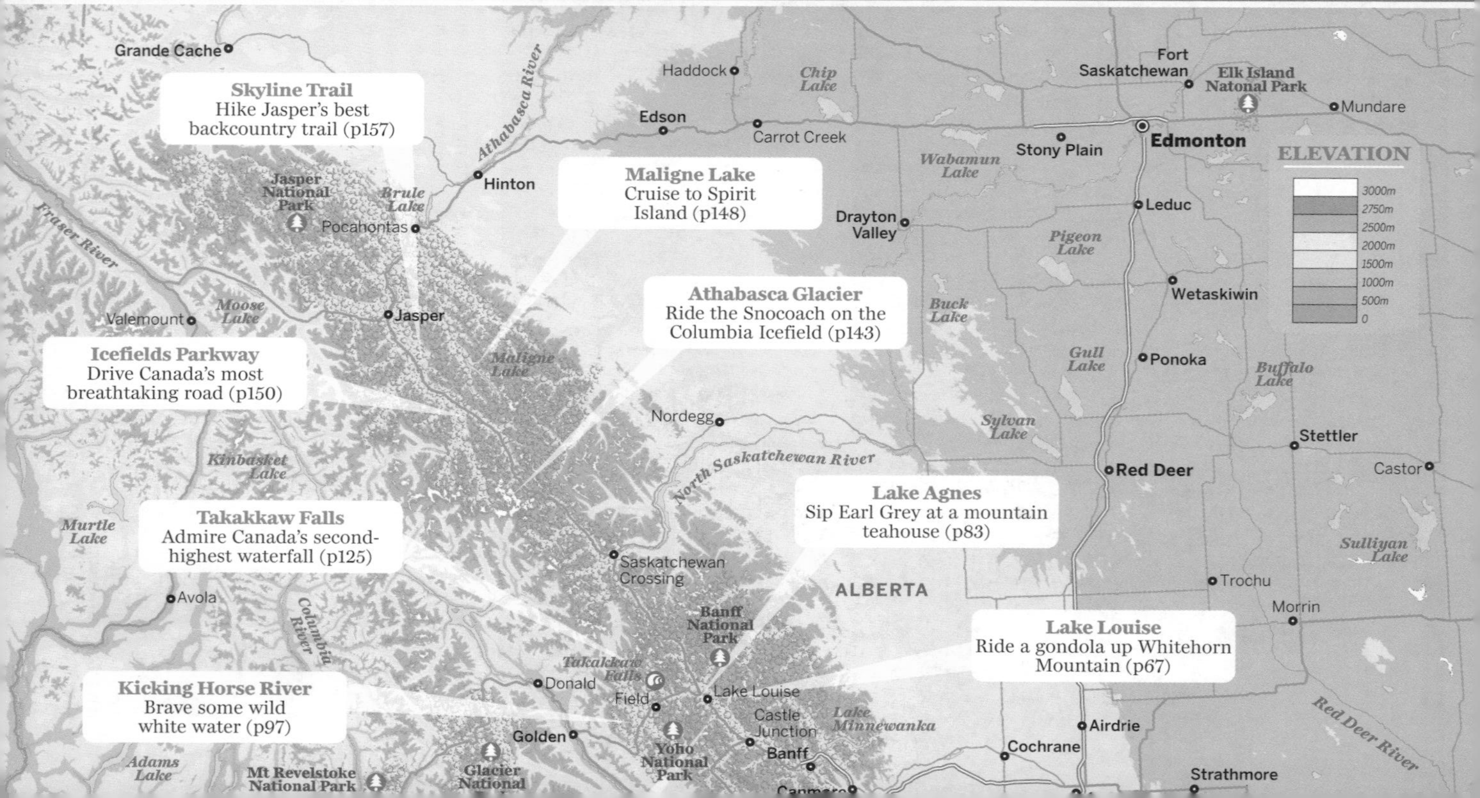

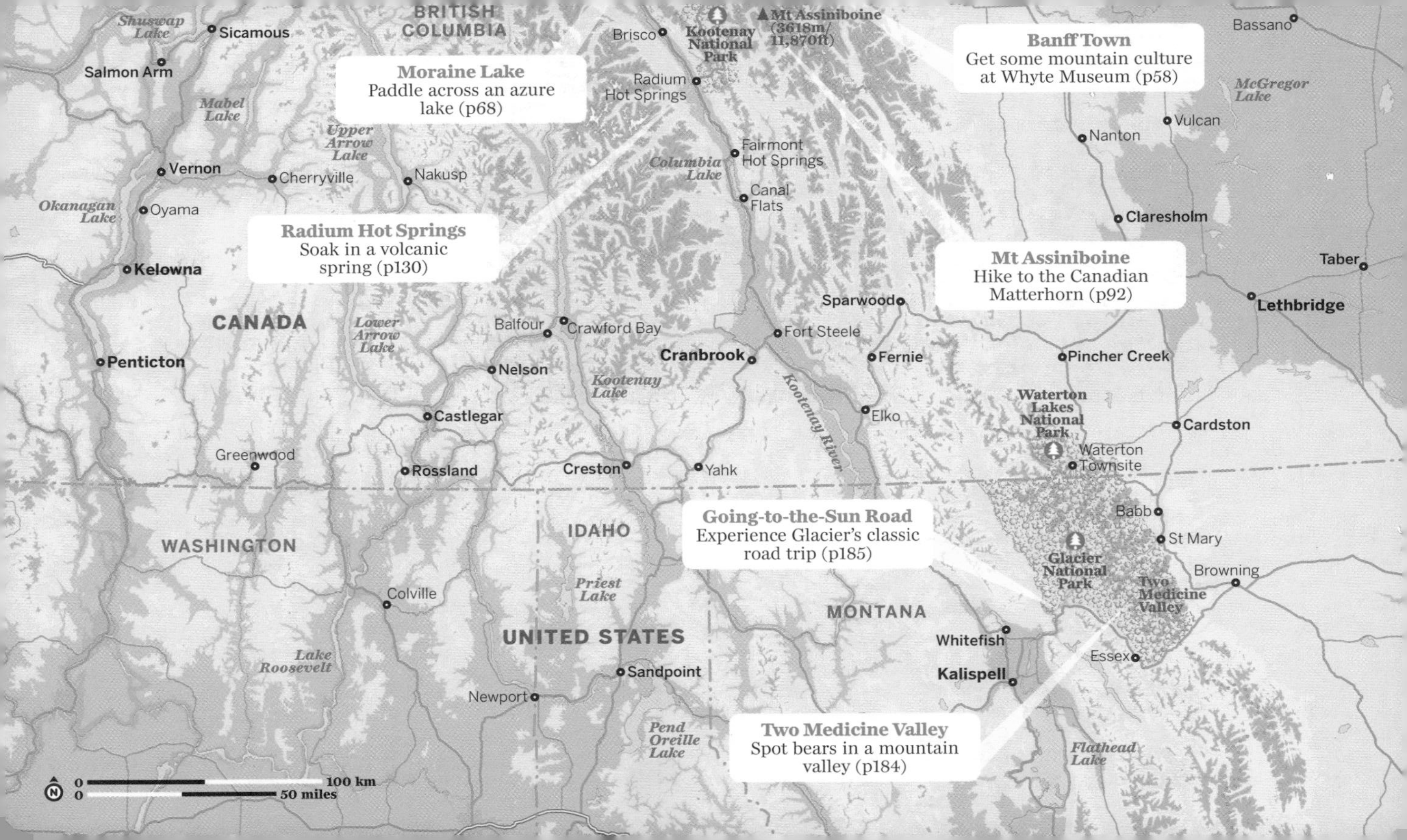

Banff Town
Get some mountain culture at Whyte Museum (p58)
Moraine Lake
Paddle across an azure lake (p68)
Radium Hot Springs
Soak in a volcanic spring (p130)
Mt Assiniboine
Hike to the Canadian Matterhorn (p92)
Going-to-the-Sun Road
Experience Glacier's classic road trip (p185)
Two Medicine Valley
Spot bears in a mountain valley (p184)
BRITISH COLUMBIA
CANADA
WASHINGTON
IDAHO
MONTANA
UNITED STATES
Shuswap Lake
Sicamous
Salmon Arm
Mabel Lake
Upper Arrow Lake
Vernon
Cherryville
Nakusp
Okanagan Lake
Oyama
Kelowna
Penticton
Lower Arrow Lake
Balfour
Crawford Bay
Nelson
Kootenay Lake
Castlegar
Greenwood
Rossland
Creston
Yahk
Brisco
Kootenay National Park
Mt Assiniboine (3618m/ 11,870ft)
Radium Hot Springs
Fairmont Hot Springs
Columbia Lake
Canal Flats
Sparwood
Fort Steele
Cranbrook
Fernie
Kootenay River
Elko
Bassano
McGregor Lake
Vulcan
Nanton
Claresholm
Taber
Lethbridge
Pincher Creek
Cardston
Waterton Lakes National Park
Waterton Townsite
Babb
St Mary
Glacier National Park
Two Medicine Valley
Browning
Whitefish
Kalispell
Essex
Flathead Lake
Colville
Priest Lake
Lake Roosevelt
Sandpoint
Newport
Pend Oreille Lake
0 100 km
0 50 miles

20 TOP EXPERIENCES

Skyline Trail

1 Cross-park views of Jasper are par for the course on the widely celebrated Skyline Trail (p157). It could have had any number of descriptive names conferred upon it – the Homeric path, the celestial walk, the resplendent ramble, but instead its name describes exactly how it is: a 45.8km (28.7-mile) promenade through Jasper's splendidly glaciated high country that offers kilometer after kilometer of seemingly endless skyline. Is there a more spectacular hike anywhere in North America? Possibly not.

Lake Louise Gondola

2 For an instant rush of mountain scenery, nothing beats a ride in the Lake Louise Gondola (see boxed text, p67). In just 14 vertigo-inducing minutes, you'll be whisked up to the viewing station at a sky-topping altitude of 2088m (6850ft), from where you'll be treated to a 360-degree view of the peaks and glaciers encircling Lake Louise. It's a fantastic lookout in its own right, and if you're really lucky you might be able to spot grizzlies wandering along the avalanche slopes of Whitehorn Mountain nearby.

1

ANDREW BAIN/LONELY PLANET IMAGES ©

2

JULIA CATT PHOTOGRAPHY/ALAMY ©

Icefields Parkway

3 There are amazing road trips, and then there's the Icefields Parkway (p73). This iconic highway unfurls for 230km (143 miles) between Lake Louise and Jasper, and takes in some of the most mind-blowing mountain panoramas anywhere on the Continental Divide. En route you'll pass cerulean lakes, crashing cascades, gleaming glaciers and the largest area of unbroken ice anywhere in North America, the mighty Columbia Icefield. It's a true trip of a lifetime, so fuel up, sit back and let one of the world's great scenery shows unfold.

Moraine Lake

4 Canoes have been the preferred method of transport in the Rockies since time immemorial, and they're still an ideal way to explore the region's lakes and rivers. Canoes and kayaks can be hired on many of the region's waters, but few water journeys can match Moraine Lake (p68) in the scenic stakes. Paddling out across this peacock-blue lake in a traditional canoe, gazing up to the icy summits of the Wenkchemna Peaks, you'll feel like you've been transported back in time to the days of the early pioneers and voyageurs.

PHOTOLIBRARY/GETTY ©

LAWRENCE WORCESTER/LONELY PLANET IMAGES ©

PHOTOLIBRARY/GETTY ©

Going-to-the-Sun Road

5 The start's inauspicious enough: a sign-posted turning off US 2, the blink-and-you'll-miss-it village of West Glacier, followed by a serendipitous plunge into dense forest around Apgar. It's only on the shores of Lake McDonald that the views start getting better and better, until you feel as if the Going-to-the-Sun Rd (p179) really is – well – going to the sun. The highpoint is Logan Pass on the Continental Divide; after that it's all downhill to St Mary, amid more jaw-dropping scenery and potent lessons in glacial erosion.

Canmore Nordic Centre

6 The Rockies' rugged landscape of mountains and valleys makes perfect terrain if you're into mountain biking. Many of Banff and Jasper's trails are designated as multi-use, meaning they're open to hikers and horseback riders as well as cyclists, but for the best biking head for the groomed trails of the Canmore Nordic Centre (p116). There are more than 65km (40 miles) of routes to explore, ranging from easy rolls to epic single-tracks, and the regular skills clinics can help you get the most out of your ride.

LEE FOSTER/LONELY PLANET IMAGES ©

Radium Hot Springs

7 If it weren't for the geothermal springs that bubble up from beneath the mountains, Banff and its neighboring national parks may never have come into existence. The craze for spa bathing was instrumental in attracting early visitors to the park during the late 19th century; while the original site at the Cave & Basin Historical Site is now off-limits to bathers, you can still take an outdoor dip at the twin pools of Radium Hot Springs (p131), as well as its sister springs in Banff and Jasper.

Jasper Tramway

8 It probably wouldn't happen today, but back in the 1960s, in an era when mechanical geeks were experimenting with fancy new gimmicks, the Jasper park authorities built this high-speed cable car (p145) to a lofty knoll on 2466m (8088ft) Whistlers Mountain. Hiking purists may disapprove, but the tramway provides an easy way for people of all ages and abilities to enjoy the beautiful alpine tundra.

Maligne Lake

9 Beyond its oft-visited northern shore, Maligne Lake (p148) remains a wilderness lake bequeathed with the kind of grandiose scenery that early explorers such as Mary Schäffer would still recognize. The only way to penetrate this watery kingdom's southern reaches is to hike in through backcountry, venture out solo on a kayak, or – for more relaxed day-trippers – enjoy it communally on a daily boat launch. The object of everyone's longing is the calendar-cover view of tiny Spirit Island backed by an amphitheater of appropriately 'rocky' mountains.

WITOLD SKRYPCZAK/LONELY PLANET IMAGES ©

Tonquin Valley

10 In winter Jasper's visitors drop to a trickle, with the majority never venturing far beyond the comforting hub of Marmot Basin. What they're missing is some of the best icy backcountry in Canada. The Tonquin Valley (see boxed text, p165) – already well known to summer hikers and horseback riders – is a snow-blanketed nirvana equipped with a sprinkling of lodges where you can practice the energetic art of hut-to-hut skiing common in the Alps. Characterized by manageable elevation and a minimal avalanche risk, it's a 'haute route' without the height, or the danger.

PHOTOLIBRARY/GETTY ©

Mt Assiniboine

11 If it's a taste of the wilds you're yearning for, Assiniboine (p129) is where you'll find it. The mountain's rocket-profile peak marks the start of some of the finest backcountry trails anywhere in the Canadian Rockies. With its secret lakes, soaring mountains and remote backcountry campgrounds, Assiniboine feels like another world compared to the busy trails of Banff. It takes some effort and dedication to get here, though – you'll need legs of steel, sturdy boots, proper supplies and, of course, a sense of adventure.

Whyte Museum of the Canadian Rockies

12 Visiting a museum might not be high on your priority list when visiting a national park, but don't miss the chance to visit the excellent Whyte Museum (p58). Founded by the artists Peter and Catharine Whyte, the museum houses one of the best collections of mountain art in western Canada. It explores the history and culture of the Rockies through a varied collection of artifacts, ranging from vintage photographs to Stoney craftwork, and runs guided tours of Banff's most historic buildings.

11

DANITA DELIMONT/ALAMY ©

TOM UHLMAN/ALAMY ©

MARK NEWMAN/LONELY PLANET IMAGES ©

Bears in Two Medicine Valley

13 Bear sightings inspire the whole gamut of adrenaline-fuelled feelings in humans, from fascination, intrigue and reverence, to shock and blind fear. You can grab a cocktail of all five in the Two Medicine Valley (p184), once one of Glacier National Park's more accessible haunts but, in the days since car traffic diverted to the Going-to-the-Sun Rd, a deliciously quiet corner preferred by hikers, solitary fishers and – er – bears. Last count the park had in the vicinity of 400 grizzlies and substantially more black bears. Do you feel lucky?

Wildlife Watching

14 Black and grizzly bears may be the holy grail for wildlife spotters, but there are plenty of other animals (p39) to seek out, too. The parks support a hugely diverse range of species, from elk and bighorn sheep to mountain goats, marmots and moose, not to mention an entire aviary of unusual birds. The best time to see wildlife is always at dawn or dusk – bringing along decent binoculars and a telephoto lens will help you get the perfect view. Bighorn sheep

Kicking Horse River

15 There are few activities that induce a more white-knuckle, heart-in-mouth, seat-of-the-pants adrenaline hit than hurtling downriver in an inflatable raft armed with nothing but a paddle and a prayer. Despite the apparent danger, white-water rafting (p38) is actually well within the capability of most people. Guided trips are run on many rivers, including the Bow, Kananaskis and Kicking Horse, and while you're guaranteed to get soaked to the skin, you're sure to have a huge grin on your face once you're finally back on terra firma.

Athabasca Glacier

16 Driving on a glacier: sounds more like the kind of stunt pulled on a testosterone-fuelled TV show than something you could actually do, right? Wrong. At Jasper's humungous Columbia Icefield (p143), specially adapted Snocoaches crawl and crunch across the Athabasca Glacier, affording amazing views of crevasses, seracs and an endless horizon of ice. You'll even get the chance to disembark briefly and set foot on the 400-year-old snow. The so-called Ice Explorers leave every 15 to 30 minutes from the Columbia Icefield Centre in summer.

15

16

MICHAEL WEBER/IMAGEBROKER ©

17

DAVID TOMLINSON/LONELY PLANET IMAGES ©

Takakkaw Falls

17 First Nations people had it right when they named this thundering waterfall (p125): Takakkaw translates as 'it is magnificent' from the Cree language, and you'll probably find yourself thinking the same thing when you first set eyes on it. At a total height of 384m (1259ft), Takakkaw is the second-highest waterfall in Canada, topped only by Della Falls on Vancouver Island. A trail leads through pine forest to the base of the falls, affording grand views across the valley toward Cathedral Mountain and the rest of Yoho National Park.

Afternoon Tea at Lake Agnes

18 After slogging all day on the mountain trails around Lake Louise, what could be more civilized than a cup of Earl Grey and a slice of homemade chocolate cake? The historic teahouse at Lake Agnes (p83) has been serving refreshments to weary walkers for over a century; it was originally built in 1901 as a lodge for the Canadian Pacific Railway, and it now makes an ideal stop-off for parched hikers tackling the trail to the summit of the Big Beehive.

Waterton's Carthew-Alderson Trail

19 Waterton's diminutive size means that everything's close at hand, from the local cinema and afternoon tea in the Prince of Wales Hotel to the Carthew-Alderson Trail (p213), your highly prized 'day pass' into flower embellished high-alpine tundra with barely a tree to break the vista. Even better, you don't need a cable car to get there! Just catch the early hiker's shuttle to Cameron Lake, climb 4km (2.5 miles) through scented pine forest and you're there – on top of the world, or feeling like it.

The Burgess Shale

20 Hard as it may be to believe, the land that now makes up the Rockies once lay at the bottom of a vast ancient sea, and the mountains around Mt Burgess in Yoho National Park are littered with the fossilized remains of many weird creatures from Earth's early history. These fossil beds were discovered by Charles Walcott in 1909, and are now known as the Burgess Shale (see boxed text, p125); they represent a priceless treasure trove for paleontologists and can be visited on a guided hike from the nearby town of Field.

19

ALEXANDRA KOBALENKO/ALL CANADA PHOTOS/CORBIS ©

20

MARK UNRAU/ALL CANADA PHOTOS/GETTY ©

need to know

Entrance Fees

» Banff/Jasper day pass: adult C$9.80, group/family C$19.60

» Glacier weekly pass (summer): per vehicle US$25

Number of visitors (2010)

» Banff: 3,174,043

» Jasper: 1,976,928

» Glacier: 2,200,048

When to Go

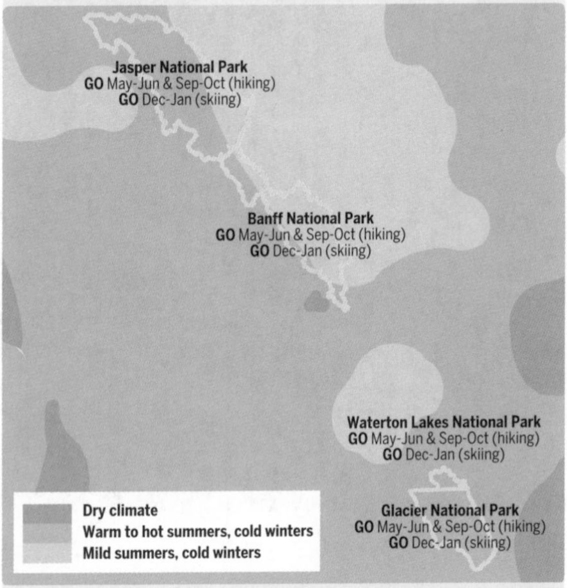

High Season

» July and August are busiest months

» Mainly warm weather and sunny skies, but be prepared for sudden thunderstorms

» Trail closures and hiking restrictions during buffaloberry season (mid-July onwards)

Shoulder Season

» Spring comes late, with snow lingering until May or June

» Many lakes are frozen and some trails remain closed until early summer

» June is the wettest month in Banff and Jasper

Low Season

» Late March to May is the quietest season

» Accommodations can be cheap, but many campgrounds, trails and activities are closed

Your Daily Budget

Budget less than

C$100

» Dorm room in hostel C$30-40

» Self-catering from supermarkets C$20

» Hiking on local trails using public transport

Midrange

C$200–300

» Double room C$120-180

» Lunch and dinner with drinks C$50

» One day's compact car hire C$50

Top End over

C$400

» Suite in luxury hotel or lodge C$300

» Three-course meal with wine C$80-100

» Guided minibus tour C$100

Year founded
» Banff: 1885
» Jasper: 1907
» Glacier: 1910

Money
» ATMs: several around Banff, Jasper and Glacier townsites, scarce elsewhere.
» Credit and debit cards: accepted practically everywhere.

Cell phones
» Coverage is patchy outside townsites.
» Phone must be compatible with Canadian/US network.
» Beware of roaming charges.

Driving
» Most major roads are sealed, some minor roads are gravel/dirt.
» Some roads closed during heavy snowfall.
» Snow tires/chains required in some areas.

Websites

» **Lonely Planet** (www.lonelyplanet.com/canada/alberta/banff-and-jasper-national-parks, www.lonelyplanet.com/usa/rocky-mountains/glacier-national-park) Hotel bookings, traveler forum and more.

» **National Parks Canada** (www.pc.gc.ca) Comprehensive info for Canada's national parks.

» **US National Parks** (www.nps.gov) US parks including Glacier.

» **Travel Alberta** (www.travelalberta.com) Alberta-wide site.

» **Hike Alberta** (www.hikealberta.com) Online trail guide.

Exchange Rates

Australia	A$1	C$1.04	US$1.09
Canada	C$1	C$1	US$1.04
Eurozone	€1	C$1.36	US$1.43
Japan	¥100	C$1.24	US$1.29
New Zealand	NZ$1	C$0.84	US$0.87
UK	£1	C$1.56	US$1.63
USA	US$1	C$0.96	US$1

For current exchange rates see www.xe.com.

Important Numbers

Banff Information Centre	☎403-762-1550
Jasper Information Centre	☎780-852-6176
Glacier National Park Headquarters	☎406-888-7800

Opening Dates

» **Banff**
Hwy 1 between Banff to Lake Louise open year-round.
Minor roads snowbound in winter.
High trails closed till at least mid-June.

» **Jasper**
Icefields Parkway between Lake Louise and Jasper closes during heavy snowfall.
Minor roads snowbound between December and May.
Most trails open by late June.

» **Glacier**
Key roads (eg Going-to-the-Sun Rd) closed till May or June.

Coping with Crowds

Summer crowds can be a real problem in the national parks, especially around key sights such as Lake Louise, the Banff Gondola, Moraine Lake and Johnston Canyon in Banff, and Maligne Lake, the Miette Hot Springs and the Athabasca Falls in Jasper, and along Glacier's Going-to-the-Sun Rd.

The best way of avoiding the crowds is to set out early or late – ideally before 9am and after 6pm, which are also the best times for seeing wildlife. Take minor roads wherever you can and don't stick to the roadside viewpoints – you'll have a better shot at solitude (and often much better views) by leaving the car and exploring the trails. Avoid visiting in July and August – the light and weather are just as good in May, September and October, but the trails and sights are much quieter.

what's new

For this new edition, our authors have hunted down the fresh, the transformed, the hot and the happening. These are some of our favorites. For up-to-the-minute recommendations, see lonelyplanet.com/canada/alberta/banff-and-jasper-national-parks and lonelyplanet.com/usa/rocky-mountains/glacier-national-park.

Legacy Trail between Canmore & Banff

1 This new paved bike trail opened in 2010 and enables you to cycle all the way from Banff to Canmore. It runs for 25km (15.5 miles) from Banff Ave to Banff's East Gate, with a short stretch on Hwy 1 into Canmore. It's proved a big hit with hikers and rollerbladers, as well as cross-country skiers looking to stay in shape in summer.

Bike 'n Hike Shuttle in Banff

2 There's now a handy new way to reach some of the major trailheads in and around Banff thanks to a new 'Bike 'n Hike' shuttle service provided by White Mountain Adventures.

A Facelift for the Cave & Basin

3 The history of the national parks in Canada began when three brothers discovered an underwater cave and natural hot spring near Banff in 1883. To mark Park Canada's 125th birthday in 2010, the site where it all began is getting a C$13.8m overhaul.

Online Campground Reservations

4 It's now possible to make online reservations at Banff and Jasper's most popular campgrounds, including Tunnel Mountain, Lake Louise, Wapiti, Wabasso and Pocahontas.

Beer Brewing in Banff

5 Banff now has its own microbrewery on Banff Ave. It's a sister operation to Jasper Brewing; all the beers are brewed using spring water straight from the mountains.

Snowy Pursuits

6 The Rockies' ski resorts are fast catching up with Whistler. Recent additions include the region's longest high-speed quad chair lift at Marmot Basin in Jasper, and its first-ever 'snow-tube' park at Mt Norquay in Banff.

A New Bridge across Kicking Horse Canyon

7 Spanning 405m (1328ft) above the Kicking Horse River, the graceful new four-lane bridge on Hwy 1 in Yoho National Park was one of Canada's largest-ever construction projects and cost C$130 million to build.

New Wildlife Crossings over the Trans-Canada Highway

8 There are currently 24 underpasses and four overpasses over the Trans-Canada Hwy between Banff and Lake Louise, but plans are afoot for more in future years. A recent study showed they've been used 220,000 times since the first one opened in 1996.

Communitea Café in Canmore

9 Canmore's new community cafe is run along ethical, organic, veggie-friendly lines. It hosts gigs, readings and events and brews some of the best coffee in the Bow Valley.

if you like...

Wildlife Watching

Whether it's glimpsing a golden eagle soaring overhead or hearing the hooting call of a hoary marmot, getting up close and personal with the wildlife of the Rockies is always an unforgettable experience.

Vermilion Lakes A series of tranquil lakes within easy reach of Banff Town, where you can often spot elks grazing with their calves (p63)

Bow Valley Parkway Running parallel to the Trans-Canada Hwy, this old forest road is a great place to see wildlife from your car (p69)

Lake Louise Gondola Grizzly bears can often be seen on the surrounding avalanche slopes (see boxed text, p67)

Many Glacier One of the best places in Glacier to see bears (black and grizzly), as well as mountain goats, bighorn sheep and moose (p204)

Maligne Lake Road Another good route to cruise with your car – keep your eyes peeled for elusive woodland caribou (see boxed text, p138)

Lookouts & Views

The mountains may look impressive from the valley floor, but to really appreciate their splendor you need to get up high. You can catch a gondola to the top in Banff and Lake Louise, but you'll appreciate the rewards much more if you take a hike.

Sulphur Mountain Quite possibly the most famous view in Banff National Park (p60)

Castle Lookout An old fire lookout halfway up Castle Mountain, with a great vantage point over the entire Bow Valley (p79)

Fairview One of the best (and highest) viewpoints of Lake Louise (p84)

Whistlers Mountain Hike or catch a cable car up to Jasper's best-loved viewpoint amid a backdrop of high alpine tundra (p145)

Parker Ridge Gaze across the Saskatchewan Glacier from this windy ridge halfway along the Icefields Parkway (p89)

Going-to-the-Sun Road This amazing road boasts 85km (53 miles) of nonstop views (p179)

Glaciers

The landscape of the Rockies quite literally owes its existence to its majestic glaciers: the mountains and valleys were carved out over the course of thousands of years during the last Ice Age.

Athabasca Glacier This grand glacier is part of the enormous Columbia Icefield, North America's largest area of ice outside the polar regions (p143)

Grinnell Glacier See Glacier's most accessible ice river from atop the Continental Divide, or tackle it from below on a trail from Many Glacier (p184)

Saskatchewan Glacier This spur tongue from the Columbia Icefield sits at the head of an amazing river valley. It's best seen from Parker Ridge (p89)

Stanley Glacier Hike through burned forest to this classic 'hanging valley' glacier in Kootenay National Park (p130)

Jackson Glacier One of 25 fast-disappearing icefields in Glacier National Park. Don't miss the lookout on Going-to-the-Sun Rd (p182)

» Athabasca Glacier (p143), Jasper National Park

Adventure Activities

There's no end of ways to get your pulse racing in the Rocky Mountains, whether you prefer hurtling down the slopes on a mountain bike or braving the white-water rapids of the Kicking Horse River. Many activity providers offer a package of activities so you can try out several sports in just a single day.

Skiing & snowboarding Tackle heart-stopping slaloms and off-piste thrills in Banff's Big Three resorts, or head for Jasper for quieter runs (p40)

White-water rafting The wild rapids of the Kicking Horse, Athabasca, Flathead and Kananaskis Rivers are an irresistible draw for white-water junkies (p38)

Caving Explore a secret world of stalactites and underground pools in the Rat's Nest Cave near Canmore (p118)

Mountain biking Race along the exciting singletracks and groomed trails at the Canmore Nordic Centre (p116)

Ice-climbing Clamber up a frozen wall in Maligne Canyon (p147)

Lakes & Waterfalls

Electric-blue lakes and booming cascades are dotted all over the mountain parks. Some are well-known, while others lie well off the beaten track; aim to visit early or late in the day when the colors are at their most vivid.

Lake Louise Without doubt one of the most iconic vistas in Canada, as long as you don't mind sharing it with the crowds (p67)

Johnston Canyon See three waterfalls in a single canyon, but don't expect to be on your own (p69)

Lake McDonald Take a trip or paddle a canoe across the waters of Glacier's stateliest lake (p183)

Lake Minnewanka Catch a cruise across the largest lake in Banff National Park (p98)

Maligne Lake Jasper's most famous lake is also one of its most beautiful (p148)

Takakkaw Falls This enormous waterfall in Yoho National Park drops 384m (1259ft) to the valley floor (p125)

Backcountry Hikes

For many hikers, you can't even begin to understand the mountains till you've slept out in the wild under an endless canopy of stars. With some of North America's most unspoilt backcountry on your doorstep, it'd be criminal not to take their advice.

Egypt Lake A popular and achievable overnight trip through Banff's backcountry to a string of lovely mountain lakes (p90)

Skoki Valley Explore a hidden valley near Lake Louise, and kip in the Rocky Mountains' oldest ski lodge (p90)

Mt Assiniboine The crème de la crème of backcountry hikes, centring around the pencil-point peak colloquially known as the Matterhorn of the Rockies (p92)

Skyline Trail Rated by many as one of the best overnight hikes in Canada, with fantastic Jasper views and a pleasant chalet to sleep in (p157)

Gunsight Pass Trail Crisscross the Continental Divide before staying overnight in the historic Sperry Chalet (p194)

If you like... mountain biking, in summer the Kicking Horse Mountain Resort near Golden opens up its tailor-made trail system with a wealth of testing singletracks and downhills (p133)

Hot Springs

After a long day of exploring, there's nothing quite as soothing as lying back in the super-heated waters of a geothermal spring. There are four main ones to discover, although you can only actually bathe in three.

Cave & Basin National Historic Site The first springs to be discovered in the Rockies are now inaccessible to bathers to protect the critically endangered Banff Springs snail (p62)

Banff Upper Hot Springs The national park's oldest geothermal spa is still its most popular. In summer aim for an early morning or late-night dip to dodge the crowds (p61)

Radium Hot Springs Twin pools to indulge in (one hot, one cool), both with wonderful mountain views on every side (p131)

Miette Hot Springs Jasper's natural springs offer a much quieter alternative to Banff, so if you prefer to bathe in peace, these are probably the ones for you (p148)

Quiet Spots

Crowds can be a problem in the mountain parks, especially in the peak months of July and August, but that doesn't mean you can't find solitude. Here are some places where you're guaranteed to be far from the madding crowd.

Tonquin Valley No road access means guaranteed tranquility in this remote Jasper valley (p158)

Sunshine Meadows The high-altitude trails of this mountain meadow feel empty even on the busiest summer days (p66)

Consolation Lakes These twin tarns are less than an hour's walk from Moraine Lake, but feel a world away from its hustle and bustle (p81)

Two Medicine Valley No hotels, no restaurants, but plenty of wildlife and practically zero crowds (p184)

Kananaskis Country Relatively few people explore the provincial parks that make up K-Country, so you'll probably just be sharing the trails with the locals (p121)

History & Heritage

The national parks may only be a century or so old, but humans have been living in and exploring the Rockies for thousands of years. Getting to grips with the region's history and heritage is both fascinating and fun.

Banff Park Museum A wild menagerie of stuffed beasts and animal heads adorn the walls of Banff's oldest museum (p59)

Whyte Museum of the Canadian Rockies Mountain art takes centre stage at this excellent museum in Banff (p58)

Native American speaks Regularly held at the St Mary Visitor Center in Glacier (p220)

Railway heritage Train enthusiasts will find plenty to pique their interest, from Yoho's ingenious Spiral Tunnels (p126) to Jasper's historic train station building (p145)

Buffalo Nations Luxton Museum Some of the fiberglass displays might be tacky, but this Banff museum also has some intriguing examples of First Nations costume, art and craftwork (p63)

month by month

Top Events

1. **Banff Summer Arts Festival**, August
2. **North American Indian Days**, July
3. **Jasper Heritage Rodeo**, August
4. **Banff Winter Festival**, January
5. **Canmore Highland Games**, September

January

Chilly temperatures and crisp snow transform the mountain parks into a winter wonderland. The slopes around Banff and Jasper are busy with skiers and snowboarders.

Ice Magic

During this annual competition, held in January at the Fairmont Lake Louise, teams of ice carvers battle it out to create sculptures fashioned from 136kg (300lb) blocks of ice.

Banff/Lake Louise Winter Festival

This winter-themed knees-up has been an institution in Banff since 1916. Street parades, sled competitions and ski contests hit town in January and February, and there's always a big party to wrap up the celebrations.

Jasper in January

Jasper's atmospheric winter festival hosts plenty of family-friendly events, including cross-country skiing, sleigh rides, skating and a chili cook-off.

February

Winter holds the mountains in an icy grip, with frequent snowfalls and sub-zero temperatures still the norm.

Canmore Winter Carnival

This boisterous festival shakes off the winter blues with log-sawing, ice-carving and beard-growing contests, but the Trapper's Ball is the highlight.

March

Little has changed in the mountains by March: snow and ice still cloak the landscape, with the spring thaw still months away.

Polebridge Iditarod

Mushers and husky teams compete to claim the fastest time at this annual dog-sledding competition held in Polebridge, Montana.

April

Late April sees the first hints of spring – snowmelt at lower elevations and the odd warm sunny day – but don't put away the winter woollies just yet.

Big Mountain Ski Annual Furniture Races

Settees with skis and beds on sleds take to the slopes in this zany downhill furniture race in Whitefish in April.

May

The snows finally begin to thaw and spring creeps into the Rockies in mid- to late May. It's still cold though; most lakes stay frozen until June.

Canmore Children's Festival

Pageantry, puppet shows, workshops and magic displays keep young minds entertained at this children's party (www.canmorechildrensfestival.com).

July

Summer settles in by July, and everyone starts to look forward to long days of hiking, biking and other outdoor activities. Colorful blooms carpet the mountain meadows, and most trails are open.

Canada Day

Food booths, fireworks and outdoor concerts in celebration of the nation. Events take place in Banff, Jasper and Glacier on July 1.

North American Indian Days

The largest of several celebrations held on the Blackfeet Indian Reservation throughout the year, this July event has displays of traditional drumming and dancing and the crowning of the year's Miss Blackfeet.

Canmore Folk Festival

Top folk acts descend on Canmore for this lively music festival, held every year since 1978 over the Heritage Weekend. The main stage is in Centennial Park, but there are extra gigs at many cafés and bars round town, too.

August

The hottest month of the year coincides with a host of special events, as well as the Rockies' busiest tourist season. The weather is mostly hot and dry, but watch out for thunderstorms.

Banff Summer Arts Festival

Culture takes center stage for this month-long showcase of artistic activity at the Banff Centre, hosting everything from opera, theater and street performance to art exhibitions. It kicks off in late July and runs through August.

Jasper Heritage Rodeo

Since 1926 bull-riders, steer-wrestlers and calf-ropers have been congregating in Jasper for this annual hoedown and rodeo (www.jasperheritagerodeo.com), held in mid-August.

Banff Dragon Boat Festival

Crews paddle elaborately carved dragon boats across Lake Minnewanka in this exciting boat race, while spectators cheer them on from the lakeshore.

Doors Open Banff

Visitors are invited to explore some of Banff Town's historic monuments and heritage buildings, with special guided tours run by the Whyte Museum.

September

Fall brings a blaze of color to the mountain parks, making it one of the most spectacular seasons for hiking – especially since the summer crowds have left for home. Days remain warm, but the nights are getting chilly.

Banff International String Quartet Competition

A world-famous contest for the cream of the world's classical string quartets, held at the Banff Centre.

Canmore Highland Games

Canmore celebrates its Scottish roots with a day of caber-tossing, piping, drumming, sheepdog trials and a traditional ceilidh to round things off.

Lake Louise Fall Festival

Lake Louise hosts a series of events to mark the arrival of fall, ranging from guided walks to photography exhibitions. Many local restaurants have special fall-themed menus.

November

Winter is knocking on the door in November, which usually sees the first snowfall of the season and the opening of some of the area's higher ski resorts.

Banff Mountain Film & Book Festival

Since the mid-1970s, this three-day film and literature festival has celebrated the spirit of mountain adventure through films, videos, readings and lectures.

Winterstart

This Banff street party is popular with the snowboarding and winter-sports crowd, and includes the Ski Big Three Rail Jam and Santa's Parade of Lights.

itineraries

Whether you've got six days or 60, these itineraries provide a starting point for the trip of a lifetime. Want more inspiration? Head online to lonelyplanet.com/thorntree to chat with other travelers.

Two Weeks

Rocky Mountain Roadtrip

This once-in-a-lifetime trip takes in the best of the Rocky Mountain parks. Start out with three days exploring **Glacier** and the magnificent mountain scenery around Going-to-the-Sun Rd and Many Glacier. On day four, head north across the Canadian border for **Waterton Lakes** and a hike along the iconic Carthew-Alderson Trail. Spend the next day driving north to **Banff**, your base for the next four days. How you divide the time is up to you, but make sure you factor in the gondola ride up Sulphur Mountain, wildlife spotting around Vermilion Lakes and the Bow Valley Parkway, a boat trip across Lake Minnewanka and at least one day hike. Day 10 is set aside for more mind-blowing scenery around Lake Louise and Moraine Lake, followed on day 11 by a drive up the **Icefields Parkway** – it won't take long for you to realize why it's often dubbed the world's most spectacular road. Round the trip off with three days in **Jasper**, including a cruise on Maligne Lake, a day hike, a ride on the Jasper Tramway and a dip in Miette Hot Springs.

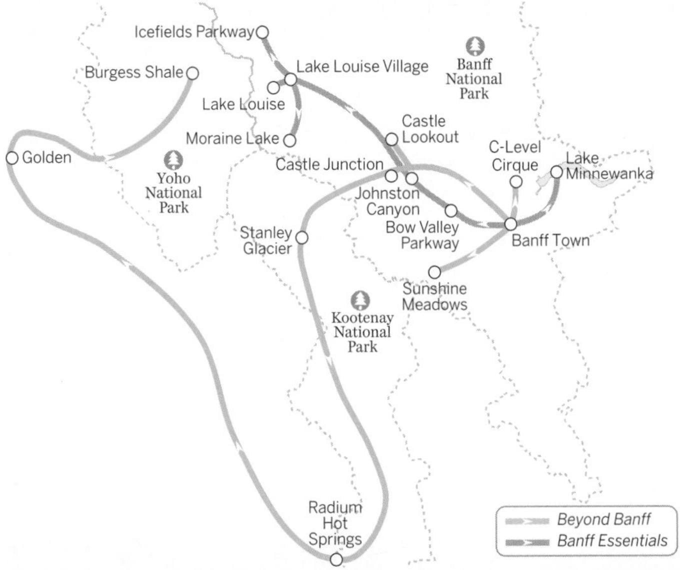

One Week
Beyond Banff

This itinerary takes in some of Banff's top day hikes, and then heads into the neighboring national parks. For the first few days, base yourself in **Banff Town** and spend the time breaking in those boots: you could hike up to a hidden icefield at the **C-Level Cirque**, admire the Bow Valley from **Castle Lookout**, or trek through the colorful wildflowers of **Sunshine Meadows**.

From Banff, head west across the Alberta–British Columbia border into **Kootenay National Park**. This is one of the most fire-prone areas of the Rockies: you'll still be able to see the damage wrought by the last big burn in 2003. Take the time to hike up to **Stanley Glacier** before chilling in the 'hot' and 'cool' pools of **Radium Hot Springs**, both fed from a volcanic spring hidden deep beneath the mountainside.

From Radium, the route loops north via **Golden**, a lively little town known for its outdoor sports, especially mountain biking and skiing. From here, the road heads east along the Kicking Horse Valley into **Yoho National Park**, where you can spend the remaining few days admiring the sights: don't miss Emerald Lake, Takakkaw Falls and a guided walk to the fossil fields of the **Burgess Shale**.

Five Days
Banff Essentials

With five days you should have just enough time to see Banff's key sights. Kick off with a day exploring **Banff Town**, a lively mini-metropolis with a cosmopolitan mix of shops, bistros, pubs and museums. Check in for some chateau luxury at the historic Fairmont Banff Springs Hotel, followed by a day exploring **Lake Minnewanka**, canoeing on the Bow River and relaxing in the Upper Hot Springs Pool.

On day three, drive out of Banff and detour off the Trans-Canada Hwy and onto the **Bow Valley Parkway**. Keep your eyes peeled for wildlife, and don't miss the famous waterfalls of **Johnston Canyon**. By mid-afternoon, you'll reach the iconic sight of **Lake Louise** and nearby **Moraine Lake**, both renowned for their sapphire-blue waters and stunning mountain settings. Sleep in style at the smart Deer Lodge, and spend day four stretching your legs, either on the dramatic trail along the Plain of Six Glaciers, or on the steep climb to Lake Agnes and the Beehives.

On day five, drive along the breathtaking **Icefields Parkway**, passing jagged peaks, mighty glaciers and sparkling lakes en route to Num-Ti-Jah Lodge, one of the Rockies' most famous mountain retreats.

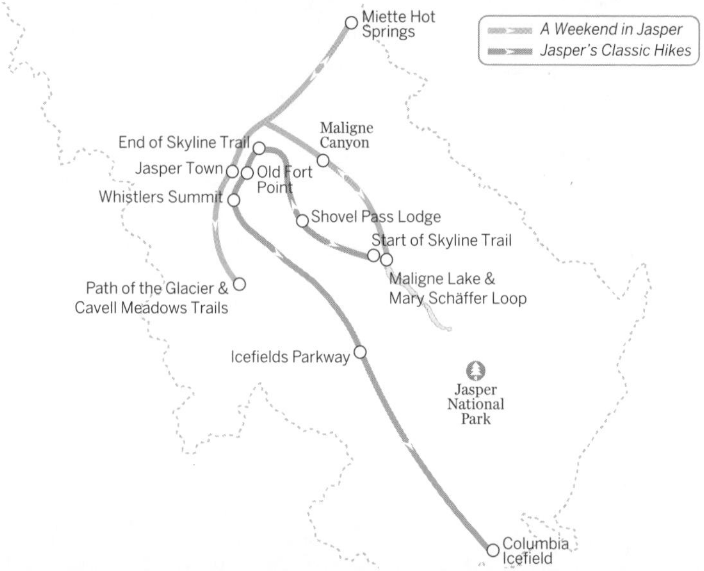

One Week

Jasper's Classic Hikes

You've seen Jasper's must-see sights, so now's the time to try some more challenging hikes. Pitch a tent at Wapiti Campground and warm up with a hike up to **Old Fort Point** or **Whistlers Summit**.

Now you're trail-ready, it's time for the real challenge. Jasper has some of the finest backcountry anywhere in Canada, and you simply won't be able to appreciate the splendor of the park unless you spend a few nights in the wild. The two- to three-day **Skyline Trail** is without doubt one of North America's premier overnight hikes, taking in everything from snowy peaks and glacial lakes to lofty passes with mind-boggling views. You don't even have to rough it thanks to the cozy **Shovel Pass Lodge**.

After the exertion, it's time to sit back and let the views come to you. Spend a day driving south along the Jasper section of the **Icefields Parkway**, and finish up with a visit to the **Columbia Icefield**, the largest area of ice this side of the North Pole. Most people trundle up in a Snocoach, but a guided walk will give you an even more memorable perspective.

Three Days

A Weekend in Jasper

Even with only a weekend at your disposal, it's still possible to get a taste of what makes Jasper special. Base yourself in **Jasper Town**, either at the swish Park Place Inn or the more traditional Patricia Lake Bungalows. On the first day, tick off the townsite: get an early morning ticket for the Jasper Tramway, visit the town museum, pick up lunch from the Bear's Paw Bakery, then spend an afternoon at Patricia and Pyramid Lakes. Stroll along the Discovery Trail as the sun sets, with a smart dinner at Evil Dave's.

On day two, pack a picnic from Patricia St Deli and drive along Maligne Lake Rd – a hotspot for wildlife. Explore the crashing cascades of **Maligne Canyon**, and then head for nearby **Maligne Lake** for a guided cruise to tiny Spirit Island and an early evening walk on the **Mary Schäffer Loop**.

On your last day, it's time to hit the trail. Jasper has lots of day hikes, but you'll be hard pushed to top the spectacular **Path of the Glacier and Cavell Meadows Trails**. Reward yourself with an evening soak at **Miette Hot Springs**, followed by a farewell drinks and dinner at Jasper Brewing Company.

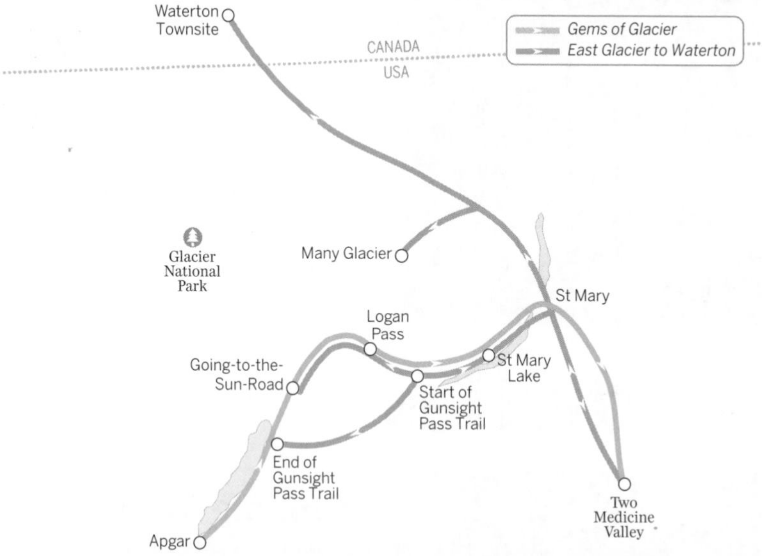

Three Days

Gems of Glacier

With only three days in Glacier, you'll have to get your skates on. Use one of the hotels or motels around **Apgar** as your launchpad: the Lake McDonald Lodge is the luxury choice, but the Village Inn is cheaper and cozier.

From here, you'll be perfectly placed to venture east into the national park. On day one, explore around Apgar, West Glacier and nearby Lake McDonald, perhaps taking a walk among ancient rainforest on the Trail of the Cedars, or admiring mountain scenery on the Avalanche Lake Trail.

On day two, travel east along the **Going-to-the-Sun Road**, one of America's most stunning stretches of asphalt. You can take your own vehicle or jump aboard one of the vintage Red Jammer buses, which have been trundling along the road since 1936. Stop to see the sights: the tumbling cascades of Bird Woman Falls and the Weeping Wall, the dramatic stretch of highway over Logan Pass, and the Jackson Glacier Overlook, which affords a knockout view of one of the park's namesake glaciers.

Stay overnight at the Rising Sun Motor Inn on the shores of **St Mary Lake**, and spend your last day hiking trails and spotting wildlife in **Two Medicine Valley**.

One Week

East Glacier to Waterton

A week allows more time to hike Glacier's trails and travel north into Waterton Lakes. **St Mary**, on the park's east side, makes a convenient base to begin with, with several hotels, motels and frontcountry campsites to choose from.

Spend the first couple of days exploring north and south around **Going-to-the-Sun Road**. **Two Medicine Valley** is a short drive south of St Mary, while **Logan Pass** lies to the west: both are fantastic areas for walking and wildlife watching. To get underneath Glacier's skin, however, a backcountry hike is essential – and there's none finer than the **Gunsight Pass Trail**, which runs through 32km (19.8 miles) of pristine backcountry from Jackson Glacier Overlook to the east side of Lake McDonald. Frequent buses on Going-to-the-Sun Rd mean you don't even need to worry about transport.

Then it's north for a couple of days in **Many Glacier**, arguably the national park's most beautiful valley. Reward yourself with a stay in the Many Glacier Hotel, overlooking the sparkling waters of Swiftcurrent Lake.

Finish up with some more hiking and sightseeing in **Waterton**: don't miss the classic Carthew-Alderson Trail and the equally impressive tramp to Crypt Lake.

Activities

Hike Grades

Throughout this book we've written detailed descriptions of our favorite hikes. For ease of use and to help you decide which one to take, we've graded them into three difficulty levels.

Easy Mostly flat, simple walking on clearly defined trails, suitable for families and inexperienced hikers. Some may be paved and suitable for wheelchair users or people with reduced mobility.

Moderate These hikes will feature significant elevation gain, and include steep sections and possibly some ungroomed areas of trail (such as rubble, stones or moraines). Suitable for any hiker with an average level of fitness.

Difficult Expect very steep climbs, sections of exposed and unmaintained trail, challenging terrain and occasional route-finding. These hikes are for experienced hikers, and will entail long days and significant distances. Pack equipment appropriately.

Planning Your Trip

Experiencing the great outdoors is undoubtedly one of the top reasons to visit the Rockies. Whether it's plummeting down the slopes on a mountain bike or climbing up them on a classic hike, the mountain parks present a wealth of ways to expend your energy and get the most of the spectacular scenery.

When to Go

When you choose to visit the mountain parks depends on what you want to do. Winter is long in the Rockies, with snow covering the landscape for up to six months of the year (from around November to May). Most summer activities take place between May and September, although the exact periods vary according to seasonal conditions.

Summer Activities

» **June–September** This is the peak activity season, and usually offers the most reliable weather. Most trails are open by late June or early July. It's worth saving longer overnight hikes for the warmer temperatures of late July and August.

» **July–August** By far the busiest times on the trails, so if you prefer to walk in solitude, the shoulder months are a better bet.

» **September–October** Both great months to visit, as fall brings a sea of autumnal colors to the parks and most trails are comparatively quiet.

Winter Activities

» The ski season usually runs from late November until April, but can open early or late depending on seasonal conditions.

» Some hiking trails stay open in winter – but you'll need to master the art of snowshoes!

Outdoor Activities

Hiking & Backpacking

If there's one activity that sums up the spirit of the Rockies, it's hiking. No matter where you travel in the parks, there's a trail nearby that'll whisk you up spectacular mountains, into picturesque forests or down a dramatic gorge.

The Rockies are a destination *par excellence* for experienced hikers, but have plenty to offer novice walkers, too. Some trails have interpretive signs that are ideal for families, while others feature paved sections designed for people with limited mobility.

We've detailed many of our favorite hiking routes in this book. A good-quality topographical map of the area you're hiking in is essential – the Gem Trek maps (see p257) are the best for the Canadian parks.

For general advice on keeping safe on the trail and what to bring, see our dedicated Health chapter on p266 and our Equipment chapter on p272.

Day Hikes

Most walks in this book are classed as 'day hikes,' a term that covers everything from an hour-long woodland stroll to an eight-hour haul to a mountain pass. Any route that takes less than eight hours to complete, or covers a round-trip of less than 24km (15 miles), is generally practical for a day hike.

You might not quite reach the edge of the true wilderness in a single day, but you can still experience an astonishing variety of terrain and enjoy plenty of wonderful views.

It's always worth reading up on your chosen route before you set out to make sure it suits your ability level and that you know what to expect from your day on the mountain. Latest trail reports and wildlife warnings are available from park visitor centers or online from the national park websites.

Overnight Hikes

For a true wilderness experience you have to spend a few nights out in the wild. There are hundreds of backcountry routes scattered around the parks. Some string together a few day hikes with a night in a backcountry campground, while others are multiday epics that venture into distant and little-visited corners of the national parks.

» Trips can last anywhere from a couple of days to a couple of weeks.

» Overnight hikes require a wilderness pass and backcountry campground reservations – see destination chapters.

» The majority of overnight hikes are within the capabilities of most hikers, as long as you're properly equipped and reasonably fit.

» You'll need to pack in food, a tent and sleeping bag, first-aid supplies and all other equipment, and pack out all your rubbish.

» See the Clothing & Equipment chapter (p272) for advice on recommended gear.

TOP AREAS FOR OVERNIGHT HIKES

» Skoki Valley, Banff (p90)

» Egypt Lake, Banff (p90)

» Mt Assiniboine, Banff (p92)

» Kananaskis Country (p123)

» Tonquin Valley, Jasper (p158)

» Skyline Trail, Jasper (p157)

» Gunsight Pass, Glacier (p194)

» Lake O'Hara, Yoho (p128)

» Northern Highline-Waterton Valley (p195)

Responsible Backcountry Hiking

The general rule in the backcountry is to leave everything as you find it – the **Leave No Trace** (www.leavenotrace.ca) website has some excellent advice on ways to reduce your impact on the environment. Key points:

» Pitch on sites previously used by other campers to avoid unnecessary damage to the landscape.

» Keep your campsite clean to avoid attracting animals.

» Store food, toiletries and cooking equipment in bear-proof lockers if available, or suspend them between two trees at least 4m (13ft) above the ground and 1.3m (5ft) from each trunk.

» Use biodegradable soap and wash dishes well away from rivers and streams.

HIKING IN BANFF NATIONAL PARK

NAME	REGION	DESCRIPTION	DIFFICULTY
Fenland Trail & Vermilion Lakes	Banff Town	Flat woodland trail leading to network of lakes where you'll often spot grazing elk	Easy
Sundance Canyon	Banff Town	Wild canyon walk reached via paved riverside trail; easy bike ride from Banff	Easy
Bow Falls & the Hoodoos	Banff Town	Riverside walk to Banff's most famous waterfalls and a landscape of weird rock towers	Easy
Sulphur Mountain	Banff Town	Steep hike up flank of Sulphur Mountain with wrap-around views	Moderate
Cascade Amphitheatre	Banff Town	High-level trail across ski fields to classic glacial cirque hidden among mountains	Moderate-difficult
Castle Lookout	Bow Valley Parkway	Mountainside path to abandoned fire lookout overlooking Bow Valley	Moderate
Johnston Canyon & the Inkpots	Bow Valley Parkway	Visits Bow Valley's best-known waterfalls and continues to colorful mountain tarns	Moderate
Parker Ridge	Icefields Parkway	Switchbacking climb to stunning knife-edge ridge above Saskatchewan Glacier	Moderate
Peyto Lake & Bow Summit Lookout	Icefields Parkway	Busy trail to lookout above Peyto Lake, leading to quieter climb to old fire lookout	Moderate
Bow Glacier Falls	Icefields Parkway	Start at Num-Ti-Jah Lodge and walk across boulders and moraines to impressive glacial cascade	Easy-moderate
Sunset Lookout	Icefields Parkway	Little-used trail to superb fire lookout with views of rivers, glaciers and peaks	Moderate
Helen Lake	Icefields Parkway	Often-overlooked route up to lake-filled mountain meadow with vistas of Icefields Parkway	Moderate
Plain of Six Glaciers	Lake Louise	Superb walk to glacier viewpoint, with option to stop at historic teahouse	Moderate
Lake Agnes & the Beehives	Lake Louise	Steep walk to Lake Louise's most famous teahouse and lofty summit high above	Moderate-difficult
Saddleback & Fairview	Lake Louise	Double summit trail from shores of Lake Louise to above-the-clouds viewpoint at top of Fairview	Moderate-difficult
Skoki Valley	Lake Louise	True classic of the Rockies, exploring one of the most beautiful backcountry valleys near Lake Louise	Moderate-difficult
Paradise Valley & the Giant's Steps	Lake Louise	Difficult Lake Louise trail, hiking through wild valley frequented by goats, marmots and grizzly bears	Difficult
Stewart Canyon	Lake Minnewanka	Flat lakeshore trail to hidden forest canyon; canoeing possible	Easy
C-Level Cirque	Lake Minnewanka	Hike past old mine-workings to ice amphitheater high above Lake Minnewanka	Moderate
Consolation Lakes Trail	Moraine Lake	Escape Moraine Lake crowds into wild mountains past glassy lakes	Easy
Larch Valley & Sentinel Pass	Moraine Lake	Wildflowers and native larches in mountain meadow overlooking Ten Peaks, with add-on to high-level pass	Moderate
Garden Path Trail & Twin Cairns Meadow	Sunshine Meadows	Wonderful walk through high mountain meadows and past lakes	Easy
Healy Pass	Sunshine Meadows	Rewarding walk that affords fantastic glimpses over Continental Divide	Moderate-difficult
Egypt Lake	Sunshine Meadows	Great option for first-timers in backcountry, taking in lakes and moderately demanding mountains	Moderate-difficult
Mt Assiniboine	Sunshine Meadows	Unforgettable journey into wild backcountry around shining pinnacle of Mt Assiniboine	Difficult

Wildlife Watching · *Great for Families* · *Rock Climbing* · *Fishing* · *Waterfall* · *Restrooms* · *Drinking Water*

DURATION	ROUND-TRIP DISTANCE	ELEVATION CHANGE	FEATURES	FACILITIES	PAGE
30min	2.1km (1.3 miles)	Negligible	Wildlife, Family	Public Transport to Trailhead	p75
1hr	2km (1.2 miles)	145m (476ft)	Family, Water feature	Picnic Sites	p75
3hr	10.2km (6.4 miles)	60m (197ft)	Family, Water feature	Restrooms, Public Transport to Trailhead, Picnic Sites	p74
4hr	11km (6.8 miles)	655m (2149ft)		Restrooms, Public Transport to Trailhead, Picnic Sites, Grocery Store Nearby, Restaurant Nearby	p77
6hr	15.4km (9.6 miles)	640m (2100ft)	Wildlife		p78
3-4hr	7.6km (4.7 miles)	520m (1706ft)	Climbing	Grocery Store Nearby	p79
4hr	10.8km (6.7 miles)	215m (705ft)	Wildlife, Water feature	Restrooms, Drinking water, Restaurant Nearby	p78
2hr	4km (2.5 miles)	250m (820ft)		Restrooms	p89
2hr	6.2km (3.8 miles)	245m (803ft)		Restrooms	p87
3hr	7.2km (4.4 miles)	155m (509ft)	Family, Water feature	Restrooms, Drinking water, Restaurant Nearby	p86
3hr	9.4km (5.8 miles)	250m (820ft)			p89
4hr	12km (7.6 miles)	455m (1493ft)	Wildlife	Restrooms	p88
4-5hr	13.5km (8.4 miles)	365m (1198ft)		Restrooms, Restaurant Nearby	p82
4hr	10.8km (6.6 miles)	495m (1624ft)		Restrooms, Picnic Sites, Restaurant Nearby	p83
5-6hr	10.2km (6.4 miles)	1013m (3323ft)	Climbing	Restrooms, Restaurant Nearby	p84
4 days	50.6km (31.4 miles)	Up to 1136m (3727ft)	Wildlife	Restrooms, Drinking water, Backcountry Campsite	p90
6-7hr	20.3km (12.6 miles)	385m (1263ft)	Wildlife, Climbing		p85
2hr	5.6km (3.5 miles)	Negligible	Family, Fishing	Restrooms, Picnic Sites, Restaurant Nearby	p76
4hr	8.8km (5.4 miles)	455m (1493ft)		Restrooms	p77
2hr	6km (3.8 miles)	65m (213ft)	Wildlife, Family, Fishing		p81
4-5hr	11.6km (7.2 miles)	725m (2379ft)			p84
3½hr	8.3km (5.1 miles)	Negligible	Family	Restrooms, Public Transport to Trailhead, Restaurant Nearby	p79
6-7hr	18.4km (11.4 miles)	650m (2132ft)		Restrooms, Public Transport to Trailhead, Restaurant Nearby	p80
3 days	24.8km (15.4 miles)	Up to 655m (2149ft)	Wildlife, Family, Fishing	Drinking water, Public Transport to Trailhead, Ranger Station, Backcountry Campsite, Picnic Sites	p90
4-5 days	53.3km (33.1 miles)	Up to 695m (2280ft)	Wildlife	Public Transport to Trailhead, Ranger Station, Backcountry Campsite	p92

Public Transport to Trailhead · *Ranger Station* · *Backcountry Campsite* · *Picnic Sites* · *Grocery Store Nearby* · *Restaurant Nearby*

» A portable stove is more eco-friendly than a campfire as it prevents unnecessary scorching of the ground.

» If you do have a fire, don't cut anything down to burn as fuel – dead wood is OK, green wood certainly isn't.

» Heed any fire restrictions that may be in place.

» If you get caught short on the trail, move well away from the path and at least 70m (230ft) from any water source, dig a hole, do the deed and cover it with dirt. Pack out toilet paper in a sealed bag.

Rules & Permits

No matter where you're hiking, you'll need a valid park pass and, if you're exploring the backcountry, backcountry campground reservations and a wilderness permit for each night of your stay. All these can be arranged through visitor centers.

It's also a good idea to leave a full trip itinerary with park staff if you're traveling in remote country or doing any hazardous activities (such as mountaineering or rock climbing). Remember to sign in once you're back, otherwise you will be listed as missing and a search party will be sent out to find you.

It's extremely important to stay on the trails – cutting across switchbacks, avoiding muddy patches and tramping trail fringes causes unnecessary 'braiding' of the path and damages the fragile alpine environment.

Trail Guides

A standalone hiking guide can be a useful purchase, as they have extra space to detail precise trail distances, marker points, full elevations and compass bearings for specific routes. There are lots of different guides to choose from; the following are just some of our favorites.

Standard hiking textbook *The Canadian Rockies Trail Guide* by Brian Patton and Bart Robinson celebrated its 40th birthday in 2011, and it's still many people's preferred guide. Simple layout, no-nonsense text and trail descriptions for 229 hikes are all user-friendly, although the black-and-white format looks dated.

HIKING IN JASPER NATIONAL PARK

NAME	REGION	DESCRIPTION	DIFFICULTY
Beauty Creek & Stanley Falls	Icefields Parkway	Popular waterfall off the Icefields Parkway reached on a surprisingly straightforward and rewarding hike	Easy
Path of the Glacier & Cavell Meadows Trails	Icefields Parkway	See Angel Glacier resting atop a lake with icebergs while the meadows offer amazing views	Moderate-difficult
Geraldine Lakes	Icefields Parkway	A rocky scramble through staircaselike valley replete with lakes and waterfalls	Moderate-difficult
Tonquin Valley	Icefields Parkway	Wildlife, lush meadows and sparkling lakes, all in the shadow of the Ramparts	Difficult
Mina & Riley Lakes Loop	Jasper Town & Around	Takes you into the woods to remote lakes	Easy-moderate
Whistlers Summit	Jasper Town & Around	A long walk up a steep hill through three different life zones	Difficult
Mary Schäffer Loop	Maligne Lake Area	Holds the famous view first seen by Mary Schäffer	Easy
Moose Lake Loop	Maligne Lake Area	Offers a peaceful, verdant forest and the chance to spot a moose	Easy
Beaver, Summit & Jacques Lakes	Maligne Lake Area	One of the park's simplest 'long' hikes with wide paths and peek-a-boo mountain views	Easy-moderate
Skyline Trail	Maligne Lake Area	The Rockies' premier backcountry trail, offering infinite views across the mountains	Moderate-difficult
Opal Hills Loop	Maligne Lake Area	A steep grunt up to the flower-filled meadows above Maligne Lake	Difficult
Sulphur Skyline	North of Jasper Town	A short sharp hike up to a lofty ridge with spectacular views	Moderate-difficult

Wildlife Watching · *Great for Families* · *Fishing* · *Waterfall* · *Restrooms* · *Drinking Water*

The full-color *Classic Hikes in the Canadian Rockies* by Graeme Pole is more useful if you're after some context on your hike, with glossy photos of views, sights, wildflowers, and flora and fauna. The book is handily divided into color-coded sections for each national park.

The opinionated *Don't Waste Your Time in the Canadian Rockies* by Kathy and Craig Copeland rates hikes into four categories (Premier, Outstanding, Worthwhile and Don't Do). Some of the choices are controversial, but it certainly helps you narrow your selection.

Going Solo

For many people it's the chance for solitude that makes the idea of hiking in the mountains so irresistible, but it's worth thinking carefully if you're heading out solo. If you'd prefer not to go alone, ask around at local hostels and visitor centers to see if you can find some like-minded hikers or an organized walk to tag along with.

Walking alone (especially in the backcountry) is inherently more risky – your chance of encountering wildlife is greater, there's no one to go for help if you get into trouble or sprain an ankle, and no one to blame if you get lost due to bad navigation skills! If you do decide to hike alone, take the following precautions:

» Pack a compass and a good trail map, and make sure you're familiar with basic navigation techniques.

» Look out for recent wildlife warnings at trailheads, which will also be posted in park visitor centers.

» Pay attention to group access restrictions and seasonal trail closures around Lake Louise in summer.

» Let someone know where you're planning on hiking and what time you expect to be back.

» Sing loudly on the trail, shout and clap your hands to warn animals of your approach.

» Be particularly wary about wildlife around noisy streams or dense forest.

» Carry bear spray in an easily accessible place, and make sure you know how to use it. Also check expiry dates on the canister.

DURATION	ROUND-TRIP DISTANCE	ELEVATION CHANGE	FEATURES	FACILITIES	PAGE
1hr	3.2km (2 miles)	Negligible			p153
3hr	9.1km (5.6 miles)	400m (1300ft)			p152
3-4hr	10km (6.3 miles)	407m (1335ft)			p151
2-3 days	53.2km (33 miles)	710m (2329ft)			p158
3hr	9km (5.6 miles)	160m (525ft)			p153
3½hr	7.9km (4.9 miles)	1280m (4125ft)			p154
45min	3.2km (2 miles)	Negligible			p155
45min	2.6km (1.6 miles)	Negligible			p155
6-7hr	24km (15 miles)	90m (300ft)			p156
2 days	45.8km (28.7 miles)	1400m (4526ft)			p157
3hr	8.2km (5.1 miles)	460m (1509ft)			p155
3hr	8km (5 miles)	700m (2297ft)			p156

Public Transport to Trailhead · Ranger Station · Backcountry Campsite · Picnic Sites · Grocery Store Nearby · Restaurant Nearby

HIKING IN GLACIER NATIONAL PARK

NAME	REGION	DESCRIPTION	DIFFICULTY
Sun Point to Virginia Falls	Going-to-the-Sun Rd	Sun-dappled valley trail to a trio of beautiful waterfalls	Easy
Hidden Lake Overlook Trail	Going-to-the-Sun Rd	Quick scamper to a spectacular lookout	Easy-moderate
Avalanche Lake Trail	Going-to-the-Sun Rd	Very popular forested walk to a stunning lake	Easy-moderate
Highline Trail	Going-to-the-Sun Rd	Phenomenal alpine scenery all the way to the Granite Park Chalet	Moderate
Piegan Pass	Going-to-the-Sun Rd	A forest, a meadow, a glacier, a pass and a descent through a wildlife corridor	Moderate-difficult
Gunsight Pass Trail	Going-to-the-Sun Rd	See snowfields, glaciers, lakes and more over two riveting days	Moderate-difficult
Northern Highline-Waterton Valley	Going-to-the-Sun Rd	Continuation of Highline Trail along the Continental Divide toward the Canadian border	Moderate-difficult
Mt Brown Lookout	Going-to-the-Sun Rd	Glacier's steepest day hike to a lofty historic lookout on Mt Brown	Difficult
Swiftcurrent Lake Nature Trail	North of Going-to-the-Sun Rd	From civilization to bear-infested wilderness in less than 60 seconds	Easy
Iceberg Lake Trail	North of Going-to-the-Sun Rd	Leads to one of the most impressive glacial lakes in the Rockies	Easy-moderate
Quartz Lakes Loop	North of Going-to-the-Sun Rd	Rare North Fork loop trail in one of Glacier's most remote corners	Moderate
Swiftcurrent Pass Trail	North of Going-to-the-Sun Rd	Pleasant valley ramble followed by sharp climb to the Continental Divide	Moderate-difficult
Dawson-Pitamakin Loop	South of Going-to-the-sun Rd	A lengthy but rewarding hike around the true 'Crown of the Continent'	Difficult

Wildlife Watching *Great for Families* *Waterfall* *Restrooms* *Drinking Water* *Public Transport to Trailhead*

Biking

While parks authorities have cracked down on a number of unauthorized bike trails in recent years, there are still plenty of routes open to mountain bikers in Banff, Lake Louise, Kananaskis and Jasper. Waterton Lakes also has a small selection of routes, but mountain biking is banned on all trails in Glacier.

There are also dedicated bike parks at the Canmore Nordic Centre (p116) and the Kicking Horse Mountain Resort (p133) in Golden, which has its own cyclist-friendly gondola and a huge network of mountain trails.

Road riding is most popular along the Bow Valley Parkway, Minnewanka Loop and the Icefields Parkway, but you won't get away without tackling a few hills.

Preparation, Equipment & Safety

» Rent bikes and equipment in Banff, Jasper, Waterton, Kananaskis, Canmore and Golden.

» Always wear a helmet, take a puncture repair kit and/or spare inner tubes, and a basic trail tool kit including hex keys, screwdrivers and chain tool.

» Many rental companies offer shuttle services to trailheads or guided trips along classic routes in the parks.

DURATION	ROUND-TRIP DISTANCE	ELEVATION CHANGE	FEATURES	FACILITIES	PAGE
4hr	11.5km (7 miles)	90m (300ft)			p188
2hr	5km (3.2 miles)	150m (494ft)			p187
2½hr	6.4km (4 miles)	145m (475ft)			p187
7½hr	18.7km (11.6 miles)	255m (830ft)			p189
6hr	20.5km (12.8 miles)	509m (1670ft)			p190
2 days	32km (20 miles)	930m (3000ft)			p194
2-3 days	46km (28.8 miles)	1280m (4200ft)			p195
6hr	17.3km (10.8 miles)	1318m (4325ft)			p190
1hr	4km (2.5 miles)	Negligible			p191
5½hr	14.5km (9 miles)	370m (1190ft)			p191
7hr	20.5km (12.8 miles)	765m (2470ft)			p193
6hr	12km (7.6 miles)	650m (2100ft)			p192
8hr	30km (18.8 miles)	910m (2935ft)			p191

Ranger Station · *Backcountry Campsite* · *Picnic Sites* · *Grocery Store Nearby* · *Restaurant Nearby*

» Trail conditions vary widely, from flat, paved trails to technical singletracks with hazards such as branches, rocks and knotted roots. Do your research before you set out.

» Bikers are particularly prone to surprise bear encounters due to the speed and silence with which they travel. Make plenty of noise, slow down in dense forests, and take extra care near rivers and on windy days.

Fishing

With hundreds of waterways and lakes open for angling, the mountain parks are unsurprisingly a paradise for aspiring anglers. Arctic grayling, rainbow trout, brown trout, brook trout, lake trout, northern pike, mountain whitefish and lake whitefish are all abundant, although some species (such as bull trout, cutthroat trout and kokanee salmon) have suffered a major decline in recent years and are protected by law.

The most popular angling areas include the Bow River and Lake Minnewanka in Banff; Maligne Lake, Pyramid Lake and Princess Lakes in Jasper; and Lake McDonald and St Mary Lake in Glacier.

Rules, Regulations & Seasons

To fish anywhere in Banff and Jasper, you will need to buy a fishing permit, available from park visitor centers. The free *Fishing*

HIKING IN WATERTON LAKES NATIONAL PARK

NAME	REGION	DESCRIPTION	DIFFICULTY
Carthew-Alderson Trail	Cameron Lake	Memorable hike offers beautiful scenery and sweeping views	Moderate
Rowe Lakes	Waterton townsite	A foray to the cusp of Waterton's backcountry that'll have you returning for more	Easy-moderate
Tamarack Trail	Waterton townsite	Waterton's big backcountry adventure through glacial moraines and kaleidoscopic wildflower displays	Moderate-difficult
Crypt Lake Trail	Waterton townsite	Involves tunnel crawling and a cable-assisted walk along sheer cliffs	Difficult

Wildlife Watching *Fishing* *Restrooms* *Drinking Water* *Public Transport to Trailhead* *Ranger Station*

Regulations Summary will be included with your permit, detailing angling seasons, catch limits and other useful information. There's also a handy pictorial key for helping to identify your fish: it's important to be sure about your catch, as you'll be fined if you're caught in possession of one of the protected species by park authorities. If in doubt, catch-and-release is the way to go.

No fishing permit is required across the border in Glacier. Casting on the park's boundaries may require a Montana state fishing license, and waters on Blackfeet Indian Reservation land (such as part of Lower Two Medicine Lake) require permits from the reservation.

» The season in Canada generally runs from June to September, with a slightly longer season in Glacier.

» It's illegal to fish with natural bait, chemical attractants or lead tackle.

» You cannot have more than one line in the water at a time and may not fish from two hours after sunset to one hour before sunrise.

» Some waters are catch-and-release zones only, while most others have catch limits for particular species.

» Consider employing a local guide, who can provide gear and tackle, help you find the choicest waters and make sure you stay within the rules.

Horseback Riding

People have been taking pack trips around these parts since the days of the earliest settlers, and the horseback tradition remains strong to this day. Many trails in Banff, Jasper and Glacier are open to horseback riders as well as hikers, and horses are also welcome at many backcountry campgrounds and lodges, so there's plenty of opportunity for day trips as well as more adventurous backcountry expeditions.

Most people choose to saddle up with a local guiding company, but it's possible to bring along your own steed. See p49 for information on horse trails and equestrian facilities. If you're trotting off into the Canadian backcountry, you'll need a grazing permit in addition to your wilderness pass. Comprehensive listings of pack-trip companies and outfitters are available from:

Alberta Outfitters Association (☎403-722-2692; www.albertaoutfitters.com)

Montana Outfitters & Guides Association (☎406-449-3578; www.montanaoutfitters.org)

White-Water Rafting & Float Trips

The Rockies have some of the best white water in Canada. Rapids systems are graded into six degrees of difficulty, ranging from I (easy) to VI (near-impossible): most local activity companies tackle rapids rated between I and III. Equipment, safety gear and trained guides are all supplied, and though it can be pretty white-knuckle at times, in general white-water rafting is safe – although you'll obviously need to be able to swim, and be prepared to get very wet.

More sedate float trips on rivers are ideal for families and often provide a good way of spotting water birds and wildlife. The raft-

DURATION	ROUND-TRIP DISTANCE	ELEVATION CHANGE	FEATURES	FACILITIES	PAGE
6hr	19km (11.8 miles)	610m (1968ft)			p213
3hr	8km (5 miles)	250m (820ft)			p212
2 days	31.6km (19.6 miles)	1460m (4700ft)			p215
6hr	17.2km (10.3 miles)	710m (2329ft)			p214

Backcountry Campsite

ing season is May through September, with highest river levels (and therefore the most rapids) in spring.

The best areas for rafting are along the Kicking Horse and Kananaskis Rivers; Canmore and Golden both have plenty of operators who run trips. Jasper also has its own network of white-water rivers, while in Glacier, the Middle and North Forks of the Flathead River offer the best stretches of white-water for rafting.

Canoeing & Kayaking

First Nations people have been using canoes for thousands of years (an example followed by the early European settlers and 'voyageurs'), and canoeing and kayaking are still the best ways to get out on the water.

Nonmotorized boats (including canoes, dinghies and kayaks) are allowed on nearly all waterways in the Canadian parks, but motorboats are banned except on Lake Minnewanka. The rules are less strict in Glacier, with most waterways open to boats.

» Canoes and kayaks are readily available for hire at many lakes; expect to pay around C$30 to C$40 per hour, including life jackets, paddles and boat hire.

» Banff's best places for canoeing are Lake Louise, Moraine Lake, Bow River and Vermilion Lakes. Cruises are offered on Lake Minnewanka. You can also paddle on Emerald Lake in Yoho.

» In Jasper, Maligne Lake offers superb canoeing and commentated cruises to Spirit Island. Pyramid Lake is another good spot.

» In Glacier, hire boats and cruises are offered on Lake McDonald, St Mary, Swiftcurrent Lake and Josephine Lake.

» In Waterton, Cameron Lake is the best lake for sailing, with rowboats, kayaks and canoes for rent.

Wildlife Watching

With a rich and varied animal population ranging from bighorn sheep to wolverines, elk and grizzly bears, you should have plenty of opportunities to glimpse the parks' wilder residents. As always, the best times for wildlife watching are dawn and dusk. You'll have more luck away from major roads, especially around the more remote areas of Jasper and Glacier, but even in Banff you're bound to cross paths with at least a few wild animals.

In general, wildlife tends to go wherever humans don't, so the quieter areas of Kananaskis and Kootenay are likewise excellent places for wildlife seekers. Kananaskis is also famous for the annual migration of around 6000 golden eagles, which takes place through the valley every fall.

Wild animals can be highly unpredictable, and often perceive humans as a threat, so be careful not to get too close (even seemingly harmless animals such as elk can be dangerous, especially during calving season). A good pair of binoculars or a telephoto lens will help you see the show from a distance.

Rock Climbing & Mountaineering

With so many peaks and rock faces to tackle, Banff and Jasper are both well-known destinations for rock climbers, but the mountainous terrain is generally challenging and technical and mostly more suited to experienced alpinists than novices.

With many mountains that top out above 3050m (10,000ft), frequent rockslides and notoriously changeable weather conditions, it's not a place to be taken lightly – rookie climbers should definitely take an organized tour and even experienced climbers should consider employing the services of a local mountain guide.

The **Alpine Club of Canada** (www.alpineclubofcanada.ca) and the **Association of Canadian Mountain Guides** (www.acmg.ca), both based in Canmore, provide general advice on climbing in the Rockies and can help put you in touch with local mountain guides.

Skiing & Snowboarding

While perhaps not quite on a par with Whistler, Banff and Jasper have a growing reputation for winter sports – and with more than five months of snow every year, and, of course, no shortage of mountains, it's hardly surprising.

Banff & Jasper

The three main resorts in Banff are Mt Norquay, Lake Louise and Sunshine Village, collectively known as the **Big Three** (www.skibig3.com). Lift passes covering all three resorts are available, or you can buy individual resort passes if you only have a limited time in the mountains.

In Jasper, the main skiing center is **Marmot Basin** (www.skimarmot.com), along the Icefields Parkway. The slopes and facilities are generally a little quieter than in Banff, so Marmot makes a good destination if this is your first time on the snow.

The facilities at all four resorts are excellent, with ski and snowboarding schools, childcare facilities, terrain parks and halfpipes for snowboarders, as well as public transportation to the slopes and lots of groomed and powder runs.

The bars and restaurants in the townsites of Banff and Jasper are also within easy reach, so you'll have plenty to keep you busy once your day on the snow is over.

Other Resorts

Though less well-known than Banff and Jasper, there are a couple of other resorts that are just a short drive away. **Nakiska** (www.nakiska.com) in Kananaskis Country, about an hour's drive south of Canmore, was originally developed for the 1988 Winter Olympics, and still has a good reputation among skiers and snowboarders. It's usually a lot quieter than Banff, but has fewer runs and simpler facilities. Shuttle buses run throughout the ski season from Banff and Canmore. Its sister resort at Fortress Mountain remains closed for the foreseeable future.

The **Kicking Horse Mountain Resort** (www.kickinghorseresort.com), near Golden, is the Rocky Mountains' newest ski resort (and one of the only ones to be granted development permission in the last 20 years). With more than 1120 skiable hectares, over 120 runs and a vertical drop of 1260m (4133ft), it's also fast becoming one of the best.

TOP SPOTS FOR WILDLIFE

Experienced wildlife watchers know that seeing animals in their natural habitat requires planning, preparation, patience – and plenty of luck. More often than not, it simply comes down to being in the right place at the right time of day. Here are some of the key areas to try, along with the animals you're most likely to see:

- **Vermilion Lakes, Banff** Elk
- **Lake Minnewanka, Banff** Bighorn sheep, mountain goats, pika, ground squirrels
- **Bow Valley Parkway, Banff** Elk, moose, occasionally black bears
- **Smith–Dorrien Highway, Kananaskis** Mountain goats, bighorn sheep
- **Lake Louise Gondola, Banff** Grizzly bears on the avalanche slopes
- **Emerald Lake Area, Yoho** Moose, black and grizzly bears
- **Icefields Parkway, Jasper** Elk, moose, marmots, bighorn sheep
- **Maligne Lake Road, Jasper** Moose, mountain goats, occasionally wolves
- **Tonquin Valley, Jasper** Moose, bighorn sheep, marmots, some bears
- **Many Glacier, Glacier** Mountain goats, black and grizzly bears
- **Two Medicine Valley, Glacier** Grizzly bears

EXTREME PURSUITS

Looking for some extra adrenaline? No problem – the mountain parks have plenty of ways to get your blood pumping.

» Live out your Jack London fantasies on a **dogsledding expedition** (p118)

» Plumb the depths of the **Rat's Nest** (p118) cave system

» Challenge the rapids on the **Kicking Horse** and **Kananaskis Rivers** (p97)

» Slide down the mountain on an inflatable **snowtube** (p99)

» Soar through the skies on a **heli-hiking** (p98) expedition

» Clamber aboard a snowcat for some **cat-skiing** (p135)

» Scramble around the peaks of **Mt Edith Cavell** (p163) or **Canmore** (p98)

» Hurtle at over 50km/h (30mph) on a death-defying **zip-line** (p133)

Whitefish Mountain Resort (www.skiwhitefish.com), 11km (7 miles) south of Whitefish, is another prime ski destination, with the excellent Fishbowl terrain park, a vertical drop of 717m (2353ft) and 93 marked trails spread over a massive 1215 hectares (3000 acres). Look out for the annual Furniture Race (p24) down the slopes of Big Mountain, which really has to be seen to be believed.

Cross-Country Skiing

While most skiers choose to bomb down the mountainside, an increasing number of people are taking to the more sedate form of cross-country skiing (known in Europe as telemarking) as a way of experiencing the parks in their wintry glory.

Cross-country skiers have the chance to explore the empty backcountry deep into midwinter; many trails around Banff, Lake Louise and Jasper are specifically kept open for use by cross-country skiers from December through March, with a more limited range of trails also open in Glacier, Waterton, Kananaskis and Yoho.

» Park authorities supply trail maps of open routes, and you'll find lessons and equipment rental from most outdoor activity operators and some ski schools.

» Trails aren't always signposted and can be difficult to make out under heavy snow cover. Check trail conditions before you set out.

» Cross-country skiers need to be alert to the dangers of avalanches, especially in remote areas.

» Carry with you emergency supplies, an avalanche beacon, a full repair kit, a compass and a detailed topographical map on any cross-country skiing trip.

Snowshoeing

Snowshoeing has been practiced by Aboriginal people in the Rockies for hundreds of years, and it's one of the easiest and most enjoyable ways to explore the winter wilderness (although walking around with two glorified tennis rackets strapped to your feet certainly takes some getting used to).

Many of the trails kept open for cross-country skiers also have parallel tracks for snowshoers, and there are other routes to explore around the townsites in Jasper, Banff and Glacier. As always, parks staff can help with route maps and condition reports for current trails.

Snowshoes can be hired from outdoor equipment stores and activity providers in Banff, Jasper and Glacier.

Travel with Children

Best Activities for Kids

Hiking
Hitting the trails is the best way to appreciate the national parks.

Canmore Nordic Centre
Discover 60km (37 miles) of trails at this purpose-built bike park.

Snocoach Tour
Trundle up the Athabasca Glacier in an all-terrain Snocoach.

Canoeing on Moraine Lake
Paddle across the waters of this idyllic mountain lake.

Hot Springs
Kids will love the hot springs in Banff, Jasper and Radium.

Gondola Rides
Zip up the mountainside in style in Banff, Jasper and Lake Louise.

Horseback Riding
Trot through the Rockies and tuck into a trailside cookout.

Wildlife Watching
From marmots to moose, the Rockies are a paradise for wildlife spotters.

White-water Rafting
Get wet and wild on the Bow and Kicking Horse Rivers.

Banff, Jasper & Glacier for Kids

Sights & Attractions

The national parks are fantastic places to explore as a family. Seeing nature through your kids' eyes will give you a whole new perspective on the experience. It'll certainly take some extra planning, but with a bit of pre-trip research you'll find hundreds of family-friendly destinations and activities scattered around the parks – from ranger programs and nature walks to trailside cookouts around an open fire.

Inevitably, it's the outdoor pursuits that are going to be the real attraction. Wildlife walks, white-water rafting, canoeing and horseback riding are all popular family pastimes, and most activity providers are well set up for dealing with kids. Throughout this book, hotels, sights and activities that we think are particularly child-friendly are marked with the icon.

Children qualify for discounted entry to nearly all sights (generally around half-price for ages five to 15, while under-fives often go free). Family tickets, which usually include entry for two adults and two children, are also available for many tours and sights.

Hiking

Hiking is one of the best all-round family activities. Many of the trails around the parks

TOP HIKES FOR KIDS

» Johnston Canyon (p78)

» Sundance Canyon (p75)

» Consolation Lakes (p81)

» Garden Path Trail (p79)

» Mary Schäffer Loop (p155)

» Moose Lake Loop (p155)

» Crypt Lake Trail (p214)

» Avalanche Lake Trail (p187)

» Swiftcurrent Lake Nature Trail (p191)

are well maintained and easily within the scope of active kids. They'll probably even be capable of tackling some of the shorter overnight hikes, and staying out in the backcountry and cooking dinner over an open campfire is an experience they'll likely never forget.

Trails that combine the sights are usually more fun for inquiring young minds, so try to find walks that take in a mix of forest, mountain, river and canyon, or those that wind their way through well-known wildlife habitats. Several trails have interpretive panels to help you understand the geographical features, flora and fauna.

If the kids are interested in nature, it might be a good idea to join an organized hike. Many local guides are accredited by the Mountain Parks Heritage Interpretation Association (MPHIA) and can help children really engage with the natural world they're walking through. The main tour operators in Banff run morning and evening wildlife tours on which you'll have a good chance of spotting elk, moose, bighorn sheep and other animals.

Remember to take along all the necessary supplies, including plenty of water, hats, sun lotion, blister cream and, most importantly, something nice to eat once you reach the end of the trail. Good-quality waterproofs will also come in handy in case of sudden rainstorms.

Biking

Biking is another great activity for kids. Most bike-rental companies offer children's bikes, child helmets and protective pads, as well as child chariots and 'tag-a-longs' for younger children.

One of the best areas for biking is at the Canmore Nordic Centre (p116), which has a huge system of trails catering for all ages and abilities. The Kicking Horse Mountain Resort (p133) is also great for mountain biking in summer, and there are many trails around the townsites in Banff and Jasper that are ideal for families.

Canoeing & Rafting

Canoeing is one of the most enjoyable ways to explore the parks' spectacular lakes: canoes are readily available for hire on Lake Louise, Moraine Lake, Emerald Lake and many others throughout the summer months. For more thrills, white-water rafting on the Kicking Horse and Bow Rivers is guaranteed to get big smiles – but if you want to try out the sport in a more sedate way, family-friendly 'float trips' are offered on many rivers. All canoeing and rafting companies provide suitable boats for kids, or spaces in adult boats, along with child-sized life vests.

If you prefer to let someone else do the steering, there are scenic boat cruises on Lake Minnewanka, Maligne Lake and several of Jasper's lakes.

Horseback Riding

Seeing the parks from the saddle is another exhilarating way for kids to explore. Most horse-trip companies provide small ponies and child-friendly saddles, and cater for complete novices as well as experienced riders.

Holiday on Horseback (☎403-762-4551; www.horseback.com) has lots of easy rides in Banff and also offers a great evening trail cookout (complete with BBQ steak and homemade baked beans).

You can usually visit the horses at Spray River Corral and the Warner stables (p98), near the Cave and Basin in Banff; phone ahead to check the stables are open for visitors.

Jasper also has plenty of potential for horseback riding, with popular day trails around Lake Annette and Lake Patricia, and longer trips into Tonquin Valley and Maligne Pass. For full details, see p163.

Skiing, Snowboarding & Other Winter Activities

In winter, skiing and snowboarding are the main outdoor pastimes. All of the ski resorts in Banff, Jasper and Kananaskis, as well as Whitefish Mountain Resort near Glacier,

RAINY-DAY ACTIVITIES

Bad weather can put a dent in even the best-laid plans, so here are a few ideas on what to do when the sun won't play ball.

Banff Park Museum Get spooked out by all the stuffed beasties.

Lux Cinema in Banff Top place for catching the latest flicks.

Jasper Aquatic Center Get wet in Jasper's municipal pool.

Ice-skating Public skating sessions are offered at the Fenlands (otherwise known as the Banff Recreation Centre).

Banff Skatepark Plenty of bowls, rails and ramps to grind.

Hot Springs in Banff, Jasper and Radium You're already wet, so why mind the rain?

Museum of the Plains Indian Learn about First Nations Culture at this interesting museum on the Blackfeet Indian Reservation.

have runs that are specially tailored for younger users. Child-size skis, snowboards, goggles and gear are all available for hire.

Most resorts offer ski lessons and snowboard schools, as well as day-care and babysitting services. For more info, the website for Banff's **Big Three** (www.skibig3.com) ski resorts will give you some idea of what's on offer.

Cross-country skiing and snowshoeing are both really fun, unusual ways to explore the winter landscape: Jasper's Tonquin Valley and the Lake Louise area are both good places to start. Ice-skating is sometimes possible on some of the park's lakes in winter, depending on seasonal temperatures.

Ranger Programs

Glacier operates the National Parks Service's excellent **Junior Ranger Program** (www.nps.gov/learn/juniorranger.htm), in which kids pick up a free ranger booklet from park visitor centers. The booklet contains activities, questionnaires, quizzes and games to complete during their stay; they'll earn a Junior Ranger badge and a certificate when the book is completed.

There's no age limit for the program – it's not entirely unknown for parents to get carried away and complete a book of their own in pursuit of that all-important ranger's badge. Before you even set out for the national park, kids can sign up to become a 'WebRanger' at www.nps.gov/webrangers, where there are plenty of online games, puzzles and activities to pique their interest.

In Banff and Jasper, **Junior Naturalist Walks** are run in summer by the Friends organizations. These short events usually last for a couple of hours and combine games and outdoor activities with nature talks and short trails.

Friends of Banff also conducts a regular nature walk around Vermilion Lakes, and rents out 'Discovery Packs,' which include binoculars, field wildlife guides, a bird checklist and a map of Banff. Contact **Friends of Banff** (☎403-762-8918; www.friendsofbanff.com) and **Friends of Jasper** (☎780-852-4767; www.friendsofjasper.com) for more information.

Parks Canada also provides regular educational programs at main campgrounds in Banff, Jasper, Waterton and Kootenay, with slide shows, talks, films and activities exploring many aspects of the parks, including wildlife, natural history and geology. In West Glacier, the National Park Visitor Center holds regular ranger talks and educational slideshows throughout summer, and the Discovery Cabin in Apgar Village holds Junior Ranger programs in July and August.

Children's Highlights

Banff & Around

» **Banff Gondola** Ride the sky-topping cable car to the top of Sulphur Mountain.

» **Bow River** Rafting and kayaking potential aplenty.

» **Lake Louise** Hike up for afternoon tea at the Lake Agnes Tea House.

» **Rat's Nest Cave** This cave system near Canmore has over 65km (40 miles) of underground tunnels to explore.

» **Boo the Grizzly Bear** The Rocky Mountains' only captive grizzly bear lives at the Kicking Horse Mountain Resort, near Golden.

» **Rocky Mountain Buffalo Ranch** Say hello to native buffalo at this working ranch near Golden.

» **Cows Ice Cream** Banff Ave is the only place where you can buy a Cows cone outside of Prince Edward Island.

Jasper

» **Maligne Lake** Jump aboard a cruise boat to Spirit Island.

» **Jasper Tramway** More gravity-defying cable cars.

» **Columbia Icefield Centre** Learn all about North America's largest icefield.

» **Jasper Town Trails** Hike or pedal the scenic trails around Jasper's townsite.

» **Miette Hot Springs** Splash around in geothermaly heated waters.

Glacier & Waterton

» **Going-to-the-Sun Road** Ride this spectacular road in a vintage 'jammer' bus.

» **Native American Speaks** Watch First Nations culture in action at the St Mary Visitor Center.

» **Many Glacier Valley** Top spot for wildlife and glacier-spotting.

Planning

Accommodations

Most hotels will happily accept kids, and many places allow children under a certain age to stay in their parents' room for no extra charge (the exact age varies according to the hotel, but it's usually under 12, 15 or 16). Extra pull-out beds are often available; otherwise ask for a triple-bed or family room.

» Consider staying in a hotel that has facilities such as games rooms, saunas and swimming pools to fend off boredom once the day's activities are done.

» Hostels can be great for families – booking out a whole dorm is usually far cheaper than an equivalent hotel room, and the big HI hostel in Banff has private self-catering cabins that are ideal for families.

» Many cabin complexes and some hotels have self-catering suites with fully equipped kitchens that are ideal for families.

» Larger campgrounds such as Tunnel Mountain, Johnston Canyon and Lake Louise in Banff, or Whistlers or Wapiti in Jasper host regular interpretive programs and activity sessions for children.

Dining

Most restaurants in the parks are fairly kid-friendly, with the exception of some of the more upmarket establishments. Kids' menus are widespread, especially in hotels and the main town restaurants, and staff are usually pretty understanding about kids sharing their parents' main meals.

A few restaurants even have small play areas kitted out with toys, coloring books

WHAT TO PACK

For Babies & Toddlers

☐ Back sling or child-carrier rucksack – perfect for hiking the trails and keeping your hands free.

☐ Portable changing mat, plus hand-wash gel, disinfectant, talc and other essentials – as trail toilets are very basic.

☐ Child's car seat – to avoid the extra expense and hassle of arranging a car seat from your rental company.

☐ Stroller and rain-cover – the cover is essential in case of bad weather.

For Five to 12 Year Olds

☐ Rain gear – a good raincoat and plenty of warm layers will be indispensable.

☐ Proper footwear – a pair of boots (or at the very least decent trail shoes) are important to avoid sprained ankles and to keep feet dry. Sneakers are not a good idea.

☐ Nature guides – essential for helping to identify wildflowers, birds and animals on the trails.

☐ Binoculars – for long-distance wildlife watching.

☐ First-aid kit – including disinfectant, antibiotic cream, Band-Aids, blister cream and moleskin patches for hot spots in boots.

☐ Spare batteries – for torches, games etc.

and activities where the kids can entertain themselves until the meals turn up.

Driving

Driving distances from the airports (and in the parks themselves) can be long. While the scenery is impressive, even mountains can get a little tiresome: try to break up the journey with regular stops, and combine long trips with other activities such as short hikes and sightseeing excursions.

» In Canada and the US, it's a legal requirement that children under six and weighing less than 40lb (18kg) – 60lb (27kg) in the US – are secured in a properly fitted child-safety seat.

» Drivers are responsible for ensuring that other passengers are safely secured and wearing seat belts. Safety seats for toddlers and children are available from all the major rental companies, but you'll incur an extra charge (usually around C$6 to C$10 per day). You'll need to reserve them at the time of booking.

Travel with Pets

Best Spots for Dogs

Sundance Trail, Banff
A flat, paved trail near Banff Town that's shared with walkers, cyclists and horseback riders.

Marsh Loop, Banff
This pleasant dirt trail is usually peaceful and offers lovely views of the Bow River.

Lake Minnewanka, Banff
The lakeshore makes a perfect place for a family picnic.

Johnson Lake, Banff
A quiet lakeside trail that's often shared with summer sunbathers.

Mary Schäffer Loop, Jasper
Part-wooded walk on the eastern shoreline of Maligne Lake.

Lake Annette, Jasper
You can follow a paved trail around Lake Annette, but be on the lookout for elk and deer.

Moose Lake Loop, Jasper
Offers a quick escape from the Maligne Lake crowds.

Rules & Regulations

» In Banff and Jasper, dogs are allowed on most trails and at most campgrounds (both front and backcountry), but you're required to keep them securely leashed at all times.

» In Glacier, dogs are banned from *all* park trails, but are allowed in drive-in campgrounds, along park roads open to vehicles and in most picnic areas.

» You are required by law to clean up after your dog, so remember to bring along a couple of plastic bags or a pooper-scooper.

» Bring along all the necessary supplies, including food, and any medications, as they'll be almost impossible to buy outside the townsites.

» Guide and service dogs should wear reflective vests to indicate their working status.

Border Crossings

For many people, visiting the national parks is very much a family affair and often that doesn't just mean mom, pop and the kids. Plenty of people also decide to bring their pets along on their park adventure, but you definitely need to be prepared for the added complications that come with having your furry companion in tow.

The same rules and regulations apply to dogs of all sizes, regardless of whether they're a dachshund or a Doberman. If you're crossing the US–Canada border, you may be asked for a pet-health certificate and/or rabies certificate issued by an accredited veterinarian.

For exact rules, consult the relevant government agency.

Canadian Food Inspection Agency (http://www.inspection.gc.ca/english/anima/imp/petani/petanie.shtml)

US Department of Agriculture (http://www.aphis.usda.gov/animal_welfare/pet_travel/pet_travel.shtml)

Health & Safety

In addition to the official rules, it's also worth considering how dogs will be perceived by any wild animals you might meet out on the trail. To elk, caribou and moose, dogs will probably be perceived as a threat, while to other beasties (such as cougar and bears) they might resemble prey. Either way, bringing your dog along the trail puts you at increased risk in the event of an animal encounter – previously placid bears have been known to become enraged due to the noise of a barking dog.

» Ticks are a common parasite in the Rockies, especially in spring. Check your dog's coat carefully for ticks after any long walk, and remove any you find. For more info, see p268.

» Make sure you keep your dog on a leash at all times, and discourage them from eating berries, fungi or other unknown plants.

» Urinating near streams and water sources is a major cause of giardia and other water-borne parasites, so try to discourage your dog from doing so.

Choosing Accommodations

It's important to think about two things before you bring along your pet to the parks: what they'll do while you're out on the trail or exploring the sights, and where they'll stay overnight. Leaving your dog leashed up for hours on end isn't much of a holiday for them – so it's best to decide beforehand what kind of trip you're planning on, and how bringing a pet will fit into those plans.

Relatively few hotels in Banff and Jasper accept dogs; those that do will probably charge an extra fee on top of the standard room rate. Most campsites accept dogs, but unless they're very obedient, they should always be securely tethered. In Glacier, no hotels accept pets. Campsites will accept them (as long as they're kept on a lead).

Throughout this book we have marked particularly pet-friendly places with a 🐾 icon. There's also a useful online directory of animal-friendly accommodations in Canada at **Pet Friendly** (www.petfriendly.ca).

Veterinarians

Veterinary services are nonexistent outside the main town areas.

Alberta Veterinary Medical Association (www.avma.ab.ca) Online listings of veterinary services.

Banff Veterinary Services (☎403-762-3611; petcare@canmorevet.com; 140 Hawk Ave, Banff)

Bow River Veterinary Centre (☎403-678-9595; 1510 Railway Ave, Canmore)

Canmore Veterinary Hospital (☎403-678-4425; 502 Bow Valley Trail, Canmore)

Jasper Veterinary Clinic (☎780-852-5551; jaspervetclinic@telus.net; 6 Stan Wright Dr, Jasper)

Pincher Creek Veterinary Clinic (☎403-627-3900; 1124 Waterton Ave, Pincher Creek)

Whitefish Animal Hospital (☎406-862-3178; www.whitefishanimalhospital.com; 245 W 2nd St, Whitefish)

Kennels

The two veterinary services in Canmore have limited boarding facilities for pets.

Three Dog Ranch (☎406-862-3913; www.threedogranchmontana.com; 5395 Hwy 93, Whitefish) Grooming, day and overnight care, and pet store 3.3km (2 miles) south of Whitefish, Montana.

Veronica's Dog Grooming (☎403-762-3647; www.veronicasdoggrooming.com; 114 Eagle Cres, Banff) Dog and cat grooming and overnight stays.

Lost & Found

If you have lost or found an animal, contact the relevant authorities as soon as possible.

Banff Animal Control (☎403-762-1218)

Canmore Animal Services (☎403-678-4244)

Jasper Animal Control (☎780-852-5514)

Royal Canadian Mountain Police (RCMP; ☎403-678-5516) For emergencies in Banff and Canmore outside business hours.

DOGGIE DOS & DON'TS

- ☐ Do keep dogs leashed at all times
- ☐ Do keep them quiet and under control in campgrounds
- ☐ Do check them regularly for ticks, fleas and other parasites
- ☐ Do bring extra water, food and supplies
- ☐ Don't let them eat berries and plants on the trail
- ☐ Don't let them run off into the undergrowth, especially in grassy meadows or wooded areas
- ☐ Don't leave them locked up in hot cars or RVs
- ☐ Don't let them bark at horses
- ☐ Don't assume everyone likes dogs

Horse Trails & Equestrian Facilities

Many trails in Banff, Jasper and Glacier are open to horses, but seasonal conditions such as mud, swollen rivers, snow cover and wildlife activity means this can change at short notice. Some areas are also permanently closed to horse use, and in the backcountry there are strict quotas to prevent overuse and to protect wilderness areas. Contact park authorities for the latest advice on which routes are and are not open to horses, or consult the websites detailed below.

If you just fancy a quick day ride, or you don't want the hassle of transporting your own horse to the park, contact one of the commercial horse guiding companies (see p38), some of which will let you bring your own animal on organized trips and provide stabling facilities.

For more information and advice, pick up the free *Horse User's Guide* from park offices, contact the local **warden's office** (☎Banff 403-762-1470, Jasper 780-852-6167), or consult the following websites:

Banff (www.pc.gc.ca/pn-np/ab/banff/activ/activ6a_e.aspx)

Jasper (www.pc.gc.ca/pn-np/ab/jasper/activ/activ6.aspx)

Glacier (www.nps.gov/glac/planyourvisit/privatestockuse.htm)

Permits & Corrals

» If you're trekking into the Canadian backcountry, you'll need a wilderness pass (C$9.80) as well as a grazing permit (C$1.90) for each night.

» In Glacier, backcountry permits are free, but advance reservations incur a levy of US$20.

» Most backcountry campgrounds in Canada accept horses, but some in Glacier are closed to horse use. Discuss your route and make advance reservations with park staff.

» In Banff, public corrals are available at Pipestone River, Mosquito Creek and 2km (1.2 miles) east of Saskatchewan Crossing along Hwy 11.

» In Jasper, there are corrals at the trailheads at Portal Creek, Poboktan, Beaver Creek, Maligne Pass, Whirlpool River, Nigel Creek, Dorothy Lake, Miette Lake and Miette Hot Springs.

» In Glacier the corrals are not for public use, though there is one small exception. The Many Glacier corral can be used as an overnight stop for riders undertaking the Continental Divide Trail.

» Depending on the corral, maximum stays are usually between 48 and 72 hours.

regions at a glance

Which national park you visit really depends on two things: what you want to see and how much time you have to spare. The vast majority of visitors kick off their stay in Banff, thanks to its comprehensive facilities, plentiful restaurants and family-friendly activities, not to mention easy access to wonderful trails.

If you have a bit more time for your trip, Jasper is the next natural stop, particularly if you're interested in wildlife watching and backcountry hiking. Glacier receives far fewer visitors than the other two parks, so it's the best option if you prefer the trails to be quiet and the crowds to be few and far between.

Banff

Day Hikes ✓✓✓
Mountains ✓✓✓
Snow Sports ✓✓

Scenic Wonders
There's a good reason that Banff is Canada's most popular national park – it's home to some of the most fabulous mountain scenery in the Rocky Mountains. Gleaming glaciers, snow-dusted peaks, roaring rivers: Banff's got it all.

Landmark Lakes
Banff's lakes are impossible to miss, reflecting a myriad of colors under ever-changing skies, from vivid turquoises to emerald greens and fiery oranges. Lake Louise and Moraine Lake draw the biggest crowds, but there are many more to discover.

Hot Springs
Banff is synonymous with its geothermal springs. They were the park's main attraction for early visitors, and they're still a highlight. Sit back in the naturally heated hot pools and drink in the wraparound mountain views.

p54

Jasper

Day Hikes ✓✓✓
Wildlife ✓✓✓
Lakes ✓✓

Backcountry Hiking

If it's walking in the wilderness you're after, Jasper boasts some of the best backcountry hikes in North America. The Skyline Trail and the Tonquin Valley are two of the best-known trails, but there are tons more to explore.

Dramatic Drives

The stretch of Hwy 1 between Banff and Glacier, colloquially known as the Icefields Parkway, is often referred to as the world's most spectacular road. It's certainly one you won't forget in a hurry: glimpse glaciers, lakes, mountains and wildlife without ever leaving your automobile.

Biking & Horseback Riding

Mountain bikers rave about Jasper's challenging singletracks, and they're ideal if you prefer to see your scenery from the saddle. A popular trail network leads out directly from the townsite, and is also open to hikers and horseback riders.

p137

Glacier

Day Hikes ✓✓
Wildlife ✓✓✓
Glaciers ✓✓✓

Glaciers

For many people, the main reason for visiting Glacier is the chance to see its famous icefields. But you'd better be quick – experts think that they could have all disappeared within a matter of decades due to climate change.

Wildlife Watching

If you're keen on wildlife, you're in for a treat in Glacier. The combination of relatively few visitors and plenty of remote backcountry means that it's one of the best parks for spotting wild animals, including bighorn sheep, mountain goats and a healthy population of grizzly bears.

Boating

Six historic boats ply five different lakes in Glacier, but if you prefer to explore under your own steam, there's plenty of opportunity for kayaking and canoeing too.

p176

Every listing is recommended by our authors, and their favourite places are listed first

Look out for these icons:

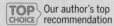

TOP CHOICE Our author's top recommendation

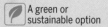

A green or sustainable option

FREE No payment required

BANFF NATIONAL PARK....54

See the Index for a full list of destinations covered in this book.

On the Road

Banff National Park

Includes »

Best Hikes

» C-Level Cirque (p77)
» Plain of Six Glaciers (p82)
» Larch Valley (p84)
» Parker Ridge (p89)

Best Places to Stay

» Blackstone Mountain Lodge (p119)
» Num-Ti-Jah Lodge (p108)
» Skoki Lodge (p109)
» Fairmont Banff Springs (p102)

Why Go?

Ever since it was founded way back in 1883, Banff National Park has proved an irresistible draw for people looking to experience the wonders of the Canadian wilderness, and with some of the world's most mind-blowing mountain scenery right on its doorstep, it's not hard to see why. From the sapphire-blue waters of Lake Louise to the glittering glaciers of the Icefields Parkway, Banff is without doubt one of the jewels of the Canadian Rockies, a fact that was underlined when the park was declared a World Heritage site by Unesco in 1984. And while over 3 million visitors pass through the park gates every year, making it by far and away Canada's most popular national park, it's still easy to give the crowds the slip: just strap on your boots, hit the nearest trail and you'll soon find out what makes Banff such an unforgettable place.

When to Go

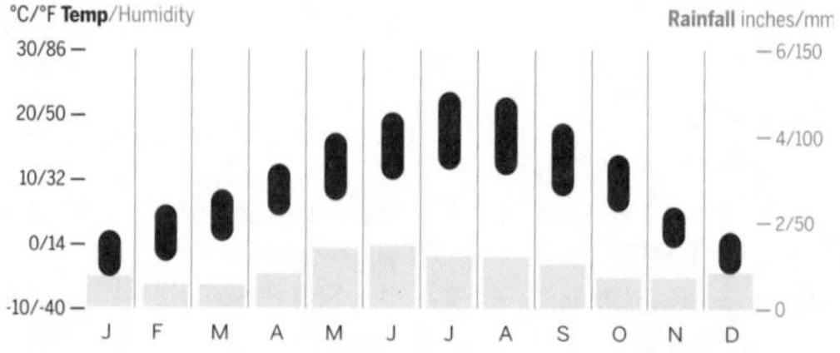

July Warm, settled weather makes this the prime month for hiking and sightseeing.

Late September The summer crowds die down and the forests are at their most colorful.

November The winter season begins with a bang at the lively Winterstart sports festival.

Entrances

There are four main road entrances into Banff National Park. All are open year-round, weather permitting. The main East Gate is on Trans-Canada Hwy 1, 7km (4.3 miles) west of Canmore, and has manned tollbooths where you can purchase park passes (they all accept cash, check and plastic). If you already have a pass, you can use the right-hand lane to avoid queuing at the tollbooths. The other park entrances are on Trans-Canada Hwy 1 eastbound from Yoho National Park; Hwy 93 eastbound from Kootenay National Park; and Hwy 93 southbound from the Icefields Parkway. If you're driving, remember to hang your pass from your rear-view mirror so that park staff know you've already paid. For details on current park pass prices, see p56.

DON'T MISS

For quick access to some of Banff's most spectacular sky-top scenery, there's nowhere better than **Sunshine Meadows**. During winter this high-altitude alpine area is home to one of Banff's most popular ski and snowboard resorts, but in summer the warming weather opens up a wonderful network of hiking trails blessed with some of the loveliest scenery anywhere in the national park. The best months to visit are July and August, when the high meadows are awash with vividly colored wildflowers. September is another good month to visit, as the trails are much quieter and the landscape takes on more autumnal hues. Whenever you visit, don't miss the truly unforgettable panorama from **Standish Ridge**, offering a 360-degree view across the Great Divide.

You can hike up to the trailheads from the Sunshine parking lot, but the easier option is to catch one of the frequent shuttle buses provided by White Mountain Adventures. For more information on the Sunshine Meadows area, see p66, and our detailed day hikes on p79.

When You Arrive

- Buy your park pass from the tollbooths at Banff's East Gate or a park visitor center.
- Check the latest trail reports at the Banff Information Centre or online at www.pc.gc.ca/apps/tcond/cond_e.asp?opark=100092
- Most campgrounds operate on a first-come, first-served system: arrive early at your chosen site (ideally well before check-out at 11am) for the best chance of securing a pitch.

PLANNING TIPS

Accommodations in Banff and Lake Louise are expensive and scarce in summer; so book early. To cut costs, avoid peak months or stay outside the park. Some Lake Louise trails require hikers to walk in groups of four in summer.

Fast Facts

- Area: 6641 sq km (2564 sq miles)
- Highest elevation: 3618m (11,870ft)
- Lowest elevation: 1310m (4297ft)

Reservations

Accommodations bookings are handled by the **Banff Tourism Bureau** (☎403-762-8421; www.banfflakelouise.com). For advance reservations at Tunnel Mountain and Lake Louise campgrounds, contact the **Parks Canada campground reservation service** (☎1-877-737-3783; www.pccamping.ca/parkscanada/en). For backcountry campground reservations and wilderness passes, contact the **Banff Information Centre** (☎403-762-1550; banff.vrc@pc.gc.ca).

Resources

- Parks Canada: www.pc.gc.ca/eng/pn-np/ab/banff/index.aspx
- Friends of Banff: www.friendsofbanff.com
- Banff Town website: www.banff.ca

Orientation

Banff National Park lies along the eastern edge of the Rocky Mountains and the Continental Divide, nestled on the border between the provinces of Alberta and British Columbia. Covering more than 6641 sq km (2564 sq miles), the park stretches from its southeastern border (west of Canmore) northwest to the border with Jasper National Park. Trans-Canada Hwy 1 travels through the center of the park along the banks of the Bow River and connects the major sights. The scenic Bow Valley Parkway runs parallel to the main highway between Banff and Lake Louise.

The southern section of the park is by far the busiest area, with the vast majority of visitor services concentrated around the park's two conurbations, Banff and Lake Louise. Banff is the main visitor hub, crammed to bursting with outdoors stores, shops, bars, hotels and restaurants (plus plenty of tourists). North of town is Lake Minnewanka, the park's largest lake, and Mt Norquay, a popular winter-sports destination. Sunshine Meadows, another popular skiing area, is to the west.

Lake Louise Village lies 58km (36 miles) northwest of Banff along Trans-Canada Hwy 1 and has limited services, including a gas station, a post office, a grocery store, a bookstore and an outdoors supplier, plus several large hotels. Lake Louise itself is about 8km (5 miles) west of the village, while Moraine Lake is 13km (8 miles) to the south. North of Lake Louise, the Icefields Parkway heads northwest, entering Jasper National Park after 122km (75.6 miles), beyond the high Sunwapta Pass.

Park Policies & Regulations

PARK PASSES

Anyone intending on stopping in Banff or driving along the Icefields Parkway will require a National Park Pass. If you're staying longer than a few days, the annual pass is by far the best value: it currently costs C$67.70 for an adult, C$33.30 for a

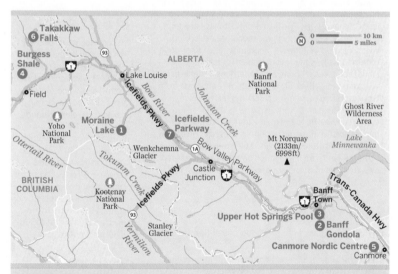

Banff Highlights

1. Guide a canoe across the crystal-blue surface of **Moraine Lake** (p68)
2. Catch a lift to the top of Sulphur Mountain on the **Banff Gondola** (p60)
3. Soak your bones in the hot mineral waters of the **Upper Hot Springs Pool** (p61)
4. Investigate some of the world's most ancient fossils on a guided hike to the **Burgess Shale** (see the boxed text, p125)
5. Pedal the network of off-road trails at the **Canmore Nordic Centre** (p116)
6. Marvel at the splash of **Takakkaw Falls** (p125)
7. Take an unforgettable road trip along the **Icefields Parkway** (p68)

child aged six to 16, C$57.90 for a senior aged over 65 or C$136.40 for a family (up to seven people traveling in one vehicle). The pass covers entry to all of Canada's national parks and remains valid for a year. Daily passes cost C$9.80/4.90/8.30/19.60 per adult/child/senior/family.

Passes can be purchased in advance at www.achatsparcs-parksstore.ca/en/purchase anationalpass or by calling the **Parks Canada reservation service** (☎1-800-748-7275), or at national park visitor centers.

For information on wilderness passes, see the boxed text, p91.

NATURE & WILDLIFE

It is illegal to remove any natural or cultural artifacts from the park, including rocks, stones, minerals and fossils as well as antlers, nests, bird eggs, plants, cones and wildflowers. Tree bark should also be left in situ to avoid the spread of the mountain pine beetle and other tree parasites. Pets must be kept on a leash at all times and are not allowed in backcountry shelters. Hunting and firearms are not permitted anywhere in the park. Most importantly, stay on the trails and avoid cutting across switchbacks, which causes unnecessary erosion and damages fragile plants.

Dangers & Annoyances

Banff is generally one of the safest of the national parks, but as always, you should take the necessary precautions to avoid unexpected wildlife encounters. Carry bear spray, make noise on the trail and hike in groups wherever possible. Pay attention to trail closures and group access restrictions, especially around the Lake Louise area in summer.

It's also important to take extra care on the road, as road and railway collisions are still the number one cause of death for wildlife in Banff.

If you're hiking and leaving your vehicle at a trailhead (especially overnight), make sure you don't leave any valuables on display.

SIGHTS

In terms of pure scenic splendor, few corners of Canada can hold a candle to Banff. Founded in 1887, Canada's oldest national park is home to some of the most majestic scenery anywhere in the Rockies: a big-sky panorama of craggy peaks, dense forests, roaring rivers, iridescent lakes and, of course, enough trails to fill a lifetime of hiking. Little wonder, then, with around 3 million visitors every year, it's by far and away Canada's most popular national park.

Banff Town

For many first-time visitors, the busy townsite of Banff comes as something of a surprise. Framed by lofty peaks and bisected by the Bow River, it's a bustling commercial and administrative hub for the wider national park. The town's history stretches back over a century, but you'll have to look hard to spot the heritage buildings among the shopping malls and purpose-built hotels: modern-day Banff is a long way from the ramshackle frontier town frequented by Bill Peyto, Jimmy Simpson, Mary Schäffer and other early pioneers.

While the town itself might not have much period character, Banff makes an excellent base for exploring the rest of the national park, with a wealth of restaurants, hotels and activities, and easy access to all of the main sights (including Lake Louise, around an hour's drive to the north). The town gets very busy in summer, though, so be prepared for traffic jams and pedestrian congestion.

Banff Avenue STREET

(Map p64) A little over a century ago, Banff Ave *was* Banff. While most of the other towns that sprang up along the Bow Valley in the 19th century were developed to exploit the area's natural resources (mainly coal, silver and other minerals), Banff was envisioned from the outset as a tourist center. Initially, the central street was home to little more than a handful of hotels, homesteads and trail outfitters, but the town slowly began to develop following the arrival of the Canadian Pacific Railway (CPR) in 1885 and the opening of the landmark Banff Springs Hotel on the banks of the Bow River in 1888.

Though much of the original architecture of Banff Ave is modern, it's still possible to make out a few of the historic buildings that would have greeted early visitors. The most obvious is the timber-framed Banff Park Museum, which has hardly changed since its construction in 1903. Further along the street, look out for the **Cascade Dance Hall** at No 120 (built in 1920), the original

Banff National Park

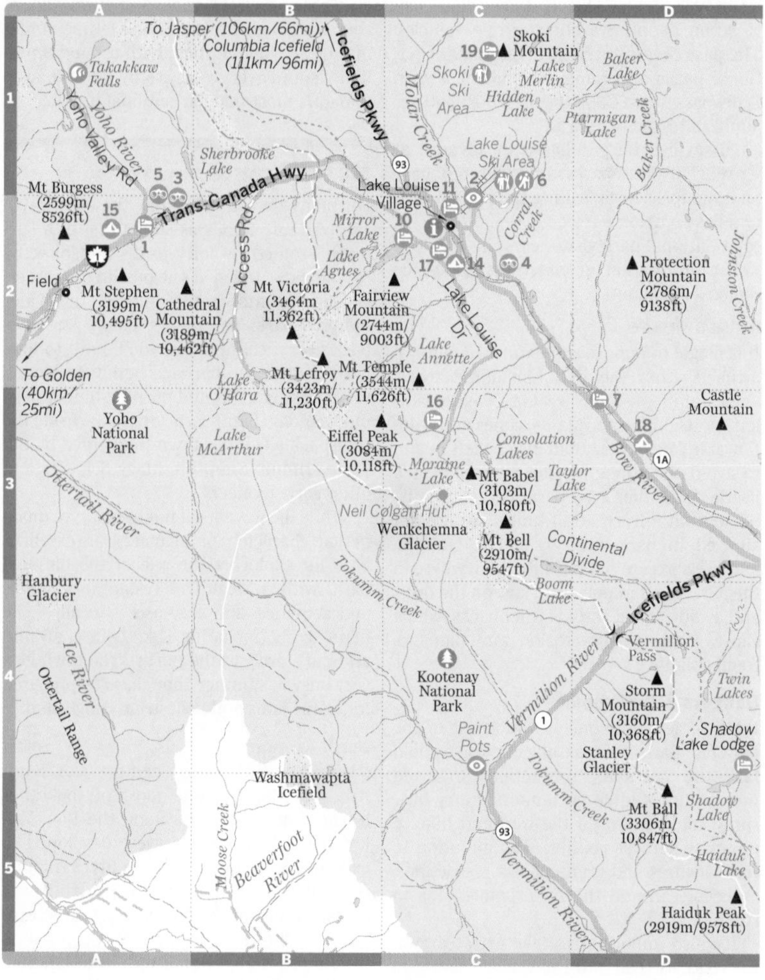

Brewster Transportation Building at No 202 (built in 1939, now occupied by the Rose & Crown pub), the **Banff School Auditorium** (built in 1939, now occupied by the Banff Information Centre) and **St Paul's Presbyterian Church** at No 230 (built in 1930).

There are several more historic houses around town that are worth seeking out – the Banff Information Centre can supply you with a free leaflet, *Walking Through Banff's History*, which points out the town's most important buildings. Alternatively, you can join one of the Whyte Museum's guided tours.

TOP CHOICE Whyte Museum of the Canadian Rockies MUSEUM

(Map p64; www.whyte.org; 111 Bear St; adult/child under 6yr/senior & student/family C$8/free/5/20; ⏲10am-5pm) Founded by the artists Peter and Catharine Whyte, who spent most of their lives living and working in Banff and the Canadian Rockies, the Whyte Museum opened its doors in 1968 in a modest building shared with the Banff public library. The original displays were based around an assortment of local artifacts belonging to the Whytes, but over 40 years the museum has assembled a huge collection of paintings,

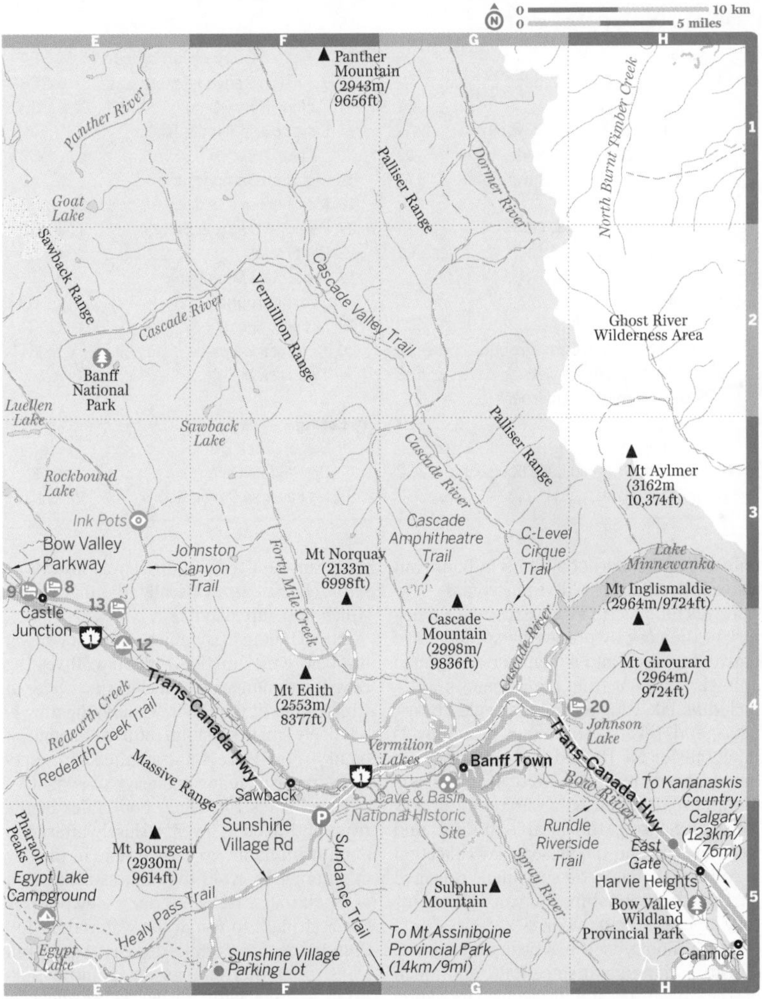

artwork and cultural exhibits relating to the Rockies' heritage.

The heart of the museum is the permanent display exploring the Whytes' fascinating life together. Among the exhibits are a reconstruction of their mountain cabin, Catharine's Paris-designed wedding dress, Peter's military uniform and an entrancing collection of First Nations costumes belonging to their friend, the Stoney Chief Walking Buffalo. There are also plenty of the Whytes' paintings on display, alongside temporary exhibitions drawn from the museum's archives.

The museum also runs several **guided tours** around Banff, including the 1½-hour Historic Banff walk and a 45-minute Heritage Homes tour. Tours cost C$8 for adults, and run several times daily from June to September.

Banff Park Museum MUSEUM

(Map p62; 93 Banff Ave; adult/child/senior/family C$3.90/1.90/3.40/9.80; ⏲10am-6pm mid-May–Sep, 1-5pm Oct–mid-May, guided tours 3pm summer) Housed in a striking wooden building built in 1903 in the fashionable 'railway pagoda' style, the Banff Park Museum is not

Banff National Park

Sights

1 Cathedral Mountain Lodge....A2
2 Lake Louise Gondola....C2
3 Lower Spiral Tunnel Viewpoint....A2
4 Morant's Curve Viewpoint....C2
5 Upper Spiral Tunnel Viewpoint....A1

Activities, Courses & Tours

6 Fish Creek Trailhead....C1

Sleeping

7 Baker Creek Chalets....D3
Castle Mountain Campground....(see 9)
8 Castle Mountain Chalets....E3
9 Castle Mountain Wilderness Hostel....E3
Deer Lodge....(see 10)
10 Fairmont Chateau Lake Louise....C2
11 HI Lake Louise....C2
12 Johnston Canyon Campground....E4
13 Johnston Canyon Resort....E3
Kicking Horse Campground....(see 15)
14 Lake Louise Tent & Trailer Campgrounds....C2
15 Monarch Campground....A2
16 Moraine Lake Lodge....C3
17 Paradise Lodge & Bungalows....C2
Post Hotel....(see 11)
18 Protection Mountain Campground....D3
19 Skoki Lodge....C1
20 Two Jack Lakeside....H4
Two Jack Main....(see 20)

Eating

Baker Creek Bistro....(see 7)
Bill Peyto's Café....(see 11)
Mt Fairview Dining Room....(see 10)

only one of the oldest buildings in Banff, but also one of Alberta's oldest museums.

It was founded to explore the natural history of the park by preserving specimens of native creatures, and a menagerie of stuffed animals stare out from the museum's walls, including elk, cougars, golden eagles, bears, pikas and several enormous bison heads (look out for Sir Donald, the patriarch of a buffalo herd that once lived near Cascade Mountain). The museum's first curator was Norman Sanson, the local naturalist and weatherman, and the present-day collection is still largely based on specimens collected during his curatorship. You can still see his cozy office on the 1st floor.

The building itself has been classified as a historic monument since 1985, and much of the furniture and finishing (including the museum's glass-fronted display cases) are original. The ingenious lantern window at the top of the building was designed to provide natural light for both the upper and lower floors.

Bow Falls WATERFALL

(Map p62) One of Banff's most notable natural features is the mighty Bow River, which flows right through the center of town. The river begins 100km upstream as meltwater from the Bow Glacier, flowing south through Banff en route to the prairies and Hudson Bay far beyond. The river has been known to First Nations people for well over 10,000 years; to the Cree Nation, it was known as *manachaban sipi* (literally 'the place from which bows are taken').

About 500m (0.3 miles) south of town, just before the junction with Spray River, the Bow River plunges into a churning *melée* of white-water at Bow Falls. Though the drop is relatively small – just 9m (30ft) at its highest point – Bow Falls is a dramatic sight, especially in spring following heavy snowmelt.

Paved trails run along both sides of the river, and make a lovely leisurely afternoon stroll from Banff; go early or late in the day in summer to avoid the endless procession of coach tours. The **west bank viewpoint** is the best place to watch the waterfall in full thundering flow, while the east bank trail leads to another famous viewpoint at **Surprise Corner**, with a view across the falls toward the Fairmont Banff Springs hotel. It also marks the start of the Hoodoos Trail (p74), which leads along the Bow River to a landscape of bizarre rock pillars shaped by eons of natural erosion.

Banff Gondola CABLE CAR

(off Map p62; www.explorerockies.com/banff-gondola; Mountain Ave; adult/child 6-15yr C$29.95/14.95; 8:30am-9pm late May-Aug, 8:30am-6:30pm Apr & Sep, reduced hr rest of yr) It's a pretty lazy way of getting to the mountaintops, but for instant access to glorious views you really can't top the Banff Gondola. From the car park next to the Upper Hot Springs, the cable car whisks you 698m (2292ft) in just eight minutes, right to the top of Sulphur Mountain, 2281m (7468ft) above sea level.

You'll find a couple of pricey restaurants and shops at the top, but for the best views you should follow the spectacular **Banff Skywalk**, a 1km (0.6-mile) walkway that leads along the summit ridge, providing mind-blowing views of Banff Town and the surrounding peaks. En route, the walkway visits Sulphur Mountain's **Cosmic Ray Station** (one of nine sites built across Canada in 1958 to study interstellar rays). Nearby is the historic weather station on **Sanson's Peak**, named after the meteorologist and museum curator Norman Sanson, who hiked up here at least once a week between 1896 and 1931 to take weather readings. You can follow in Sanson's footsteps on the Sulphur Mountain Trail (see p77), but don't expect anyone to clap you on the back – they'll be much too busy taking photos of the view.

BANFF MUSEUM PASS

The **Banff Heritage Passport** (adult/child 6-16yr/senior & student C$10/6/7) covers entry to the Whyte Museum and the Banff Park Museum, and includes a 50% discount to the Buffalo Nations Luxton Museum. It can be bought at any of the participating museums or from Brewster Tours (p100).

The easiest (and greenest) way to get to the gondola is to catch Route 1 on the Roam bus (p115); alternatively, you can hunt for a spot in the enormous car park.

Upper Hot Springs Pool HOT SPRING
(www.hotsprings.ca; Mountain Ave; adult/child & senior/family C$7.30/6.30/22.50; ⌚9am-11pm mid-May–mid-Oct, 10am-10pm Sun-Thu, 10am-11pm Sat & Sun mid-Oct–mid-May) Banff quite

THE BIRTH OF A NATIONAL PARK

Canada's present-day national-park system can trace its origins back to the discovery of three geothermally heated springs near Banff in the autumn of 1883. Although First Nations people had known about the hot springs around Banff for well over 10,000 years, the first white man to set eyes on them was James Hector, who recorded the springs on the Palliser expedition of 1859, probably following the advice of local Stoneys. Two surveyors working for the Canadian Pacific Railway revisited the springs in 1874, but it was brothers Tom and William McCardell, and their partner Frank McCabe, that changed the history of the springs for good.

In the autumn of 1883, they crossed the marshy area to the west of present-day Banff and stumbled across a series of deep chambers filled with naturally hot water. When William was lowered by his companions into one of the caves, he's reported to have described it as being 'like some fantastic dream from a tale of the *Arabian Nights*.' They smelled much more than just the odor of the sulfurous water – with the fashion for spa bathing still in full swing in Europe, and hot water on tap still an undreamt-of luxury, there was the whiff of money around the hot springs. The three companions staked a claim on the area, though ownership soon degenerated into legal wranglings over mineral rights and land claims, forcing the government to step in and declare the springs the property of Canada – sowing the seeds for the birth of Banff National Park and the National Park Act, eventually enacted in 1930.

The springs themselves proved to be just the money-spinner the three companions had hoped, although none of them saw any of the proceeds. Victorians and First Nations peoples alike believed the waters had healing properties (supposedly good for everything from arthritis to stinky feet) and within a few short years resort spas had sprung up all across the foot of Sulphur Mountain.

By the early 1900s, the precious water was being pumped to a health sanatorium on the site of present-day Canada Pl, while companies were bottling the water for export to the distant corners of Canada. There were even bars along Banff Ave where customers could take a tot of gin or rum along with a splash of mineral water. And though the medicinal properties of the waters have never quite been proven, there's no doubt that sinking into the hot waters with a view of the surrounding mountains is a fantastically soothing experience.

Banff Town

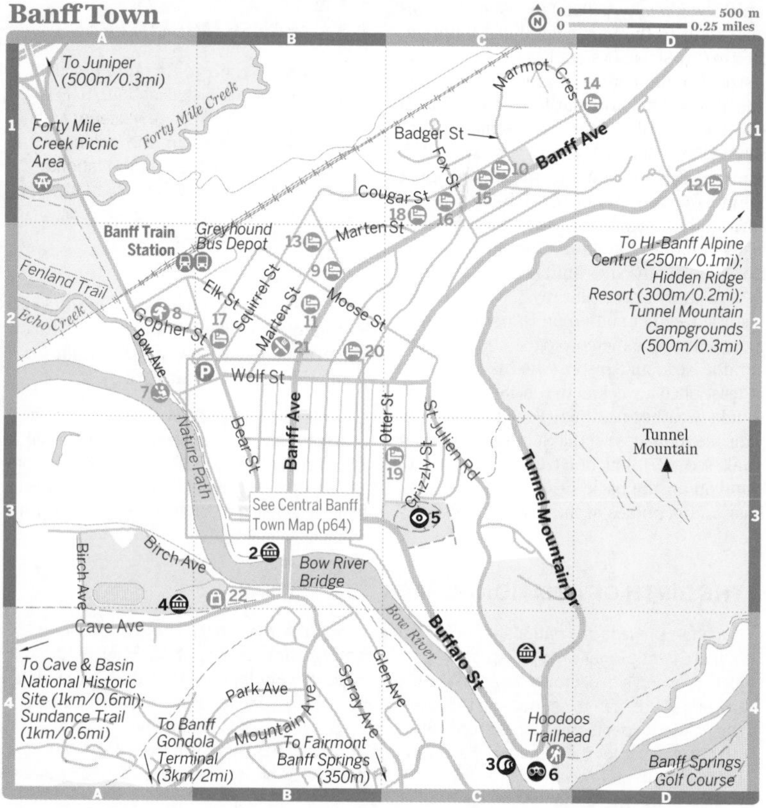

literally wouldn't be Banff if it weren't for its hot springs, which gush out from 2.5km (1.5 miles) beneath Sulphur Mountain at a constant temperature of between 32°C (90°F) and 46°C (116°F). It was the hot springs that drew the first tourists to Banff, and you can still sample the soothing mineral waters at the Upper Hot Springs Pool, near the Banff Gondola.

Several hotels once occupied the site where the present-day Hot Springs Pool stands – Dr RG Brett's Grand View Villa, built in 1886, was joined by the Hydro Hotel in 1890 but both establishments burnt down and were replaced in the 1930s by a new bathhouse in the fashionable art deco style.

Renovations have since masked some of the bathhouse's period elegance, but the hot springs still rank as one of those not-to-be-missed Banff experiences – there aren't many places in the world where you can take a hot bath with a mountain view as spectacular as this.

The pools get busy in season, so aim for a late dip if you prefer to have the water to yourself (alternatively, you can hire the whole thing for C$269.80 per hour). Towels, lockers and swimsuits are available for hire, and the **Pleiades Spa** (per 30min/hr C$55/85) offers treatments such as shiatsu, hot-stone massage and reiki.

Cave & Basin National Historic Site

HISTORIC SITE

(Map p58; www.pc.gc.ca/eng/lhn-nhs/ab/caveandbasin/natcul.aspx) The three sulfurous springs discovered by McCabe and the McCardell brothers now form part of the Cave & Basin National Historic Site, although bathing in the hot springs themselves is no longer allowed, in order to protect the critically endangered Banff Springs snail.

The entire site (including the replica of the original 1887 bathhouse) is currently undergoing a major restoration program and will

Banff Town

Sights

1 Banff Centre ... C4
2 Banff Park Museum ... B3
3 Bow Falls ... C4
4 Buffalo Nations Luxton Museum ... A3
5 Old Banff Cemetery ... C3
6 Surprise Corner Viewpoint ... C4

Activities, Courses & Tours

7 Blue Canoe ... A2
8 Brewster ... A2

Sleeping

9 Banff Aspen Lodge ... B2
10 Banff Caribou Lodge ... C1
11 Banff Ptarmigan Inn ... B2
12 Buffalo Mountain Lodge ... D1
13 Buffaloberry ... B2
14 Bumper's Inn ... D1
15 Charlton's Cedar Court ... C1
Driftwood Inn ... (see 11)
16 Fox Hotel ... C1
17 Poplar Inn ... B2
18 Royal Canadian Lodge ... C1
19 Thea's House ... C3
20 Treetops ... B2

Eating

Bumper's ... (see 14)
Evergreen ... (see 18)
21 Safeway ... B2

Shopping

22 Banff Indian Trading Post ... B3

remain closed until summer 2012. Check with the Banff Information Centre for updates.

Marsh Loop NATURE RESERVE
This popular loop trail begins near the Cave & Basin National Historic Site and meanders through one of Banff's most important areas of natural marshland. It's an excellent spot for bird-watching: keep your eyes peeled for red-winged blackbirds, green-winged teals and yellowthroats, as well as colorful butterflies and dragonflies. Part of the route follows a wooden boardwalk and leads to a **fish-viewing platform** and a **bird hide**. For a longer walk, you could continue on the trail to Sundance Canyon (p75).

South of the Marsh Loop, a band of forest on the flanks of Sulphur Mountain has been designated as the Middle Springs Wildlife Corridor to allow large mammals (including bears, wolves and cougars) to migrate across the valley without having to enter the townsite. The area is permanently off-limits to people, but animals don't always respect the boundaries, so look out for wildlife warnings and trail closures around Marsh Loop and Sundance Canyon.

Buffalo Nations Luxton Museum MUSEUM
(Map p62; ☎403-762-2388; 1 Birch Ave; adult/child/senior/family C$6/2.50/4/13; ⏰10am-7pm mid-May–mid-Oct, noon-5pm mid-Oct–Apr) Founded by Norman Luxton and built to resemble a frontier fort, this museum explores the culture of the First Nations from the Rockies and the Northern Plains. Some of the waxwork reconstructions are a bit tacky (check out the 'sun-dance' tableau), but on the whole it's an interesting introduction to First Nations culture.

The displays of traditional costumes, weapons and tools are particularly good – look out for the 'protection pouches' filled with sacred items, which tribal people would have worn to keep them safe in battle and ward off evil spirits. There's also an intriguing gallery of peace pipes, and some beautifully simple buckskin dresses, bags and rifle cases, all decorated with intricate beadwork that would have required hundreds of hours of work to complete.

Vermilion Lakes NATURE RESERVE
(Map p58) Northwest of the townsite, this trio of tranquil lakes is another great place for wildlife spotting – elk, beavers, bald eagles and ospreys can often be seen around the lakeshore, especially at dawn and dusk. A paved driveway runs along the lake's southern side for 4.5km (2.8 miles), but the proximity of the Trans-Canada Hwy means that it's not as peaceful as it could be. A good pair of binoculars and a telephoto lens for your camera will definitely come in handy for seeing the wildlife.

Old Banff Cemetery CEMETERY
(Map p62) Banff's shady cemetery is worth a visit, especially if you're interested in the town's history. Some of the gravestones date back to the 1890s; among the famous names buried here are the pioneering trail guides Tom Wilson (who discovered Lake Louise), Jim Brewster (the founder of Brews-

Central Banff Town

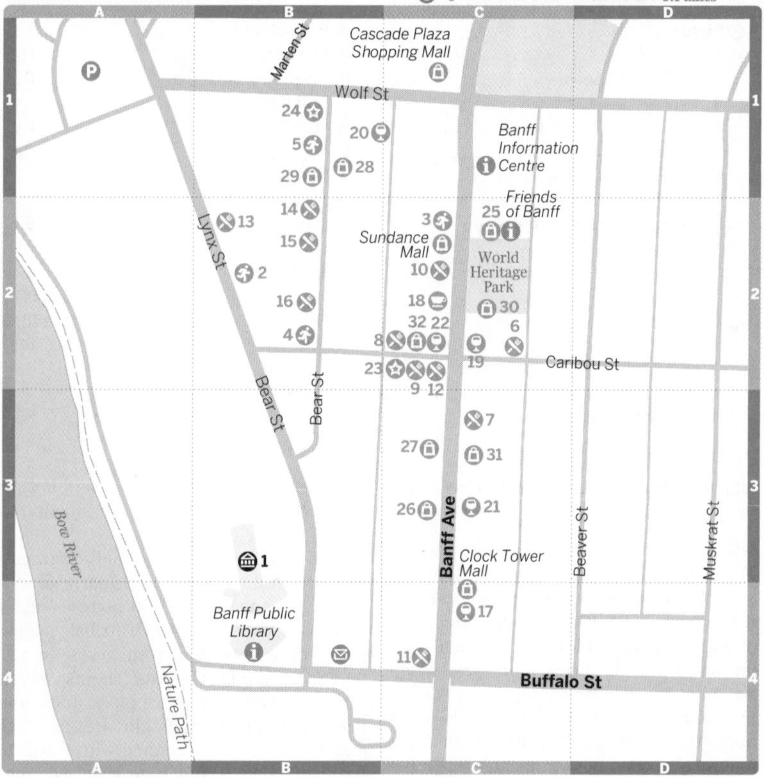

ter Transportation) and Bill Peyto (see the boxed text p87); the artists Peter and Catharine Whyte; and the frontierswoman, naturalist and writer Mary Schäffer-Warren, whose house can be seen just across the street from the cemetery.

Tunnel Mountain MOUNTAIN

(Map p62) It might be Banff's smallest mountain, but Tunnel Mountain (1692m/5551ft) is still one of the town's most recognizable landmarks. The mountain's distinctive rippled profile looms up to the east of town, and was known to the Stoney people as *tatanga* (buffalo), as it resembles a sleeping buffalo when seen from the north and east.

The mountain gets its modern name courtesy of the CPR surveyor Major AB Rogers who, while laying the groundwork for the arrival of the railway in Banff in 1882, devised a hare-brained plan to blast a 275m (300yd) tunnel through the base of the mountain to avoid the twists and turns of the Bow River. Incensed at the projected cost, Rogers' superiors ordered him to find an alternative, and the railway was subsequently rerouted north of the mountain at a fraction of the original price.

From the north side of St Julien Rd, a short, twisty **trail** (4.3 km/2.6 miles, 300m/984ft elevation gain) switchbacks up the mountainside to Tunnel Mountain's summit, offering an airy view west over Banff Town and the Sundance Range, north to Mt Norquay and Cascade Mountain, and south toward the shark-fins profile of Mt Rundle.

Banff Centre ARTS VENUE

(Map p62; www.banffcentre.ca; 107 Tunnel Mountain Dr; tickets C$10-25) Perched on the side of Tunnel Mountain, Banff's flagship arts venue hosts a varied program of concerts, lectures, exhibitions and events throughout the year. It's also the main focus for big cultural events, including the Banff Summer Arts Festival in July, the Banff International String Quartet

Central Banff Town

Sights

1 Whyte Museum of the Canadian Rockies B3

Activities, Courses & Tours

2 Banff Adventures Unlimited B2
3 Discover Banff Tours C2
Hydra River Guides .... (see 2)
4 Ski Stop B2
5 Snowtips/Bactrax B1
Warner Guiding & Outfitting .... (see 31)

Eating

Bear St Tavern .... (see 15)
6 Bruno's Bar & Grill C2
7 Cows C3
8 Coyote's Deli & Grill C2
9 Eddie Burger & Bar C2
10 Grizzly House C2
11 Le Beaujolais C4
12 Maple Leaf C2
13 Melissa's B2
Nourish .... (see 3)
14 Saltlik B2
15 The Bison B2
16 Wild Flour Café B2

Drinking

17 Banff Ave Brewing Company C4
18 Evelyn's Coffee Bar C2
Evelyn's Coffee Bar .... (see 24)
Lik Lounge .... (see 14)
19 Rose & Crown C2
20 St James's Gate B1
21 Tommy's Neighborhood Pub C3
22 Wild Bill's Legendary Saloon C2

Entertainment

Aurora Club .... (see 17)
23 Hoodoo Lounge C2
24 Lux Cinema B1

Shopping

25 Bear & Butterfly C2
26 Chocolaterie Bernard Cabellaut C3
27 Monod Sports C3
28 Mountain Magic B1
29 Mountain Magic Sports B1
30 Rocky Mountain Soap Company C2
31 Trail Rider Store C3
32 Viewpoint C2

Competition in August and the Banff Mountain Film Festival in November.

The site is about 1.5km (0.9 miles) from downtown Banff. A new route on the Roam Bus (p115) is currently being trialled between Banff Ave and the Banff Centre: for the latest updates, see www.banffcentre.ca/about/directions-maps/.

Fairmont Banff Springs HISTORIC HOTEL
(off Map p62; www.fairmont.com/banffsprings; Spray Ave) Looming up beside the Bow River, the Banff Springs is a local landmark in more ways than one. Originally built in 1888, and remodeled in 1928 to resemble a cross between a Scottish baronial castle and a European chateau, the turret-topped exterior conceals an eye-poppingly extravagant selection of ballrooms, lounges, dining rooms and balustraded staircases that'd make William Randolph Hearst green with envy.

Highlights include an Arthurian great hall, an elegant, wood-paneled gentleman's bar and the gorgeous hot-springs spa. Even if you're not staying here, you're welcome to wander around, and it's worth splashing out on a coffee or a cocktail in one of the four (count 'em!) lounges. The hotel is best seen in winter, when the lights of its 700-odd rooms twinkle out from under a thick crust of snow. For info about staying here, see p102.

Banff Springs Golf Course GOLF COURSE
(off Map p62; ☎403-762-6801; www.fairmont.com; ⏰May-Oct) Laid out in 1928 and impressively located in the shadow of Mt Rundle and Sulphur Mountain, this is one of the Rockies' most famous fairways. You'll need to dress up for the occasion; no denim, no sweats, dress shorts only and collared shirts required for men. Shoe and club rentals are available.

Even if you're not planning on a round, the road through the golf course makes a lovely bike ride, and is also a good place for spotting elk, especially at dawn and dusk.

Around Banff Town

LAKE MINNEWANKA

Cradled high above town between the Palliser and Fairholme Ranges, Lake Minnewanka (Map p58) is the largest body of water in the national park – 24km (15 miles) long, 142m (465ft) deep and barely a few degrees above freezing. Known to Stoney people as *minn-waki* ('the lake of the spirits'), the lake was believed to be haunted by the spirits of the dead, perhaps explaining why early Europeans referred to it as Devil's Lake.

The lake has been dammed three times at its western end: in 1895, 1912 and finally in 1941, when the lake level was raised by around 30m, completely submerging the lively summer settlement of Minnewanka Landing, which boasted four avenues and three streets lined with hotels, shops and saloon bars. Today the drowned town is off-limits to everyone except scuba divers, so you'll have to content yourself with a picnic or a stroll along the lakeshore. There's a small seasonal café next to the car park serving sandwiches, drinks, ice creams and other snacks. Bighorn sheep can often be seen grazing along the lakeshore.

Minnewanka is the only lake in Banff that allows motorboats. You can rent **motor launches** (per hour C$49, additional hours C$30; ⏱Jun–mid-Oct) from the boathouse, or take a trip with **Banff Lake Cruises** (www.explorerockies.com/minnewanka; adult/child C$45/20; ⏱hourly 10am-6pm mid-Jun–Sep, fewer sailings early Jun & late Sep), which offers 1½-hour cruises that include a commentary on the history, geology and mythology of the lake, and a visit to the glacial pass known as the Devil's Gap.

Minnewanka also marks the start of several hikes. The gentle trail to Stewart Canyon (p76) is a great family option, while hardier walkers might want to tackle **Aylmer Lookout** (11.8km/7.3 miles one way, 560m/1837ft elevation gain) or continue on to **Aylmer Pass** (13km/8 miles one way, 810m/2657ft elevation gain). Note that the Aylmer trails are closed during the buffaloberry season between mid-July and September, as it's a frequent hangout for grizzly bears.

The driving tour on p71 covers all of the other sights around the lake.

MT NORQUAY

One of Banff's 'Big Three' ski resorts, **Mt Norquay** (Map p58; www.banffnorquay.com) is the nearest ski hill to town and offers 28 groomed runs during the main season between November and mid-April. Norquay has been a popular downhill destination since the 1920s; the mountain was named after John Norquay (premier of Manitoba from 1878 to 1887), who supposedly made the first summit ascent following the end of his premiership in 1887. For info on skiing the mountain, see p98.

The ski area parking lot at the top of the mountain marks the start of two hikes: the long slog to **Cascade Amphitheatre**, and the shorter trail to the top of **Stoney Squaw Mountain** (4.2km/2.6 miles round-trip, 190m/623ft elevation gain), from where there's a superb panorama across the Bow Valley and Vermilion Lakes.

SUNSHINE MEADOWS

Straddling the Continental Divide and the border between Alberta and British Columbia, Sunshine Meadows is an expanse of high alpine meadowland stretching for 15km (9.3 miles) between Citadel Pass and Healy Pass.

In winter it's one of Banff's most popular ski areas, but in summer, once the snows thaw, it marks the start of several fantastic hiking trails that are particularly renowned for their colorful wildflowers, including the Garden Path Trail (p79) and Healy Pass (p80). The Sunshine area also allows access to popular backcountry routes into Egypt Lake and Mt Assiniboine Provincial Park, but at an altitude of about 2300m (7545ft) it's not an easy place to reach, particularly since the ski gondola up to the village doesn't run in summer, leaving you with a 6.5km (4 mile) climb up from the Sunshine parking lot.

Thankfully, there is another option. **White Mountain Adventures** (☎403-760-4403; www.whitemountainadventures.com; ⏱mid-Jun–Oct) operates a shuttle bus along the mountain access road, departing from the Sunshine parking lot (adult/child 3 to 12 years C$26/15) eight times daily between 9am and 4:45pm, and from Sunshine Village back down the mountain once hourly from 9:15am to 4:30pm. During July and August, there's also an extra bus up the mountain at 8am and down at 5:30pm.

If you don't have your own transport, you could catch the daily connection from Banff (adult/child 3 to 12 years C$55/30), which leaves between 8:15am and 8:30am. There are return buses to Banff at 2:30pm and 4:30pm. Hikers coming from the backcountry can also purchase a one-way ticket down the mountain for C$15. The fare is the same for adults and children.

You can book a place on the shuttle bus online at www.sunshinemeadowsbanff.com/sunshine_meadows/shuttle.htm or by calling ☎403-762-7889.

To reach the Sunshine parking lot, drive west from Banff for 8km (5 miles) and look out for the Sunshine Village exit. From the turnoff, it's another 7m (8 yards) to the parking lot.

BOW VALLEY PARKWAY

While most people zoom up busy Trans-Canada Hwy 1 with nothing but views of truck tailgates and overtaking automobiles, wiser souls swing over onto the quieter and much more scenic Hwy 1A, otherwise known as the Bow Valley Parkway (Map p58), which runs for 51km (31.6 miles) nearly all the way north to Lake Louise. The route is hemmed in by thick fir forest and mountains, with regular viewpoints looking out across the Bow Valley. It's a great spot to look out for wildlife, especially elk, bighorn sheep and even the occasional moose, but take things slow: the regular speed limit is 60km/h (37mph), dropping down to 30km/h (19mph) at certain sections to avoid wildlife collisions.

There's a detailed driving tour covering sights along the Bow Valley Parkway on p69. If you're short on time, at the very least make sure to visit the thundering waterfalls of **Johnston Canyon**, where a suspended catwalk tracks along the canyon wall to a series of viewpoints overlooking the Lower and Upper Falls. It's one of Banff's most popular sights, and the car park is often full by mid-morning: save it for an early morning or late-evening visit. A little further along the parkway is the lookout point at **Castle Mountain**, one of Banff's most recognizable mountain peaks.

The eastern section of the road between Fireside Picnic Area and Johnston Canyon is closed from 6pm to 9am during spring mating season (March to late June).

Lake Louise & Around

If you're still searching for the quintessential Rocky Mountains view, you'll have to work pretty hard to find anywhere more beautiful than Lake Louise. Fifty-eight kilometers (36 miles) north of Banff, this glittering glacial lake is one of Canada's most iconic sights, hemmed in on every side by saw-tooth mountains, snowy slopes and thick forest. Favored by photographers, hikers, sightseers and grizzly bears alike, it's also one of the national park's busiest corners, but even on the most hectic days you can normally find some peace and tranquility by striding out along the lakeshore or tackling one of the area's fantastic day hikes.

The lake itself is an 8km (5-mile) drive uphill from Lake Louise Village just off Trans-Canada Hwy 1, where you'll find most facilities, including the visitor center, post office, grocery and other shops.

LAKE LOUISE

Arguably the most famous sight in Banff National Park – if not the whole Canadian Rockies – the gleaming blue bowl of Lake Louise (Map p58) has been an essential item on every visitor's itinerary since the 1890s. Stoney people knew about the lake long

DON'T MISS

LAKE LOUISE GONDOLA

For a bird's-eye view of the Lake Louise area – and a good chance of spotting grizzly bears on the avalanche slopes – climb aboard the **Lake Louise Gondola** (Map p58; www.lakelouisegondola.com; adult/child 6-15yr/child under 5yr C$26.75/13.40/free; ⏲9am-6:30pm Aug, to 5:30pm late June-July, to 4:30pm Sep, to 4pm mid-May–late June), which crawls up the side of Whitehorn Mountain via an open ski lift or enclosed gondola to a dizzying viewpoint 2088m (6850ft) above the valley floor. Look out for the imposing fang of 3544m (11,626ft) Mt Temple piercing the skyline on the opposite side of the valley.

At the top of the mountain there are free hourly interpretive programs exploring grizzly bears and the history of the Lake Louise area, plus a 45-minute **guided nature walk** (tickets C$5; ⏲11am, 1pm & 3pm), or you can wander around several short marked trails. Back at the bottom, snacks and light meals are available at the **Lodge of the Ten Peaks** (buffet lunch adult/child 6-15yr/child under 5yr C$19.30/12.30/4.10, incl gondola ticket C$33.25/19/4.10; ⏲8am-5:30pm mid-May–Sep). See the website for opening hours during the ski season.

The gondola is about 2km east of Lake Louise Village. Complimentary shuttle buses run several times daily from the Fairmont Chateau Lake Louise, Deer Lodge, Lake Louise Tent & Trailer Campgrounds and Samson Mall. For information on bus departure times, visit www.lakelouisegondola.com/contact_us.php.

before the first European settlers arrived, but the first white man to 'discover' it was the railway surveyor and pack guide Tom Wilson, who was taken to the 'Lake of Little Fishes' by native guides in 1882. Originally known as Emerald Lake, it was later renamed in honor of Princess Louise Caroline Alberta, Queen Victoria's fourth daughter and wife of the then Canadian governor-general.

Roughly 2km (1.2 miles) end-to-end and 70m (230ft) deep, the lake is famous for its searingly blue water, caused by light reflecting off tiny particles of 'rock flour' (glacial silt) carried down from the mountain glaciers. On still days the lake becomes a shimmering mirror for the surrounding scenery; it's best seen early or late in the day, when the vibrant colors of the lake are strongest. In winter the scene is transformed into a wonderland of powder-white ice and snow-cloaked peaks. The surface of the lake often freezes over and skaters glide across it, wrapped up tight against the biting mountain cold.

It's since become one of the park's most famous (and busiest) attractions, and the lakeshore inevitably gets crushingly crowded on summer days. Visit as early as possible to avoid the squash, and spend the rest of the day exploring the nearby attractions of Moraine Lake and the Lake Louise Gondola.

You can usually escape the coach loads of sightseers milling around in front of the Fairmont Chateau Lake Louise by following the lakeshore trail, which tracks through forest along the northern side of the lake, offering fabulous vistas of Fairview Mountain and the Victoria Glacier. A spur trail leads steeply up the mountainside to the famous Lake Agnes Teahouse and the Big Beehive (see p83), but it's a long slog, so you'll need good shoes and plenty of water. Further along the lakeshore trail, you can continue up the valley on the Plain of Six Glaciers walk (p82). There are several more classic hikes leading off around Lake Louise, including the steep climbs up Saddleback (2330m/7644ft) and Fairview Mountain (2744m/9003ft), which both brood along the lake's southern shore.

For something more sedentary, you can hire canoes from the **Lake Louise Boathouse** (Map p58; per hr C$55; ⏲10am-6pm Jun–mid-Oct). Sculling through the water, far from the crowds, you'll be rewarded with a sense of the silence and natural majesty that must have greeted Tom Wilson when he first laid eyes on the lake.

MORAINE LAKE

Reached by a twisting 13km (8-mile) road that's only open from June to October, the mountainous panoramas around Moraine Lake (Map p58) are arguably even more stunning than those at Lake Louise. Backed by the dagger-point peaks of the Wenkchemna Range, all of which top out over 3000m (10,000ft), Moraine Lake is another sparkling blue lake that's fed by glacial runoff from the surrounding mountains. It's one of the best-known views in the Rockies, and graced the back of the C$20 bill from 1969 to 1986.

The mountains were originally named in 1894 by the explorer Samuel Allen, using the numbers one to 10 in the Stoney language ('wenkchemna' means 10). All but two of the mountains have since been renamed, but you'll still see some guidebooks and maps using the original Stoney names.

At the eastern end of the lake is the **Moraine Lake Rockpile**, a massive heap of boulders of somewhat uncertain origin: some geologists think it was created by an ancient avalanche, while others believe it was formed by the long-gone glacier that carved out the rest of the valley. A paved trail leads up to a series of viewpoints at the top of the rockpile, offering a panoramic vista across the lake and the Wenkchemna Peaks beyond. On his first climb up the rockpile in 1899, early adventurer Walter Wilcox wrote: 'No scene has ever given me an equal impression of inspiring solitude and rugged grandeur.' It's hard to argue.

A part-paved trail leads off around the lake's northern shore, linking up with the branch trail to Larch Valley (p84) and Eiffel Lake. Another trail leads southeast from the rockpile to Consolation Lakes (p81).

Alternatively, you can explore the lake in the manner of the old voyageurs by hiring a **canoe** (⏲10am-6pm summer) from the boathouse next to Moraine Lake Lodge.

Icefields Parkway

The **Icefields Parkway** (Map p70; www.icefieldsparkway.ca; Hwy 93) is often referred to locally as the 'world's most spectacular road', and it's tough to argue. Stretching for 230km (142.6 miles) north from Lake Louise all the way to Jasper, the road climbs through an amazingly diverse range of Rocky Mountain scenery, from surging rivers and high alpine

THE 10 PEAKS

From east to west, here are the 10 Wenkchemna Peaks (with the Stoney name in brackets):

» Mt Fay (Heejee, 3235m/10,613ft)

» Mt Little (Nom, 3139m/10,300ft)

» Mt Bowlen (Yamnee, 3071m/10,076ft)

» Tonsa (3054m/10,020ft)

» Mt Perren (Sata, 3051m/10,010ft)

» Mt Allen (Shappee, 3301m/10,830ft)

» Mt Tuzo (Sagowa, 3245m/10,646ft)

» Deltaform Mountain (Saknowa, 3424m/11,233ft)

» Neptuak Mountain (3237m/10,620ft)

» Wenkchemna Peak (3206m/10,518ft)

glaciers to mountain passes and brilliant blue lakes.

Much of the route was established in the 1800s by First Nations people and fur traders looking for easy trading routes through the mountains, and the road itself was constructed in several stages before opening in the 1940s and being improved in the early 1960s.

About the only way to explore the parkway is by car; we've put together a driving itinerary (p73) that strings together all the key sights. The road's most famous sights include the **Crowfoot Glacier** (so called for its three-pronged face, although one of the clawlike 'toes' has since disappeared), the turquoise sweep of **Peyto Lake** and nearby **Bow Lake**, and the enormous expanse of the **Columbia Icefield**, the largest area of unbroken ice in North America, just across the border into Jasper over Sunwapta Pass (see the boxed text, p143).

Accommodations on the parkway are limited; apart from campgrounds at Rampart Creek, Mosquito Creek and Waterfowl Lakes, and a historic lodge established by the famous Rockies character Jimmy Simpson, about the only options are an overpriced motel at Saskatchewan Crossing and hostels at Mosquito Creek and Rampart Creek. You'll be better off overnighting in Lake Louise and Jasper, both handily situated at opposite ends of the parkway.

The speed limit on the parkway is 90km/h (56mph), with reduced speeds around Saskatchewan Crossing and the Columbia Icefield. The road often becomes impassable in winter due to heavy snow, and chains or all-season tires are advisable between October and May. Regardless of the time of year, you'll also need a valid National Park Pass for everyone in your vehicle in order to drive on the parkway.

DRIVING

Around Banff

The Bow Valley Parkway

Duration 2-2½ hours one way

Distance 52km (32.2 miles)

Speed Limit 60km/h (37mph) dropping to 30km/h (19mph) at certain points

Start Banff

Finish Lake Louise

Nearest Towns Banff (p57), Lake Louise (p67)

Summary This is a peaceful drive along one of the park's most picturesque minor roads, with an excellent chance of spying wildlife.

If you prefer scenery to speed, this leisurely drive between Banff and Lake Louise is a must-do. The Bow Valley Parkway runs parallel to the Trans-Canada Hwy practically all the way to Lake Louise, but it's an altogether more tranquil drive. It's particularly well known for its wildlife: you'll have a great chance of spotting elk and bighorn sheep, especially early and late in the day, and if you're really lucky, you might even spot an elusive moose or black bear. Needless to say, this also makes the Bow Valley Parkway a hot spot for collisions with animals, so keep your speed well down and keep your eyes peeled for wildlife on the edge of the road. The road's eastern end between the Fireside Picnic Area and Johnston Canyon is closed from 6pm to 9am during spring mating season (March to late June).

From Banff Town, head west on Trans-Canada Hwy 1 toward Lake Louise, taking the exit for Bow Valley Parkway at 5km (3.1 miles). The road curves into forest, passing the **Muleshoe Wetlands** and the **Sawback Range**, which underwent a prescribed burn in 1993. Interpretive panels along the route explain the science behind forest fires.

Icefields Parkway

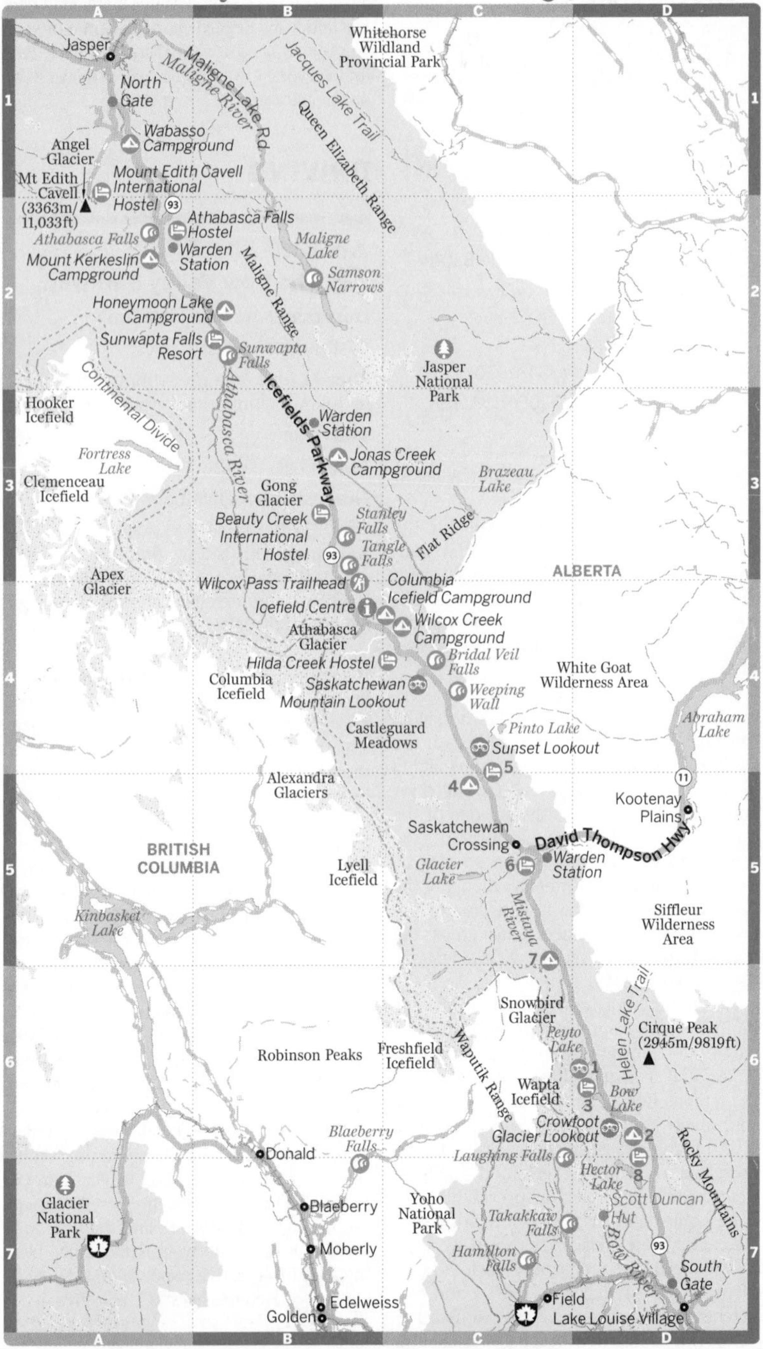
0 20 km
0 10 miles
Jasper
North Gate
Maligne Lake Rd
Maligne River
Jacques Lake Trail
Whitehorse Wildland Provincial Park
Queen Elizabeth Range
Wabasso Campground
Angel Glacier
Mt Edith Cavell (3363m/11,033ft)
Mount Edith Cavell International Hostel
93
Athabasca Falls Hostel
Athabasca Falls
Warden Station
Mount Kerkeslin Campground
Maligne Lake
Samson Narrows
Maligne Range
Honeymoon Lake Campground
Sunwapta Falls Resort
Sunwapta Falls
Jasper National Park
Continental Divide
Athabasca River
Icefields Parkway
Hooker Icefield
Warden Station
Fortress Lake
Jonas Creek Campground
Brazeau Lake
Clemenceau Icefield
Gong Glacier
Beauty Creek International Hostel
Stanley Falls
Flat Ridge
Tangle Falls
ALBERTA
Apex Glacier
Wilcox Pass Trailhead
Columbia Icefield Campground
Icefield Centre
Wilcox Creek Campground
Athabasca Glacier
Hilda Creek Hostel
Bridal Veil Falls
White Goat Wilderness Area
Columbia Icefield
Saskatchewan Mountain Lookout
Weeping Wall
Abraham Lake
Castleguard Meadows
Pinto Lake
Sunset Lookout
5
4
Alexandra Glaciers
11
Kootenay Plains
Saskatchewan Crossing
David Thompson Hwy
BRITISH COLUMBIA
Lyell Icefield
Glacier Lake
6
Warden Station
Mistaya River
Siffleur Wilderness Area
Kinbasket Lake
7
Helen Lake Trail
Snowbird Glacier
Peyto Lake
Cirque Peak (2945m/9819ft)
Robinson Peaks
Freshfield Icefield
Waputik Range
1
Wapta Icefield
3
Bow Lake
Crowfoot Glacier Lookout
2
Rocky Mountains
Blaeberry Falls
Donald
Laughing Falls
Hector Lake
8
Glacier National Park
Blaeberry
Yoho National Park
Scott Duncan Hut
Takakkaw Falls
Bow River
93
Moberly
Hamilton Falls
South Gate
1
Field
Edelweiss
Golden
Lake Louise Village

Icefields Parkway

Sights

1 Bow Summit Lookout D6
Saskatchewan Crossing .... (see 6)

Sleeping

2 Mosquito Creek Campground D6
3 Num-Ti-Jah Lodge D6
4 Rampart Creek Campground C5
5 Rampart Creek Hostel C4
6 The Crossing C5
7 Waterfowl Lakes Campground C5
8 Wilderness Hostel D7

Eating

Num-Ti-Jah Lodge .... (see 3)

At around 15km (9.3 miles) the road divides briefly (supposedly thanks to a lazy construction worker) before passing **Johnston Canyon** at 18km (11.2 miles); for hiking info, see p78. Just west is a viewpoint overlooking the grassy **Moose Meadows**, once a favorite moose hangout, but now more often frequented by elk.

Around 5km (3.1 miles) further west, look out for a **panel** marking the site of Silver City, one of several boom towns that briefly flourished around the Bow Valley during a series of mineral rushes in the 1880s and '90s. Silver City lasted barely two years; 3000 prospectors flocked to the site in 1883 after silver was said to have been found here, but the town collapsed in 1885 when it transpired that the discovery was nothing more than a moneymaking ruse propagated by unscrupulous entrepreneurs.

At 24.5km (15.2 miles) you'll pass **Castle Mountain Junction**, where a branch road heads over the Trans-Canada Hwy toward Kootenay National Park. There's a small gas station, general store and chalet complex next to the junction that makes a good place to pick up drinks, snacks and ice creams.

Directly east of the junction rises the craggy profile of **Castle Mountain**, so named for its 'castellated,' fortress-like appearance, created by a combination of geological forces and natural erosion. After WWII the mountain was briefly renamed Mt Eisenhower in honor of the US general, but locals were far from keen on the change and it was restored to Castle Mountain in 1979, although the stand-alone pillar at the southern end is still known as Eisenhower Peak.

Another 6km (3.7 miles) on, you'll pass a small **monument** that marks the site of a former prison camp that housed Ukrainian immigrants during WWI. Nearby is another pullout with grand views of Mt Whymper and the important wildlife corridor across the Vermilion Pass.

Continuing west toward Lake Louise, look out for a **viewpoint** looking west toward Storm Mountain, before crossing Baker's Creek en route to the viewpoint at **Morant's Curve**, a site much favored by the Canadian Pacific Railway (CPR) and *National Geographic* photographer Nicholas Morant (1910–99), whose images helped publicize Banff during its early days as a national park.

The Bow Valley Parkway ends after 47km (29.1 miles) at a T-junction. The right turn heads toward the Lake Louise Gondola (see the boxed text, p67), while the left turn heads toward Lake Louise and Trans-Canada Hwy 1.

Minnewanka Loop

Duration 1-1½ hours round-trip

Distance 16.5km (10.2 miles)

Speed Limit 50km/h (31mph)

Start/Finish Banff

Nearest Town Banff (p57)

Summary A circular route taking in a trio of the park's loveliest lakes.

This loop makes a good morning or afternoon drive. There are great views of Cascade Mountain, the Palliser Range and the Fairholme Range and, if you wish, you can break up the drive with a hike to Stewart Canyon, Johnson Lake or C-Level Cirque. As with other high roads, this route is closed for snow cover from November to mid-April or May.

Heading west from Banff Town along Banff Ave, follow signs for Lake Minnewanka. You'll cross under Trans-Canada Hwy 1 and begin to climb along the lower flanks of Cascade Mountain; look out for waterfalls tumbling down the mountainside after heavy rain. On the right is **Cascade Ponds**, a picnic area around small pools of water.

Drive past the right-hand turn signed to Johnson Lake and continue north into the treeline, toward the stacked-up spires of the Palliser Range. At roughly 3km (1.9 miles), look out for the right-hand turn to **Lower Bankhead**, where you can wander around the ruins of an abandoned mining town constructed by the CPR to exploit the rich coal deposits hidden deep beneath Cascade Mountain. Founded in 1903, Bankhead was once home to around 1000 people, and boasted electric power, running water, a school, a theatre and even a couple of tennis courts. A disastrous post-war collapse in coal prices and a series of costly labor strikes forced the closure of the mine in 1922. Many of the town's buildings were subsequently moved to Banff or Canmore, including the Bankhead train station, which can still be seen on Tunnel Mountain Dr.

Precious little now remains of this once-thriving industrial town, save for the old transformer house, the miners' lamp house and the footings of a few other key buildings. A self-guided trail winds its way around the ruins: look out for the huge slag-heaps of coal left behind after the mine's closure, spotted with wild rhubarb planted by the Chinese laborers who once lived nearby. The actual mine was located up the hill at Upper Bankhead, now the trailhead for C-Level Cirque (p77).

After 6km (3.7 miles) you'll arrive at **Lake Minnewanka** (p65). Time your arrival right and you'll be able to jump on a boat for a trip around the lake, wander along the shoreline or just stop for something cold from the lakeside snack shack.

From Lake Minnewanka, follow the road across the top of the lake dam toward **Two Jake Lake**, another popular spot with picnickers and sunbathers. The jagged mountain that looms up behind the lake is **Mt Rundle**, actually a crinkled ridge of peaks, which runs for 12km south all the way to Canmore. It's named after Robert Rundle, a Methodist missionary who spent much of his life working with First Nations tribes in the Bow Valley during the 1800s.

A little further on, 11km (6.8 miles) along the route, is the junction for **Johnson Lake**, another lakeside getaway for locals looking to escape the Banff bustle. If it's sunny, you can join people sunbathing around the lakeshore, or wander around the lake trail on cloudier days. Brave souls sometimes take the plunge into the lake's chilly waters, but you'll need a steely constitution (and preferably a wetsuit) to join them, as it stays chilly well into high summer.

From here the road trundles downhill and rejoins the main loop road. Turn left to head back to Banff.

WILDLIFE CROSSINGS

As you drive north from Banff toward Lake Louise along the Trans-Canada Hwy, look out for the four arched overpasses spanning the road. They're not for humans, but are actually wildlife crossings, which have been specially designed to allow Banff's animals to cross the road without fear of getting mown down by a passing truck or recreational vehicle (RV).

Trans-Canada Hwy 1 sits slap bang in the middle of several key 'wildlife corridors' (migratory routes between seasonal habitats) that crisscross the Bow Valley. Thousands of animals have been killed while trying to cross the highway over the years, especially since the road was twinned in 1981, and collisions with vehicles remain the number one cause of wildlife fatalities in the national park.

In order to reduce the risk of accidents and protect the park's increasingly fragile animal population, the wildlife crossings were built at a cost of around C$1 million each, alongside 24 other underpasses that tunnel beneath the road at various points.

They seem to be working: according to a recent study, 11 different species of large mammals have used the crossings in excess of 220,000 times since 1996. Intriguingly, animals seem to have adapted to the crossings at different speeds: elk and deer began using them almost straight away, while it took as much as five years for more wary species such as bears and wolves to adapt to them.

Different species also seem to have preferences for the types of bridges they like to use: elk, moose, wolves and grizzly bears seem to like crossings that are high, wide and short, while black bears and cougars prefer them long, low and narrow.

A new project is currently underway to monitor exactly which animals are using the crossings and how often, using DNA from barbed-wire fur traps positioned at the crossing entrances. Once the data has been collected and analyzed, it's very likely that there could be several more crossings built around the Lake Louise area over the next few years. Watch this space – or rather, watch this road.

Around Lake Louise

Into the Icefields

Duration 3-4 hours one way

Distance 230km (143 miles) from Lake Louise to Sunwapta

Speed Limit 90km/h (56mph)

Start/Finish Lake Louise

Nearest Town Lake Louise (p67)

Summary This has to be one of Canada's most scenic stretches of blacktop, taking in some of the nation's most dramatic mountains, lakes and glaciers.

This once-in-a-lifetime road trip starts in Lake Louise and follows the southern section of the **Icefields Parkway** to the Saskatchewan Crossing, near the border with Jasper National Park. It's a long route, so set out early and leave yourself plenty of time to enjoy the drive. Make sure you set out with a full tank, as the only gas stations en route are at Lake Louise or Saskatchewan Crossing. The road is officially open year-round, but is often closed due to snow between November and April.

Start at Lake Louise and head north along Hwy 1 to the signed turnoff to Jasper. You'll reach a parks tollbooth 2km (1.2 miles) north of the junction; as you'll already have your parks pass, you can zip through without stopping.

To the west rises the **Waputik Range**, dominated by 2755m (9039ft) Waputik Peak, overlooking the winding Bow River. Around 16.1km (10 miles) from the start of the parkway you'll reach **Hector Lake**, named after James Hector, a geologist and naturalist who accompanied the historic Palliser Expedition to chart unexplored areas of western Canada between 1857 and 1860.

At 33km (20.5 miles), look out for the **Crowfoot Glacier**, nestled on the rocky flanks of Crowfoot Mountain above ice-blue **Bow Lake**. The glacier was named for its three clawlike 'toes,' but unfortunately its lowest toe had melted by the 1940s.

At the northern end of Bow Lake is **Num-Ti-Jah Lodge** (p108), built by the famous trailsman Jimmy Simpson, who was born in England in 1895 but went on to become one of the Rockies' best-known explorers, adventurers and guides. The lodge makes an ideal stop for lunch, and you can always

Into the Icefields

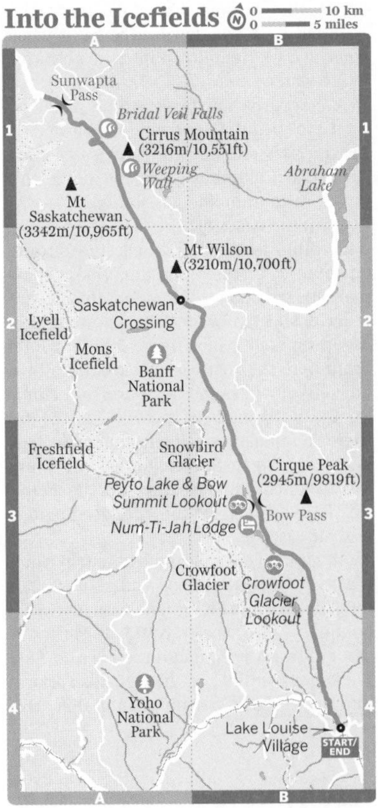

burn off the calories by following the trail to **Bow Falls** (p86).

From Bow Lake, the road climbs toward **Bow Pass**, which at 2069m (6788ft) is the highest point on the parkway. Nearby you'll find the turnoff to the busy **Peyto Lake Viewpoint**, named after the park warden Bill Peyto (see the boxed text, p87). A 400m (0.2-mile) wooded trail leads from the parking lot to a decked viewpoint that looks out over the sapphire-blue lake. It's usually packed, but there's a quieter viewpoint further on, near the path to Bow Summit Lookout.

Back in the car, head 6km (3.7 miles) further north to a pullout overlooking Snowbird Glacier, which clings to the edge of Patterson Mountain like an avalanche frozen in mid-motion. Further north is the parking lot for **Mistaya Canyon** (p86), reached by a 500m (0.3-mile) walk from the pullout. Carved out by the Mistaya

River, the curving limestone canyon is spanned by a wooden bridge from where you can look right down into the pounding white water.

A short drive northwest brings you to the **Saskatchewan Crossing**, established by fur trappers crossing the Rockies en route to British Columbia, and now home to a motel, restaurant and gas station.

From the Crossing, the road crosses river flats (often frequented by elk and birdlife) en route to Cirrus Mountain, where snow-melt streams down the mountainside, creating a sheet of waterfalls known as the **Weeping Wall**, which freeze solid in winter. From here the road sweeps around a huge hairpin known as the **Big Bend** and climbs up the aptly named **Big Hill**; at the top there's a fantastic viewpoint that looks back down the North Saskatchewan Valley and Mt Saskatchewan. Nearby are the **Bridal Veil Falls**, named for the interlaced pattern of their cascade.

At 230km (143 miles) into the trip, you'll reach **Sunwapta Pass**, which is 2023m (6637ft) above sea level. The pass marks the boundary with Jasper National Park; you can either retrace your route back to Lake Louise, or continue on the Icefields Parkway into Jasper (for a continuation of this drive, see p151).

DAY HIKES

While you can see many of Banff's sights from an automobile, to really appreciate the park's beauty you'll have to strap on the hiking boots and take to the trail. Even if you're not a frequent hiker, you really must try to build at least one or two walks into your itinerary – there are trails to suit all levels, from easy rambles to full-blown epics that will test even the fittest walkers. All the walks detailed in this section are within reach of reasonably fit walkers, and are suitable for families unless otherwise indicated.

Plenty of people tackle the trails in T-shirts and sneakers, but even on the simplest trails, it pays to be better prepared. Wear decent boots (ideally with a high ankle to avoid sprains); take plenty of water and trail snacks; and pack warm, layered clothing and waterproofs in case the weather takes a turn for the worse.

There's a handy run-down of Banff's best day hikes on p32.

Banff Town & Around

Bow Falls & the Hoodoos

Duration 3 hours round-trip

Distance 10.2km (6.4 miles)

Difficulty Easy

Start/Finish Buffalo St, Banff Town

Elevation Change 60m (197ft)

Nearest Town Banff (p57)

Transportation Bus

Summary A scenic stroll from Banff, tracking the Bow River through woodland all the way to the Hoodoos.

Despite its proximity to downtown Banff, this easy ramble quickly leaves both traffic noise and tourists behind and delves into the forests and rivers west of the main town, ending at the otherwordly landscape of rocky pillars known as the Hoodoos.

Start out on Buffalo St and follow the road east to the start of the gravel trail beside the river, a popular jaunt for Banff cyclists and joggers. The flat trail tracks the Bow River for about 1.2km (0.7 miles), where it reaches a set of two staircases up to the **Surprise Corner viewpoint** and parking lot, looking out over the rushing white water of **Bow Falls**. You could turn around and retrace your steps here, but it's worth carrying on to the Hoodoos.

From the parking lot, the trail descends through larch and pine woodland and again runs parallel to the river, passing several inlets and small beaches en route to a wide, open grass meadow at around 3km (1.9 miles), from where there are fine southerly views to Mt Rundle on the opposite side of the river.

From here the trail climbs gently up onto the canyon side above the river, with great views across the Bow Valley – make sure you stick to the main trail, as several faint sub-trails veer off along the riverbank and are much tougher going. After 5.1km (3.2 miles) you'll reach the **Hoodoos interpretive trail**, from where you can look out over the Hoodoos rising above the snaking course of the Bow River. The Hoodoos themselves are predominantly made of limestone, with a hard cap of magnesium-rich rock at the top; eons of wind and rain have carved them into a complex topography of twisted towers and weird spires.

GUIDED HIKES

If you're looking for someone to help you interpret the scenery, there are lots of hiking guides in the Banff area. Make sure your guide is accredited by the Mountain Parks Heritage Interpretation Association (MPHIA) for that extra seal of quality.

Great Divide (☎403-522-2735; www.greatdivide.ca; half-day hikes adult/child 6-16yr C$59/39, full-day hikes C$89/59) Run by a knowledgeable husband-and-wife team based in Lake Louise, this company offers guided walks focusing on nature and wildlife. There are scheduled hikes throughout summer; on other days the first to book gets to choose the route (although others are welcome to tag along if there's space). Maximum group size is eight people.

Mahikan Trails (☎403-609-2489; www.mahikan.com; half-day custom hikes C$340 for 4 people, full day C$600) This company combines guided hikes with an introduction to First Nations culture, including tracking, wood lore and traditional bushcraft skills, such as rope-making, native medicine and navigation.

White Mountain Adventures (☎403-760-4403; www.whitemountainadventures.com; half-day hikes for 6 people C$330, full day C$450) A well-regarded hiking and adventure guiding service, with charter trips along popular Banff trails, covering nature spotting, local history and other points of interest. It also offers easy picnic trips (C$75 per person) to Johnson Lake.

Return along the same route or, if your legs are feeling the strain, catch a bus back to Banff from Tunnel Mountain Dr.

Fenland Trail & Vermilion Lakes

Duration 30 minutes round-trip

Distance 2.1km (1.3 miles)

Difficulty Easy

Start/Finish Forty Mile picnic area, Banff

Elevation Change None

Nearest Town Banff (p57)

Transportation Car/foot

Summary Quiet forest walk that follows the green Echo and Forty Mile Creeks through the fenlands.

Popular with Banff cyclists and joggers, this short trail travels through a variety of natural habitats: woodland, marsh, fen, riverbed and wetland. Begin the trail at the Forty Mile picnic area, just north of the 'Welcome to Banff' sign on Lynx St. If you're coming from downtown, there's a connecting trail on the left side of Lynx St, just over the rail tracks. Bring along some mosquito repellent as the biting bugs can be rampant along here, and pick up one of the free trail leaflets from the start of the trailhead.

The flat dirt trail travels through the trees and crosses several wooden bridges where you can view the river and the rich fenland; look out for wooden posts that match points of interest on the trail leaflet. It's a rich habitat for wildlife – listen for tapping woodpeckers, whistling chickadees, honking Canada geese and bugling elks in autumn. Try also to spot the many flowers and plants that thrive in the fenland – sedges, grasses, willows, poplars and dogwoods all flourish in the nutrient-rich groundwater. The only drawback is the constant thrum of traffic traveling along the Trans-Canada Hwy nearby, but it does at least give you a sense of how the local wildlife must feel about the racket on the main road.

If you want a longer hike, you can extend the walk by crossing the large bridge about halfway around the loop and heading left down the road to the **Vermilion Lakes** (p63), a wetland that's popular with wildlife-spotters. The lakes are a 4km (2.5-mile) round-trip. In late May and early June the trail is often closed due to aggressive female elk, which use the area for calving.

Sundance Canyon

Duration 1 hour round-trip

Distance 2km (1.2 miles)

Difficulty Easy

Start/Finish Sundance Trail

Elevation Change 145m (476ft)

Nearest Town Banff (p57)

Transportation Hike/bike

Summary A delightful route around a river canyon, with views of a gushing waterfall, rugged mountains and the Bow Valley.

To reach this canyon walk, you'll need to hike or bike along the **Sundance Trail** (p94) from the Cave & Basin National Historic Site or the Marsh Loop. The route's mainly through thick forest so the views are fairly limited, but it's usually a lot quieter than many trails around Banff. Check at the park office for wildlife warnings, as bears sometimes wander into the canyon from the nearby Middle Springs Wildlife Corridor.

The trail starts at the bike lock-up at the base of the canyon and passes steeply up the left side of a tumbling waterfall. After crossing the wooden bridge and scrambling up a section of rocks and boulders, you'll come out on the mainly flat, sun-dappled trail, which tracks a bubbling stream through the wooded canyon. In summer it's always filled with birdsong and butterflies, and the shady forest makes a rich habitat for lichen, mosses and wildflowers: take along a nature guide to help you spot the species.

After crossing a couple more wooden bridges the trail loops back on itself and after about 1.6km (1 mile) reaches a **lookout point**, from where there are views across the Bow Valley and distant mountain peaks – look closely and you can even see the twisting outline of Hwy 1. From here the trail descends through switchbacks to the bike lock-up.

Johnson Lake

Duration 45 minutes round-trip

Distance 3km (1.9 miles)

Difficulty Easy

Start/Finish Johnson Lake parking lot

Elevation Change None

Nearest Town Banff (p57)

Transportation Car

Summary More an amble than a hike, this walk circles around the shore of a popular recreational lake, mixing wooded and open-air sections, with the option of a paddle in the water when the weather's warm.

Compared to nearby Lake Minnewanka, Johnson Lake is little more than a pond, but on warm summer days it's the nearest thing Banff has to a seaside getaway: sun worshippers and beach bums throng to the lake to lounge around in the sunshine. Ringed by fir forest and encircled by an easy trail with views of Cascade Mountain, Johnson Lake makes a lovely place to combine a lakeside picnic with a leisurely stroll. To reach the lake, follow Lake Minnewanka Rd north of Hwy 1 and take the first right. The next junction is signposted right to Johnson Lake.

From the parking lot, follow the trail past a few picnic tables down to the lakeshore, and pick up the trail on the lake's right (southern side). Initially you'll pass through a grassy section overlooked by power lines from the nearby hydroelectric dam, but the dirt trail soon passes into the fir and spruce woods by the lakeshore.

The trail emerges at an earthen dike on the eastern edge of the lake after about 1.6km (1 mile). The forest to the east is one of the few areas of unmanaged woodland left in Banff National Park, with many old Douglas fir trees. Johnson Lake itself sits in the montane zone, a subalpine area that makes up just 3% of the park's landscape but provides a crucial, vegetation-rich habitat for wildlife. Look out for birds and insects as you walk, and see if you can spot any trout or spotted frogs in the water.

On the northern side of the lake, the trail sticks close to the water and passes a small marshy section formed by a tributary off the main lake. Nearby is a shady area under the trees that makes an excellent spot to stop and tuck into your picnic. From here it's a short walk back to the parking lot.

Stewart Canyon

Duration 1½-2 hours round-trip

Distance 5.6km (3.5 miles)

Difficulty Easy

Start/Finish Lake Minnewanka parking lot

Elevation Change None

Nearest Town Banff (p57)

Transportation Car

Summary A level hike that takes in the north shore of Lake Minnewanka plus an impressive river canyon.

With several of the trails around Lake Minnewanka closed during buffaloberry season due to grizzly bear activity – including the hike to Aylmer Lookout – the easy walk up to **Stewart Canyon** is the area's best option for a summer hike.

The trail starts from the recreational area near the boat ramp on the west side of the lake, and travels for a few hundred meters (approximately 300yd) along a flat, paved section past picnic tables and BBQ shelters. The trailhead proper is marked by an information panel, where you'll find notices about trail closures during the buffaloberry season.

From here the trail passes onto a wooded dirt track offering views of the turquoise lake; it's just about passable for sturdy wheelchairs, but becomes increasingly rooty and rocky the further you travel. The trail tracks into pleasant forest, heading over a wooden bridge above the **Cascade River** at 1.6km (1 mile). On the far side of the river, there's a fork in the trail: the right-hand branch leads up to Aylmer Pass, so take the left fork.

The trail follows the canyon side for another 1.2km (0.7 miles) before reaching another fork. The route to the right leads down into a river gully where you can clamber across boulders and rocks to the bottom of the canyon and the edge of the Cascade River. The canyon itself is named after George Stewart, first superintendent of Canada's first national park. The water level here has risen by about 25m (80ft) since Lake Minnewanka was last dammed in 1941.

Retrace your steps back to the Minnewanka parking lot.

Sulphur Mountain

Duration 4 hours round-trip

Distance 11km (6.8 miles)

Difficulty Moderate

Start/Finish Banff Gondola terminal

Elevation Change 655m (2149ft)

Nearest Town Banff (p57)

Transportation Bus

Summary Savor your superiority over the gondola-goers after climbing this challenging mountain, with outlooks on Banff Town and Mt Rundle.

If you want to test your calf muscles, this leg-sapping route up the side of **Sulphur Mountain** is just the ticket. While mere mortals ride to the top on the gondola (which you'll glimpse occasionally as you ascend the mountain), the sense of achievement you'll get by arriving on foot is worth the climb.

The trail starts at the northwest end of the gondola parking lot, near the Upper Hot Springs Pool. You start climbing almost immediately on the well-marked trail (a daily workout for some of Banff's fitter residents), with viewpoints of Mt Rundle and Banff as you ascend. Most of the trail is along well-graded switchbacks and becomes increasingly steep the further you go; the last section, where the trail arrows straight up the mountainside, is really tough going.

Once at the top, grab an ice cream at the gondola station as a reward and stroll along to **Sanson Peak**, where you'll find Norman's old weather station and great views over the whole valley.

Hikers used to get a free trip back down on the gondola, but now you'll have to pay half the standard fare, so you might as well just make the downhill trudge instead.

C-Level Cirque

Duration 4 hours round-trip

Distance 8.8km (5.4 miles)

Difficulty Moderate

Start/Finish Upper Bankhead parking lot

Elevation Change 455m (1493ft)

Nearest Town Banff (p57)

Transportation Car

Summary Throw your own echo into the silent peaks around a natural amphitheater – if you've still got the energy after the climb.

This popular trail starts out from the Upper Bankhead parking lot, 3.5km (2.2 miles) from Hwy 1 along Lake Minnewanka Rd. It's relatively short but steep, and the cirque itself makes a worthy reward for the climb: a deep glacial bowl carved out by a long-gone glacier and surrounded by jagged mountaintops. Snow lingers in the cirque well into summer: if you're hiking here in early spring, there is a danger of avalanches, so it's worth checking at the park office on trail conditions before you set out.

The route starts from the west side of the parking lot and climbs for about 20 minutes through green forest, often sprinkled with violets, calypso orchids and clematis in summer, before reaching the first remains of the old anthracite coal mine of **Lower Bankhead** (p71); the C-Level in the hike's name refers to the level where the miners once worked.

You'll pass more abandoned mine workings and capped-off shafts as the route climbs; if you're here alone, it can be a rather spooky place, even in blazing sunshine.

After around 45 minutes of climbing, the forest thins out and you'll begin to catch glimpses back toward Banff Town, Mt Rundle and the nearby lakes, and pass through a few sections with steep drop-offs. A little over an hour into the hike, you'll emerge into the **C-Level Cirque** itself.

Pikas, golden-mantled ground squirrels and the occasional hoary marmot can often be seen scurrying beside the path as you continue along the rough trail along the edge of the cirque, before joining up with the last steep, rubbly section up to the **lookout knoll**. Rest here and admire the fabulous views stretching back down the valley toward Banff and the Bow River.

Cascade Amphitheatre

Duration 6 hours round-trip

Distance 7.7km (8.2 miles) one way

Difficulty Moderate-difficult

Start/Finish Mt Norquay parking lot

Elevation Change 640m (2100ft)

Nearest Town Banff (p57)

Transportation Car

Summary Huge views and a technical hike make this trail a good option if you're after something challenging.

You'll start out high and keep on getting higher on this mountain trail into a hanging valley beneath **Cascade Mountain**, carved out by glaciers that melted away long ago. It's a favored hangout for marmots and pikas, and a well-known spot for appreciating alpine wildflowers in late July and early August, but it's tough going and largely through forest, so you won't get too many views until the end. It might be a bit too much for younger walkers.

Head up Mt Norquay Rd from Banff Town all the way to the ski lodge parking lot; the trail starts near the entrance. You'll traverse a service road and pass the Mystic chair lift, then descend into lodgepole pine forest. Continue straight ahead at the Mystic Pass/Forty Mile Summit junction. After 3km, you'll reach the banks of Forty Mile Creek; keep to the right and cross over the bridge.

From here the real climb begins as the trail continues through the forest to a junction with the Elk Lake Summit Trail at 4.3km (2.7 miles). Keep right and catch your breath ahead of a series of brutal switchbacks that carry you 2.3km (1.4 miles) up the pine-forested western slope of the mountain.

Just before arriving at the valley, the trail levels off and a number of faint paths head to the right. These lead to the summit ridge, which is suitable for mountaineers only, so stick to the main path until you emerge at a lovely alpine meadow, which is dotted with white anemone and yellow lilies in summer.

The trail becomes indistinct but continues for about 1km (0.6 miles) to the upper end of the amphitheater, where the vegetation thins out and boulders litter the ground. Rest here for a while and you'll be able to watch marmots and pikas scurrying between the rocks.

Johnston Canyon & the Inkpots

Duration 4 hours round-trip

Distance 10.8km (6.7 miles)

Difficulty Moderate

Start/Finish Johnston Canyon parking lot

Elevation Change 215m (705ft) to Inkpots

Nearest Town Banff (p57)

Transportation Car

Summary A classic canyon hike past two of the park's most impressive waterfalls, with an optional add-on to five colorful springs in an alpine meadow.

The paved path through **Johnston Canyon** to its twin waterfalls is one of Banff's highlights, which means it's nearly always jammed with people – but don't let its popularity put you off. It's a must-see destination, and you can usually beat the worst of the crowds by turning up early – if you arrive before 9am you'll usually have the canyon practically to yourself.

The asphalt trail cuts through the center of the lush canyon, traversing several suspended catwalks high above the surging waters of Johnston Creek, which has carved out the canyon from the surrounding limestone rock. Shaded by trees, the towering canyon walls are covered with mosses, lichen and ferns, and black swifts can often be seen darting around the treetops during their nesting season from late June to September. It's also a great walk to do in the rain, as a downpour only adds to the spectacular force of the falls.

The first paved section (suitable for wheelchairs) leads to the **Lower Falls** after 30 minutes. Here you can duck through a natural cave right into the spray of the falls – be prepared to get wet, and bring a waterproof bag to protect your camera. The route to the Upper Falls (about 45 minutes from the Lower Falls) is steeper and crosses a few staircases, passing the mineral and algae-encrusted wall known as the **Travertine Drape**. You can descend to another platform viewpoint at the bottom of the **Upper Falls**, but it's worth continuing on up the trail for a reverse view of the falls as they plunge over the cliff edge into the canyon below.

Most people turn back at this point, but they're missing out on another nearby natural marvel: the colorful ponds known as the **Inkpots**. From the Upper Falls, the trail climbs fairly steeply through the forest for 3km (1.9 miles) and then descends into a vast mountain meadow. Here you'll find the six Inkpots, encircled by snowcapped mountains: the pools get their name from the bright blue-green water that bubbles up from natural springs deep inside the mountain.

From the Inkpots, trails lead deep into the backcountry: northeast along Mystic Pass and Forty Mile Creek, and northwest along Johnston Creek (often used by bears as a drinking hole). Both are overnight trips, so you'll need proper supplies and a wilderness pass to tackle either trail.

Castle Lookout

Duration 3-4 hours

Distance 7.6km (4.7 miles)

Difficulty Moderate

Start/Finish Castle Mountain parking lot

Elevation Change 520m (1706ft)

Nearest Town Banff (p57)

Transportation Car

Summary A steep trail to an abandoned fire lookout beneath Castle Mountain, offering grand views across the Bow Valley.

Although it's a tiring climb and most of the trail is in thick lodgepole pine forest, the final view from this old fire lookout is a knockout, offering one of the best panoramas in the entire Bow Valley.

The trailhead is halfway along the Bow Valley Parkway, a 4km (2.5-mile) drive on from **Castle Junction**. From the parking lot, pick up the trail into the forest and start your ascent up the switchbacks. At around 1.5km (0.9 miles) you'll pass a ramshackle cabin, left over from the days when Castle Mountain was a bustling center for miners and prospectors. Another series of switchbacks carries you up and out toward the treeline, emerging onto the rocky cliffs and steep escarpments that are so characteristic of Castle Mountain. In summer the upper trail is often awash with wildflowers, especially calypso orchids, arnica and the lovely blue clematis.

At 3.8km (2.4 miles), the trail breaks out above the forest onto an open plateau. This was the site of the **Castle Lookout**, a fire watchtower built by conscientious objectors in the 1940s. The site was abandoned in the 1970s, and now nothing remains except the lookout's concrete foundations.

Fittingly for a fire lookout, the wide-open views over the Bow Valley are stunning. Jagged mountains cut across the horizon: look out for the dog-tooth profiles of Storm Mountain to the west and Mt Temple to the north, and the distant peaks of the Sundance and Fairholme Ranges to the southeast. Behind you, the hulking form of Castle Mountain juts skywards; its shattered cliffs are popular with rock climbers, who have constructed a basic climbing hut a little further on the trail toward the face.

From the lookout, retrace your steps back through the forest to the parking lot, and remember to check yourself carefully for ticks if you're hiking here in May and June.

Garden Path Trail & Twin Cairns Meadow

Duration 3½ hours round-trip

Distance 8.3km (5.1 miles)

Difficulty Easy

Start/Finish Sunshine Village parking lot

Elevation Change None from ski area, 655m (2148ft) from parking lot

Nearest Town Banff (p57)

Transportation Bus

Summary The easiest of the hikes from Sunshine Village takes in lakes, flowers and a viewpoint of Simpson Pass.

This might be the easiest option in Sunshine Meadows (p66), but it's certainly not short on views. The flat, well-marked trail leads past three glimmering alpine lakes and lush meadows filled with summer wildflowers, leading to a grandstand lookout above the Continental Divide. Watch out for ground squirrels bounding around the pathway and take along a guidebook to help you check off the summer blossoms.

Catch the bus from the parking lot to the Sunshine Village ski area. The trailhead starts on the southern side of the ski area, passing underneath the line of the main gondola up to Standish Ridge (look out for the log cabin at the start of the trail).

From here it's a gentle 10-minute climb up to the first fork, where you should stay right. At the top of the hill, you enter the alpine meadows, sprinkled with mountain flowers and larch trees; you'll soon reach the summit of the Great Divide and cross over into British Columbia. At the next junction, keep right; the left fork leads to Quartz Hill to the soaring Citadel Pass.

Over the crest of the hill, the terrain rolls downwards to **Rock Isle Lake**, so called for the distinctive wooded islet that juts out from the middle of the water. Above the lake there's a good **lookout** with views of Standish Ridge to the right and Quartz Hill to the left, with a distant glimpse of the snowy pinnacle of Mt Assiniboine.

Rejoin the trail and head left at the next junction. The path winds through larch trees and pebble-filled streams en route to the Grizzly and Larix Lakes Loop. Continue over the next junction for **Grizzly Lake**, and follow the lakeshore to the **Simpson Valley Lookout**. The pass is named after George Simpson, governor of the Hudson's Bay Company, who made the first foray along the valley in 1841. From the viewpoint, the trail loops around green-blue **Larix Lake** and rejoins the main Garden Path Trail.

You could return to Sunshine Village the way you came, but for better views head back via **Twin Cairns Meadow**. Turn left at the first junction after Rock Isle Lake, signposted to Standish Viewpoint. It's worth detouring 500m (0.3 miles) off the main trail to reach the **Standish Ridge viewpoint**, which offers a 360-degree panorama encompassing Citadel Pass, Simpson Valley and Healy Pass.

Descend back to the main trail and turn right (north) across Twin Cairns Meadow. After 2km (1.2 miles) you reach a T-junction; take a detour left to **Monarch Viewpoint** (100m), which has excellent views of Mt Assiniboine on a clear day. Turn back from the viewpoint and follow the path back down to Sunshine Village, 1.6km (1 mile) away, via a winding trail through the woods.

Healy Pass

Duration 6-7 hours round-trip

Distance 18.4km (11.4 miles)

Difficulty Moderate-difficult

Start/Finish Sunshine Village parking lot

Elevation Change 650m (2132ft)

Nearest Town Banff (p57)

Transportation Bus

Summary Wildflowers, forest and lofty mountain ramparts combine on this varied hike, which ascends from the valley floor right onto the rooftop of Sunshine Meadows.

If the Sunshine Meadows area has whetted your appetite, try this more challenging route up **Healy Pass**, which traverses lush meadows with an uninterrupted vista of peaks and lakes. It's ideally undertaken late in the season, when the weather's best and your legs are up to the effort.

The trailhead begins at the Sunshine Village parking lot, near the gondola base station. It leads up a rocky service road, passing into forest after 800m (0.5 miles). From here the trail crosses Sunshine Creek and ascends steadily along Healy Valley, canopied by spruce and fir trees. Look out for red squirrels, woodpeckers, chickadees and Clark's nutcrackers in the trees. The trail then leads along Healy Creek, reaching the Healy Creek campground after 5.7km (3.5 miles).

From here the forest opens up and the trail levels off into a more gradual climb as it enters the open meadows, alive with wildflowers throughout July and August. You'll pass the junction for Simpson Pass Trail on the left, where it's possible to make a circular loop via Simpson Pass and Healy Meadows; alternatively, stick to the main trail and continue for a further 1.5km (0.9 miles) all the way to Healy Pass.

Perched at 2330m (7644ft) atop the escarpment of Monarch Ramparts, this is one of the Rockies' great views. It's only 1km (0.6 miles) from the Great Divide, and looks over some of the region's most dramatic sights, including the witch's-hat peak of Mt Assiniboine far to the southeast. To the west are Egypt, Mummy and Scarab Lakes, shining brightly beneath the Pharaoh Peaks, and to the north, the aptly named Massive Range broods along the horizon. You might even spy grizzlies and black bears on the open meadows around the pass.

From here the trail continues west toward Egypt Lake, an overnight route covered on p90. If you're not planning on camping overnight, bid your farewells to the pass and retrace your steps back down to Sunshine Village. If time allows, you could take the optional detour via Simpson Pass on the way down.

Lake Louise & Around

Consolation Lakes Trail

Duration 2 hours round-trip

Distance 6km (3.8 miles)

Difficulty Easy

Start/Finish Moraine Lake

Elevation Change 65m (213ft)

Nearest Town Lake Louise (p67)

Transportation Car

Summary It's only a short uphill stroll from Moraine Lake, but this trail still offers a taste of the wild Rockies.

Most people never get much further than the Moraine Lake shoreline, but to reach the real scenery you really do have to stretch your legs. This short trail winds through rocks and boulders to a duo of sparkling mountain lakes backed by brooding cliffs. The walk is straightforward, although you will need proper hiking boots – the trail gets very muddy in spring and

HIKING RESTRICTIONS AROUND LAKE LOUISE

The Lake Louise area is one of three key grizzly bear habitats in Banff National Park, and supports a number of grizzly sows and their cubs. To avoid bear encounters, park authorities often impose group access restrictions in summer on several trails around Lake Louise, including the Consolation Lakes Trail, Larch Valley, Sentinel Pass, Paradise Valley and Wenkchemna Pass.

Under the rules, hikers are required by law to travel in tight groups of at least four people, and take the usual precautions to avoid bear encounters (make noise on the trail, carry bear spray etc). Other routes (including the Moraine Lake Highline Trail) may also be closed according to bear activity – check ahead with park staff. If you're caught breaching the 'group of four' rule, you'll be up for a hefty fine, so stick to the rules: they're there for your own safety.

The timetable varies every year according to bear activity and the berry season, but usually begins around mid-July and lasts until early September. Restrictions are clearly posted in park offices and at trailheads.

If you're short on numbers, the Lake Louise Visitor Centre keeps a logbook where you can leave your details to get in touch with other hikers to make up the required numbers. Or leave your details at one of the local hostels or just hang around the trailheads at the start of the day – you're bound to find another group who won't mind you tagging along.

Consolation Lakes Trail

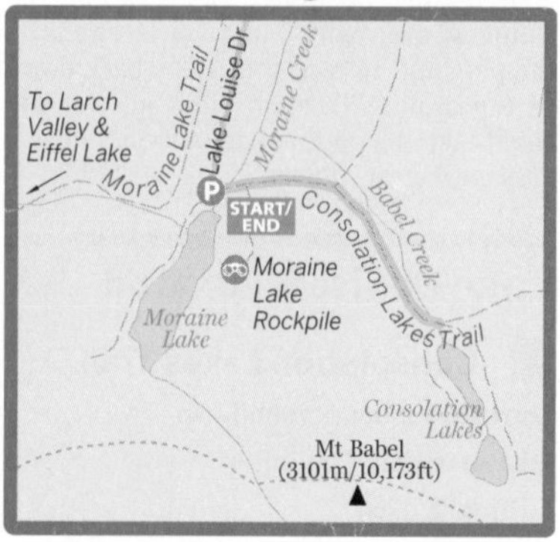

autumn, and traverses an area of rough, rocky boulders en route to the lakeshore. Note also that the Consolation Lakes are prime bear habitat, and fall under group access restrictions in summer (see the boxed text, p81).

Heading east from the parking lot, follow signs for the Consolation Lakes. You'll pass a small bridge and skirt the back of the rockpile, crossing over a rocky moraine before ascending into pine forest. This section of the trail offers great views up the side of Mt Babel and back over the shoreline peaks of Moraine Lake.

For the next 1.6km (1 mile), the trail winds by the trees along the shores of the clattering **Babel Creek**. Some sections get very muddy after snowmelt and heavy rain, but try not to take any shortcuts off the main path, as it damages the fragile forest habitat.

You'll reach the Consolation Lakes after 3km (1.9 miles), tucked into the base of a distinctive U-shaped glacial valley dotted with rough boulders, scree and smashed rocks, which make for difficult walking. Take extra care as you cross the rocks toward the lakeshore. The valley is trammeled by Panorama Ridge to the east, Mt Bell to the southeast and the sharp peaks of Mt Quadra and Bident Mountain at the northern side of the lake. The icy monsters to the west are Mt Fay (3235m/10,613ft) and Mt Babel (3101m/10,173ft).

The trail to the Upper Lake crosses some treacherous areas of boulders and scree, so unless you're an experienced scrambler, it's best to settle for the views from the lower lake before heading for home.

Plain of Six Glaciers

Duration 4-5 hours round-trip

Distance 13.5km (8.4 miles)

Difficulty Moderate

Start/Finish Fairmont Chateau Lake Louise

Elevation Change 365m (1198ft)

Nearest Town Lake Louise (p67)

Transportation Car

Summary One of the Lake Louise classics, ending at a historic teahouse with views across the Victoria and Lefroy Glaciers.

This classic hike from Lake Louise punches up the rubble-strewn glacial valley to the foot of Victoria and Lefroy Glaciers, twin tongues of glittering ice jammed between regal peaks. It's a jaw-dropper of a hike that'll leave you breathless in more ways than one. You'll need sturdy boots, warm layers and a good rain shell; walking poles are useful for keeping yourself upright on the shifting moraines. The trail is often one of the last to open after spring due to snow and avalanche danger: check at the park office before you start out.

Follow the paved shoreline walk from the Fairmont Chateau Lake Louise for 2km (1.3 miles) to the lake's southwestern end, and then head along the edge of the river flats, watching as the glacial creek feeding the lake becomes a torrent. The trail climbs steadily through forest, emerging occasionally to give you views of the glacial ravine. At 3.3km (2 miles) and again at 4km (2.5 miles), you'll meet trails branching off to the right, leading to the highline trail to the Big Beehive and Lake Agnes. Ignore these and press on up the valley, as the tree cover gradually thins out and you emerge onto switchbacks. You'll have plenty of opportunity to stop and catch your breath, as well as to gaze at the rapidly approaching glaciers to the southwest and the ice-strewn slopes of Mts Lefroy and Victoria. Keep your ears open for the rumble of avalanches crashing off the distant Victoria Glacier, especially late in the morning.

After two hours and 5.5km (3.4 miles) of climbing, you'll reach the **Plain of Six Glaciers Teahouse** (lunch C$5-10; ⏲8am-6pm Jun–mid-Oct), constructed in 1927 as a way station for Swiss mountaineering guides leading clients up to the summit of Mt Victoria.

THE DEATH TRAP

At the crest of Victoria Glacier on the Plain of Six Glaciers hike, look out for the tiny speck of Abbot Hut, a refuge built in 1922 by the pioneering guide Edward Feuz Jr as a shelter for mountaineers. It's Canada's highest national historic site, and is now maintained by the Alpine Club of Canada. The pass (and the hut) are named after Philip Abbot, an experienced American mountaineer who set out with three friends to make the first successful ascent of Mt Lefroy in 1896, but tragically became the first climbing fatality in North America when he slipped on loose snow on the final section of the ascent and fell to his death. The narrowest section of the glacier up to the hut is known as the Death Trap, receiving its ominous name while Feuz and his companions were building the Abbot Hut; the entire construction team were caught in one of the frequent avalanches and swept back down the glacier. Despite having narrowly escaped with his life, Feuz is said to have been unruffled by the experience – his only complaint was that he had lost his favorite pipe in that 'damned avalanche.'

Nestled in a quiet glade, the twin-level log chalet looks like something out of the pages of *Heidi*, and dishes up homemade sandwiches, cakes, gourmet teas and hot chocolates to a steady stream of puffed-out hikers.

Despite its allure, sensible walkers leave the treats of the teahouse for the return walk, as the main hike isn't over yet. From the clearing, the trail leads a further 1.6km (1 mile) uphill to the **Plain of Six Glaciers** itself, tracking a rubbly ridge that can be slippery in wet weather and is exposed to vicious winds funneled up the valley.

Although there's nothing to mark it, you'll know you've reached the lookout when you have a grandstand view of the front edge of the **Victoria Glacier** and can see back down the valley to Lake Louise and the chateau. In the 1800s the glacier covered most of the surrounding area. From the lookout, a path leads up the face of the moraine to the cliff edge and a small waterfall; it's very slippery, so only tackle it if you're a competent scrambler. You should see the cleft of Abbot Pass from the top. Once you've admired the views, retrace your steps down the moraine and visit the teahouse before heading back down the valley. If your legs are up to it, you could detour along the signposted highline trail, which links up with the route to Lake Agnes and the Big Beehive.

Lake Agnes & the Beehives

Duration 4 hours round-trip

Distance 10.8km (6.6 miles)

Difficulty Moderate to Lake Agnes, moderate-difficult to Big Beehive

Start/Finish Fairmont Chateau Lake Louise

Elevation Change 495m (1624ft)

Nearest Town Lake Louise (p67)

Transportation Car

Summary The walk that practically everyone who visits Lake Louise wants to do. It's crowded but the sights are unmissable, visiting a historic teahouse, two mountain lakes and a fantastic cloud-level lookout.

This is one of the most popular walks in the Lake Louise area, so it's worth doing early or late in the day to beat the crowds. It's a fine, well-marked route taking in forest trails, hidden lakes and scenic viewpoints, as well as a famous teahouse – but it is formidably steep (especially around the Big Beehive), so bring plenty of water and take regular rests. You can either make it a stand-alone hike or combine it with the Plain of Six Glaciers hike.

Begin on the Lake Louise shoreline trail, and take the fork on the right after about 800m (0.5 miles) as it ascends into forest. The path zigzags through the trees for about 45 minutes, with occasional views back over the lake to Fairview Mountain, before emerging at the glassy surface of **Mirror Lake**, famous for its photogenic reflection of the Big Beehive. The lake makes a good place to refuel before continuing on the steep climb to Lake Agnes itself.

The trail divides at Mirror Lake. You can reach the lake via the right-hand trail, but the most straightforward route is to take a left from the lake and then an immediate right after about 100m for the direct climb to the teahouse (left here leads on to the Plain of Six Glaciers hike). It's a steep slog through the forest for a further 15 minutes, but you'll have good views of the mountains as the trees begin to thin out. The final section passes a waterfall and traverses a near-vertical set of wooden stairs before emerging at the lake and the teahouse.

Lake Agnes itself is named after Lady Susan Agnes Macdonald (wife of former prime minister Sir John Macdonald), who made the climb to the lake in 1890. There's been a **teahouse** (⌚9am-6pm Jun-Aug, 10am-5:30pm Sep) here since 1901, but the present building is actually a replica built in 1981: it serves a huge selection of exotic teas ranging from golden monkey to 'Imperial Keernun' sacred blend, but tables can be scarce at peak times. Soups, cakes and sandwich platters are also available if you're after something more substantial.

Once you've fuelled up at the teahouse, you can either take an optional detour to the top of the **Little Beehive** (105m/344ft elevation gain) before heading around the right side of the lake en route to its bigger brother, the **Big Beehive** (135m/442ft elevation gain), which you'll reach after 1.6km (1 mile) of relentless, leg-shredding switchbacks. Needless to say, the summit rewards the effort: you'll enjoy a sky-topping vantage of the entire Lake Louise area, with the Slate Range to the northeast, the Bow Valley southeast and Lake Louise and its surrounding peaks way below. It's a truly unforgettable lookout, but you'll need a head for heights.

From the top, you can either retrace your steps to Lake Agnes, or descend south toward the Plain of Six Glaciers trail.

Saddleback & Fairview

Duration 5-6 hours round-trip

Distance 7.4km (4.6 miles) to Saddleback, 10.2km (6.4 miles) to Fairview

Difficulty Moderate-difficult

Start/Finish Lake Louise

Elevation Change 600m (1970ft) to Saddleback, 1013m (3323ft) to Fairview

Nearest Town Lake Louise (p67)

Transportation Car

Summary Big vistas from two of Lake Louise's most famous viewpoints, but tough going all the way to the top.

This hike starts out steep and just keeps getting steeper, climbing to a famous pass between Fairview and Saddle Mountain, and an even more famous summit lookout. There's no getting around the elevation gain, but at least you'll feel like you've earned the view.

Start at the viewpoint in front of the Fairmont Chateau Lake Louise, and follow signs pointing to Saddleback. After around 300m, you'll reach a junction: the left fork joins up with the Moraine Lake Highline Trail (p96), while the right fork emerges at a viewpoint above the lake. The main trail lies dead ahead. It climbs sharply along a snaking trail, ascending relentlessly through spruce and larch forest all the way to the **Saddleback** at 3.7km (2.3 miles).

The landscape of Lake Louise opens up like a panoramic picturebook once you finally reach the top of the pass. It's a superb place to tick off some of the main peaks around Lake Louise: south is Mt Temple (3544m/11,626ft), southwest are Sheol Mountain (2779m/9117ft) and Haddo Peak (3070m/10,072ft). A compass and a topo map are useful to help identify each mountain.

Directly north of the pass is the trail to the top of **Fairview** (2744m/9003ft), the craggy peak that dominates the southern side of Lake Louise. You don't necessarily have to tackle the path to the top, but it's worth the toil if you're up to it. Basic scrambling skills and sturdy boots with plenty of grip will come in handy, as some sections can be rocky and slippery. Once you reach the top, you'll realize exactly how the mountain came by its name.

Larch Valley & Sentinel Pass

Duration 4-5 hours round-trip

Distance 8.6km (5.3 miles) to Larch Valley, 11.6km (7.2 miles) to Sentinel Pass

Difficulty Moderate

Start/Finish Moraine Lake

Elevation Change 535m (1755ft) to Larch Valley, 725m (2379ft) to Sentinel Pass

Nearest Town Lake Louise (p67)

Transportation Car

Summary A popular trail through larch forest and alpine meadows with wonderful views of the Wenkchemna Peaks.

Another of Lake Louise's quintessential hikes, this route offers one of the best outlooks of the Valley of the Ten Peaks and travels through some of the park's finest larch

Larch Valley & Paradise Valley

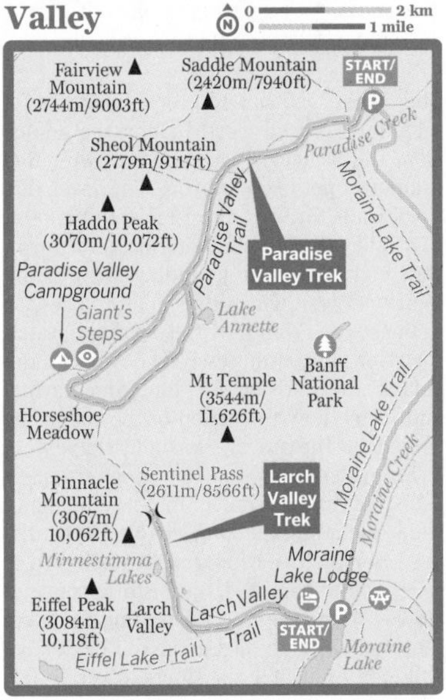

forests. Snow lingers at higher elevations well into spring, so it's best visited in fall when the valley turns into a sea of autumnal colors. Strong hikers can extend the walk for an impressive mountain panorama at Sentinel Pass.

Start on the Moraine Lake Trail and veer right at the signpost for Larch Valley into dense forest, traveling up a set of switchbacks that gain over 350m (1148ft) in 2.5km (1.6m miles).

At the first junction, the left trail leads to **Eiffel Lake** (another great destination that's often quieter than the Larch Valley trail). Follow the right-hand turn and climb further into the fragrant forest, emerging after about 3.5km (2.2 miles) into the wide-open spaces of **Larch Valley**. The meadows are famous for their wildflowers, but the high-alpine habitat is extremely fragile, so don't step off the main trail if you can possibly help it.

From here, the path breaks above the treeline and continues to the little **Minnestimma Lakes** at about 4.5km (2.8 miles). From here, there's an amazing view of eight of the 10 Wenkchemna peaks, as well as the white mass of the **Fay Glacier**.

Most hikers end the walk here, but if the weather's good and your legs are feeling strong, you could continue up and over the 2611m (8566ft) **Sentinel Pass**, one of the highest maintained passes in the Canadian Rockies. It's a hard, tiring trail that crosses slippery areas of talus and scree: don't even think about tackling it in snow or heavy rain, as the weather can turn suddenly. Check the forecasts before you set out, and bring layers and waterproofs.

From the top of the pass, experienced hikers can make a truly epic circle down into adjacent **Paradise Valley**, but you'll be stranded at the other end unless you've got two vehicles.

Note this route falls under group access restrictions (see the boxed text, p81).

Paradise Valley & the Giant's Steps

Duration 6-7 hours round-trip

Distance 20.3km (12.6 miles)

Difficulty Difficult

Start/Finish Paradise Valley parking area, Moraine Lake Rd

Elevation Change 385m (1263ft)

Nearest Town Lake Louise (p67)

Transportation Car

Summary An unforgettable route along a remote mountain valley, rated by many seasoned hikers as one of their favorite destinations in the Canadian Rockies.

Paradise Valley goes head to head with Larch Valley in the scenic stakes. It's a showstopper, tracing a route past ice-crowned summits, delicate cornices, scree slopes and a natural rock cascade called the Giant's Steps. This is prime grizzly habitat, so group access restrictions may be in force (see the boxed text, p81) – take care and make extra noise. Trails were rerouted in 2007 to reduce the risk of bear encounters. It's also a route for experienced hikers.

The trailhead starts at a small parking lot about 2.5km (1.6 miles) along Moraine Lake Rd. The first section travels gently through forest, tracking the course of Paradise Creek. At 1.1km (0.7 miles) from the trailhead, you'll cross the **Moraine Lake Highline Trail** (p96) between Lake Louise and Moraine Lake; turn right (north), then almost immediately left (west) for Paradise Valley.

The trail then crosses the creek a couple of times before passing the right-hand fork to **Saddleback** (p84) at 4.2km (2.6 miles).

Ignore the junction and continue west toward **Lake Annette**, which you'll reach at around 5.8km (3.6 miles). This peaceful lake feels thrillingly remote, surrounded by lonely mountains and silent forest that remain snowclad until well into July. It also offers soaring views of nearby **Mt Temple** (3544m/11,626ft), the highest peak around Lake Louise, and the third highest in Banff National Park.

From the lake, the trail rolls southwest toward the head of the valley, dominated by the dramatic Horseshoe Glacier and a cluster of impressive peaks. The tallest of all is **Mt Hungabee** (3493m/11,460ft), which means 'chieftain' in the Stoney language. As you continue southwest, the specter of **Pinnacle Mountain** appears to the south, while to the northwest across the valley, the glacier-flanked slopes of **Mt Lefroy** (3423m/11,230ft) loom above a sparkling blue glacial lake. This section is one of the most dramatic in the entire national park: take your time and don't forget to take plenty of pictures.

At 8.5km (5.2 miles), you'll reach a right-hand fork leading to the northwest. Take the turning and follow the path down toward a bridge over Paradise Creek. Soon afterwards, you'll reach another junction: straight ahead takes you to the little Paradise Valley Campground, while the right-hand fork leads to the tumble of rock slabs known as the **Giant's Steps** after about 300m. Check ahead at the park office if you're planning on camping, as the campground is closed whenever there's bear activity in the valley.

From the Giant's Steps, you can either retrace your steps or make an optional loop around the edge of **Horseshoe Meadow** (keep an extra eye out for bears here). On the south side of the meadow, you'll pass the connector trail south to **Sentinel Pass** (p84), while the main trail leads northeast back toward Lake Annette.

Icefields Parkway

Mistaya Canyon

Duration 30 minutes round-trip

Distance 1km (0.6 miles)

Difficulty Easy

Start/Finish Mistaya Canyon lay-by

Elevation Change None

Nearest Town Saskatchewan Crossing (p74)

Transportation Car

Summary An easy walk to one of the park's most picturesque river canyons.

This short trail barely even qualifies as a hike, but it's well worth taking the detour from the Icefields Parkway to discover this dramatic, potholed canyon. The level dirt track leads through forest for around 500m (0.3 miles) before emerging on the canyon wall high above the pounding swirl of the **Mistaya River**, which rises in Peyto Lake far to the south. From the bridge you can watch the river plunge impressively down into the curves and curls of the limestone ravine, and watch how the action of the water has carved out the canyon's tortuous shape.

From the far side of the bridge the path leads on to two much more challenging trails, including the long slog up to the disused **Sarbach fire lookout**, a 10.6km (6.6-mile) round-trip; and the historic route to **Howse Pass**, the first fur-trading route established through the Canadian Rockies. It's 4.3km (2.7 miles) to the Howse River.

Bow Glacier Falls

Duration 3 hours round-trip

Distance 7.2km (4.4 miles)

Difficulty Easy-moderate

Start/Finish Num-Ti-Jah Lodge

Elevation Change 155m (509ft)

Nearest Town Lake Louise (p67)

Transportation Car

Summary Cross river flats and moraine fields to reach an impressive glacier-fed waterfall.

When Jimmy Simpson used to lead his guests along this well-worn walk in the early 1900s, the Bow Glacier still filled much of the basin at the end of the trail. These days it's shrunk into the mountains, leaving a boulder-filled valley and the clattering Bow Glacier Falls in its wake. It's an easy and rewarding jaunt, with just one steep section and a fine finish as you cross the moraine moonscape up to the face of the falls. It's a good one to consider on rainy days, when the cascade is at its most powerful.

The trailhead starts just behind Jimmy Simpson's former hotel, **Num-Ti-Jah Lodge**, 37km (23 miles) from the southern end of the Icefields Parkway. The first section winds along the lakeshore, with views of Crowfoot Mountain and the Wapta Glacier. After 2km (1.2 miles) you reach the edge of the lake, and follow the path southwest across a rock bed. To your right are two narrow **waterfalls** streaming down the cliff face. Follow the cairns across the rocky terrain, heading for a distant staircase and the canyon mouth.

After 3.5km (2.2 miles) the steep staircase leads you up a forested ridge alongside the canyon; watch your step if it's been raining, as there are no handholds and there's a long drop to your left. About halfway up you'll pass a massive boulder jammed into the valley, which climbers have to cross in order to follow the route to the high-altitude Bow Hut, the starting point for many ascents.

After 10 minutes or so the staircase ends and the trail leads onto the edge of the huge moraine field, sprinkled with boulders, rocks and stones and backed by the distant crash of the **Bow Glacier Falls** plunging 100m (328ft) over the edge of the valley. Cairns mark the route across the valley to the falls themselves; walking poles will come in handy here, as it's usually slippery underfoot. Finish up with a drink and a picnic beside the cascade before retracing your steps back to the lake.

Peyto Lake & Bow Summit Lookout

Duration 2 hours round-trip

Distance 6.2km (3.8 miles)

THE MOUNTAIN MAN

Driving into Banff you might notice a distinctive face staring at you from the town-limits sign, sporting a jaunty hat, a drooping meerschaum pipe and a rather splendid handlebar moustache. Meet 'Wild' Bill Peyto, one of the great characters of the Canadian Rockies and the original wild man of the mountains.

Born in Kent, England, in 1869, young William was the third eldest of a family of nine children. Having left the cramped environs of the Peyto household at 17, Bill set out to find his fortune in Canada, arriving in Halifax in 1887, where he initially found work as a railway laborer, part-time rancher and government employee. But it wasn't long before Bill found his true calling – as a mountain guide working for the packing and outfitting business owned by Tom Wilson.

Over the next decade he proved himself a skilled trapper, huntsman and alpinist, exploring Mistaya Valley and Peyto Lake, making the first successful ascent of Bow Summit in 1894 and notching up the first (failed) attempt at Mt Assiniboine the following year (he eventually scaled it in 1902). He even found time for some book-larnin', schooling himself in paleontology and geology using secondhand textbooks. Within a matter of years he had become one of the most skilled amateur naturalists in the Rockies.

He was also a notorious showman with an eye for a natty outfit. One of his clients, Norman Collie, painted a vivid picture of Wild Bill: 'Peyto assumes a wild and picturesque though somewhat tattered attire. A sombrero, with a rakish tilt to one side, a blue shirt set off by a white kerchief (which may have served civilization for napkin), and a buckskin coat with a fringe border add to his cowboy appearance. A heavy belt containing a row of cartridges, hunting knife and six-shooter as well as the restless activity of his wicked blue eyes, give him an air of bravado...'

As his reputation grew, so did the stories that surrounded him. According to one famous legend, Bill once strolled into a saloon with a wild lynx strapped to his back to scare off the other punters (apparently he liked to drink in peace). Another tall tale maintains that he had a habit of setting man-traps inside his cabin in order to catch thieves helping themselves to his stores.

He was also a man with a conscience. He fought in the Boer War, became one of the very first park wardens in 1913 and later served with the 12th Mounted Regiment in WWI, sustaining wounds at Ypres in 1916 and enduring a long convalescence in England before returning to his park duties. He continued to serve as a warden until he retired in 1936 to care for his wife, Ethel Wells; she died in 1940, and Bill followed three years later.

You can still visit one of Bill's original log cabins on the grounds of the Whyte Museum in Banff, and his action-packed diary – which is appropriately titled *Ain't It Hell: Bill Peyto's Mountain Journal* – is available from the museum shop.

Difficulty Moderate

Start/Finish Peyto Lake parking lot

Elevation Change 245m (803ft)

Nearest Town Saskatchewan Crossing (p74)

Transportation Car

Summary An old fire road passing the famous Peyto Lake viewpoint up to an abandoned fire lookout high above the Bow and Mistaya Valleys.

You'll have plenty of company along the first part of this trail; practically every visitor to the Icefields Parkway stops to take in the sights from the **Peyto Lake Lookout**, which you'll reach after an easy 15 minutes through the forest from the main parking lot. Leave behind the crowds on the main wooden lookout and continue on to a three-way junction; left leads to the upper parking lot, while the right and middle trails continue on a forested loop with interpretive signs detailing various aspects of the alpine environment. Take the middle trail and look out for an unmarked dirt road on your left after about 1km (0.6 miles), zigzagging uphill toward the lookout. Soon you'll reach a **plateau** on the right with much better views across the lake than you'll get from the main viewpoint. Stop here for a while to appreciate the scenery, with mountain sentinels standing on either side of the glittering blue water and a string of smaller waterways leading off into the distance at the far end of the valley.

From here the trail continues to climb, with wildflowers replacing the increasingly scarce trees. At 2.5km (1.5 miles) the road dips into a rocky bowl, often frequented by sunbathing marmots and bisected by a tinkling stream. Cross the bowl and set out on the last ascent of 500m (0.3 miles), crossing two hills to the **Bow Summit Lookout**. North is Mistaya Valley rising up to Bow Pass; east is Cirque Peak, and southeast across the Bow Valley is the great sweep of Crowfoot Glacier.

Helen Lake

Duration 4 hours round-trip

Distance 12km (7.4 miles)

Difficulty Moderate

Start/Finish Helen Lake parking lot

Elevation Change 455m (1493ft)

Nearest Town Saskatchewan Crossing (p74)

Transportation Car

Summary Steep route leading up to a hidden valley renowned for its glorious display of summer wildflowers.

This is one of the most beautiful high-altitude valleys along the Icefields Parkway and, in summer, it's also one of the top places to see a Technicolor display of Canadian wildflowers. You'll have a real sense of solitude at the top, and the mountain panoramas of Cirque Peak and Dolomite Peak are outstanding. It's best done in good weather; you're quite exposed on the trail and at the top, and the views are disappointing if it's sheeting with rain. The high mountain meadows also remain snowbound until well into July. Bears are also fairly common visitors to the area, so hike in a group and make plenty of noise on the trail.

The trailhead is 33km (20.5 miles) along the parkway, near the turnoff to the Crowfoot Glacier viewpoint. From the Helen Lake parking lot, follow the dirt trail through spruce and fir for the 3km (1.9-mile) ascent. As the forest thins, you'll be treated to fine views of **Crowfoot Glacier** and **Bow Lake** across the valley.

Near the top of the ascent, an area of old burned forest slowly levels out into an ancient glacial valley, spotted with stands of pine and larch, and carpeted with vivid displays of wildflowers between July and August. The trail winds across a couple of creeks and leads past a massive rockslide, where you'll often be able to spot marmots squeaking among the rocks, before rising up and over a flat plateau of heather and alpine grass all the way to **Helen Lake** at 6km (3.7 miles).

The lake offers a superb viewpoint back down the valley. To the north is the lumpy prominence of **Cirque Peak**, and to the east are the chimneylike stacks of **Dolomite Peak** along the horizon, named by early explorers for its resemblance to the Dolomite Mountains of northern Italy. Break the hike here and savor the solitude; few hikes give you such a sense of the age and silent power of the country.

For a longer walk, strong hikers could continue northeast from the lake for the lonely lookout of **Dolomite Pass**, reached after another 2.9km.

Parker Ridge

Duration 2 hours round-trip

Distance 4km (2.5 miles)

Difficulty Moderate

Start/Finish Parker Ridge parking lot

Elevation Change 250m (820ft)

Nearest Town Saskatchewan Crossing (p74)

Transportation Car

Summary If you want to see a glacier in all its glory, you can't beat this steep ascent onto the crest of an impossibly scenic ridge near the Banff–Jasper border.

If you only do one hike along the Icefields Parkway, make it Parker Ridge. It's short enough to crack in an afternoon, but leads to one of the most impressive lookouts of any of Banff's day hikes, with a grandstand view of Mt Saskatchewan, Mt Athabasca and the gargantuan Saskatchewan Glacier. Bring warm clothing and a decent coat, as the wind on the ridge can be punishing.

The first part of the walk is pretty uneventful. From the parking lot the trail runs through a narrow wood before emerging on the hillside and entering a long series of switchbacks. As you climb, you look down onto the main road as it recedes into the distance, and every step improves the panorama of mountains across the valley. Near the top, the trail turns briefly nasty, ascending sharply before you finally stumble over the **crest** of the ridge at 2km (1.2 miles), puffed out and panting, to be greeted by an arctic blast of wind and an explosive panorama of peaks and glaciers.

On the right loom Mts Athabasca and Andromeda, and just to their left is the gleaming bulk of the Saskatchewan Glacier, which lurks at the end of a deep valley. At almost 13km (8-miles) long, the glacier is one of the longest in the Rockies, but it's actually just a spur from the massive 230-sq-km (88-sq-mile) Columbia Icefield that lies to the north. For the best views, follow the trail southeast along the edge of the ridge and stop at one of the unmarked **viewpoints**.

On the way back down the trail, you can swing left onto a narrow spur trail, which climbs for 15 minutes to another ridge crest, marked by rough cairn shelters where you can escape the wind and look down over the parkway. Retrace your steps and rejoin the main trail for the descent to the parking lot.

Sunset Lookout

Duration 3 hours round-trip

Distance 9.4km (5.8 miles)

Difficulty Moderate

Start/Finish Sunset Lookout parking lot

Elevation Change 250m (820ft)

Nearest Town Saskatchewan Crossing (p74)

Transportation Car

Summary An abandoned fire lookout commanding unbroken views of the North Saskatchewan Valley.

This remote trail is just a few kilometers from the northern border of Banff National Park, and it feels a long way from anywhere. It's mainly used as an access route for backpackers on the way to Pinto Lake and the wilderness area beyond, but the first section gives you a sense of adventure without actually having to camp out overnight.

From the parking lot on the east side of the parkway, 16.5km north of Saskatchewan Crossing, the trail climbs sharply through lodgepole pine forest, roughly following the course of **Norman Creek**. In late July the forest is thick with buffaloberry bushes, so it's a favorite feeding ground for hungry grizzlies – check for trail closures before you start out, and make noise to avoid surprise encounters. The path leads past a dramatic canyon carved out by Norman Creek, before zigzagging back into forest and reaching the left-hand junction for the lookout at around 2km (1.2 miles).

From here, it's another 1.5km (0.9 miles) to the **lookout site**, dangling high above the forest. Far below are the **Graveyard Flats**, crisscrossed by the neighboring Alexandra and North Saskatchewan Rivers. A roll call of remote mountains looms on each horizon, including **Mt Saskatchewan** to the west and faraway **Bow Peak** to the south. The lookout itself operated between 1943 and 1978; you can still make out its foundations and the remains of cables that were once connected to the lookout's lightning conductor.

Back at the main trail, you can either turn right back to the parking lot, or turn left and strike out for **Sunset Pass**, 7.6km (4.7 miles) from the trailhead. Beyond lies some of Banff's wildest backcountry, including Pinto Lake and the White Goat Wilderness Area.

OVERNIGHT HIKES

Banff's day hikes offer ample adventure for most people, but for a real appreciation of the park's wild side you've got to head into the backcountry. With a network of trails crisscrossing the high mountains, and a selection of routes ranging anywhere from two days to several weeks, there are enough backcountry trips here to satisfy the most mile-hungry hiker; the real challenge lies in choosing which one to do.

You don't necessarily have to submit a full trip itinerary when you purchase your wilderness pass, but it's often a good idea; if you're not back by the specified date, a search party will set out to look for you, so it's *vital* that you report back to park authorities once your trip is finished to avoid triggering a false alarm.

Wild camping is only permitted in certain remote areas – contact the Banff Information Centre for details. In the backcountry, you have to pack out all your garbage by law.

The hiking chart on p32 provides a quick overview of all the backcountry hikes covered in this section.

Egypt Lake

Duration 3 days round-trip

Distance 24.8km (15.4 miles) round-trip to Egypt Lake, 40.8km (25.4 miles) via Twin and Arnica Lakes

Difficulty Moderate-difficult

Start/Finish Sunshine parking lot

Nearest Town Banff (p101)

Transportation Bus or car

Summary An ideal introduction to the world of the backcountry, crossing meadows and a mountain pass en route to a network of glittering lakes.

This backcountry classic starts out as a standard day hike to **Healy Pass** and just keeps on going. Rather than turning back once you've crossed the Continental Divide, you'll continue on for another 3km (1.9 miles) to reach the high mountain tarns around **Egypt Lake**. Time it right and you'll be greeted with a profusion of wonderful summer wildflowers or autumnal trees. Whenever you choose to come, you'll have a sweeping panorama of the Monarch Ramparts, the Ball Range and the Alberta–British Columbia border. Best of all, it's relatively straightforward for a backcountry hike, which unfortunately also means it can get crowded in season.

DAY 1: HEALY PASS TO EGYPT LAKE CAMPGROUND

4 HOURS, 12.4KM (7.7 MILES)

Start out on the Healy Pass hike (p80) from the Sunshine parking lot and, once you crest over Healy Pass, continue northwest into forest, passing Pharaoh Creek at 3km (1.9 miles). A little further on, you pass a trail on the right to Egypt Lake Warden Cabin, then cross a bridged creek into a meadow, where you'll find your overnight spot of Egypt Lake Campground and Shelter. Book well ahead for both in season.

Several spur trails radiate out from the campground and provide excellent day-hike options, including the 4.2km (2.6 miles) to Natalko (Talc) Lake, and the 2.8km (1.7-mile) trail to Pharaoh and Black Rock Lakes.

DAY 2: EGYPT LAKE CAMPGROUND TO SHADOW LAKE

5-6 HOURS, 14.4KM (8.9 MILES)

Ringed by forest and the Pharaoh Peaks, **Egypt Lake** is one of the loveliest high-altitude lakes in the park. It can be visited as a day hike from the Egypt Lake Campground, or as stage two of the main hike. You can add in sidetrips to **Scarab Lake** and **Mummy Lake** and an ascent of **Whistling Pass**, supposedly named for the hooting hoary marmots that live there, although it could equally be named for the whistling wind that often whips across the top of the pass. From here, it's another 5.3km (3.2 miles) to **Shadow Lake**, where you can overnight at the campground or backcountry lodge.

DAY 3: SHADOW LAKE TO VISTA LAKE TRAILHEAD

5-6 HOURS, 14KM (8.7 MILES)

From Shadow Lake, you have a choice of routes back to civilization. You could head northeast for 13.9km (8.6 miles) along **Redearth Creek**, but the more scenic option is the 14km (8.7-mile) route over **Gibbon Pass** via Twin Lakes and Arnica Lake, which ends at the Vista Lake/Twin Lakes trailhead on Hwy 93 in Kootenay National Park. Obviously, if you take this option, you'll need to arrange for someone to pick you up.

Skoki Valley

Duration 4 days round-trip

Distance 50.6km (31.4 miles) round-trip

Difficulty Moderate-difficult

STAYING IN THE BACKCOUNTRY

Camping

There are over 50 campgrounds dotted around the Banff backcountry, but they're generally a lot more basic than the national park's other camping areas. Cleared sites, tent pads and pit toilets pretty much sum up the facilities; some also have bear-proof bins or food storage cables. You'll need to pack in everything else (including food, fuel, water-treatment equipment and other supplies). You'll also need to pack everything out again once your trip's finished (including all your rubbish).

All overnight stays in the backcountry require a **wilderness pass** (per day/year C$9.80/68.70), available from park visitor centers. You'll need to indicate which campgrounds you intend to use when you purchase your pass; reservations are accepted up to three months in advance for a C$11.70 fee, and you *must* stick to these campgrounds once you've booked them. Trail and campground numbers are strictly limited, so you might well find your route is booked out unless you plan ahead, especially in July and August. The maximum stay at any one site is three days.

Beyond the backcountry, wild camping is permitted in some areas. Make sure your campsite is 5km (3.1 miles) from any trailhead, 50m (164ft) off the trail and 70m (229ft) from any water source, and take the usual precautions against bears and forest fires.

Shelters

Parks Canada operates two backcountry trail shelters, one at Egypt Lake and another at Bryant Creek. Both are extremely rustic and offer little more than a roof over your head. You'll need to be completely self-sufficient, with your own bedding, food and cooking equipment. You can book spaces at the shelters when you purchase your wilderness pass.

Alpine Club of Canada Huts

The Alpine Club of Canada operates several remote huts for climbers and mountaineers that are also open to backcountry walkers. They range from basic portacabins to historic log huts. Most have mattresses, cooking stoves and utensils, but you'll need your own sleeping bag, food and other supplies (including toilet paper and matches).

Reservations are required at all huts and can be made through the **Alpine Clubhouse** (☎403-678-3200; www.alpineclubofcanada.ca; Indian Flats Rd, Canmore; per night member/nonmember C$30/36) up to a month in advance. Following are the key Alpine Club of Canada huts:

Abbot Pass Hut (⏲summer) Sleeps 24 and is perched atop a difficult glacier climb at the end of the Plain of Six Glaciers.

Castle Mountain Hut (⏲summer) Sleeps six and is located halfway up Castle Mountain. It's mainly used by rock climbers.

There's also a string of huts along the Wapta Icefield, allowing adventurers to complete the so-called Wapta Traverse. These include **Peyto Hut** (⏲summer & winter), which sleeps 18 in summer and 16 in winter; **Bow Hut** (⏲summer & winter), sleeping 30; and **Neil Colgan Hut** (⏲summer & winter), the highest habitable structure in Canada, sleeping up to 18 in summer.

Lodges

For a bit of extra comfort in the backcountry, there are two historic mountain lodges at Skoki and Shadow Lake (see p109).

Start/Finish Fish Creek trailhead

Nearest Town Lake Louise (p67)

Transportation Bus/car

Summary A dreamy landscape of high mountains and lakes awaits around the Skoki Valley.

It might not have the lush greenery of some of Banff's other backcountry destinations, but for the desolate beauty of its high mountains and truly unparalleled views, **Skoki Valley** is a gem. The Skoki area has been a popular skiers' hangout since the 1930s, but these days it has also become a regular haunt of summer hikers, especially for those visitors itching to try out a night at Skoki Lodge, one of Banff's most historic ski lodges.

You can expect a mix of mountain landscapes en route – meadow, peaks, lakes and barren rock – and a massive sense of achievement once you're done.

DAY 1: FISH CREEK TRAILHEAD TO MERLIN MEADOWS

8 HOURS, 17.8KM (11.1 MILES)

The first day is a full-blown, hard mountain hike, so start as early as possible to be sure of camping in daylight. The trip starts out at an elevation of 1690m (5545ft), with the first steep, wooded section following Temple Fire Rd for 3.9km (2.4 miles). It reaches a trail lodge and crosses a ski slope before ascending to a meadowy area with great views of the Slate Range after around 6.5km (4 miles). At 7.1km (4.4 miles) you'll pass Halfway Hut, a day shelter once used by skiers heading for Skoki Lodge, and the Hidden Lake campground, where you can take an overnight break if you wish.

Most people push on to **Boulder Pass** at 8.6km (5.3 miles), situated above Ptarmigan Lake with a view of Ptarmigan Peak, Redoubt Mountain and Mt Temple to the southwest. Take a break here and admire the vista, then continue north via **Deception Pass**, looking out for the Skoki Lakes on your left before reaching Skoki Lodge after 16.4km (10.2 miles). Base yourself at the lodge or nearby Merlin Meadows Campground, another 1.2km northwest.

DAY 2: MERLIN MEADOWS TO RED DEER LAKES

6 HOURS, 11.4KM (7 MILES)

On the second day, backtrack the 1.2km (0.7-mile) trail and explore the high mountain scenery around Skoki Lodge, including the 6.2km (3.8-mile) round-trip to **Merlin Lake**. Back at the lodge, head south and take the left-hand (east) fork along the 'Jones Pass' Trail, which skirts past the southern flanks of Skoki Mountain.

Spend the night at Red Deer Lakes Campground, a walk of 4km (2.5 miles) from the lodge.

DAY 3: RED DEER LAKES TO HIDDEN LAKE

6-7 HOURS, 11.7KM (7.3 MILES)

On day three, head south through the alpine meadows around Oyster Creek and Cotton Grass Pass, before veering westwards along the northern shore of **Baker Lake** and rejoining the main Skoki trail just south of **Deception Pass**. On the way back down the valley, you'll have a fine outlook of Ptarmigan Peak (3059m/10,035ft) to the west and Redoubt Mountain (2902m/9520ft) to the south. Camp at the Hidden Lakes Campground, near the Halfway Hut.

DAY 4: HIDDEN LAKE TO FISH CREEK TRAILHEAD

2-3 HOURS, 9.7KM (6 MILES)

On the last day, take an early evening jaunt up to **Hidden Lake** itself (2.6km/1.6-mile round-trip), a classic glacial tarn nestled among craggy peaks. Rejoin the main trail and hike back to the start point at Fish Creek.

Mt Assiniboine

Duration 4-6 days round-trip

Distance 53.3km (33.1 miles), more with sidetrips

Difficulty Moderate-difficult

Start/Finish Sunshine Village

Nearest Town Banff (p101)

Transportation Bus to Sunshine Village, car from Mt Shark

Summary The *pièce de résistance* of Banff backcountry trips, carrying you far from civilization into the shadow of the Matterhorn of Canada.

This multiday hike ventures into the heart of **Mt Assiniboine Provincial Park**, an area famous not just for its pyramidal mountain, but also for its meadows, lakes and seemingly endless hiking options.

There are several routes into the park, including from Sunshine Village, from Kootenay National Park along the Simpson River Trail, and from Kananaskis Country along Bryant Creek (accessed near Mt Shark, about a 43km drive from Canmore along the gravel Smith-Dorrien/Spray Trail road). The best option is to combine the Sunshine Village–Bryant Creek trails, creating a stunning 55.7km (34.6-mile) route tracking the ridge of the Great Divide. You'll need a car at either end of the trail to avoid getting stranded; alternatively, leave your car at Mt Shark, catch a lift back and take the bus or hike up to Sunshine Meadows from the parking lot. If you're feeling really flush, you could even catch a helicopter into the park from Canmore, but that really would be cheating.

The following trip includes two days of hiking into the park, three days for sidetrips at Lake Magog, and a one- or two-day hike back out to Mt Shark. Though popular, it's still proper backcountry: taking bear precautions and packing proper supplies are essential.

DAY 1: SUNSHINE VILLAGE TO PORCUPINE CAMPGROUND

6-7 HOURS, 13.3KM (8.3 MILES)

Begin with the hike for the Garden Path Trail (p79). At the junction at 1.3km (0.8 miles), instead of continuing west toward Rock Isle and Grizzly Lake, turn south toward Citadel Pass. The trail crosses briefly into British Columbia, passing the Howard Douglas Lake and Campground en route to **Citadel Pass** at 9.3km (5.8 miles). If the weather's clear, from here you should have a great view of Mt Assiniboine spiking skywards, way off to the southeast.

At 12.3km (7.8 miles) the trail meets the junction to Porcupine Campground (where most hikers spend their first night). To reach the campground, head right (south) for another kilometer (0.6 miles).

DAY 2: PORCUPINE CAMPGROUND TO LAKE MAGOG

6-7 HOURS, 15.5KM (9.7 MILES)

On day two, head southeast from the campground for 3.5km to rejoin the main trail, which heads into the aptly named **Valley of the Rocks**. The enormous boulders that crowd this lengthy valley are left over from a long-ago rockslide, the largest anywhere in the Rockies: it feels wild and desolate at the best of times, but in bad weather seems positively unearthly. The valley runs southeast for around 6km (3.7 miles), but the rocky path makes it tough going. Also note that there is no water in the Valley of the Rocks, so make sure you're stocked up before you start out.

If the rocky traverse has worn you out, you could break overnight at Og Lake Campground; but if you feel up to it, it's worth continuing across Og Meadows for another 6km (3.7 miles) to reach **Lake Magog**, the main base for explorations around Mt Assiniboine.

There is a superb campground perched right beside the lakeshore, offering a grandstand viewpoint up the snowy slopes of Mt Assiniboine. There are also several rustic Naiset Huts and a historic lodge situated near the lake; all are heavily oversubscribed in season, so book as early as possible to be sure of a place.

DAYS 3-5: MT ASSINIBOINE PROVINCIAL PARK

With some of the Rockies' most incredible lakes and mountains right on its doorstep, Lake Magog makes an ideal base for further forays into the surrounding park.

Popular options include the twin humps of the **Niblet and Nublet** (add three to four hours, 6km/3.7 miles); the scenic loop around **Sunburst**, **Cerulean** and **Elizabeth Lakes** (add four to five hours, 9km/5.6 miles); and the tough but rewarding trail to **Og Pass** and **Windy Ridge** (add six hours, 12km/7.5 miles; colloquially known as 'The Slog from Og' for good reason).

DAY 6: LAKE MAGOG TO MT SHARK

10 HOURS, 25KM (15 MILES)

If you've managed to sort out transportation at the Mt Shark end, the best option is to head out of the park via spectacular **Wonder Pass** and **Bryant Creek** (a hike of just over 25km/15 miles from Lake Magog). It's a wonderfully scenic walk in its own right, passing the shining expanse of **Marvel Lake**, the 6th-largest lake in Banff National Park. It's a long route to do in one day, so you might feel like breaking the walk in two: there are a couple of campgrounds near the lake's eastern end (McBride's Camp and Marvel Lake), which you'll reach around 12km (7.4 miles) from Lake Magog.

Otherwise, you could just visit Wonder Pass and Marvel Lake as a day hike before retracing your route back to the trailhead across Sunshine Meadows.

BIKING

Despite the grumbles of Banff cyclists, who moan that park authorities are trying to shove them out of the park on the sly, Banff still has plenty of paved routes, singletrack and dirt trails. Mountain biking tends to be more popular than road cycling in Banff (although you'll often see hardcore road-riders slogging it out along the formidable challenge of the Icefields Parkway). The Banff Information Centre has a free leaflet detailing the main routes, while local bike shops often run organized rides and can provide tips on

BANFF BIKE & HIKE SHUTTLE

Getting to the start of a trail can be an obstacle in Banff, especially if you don't have your own car. The new **Bike 'n Hike Shuttle** (www.bikeandhike shuttle.com) run by White Mountain Adventures provides an easy way for hikers and bikers to travel from Banff and Canmore to several of the main trailheads.

Stops along the route include Goat Creek, the Canmore Nordic Centre, Bankhead, Lake Minnewanka and Cory Pass (on the Bow Valley Parkway).

Sample fares from Canmore to Banff are adult/child C$15/10 one way or C$25/20 return. From Banff to Lake Minnewanka, the fare is C$10 one way or C$15 return per person. From Banff to the Goat Creek trailhead, the fare is C$20/15 per adult/child; the bus also stops at Canmore and the Canmore Nordic Centre.

lesser-known (and not always entirely official) trails.

The free *Mountain Biking and Cycling Guide,* available at park offices, details the most popular routes, many of which are shared-use trails with horseback riders and hikers.

In addition to the routes detailed in this section, other good rides include the family-friendly, 12.5km (7.8-mile) Spray River Loop, the 28km (17-mile) roller-coaster singletrack along Rundle Riverside and the challenging 30km (18.6-mile) Lake Minnewanka singletrack to Devil's Gap.

There is also an excellent network of purpose-built bike trails at the Canmore Nordic Centre (p116).

Rentals

Snow Tips/Bactrax BIKE SHOP
(Map p64; ☎403-762-8177; www.snowtips-bactrax.com; Bear St, Banff; hire per hr C$12-16, per day C$42-60, tours per hr C$20) One of Banff's best-stocked bike shops, offering a decent range of Norco bikes for rental, and organized tours to Vermilion Lakes, Bow Falls Golf Course, and the Cave & Basin National Historic Site (24 hours notice required). It also rents out other outdoors gear, including hiking boots, day packs and tents.

Ski Stop BIKE SHOP
(Map p64; ☎403-762-5333; www.theskistop.com; Bear St, Banff; hire per hr C$12-14, per day C$42-49) Just up the road from Bactrax, this is a good snowboard-cycling crossover. Hire bikes are mostly Trance models. It also offers a shuttle service to the start of the Goat Creek trailhead; the cost is C$94.95, and includes map, shuttle and a full day's bike hire.

Rebound Cycle BIKE SHOP
(Map p117; ☎866-312-1866; www.reboundcycle.com; 902 Main St, Canmore; hire per day C$30-70) Canmore's clued-up bike store rents everything from town bikes to full-suspension rigs. Kids' bikes and chariot carriers are also available.

Trail Sports BIKE SHOP
(Map p117; ☎403-678-6764; www.trailsports.ab.ca; Canmore Nordic Centre; hire per hr/day C$15/45, kids' bikes C$5/15; ⏲9am-8pm Mon-Fri, to 6pm Sat & Sun) If you're visiting Canmore's busy trail center, you don't even need to bring your own bike: Rocky Mountain rigs are available from Trail Sports, right across from the visitor office at the Canmore Nordic Centre. It also runs guided tours around some of the center's trails.

Wilson Mountain Sports SPORTS SHOP
(☎403-522-3636; www.wmsll.com; Samson Mall, Lake Louise; hire per hr C$15-25, per day C$39-59) This outdoors shop is pretty much the only place to rent bikes in Lake Louise. Hardtails cost C$15/39 per hour/day. Kids' bikes, trail-a-bikes and chariot trailers cost C$10/20 per hour/day.

Sundance Trail & Healy Creek

Duration 3 hours round-trip

Distance 17km (10.5 miles)

Difficulty Easy

Start/Finish Banff

Nearest Town Banff (p57)

Transportation Bike

Summary Paved, mixed-use trail that's perfect for families and riders of all abilities, tracking the course of the Bow River en route to Sundance Canyon and beyond.

This gentle trail is a perfect route if you're just up for a refreshing ride through the countryside. Start out in Banff Town and cross the bridge over Bow River at the end

Sundance Trail & Sundance Canyon

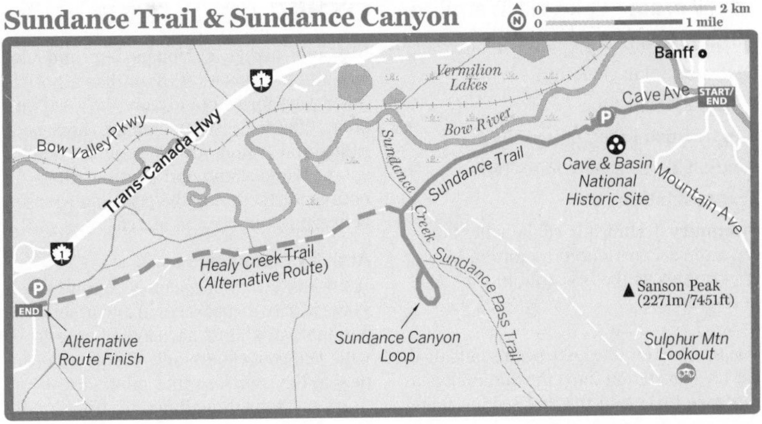

of Banff Ave. Turn left and roll along the main road or the dirt trail all the way to the **Cave & Basin National Historic Site**, where the tarmacked Sundance Trail begins just beyond the museum. It's flat and easy riding, with views of the Bow River on your right and Sulphur Mountain to your left, passing through a few sections of marsh and wetland where you'll often spy wading birds and dragonflies.

There's a dirt track on the left side of the trail that is reserved for horses, which is handy as it keeps the main trail free of horse manure. If you fancy taking a break, you'll find riverside benches dotted along the trail.

After around 2km (1.2 miles) you'll reach a junction. Left climbs gently to **Sundance Canyon**, where there's a bike rack where you can lock your wheels while you follow the canyon walk (p75). For a longer bike ride, turn right instead along the Healy Creek dirt doubletrack, which meets Hwy 1 after 4.8km (3 miles); follow the busy main road back to Banff, or reverse the route for a quieter return journey.

Goat Creek Trail

Duration 2-3 hours one way

Distance 19.1km (11.9 miles)

Difficulty Moderate

Start Whiteman's Gap

Finish Banff

Nearest Towns Banff (p57), Canmore (p116)

Transportation Car/minibus

Summary A great doubletrack between Banff and Canmore that crosses several types of terrain and winds its way between the Goat Range and Mt Rundle.

This much-recommended one-way route is best done with two vehicles, or on an organized tour that provides transportation from either end of the trailhead. There's an elevation change of 1000m (3280ft) from Canmore to Banff, so most people tend to get dropped off at Canmore and head northwest to Banff. Several bike shops offer a shuttle service to the trailhead.

It's a pretty easy ride along dirt and gravel doubletrack, with a few climbs and steep sections, as well as a fiddly bridge crossing and a few blind corners – watch out for other trail users, especially cyclists coming in the opposite direction.

The trailhead is high above Canmore at **Whiteman's Gap**, up the dirt Smith-Dorrien road past Canmore Nordic Centre. The first section travels through pine and spruce forest along the course of **Goat Creek**, with the Goat Range to the south and Mt Rundle to the north. It feels wild and rewardingly remote and you can either roll along at a leisurely pace or pin back your ears and pick up the speed.

After 9.2km (5.7 miles) you'll reach a bridge over the **Spray River** near the old fire road. Turn right at the junction to begin the second section, which travels along the fire road all the way to the Fairmont Banff Springs parking lot.

Moraine Lake via Tramline

Duration 3-5 hours round-trip

Distance 30km (17 miles)

Difficulty Difficult

Start/Finish Lake Louise Village

Nearest Town Lake Louise (p67)

Transportation Car

Summary Technically challenging but rewarding. Experienced mountain bikers rate this as the best trail in the Lake Louise area.

The trail to Moraine Lake begins outside the old Laggan station (now the Station Restaurant; see p111), and the first section follows the course of the old tram line that once ferried visitors up to Lake Louise in the early 1900s. If you want to avoid the uphill section, you could drive to the Paradise Valley parking lot (see further in this bike route) and start the ride there.

If you're tackling the tramline, park opposite the Station Restaurant. Cross the bridge and set out along the broad trail, climbing steeply to **Louise Creek** and eventually linking up with the busy Lake Louise road – take care crossing here, as traffic is fast and heavy.

Turn down Moraine Lake Rd. Look out for the Paradise Valley parking lot on the right, which also marks the start of the **Moraine Lake Highline Trail**. There's a junction about 1km (0.7 miles) from the Paradise Valley parking lot; turn left (south) to get onto the Highline.

Here's where the fun really starts: the trail zips into rocky, rooty singletrack that's tough and technical. Note this section is a grizzly favorite, and is sometimes closed during the peak buffaloberry season from mid- to late summer – check with a park office before setting out, and make lots of noise at all times to avoid any bear-shaped surprises.

From here the views and the riding are fantastic as you follow the eastern flank of Mt Temple and encounter wonderful views over the Valley of the Ten Peaks, Moraine Lake and Consolation Valley. The route is rough, narrow and exposed in places – take it easy and admire the outlook. After around 10km (6.2 miles) you'll roll down to the shore of Moraine Lake.

You can retrace the route or head back along the paved (and steep) Moraine Lake Rd to complete the loop.

OTHER ACTIVITIES

Although hiking and biking are undoubtedly the firm favorites, Banff has a host of other ways for you to explore the great outdoors. Rafting, rock climbing, horseback riding and fishing are all popular summer sports, while skiing and snowboarding are both fantastic during the peak snow season between December and March.

Activity Companies

Banff has several agencies that can book a range of activity packages in and around the national park. Most have lots of experience with younger clients and people who are new to the sports, so they offer a great way to try out something different. If you're doing a lot of activities, booking through one agency can be very convenient, but you'll often get better deals by going direct to the provider.

Banff Adventures Unlimited ADVENTURE SPORTS
(Map p64; ☎403-762-4554; www.banffadventures.com; 211 Bear St, Bison Courtyard, Banff; ⏱7:30am-9pm summer, 9am-9pm winter) Banff's main activity booking company is based in Bison Courtyard in downtown Banff. It can book a huge range of activities with experienced local operators, ranging from ATV tours to heli-hikes and rafting trips, and puts together its own combo packages (such as the 'Raft, Ride & Relax' tour, which includes a raft trip, a trail ride, BBQ lunch and dinner, and a pass to the Upper Hot Springs).

Inside Out Experience ADVENTURE SPORTS
(☎403-949-3305; www.insideoutexperience.com; Bragg Creek) Another good multi-activity provider offering mountain biking, white-water rafting, hiking and winter sports, as well as exciting combination tours involving several activities (ride and raft, saddle and paddle… you get the idea).

White Mountain Adventures ADVENTURE SPORTS
(☎403-760-4403; www.whitemountainadventures.com; 122a Eagle Cres, Banff) The owners of Sunshine Meadows also offer summer and winter activity packages, including guided day hikes, bike tours and backcountry trips. They also run the bus shuttle from Banff to Sunshine Village, and the new Bike 'n Hike Shuttle service (see p94).

Canoeing & Kayaking

Canoes and kayaks have played a pivotal role in Canada's history, so there's really no better way to explore the Banff scenery. You can hire canoes from boathouses at Lake Louise (p67) and Moraine Lake (p68), although the water is generally frozen from October to mid-May.

For experienced canoeists, the Bow River has some of the best canoeing in the Rockies – contact park staff for a free guide sheet or download it from www.pc.gc.ca/pn-np/ab/banff/activ/activ28c_e.asp. Most of the activity companies we've detailed can also organize guided kayak expeditions.

Blue Canoe CANOEING
(Map p62; ☎403-760-5465; Bow River Canoe Docks, cnr Bow Ave & Wolf St, Banff; per hr/day C$27/60) For quick trips, Blue Canoe hires canoes from its river station at the end of Wolf St. Bow River, Forty Mile Creek and the Vermilion Lakes are all just a short paddle away from downtown Banff.

White-Water Rafting

If canoeing is too sedate, then the white-knuckle sport of white-water rafting is guaranteed to provide more thrills. The area around Banff is well known for its white water, especially along the Kicking Horse, Red Deer and Kananaskis Rivers: you can opt for a swift half-day hit (from C$45 to C$100) or a multiday expedition (from around C$120 per day).

There are many companies to choose from, but it's always wise to go with a well-established operator, as white-water rafting is potentially a highly dangerous sport. All the following companies provide life jackets, instruction, experienced guides and full safety gear. Rapids are classed from I (easy) to V (expert) – the extreme Class VI is for rapids that have rarely been completed successfully.

Hydra River Guides RAFTING
(Map p64; ☎403-762-4554; www.raftbanff.com) Based in Bison Court, this well-regarded company offers three core trips along the Kicking Horse River. The most popular is the 20km (12.4-mile) 'Kicking Horse Classic' (C$105), which tackles a varied range of rapids up to Class IV, and includes a BBQ lunch. Hardier rafters could try the full-day trip (C$149), while novices might prefer the more sedate float trip (adult/child C$74/49).

It also offers combo packages including horseback riding, zip-lining and ATV driving.

Rainbow Riders RAFTING
(☎403-678-7238; www.rainbowriders.com) One of the best options for rafting on the Bow and Kananaskis Rivers. The Introductory Class (C$69) covers Class I-III rapids through the Canoe Meadows on the Kananaskis, while the Thrilling Class (C$79) covers Class II-IV rapids through the stunning Horseshoe Canyon on the Bow River. It also offers float trips (C$49) and riverboarding (C$89), which is a bit like bodyboarding on river rapids; you'll need to be a strong swimmer, but it's dangerously addictive.

Chinook Rafting RAFTING
(☎866-330-7238; www.chinookrafting.com) A great company for families and groups, run jointly with Discover Banff Tours. Family-rated tours (adult/child C$79/52) are on the Kananaskis River, while Adventurous (C$82) and Wild (C$125) tours are on the Bow and Kicking Horse Rivers; you'll need to be aged 12 or over for the more advanced trips. You can even train to be a river guide if you really catch the rafting bug.

Canadian Rockies Rafting Company RAFTING
(☎403-678-6535; www.rafting.ca) Offers everything from slow nature floats on the Bow River (adult/child/senior C$55/45/50) to full-day 'double shots' on the Kicking Horse (adult/child 12 to 15 years C$125/115). The nature float is a great way to see the Bow Falls up close.

Fishing

The fish in Banff might not be as plentiful as they were in the days of Bill Peyto and pals, but angling is still a quintessential way to experience Banff's sedate side.

A **fishing permit** (per day/year C$9.80/34.30) is required for angling anywhere in the national parks, and can be purchased at visitor centers. The *Fishing Regulations* summary details current catch allowances; it's illegal to keep many endangered native species such as bull trout, kokanee salmon and cutthroat trout.

The most popular area to fish is the Bow River, which is open year-round (although ice fishing is always banned). Ghost Lake, Johnson Lake, Lake Minnewanka, Two Jack Lake and the Vermilion Lakes are usually open mid-May to mid-September.

Banff Fishing Unlimited FISHING
(☎403-762-4936; www.banff-fishing.com) Year-round fly-fishing, spin-casting and lake fishing with experienced local guides. The full-day 'Walk and Wade' trips combine guided hikes with some of the best fishing spots on the Bow River.

Tightline Adventures FISHING
(☎403-762-4548; www.tightlineadventures.com; trips for 2 people from C$225) Specializes in dry-fly fishing for rainbow and brook trout in the Bow River, and offers walk-and-wade packages to more remote river stretches.

Lake Minnewanka Guided Fishing FISHING
(www.explorerockies.com/minnewanka/charter-fishing.aspx; half-day C$395, full day for up to 2 adults C$500; ⏲Jun-Sep) Offers guided boat trips on Lake Minnewanka for lake trout and whitefish.

Climbing

Climbers have been flocking to Banff's sky-piercing peaks and dizzying rock faces since the sport first took off in the late 1800s. Yamnuska, Mt Rundle and Ha Ling Peak are just some of the best-known ascents, but there are hundreds more to discover. Unless you're an experienced climber, it's worth employing the services of a local guide to make sure you get the most out of your experience on the mountain and stay safe at the same time.

The head office of the **Alpine Club of Canada** (www.alpineclubofcanada.ca; PO Box 8040, Indian Flats Rd, Canmore) can put you in touch with qualified guides across the Canadian Rockies.

Yamnuska ROCK CLIMBING
(☎403-678-4164; www.yamnuska.com; trips for 1 person from C$475, for 2 people C$263) Well-regarded Canmore-based company offering daily instruction courses, plus more challenging trips for intermediate and advanced climbers. From Tuesday to Saturday in July and August there's a daily climb for C$110 per person including gear and transport.

On Top Mountaineering ROCK CLIMBING
(☎1-800-506-7177; www.ontopmountaineering.com) Based in Canmore, this locally run outfit offers five-day organized climbing courses in the Rockies throughout summer for C$830 per person, which provide an ideal introduction to the sport for new climbers, and help more experienced climbers hone their skills. Alternatively, you can devise your own custom route with a private guide from C$450 for two people.

CMH Mountaineering ROCK CLIMBING
(☎800-661-0252; www.canadianmountainholidays.com) Specialist in heli-hikes and high-altitude trips, but you'll need to have plenty of cash to splash.

Horseback Riding

Exploring the Canadian Rockies would have been all but impossible without the help of the humble horse, and clopping along the trail will give you a real appreciation of how the park must first have appeared to early settlers. Many trails are open to horses: for full details consult the free *Horse Users Guide*, available from park offices.

Warner Guiding & Outfitting HORSEBACK RIDING
(Map p64; ☎1-800-661-8352; www.horseback.com; 132 Banff Ave, Banff) Warner's two stables in Banff and Spray Creek run lots of horseback riding tours. Easy half-day trips are run regularly along the Bow River, Sundance Loop, Bow Valley and the Spray River, from C$42 to C$119 per person. For an authentic frontier experience, it also offers a breakfast and evening cookout (C$107 on horseback, C$86/76 per adult/child in a covered wagon).

For something more challenging, multiday expeditions to Warner's backcountry lodges start at C$512 per person for a two-day trip. It also offers special interpretive trips geared toward photographers and wildlife enthusiasts.

Timberline Tours HORSEBACK RIDING
(☎888-858-3388; www.timberlinetours.ca; Lake Louise) This outfitter has its corral near Lake Louise, and offers 1½-hour trips along the lake (C$70), day rides up to Lake Agnes Teahouse (C$105) and the Plain of Six Glaciers (C$125), as well as full-day rides to Paradise Valley, Skoki Lodge, Baker Lake and the Moraine Lake Highline Trail (C$179). Overnight trips and pony rides are also available.

Skiing & Snowboarding

While Banff is at its busiest during summer, for many people it's the winter months that offer the main attractions. The area's reputation as one of Canada's top ski destinations ensures a steady influx of skiers and snowboarders throughout winter to the three main areas of Mt Norquay, Lake Louise and

Sunshine Village, collectively branded as the **Big Three** (www.skibig3.com; 3-day pass adult C$239.85, 7-day pass C$548.45).

Passes include gondolas, lifts and free shuttles to the ski domains, but as always you'll usually get better value if you buy them as part of an organized package tour, which includes accommodations at local hotels. The peak months are from December to January, especially during the school holidays around Christmas and New Year. For the best deals, aim to ski early or late in the season; snow lingers at many of the highest runs until late April and even early May, and discounts are often substantial for off-season packages.

All the resorts have ski schools where you can pick up the basics or graduate to more advanced skills, as well as day-care facilities for younger kids. The websites for each resort have regular snow reports and piste webcams so you can check the snow before you go.

Mt Norquay SKIING

(www.banffnorquay.com; Mt Norquay Access Rd; full day adult C$55, child 6-12yr C$17, 13-17yr C$43, senior C$43; ⏲early Dec–mid-Apr) Mt Norquay is the smallest of the Banff resorts and also one of the oldest – the first runs were established here way back in 1926. Today there are 28 runs spread out over just 76 skiable hectares (190 acres), covering a total vertical drop of 503m (1650ft). What it lacks in size it makes up in speed – Norquay is the only Banff resort with 'expert'-rated runs, the longest of which is an impressive 1627m (5337ft). Some of the double black diamond runs on the North American lift will turn your hair whiter than the mountain snow.

There's also a terrain park for snowboarders, and classes in advanced techniques are available at the Snow Sport Centre. Norquay's latest innovation is 'snow-tubing,' which involves hurtling down the mountain on an inflatable tire; it's currently the only resort in Banff with a purpose-built tube park.

Sunshine Village SKIING

(www.skibanff.com; full day adult C$76.14, child 6-12yr C$26.42, 13-17yr C$54.28, senior C$61.26; ⏲mid-Nov–mid-May) If restricted time or funds mean that you can only ski one resort in Banff, Sunshine Village is probably the best to choose. Sunshine's ski area is much larger than Norquay at a total of 1358 hectares (3358 acres), divided between 107 runs and the 6-hectare (15-acre) Rogers Terrain Park. With such a huge area, the resort can comfortably handle several thousand skiers and still feel relatively uncrowded.

All the runs are at high elevations (over 2133m/7000ft), so snow conditions are nearly always reliable on the three mountains (Lookout, Standish and Goat's Eye). It's also unusual in that it only needs to manufacture a small amount of snow every year: snow pack in good years can be up to 9m (29ft), most of which is captured naturally through an ingenious system of snow-fencing.

Sunshine is only around 15km (9.3 miles) from downtown Banff, so many ski packages use off-mountain accommodations and use shuttle buses to get you up to the resort. If you prefer to be closer to the snow, Sunshine also has Banff's only ski-in, ski-out hotel at the Sunshine Inn.

Lake Louise SKIING

(www.skilouise.com; full day adult C$69, child 6-12yr C$22, 13-17yr C$48; ⏲Nov-May) The largest of the Big Three resorts is Lake Louise, offering over 1699 skiable hectares (4200 acres) divided between 139 runs. It's probably the best for families, with a good spread of beginner-rated (25%) and intermediate-rated (45%) runs. The longest (8km/4.9 miles) is on the Larch Face, and there are lots of beginner runs on the Front Side/South Face, especially around the base area. There's plenty of powder and off-piste skiing for advanced riders too, as well as a snowboard park.

Lake Louise's average snowfall is only around half that of Sunshine Village, however, meaning that snow machines are often used to supplement the natural snowpack.

Cross-Country Skiing

It might not have the adrenaline edge of downhilling, but cross-country skiing has a long mountain heritage and it's about the only way to explore the national park's trails in winter. It's one of Canada's fastest-growing sports, and you'll even see people practicing their skills in the summer months (using rollerblades rather than skis).

Over 80km (50 miles) of trails are groomed by park authorities specifically for the use of cross-country skiers, including the Spray River Loop, Cave and Basin Trail, Cascade Fire Rd and the Golf Loop near Banff, and the Moraine Lake Rd and Lake Louise Shoreline Trail near Lake Louise Village.

Check with Parks Canada to see which trails are open before you set out, as heavy snowfall means that trails are sometimes closed at short notice.

Cross-country gear can be rented at any of the ski stores in Banff, and most local activity agencies (see p96) can help book taster sessions if you're a first-timer.

Other Winter Sports

Strapping on skis isn't the only way to explore Banff's winter wonderland. **Ice-skating** is often possible at various spots, depending on seasonal conditions. The Fairmont hotels in Lake Louise and Banff both maintain small skating areas, as does the Banff Recreation Center. Vermilion Lakes, Johnson Lake and Lake Minnewanka often have skateable ice, but check with a park office first.

Another way to get out into the backcountry in winter is on **showshoes**, which are thought to have been used by First Nations people in the Rockies for hundreds of years. Most local mountaineering and activity companies offer taster sessions in both snowshoeing and ice-skating, and can also arrange guided **ice-climbing** trips for intermediate and advanced climbers.

TOURS

Unless you're really short on time or are traveling without your own vehicle, there's no real need to splash out on a guided tour – but if you prefer to let someone else do the organizing (and the driving), a minibus trip can be a good way of packing in the sights. Most companies offer pick-up and drop-off from your hotel, and include lunch in their full-day tours.

Brewster Tours

Founded way back in 1892 by the entrepreneurial Brewster brothers Bill and Jim, **Brewster** (Map p62; ☎403-762-6750; www.brewster.ca; 100 Gopher St, Banff) is one of Banff's oldest guiding firms and is still one of the town's busiest tour operators. Today it also operates three of the park's most lucrative sights, including the Banff Gondola, Lake Minnewanka Boat Tours and the Columbia Icefield.

In the early days visitors were ferried around by packhorse and mule train, but these days the transportation is rather plusher: Brewster's tours are run in large motor coaches, complete with air-con and guided commentary. The big buses feel a bit impersonal compared to smaller operators, and remember that stopping times (especially on the full-day tours) at the sights are whistle-stop brief.

Tour options include the following:

Evening Wildlife Safari (adult/child C$39/25; 2hr tours) Wildlife-spotting tour around the Marsh Loop and Vermilion Lakes.

Discover Banff Tour (adult/child C$50/25; 3hr tours) Stops at the Hoodoos, the Cave and Basin, Surprise Corner and Tunnel Mountain. Adding on the gondola costs C$29.95/14.95 extra per adult/child.

Lake Louise Tour from Banff (adult/child C$62.95/31.95; 6.5hr tours) Travels along the Bow Valley Parkway via Johnston Canyon and Castle Mountain to Lake Louise.

Discover Grizzly Bears (adult/child C$159/89; 10hr tours) Travels via Yoho to the Kicking Horse Resort near Golden, where you can meet the resident grizzly, Boo.

If you're planning on visiting more than one of Brewster's attractions, buying an **Explorer Package** can be a good way to save cash compared to the cost of buying individual tickets (especially for families). By way of illustration, the cost of individual tickets to all three attractions comes to adult/child C$124.90/59.90, but the Ultimate Rockies Explorer Pass costs C$99.95/44.95 – a saving of almost C$25/15 per adult/child.

Current prices (all excluding GST):

Banff Explorer (adult/child C$69.95/33.95) Banff Gondola and Lake Minnewanka Cruise.

Alpine Explorer (adult/child C$79.95/43.95) Columbia Icefield and Lake Minnewanka Cruise.

Mountain Explorer (adult/child C$68.95/38.95) Banff Gondola and Columbia Icefield.

Ultimate Rockies Explorer (adult/child C$99.95/44.95) Includes all three attractions.

Discover Banff Tours

Besides Brewster, **Discover Banff Tours** (Map p64; www.banfftours.com; Sundance Mall, 215 Banff Ave, Banff) is the other big tour operator located in Banff. It operates smaller buses than Brewster, so things feel a bit less regimented – you can even hire your own personal guide (half-/full day C$325/450). In summer scheduled trips include the following:

Discover Banff & its Wildlife (adult/child under 5yr/6-12yr C$52/free/30; 3hr tours) A great tour for wildlife, with stops around Banff, Vermilion Lakes and the Bow Valley Parkway. Special morning and evening wildlife safaris also available.

Lake Louise (adult/child under 5yr/6-12yr C$64/free/35; 6hr tours) Commentated bus ride to Lake Louise, with five hours to spend exploring the lake. Shorter tours to Lake Louise and Moraine Lake are also available.

Glacier Trail (adult/child under 5yr/6-15yr C$154/free/79; 7hr tours) Stops at Lake Louise en route to the Icefields Parkway, with a trip onto the Columbia Icefield included.

Grizzly Bear Tour (adult/child under 5yr/6-12yr C$159/free/89; 6hr tours) Via Yoho to the Kicking Horse Resort grizzly center.

Other Tours

GyPSy GPS TOURS

(www.gpsguide.com; per day/week C$39/219) These audioguides offer GPS-based tours to sights across the Rockies and western Canada. They're a good option if you prefer to devise your own route, but the commentary is fairly basic. Units can be rented from Discover Banff Tours or the Tourism Calgary desk at Calgary airport.

SLEEPING

With enough hotel rooms to rival a town three times its size, finding a place to sleep in Banff certainly isn't a problem, but finding somewhere that'll suit your budget is a trickier proposition. Banff's room rates are notoriously expensive and take a hefty upward hike in the peak seasons, especially between June and August.

While there are usually discounts and package deals for stays of a week or more, accommodations will still be your biggest outlay during your stay in the park – which explains why so many visitors choose to cut costs by camping or hiring recreational vehicles (RVs). Renting a condo or vacation apartment can be another good way to keep costs down, especially if you're staying mainly in one area.

Banff

Camping

Tunnel Mountain CAMPGROUND $

(off Map p62; Tunnel Mountain Dr; kiosk 7am-midnight) Banff's massive main campground is split over three separate 'villages' halfway up the slope of Tunnel Mountain. All told, the combined area offers over 1000 sites, but still manages to fill to capacity in summer thanks to its convenient location just a quick drive from downtown Banff. All three areas have flush toilets, proper showers and wheelchair-accessible sites, making them suitable for pretty much everyone – but you might be better off elsewhere if you're looking for tranquil camping.

Tunnel Mountain Trailer Court

(campsites C$38.30; May-late Sep;) The nearest to town along Tunnel Mountain Dr, the trailer court is solely dedicated to trailers and RVs, with full hookups (water, power and sewage). Each site occupies its own terraced pullout and some are shaded by overhanging trees, so there's a bit of privacy and seclusion even between neighboring sites. Fires are not permitted. It's one of the busiest RV sites in the whole park, though, so reserve well ahead.

Tunnel Mountain Village Two

(campsites C$32.30; year-round;) Next door to the trailer court, Village Two occupies an open, grassy field with 188 paved spaces for tents and RVs, some of which have power hookups. There's not much tree cover, which means it's rather exposed and at times can get quite windy, although the views are pretty fine; it also means you'll need to get friendly with your neighbors when it's full.

Tunnel Mountain Village One

(tent sites C$27.40; May-late Sep;) Located 1.5km (0.9 miles) further up the road from Banff, Village One offers a more authentic backwoods experience, with 618 tent sites spread out among the pines, divided between 10 discrete loops (A–G), each served by its own washroom block. This one's the favorite for seasoned campers, but it can be a little noisy when it's full – campfires, singsongs and marshmallow toasting are the order of the day. Views are mostly obscured by the trees, but some of the upper loops overlook the slopes of Mt Rundle.

BANFF CAMPGROUNDS

Banff has 13 frontcountry campgrounds catering for tents, recreational vehicles (RVs) and camper vans. Most are open from around June to mid-September, although Tunnel Mountain Village Two, Lake Louise Trailer and Mosquito Creek campgrounds are open year-round. For full details on the facilities at Banff's campgrounds, see p104.

Advance reservations are currently only available at the large campgrounds on Tunnel Mountain and at Lake Louise; contact the **Parks Canada campground reservation service** (☎1-877-737-3783; www.pccamping.ca/parkscanada/en/; ⏰7am-7pm), which books sites up to 24 hours in advance for a fee of C$10.80 in addition to regular camping fees.

Sites at all other campgrounds are allocated on a first-come, first-served basis, so the best way to claim a spot is to turn up early (well before the official 11am checkout time) or check with parks staff about which campgrounds currently have availability. Banff Park Radio (101.1FM) also releases regular bulletins on campgrounds with available sites. It's a good idea to stay in one place over weekends; sites are generally easier to come by on Thursday and Friday.

Checkout at all campgrounds is 11am and there's a maximum stay of 14 nights. You can have one tent and up to two vehicles at one campsite. At larger campgrounds you'll need to pay fees at the entry kiosk, but at smaller campgrounds, you'll have to self-register: find a vacant site first, then go to the self-registration shelter, remembering to enter your name, site number, license plate and duration of stay on the envelope along with the relevant fees. If it's late when you arrive, you can do this in the morning, or sometimes staff will come around and collect your fees in person in the morning.

Fires are usually allowed at campsites where there's a fire pit – you'll need to buy a **fire permit** (C$8.80, incl wood) from the campground entrance. Watch for fire restrictions during dry periods.

As in the backcountry, it's good practice to try and keep your campsite tidy. Dump stations, bear-proof garbage containers and recycling bins are available at many of the campgrounds.

Lodging

Banff has accommodations to suit all budgets and tastes, from hostels and home stays to fancy hotels with all the luxury trimmings. Hotel rates fluctuate wildly according to the season, with prices spiking considerably during summer and school holidays. The prices we've quoted are for peak season unless otherwise indicated.

If you're looking to save some cash, staying in local B&Bs is usually much cheaper than an equivalent hotel room; ask about weekly rates, and check their policy on pets and kids before booking. Contact the Banff Information Centre for a full list.

If you're stuck for a place to sleep, the following organizations can help find available rooms:

Banff Central Reservations (☎403-277-7669; www.banffinfo.com) Commercial agency with links to preferred hotels.

Banff Tourism Bureau (Map p64; ☎403-762-8421; www.banfflakelouise.com; 224 Banff Ave)

TOP CHOICE **Thea's House** B&B $$$
(Map p62; ☎403-762-2499; www.theashouse.com; 138 Otter St; r C$225-250; wifi) If you're looking for somewhere with quirkiness and character, look no further than Thea's. It's run with serious style by its owners Jami and Greg Christou. The feel's light, sexy and modern: glossy fir floors, hand-built wooden beds, Aveda bath goodies and big gas fires in the rooms, with little extras such as complimentary juice, coffee and DVDs in the guest lounge. Breakfast is a treat, too: continental croissants supplemented by pancakes, eggs benny, French toast and potato rosti.

Fairmont Banff Springs HOTEL $$$
(off Map p62; ☎403-762-2211; www.fairmont.com/banffsprings; Spray Ave; r C$379; ❄ wifi 🏊 👶) Slap down the platinum and prepare to be preened – you've just checked into one of Canada's landmark hotels. Built in 1888, the Banff Springs juts out above the Bow River like a fairy-tale European chateau, and was designed to offer the last word in luxury for its guests: grand halls, stately staircases

and balustraded landings, not to mention a Gothic great hall and evening ballroom. As always with celebrity hotels, the plush rooms are eye-wateringly expensive and standards can be variable: don't be afraid to haggle for the best you can get. And if you can't afford the price tag, you could always just settle for afternoon tea.

Fox Hotel HOTEL **$$$**

(Map p62; ☎403-760-8500; www.bestofbanff.com/fox-hotel-suites; 461 Banff Ave; d C$179, ste C$249-489;) The Fox is one of the top hotels in Banff. The decor is a welcoming mix of cozy and contemporary: gingham-check bedspreads and rustic touches meet flat-screen TVs and flashy wallpapers. The basic rooms are small, so it's worth bumping up to a suite: some have kitchen nooks, others separate lounges, while the premium-rate suites have a romantic loft bedroom. Ask for a room at the rear for the least noise.

Buffalo Mountain Lodge HOTEL **$$$**

(Map p62; ☎1-800-661-1367; www.crmr.com/buffalo; 700 Tunnel Mountain Dr; lodge rooms C$279, premier rooms C$339;) Three hectares (9 acres) of private grounds make this lodge-hotel complex on Tunnel Mountain one of Banff's most pleasant mountain retreats. The lodge-style rooms combine rustic-chic with mod-cons: timber beams, clawfoot tubs, fieldstone log fires and underfloor heating in the bathrooms. You don't even have to go into town for dinner thanks to the in-house Cilantro Mountain Café.

Hidden Ridge Resort RESORT **$$$**

(off Map p62; ☎403-762-3544; www.bestofbanff.com/hidden-ridge-resort; 901 Coyote Dr; 1-bed condo C$189-209, family condos C$389-449;) Half hotel, half self-catering resort, the Hidden Ridge is a great option for families, with modern condos and A-frame chalets available in multiple configurations. The basic chalets boast wood-burning stoves, galley kitchens and mountain-view porches, while at the top end you can splash out on Jacuzzis and cozy loft bedrooms for the kids. There's even a forest hot tub if you're valiant enough to brave the mountain air.

HI-Banff Alpine Centre HOSTEL **$$**

(off Map p62; ☎403-762-4123; banff@hihostels.ca; 801 Hidden Ridge Way; dm C$34-40, r C$107-133, r with washroom C$127.50-150, cabins C$149-170;) Banff's timber-clad HI hostel is conveniently placed on lower Tunnel Mountain, and is by far the best budget option in town. The rooms are standard hostel-style – pine bunks, generic color schemes – but they're squeaky clean. Private rooms and self-contained cabins are available for more privacy. Facilities include a log-fired lounge, an on-site pub, an ice wall and the excellent Cougar Pete's kitchen-café. Residents also travel free on Roam buses.

Poplar Inn B&B **$$**

(Map p62; ☎403-760-8688; www.thepoplarinn.ca; 316 Lynx St; d C$125-175) Two sweet rooms in a heritage home just steps from Banff Ave. Both have luxury touches such as Egyptian cotton sheets and sliding doors onto private garden patios. The lovely breakfast of muffins, cinnamon buns and chocolate croissants is served in one of the house's turrets.

Banff Ptarmigan Inn HOTEL **$$**

(Map p62; ☎403-762-2207; www.bestofbanff.com/banff-ptarmigan-inn; 337 Banff Ave; d C$139-174;) It lacks the wow factor of Banff's top-end hotels, but for value the Ptarmigan Inn is a top choice. There's little to choose between the standard, superior and premium rooms (floral throws, framed watercolors and beige shades are standard throughout), though extra cash buys extra space and perhaps a mountain view. Facilities include whirlpools, sauna and steam room, and breakfast is included.

Driftwood Inn MOTEL **$**

(Map p62; ☎403-762-4496; www.bestofbanff.com/tdi; 337 Banff Ave; d C$99;) This might not be the mountain retreat of your dreams, but for staying in Banff on a budget, the Driftwood beats all comers. Next door to the Banff Ptarmigan Inn (and sharing use of its facilities), the Driftwood is a generic motel with a bare minimum of frills, but if you can look past the dated decor and the occasional dustball, its rates offer just about the best value in town.

Banff Aspen Lodge HOTEL **$$**

(Map p62; ☎403-762-4401; www.banffaspenlodge.com; 401 Banff Ave; r C$169-229;) Despite its boxy exterior and equally boxy rooms, the Banff Aspen is still worth investigating. Inside it feels up-to-date and uncluttered: rooms are finished in slate grays and sharp pine, and most have a balcony overlooking Banff Ave. Economy rooms are on the ground floor; bumping up to Superior buys more space, but won't shut out the constant thrum of traffic noise. A couple of hot tubs are available downstairs for guests' use.

BANFF NATIONAL PARK CAMPGROUNDS

CAMPGROUND	LOCATION	DESCRIPTION	NO OF SITES	ELEVATION
Tunnel Mountain Trailer Court	Banff	Dedicated RV and trailer site with full hookups	321	1440m (4725ft)
Tunnel Mountain Village One	Banff	Large, forested, tent-only campground, popular with families but can get overcrowded	618	1440m (4725ft)
Tunnel Mountain Village Two	Banff	Mixed-use campground that's handy for Banff Town but feels a little exposed to the elements	188	1450m (4760ft)
Castle Mountain	Bow Valley Parkway	Small woodland campground that's handily located near a grocery store	43	1450m (4760ft)
Johnston Canyon	Bow Valley Parkway	One of the park's most scenic and best-equipped campgrounds, with lots of day hikes on its doorstep	132	1430m (4700ft)
Protection Mountain	Bow Valley Parkway	Popular with hikers thanks to its proximity to trailheads; amenities include recycling and kitchen shelters	89	1450m (4760ft)
Mosquito Creek	Icefields Parkway	Very basic, tree-lined campground in the shadow of Mt Hector, at the southern end of the Icefields Parkway	32	1850m (6070ft)
Rampart Creek	Icefields Parkway	The last frontcountry campground south of the Jasper border; rudimentary but peaceful	50	1450m (4760ft)
Waterfowl Lakes	Icefields Parkway	The best equipped of the Icefields Parkway campgrounds, with recycling bins, piped water and food storage	116	1650m (5410ft)
Lake Louise Tent Campgrounds	Lake Louise	Tent campground next door to the RV campground, protected by an electric bear-proof fence	206	1540m (5050ft)
Lake Louise Trailer Campgrounds	Lake Louise	RV-friendly campground that keeps 30 sites open in winter	189	1540m (5050ft)
Two Jack Lakeside	Lake Minnewanka	Beautiful and very popular lakeside campground with private, secluded sites	74	1460m (4790ft)
Two Jack Main	Lake Minnewanka	Scattered pleasantly under the trees, but the lack of shower facilities is a drawback	380	1460m (4790ft)

Drinking Water *Flush Toilets* *Great for Families* *Grocery Store Nearby*

Banff Caribou Lodge HOTEL **$$**
(Map p62; 403-762-5887; www.bestofbanff.com/banff-caribou-lodge; 521 Banff Ave; r C$169-199;) The bland timber-and-concrete facade is still in situ, but the Caribou is slowly getting a much-needed overhaul. Standard rooms are plain, with leaf-print bedspreads and motel-issue furniture: the roomier loft suites are more luxurious, with a lounge and fireplace downstairs, and a Jacuzzi and sleeping area upstairs. The Keg Steakhouse and Red Earth Spa make it a more attractive package, and the rates are reasonable even in season.

Buffaloberry B&B **$$$**
(Map p62; 403-762-3750; www.buffaloberry.com; 417 Marten St; r C$335;) This premium B&B makes a comfortable place to stay, but you'll have to pay for the privilege. The four bedrooms are heavy on homey charm and country fabrics, and under-floor heating and nightly turn-down treats keep the pamper factor high – but it's pricey for what you get.

Charlton's Cedar Court MOTEL **$$**
(Map p62; 403-762-4485; www.charltonscedarcourt.com; 513 Banff Ave; d C$154, ste C$169-185)

OPEN	RESERVATIONS NEEDED?	DAILY FEE	FACILITIES	PAGE
May-Sep	yes	C$38.30		p101
May-Sep	yes	C$27.40		p101
year-round	yes	C$32.30		p101
Jun-Sep	no	C$21.50		p106
Jun-Sep	no	C$27.40		p106
Jun-Sep	no	C$21.50		p106
year-round	no	C$17.60		p108
Jun-Sep	no	C$15.70		p108
Jun-Sep	no	C$21.50		p108
Jun-Sep	yes	C$27.70		p107
year-round	yes	C$32.30		p107
May-Sep	no	C$27.40		p106
May-Sep	no	C$21.50		p106

Restaurant Nearby *Payphone* *Summertime Campfire Program* *RV Dump Station*

Yes, it's a bit old-fashioned, but this motel complex on Banff Ave has some of the most consistent rates in town. Cheaper rooms are dowdy, so better to opt for one of the larger split-level suites, some of which have kitchenettes and mezzanine sleeping areas. Luxury it ain't, but it's a reasonable downtown base.

Treetops B&B **$$**
(Map p62; ☎403-762-2809; www.banfftreetops.com; 336 Beaver St; d C$125-140) Two inviting rooms in a timber house just off Beaver St.

Bumper's Inn MOTEL **$$**
(Map p62; ☎403-762-3386; www.bumpersinn.com; 603 Banff Ave; r C$125-140) Basic, bog-standard motel, worth considering for its knock-down rates if you're stuck for somewhere to stay.

Juniper HOTEL **$$**
(off Map p62; ☎403-762-2281; www.thejuniper.com; 1 Juniper Way; r C$169-229;) Purpose-built, pet-friendly hotel with modern rooms, let down by the constant traffic noise from nearby Hwy 1.

Lake Minnewanka

Camping

The twin campgrounds around Lake Minnewanka are perennially popular thanks to their peaceful wooded setting.

Two Jack Lakeside CAMPGROUND **$**
(Map p58; Minnewanka Loop Dr; campsites C$27.40; ⏲mid-May–mid-Sep) With just 74 sites, the lakeside campground offers some of Banff's most exclusive camping. There are fantastic views, particularly if you can grab a site overlooking the lake itself, and the comprehensive facilities (lockers, flush toilets, showers) and limited numbers of campers make it all the more attractive.

Two Jack Main CAMPGROUND **$**
(Map p58; Minnewanka Loop Dr; campsites C$21.50; ⏲mid-May–Sep) If the lakeside campground is full (and it probably will be), Two Jack's main campground is a very pleasant fallback. The 380 pitches are spread out spaciously under the trees just up the road from the lakeside campground, but the lack of showers and laundry facilities is a big drawback.

Bow Valley

Set midway between Banff Town and Lake Louise Village, the Bow Valley gives you a chance to experience the wilderness and is also handy for an early start on day hikes.

The only negative to staying in the Bow Valley is the proximity of the CPR train line, which runs right along the length of the valley all the way to Lake Louise. The melancholy blast of a distant train horn sounds romantic around a campfire at dusk, but you might not feel quite so charitable when it wakes you up at 3am.

Camping

Johnston Canyon Campground CAMPGROUND **$**
(Map p58; Bow Valley Parkway; campsites C$27.40; ⏲early Jun–mid-Sep; 📶) For that authentic backwoods camping feel, this lovely creekside campground opposite the parking lot for Johnston Canyon is tough to top. It strikes just the right balance between facilities and camper freedom. The 132 sites are spacious and fairly private and you won't feel nearly as hemmed in as at some of Banff's bigger campgrounds. Flush toilets and hot and cold water are available at all the five washroom blocks, but only two have showers. Most sites are suitable for RVs.

Castle Mountain Campground CAMPGROUND **$**
(Map p58; Bow Valley Parkway; campsites C$21.50; ⏲early Jun–mid-Sep) A small self-registration campground of only 43 sites, handily placed among pine forest near the Castle Mountain store. It's beautifully secluded, with sites arranged around one long woodland loop, but there's only one wash block and annoyingly it doesn't have any showers. Nevertheless, the lovely surroundings and limited sites means it fills up fast.

Protection Mountain Campground CAMPGROUND **$**
(Map p58; Bow Valley Parkway; campsites C$21.50; ⏲Jun-Sep) A basic site further up the Bow Valley Parkway from Castle Mountain and offering similar facilities (or lack thereof). With 89 sites, no hookups, showers or laundry facilities, and a relatively long journey to Banff and Lake Louise, it's often quieter than the other Bow Valley campgrounds, and you can usually find a spot even at the busiest times.

Lodging

Baker Creek Chalets CABINS **$$$**
(Map p58; ☎403-522-3761; www.bakercreek.com; Bow Valley Parkway; cabins C$295-335) Set on a quiet glade near Baker Creek, this cabin complex has a choice of single-story chalets, deluxe twin-level loft cabins, or suites inside the main lodge. The style is deliberately old country – wood panels, porches, stoves – but the rates are quite pricey for what you get. Still, kids will absolutely *love* the wooden ladders up to the loft beds in the twin-level loft cabins.

Johnston Canyon Resort CABINS **$$**
(Map p58; ☎403-762-0868; www.johnstoncanyon.com; Bow Valley Parkway; cabins C$149-259; ⏲May-Oct) Built in the late 1920s to accompany the nearby teahouse (now a restaurant), these dinky log cabins trade heavily on their proximity to Johnston Canyon. Despite their heritage appearance (complete with porch and smoking chimneys), the interior decor wouldn't look out of place in a modern motel. The four-person classic bungalows have two separate bedrooms as well as cooking facilities, so they're great for families.

Castle Mountain Chalets CABINS **$$**
(Map p58; ☎403-762-3868; www.castlemountain.com; Castle Junction; chalets C$149-239; 🐾) Right next door to the Castle Mountain store, these

log chalets are plain inside but offer a surprising amount of mod-cons, including DVD players, dishwashers, wood-burning stoves and even iPod clock-radios. At C$239, the top double-room chalets are great value for families or two couples, but work out expensive for solo or duo travelers. The site itself is quite cramped and can be noisy, with the busy lanes of Hwy 1 just to the west.

Castle Mountain Wilderness Hostel HOSTEL $

(Map p58; ☎403-670-7580; cr.castle@hihostels.ca; Castle Junction; dm C$23; ⏲year-round, check-in 5-10pm, closed Wed winter) Like Rampart Creek (p108) and Mosquito Creek (p108), this is more a backcountry cabin than a facility-packed backpackers. There's a simple kitchen, a couple of gender-sorted dorms and a snug common room set around a log-burning stove, with large windows looking out onto mountainous countryside. Don't be surprised if you spy an elk or two grazing outside – it's all part of the backwoods vibe. It's a short drive south from Castle Mountain Junction.

Lake Louise

No matter which way you cut it, staying around Lake Louise is going to make a hefty dent in your wallet. The premium location means local hotels can charge ludicrously inflated prices, especially in summer; and considering the eye-watering cost, standards are largely disappointing. Unless there's a really good reason to stay here, you're better off basing yourself in Banff or Yoho and visiting on a day trip.

Camping

Lake Louise Tent & Trailer Campgrounds CAMPGROUND $

(Map p58; Lake Louise Village; tent sites C$27.70, campsites incl trailers C$32.30; ⏲tent park Jun-late Sep, trailer park year-round; wi-fi) Lake Louise's huge campground (actually separate tent and RV sites with one access gate) is over 4km (2.5 miles) from the lake and 1km (0.6 miles) from the village, but as it's the only place for campers and RVs nearby, it's nearly always busy. It's certainly not as pretty or private as some of Banff's other campgrounds, and nearly all the sites suffer from constant traffic noise thanks to the nearby highway. Online booking is available (see the boxed text, p102).

Lodging

HI Lake Louise HOSTEL $

(Map p58; ☎403-670-7580; www.hihostels.ca; Village Rd, Lake Louise Village; dm C$30.25-42, r C$95-120; @ wi-fi) A flagship HI hostel built in the chalet style that's *de rigueur* around Lake Louise. With facilities ranging from an in-house sauna to complimentary wi-fi for guests, it's one of Canada's most impressive hostels; look out for special activity-and-accommodations packages in summer and winter. As always, the rooms are small, bland and basic, but for these prices they're a steal. Hot meals are on offer in the on-site Bill Peyto's Café.

Paradise Lodge & Bungalows LODGE, HOTEL $$$

(Map p58; ☎403-522-3595; www.paradiselodge.com; 105 Lake Louise Dr; cabins C$261-383, r C$333-381) A choice of timber cabins or cozy lodge rooms just a quick spin from Lake Louise. The olde-worlde cabins are named after mountain peaks and feature rickety furniture, wood-clad walls and cute gingerbread windows, but as always in Lake Louise, they're a bit too simple to justify the sky-high prices. The lodge rooms are smarter but less fun, although the private kitchens are a bonus.

Deer Lodge HOTEL $$$

(Map p58; ☎403-522-3991; www.crmr.com/deer; 109 Lake Louise Dr; r C$280-300; ❄ wi-fi ≋) Run by the owners of Buffalo Mountain Lodge and Emerald Lake Lodge, this chic lodge-hotel is one of the most upmarket places to stay in Lake Louise. The hotel's history stretches back almost a century, and the interior is a mix of old and new: taupe bedspreads and tasteful tones blended with vintage pieces of furniture and antique lamps. For the most character, opt for a room in the Heritage Wing or the hotel tower, and expect to pay a premium for the privilege. The new rooftop hot tub offers divine mountain views.

Fairmont Chateau Lake Louise HOTEL $$$

(Map p58; ☎403-522-3511; www.fairmont.com/lakelouise; Lake Louise Dr; d from around C$449; ❄ wi-fi) Like its sister hotel in Banff, you're renting a slice of history when you stay at the Chateau Lake Louise, but sadly most of the hotel's original 1920s elegance has been swept away in successive renovations. It all feels depressingly corporate these days, and despite the extravagant decor, designer shops and snooty service, you can't help but feel it's a place that lost its soul long ago.

Post Hotel HOTEL $$$
(Map p58; ☎403-522-3989; www.posthotel.com; Village Rd, Lake Louise Village; r C$385-850; ❄📶) You'll need a second mortgage to afford a mountain view at this modern hotel in Lake Louise Village.

Moraine Lake Lodge HOTEL $$$
(Map p58; ☎403-533-3733; www.morainelake.com; Moraine Lake; r C$349-489; ⊙Jun-Oct; ❄) The only hotel with a view of Moraine Lake, but expect tiny rooms at toe-curling prices.

Icefields Parkway

Camping

The campgrounds along the Icefields Parkway are a lot more basic than many in Banff, but they're ideal if you want to escape the campfire smoke and crowds of the busier sites.

Mosquito Creek Campground PRIMITIVE CAMPGROUND $
(Map p70; Icefields Parkway; campsites C$17.60; ⊙year-round) Tucked under Mt Hector in a wooded creekside setting, this tiny 32-site campground is about as simple as they come – pit toilets and a hand pump for water just about sum up the facilities, but it's a wonderful spot for those who are seeking seclusion. And, despite the name, mosquitoes don't seem to be too much of a problem (hardly surprising given the nighttime temperatures!).

Rampart Creek Campground PRIMITIVE CAMPGROUND $
(Map p70; Icefields Parkway; campsites C$15.70; ⊙Jun-Sep) The northernmost campground in Banff is a primitive affair, but handy for the Columbia Icefield. The mountain views are particularly grand and it's often a good spot for wildlife – don't be surprised if the odd elk or bighorn sheep putters past your tent. There's well water, dry privies and kitchen shelters on-site, plus a fire-free loop if you're sick of smelling other people's smoke.

Waterfowl Lakes Campground CAMPGROUND $
(Map p70; Icefields Parkway; campsites C$21.50; ⊙mid-Jun–late Sep) The best serviced of the parkway campgrounds, Waterfowl Lakes is nicely situated at the head of the lake and has lots of large, wooded, wheelchair-accessible sites and surprisingly fancy facilities, including flush toilets and BBQ shelters.

Lodging

TOP CHOICE **Num-Ti-Jah Lodge** HOTEL $$$
(Map p70; ☎403-522-2167; www.num-ti-jah.com; Icefields Parkway; d mountain/lake view from C$205/220, incl meals C$403.89/418.89; ⊙Dec–mid-Oct) This is the real deal – a genuine historic mountain lodge, built by the pioneering backwoodsman Jimmy Simpson, a man who did much to popularize the Rockies and who laid the foundations for the modern-day practice of mountain guiding. Picturesquely nestled on the shores of Bow Lake, overlooking Crowfoot Mountain and the Wapta Icefield, it's the kind of place where every crevice hides a historic secret. Huge animal skins, dog-eared photos and wonky bits of furniture litter the library and downstairs lounge, while elk heads and snowshoes hang from the walls, commemorating Simpson's life in the great outdoors. Haphazard staircases lead up to the plain, pine-paneled rooms, all free of TVs and phones and laid out in charming, higgledy-piggledy fashion. It might be a bit pricier than it was in Jimmy Simpson's day, but then again, how often do you get to sleep in a genuine Rocky Mountains landmark?

Mosquito Creek Wilderness Hostel HOSTEL $
(Map p70; ☎403-670-7580; cr.mosquito@hihostels.ca; Icefields Parkway; dm C$23; ⊙year-round snow permitting, reception 5-10pm) Tucked away under trees near the campground, this small 34-bed HI hostel was built to house German POWs during WWII, and these days makes a charming backcountry hostel. There's a rustic sauna, a stove-lit lounge and a pocket-sized (propane-powered) kitchen where you can cook up communal grub. Dorms are single gender.

Rampart Creek Hostel HOSTEL $
(Map p70; ☎403-670-7580; cr.rampart@hihostels.ca; Icefields Parkway; dm C$23) These 12 gingerbread cabins collected around a wood clearing are much loved by climbers and hikers looking to get out into the real backwoods. An HI hostel, the facilities are similar to Mosquito Creek – plain dorm cabins, a shared lounge, a wood-fired sauna and a lively communal kitchen. It's a little shabby in spots but livened up by a great climbing library and a decidedly offbeat chap in charge.

The Crossing MOTEL $$
(Map p70; ☎403-761-7000; www.thecrossingresort.com; cnr Hwy 11 & Icefields Parkway; s & d

C$159-179, tr C$174-194, q C$189-209; ⏲mid-Mar–Nov) Apart from the Num-Ti-Jah, this dull motel is your only option on the Icefields Parkway. The bog-standard units are arranged around a central courtyard, which is also home to the only café, pub and shop for kilometers around.

Backcountry

Lodging

Traveling in the backcountry doesn't necessarily have to mean roughing it. In the early days of Banff's history, the only people who could afford to explore the national park were wealthy adventurers, and they often expected a bit more comfort than a pup tent and an open campfire. Consequently, a number of backcountry lodges were built by the early trail guides to cater for their guests, several of which are still in use today.

Skoki Lodge HOTEL **$$$**
(Map p58; ☎403-522-3555; www.skoki.com; r per person C$169-263, 2-night minimum stay) The first ski lodge ever built in the Canadian Rockies remains one of the most atmospheric places to stay in the whole national park. Built in 1931 overlooking a glorious high mountain valley, and briefly managed by Peter and Catharine Whyte (who founded Banff's Whyte Museum), the lodge is reached after an 11km (6.8-mile) climb from Lake Louise via Deception Pass (see the Skoki Valley hike, p90). As you'd expect, the decor's rough and ready – log walls, rustic bunks, kerosene lamps, and water jugs for washing – but that's all part of Skoki's special charm. Rates include meals cooked up by the lodge chef. If you really want an adventure, you can even snowshoe or ski to the lodge in midwinter.

Shadow Lake Lodge CABINS **$$**
(☎403-762-0116; www.shadowlakelodge.com; cabins per person summer C$196-202, 2-night minimum stay) Twelve sweet timber cabins just a stone's throw from Shadow Lake, 13.2km (8.2 miles) from the Redearth Creek trailhead. Though it lacks the heritage kick of Skoki, the cabins are a little roomier and more private (complete with solar-powered lighting and propane heating). You'll even be treated to afternoon tea and a glass of champagne during your stay, as three gourmet meals are included in the price.

EATING

Banff is brimming with places to pamper your palette. Choices are a lot more limited the further you travel north along Hwy 1; Lake Louise has a few options, including a great restaurant in the former Laggan train station, but around the Icefields Parkway you'll have to rely on your own supplies.

For the reviews in this section that appear with telephone numbers, you'd be wise to make reservations.

Banff Town

TOP CHOICE **Maple Leaf** GOURMET CANADIAN **$$$**
(Map p64; ☎403-760-7680; www.banffmapleleaf.com; 137 Banff Ave; lunch & dinner mains C$28-40; ⏲lunch & dinner) This fine-diner takes every opportunity to showcase its Canadian credentials. A big birch-bark canoe dangles above the entrance, local artwork hangs on the walls and the menu revolves around home-sourced ingredients (Quebecois foie gras, Albertan meat and game, British Columbian shellfish and salmon). The feel is formal to match the food: glossy wood, crisp white tablecloths, and candles on the tables.

Saltlik STEAKHOUSE **$$$**
(Map p64; ☎403-762-2467; www.saltlik.com; 221 Bear St; mains C$15-28; ⏲lunch & dinner) A contemporary take on the steakhouse, both in design and dining. Shiny wood, murals and mood lights create a swish dinner club atmosphere, and the menu revolves around rancher salads, club sandwiches, sticky ribs and enough varieties of steak to sate the most discerning carnivore.

The Bison AMERICAN **$$$**
(Map p64; ☎403-762-5550; www.thebison.ca; Bison Courtyard, 211 Bear St; mains C$19-44; ⏲breakfast, lunch & dinner) Modern American bistro food is the order of the day at the Bison, which makes a fine place for all-day dining – whether you're tucking into a duck and goat's cheese benny for lunch, or a Springbank bison striploin for supper. It's more a laid-back bistro than a gourmet restaurant, and the feel throughout is relaxed rather than ritzy. Best of all, the mountain-view patio is a real beauty.

Bear St Tavern PUB, PIZZA **$$**
(Map p64; www.bearstreettavern.ca; 211 Bear St; mains C$11-17; ⏲from 11:30am; 👪) Run by the owners of the Bison, this brew-pub hits a

double whammy: practically perfect pizza washed down with a practically perfect pint. Food is designed for sharing: Banffites head here in their droves for a plate of pulled pork nachos or a wild-mushroom pizza, accompanied by a pitcher of locally brewed ale. The patio overlooking Bison Courtyard soaks up the rays when the sun shines, or you can duck into the cozy tavern if the weather won't play ball.

Evergreen CANADIAN $$$

(Map p62; ☎403-762-3307; 459 Banff Ave; mains C$26-40; ⏲lunch & dinner) Hotel restaurants can be hit-and-miss, but the Evergreen inside the Royal Canadian Lodge is consistently good – provided you like formal fine dining and can look past the rather dated decor. Chef Hans Hacker's modus operandi is to combine classic Italian and French dishes with Canadian produce; expect plenty of words like *millefeuille*, *confit* and *dauphinoise* on the menu, and dress smartly to match the starchy service.

Coyote's Deli & Grill CAJUN $$$

(Map p64; www.coyotesbanff.com; 206 Caribou St; breakfast C$5-10, mains C$17-29; ⏲lunch & dinner) Southwestern, Cajun and Mexican flavors underpin the menu at this small, ever-busy restaurant just off Banff Ave. Most of the dishes have a spicy kick, such as Alverta tenderloin in a chili béarnaise, or blue-corn chicken enchilada with a chili sauce.

Wild Flour Café ORGANIC CAFÉ $

(Map p64; 211 Bear St; mains C$4-10; ⏲7:30am-6pm) Bringing a bit of boho west-coast spirit to Banff, this wholefood café is a great option for coffee, cakes and light lunches. Fairtrade coffees, homemade paninis, super-food juices and organic soups are chalked up on blackboards above the espresso machines, and the counter is crammed with all kinds of unusual cakes and pastries. Get there early on sunny days if you want to snag one of the sidewalk tables.

Eddie Burger & Bar BURGERS $$

(Map p64; www.eddieburgerbar.ca; 6/137 Banff Ave; burgers C$12-20; ⏲lunch & dinner; 👪) Sometimes nothing hits the spot like a burger, and Eddie's serves up some of the best in town. It's decked out in authentic diner style, and as you'd expect, all the classics are on the menu. If you're feeling a bit more adventurous, you might like to try one of Eddie's 'Signature' burgers, such as elk burger with avocado, gouda cheese and pesto mayo.

Melissa's DINER $$

(Map p64; www.melssteak.com; 218 Lynx St; breakfast C$8-16, dinner mains C$17.95-28.95; ⏲breakfast, lunch & dinner; 👪) For decades there's only been one address in Banff for a hearty breakfast or a T-bone, and that's Melissa's. This is very much a diner from the old school – check tablecloths, friendly waitresses and sauce bottles on the table – but if you're craving hearty food just like mom used to make, Melissa's is undoubtedly the place.

Grizzly House EUROPEAN $$$

(Map p64; www.banffgrizzlyhouse.com; 207 Banff Ave; fondues per person C$26.95-79.95; ⏲lunch & dinner) This odd restaurant specializes in exotic meats, from beef and buffalo to shark and rattlesnake, cooked fondue-style at your table, either in hot oil or on a hot rock. It's dark, dingy and gets very smoky when everyone's sizzling, but at the very least it'll be an experience to tell your friends about. Check out the working phone beside your table, left over from the restaurant's days as a disco in the 1970s.

Le Beaujolais FRENCH $$$

(Map p64; ☎403-762-2712; 212 Buffalo St; lunch mains C$15-25, dinner mains C$32-38; ⏲dinner, & lunch on Sat & Sun) Classic Gallic cooking is the *raison d'être* at the Beaujolais: lobster bisque, boeuf bourgignonne and, of course, *escargots* (snails) and *cuisses de grenouilles* (frogs' legs). As you'd expect, the food is rich and indulgent, but the slightly stuffy atmosphere might not be to everyone's taste.

Nourish VEGETARIAN $$

(Map p64; www.nourishbistro.com; Upper Level Sundance Mall, 215 Bear St; mains C$10-18; ⏲lunch & dinner, closed Tue) Nourish has carved out a devoted following in Banff thanks to its veggie food. The menu revolves around fairly conventional standards such as portobello-mushroom melts and oven-baked falafels, but the odd location on the top level of Sundance Mall is a letdown.

Cows ICE CREAM $

(Map p64; 134 Banff Ave; ⏲11am-7pm Mon-Thu, 10am-9pm Fri & Sat, 10am-7pm Sun; 👪) Moo Crunch, Wowie Cowey and Turtle Cow are just some of the weird and wonderful flavors concocted by this renowned Canadian ice-cream maker. You might as well make the most of it, too, as the only other Cows in western Canada is a few hundred kilometers away in Whistler, British Columbia.

Bruno's Bar & Grill BURGERS $
(Map p64; 304 Caribou St; mains C$6-10; breakfast, lunch & dinner) Named after the champion skier and photographer Bruno Engler, this cozy burger bar does a decent line in burgers, wraps and all-day breakfasts.

Safeway SUPERMARKET $
(Map p62; cnr Elk & Marten Sts; 8am-11pm) Banff's largest supermarket has the best selection for campers and self-caterers.

Bumper's DINER $$
(Map p62; 603 Banff Ave; mains C$10-20; from 5pm;) Simple steakhouse diner at the top end of Banff Ave.

Bow Valley Parkway

Baker Creek Bistro EUROPEAN $$$
(Map p58; 403-522-2182; Bow Valley Parkway; mains C$20-35; dinner) This attractive cabin restaurant is located inside the Baker Creek Chalet complex and is pretty much the only place to eat on the Bow Valley Parkway. Good thing it's decent: executive chef Shelley Robinson blends seasonal local produce with European influences. It's as good for a light tapas lunch as for a sit-down dinner, and the forest setting is really lovely.

Lake Louise

TOP CHOICE **Station Restaurant** EUROPEAN $$$
(403-522-2600; 200 Sentinel Rd; lunch C$9-17, dinner C$18-36; 11:30am-midnight) Locations don't get much more special than this. Back in the days when Lake Louise was still known as Laggan and steam trains chugged up the Bow Valley, this place was the village's main station, and the CPR tracks still run right outside its windows. The heritage 1909 building has been lovingly restored, complete with magnificent leaded windows, creaky floors, original fireplaces and vintage furniture, and the menu is stuffed with classy European fare. For a really memorable meal, you can even hire one of the restored Delamere or Killarney railway dining cars just behind the station.

Caribou Lounge INTERNATIONAL $$
(403-522-3991; 109 Lake Louise Dr; mains C$12-23; breakfast, lunch & dinner) The more relaxed of the two restaurants at the Deer Lodge is one of the nicest places for lunch around Lake Louise, with a selection of light dishes such as flatbread pizzas, salmon linguine and ranch burgers, and proper afternoon tea served with dainty cakes. The lounge has the same heritage feel as the rest of the lodge, but the real selling point is the magnificent view of Victoria Glacier from the outside patio.

Mt Fairview Dining Room GOURMET CANADIAN $$$
(Map p58; 403-522-3991; dining room mains C$26-40; lunch & dinner) The Deer Lodge's main restaurant is an altogether glitzier affair than the Caribou – crisp tablecloths and razor-edge napkins are *de rigueur*, so it's definitely not somewhere to pitch up in T-shirt and sneakers. It's the kind of place where the presentation is almost as important as the food; think delicate stacks of caribou medallions perched atop crispy gratins, or chargrilled lake fish served with a pea-shoot risotto. Dress smartly and expect a sizable bill.

Trailhead Café SANDWICHES $
(Samson Mall, Lake Louise Village; sandwiches & omelets C$6-10; 8am-5:30pm) Pick up some trail supplies at this bustling sandwich bar in Lake Louise Village. Sandwiches, bagels and wraps are made to order, and there's a selection of juices, cakes and pastries on the counter.

Bill Peyto's Café CAFÉ $
(Map p58; HI Lake Louise, Village Rd, Lake Louise Village; mains C$5-12; 7am-10pm summer, to 9pm winter) You can fill up for next to nothing at the HI's in-house café, so expect queues when the hostel's full. The menu is certainly nothing fancy, but if a bowl of chili or a baked potato is all you're after, Peyto's definitely hits the spot.

Village Market SUPERMARKET $
(Samson Mall, Lake Louise Village; 6am-8pm) Supermarket selling general groceries and food supplies inside Samson Mall.

Laggan's Mountain Bakery PIES, SANDWICHES $
(Samson Mall, Lake Louise Village; 6am-8pm) Nowhere near as good as it once was, but if you're stuck, the pies and sandwiches are just about passable.

Icefields Parkway

Num-Ti-Jah Lodge CANADIAN $$
(Map p70; 403-522-2167; www.num-ti-jah.com; Icefields Parkway; lunch mains C$14-25, dinner mains C$18-40; lunch & dinner) The Num-Ti-Jah's delightfully down-home restaurant

serves hale and hearty food (steaks, pastas, fish and game) in a gorgeous log dining room overlooked by the requisite moose heads and elk horns. Priority goes to guests, so if you're staying elsewhere make sure you reserve ahead.

DRINKING & ENTERTAINMENT

TOP CHOICE Banff Ave Brewing Company BREWERY
(Map p64; www.banffavebrewingco.ca; 110 Banff Ave;) Banff's only microbrewery is a must-visit for brewheads. Founded in 2010 and located inside the Clocktower Mall, it has rapidly become one of the town's favorite meeting spots. All the beer is brewed using natural water from the Rockies and a minimum of industrial additives. Choices range from light Czech-style Czuggers Pilsner to strong, dark Reverend Rundle Stout and the hoppy (and marvelously named) Head Smashed IPA.

Rose & Crown PUB
(Map p64; 202 Banff Ave; 11am-late) The Rose & Crown is one of the town's oldest drinking holes and is still as popular as ever. Expect a lively pub atmosphere, lots of beers on tap and regular live bands at weekends.

Lik Lounge BAR
(Map p64; 221 Bear St; 11am-2am) The downstairs bar at the Lik brings some big-city style to Banff. It suits several moods: predinner drinkers mingle here for pricey cocktails, while sports fans down pitchers of beer while catching the game on the big-screen TV.

Wild Bill's Legendary Saloon BAR
(Map p64; 201 Banff Ave; 11am-late) Down at Wild Bill's, country tunes sing out from the jukebox while Stetson-wearing line dancers and two-steppers shuffle to the beat. This lively saloon bar is also a popular venue for touring bands.

Tommy's Neighborhood Pub PUB
(Map p64; 120 Banff Ave; from around 11am) Basement pub in the British tradition, ideal for homey pub grub, draft beer and a game of darts.

Evelyn's Coffee Bar CAFÉ
(Map p64; 119, 201 & 215 Banff Ave; 7am-11pm) Popular local café chain with locations on Banff Ave and one at 229 Bear St.

St James's Gate IRISH PUB
(Map p64; 205 Wolf St) Banff's largest Irish pub has 30 beers, 50 scotches and draft Guinness on tap.

Lux Cinema CINEMA
(Map p64; 403-762-8595; 229 Bear St; adult/child C$9.50/5.50) The town's main cinema, showing all the latest mainstream studio releases and one-off films during the annual Banff Mountain Film Festival.

Hoodoo Lounge CLUB
(Map p64; www.hoodoolounge.com; 137 Banff Ave; Mon-Sat) Banff's main club has nights to suit all tastes – house, dance and jun-

MR BANFF

Early Banff had its fair share of larger-than-life characters, but few were as colorful as **Norman Luxton** (1876–1962). Known to residents as 'Mr Banff,' Luxton was an amateur taxidermist, gold prospector, explorer and trader, not to mention a globe-trotting seaman: in 1901 he embarked on a 16,000km (10,000 mile) trip across the Pacific in a dugout canoe called Tilikum with his companion Captain Jack Voss, before being forced to abandon the expedition after five months due to ill health.

He returned to Banff to recuperate and subsequently played a key role in the town's development as a tourist center. Among other things, Luxton founded the Lux Cinema, ran the King Edward Hotel on Banff Ave, published the *Crag & Canyon* newspaper and established the Sign of the Goat Curio Shop (now the Banff Indian Trading Post).

He was fascinated by First Nations culture throughout his life, and in 1953 founded the Luxton Museum of the Plains Indian (now the Buffalo Nations Luxton Museum) to house his enormous collection of native artifacts. He was even made an honorary chief by the Stoney tribe, who gave him the name 'Chief White Shield.'

The Whyte Museum runs a special guided tour exploring Luxton's former home and garden on Beaver St.

gle at weekends, and themed party nights throughout the week.

Aurora Club CLUB
(Map p64; www.aurorabanff.com/index.aspx; 110 Banff Ave; ⏲Wed-Sat) The town's other late-night venue is part lounge-room bar, part club.

SHOPPING

Banff Town

Bear & Butterfly GIFTS
(Map p64; 214 Banff Ave) This gift store is run by the **Friends of Banff** (www.friendsofbanff.com), and sells local craftwork, pottery, artwork, books and other souvenirs to fund its activities in and around the national park, including Park Radio.

Banff Indian Trading Post GIFTS
(Map p62; www.banffindiantradingpost.com; cnr Cave & Birch Aves) Established by Norman Luxton, the old Sign of the Goat store is still the first place to head if you're after some First Nations crafts, including beadwork, deer-hide gloves, antler-handled hunting knives and 'dreamcatchers.' Some of the stuff is pretty tacky and of dubious provenance, so choose carefully.

Monod Sports OUTDOOR EQUIPMENT
(Map p64; www.monodsports.com; 129 Banff Ave; ⏲10am-9pm) This is Banff's oldest outdoor-equipment supplier, and still the best. Women's and men's clothing from big brands such as Patagonia, Arcteryx, Icebreaker, Columbia and North Face, supplemented by dedicated sections for rucksacks, equipment and footwear. Note that prices for outdoors goods in Banff tend to be quite high, so it's probably best to make the big purchases before you leave home.

Mountain Magic OUTDOOR EQUIPMENT
(Map p64; www.mountainmagic.com; ⏲8am-9pm Mon-Sat, to 6pm Sun) Sportswear (225 Bear St); Technical Clothing (220 Bear St) A good outdoors shop mainly geared toward climbers and cyclists. Note the separate stores for technical clothing and sportswear, right across the street from each other.

Trail Rider Store CLOTHING
(Map p64; 132 Banff Ave) Pick up all the Brokeback fashion you'll ever need for looking the part in the saddle, from Stetsons, chaps and plaid shirts to handmade leather cowboy boots.

Viewpoint BOOKS, GIFTS
(Map p64; 201 Caribou St) Mainly sells glossy photo books, as well as books on Banff's local history, geology and wildlife.

Rocky Mountain Soap Company BEAUTY
(Map p64; www.rockymountainsoap.com; 204 Banff Ave; ⏲10am-9:30pm Sun-Thu, to 10pm Fri & Sat) Banff branch of the Canmore-based beauty company, selling natural soaps, lotions and creams.

Chocolaterie Bernard Callebaut CHOCOLATES
(Map p64; www.bernardcallebaut.com; 111 Banff Ave) Gourmet chocolate maker with over 48 flavors to choose from.

Lake Louise

Wilson Mountain Sports OUTDOOR EQUIPMENT
(www.wmsll.com; Samson Mall; ⏲8am-8pm) Huge outdoor sports, snow-wear and clothing store in Lake Louise Village, which often has good sales in the off season.

INFORMATION

Emergency

Emergencies (☎911) For fire, mountain rescue and other emergencies.

Park Warden Office (☎emergencies 403-762-4506, nonemergencies 403-762-1470; 216 Hawk Ave, Banff) For park-related matters and to report wildlife sightings (especially bears, cougars, wolverines and lynx).

Internet Access

Banff Public Library (Map p64; 101 Bear St, Banff; per 30min C$1; ⏲10am-8pm Mon-Thu, to 6pm Fri & Sat, 1-5pm Sun)

Cyberweb Internet Café (Basement, Sundance Mall, 215 Banff Ave, Banff; per 10min C$1; ⏲9am-midnight)

Media

Crag & Canyon (www.banffcragandcanyon.com) Free local newspaper published Tuesday.

Park Radio (101.1/103.3FM; www.friendsofbanff.com/park-radio) Not-for-profit radio station with regular trail reports, weather bulletins and other park news.

Rocky Mountain Outlook (www.rmoutlook.com) Canmore-based paper that covers general Banff news. Published Thursday.

USEFUL NUMBERS

The following telephone numbers might come in useful during your stay:

Avalanche Hazards (☎403-762-1460) Recorded message detailing areas at high risk of avalanche.

Banff Weather Office (☎403-762-2088) For the latest weather forecast and warnings.

Road Conditions (☎403-762-1450) Provided by Rocky Mountain National Parks.

Trail Conditions (☎403-760-1305) Trail reports, wildlife warnings and closures (recorded message).

Medical Services

Mineral Springs Hospital (☎403-762-2222; www.banffmineralspringshospital.ca; 305 Lynx St, Banff; ⏰24hr) Medical emergencies.

Money

Alberta Treasury Branch (317 Banff Ave, Banff)

Bank of Montreal (107 Banff Ave, Banff)

CIBC (98 Banff Ave, Banff)

Post

Banff Post Office (Map p64; 204 Buffalo St, Banff)

Tourist Information

Banff Information Centre (Map p64; ☎403-762-1550; banff.vrc@pc.gc.ca; 224 Banff Ave, Banff; ⏰8am-8pm summer, 9am-7pm mid-May, late spring & early autumn, 9am-5pm winter) The main park visitor center can answer practically any question you care to ask. It also distributes info leaflets and trail maps, sells wilderness passes and provides latest bear sightings, trail reports and weather forecasts.

Banff Tourism Bureau (Map p64; ☎403-762-8421; www.banfflakelouise.com; 224 Banff Ave, Banff; ⏰9am-5pm spring & autumn, 8am-8pm summer, 9am-4pm winter) Opposite the Parks desks in the Banff Information Centre, this info desk provides advice on accommodations, activities and attractions.

Friends of Banff (Map p64; ☎403-762-8911; www.friendsofbanff.com; Bear & Butterfly, 214 Banff Ave, Banff) A nonprofit organization that provides educational programs, guided walks and general information on the park. It also operates Banff Park Radio (101.1FM/103.3FM in English/French).

Lake Louise Backcountry Trails Office (☎403-522-1264; Lake Louise Visitor Centre, Lake Louise Village) Specialist advice on exploring the backcountry area around Lake Louise.

Lake Louise Tourism Bureau (☎403-762-8421; Lake Louise Visitor Centre, Lake Louise Village; ⏰9am-7pm summer only) Information on activities and accommodations in Lake Louise Village.

Lake Louise Visitor Centre (Map p58; ☎403-522-3833; ll.info@pc.gc.ca; Lake Louise Village; ⏰8am-8pm summer, 9am-5pm spring & autumn, 9am-4pm winter) Located next to Samson Mall.

Websites

Head to **Lonely Planet** (www.lonelyplanet.com/canada/alberta/banff-and-jasper-national-parks) for planning advice, author recommendations, traveler reviews and insider tips.

GETTING THERE & AWAY

Most visitors arrive in the park by car, although regular shuttle services travel to Banff and Lake Louise from the airport (p261). The only buses to the main sights and trailheads are provided by private sightseeing companies and bike/hike shuttles.

For full details on traveling between the national parks, see p261.

Bus

The **Banff Airporter** (☎888-449-2901; www.banffairporter.com) airport shuttle bus runs 12 times daily from Calgary airport to Banff (one-way adult/child five to 12 years C$53/26.50) and Canmore (C$50.35/25.18). Buses provide door-to-door service to/from Banff hotels.

The **Brewster Airport Shuttle** (www.explorerockies.com/airport-shuttles) has six daily buses from Calgary airport to Banff (one-way adult/child six to 15 years C$49.95/24.95) and Lake Louise (C$69.95/34.95). One bus continues to Jasper (C$129.95/64.95). Free wi-fi is available on board.

Greyhound (Map p62; ☎1-800-661-8747; www.greyhound.ca) offers a long-distance bus service five times daily to/from Calgary via Canmore and Banff, and four times daily to/from Banff via Lake Louise, Field, Golden and Vancouver. Buses stop at Canmore Visitor Centre, Banff train station and Samson Mall in Lake Louise. A surcharge of C$3 is added to all routes on weekends, and discounts are available by buying online.

Note that Greyhound buses do not currently stop at Calgary airport, so you'll also have to factor in the cost for a taxi or shuttle from the airport to the Calgary bus depot. See p62 for further details.

Sample fares:

DESTINATION	ADULT ONE-WAY FARE
Banff–Calgary	C$27.30
Banff–Canmore	C$10.86
Banff–Lake Louise	C$16.10
Banff–Vancouver	C$128.30
Canmore–Calgary	C$23.60

Car

If you're arriving by air, the easiest option is to rent a car at either Calgary or Edmonton airports (but note that airport rentals incur a surcharge; see p262). Major car-hire companies with offices in Banff include the following:

Avis (☎403-762-3222; cnr Wolf St & Banff Ave; ⏲8am-4:30pm Mon-Sat, to noon Sun)

Budget (☎403-226-1550; 202 Bear St; ⏲8am-5pm Mon-Fri, to 3pm Sat, to 2pm Sun)

Enterprise (☎403-762-2688; cnr Lynx & Caribou Sts; ⏲8am-5pm Mon-Fri)

Train

Banff's train station is just outside town on Railway Ave. The only passenger trains that stop there are run by **Rocky Mountaineer** (☎800-665-7245; www.rockymountaineer.com), which usually has one service daily between Banff and Lake Louise. For full details on train services to Jasper and beyond, see p263.

GETTING AROUND

Bicycle

Banff is well geared for cyclists, with plenty of bike shops and rental companies dotted around the main town. Very few trailheads have cycle racks, but many rental companies offer shuttle services to main trails.

Bus

Since 2008, Banff has been the proud owner of a shiny new fleet of hybrid electric-biodiesel buses known as **Roam** (☎403-762-1215; www.banff.ca/locals-residents/public-transit-buses/roam.htm). There are three routes that run roughly half-hourly between 6:15am and 11:30pm in summer, with a reduced service in winter. Single adult tickets cost C$2. Tickets for seniors and children between six and 12 years cost C$1. Kids under six are free. A one-/three-day pass valid for all three routes costs C$5/12.

ROUTE 1 Banff Ave to Sulphur Mountain and the Banff Gondola.

ROUTE 2 Tunnel Mountain campgrounds to the Fairmont Banff Springs hotel, with stops on Tunnel Mountain Dr, Wolf St, Otter St, Banff Ave and Spray Ave.

ROUTE 3 Banff Ave to Banff Centre via Surprise Corner.

The **Banff Connector** (☎1-888-449-2901; www.banffconnector.com) is a scheduled minibus service between Banff and Canmore (adult one way/return C$15/20, child six to 12 years C$7.50/15). It's essentially the same service as the Banff Airporter, so there are 12 buses daily in both directions, with door-to-door drop-offs in Banff, and a stop in Canmore at the Radisson Hotel.

Car

Trans-Canada Hwy 1 runs straight through the center of the park via Canmore, Banff and Lake Louise. The single-lane Bow Valley Parkway (Hwy 1A) runs parallel to Hwy 1, and is closed in spring from 6pm to 9am to protect wildlife.

» Speed limits are usually 90km/h (56mph) for major roads, and 60km/h (37mph) on secondary roads unless otherwise indicated.

» Outside Banff and Lake Louise, the only gas stations are at Castle Mountain Junction and Saskatchewan Crossing.

» Most parking lots at trailheads and in Lake Louise and Banff Town are free.

Taxi

Due to the distances between sights, taxis aren't a very practical way of getting around, although they can make an economical way of getting to trailheads for families and groups of more than three people. Try the following companies:

Banff Taxi (☎403-762-4444)

Lake Louise Taxi (☎403-522-2020)

Legion Taxi (☎403-762-3353)

Mountain Taxi (☎403-762-3351)

AROUND BANFF NATIONAL PARK

Although many visitors never venture much beyond Banff, it's well worth taking the time to explore outside the park's borders. Banff is surrounded by several other spectacular national and provincial parks, all blessed with the same kind of sky-high scenery as their better-known neighbor, but with the added advantages of having far fewer visitors and quieter trails. Kananaskis and Yoho are the locals' tips for hiking, while Golden is the center for adventure sports, and backcountry walkers head for the remote trails around Mt Assiniboine Provincial Park.

Canmore

Nestled beneath the spiky trio of snow-crested mountains known as the Three Sisters, the lively little town of Canmore has changed almost beyond recognition over the last couple of decades. Perched on the banks of the fast-flowing Bow River, Canmore originally grew up as a center for the local coal-mining industry, but following the closure of the last working mine in 1979, the town has slowly reinvented itself as a gateway town for Banff National Park and a center for outdoor activities. It's quieter, cheaper and much more chilled than Banff Town, and makes the perfect launch-pad for exploring both the eastern sections of the national park and the mountains and lakes of Kananaskis Country (p121), a short drive to the south.

Canmore is 24km (15 miles) east of Banff Town and 7km (4.3 miles) from the park's East Gate along Hwy 1. Many of the hotels are located along the Bow Valley Trail, which runs roughly parallel to Hwy 1. Most shops, services and restaurants are along Main St (8th St), which runs west from Railway Ave.

Sights & Activities

Big Head SCULPTURE

At the end of Main St, half-buried in gravel by the Bow River, sits the impressive sculpture known as the Big Head (for reasons that will soon become obvious once you see it). Created by the artist Al Henderson, the sculpture was inspired by Canmore's name; the original town of Canmore in northwest Scotland was called *ceann mór*, a Gaelic word meaning great head or chief. The sculpture has become a much-loved landmark, and the head's shiny pate is sometimes adorned to mark town festivities. It sometimes even gets its very own woolly toque in winter.

Canmore Museum & Geoscience Centre MUSEUM

(www.cmags.org; 907 7th Ave; adult/child & senior C$5/3; ⏲noon-5pm Mon & Tue, 10am-5pm Wed-Sun summer, noon-5pm Mon-Fri, 11am-5pm Sat & Sun winter) The town's small museum has an intriguing collection of exhibits and photographs relating to Canmore's coal-mining history and the story of the 1988 Olympics.

The museum also runs the **North West Mounted Police Barracks** (601 8th St; ⏲1-5pm Mon & Tue, 10am-5pm Wed-Sun summer, noon-4pm Sat & Sun winter), the oldest surviving barracks in western Canada. Built in 1893, it was used by the Mounties until 1929, and is now home to a small display of Mounties-themed memorabilia and a quaint tearoom.

TOP CHOICE **Canmore Nordic Centre** MOUNTAIN BIKING

(www.canmorenordiccentre.ca) Nestled in the hills to the west of town on the way to the Spray Lakes reservoir, this huge trail center was originally developed for the Nordic events of the 1988 Winter Olympics. It's now one of the best mountain-bike parks in western Canada, with over 65km (40 miles) of groomed trails developed by some of the nation's top pedal-heads and trail designers.

There are graded routes to suit all abilities, from easy rides to technical singletracks and full-on downhills. You can bring your own bike, or hire one from **Trail Sports** (☎403-678-6764; www.trailsports.ab.ca; ⏲9am-8pm Mon-Fri, to 6pm Sat & Sun), opposite the center's day lodge. The center also offers guided rides and skills clinics (C$60 for 1½ hours) with certified instructors.

If biking is not your thing, most of the center's trails are also open to walkers, orienteerers and roller-skiers, and in winter some are specially groomed for cross-country skiers. Whatever the time of year, take precautions to avoid wildlife encounters, as the trails cross through areas of backcountry that form part of the Bow Valley Wildlife Corridor, and you might find that grizzlies, black bears and ungulates have decided to use the trails, too.

The center is a 3.6km (2.2-mile) drive from Canmore on Spray Lakes Rd. Take Rundle Dr across the river, continue south along Three Sisters Dr and follow signs to the Canmore Nordic Centre.

For bike rentals in Canmore, see p94.

Legacy Trail BIKING

After years of pressure from residents, the new paved Legacy Trail connecting Banff and Canmore was finally opened in 2010, allowing walkers, cyclists and rollerbladers to commute between the towns without having to endanger themselves on the high-speed lanes of the main highway.

The path starts near Banff Ave and runs for 25km (15.5 miles) all the way to Banff's East Gate, with a small section of road-riding as it nears Canmore. It travels parallel to Hwy 1 for nearly the whole route, so it's not

Canmore

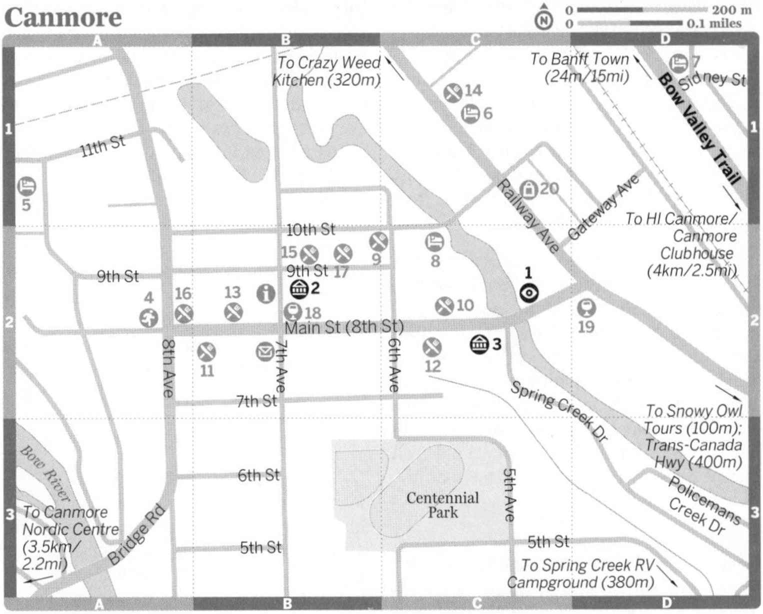

Canmore

Sights

1 Big Head ... C2
2 Canmore Museum & Geoscience Society ... B2
3 North West Mounted Police Barracks ... C2

Activities, Courses & Tours

4 Rebound Cycle ... A2

Sleeping

5 Canadian Artisans ... A1
6 Canmore Crossing ... C1
7 Lady Macdonald Country Inn ... D1
8 Paintbox Lodge ... C2

Eating

9 Communitea ... B2
10 Grizzly Paw ... C2
11 Mountain Mercato ... B2
12 Old School Bus ... C2
13 Rocky Mountain Bagel Company ... B2
14 Safeway ... C1
Sobey's ... (see 20)
15 Trough ... B2
16 Wood Steakhouse & Lounge ... A2
17 Zona's ... B2

Drinking

18 Canmore Hotel ... B2
19 Rose & Crown ... D2

Shopping

20 Sobey's ... C1

always the most peaceful bike ride – but at least you can cycle safely without living in constant fear of getting mown down by a passing truck.

Grassi Lakes Trail HIKING

There are plenty of trails within easy reach of town, including the popular 3.8km (2.4-mile) round-trip to **Grassi Lakes**, named after Lawrence Grassi, one of Canmore's founding fathers. Other options include trails to Cougar Creek and Grotto Canyon (both around 4km/2.5 miles), the sky-high ascent of Ha Ling Peak (5.6km/3.5 miles) and an airy scramble to the mountain of Lady Macdonald (8km/5 miles), which passes an abandoned teahouse en route. Trail maps and route advice are available from the Canmore Visitor Centre.

Inside Out Experience ADVENTURE SPORTS
(www.insideoutexperience.com; float trips from C$49, raft trips from C$75; ⏲May-late Sep) This experienced activity company runs adrenaline-fuelled white-water rafting expeditions on many local rivers (including unusual options such as the Elbow and Red Deer Rivers), as well as combo trips including biking, hiking and horseback riding. Rafting trips start from around C$77/62 per adult/child.

Alpine Helicopters HELICOPTER FLIGHTS
(www.alpinehelicopters.com; 91 Bow Valley Trail) Canmore is a busy base for scenic chopper flights over Spray Lakes (12 minutes; C$109 per person), the nearby Goat and Sundance Ranges (30 minutes; C$219) and Mt Assiniboine (30 minutes; C$249). Flights are weather dependent, so it's always best to have a back-up plan in case the clouds roll in. The heliport is just south of town on the Bow Valley Trail.

Canmore Cave Tours CAVING
(☎403-678-8819; www.canmorecavetours.com; ⏲year-round) Buried deep beneath the Grotto Mountain near Canmore is a system of deep caves known as the Rat's Nest. Canmore Cave Tours runs guided trips into the maze of twisting passageways and claustrophobic caverns. There are two core trips: the Explorer Tour (adult/child C$109/99), a 4.5-hour trip that involves around two hours underground; and the longer Adventure Tour, a six-hour trip that features an 18m (15ft) abseil and ends at the Grotto, a stalactite-filled chamber with a crystal-clear underground pool.

There's a minimum age of 12 years on all tours. Be prepared to get very wet and muddy, and be prepared for chilly temperatures, as the caves stay at a constant 5°C (41°F) year-round.

Dogsledding DOGSLEDDING
Following the recent controversy over dogsledding in Whistler, it's become doubly important to make sure that dogsledding companies treat their animals with respect and dignity. We're happy to say that both of the dogsledding facilities reviewed here are well run and their dogs are happy, healthy and well cared for.

Snowy Owl Tours
(☎403-678-9588; www.snowyowltours.com) Dog-sledding has been a traditional mode of travel in the Canadian Rockies for centuries, and it's a wonderful way to see the wilderness. Snowy Owl Tours offers sled trips on custom-built sleighs pulled by your own team of Siberian and Alaskan huskies. You can catch the two-hour Powder Hound Express (adult/child six to nine years/two to five years/under two years C$149/80/30/20) or go for longer four-hour (adult/child under eight years C$385/260) and eight-hour trips (C$695/495). It also offers two-day mushing courses if you really get into it.

The sledding season is usually from November to April; if you're here in summer, you can meet the dogs on a kennel tour (adult/child under 11 years C$45/35), or take a walk to Grotto Mountain with the owner's wolf-husky cross, Shaman (C$90 per person). Summer rides in wheeled sleds are also sometimes available.

Howling Dog Tours
(☎403-678-9588; www.howlingdogtours.com) This dogsledding company offers similar trips to Snowy Owl Tours. The most popular option is the two-hour Unleash the Musher Tour (C$290 for two people), which covers the basics of dogsledding and allows you to meet the hounds. Longer half-day tours and summer kennel visits are also available.

Sleeping

Camping

Booking and information for all the main campgrounds around Canmore is handled by **Bow Valley Park Campgrounds** (☎403-673-2163; www.bowvalleycampgrounds.com).

Bow River Campground CAMPGROUND $
(campsites C$23; ⏲May-Sep) The municipal campground in Canmore is very basic, so the best option if you want to camp close to town is this riverside site 1.6km (1 mile) down Hwy 1. It's sandwiched between the river and the highway, so it's not as peaceful as it could be, but it's pleasant enough if you can bag a spot by the water. Basic facilities include nonflush toilets and RV-accessible sites, but there are no hookups.

Three Sisters Campground CAMPGROUND $
(campsites C$23; ⏲mid-Apr–Nov) For prettier sites and a more peaceful atmosphere, head for this campground in the satellite town of Three Sisters, 16km (10 miles) east of Canmore. The tent spaces furthest from the highway are generally the quietest and you're handily positioned near plenty of hiking trails. RVs are welcome.

Lac des Arcs CAMPGROUND $
(campsites C$23; ⏰mid-Apr–Sep) This small site is the furthest from Canmore (25km/15.5 miles east of town), but it's also the smallest and quietest. There are only 28 sites, all surrounded by trees with their own fire pits. Its relative seclusion and the lack of power and water hookups means it's mainly used by campers.

Spring Creek RV Campground RV CAMPGROUND $
(☎403-678-5111; www.springcreekrv.ca; 502 3rd Ave; RV sites with power C$33, with water & power C$35, with full hookup C$45, extra adults & pull-throughs C$2; ⏰mid-Apr–mid-Oct) Dedicated entirely to motor homers, this open-meadow RV ground has fantastic mountain views, despite the total lack of privacy between the pitches. Nevertheless, full hookups and the handy town-edge location ensure it's usually busy.

Lodging

Canmore's hotels and B&Bs generally offer better value than most places inside the park. The **Canmore Bow Valley B&B Association** (☎403-609-7224; www.bbcanmore.com) keeps a comprehensive list of all the local B&Bs, and you'll find lots of motels and hotels along the Bow Valley Trail.

There are also a large number of apartment and condo rentals in Canmore, many of which are advertised online at B&B and holiday accommodations sites. Be careful if you're booking online, as only certain buildings and landlords in Canmore are legally permitted to provide short-term holiday accommodations.

If in doubt, it's always best to book through a reputable agency. Good places to start include **Rentals in the Rockies** (www.rentalsintherockies.com) and Canmore Holiday Accommodation (www.canmoreholidayaccommodation.com).

TOP CHOICE **Paintbox Lodge** B&B $$
(☎403-609-0482; www.paintboxlodge.com; 629 10th St; r C$159-259, 2-night minimum mid-Jun–mid-Sep & Christmas; 📶) Run by ex-Olympic skiers Thomas Grandi and Sarah Renner, this truly lavish B&B fully deserves its boutique tagline. The five suites are a super mix of country chic and luxury comfort. For maximum space ask for the Loft Suite, which sleeps four and features beamed ceilings, mountain-view balcony and sexy corner tub. All rooms share use of the mountain kitchen, kitted out with top-of-the-range Miele appliances (including an espresso machine).

Blackstone Mountain Lodge HOTEL $$
(☎1-888-830-8883; www.blackstonecanmore.ca; d C$139-249; ❄📶🏊👶) The pick of several Bellstar properties around Canmore, located a quick drive out of town on the Bow Valley Trail. It's a purpose-built hotel with a choice of traditional rooms or suites that come with their own fully equipped kitchen (complete with oven, dishwasher and washing machine), making them ideal for families. The rates are very reasonable even in summer, and there's even a hot tub and outdoor pool.

HI Canmore/Canmore Clubhouse HOSTEL $
(☎403-678-3200; canmore@hihostels.ca; Indian Flats Rd; dm nonmembers C$36, premium in peak season C$5; @📶) The old Canmore Clubhouse, run by the Alpine Club of Canada, is now affiliated with Hostelling International, and it's still the best budget bolthole this side of the Banff border. Split over two timber-clad buildings, both with full kitchens and spic-and-span dorm rooms, it's the ideal place to hook up with fellow hikers and mountaineers. You can browse the mountaineering guidebooks in the lounge, kick back in the sauna or just sit out on the deck and stare at the mountain views. There's a limited number of private rooms, so book early.

Lady Macdonald Country Inn GUESTHOUSE $$
(☎800-567-3919; www.ladymacdonald.com; 1201 Bow Valley Trail; r C$125-199, ste C$200-250) This frilly little inn wouldn't look out of place in small-town Connecticut, with its elegant verandas, turrets and wooden cladding. The rooms are dinky, each with their own style: Vermilion has views of Ha Ling and a Jacuzzi, Cascade has a gas fireplace and turret outlook, and the top Three Sisters Suite has wall-to-wall mountain views. Breakfast is included.

A Bear & Bison GUESTHOUSE $$$
(☎403-678-2058; www.bearandbisoninn.com; 705 Benchlands Trail; r C$179-279) A gabled lodge with a country vibe. Twelve rooms in all: some boast hardwood floors, chiropractic mattresses and antique dressers, others multi-jet massage tubs and private patios. Some of the decor is a bit dated, but rates include a huge breakfast (try the maple French toast or the raspberry and blueberry pancakes).

Mystic Springs APARTMENT, RESORT $$$
(www.mysticsprings.ca; chalets per week C$795-1395;) This smart Bellstar property is deliberately geared toward families, with lovely twin-floor chalets that offer all the comforts of home. They're fairly small inside, but beautifully appointed with shiny wood floors, hi-fis, top-of-the-range kitchens and multiple rooms to suit families of all sizes. There's also a communal pool and hot tub, but wi-fi is only available in the lobby. Chalets are only available for weekly rentals.

Canadian Artisans B&B $$
(403-678-4138; www.canadianartisans.ca; 1016 9th Ave; ste C$160-210) Oddball B&B tucked away in forest on the edge of Canmore. The two wood-lined suites are detached from the main house. The best is the Treehouse Suite, which has picture windows, stained-glass door panels, a futuristic shower pod and a lovely vaulted roof. The Foresthouse is a bit more cramped (especially in the bathroom-cum-bedroom department).

Canmore Crossing APARTMENT $$
(403-678-9390; www.canmorecrossing.ca; 1120 Railway Ave; ste C$189-269) This large condo complex offers self-catering apartments with up to three bedrooms and all the usual mod-cons (dishwasher, DVD, washer-dryer). The only drawbacks are the cramped layouts and the building's position right beside the railway tracks.

Eating

For such a small town, Canmore has a surprising amount of great places to dine – so many, in fact, that people often drive over from Banff solely for the pleasure to eat here.

For self-catering supplies, Canmore has two large supermarkets: **Safeway** (1200 Railway Ave) and **Sobey's** (950 Railway Ave).

TOP CHOICE **Trough** CANADIAN $$$
(403-678-2820; www.thetrough.ca; 725 Walk of Champions Way (9th St); lunch mains C$15-28, dinner mains C$32-38; lunch & dinner Wed-Mon) Canmore's slinkiest bistro is a bit tucked away on 9th St, but it's absolutely worth the effort to find. It regularly features in the Rockies' top restaurant lists, and with good reason: the food is about the best anywhere in town, mixing modern Canadian flavors with inspiration from fusion, Asian and Mediterranean cuisine. Earthy colors, wood furniture and a cute veranda patio out front complete the package.

Crazy Weed Kitchen INTERNATIONAL $$$
(403-609-2530; www.crazyweed.ca; 1600 Railway Ave; lunch mains C$12-18, dinner mains C$22-38; lunch & dinner) This flashy new bistro on the edge of Railway Ave feels more big city than small town, with its sharp designer lines, funky artwork and globetrotting menu that takes in everything from wood-fired pizza to short ribs in massaman curry and Kashmiri lamb balls. It's earned a devoted following, so book ahead.

Grizzly Paw BREW-PUB $$
(www.thegrizzlypaw.com; 622 8th St; mains C$8-14; lunch & dinner) This boisterous brew-pub is a favorite hangout for Canmore locals, especially on warm evenings when the outside patio is packed to bursting. The list of brewed beers changes constantly: regulars include Kananaskis Cream Ale, Grizzly 50 English Mild and Jacko Lantern Pumpkin Ale, plus house special sodas (our tips are the cherry cola and the traditional creamy root beer). If you're feeling peckish there's simple pub grub, including blackened chicken and Cajun burgers.

Communitea CAFÉ $
(www.thecommunitea.com; 1001 6th Ave; lunch C$6-10; 9am-5pm;) In a perfect world, this is what all cafés would be like. Locally run, ethically aware and all organic, this sweet little community café has become a Canmore institution since it opened in 2008. Homey veggie food, fresh-pressed juices and great coffee pack in the daytime punters, and the café hosts regular gigs, readings and discussions at weekends.

Zona's FUSION $$$
(403-609-2000; www.zonascanmore.com; 710 9th St; mains C$16-25; 5pm-late Wed-Sun) Just up the street from the Trough, Zona's is another fusion bistro that's popular with Canmore's late-night diners. The pan-global food is decent (if not particularly spectacular), but it's the outdoor deck and funky Moroccan souk vibe that make it worth a visit.

Mountain Mercato COFFEE, DELI $
(817 8th St; coffee C$2-5, lunch mains C$8-12; 9am-6pm Mon-Fri, 10am-7pm Sat & Sun) If you're looking for the best coffee in Canmore, this lovely deli is where you'll find it. The americanos and macchiatos are rich, strong and beautifully brewed; while you're waiting, you can browse the shelves for posh goodies, including organic fruit juices, handmade chocolates and other luxury items.

Old School Bus ICE CREAM $
(9th St; 1/2 scoops C$3.75/4.75, kid's scoop C$2.50; ⏲9am-5:30pm; 👪) Permanently parked just off Main St, this converted school bus is the place for ice cream in Canmore. The chalkboard's full of unusual flavors, including white chocolate, blackberry and peanut butter, and the milkshakes are heavenly, too.

Rocky Mountain Bagel Company SANDWICHES $
(830 8th St; bagels C$6-10; ⏲6:30am-10pm; 📶) Lunchtime queues are long at this busy bagel and coffeehouse, where the choices on the blackboard border on the bewildering. If you're stuck, choose from the house specials, or go off-piste and build your own custom creation.

Wood Steakhouse & Lounge AMERICAN $$$
(☎403-678-3404; 838 8th St; sandwiches & burgers C$15-19, mains C$22-32; ⏲11am-midnight; 👪) At the end of Main St, this sprawling bistro has the best patio anywhere in Canmore, with a panorama of Ha Ling Peak, Mt Lawrence Grassi and the Three Sisters unfolding along the horizon. The food's not quite as exciting, mainly revolving around ribs, steaks and generous burgers. Kids eat free on Sunday night.

Drinking & Entertainment

Rose & Crown PUB
(749 Railway Ave) This spit-and-sawdust British pub at the northern end of Main St looks dingy from outside, but things feel a lot more welcoming once you get out onto the riverside patio. Plentiful beers on tap make it a good place to rub shoulders with the locals, and it's also one of Canmore's main venues for live music.

Canmore Hotel PUB
(738 8th St) Boozers have been downing beers at this venerable Canmore drinking den for as long as anyone cares to remember, and the facade still looks like something out of the Old West. It often hosts touring bands.

ℹ Information

Medical Services

Canmore General Hospital (☎403-678-5536; 1100 Hospital Pl; ⏲24hr)

Post

Post Office (801 8th St)

Tourist Information

Alberta Visitor Information Centre (☎403-678-5277; www.travelalberta.com; 2801 Bow Valley Trail; ⏲8am-8pm summer, to 6pm winter) Regional visitor center just off the Trans-Canada Hwy west of town.

Canmore Visitor Centre (☎403-678-1295; www.tourismcanmore.com; 301 8th St; ⏲8:30am-5pm Mon-Sat) The main tourist office is opposite Canmore Museum.

ℹ Getting There & Away

Canmore is easily accessible by car from Banff and Calgary along Trans-Canada Hwy 1.

Bizarrely, there's no official bus service between Canmore and Banff, but the Banff Connector and Greyhound buses both stop regularly in town; see p115 for more information.

Kananaskis Country

The area collectively known as Kananaskis Country (or K-Country to the locals) covers a vast area to the south and east of Banff National Park, comprising several side-by-side provincial parks and protected areas, including Peter Lougheed Provincial Park, the Elbow Valley, Sheep Valley, Ghost River Wilderness Area and Don Getty Wildland Provincial Park.

While visitors and tourists make a beeline for Banff's trails, many Albertans prefer to hike in the K-Country, where the routes are quieter, the scenery is just as impressive and that all-important sense of wilderness is much easier to come by. It's less well known than Banff, but with a bit of research you'll find some fantastic hikes and trails, as well as plenty of sky-topping peaks, mountain lakes and outdoor pursuits.

Sights & Activities

There are two main roads through the area, which link up near the Kananaskis Lakes to form a convenient loop. The main Kananaskis Trail (Hwy 40) travels through the center of Kananaskis Valley from Barrier Lake, while the unpaved gravel Spray Lakes Trail (Hwy 742) heads northwest from the junction near Lower Kananaskis Lake all the way back to Canmore.

Gas supplies are limited in the valley, with only one (pricey) gas station near Fortress Junction. You can pick up general supplies at Kananaskis Village, about a half-hour drive from Hwy 1. Note that several subroads in the valley are closed from December to May.

Jumpingpound Demonstration Forest NATURE RESERVE
(☎403-297-8800; www.insideeducation.ca/jumpingpound; Hwy 68; ⊙May-Sep) Covering 182 hectares (450 acres) of spruce, aspen and fir, this richly forested area explores the heritage of logging and forestry practices in southern Alberta, with old sawmills and modern logging machines to see en route. You can follow a 10km (6.2-mile) driving tour or explore several walking trails, many of which travel through reforested areas as well as a 200-year-old wood.

Boundary Ranch HORSEBACK RIDING
(www.boundaryranch.com; Kananaskis Trail; short rides C$39.95-99.95, day rides from C$139.95; ⊙mid-May–mid-Oct) This experienced trail-riding ranch offers lots of options for day rides and longer pack trips, some of which also feature white-water rafting and back-country hikes.

The ranch is also home to **Rick Guinn's Steakhouse** (mains C$10-20; ⊙11am-7pm mid-May–mid-Oct), which turns out flame-grilled burgers, inch-thick steaks and smoked pork chops for its hungry horseback-riding guests (and anyone else who happens to be passing on through).

Kananaskis Country Golf Course GOLF
(www.kananaskisgolf.com; green fees C$85) This golf course is just as impressive as the one in Banff Springs, but it's much less snooty and a good deal cheaper, too. There are two courses to choose from, both backed by incredible mountain vistas. All the necessary gear (clubs, shoes and golf cart) can be rented from the clubhouse.

Nakiska SKIING
(www.skinakiska.com; ⊙Nov–mid-Apr) The K-Country's only ski resort was one of the main venues for the 1988 Winter Olympics, and it's still a popular place to hit the slopes, although the facilities and runs are a lot less developed than in nearby Banff. Shuttle buses run throughout the winter season from Canmore and Banff, making Nakiska a credible (and often quieter) alternative to the Big Three.

There are around 30 groomed runs spread out over 413 hectares (1021 acres), with plenty of scope for off-piste riding on the slopes of Mt Allan. Over two-thirds of the runs are rated intermediate, so Nakiska is a good all-round resort for most mid-level skiers. Snowboarders can also tackle the challenging **Najibska Rail Park**. The resort

WORTH A TRIP

THE SMITH-DORRIEN/SPRAY LAKES TRAIL

The Smith-Dorrien/Spray Lakes Trail (or Hwy 742 to give it its official title) is a dirt and gravel highway that runs for around 62km (38.5 miles) from the Kananaskis Lakes to Canmore. Named after a British commander of WWI, Horace Smith-Dorrien, the rough, unsealed trail passes through some of the wildest areas of the Peter Lougheed, Spray Valley and Bow Valley Wildland Provincial Parks.

The scenery is stunning, but the road is tough going, especially after heavy rain: be prepared for plenty of ruts and potholes, and go slow unless you want to wreck your rental car's suspension. There are several lakeside picnic areas en route where you can break the journey and drink in the mountain scenery. The northern section of the road into Canmore beyond Goat Creek is extremely steep, so take extra care here.

For much of its length, the road tracks the western edge of the **Spray Lakes Reservoir**, which provides much of Canmore's power through a hydro-electric dam built in 1950. Apart from the hydro-dam, the valley is almost entirely unpopulated, so it's a brilliant area for wildlife spotting: Rocky Mountain sheep, mountain goats, elk, moose and even bears can often be seen along the sides of the road, especially early or late in the day (take things slow if you want to have a chance of actually seeing anything). After dark you might even be lucky enough to hear the ghostly howl of a wolf echoing around the mountains, as the Spray Valley is a seasonal hunting ground for one of the Bow Valley's last remaining wild wolf packs.

The road also provides access to some of the K-Country's most remote trails, including the stunning **Bryant Creek route** into Mt Assiniboine Provincial Park (p129) from the Mt Shark parking lot, the 10km (6.4-mile) **Chester Lake Trail**, and the arduous 15km (9.3-mile) hike to **Burstall Pass** (five hours).

also recently added some of the Rockies' only accessible areas for glade skiing. Check the website for pricing information.

The nearby resort of **Fortress Mountain** has been closed for several years, with no sign on the horizon that it's going to reopen anytime soon – although the area recently received some extra attention when some of the snow scenes from *Inception* were filmed there.

Peter Lougheed Provincial Park HIKING

The quiet trails and backcountry areas of K-Country are superb for hikers, especially around Peter Lougheed Provincial Park, situated on the west side of Kananaskis Valley. Named after the premier of Alberta from 1971 to 1985, this remote park covers an area of 304 sq km (117 sq miles), including the **Upper** and **Lower Kananaskis Lakes** and the **Highwood Pass**, the highest-navigable road pass in Canada at 2350m (7710ft; usually open from June to October). It's an excellent area for wildlife spotting, as it's an important wildlife corridor and the valley has been subjected to very little development.

Recommended half-day hikes include the 3km (1.9-mile) trail to Boulton Creek (one hour) and the 5km (3.1-mile) hike to the natural bowl of Ptarmigan Cirque (three hours). Longer day routes include the 7.2km (4.5-mile) hike to Mt Indefatigable (four hours) and the 16km (10-mile) Upper Kananaskis Lake Circuit (five hours).

Trail leaflets and information on conditions are available from the park visitor center near Kananaskis Lakes.

Sleeping

Camping

Compared to Banff, Kananaskis' campgrounds are a haven of peace and tranquility. Book well ahead, as K-Country's backcountry trails are very popular.

There's a full listing of all the main K-Country campgrounds at www.kananaskiscountrycampgrounds.com. Reservations for most sites can be made online through the new **Alberta Campgrounds** (www.reserve.albertaparks.ca) reservation service. You'll need a wilderness permit (C$8.80) if you're planning to stay anywhere in the backcountry.

Self-catering supplies for campers are available from the small stores at Fortress Junction, Mt Kidd RV Park, Boulton Creek Trading Post and Kananaskis Village.

TOP CHOICE **Sundance Lodges** TENTS, CABINS $

(☎403-591-7122; www.sundancelodges.com; Kananaskis Trail; campsites C$29, teepees C$57-77, trapper's tents C$79; ⊙mid-May–Oct; 👪) For that authentic Canadian experience, try the hand-painted teepees and old-timey trapper's tents at this privately run campground. As you'd expect, facilities are basic – sleeping platforms and a kerosene lantern are about all you'll find inside – so you'll need the usual camping gear, but kids are bound to lap up the John Muir vibe.

Mt Kidd RV Park RV CAMPGROUND $

(☎403-591-7700; www.mountkiddrv.com; Mt Kidd Dr; RV sites with no/full hookups C$32.50/48; ⊙year-round) Halfway along the Kananaskis Valley, and handily placed for the facilities around Kananaskis Village, this place is the best option for trailer and RV campers, with full hookups and over 200 sites, plus comprehensive facilities: tennis courts, laundry, grocery store, games rooms and even a sauna.

Boulton Creek Campground CAMPGROUND $

(☎403-591-7226; standard campsites C$23, with power hookups C$35; ⊙May–mid-Oct) One of the best-equipped campgrounds and correspondingly popular, beautifully situated just to the south of Lower Kananaskis Lake. Showers, flush toilets and summer interpretive programs, plus power and water hookups, mean that it's nearly always full. There are some pull-through sites for RVs.

McLean Creek CAMPGROUND $

(☎403-949-3132; Elbow Valley; standard campsites C$23, with power hookups C$29; ⊙year-round) Another large and efficient campground near to McLean Pond and the Station Flats, just off Hwy 66 from Bragg Creek. The sites are crammed in pretty close together (especially on Loops C and D), but the facilities are comprehensive (campground theater, flush toilets, showers) and you're well placed to explore the plentiful trails nearby.

Canyon Camping CAMPGROUND $

(☎1-866-366-2267; campsites C$23; Kananaskis Lakes Rd; ⊙mid-Jun–Sep) Just a few steps from Lower Kananaskis Lake and a gorgeous little picnic area, this is a lovely mountain-view campground. Loop A has just a few sites, while Loop C is furthest from the lakeshore but usually the quietest. There are horse pits, trailer pull-throughs and a bike trail that's handy to the visitor center.

Elkwood Campground CAMPGROUND $
(☎1-866-366-2267; standard campsites C$23, with power hookups C$35; ⏲mid-May–mid-Sep) The 130 sites here, near Lower Kananaskis Lake, are fairly private, scattered around four well-spaced loops.

Lower Lake Campground CAMPGROUND $
(☎1-866-366-2267; campsites C$23; ⏲May-Nov) The 104 sites are secluded, with mountain and lake views dotted along a single trail, with a few pull-through loops for trailers. Sites are not reservable online.

Lodging

The only hotels in the valley are at Kananaskis Village, but they're both soulless corporate affairs geared toward golfers and business travelers. Unless you're happy to camp, you'll be better off basing yourself in Canmore and visiting Kananaskis on day trips.

Mt Engadine Lodge LODGE $$
(☎403-678-4080; www.mountengadine.com; Mt Shark Rd; r C$185-200, ste C$380-460, chalets C$380-660) You can't get much more rural – or more peaceful – than this remote mountain lodge, situated about 30km along the Smith-Dorrien/Spray Lakes Trail from Kananaskis Lakes. The lodge has a selection of family suites (complete with balcony and sitting room), peaceful rooms as well as detached cabins large enough for several people, all overlooking unspoilt meadows. Lodge rates include four hearty meals, including a build-your-own lunch and afternoon tea.

HI Kananaskis Wilderness Hostel HOSTEL $
(☎403-521-8421; cr.kan@hihostels.ca; Kananaskis Village; dm C$23; ⏲reception 5-11pm) The rustic exterior might fool you into thinking you'll be roughing it at this backwoods hostel, but inside you'll find shiny pine floors, plush sofas, a fire-lit lounge and a kingly kitchen. The large bunk-bed dorms are a bit institutional, and rates include linen (sleeping bags aren't allowed).

William Watson Lodge CABINS $
(☎403-591-7227; Kananaskis Lakes Rd; cabins C$30-40; ⏲year-round) This subsidized cabin complex is specially designed for visitors with disabilities, with fully accessible lodges in a quiet wood, as well as organized activities to help guests get out and explore. You'll need your own food and bedding.

ℹ Information

There are several visitor centers where you can pick up brochures, trail maps and wilderness passes.

Barrier Lake Information Centre (☎403-673-3985; ⏲8am-8pm Jun-Aug, 9am-5pm May & Sep, 9am-4pm Apr & Oct) Located 6.5km south of the junction on Hwy 1.

Elbow Valley Visitor Centre (☎403-949-2461; ⏲9:30am-4:30pm Mon-Thu, 9am-6pm Fri-Sun summer, 9:30am-4pm or 5pm shoulder seasons) Just west of Bragg Creek.

Kananaskis Country (www.tpr.alberta.ca/parks/kananaskis/flashindex.asp) Useful website for the K-Country run by the provincial government.

Peter Lougheed Information Centre (☎403-591-6322; Kananaskis Lakes Rd; ⏲9am-9pm Jul & Aug, 9:30am-4pm Apr-Jun, Sep & Oct) Near the junction with Hwy 742, north of Kananaskis Lakes.

ℹ Getting There & Away

Kananaskis Country can be reached off Trans-Canada Hwy 1 along the gravel Smith-Dorrien Rd (Hwy 742) from Canmore or the Kananaskis Trail (Hwy 40), east of Canmore. From southern Alberta, you can reach the area in summer along Hwy 40 via the Highwood Pass.

Yoho National Park

To the west of Lake Louise, the Kicking Horse River bucks and surges into the wild, ice-crowned mountains of Yoho National Park, which is largely located across the border in the neighboring province of British Columbia. Though much smaller than Banff at around 1313 sq km (506 sq miles), Yoho (from a Cree word denoting awe or amazement) is every bit as spectacular as its neighbor: hulking peaks brood along either side of the plunging Kicking Horse Valley, and spur roads twist and turn to the area's most renowned attractions, including the crashing cascade of Takakkaw Falls and the glittering, green-blue pool of Emerald Lake.

Much of Yoho is still wild, remote country, and you'll find little in the way of visitor facilities. The only real settlement is the old CPR service town of Field, 27km (16.7 miles) to the east of Lake Louise, a quaint little town that still boasts many of its original 19th-century clapboard buildings.

The main road of Hwy 1 cuts straight through the heart of the valley from Lake Louise, roughly tracing the course of the Kicking Horse River. Take care when driving, as traffic can be fast and dangerous right along the route: the section east of Field toward Lake Louise traverses a very steep gradient, and the section west toward Golden is notorious as one of the most deadly stretches of highway in western Canada. A major project to twin this section is currently underway, so expect delays in summer. Snow tires and chains are mandatory in winter.

Sights & Activities

Takakkaw Falls WATERFALL

(Map p58) Yoho has several impressive waterfalls, but none are quite as grand as Takakkaw. A thundering torrent of water tumbles from its source in the nearby Daly Glacier over a sheer cliff face for 255m (836ft), making it the second-highest waterfall in Canada. The name comes from the Cree language, and roughly translates as 'it is magnificent'; the total base-to-top height of the falls is actually 384m (1259ft), but is split into two tiers of freefall.

Takakkaw is equally impressive seen in rain or shine, and the noise at any time is quite deafening. The falls are reached via a snaking 13km (8-mile) spur road leading off Hwy 1; en route you'll pass a couple of interesting viewpoints, including the **Meeting of the Waters**, where the Yoho and Kicking Horse Rivers join into one mighty torrent. The road is steep and traverses a couple of punishing sections of switchbacks that can be extremely challenging for nervous drivers, especially if you're in an RV: be prepared to stop and let traffic pass when necessary.

At the end of the road, a trail leads for around 800m (0.5 miles) from the Takakkaw parking lot to the base of the falls. Looking back down the valley, you'll also have a grand view of the surrounding mountains, including the Vice President, Michael Peak and Wapta Mountain.

Emerald Lake LAKE

For most visitors, this vividly colored lake is Yoho's most unmissable sight. Like its sister lakes of Peyto, Moraine and Lake Louise, Emerald Lake gains its otherworldly color from sunlight bouncing off rock particles suspended in the water – the brighter the light the more vivid the color. Ringed by forest and silhouetted by impressive mountains, including the iconic profile of Mt Burgess to the southeast, it's a truly beautiful spot. It's also guaranteed to be busy: parking can be practically impossible for much of late July and August, although the crowds and coach tours usually thin out by around 6pm.

The lake also marks the start of several hikes, including the easy 800m (0.5-mile) jaunt from the parking lot to **Hamilton Falls**, and the much tougher high-level hike via the Wapta Highline.

WORTH A TRIP

THE BURGESS SHALE

In 1909 the paleontologist Charles Doolittle Walcott was exploring the slopes around Burgess Pass when he made an extraordinary discovery. Hidden among the shattered shale rocks several thousand feet above sea level, he stumbled across a huge area of fossilized remains, deposited by a bizarre menagerie of long-extinct creatures that were almost entirely unknown to science.

The Burgess Shale, as the area is now known, has proven to be one of the most important archaeological resources ever discovered. Many of the creatures buried in the beds date from around 500 million years ago, when the surrounding landscape was submerged beneath a tropical sea, and life on Earth was undergoing a series of revolutionary transformations during the so-called 'Cambrian Explosion.' The weird and wonderful creatures preserved in the Burgess Shale have provided scientists with an unparalleled window into the evolution of ancient life on Earth, and by extension our own origins.

The fossil fields have been protected as a World Heritage site since 1981, and due to their delicate nature can now only be visited on a guided hike provided by the **Yoho-Burgess Shale Geoscience Foundation** (☎800-343-3006; www.burgess-shale.bc.ca; ⊙Jul–mid-Sep). There are two core hikes, one to the original **Walcott Quarry** (adult/child under 12yr C$120/25; 10hr trip) and another to the adjacent fossil fields on **Mt Stephen** (adult/child under 12yr C$90/25; 8hr trip). Both are strenuous full-day trips with plenty of elevation gain, so you'll need to be fit and wear proper footwear. Shorter hikes tailored to seniors and kids are also offered; see the website for details.

Canoes can be rented from the lakeside **Emerald Sports & Gifts** (1hr C$20; ⌚9am-7pm summer, noon-4pm winter), and fishing is permitted from July to November.

The lake road is signed off Hwy 1 just to the southwest of Field and continues for 10km (6.2 miles) to the lakeshore. You can stop for a peek at a **natural rock bridge** over the Kicking Horse River just after the turnoff.

Kicking Horse Pass & Spiral Tunnels VIEWPOINT

The historic Kicking Horse Pass between Banff and Yoho is one of the most important passes in the Canadian Rockies. It was discovered in 1858 by the Palliser Expedition, who were tasked with discovering a possible route across the Rockies for the Canadian Pacific Railway. The first steam trains finally steamed across the pass in 1885, but the steep gradient was an enormous technical challenge: the very first train to attempt the new railway careered out of control, killing three workers, and wrecks and runaways continued to plague the railway during its first years of operation.

To cut down on accidents, an ingenious system of underground passages known as the Spiral Tunnels (Map p58) was subsequently devised by one of the CPR's Assistant Chief Engineers, JE Schwitzer, modeled on designs he had seen pioneered in the Swiss Alps. Snaking beneath the roots of Mt Ogden and Cathedral Mountain, the tunnels allowed trains to tackle the extreme gradient in stages rather than in one nightmare plunge, and drastically improved the railway's safety and reliability after they were opened in 1909. They're still in use to this day.

The main **viewing platform** (the Upper Lookout) is off Hwy 1, 8km (5 miles) east of Field. If you time it right, you can see a train exiting from the top of the tunnel while its final cars are still entering at the bottom.

Wapta Falls WATERFALL

They might not be quite as high as Takakkaw, but what they lack in stature, Wapta Falls more than make up for in noise. Named after a Nakoda word meaning 'river,' they are the largest set of falls anywhere on the Kicking Horse River, measuring 150m (490ft) across and 30m (98ft) high. They're also famous as the supposed spot where, during the historic Palliser Expedition of 1858, the geologist James Hector was kicked in the chest while trying to recover a runaway horse – an event that apparently inspired the name of one of the Rocky Mountains' most famous rivers.

The falls are reached after a gentle half-hour walk from the trailhead near the western border of Yoho. They are clearly signed off Hwy 1.

Iceline Trail HIKING

For truly unbelievable views, Yoho's infamous Iceline Trail has attained legendary status among hikers, following an airy ridgeline for 12.8km (8 miles, elevation gain 710m/2330ft) across barren extraterrestrial rock that was covered by glacial ice as recently as the turn of the 20th century. The trail affords a mind-blowing outlook of Takakkaw Falls and the Yoho Valley peaks, as well as a superb panorama over the glittering Emerald Glacier. It's a hard trail and can feel very exposed in bad weather, so save it for a settled day.

The route can be done as an out-and-back hike, but many people turn it into an overnight trip by linking up with the **Yoho Valley Loop** for a 21.1km (13.1-mile) round-trip, overnighting at one of the backcountry campgrounds at Little Yoho, Twin Falls or Laughing Falls.

Yoho Lake & Wapta Highline HIKING

Another strenuous route that ranks among the finest (and hardest) day hikes in the Rockies. The route starts at the Whiskey Jack trailhead near Takakkaw Falls, and climbs to Yoho Lake before ascending onto the sky-top flanks of Wapta Mountain. The route descends through forest and ends on Hwy 1, around 1.3km east of Field. In total it's a route of 18.3km (11.4 miles), with an elevation gain of 1010m (3314ft).

Twin Falls & the Whaleback HIKING

If waterfalls are your thing, this moderate 8.2km (5.1-mile) route from Takakkaw Falls parking lot through pine forest takes in four lovely cascades: the Angel's Staircase, Point Lace Falls, Laughing Falls and the double-tiered Twin Falls.

It's a round-trip of around seven hours, or you can extend it into an overnight trip by camping at Twin Falls Campground and following the Whaleback ridgeline back down the valley. The Whaleback crosses a seasonal bridge across the upper falls; it's sometimes swamped by snow or snowmelt, so check at the park office before setting out. The Whaleback adds on around 5km (3.1 miles) to the Twin Falls hike.

Sleeping

The best place to base yourself in Yoho is Field, which has lots of private B&Bs and rooms for rent. The visitor center keeps a comprehensive list.

Camping

Kicking Horse Campground CAMPGROUND $
(Map p58; Yoho Valley Rd; campsites C$27.40; late Jun-late Sep;) Probably the most popular campground in Yoho, in a nice forested location with plenty of space between sites, as well as all the deluxe facilities (hookup, flush toilets and wheelchair-accessible showers). The riverside sites (especially 68 to 74) are the pick of the bunch. A recent avalanche forced the closure of this campground, but it should have reopened by the time you read this.

Monarch Campground CAMPGROUND $
(Map p58; Yoho Valley Rd; campsites C$17.60; mid-May–Sep) Around 3km east of Field, and a stone's throw from Kicking Horse Campground, this is a more basic site situated in a large open meadow. Water is sourced from an on-site well and there's an outdoor BBQ shelter for alfresco cookouts.

Lodging

Kicking Horse Lodge HOTEL $$
(250-343-6303; Kicking Horse Ave, Field; d C$170, tw C$180, d with kitchen C$190, f C$250;) Run by the owners of the Truffle Pigs Café since 2008, this is Field's only hotel, and it's a decent bolthole as long as you're not too fussy about five-star luxury. The timber building has heritage charm, but the rooms are fairly simply decked out in cappuccinos and creams. Rates are expensive in high season, but drop substantially in shoulder months. The family rooms are particularly good value, with kitchens and space for six. Two rooms can accommodate pets.

Cathedral Mountain Lodge LODGE $$$
(Map p58; 250-343-6442; www.cathedralmountain.com; Yoho Valley Rd; lodges C$319-429;) These luxury log cabins have designer style in spades, but they're not nearly as secluded as you might think. Native wood furniture, soaker tubs and cedar-stocked fireplaces provide a much more luxurious feel than most cabin complexes, but the cabins are pretty small inside and packed in sardine-can tight. Train and road noise will be the main drawback for light sleepers, and if you can't live without TV, phone and wi-fi, you'd definitely better look elsewhere.

Canadian Rockies Inn GUESTHOUSE $$
(250-343-6046; www.canadianrockiesinn.com; Stephen Ave, Field; r C$125-185) Run by jovial owners Luc and Kim, who also own the shop next door, this attractive Field house has several spacious rooms for rent just a quick stroll from the Truffle Pigs Café and the Siding general store. Spotless rooms and enormous beds are the main attractions, and all the rooms have microwaves, kettles and fridges; shame they don't have proper kitchens, too.

Fireweed Hostel HOSTEL $
(250-343-6999; www.fireweedhostel.com; Stephen Ave, Field; dm C$30-40, private room C$80-125, ste C$90-160;) This small hostel in Field is a real find, beautifully finished in rustic pine, complete with snowshoes above the hearth and hiking books for perusal. The dorms are small but smart; each room has two pine bunk beds and a shared bathroom off the hallway, and have full use of a lovely kitchen and sitting room. Families or couples might like to ask for the self-contained studio suite.

Mt Stephen Guesthouse B&B $$
(250-343-6356; www.mountstephen.com; 304 Kicking Horse Ave, Field; d C$125-140) Two self-catering suites in a quirky clapboard house, both with their own private entrance. The rooms certainly aren't flashy, but they're perfectly comfy: each has a queen-size bed plus a pull-out sofa bed in the lounge, so the rates are really good if you're *en famille*. No breakfast but you'll find coffee, tea and hot chocolate in the cupboards.

Emerald Lake Lodge LODGE $$$
(403-410-7417; www.crmr.com/emerald; lodges C$375-440;) Commanding a picture-perfect 5-hectare (13-acre) site right beside the tranquil shores of Emerald Lake, and accessed by its own romantic bridge, you really couldn't ask for a better position. But these pricey lodges don't really live up to first billing. The interiors feel disappointingly old-fashioned, heavy on the frills and floral motifs, but these rooms are pretty much the only option in Yoho if you simply can't live without a lake view.

Whiskey Jack International Hostel HOSTEL $
(866-762-4122; cr.wj@hihostels.ca; Yoho Valley Rd; dm C$23; late Jun-Sep) You can almost feel the spray from Takakkaw Falls at this place – you can actually see the falls from the hostel's timber deck – but the

accommodations are simple bordering on spartan. Three nine-bed dorms and a basic kitchen are about all that's on offer, but despite the rudimentary facilities, it's usually booked out in summer.

Eating

Truffle Pigs Café FUSION **$$$**
(☎250-343-6462; Stephen Ave, Field; lunch mains C$12-16, dinner mains C$21-29; ⏰breakfast, lunch & dinner) It's the only place to eat out in Field after dark, but thankfully the Truffle Pigs shows no sign of resting on its laurels. It offers just the right blend of culinary creativity and down-home charm, with a cute cabin-like dining room that looks out across the CPR railtracks, and an offbeat menu that veers from snow crab and stick ribs to truffled potato perogies served with foie gras.

Siding CAFÉ, STORE **$**
(Stephen Ave, Field; ⏰8am-6pm, shorter hr Sat & Sun) Field's general store has been the hub of the community since the early days of the railway. It's chaotically run but cute-as-a-button, with shelves stacked high with supplies, and a small café on the side that dishes up homemade sandwiches and fresh-baked muffins to a steady local clientele.

Cilantro INTERNATIONAL **$$**
(☎250-343-6321; Emerald Lake; mains C$12-20; ⏰lunch & dinner) Once the crowds disperse, this lakeside restaurant beside the bridge to Emerald Lake Lodge makes a pleasant detour for supper. The feel is more down-to-earth bistro than fine-dining emporium, and it's all the better for it: aim for a table on the lake-view deck and tuck into seared salmon, crispy tortillas and chargrilled steaks.

Information

Yoho National Park Visitor Centre (☎250-343-6783; yoho.info@pc.gc.ca; ⏰9am-7pm summer, to 4pm winter) Just across the railway tracks from Field on the edge of Hwy 1.

Getting There & Away

Some Greyhound buses stop in Field on their way to/from Banff National Park; for full details, see p114.

Lake O'Hara

Hiking destinations don't get much more exclusive than Lake O'Hara. Hidden away among a glorious amphitheater of mountains to the south of Yoho National Park, the area is home to some of the park's most picturesque wildflower meadows and backcountry trails, but it takes an extra bit of effort to get here.

The only way into the Lake O'Hara area is via the 11km (6.8-mile) access road from the parking lot just off Hwy 1. The road is closed to public vehicles, so you'll either have to hike in on foot or try for a spot on one of the hugely oversubscribed **shuttle buses** (adult/child 6-16yr return C$14.70/7.30, max 2 bags per person; ⏰mid-Jun–Sep). The four daily buses have a total of 42 places and are always full, so you'll need to book way in advance; you'll also need to reserve well ahead to be sure of a place at Lake O'Hara's hugely popular 30-pitch **campground** (adult/child under 16yr C$9.80/free, max 3 nights per party).

Reservations for the shuttle bus and campsites at the campground can be made up to three months in advance for a C$11.70 fee by calling the **Lake O'Hara reservation line** (☎250-343-6344). Facilities in the area are very limited, although hot snacks and drinks are sold at Le Relais day shelter in season (cash only). You'll also need a valid wilderness pass to visit the Lake O'Hara area; camping fees are included if you already hold an annual wilderness pass.

If you want to stay overnight and can't get a spot at the campground, there are also two **Alpine Club of Canada Huts** (☎reservations 403-678-3200, ext 1; info@AlpineClubofCanada.ca) in Lake O'Hara: the Abbot and Elizabeth Parker. Reservations are mandatory, and include a seat on one of the inbound buses.

Even better, book into one of the gorgeously old-world cabins at **Lake O'Hara Lodge** (☎250-343-6418; www.lakeohara.com; lodges C$580-845; ⏰mid-Jan–mid-Apr & mid-Jun–Oct), where you'll be treated to home-cooked meals and hot tubs despite the fact that you're kilometers away from the outside world.

For a really exclusive experience, Lake O'Hara also provides access to the remote and fantastically wild **McArthur Valley**, which is strictly off-limits to people until August 15 to protect grizzly habitat. To visit the valley, you need to be granted one of the limited number of hiking permits that are made available each year. Phone the Field Visitor Centre for more information.

Mt Assiniboine Provincial Park

If it's a real wilderness hit you're craving, Mt Assiniboine is the place. With its ice-encrusted slopes and distinctive skyrocket profile, the pointy pinnacle of Mt Assiniboine is one of the most recognizable landmarks of the Canadian Rockies (and, at 3618m/11,870ft, the highest peak in the southern ranges).

Dubbed the Matterhorn of Canada thanks to its distinctive pyramidal shape, the mountain and the surrounding 39,050-hectare (96,494-acre) provincial park can only be reached on foot (or if you've got the cash, by chartered chopper). But you won't regret the effort it takes to get there: the high-altitude trails around the mountain and nearby Lake Magog are some of the most exquisite in the Canadian Rockies. Civilization has never felt so far away.

Most people make the trip into Assiniboine in three to five days; one in, one out and between one and three to explore the trails and mountain country around Lake Magog.

Note that most of Mt Assiniboine Provincial Park is across the British Columbia border, so you'll need a valid British Columbia backcountry permit for every night you intend to stay (C$10). If you're overnighting at a campground across the Alberta border (eg Marvel Lake on Bryant Creek), you'll also need a Banff wilderness pass plus a reservation at the relevant campground. If in doubt, check with staff at one of the park visitor centers before you set out.

You'll find general information on Assiniboine at http://env.gov.bc.ca/bcparks/explore/parkpgs/mtassini.html.

Activities

Needless to say, it's the trails that draw everyone to Mt Assiniboine. The core area centers on **Lake Magog**, with lots of easy day hikes nearby: we've detailed various options in our overnight hike to Assiniboine on p92.

Rock climbing and **mountaineering** are for experienced alpinists only. The routes are challenging and the drops are very, very long, so you need to know what you're doing. The mountain was first climbed in 1901 by a trio of mountaineers including James Outram, Christian Hasler and Christian Bohren, but the first man to conquer it solo was Lawrence Grassi in 1925.

Cross-country skiing is another way to explore the park in winter; telemarkers mostly arrive via Assiniboine Pass and need to be prepared for emergency camping and carry an avalanche beacon.

Sleeping

There are several backcountry campgrounds in Assiniboine, but most people end up pitching at either Lake Magog or Og Lake. All campsites are allocated on a first-come, first-served basis, and cost C$10 per person. Fires aren't permitted anywhere in the park.

If you're camping in Assiniboine, it's also extremely important to take precautions against bears: grizzlies and black bears often trundle through the area, so make use of the bear-proof bins at Lake Magog, Og Lake and Porcupine.

For a bit more shelter you can book a bunk in one of four **Naiset Huts** (bed C$20), which offer simple wooden beds, mattresses and a woodstove, as well as a cooking shelter with propane lights and a stove. Reservations (C$5 per night) are a good idea in summer and mandatory in winter. There's also a 15-person climbing shelter called the RC Hind Hut nestled near the northern face of Mt Assiniboine. Reservations for all huts are made through Mt Assiniboine Lodge.

Mt Assiniboine Lodge LODGE **$$$**
(☎403-678-2883; www.assiniboinelodge.com; private cabins per person C$320, lodge rooms & shared cabins per person C$260; ⏲mid-Jun–Oct & mid-Feb–mid-Apr) The only lodge in Assiniboine is also the oldest ski lodge in the Canadian Rockies, and is surrounded by mountain meadows and gloriously backed by Mt Assiniboine. The six rustic lodge rooms each sleep two people (solo travelers are usually required to share), and rates include communal meals cooked by lodge staff. At the time of writing, the lodge was closed for major renovations and is scheduled to have reopened by the time you read this. In the meantime, the lodge will continue to handle reservations for the Naiset Huts and Assiniboine campgrounds.

Getting There & Away

Forget public transportation – your only chance of a lift into Assiniboine is aboard a helicopter from the Mt Shark heliport, booked through Mt Assiniboine Lodge (C$130; Sunday, Wednesday and Friday).

Kootenay National Park & Radium Hot Springs

Stretching for just 8km (5 miles) on either side of Hwy 93 (sometimes known locally as the Kootenay Hwy or the Banff–Windermere Rd), Kootenay was founded in 1920 as a by-product of the construction of the first automobile highway across the Canadian Rockies. In exchange for helping out with the financial costs of building the road, the Canadian government claimed the slender sliver of land that now makes up the national park. Hwy 93 is the only road through the park, running for 94km (58.3 miles) from just west of Castle Junction across the Alberta–British Columbia border to Radium Hot Springs.

Due to its unusual geography, Kootenay is one of the most fire-prone areas in the Canadian Rockies; the southern section of the park toward Radium Hot Springs has been dubbed 'lightning alley' thanks to its frequent summer thunderstorms. In 2003, 17,409 hectares (43,020 acres) of forest in the northern part of the park were damaged by a huge wildfire sparked by lightning, forcing the closure of several popular areas around Tokumm Creek and Marble Canyon. The scars left by the blaze are still plain to see, and while it looks severe, it's worth remembering that wildfires are an essential part of the forest ecosystem, killing off disease and pests, clearing underbrush and weak trees and stimulating fresh growth.

Sights

Fireweed Trail NATURE TRAIL

Traveling south along Hwy 93 from Hwy 1, you'll soon start to see the effects of the 2003 forest fire, with blackened trunks and ash-gray land coating the mountainsides on either side of the road, dotted with lush green patches where the forest has started to regenerate. The Vermilion Pass area, right on the edge of the Continental Divide, was the scene of another devastating fire in 1968 and you can now take a scenic 15-minute, wheelchair-accessible walk around the Fireweed Trail, with explanatory signs detailing the role that fires play in the life of the forest.

Stanley Glacier HIKING

Further west along Hwy 93 is the trailhead to Stanley Glacier, by far the most interesting day hike anywhere in Kootenay. It's an 11km (6.8-mile) round-trip that takes in fire, forest and ice, and allows you to get right up close to one of the park's largest glaciers.

The first section of the trail winds up through burned pine forest, where you can see spectacular displays of wildflowers in summer, particularly arnica, paintbrush and fireweed. At the top of the climb, you pass into an area of old woodland that escaped the 2003 fire, before ascending into an impressive hanging valley overlooked by the crests of Storm Mountain, Stanley Peak and the sheer rock face known as the Guardwall.

On the right side of the valley, a slippery trail winds up across the boulder-strewn moraines to a fine viewpoint right beneath Stanley Glacier. It's best left for late summer, as the danger of avalanches remains high until the end of seasonal snowmelt.

Marble Canyon NATURAL FEATURE

A little further southwest, the popular trail around Marble Canyon has been revamped after a long closure to repair bridges and walkways damaged by the fire. The easy 1.6km (1-mile) loop crosses Tokumm Creek and offers great views down into the plunging limestone canyon, sculpted and shaped by the surging force of the river.

Paint Pots NATURAL FEATURE

A further 3km (1.9 miles) down Hwy 93, a short wheelchair-friendly trail leads to the rust-red **ochre ponds**, once used by First Nation tribes including the Ktunaxa (Kootenay), Stoney and Blackfoot as a source of decorative paint for adorning teepees, clothing and bodies. European settlers later used the ochre as a base for paint manufacture and a thriving mining operation was in full swing here in the early 1900s; you can still see bits of machinery scattered around the mineral beds. The Paint Pots themselves are three cold mineral springs with blue-green water that contrasts with the crimson crust of iron oxide decorating their edges.

Simpson Monument VIEWPOINT

Further south, the road crosses the Vermilion River at around 31km (19.3 miles) from the Alberta border. Shortly afterward, look out for the Simpson Monument and viewpoint on the left, which commemorates the trailblazing explorer George Simpson, who pioneered the first trail over the mountains to Banff in 1841 and later went on to run the Hudsons Bay Trading Company. The historic route he followed heads west from here along the Simpson River, and now makes a popular route into the west side of Mt Assiniboine Provincial Park.

Look out for elk, moose and mountain goats at the **Mt Wardle Animal Lick**, just south of the viewpoint. There's another animal lick near **Hector Gorge**, about 17km southwest of the Simpson Monument.

Radium Hot Springs HOT SPRINGS
(www.hotsprings.ca; Hwy 93; adult/child 3-17yr/senior/family C$6.30/5.40/5.40/19.10; hot pool 9am-11pm mid-May–early Oct, noon-9pm or 10pm rest of yr) Like its sister resort in Banff, Radium was put on the map in the late 19th century by its natural hot springs, which bubble out from beneath the mountains at a constant temperature of 44°C (111°F), cooling to a balmy 39°C (102°F) once the water reaches the 'hot' pool, and 29°C (84°F) once the water gets to the 'cool' pool.

Initially, the interest in the springs was medicinal: traces of radium dissolved from the surrounding rocks mean that the water is very faintly radioactive, and it was thought to have therapeutic value for curing everything from upset stomachs to gout. A scheme to bottle the water in the early 1900s failed, however, and the springs were subsequently developed as a spa resort. Don't fret too much about the radium in the water – it's about as radioactive as a luminous watch dial.

The twin pools themselves are pleasantly positioned beneath sheer rock faces, although the constant buzz of traffic from the nearby highway is a bit of a letdown. With a bit of luck, you might even glimpse a bighorn sheep or two while you take your dip.

Activities

Kootenay River Runners RAFTING
(1-800-599-4399; www.raftingtherockies.com; Hwy 93; half-day adult/child C$58/48, full day C$100/90, voyageur trips C$49/39) Based just outside Radium, this rafting company offers several trips on class I-III rapids on both the Kootenay and Kicking Horse Rivers and nearby Toby Creek, as well as atmospheric trips in modern 'voyageur' canoes, the multiman vessels used by early explorers to open up much of Canada.

Radium Resort GOLF
(250-347-6266; www.radiumresort.com; May-Oct) Radium is also renowned for its golf courses. There are two to choose from – the **Springs Course** (McKay St; Mon-Thu C$79, Fri-Sun C$110) and the **Resort Course** (Hwy 93/95; Mon-Thu C$47, Fri-Sun C$59) – with combined green fees if you want to play both. Cheaper green fees are offered after 2pm.

Tours

Toby Creek Adventures ADVENTURE TOURS
(250-342-5047; www.tobycreekadventures.com; Panorama; ATV trips C$199-249) Located 32km (19.8 miles) from Radium, this company offers daily ATV tours around local trails and the abandoned Paradise Silver Mine, as well as snowmobile trips in winter. The evening wildlife tours are great for photographers, too.

Sleeping

Apart from the campgrounds along Hwy 93, most of Kootenay's accommodations are in Radium, but let's be honest – it's not the most attractive place to stay in the Rockies. The visitor center can help out with suggestions if you're stuck for a bed, or just cruise around the seemingly endless motel strip looking for the 'vacancy' signs.

At the time of writing, none of Kootenay's campgrounds were accepting reservations, although Redstreak should be by the time you read this.

Camping

Redstreak Campground CAMPGROUND $
(Stanley St E, Radium Hot Springs; campsites C$27.40-38.20; Jun-Oct;) Kootenay's largest campground with 242 sites tops the list for facilities, with everything from flush toilets and hot-and-cold running water to full hookup sites, kids' playground and a small theater. It's a big, busy site, partially wooded but crisscrossed by lots of access roads; it's probably not the place if you're looking for peace and quiet, but it's only a 30-minute walk from Radium.

McLeod Meadows Campground CAMPGROUND $
(Hwy 93; campsites C$21.50; mid-May–mid-Sep;) You'll find more natural splendor at this 98-pitch campground, peacefully located on the banks of the Kootenay River just a 2.6km (1.6-mile) walk to the shores of pretty Dog Lake. Plentiful trees and spacious, grassy sites make this a fine place to pitch your canvas, especially since there are only 10 sites to each loop; aim for the higher loops for the best views. Flush toilets, bear-proof bins, fire rings, cooking shelters and RV dumps are all on-site.

Marble Canyon Campground CAMPGROUND $
(Hwy 93; campsites C$21.50; late Jun-early Sep;) This high-country 61-pitch campground is situated near the Marble Canyon trail, with similar facilities to McLeod Meadows. Most

sites have tree cover to keep you out of the wind. The eastern side has the best views.

Lodging

Kootenay Park Lodge CABINS $$
(☎403-762-9196; www.kootenayparklodge.com; Hwy 93, Vermilion Crossing; d cabins C$129-189; ⊙mid-May–late Sep) The pick of the places to stay inside the park, with a range of cute log cabins complete with verandas, fridges and two-burner hot plates to warm through your beans and trail stews. The general vibe is rusticity rather than refinement, but it makes a way nicer place to sleep than Radium. The site is at Vermilion Crossing, so you're perfectly placed for exploring the rest of Kootenay. There's also a restaurant, gift store and information center on-site.

Storm Mountain Lodge CABINS $$$
(☎403-762-4155; www.stormmountainlodge.com; Hwy 93, Castle Junction; cabins C$199-239) Originally built by the CPR in the 1920s as a 'Bungalow Camp' to attract tourists to the Rockies, these old-timey log lodges are brimming with period curios: wooden snowshoes, bison heads, hand-carved trinkets and old-fashioned claw-foot tubs. Don't expect to be pampered – there are no TVs, phones or wi-fi, and the lodge generator can be extremely erratic – but if it's a Grizzly Adams experience you're yearning for, you should feel right at home. Full meals are served at the lodge's restaurant.

Village Country Inn GUESTHOUSE $$
(☎250-347-9392; www.villagecountryinn.bc.ca; 7557 Canyon Ave, Radium Hot Springs; r C$105-125, ste C$160;) If you really have to stay in Radium, take our advice: give the motels a miss and head for this cute gabled house just off the main drag. All the rooms are decked out in country fashion with plenty of plump pillows, frilly pelmets and potted plants. The same folksy feel runs into the downstairs tearoom, where afternoon tea is served on bone china and frilly doilies.

Cedar Motel MOTEL $
(☎250-347-9463; www.cedarmotel.ca; 7593 Main St W, Radium Hot Springs; r C$74-80, extra for kitchenette C$10;) Clean, cheap and (as its name suggests) cedar-clad, this is one of the more attractive motels in Radium. The rooms are boxy but bright, with Technicolor bedspreads and large flat-screen TVs. Some have teeny kitchenettes and interjoining doorways, useful for families.

Eating

Radium's dining scene certainly isn't going to rock your world, but there are a couple of passable places on the main highway into town.

Helna's Stube AUSTRIAN $$$
(7547 Hwy 93, Radium Hot Springs; mains C$20.45-38.75; ⊙dinner Tue-Sun) Helna's offers artery-clogging food from the Austrian cookbook,

THE SWISS GUIDES IN CANADA

Following the death of Philip Abbott on Mt Lefroy in 1896, the Canadian Pacific Railway (CPR) knew it had to do something to keep mountaineering enthusiasts boarding its trains for the Rockies.

In order to reassure investors' nerves and ensure the safety of their clients in the mountains, the CPR decided to hire the services of some of Switzerland's top alpine guides, shipping them over at considerable expense with the promise of accommodations, attractive pay and – most importantly – the opportunity to be the first to claim some of the Rockies' numerous unclimbed peaks.

First to arrive in 1899 were Edward Feuz Sr and Christian Haesler, two of Switzerland's most renowned guides, followed a few seasons later by another handful of skilled alpinists, including Edward's trio of mountain-climbing sons, Ernest, Edward Feuz Jr and Walter. In order to help their new employees feel more at home, in 1911 the CPR constructed a small settlement of Swiss-style timber chalets just outside Golden, which became known to locals as the 'Swiss Village' or 'Edelweiss.' Many of the original buildings are still standing.

The Swiss guides played an important role in the development of Canadian mountaineering, and were instrumental in the formation of the Alpine Club of Canada, which was based in Golden during its early years.

Though Feuz Sr never permanently settled in Canada, he continued to visit most summers until his death in 1965, leading over 100 new routes and becoming the first man to climb 78 Canadian peaks. During his 50-year career, he never lost a client.

ZIP-LINING

Hiking too humdrum? Mountain biking too mundane? Then how about plummeting down a zip line at hair-raising speeds of up to 50km/h (31mph) while the tree tops and forests whip past far below? There are three sets of zip lines to brave near Golden, with tours provided by Banff Adventures Unlimited (see p96). Kids and wannabe paratroopers will love it, but vertigo sufferers should probably look elsewhere for their kicks. Tickets start at C$99, including transfers from Banff.

ranging from gooey fondue to authentic Wiener schnitzel. It's certainly no chocolate-box chalet, but the owners have done their best to create an Alpine atmosphere inside. Sweeter-than-sugar desserts include proper apple strudel and the house specialty of Mozart dumplings (which are filled with nougat, marzipan and chocolate-strawberry sauce).

Backcountry Jack's BURGERS $
(Hwy 93, Radium Hot Springs; mains C$8-12; ⌚11:30am-10pm Mon-Thu & Sat, to midnight Fri, to 9pm Sun) Basic cowboy grub is all you'll find at this rather shabby roadside café: spicy beans, grilled burgers, fillet steaks and chicken wings. Try the 'cowboy caviar' (otherwise known as beans and nachos).

ℹ Information

Kootenay National Park Visitor Centre (☎250-347-9505; kootenay.info@pc.gc.ca; 7556 Main St E, Radium Hot Springs; ⌚9am-7pm mid-Jun–Sep, to 5pm rest of yr) Main visitor center on the main highway through Radium Hot Springs.

Kootenay Park Lodge Visitor Centre (☎403-762-9196; info@kootenayparklodge.com; ⌚9am-6pm Jul-Sep, to 4pm or 5pm rest of yr) Located at Vermilion Lakes, 68km north of Radium Hot Springs.

ℹ Getting There & Away

From Banff, head south along Hwy 93 from Castle Junction. You can also reach the park from the south by heading north from Cranbrook on Hwy 93 to Radium Hot Springs. In Radium, the Greyhound bus depot is on Hwy 93 near the junction with Hwy 98.

Golden

The little community of Golden might be a long way from Banff's big mountains and sky-high scenery, but what it lacks in good looks it makes up for in adrenaline. It's become a popular center for outdoor activities, with everything from downhill mountain biking to white-water rafting on its doorstep, and though the town itself might not have much charm, it makes a convenient (and cheap) base for exploring Yoho to the east and the small national parks of Glacier and Mt Revelstoke to the west.

Golden is 58km west of Field along Hwy 1, 87km west of Lake Louise. The section of highway between Golden and Field is currently being twinned, so expect some delays until at least 2013.

Sights & Activities

Kicking Horse Pedestrian Bridge LANDMARK
Originally established as a logging town and supply station for the CPR (when the town was simply known as 'the Cache'), Golden is split in two by the Kicking Horse River. Just north of the main shopping thoroughfare of 9th Ave is the town's much-loved landmark, the Kicking Horse Pedestrian Bridge, which locals proudly trumpet as the longest free-standing timber bridge anywhere in Canada. Built in 2001 mainly by community volunteers, the bridge spans an impressive 46m (150ft) and weighs around 450kg (210,000lb).

Kicking Horse Mountain Resort ADVENTURE RESORT
(www.kickinghorseresort.com) The Rocky Mountains' newest ski resort is perched among the mountains to the west of Golden. Established in 2000 on the site of the small Whitetooth Ski Resort (much to the chagrin of local environmentalists), the resort has expanded rapidly over the last decade to become one of the Rockies' most popular four-season destinations.

With around 1112 hectares (2750 acres) of skiable snow in winter and a fantastic network of downhill bike trails – not to mention the second-highest vertical drop of any Canadian resort (1260m/4133ft) – this resort is a must-visit for thrill seekers.

In summer, mountain-bike passes are available on the **Golden Eye Gondola** and cost C$41/36 per adult/child seven to 18 years, or there's an afternoon-only ticket for C$29.95/24.95. Full-suspension bikes can be hired on-site from C$49.99 per day.

If you're just planning on hiking or sightseeing, full-day gondola passes cost C$25.95/15.95/69.95 per adult/child seven to 18 years/family. Combo trips are also available, which include a ride on the Catamount Chair Lift to the resort's Grizzly Bear Refuge.

The resort is 14km west of Golden in the Dogtooth Range; it's fairly well-signed, but the highway junctions in Golden can be confusing, so ask for directions in town if you get lost.

Grizzly Bear Refuge

(www.kickinghorseresort.com/mountain/activities/grizzly_bear_refuge-summer.aspx; ⏲9am-5pm Jun-Sep) If you're desperate to catch sight of a grizzly but haven't quite managed to do so in the wild, don't fret – the Kicking Horse Mountain Resort has its own resident grizzly by the name of Boo, who's lived at the resort since arriving as an orphaned cub in 2003 (his companion bear, Cari, sadly died shortly after arrival).

Whatever your take on the ethics of keeping animals in captivity, there's no question that Boo has reached a much riper age than he would otherwise have if left to fend for himself in the wild. And while he's certainly not a wild bear, Boo still has plenty of wild spirit – he's made several bids for freedom in recent years during the annual mating season, when his natural urges seem to overcome his love of the sedentary lifestyle.

While fascinating, a visit to the refuge isn't cheap. First, you need to catch the Golden Eye Gondola from Kicking Horse Village followed by the **Catamount Chair Lift** (combination lift pass adult/child 7-18yr/family C$32.95/24.95/99.95), then pay the separate admission for the **refuge** (adult/child 7-18yr/family C$20.95/14.95/59.95). Tours run hourly from 9am to 5pm, with an hour's break for lunch at 1pm. Early or late tours are best, as Boo often heads off into the trees for a snooze after lunch.

Alternatively, you could join the after-hours **Ranger Assistant Tour** (adult/child 7-18yr/family C$30/20/80), which includes an up-close introduction to Boo with one of his keepers. The visits run at 6pm after the last regular tour of the day; numbers are limited to five per visit, so book ahead.

Northern Lights Wolf Centre WILDLIFE RESERVE

(☎250-344-6798; www.northernlightswildlife.com; adult/child 6-11yr/child 12-16yr & senior/family C$12/6/9/35; ⏲9am-7pm Jul & Aug, to 6pm May, Jun & Sep, noon-6pm rest of yr) This small wildlife center is dedicated to the welfare and preservation of Canada's native wolves, and houses a small pack of gray wolves and wolf-husky crosses, all born and bred in captivity. Visits include a guided tour of the wildlife facility and an introduction to the resident wolves – although most of the viewing is rather disappointingly done through wire-frame pens, and the tours can sometimes get very busy with school groups and coach tours. If you really want a hands-on experience, you'll need to book a 1½-hour private photography tour for C$295.

The center is about a 14km (8.7-mile) drive north of Golden. Head north on Hwy 1, turn right onto Moberly Branch Rd for 2km (1.2 miles), then left onto Upper Donald Rd and follow the signs.

Rocky Mountain Buffalo Ranch WILDLIFE RESERVE

(☎1-866-400-8400; www.rockymountainbuffaloranch.com; adult/child C$12/6; ⏲10am-6pm mid-May–Oct) Just up the road from the wolf centre, in a gloriously wild spot overlooking the head of the Blaeberry Valley, this working buffalo ranch provides a unique chance to see one of North America's most symbolic animals in its natural habitat. A herd of hand-reared buffaloes roam free across the ranch, guarded by the mighty presence of Chester, the herd's 1090kg (2400lb) bull sire.

Californian owner Leo Downey is passionate about his animals and conducts guided tours of the ranch. There's also a small display of tools, weapons and musical instruments made from buffaloes' hides, horns and bones, which demonstrate the vital role this iconic animal played in the lives of First Nations people.

Leo's also a talented musician who toured with a number of bands before founding his buffalo ranch. Don't miss the chance to pick up his latest CD before you leave.

White-Water Sports

With the Kicking Horse running right through the middle of town, it's hardly surprising that Golden is a center for white-water sports. As usual, all the local operators offer a variety of runs to suit all abilities, ranging from sedate floats to heart-stopping roller-coaster rides down the rapids. All equipment, including helmets and paddles, is provided. Many operators also offer canoe trips onto the Blaeberry, Kicking Horse, Blue Water and Spillimacheen Rivers.

Alpine Rafting RAFTING
(☎1-888-599-5299; www.alpinerafting.com; Golden View Rd; half-day trips from C$79, full-day from C$109) Offers several afternoon and day trips on nearby rivers, including a special 13km ride geared toward families, and 'cat-rafting' expeditions in double-pontoon rafts.

Wet & Wild RAFTING, CANOEING
(☎1-800-668-9119; www.wetnwild.bc.ca; trips C$60-145) Offers several trips on the Kicking Horse, including two-day packages with overnight accommodations at McLaren Lodge in Golden. Also offers skidoo trips in winter.

Winter Activities

In addition to the many ski runs at Kicking Horse Mountain Resort, the slopes around Golden provide perfect territory for many other winter sports. **Chatter Creek** (www.chattercreek.ca) specializes in cat and heli-skiing in the remote high country around Chatter Creek, while **Snowpeak Rentals** (www.snowpeakrentals.com; 1025 10th Ave N; full-day tours C$345-395) organizes snowmobile and skidoo tours.

Sleeping

Dull motels and chain hotels abound in downtown Golden, but there are some lovely B&Bs and lodges within easy reach.

Vagabond Lodge LODGE $$
(☎250-344-2622; www.vagabondlodge.ca; 158 Cache Close; d from C$155;) The best value of the accommodations at the Kicking Horse Mountain Resort, this is a mountain mansion with boutique pretensions. Six of the rooms have balconies overlooking the mountains, but the best are the two split-level rooms with their own snug sleeping loft. The decor is a mix of old and new: chunky beams, well-worn settees and wooden wardrobes meet varnished wood floors, slinky leather armchairs and the odd animal head. The spacious lounge is a great place to make friends over dinner, particularly if you make use of the honesty bar.

Kicking Horse Canyon B&B GUESTHOUSE $$
(☎250-344-6848; www.kickinghorsecanyonbb.com; 644 Lapp Rd; d C$99-125) Hidden away among the hills to the east of Golden (phone for directions), this endearingly offbeat B&B takes you into the bosom of the family the minute you cross the threshold. Run by genial host Jeannie Cook and her husband Jerry (who works at the Station Restaurant in Lake Louise), it's a real mountain home-away-from-home, surrounded by private grassy grounds with views across the mountains. Rustic guest rooms (some of which share bathrooms) are in a separate timber lodge next to the main house, and meals are eaten at a communal table that's straight out of the *Waltons*. Pancakes, muffins and scrambled eggs for breakfast, too.

Canyon Ridge Lodge GUESTHOUSE $$
(☎250-344-9876; www.canyonridgelodge.com; 1392 Pine Dr; d C$99-105) Three gleaming white rooms and a smart, high-ceilinged studio suite are on offer at this lovely timber-frame home, 1km (0.6 miles) from the visitor center just off Golden Donald Upper Rd. It's beautifully finished (underfloor heating, slate-tiled private bathrooms) and there's a communal hot tub across the garden where you can soothe your aches after a day of exploring.

Golden Eco-Adventure Ranch CAMPGROUND, RV SITES $
(☎250-344-6825; www.goldenadventurepark.com; tent sites C$28, campsites C$33.60-39.20, yurts C$72.80) Spread over 160 hectares (395 acres) of mountain meadow, this great campground-cum-outdoors center feels a world away from the cramped world of municipal camping. Sites are spacious, there are full RV hookups and you can even kip in a Mongolian yurt if you're tired of your tent. The owners can help you book practically every outdoor sport you could wish for.

Hillside Lodge & Chalets CABINS $$
(☎250-344-7281; www.hillsidechalets.com; Hwy 1; 1-bed cabins C$135-160, 2-bed cabins C$230-260, ste C$205) Goldilocks would feel right at home in these dinky little cabins, pastorally set around a forest glade and equipped with potbellied stoves, hand-carved wooden furniture and sweet little porches for that pioneer feel.

Copperhorse Lodge HOTEL $$
(☎250-344-7644; www.copperhorselodge.com; ste C$180-245;) Part of the Kicking Horse complex, this groovy little number combines the ambience of a ski lodge with the amenities of an upmarket hotel: expect luxurious fabrics, picture windows, huge beds and sexy bathrooms with multijet showers.

Caribou Hostel HOSTEL $
(☎250-344-4870; www.caribou mountainadventures.ca; 1401 Adolph Johnson Rd; dm C$25, r C$60-125) Remote forest lodge that has two suites for self-caterers, one of which doubles as a

dorm room (or a bedroom for the kids) with three bunks and a private kitchen. It's in a fairly remote position in the Blaeberry Valley, about 15km (9.3 miles) from Golden, so you'll need transport. Look out for signs for the Moberley Pub.

Eating

Eleven 22 INTERNATIONAL **$$**
(☎250-344-2443; www.eleven22.ca; 1122 10th Ave S; mains C$13-24; ⊙lunch & dinner) Fusion food from across the globe finds its way onto the menu at this zingy little bistro, a quick drive from town on 10th Ave S. It's part supper lounge, part chic bar: abstract art and bold colors adorn the walls, while the chefs take their culinary cue from a bewildering array of cuisines: fiery Tex-Mex, spicy Thai, rich Italian, country Cajun.

Eagle's Eye Restaurant CANADIAN **$$$**
(☎250-439-5400; mains C$30-44; ⊙lunch daily & dinner Fri & Sat summer, hr vary at other times) At 2350m (7700ft) above sea level, the Kicking Horse Mountain Resort's flagship bistro proudly champions itself as Canada's highest restaurant, and for once the food lives up to the sky-top billing. It's a polished fine-dining experience, focusing on haute cuisine dishes (expect to see plenty of quince compotes, truffle oils and red-wine reductions on the menu). It's pricey and posh, and the wraparound views of the Purcell, Rocky and Selkirk Mountains really are out of this world. The only drawback is the effort it takes to get here, as you need to catch the gondola up from the resort. If you've already bought your gondola ticket, you'll get a C$10 voucher against lunch.

Bacchus Café CAFÉ **$**
(www.bacchusbooks.ca; 409 9th Ave N; meals C$6-12; ⊙9am-5:30pm Mon-Sat, 10am-4pm Sun) This bohemian hideaway at the end of 8th St is a favorite haunt for Golden's artsy crowd. Browse for books (new and secondhand) in the downstairs bookstore, then head upstairs to find a table for tea among the higgledy-piggledy shelves. Sandwiches, salads and cakes are all made on the premises, and the coffee is as good as you'll find in Golden.

Whitetooth Bistro INTERNATIONAL **$$**
(☎250-344-5124; www.whitetoothbistro.com; 427 9th Ave N; mains C$18-26; ⊙breakfast, lunch & dinner) It's easy to miss this town-center restaurant, as it's perched on the 1st floor of a small building opposite the post office. Classic bistro dishes form the core of chef Marcus Myerscough's menu (coq au vin, pan-fried sockeye salmon, shepherd's pie, bouillabaisse), and the wooden tables, brown leather booths and monochrome photos give it a swish urban vibe. The wine list is particularly strong on Okanagan Valley vintages.

ℹ Information

Golden Visitor Information Centre (☎250-344-7125; www.tourismgolden.com; 500 N 10th Ave; ⊙9am-5pm summer, 10am-4pm Tue-Fri winter) In a purpose-built building on the main highway into town.

ℹ Getting There & Away

About 25km (15.5 miles) west of Yoho National Park, Golden is situated next to the Trans-Canada Hwy, at the junction of Hwy 95 south. Greyhound buses pass through town twice daily.

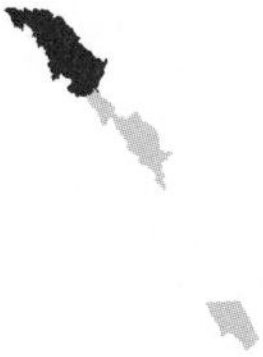

Jasper National Park

Includes »

Best Hikes

» Skyline Trail (p157)

» Tonquin Valley (p158)

» Path of the Glacier Trail (p152)

» North Boundary Trail (p161)

Best Places to Stay

» Fairmont Jasper Park Lodge (p146)

» Park Place Inn (p167)

» Athabasca Hotel (p168)

» Pyramid Lake Resort (p169)

Why Go?

In a modern world of clamorous cities and ubiquitous social media, Jasper seems like the perfect antidote. Who needs a shrink when you've got Maligne Lake? What use is Facebook when you're two days by foot from the nearest road? And, how can you possibly describe the Athabasca Glacier in a 140-character tweet? Filled with the kind of immense scenery that has turned laconic office stiffs into romantic poets, Jasper is a rugged beauty; rawer and less tourist-pampering than its southern cousin Banff, and hence host to a more ambitious, adventurous type of visitor. Its tour de force is its extensive multipurpose trail network, much of it instantly accessible from the park's compact townsite. Backing it up is abundant wildlife, colossal icefields and – for the brave – the kind of desolate backcountry that'll make you feel as if you're a good few kilometers (and centuries) from anything resembling civilization.

When to Go

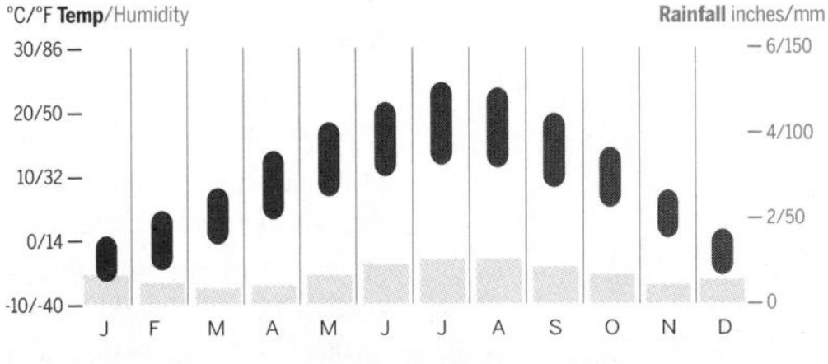

July-August The best weather for hiking Jasper's multiple trails.

September-October Quieter hiking amid autumn colors, if the weather holds.

February-March Best snow cover for skiing – both cross-country and downhill.

PLANNING TIP

Overnight stays in the backcountry require a wilderness pass (per person per night C$9.90), which you must pick up from the park office within 24 hours of heading out.

Fast Facts

» Area: 10,878 sq km (4200 sq miles)

» Highest elevation: 3782m (12,408ft)

» Lowest elevation: 985m (3232ft)

Reservations

Mandatory camping permits are available at all campground kiosks. Reservations are also recommended for backcountry camping as Parks Canada limits the number of hikers on each trail; these can be made up to three months in advance and cost C$11.85.

Resources

» Jasper National Park: www.jaspernationalpark.com

» Parks Canada: www.pc.gc.ca/eng/pn-np/ab/banff/index.aspx

Entrances

There are three main road entrances to Jasper National Park. The East Park Entrance is on Hwy 16 between Jasper and Hinton, just east of Pocahontas. The West Park Entrance is on the same highway, 24km (15 miles) west of Jasper Town, near Yellowhead Pass and the border with British Columbia and Mt Robson Provincial Park. The Icefields Parkway Entrance is south of Jasper Town on Hwy 93, on the way to Lake Louise. You must either buy or show a park pass at all entry gates.

THE WOODLAND CARIBOU

Jasper's most iconic fauna is also – ironically – one of its most endangered: the woodland caribou, better known to lovers of Father Christmas as the reindeer. Rather like the buffalo, woodland caribou were once ubiquitous in much of North America, foraging in boreal forests as far south as Idaho. But hunting and habitat loss have seen their numbers drastically diminished in recent times, leaving them banished to a small pocket of the Rockies largely contained within the confines of Jasper National Park. A member of the deer family, the woodland caribou, in contrast to its more common tundra-roaming cousins, live in smallish groups in subalpine regions where they subsist on a diet of lichen. Jasper's endangered caribou is split into two groups. A southern herd, numbering less than 100, roams the slopes around Maligne Lake and the Tonquin Valley; a more stable northern group numbering from 200 to 350 hides in the park's remote northern mountains. To see them you'll need to get lucky on the Opal Hills, Tonquin Valley or North Boundary hikes.

When You Arrive

» All visitors intending to stop off in Jasper National Park must purchase a parks pass (adult/youth/senior/family day pass C$9.80/4.90/8.30/19.60), even if it's just for a picnic or a short leg stretch.

» Passes can be procured at the Jasper Information Centre or at one of three different road entrances.

» All visitors receive the *Mountain Guide*, a magazine with maps and information on local sights.

» If you're spending a week, an annual pass (C$67.70) will work out cheaper and can be used in all national parks across Canada, including Banff and Yoho.

» The park is open year-round, though many activities and services are closed during winter.

Orientation

Jasper National Park, some 200km (125 miles) long and 80km (50 miles) wide, lies along the Continental Divide and the border between Alberta and British Columbia. The eastern Rockies span its length, topped with an amazing number of ice fields that drain into a web of rivers and lakes. In the southeast, Maligne River flows into Medicine and Maligne Lakes. In the north, the Athabasca River rages into Jasper Lake and continues south along the Icefields Parkway, following the wide Athabasca and Sunwapta Valleys. The northern third of the park is very remote, accessible only by hiking trails and rivers.

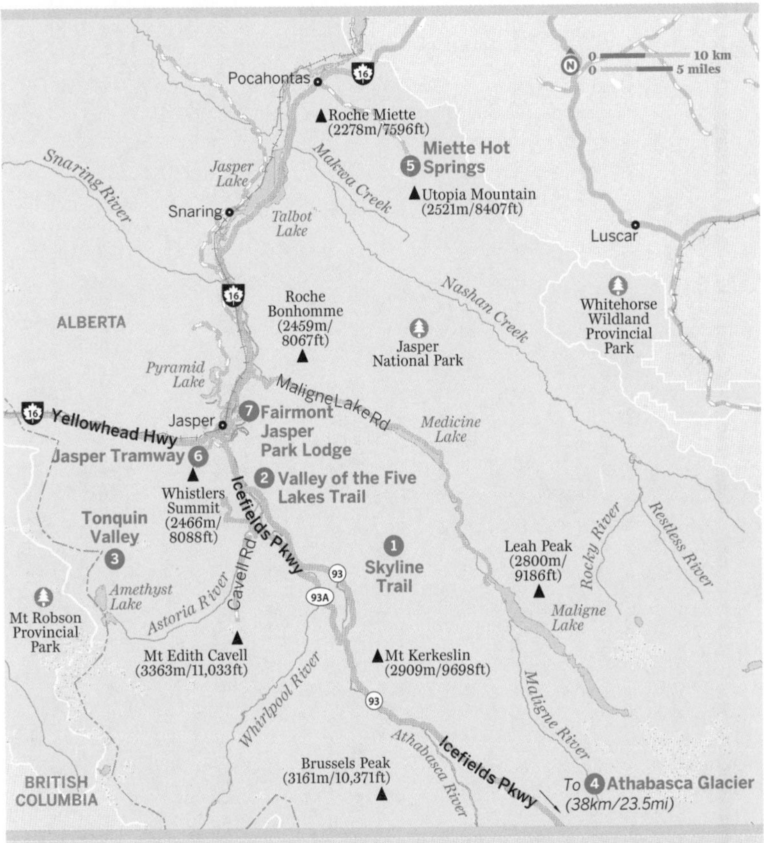

Jasper Highlights

1. Hit one of the scenic heights of North America on the spectacular **Skyline Trail** (p157)
2. Hurtle on a bike over roots, rocks and rough terrain on the hair-raising **Valley of the Five Lakes Trail** (p162)
3. Battle snow, slopes and solitude on a backcountry skiing adventure in the **Tonquin Valley** (see the boxed text, p165)
4. Take a guided hike over the solid, powerful surface of the **Athabasca Glacier** (p143)
5. Climb the steep Sulphur Skyline and contemplate your achievement afterwards in the pool at **Miette Hot Springs** (p148)
6. Give your legs a rest and tackle the less physically taxing incline of the **Jasper Tramway** (p145)
7. Earn a few hours of post-hike relaxation in the regal lobby of the **Fairmont Jasper Park Lodge** (p146)

Jasper National Park

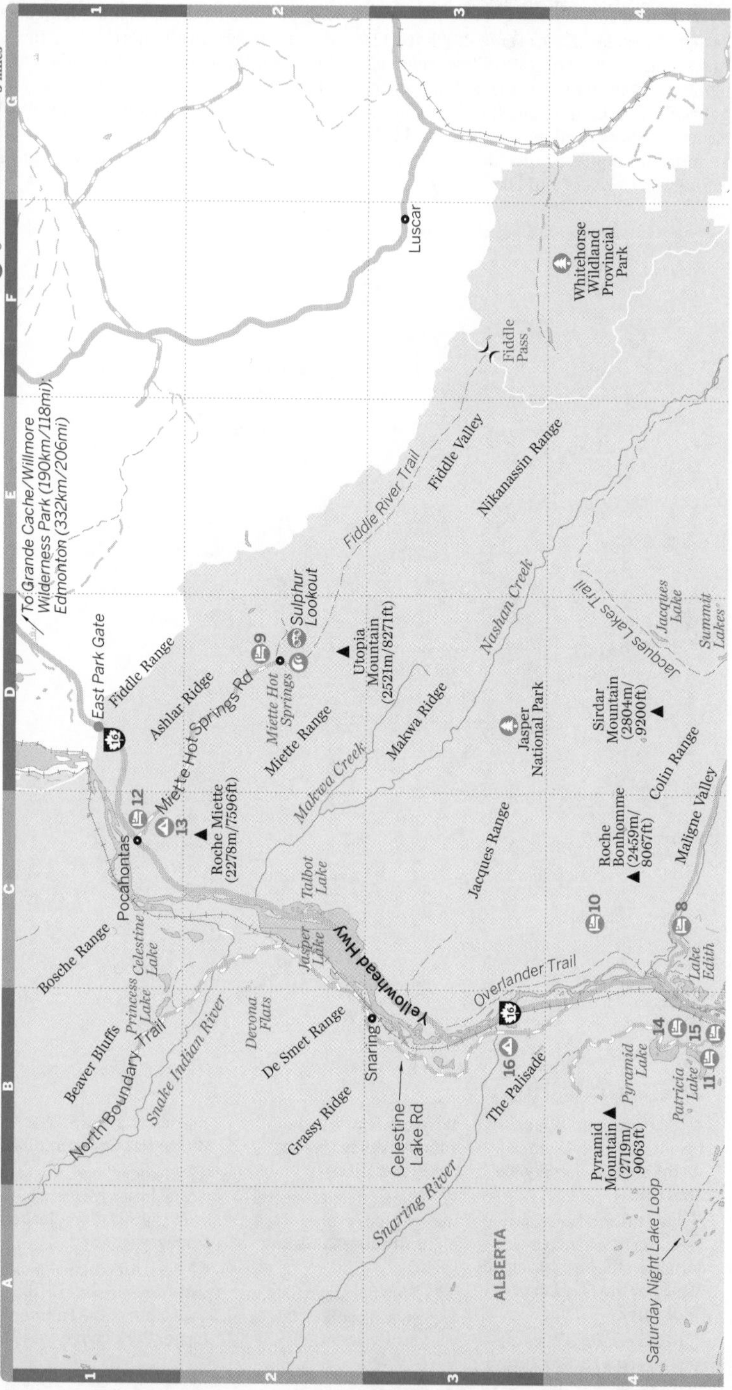

0 — 10 km
0 — 5 miles
To Grande Cache/Willmore Wilderness Park (190km/118mi); Edmonton (332km/206mi)
Luscar
Whitehorse Wildland Provincial Park
Fiddle Pass
Fiddle Valley
Fiddle River Trail
Nikanassin Range
East Park Gate
Fiddle Range
Ashlar Ridge
Miette Hot Springs Rd
Miette Hot Springs
Sulphur Lookout
Utopia Mountain (2521m/8271ft)
Miette Range
Makwa Creek
Makwa Ridge
Nasham Creek
Jasper National Park
Jacques Lakes Trail
Jacques Lake
Summit Lakes
Sirdar Mountain (2804m/9200ft)
Colin Range
Maligne Valley
Roche Bonhomme (2459m/8067ft)
Jacques Range
Roche Miette (2278m/7596ft)
Pocahontas
Talbot Lake
Jasper Lake
Yellowhead Hwy
Overlander Trail
Lake Edith
Bosche Range
Celestine Lake
Princess Lake
Beaver Bluffs
North Boundary Trail
Snake Indian River
Devona Flats
De Smet Range
Snaring
Celestine Lake Rd
Grassy Ridge
The Palisade
Pyramid Lake
Patricia Lake
Pyramid Mountain (2719m/9063ft)
Snaring River
ALBERTA
Saturday Night Lake Loop
16

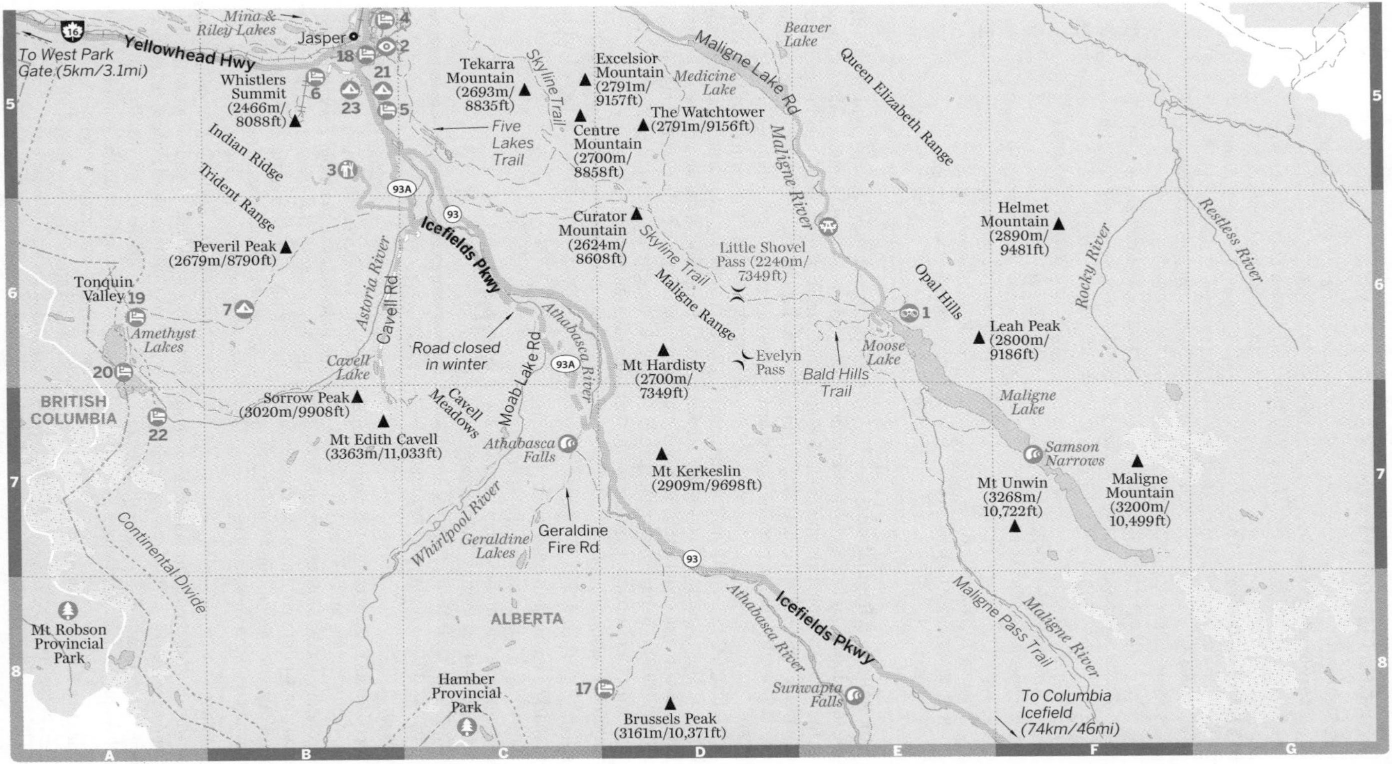
To West Park Gate (5km/3.1mi)
16
Yellowhead Hwy
Mina & Riley Lakes
Jasper
Whistlers Summit (2466m/8088ft)
Indian Ridge
Trident Range
Peveril Peak (2679m/8790ft)
Tonquin Valley
Amethyst Lakes
BRITISH COLUMBIA
Continental Divide
Mt Robson Provincial Park
Tekarra Mountain (2693m/8835ft)
Skyline Trail
Five Lakes Trail
Excelsior Mountain (2791m/9157ft)
Centre Mountain (2700m/8858ft)
The Watchtower (2791m/9156ft)
Medicine Lake
Maligne Lake Rd
Beaver Lake
Queen Elizabeth Range
Maligne River
93A
93
Icefields Pkwy
Astoria River
Cavell Rd
Cavell Lake
Sorrow Peak (3020m/9908ft)
Mt Edith Cavell (3363m/11,033ft)
Cavell Meadows
Road closed in winter
Moab Lake Rd
Athabasca River
Athabasca Falls
Whirlpool River
Geraldine Lakes
Geraldine Fire Rd
ALBERTA
Hamber Provincial Park
Curator Mountain (2624m/8608ft)
Maligne Range
Mt Hardisty (2700m/7349ft)
Little Shovel Pass (2240m/7349ft)
Evelyn Pass
Bald Hills Trail
Moose Lake
Mt Kerkeslin (2909m/9698ft)
Brussels Peak (3161m/10,371ft)
Sunwapta Falls
Opal Hills
Helmet Mountain (2890m/9481ft)
Leah Peak (2800m/9186ft)
Rocky River
Restless River
Maligne Lake
Samson Narrows
Mt Unwin (3268m/10,722ft)
Maligne Mountain (3200m/10,499ft)
Maligne Pass Trail
To Columbia Icefield (74km/46mi)
A
B
C
D
E
F
G
5
6
7
8

Jasper National Park

Sights

Park Policies & Regulations

You must have a parks pass to stop anywhere in the park, including viewpoints and short day hikes. Wilderness permits are required for backcountry hiking (see the boxed text, p138).

It is illegal to take anything from the park – from picking flowers to pocketing stones. Pets must be kept on a leash at all times and are not allowed in backcountry shelters.

Hunting and firearms are not permitted within the park.

BIKING

In marked contrast to other parks, bikes are allowed on a large number of Jasper's trails. Pick up a clearly marked map from the Jasper Information Centre. Helmets are mandatory and cyclists are required to stick to designated trails and avoid skidding.

DRIVING

Speed limits in the park are 90km/h (56mph) on major roads and 60km/h (37mph) on secondary roads. Motorists should regularly scan for wildlife either on or crossing the road. Also beware of other cars stopping or slowing down to view wildlife.

BOATING

Rowboats and canoes are allowed on many ponds and lakes within the park; electric boats are permitted on some; gas-powered boats are generally restricted.

Dangers & Annoyances

The biggest dangers are weather, rugged backcountry terrain, wildlife and avalanches. All of these dangers can be minimized with common sense and planning. Always check trail, weather and wildlife conditions before venturing out into the wilderness, and make sure you are properly equipped.

Rocky Mountain weather can turn on a dime. Prepare for all-season weather at any time of year and always carry warm layered clothing. Fickle weather conditions can also create treacherous driving conditions, even during summer.

While crime is low in Jasper, you'd be wise to always keep your car locked when unattended.

SIGHTS

Icefields Parkway

Paralleling the Continental Divide for 230km (144 miles) between Lake Louise and Jasper Town, plain old Hwy 93 is usually branded as the Icefields Parkway (or the slightly more romantic 'Promenade des Glaciers' in French) as a means of somehow preparing people for the majesty of its surroundings. And what majesty! The Parkway's highlight is undoubtedly the humungous Columbia Icefield and its numerous fanning glaciers, and this dynamic lesson in erosive geography is complimented by weeping waterfalls, aquamarine lakes, dramatic mountains and the sudden dart of a bear, elk, or was it a caribou?

Completed in 1940, most people ply the Parkway's asphalt by car, meaning it can get busy in July and August. For a clearer vision consider taking a bus or, even better, tackling it on a bike – the road is wide, never prohibitively steep, and sprinkled with plenty of strategically spaced campgrounds, hostels and hotels.

FREE Columbia Icefield Centre MUSEUM, LANDMARK

(Map p150; Icefields Parkway; early May–mid-Oct) Situated on the Icefields Parkway, close to the toe of the Athabasca Glacier, the green-roofed Icefield Centre contains a hotel, cafeteria, restaurant, gift shop, Snocoach ticket booth and Parks Canada information desk. Downstairs you'll find the fascinating Glacier Gallery, a mini-museum explaining the science of glaciers and providing a comprehensive snapshot of the area's history.

Athabasca Glacier GLACIER

(Map p150) The Athabasca is North America's most visited glacier due to its proximity to Hwy 93, aka the Icefields Parkway. Covering an area of 6 sq km (2.5 sq miles), it is a hulking relic of the last ice age, and spills stealthily off the Columbia Icefield at the rate of several centimeters per year. As recently as the 1840s this immensely powerful river of ice reached as far as the modern-day Icefields Parkway, but it has retreated over the last 150 years by more than 1.6km (1 mile), leaving behind a stony moonscape part-filled by emerald Sunwapta Lake. To reach the glacier, drive or walk 1km (0.6 miles) from the Columbia Icefield Centre to a small parking lot and the start of the short **Forefield Trail**, which takes you up to the toe of the glacier. While it is permitted to stand on a small roped section of the ice, don't follow the foolish few who cross the warning tape. The glacier is riddled with crevasses, and almost every year there is an avoidable fatality.

The safest and most environmentally congruous way to see the glacier is to go on a guided ice-walk with **Athabasca Glacier Icewalks** (www.icewalks.com), run out of the Icefield Centre. Three-hour trips (adult/child C$60/30) run daily from June to September.

Athabasca Falls WATERFALL

(Map p140) A deafening combination of sound, spray and water, Athabasca Falls is Jasper's most dramatic and voluminous waterfall. Copious visitors crowd the large parking lot and short access trail to catch a glimpse of this enduring park emblem, which is just off the Icefields Parkway, 28km (17 miles) south of Jasper Town, and at its most ferocious during summer. Despite being only 23m (75ft) high, the heavy flow volume of the Athabasca River has cut deeply into the soft limestone rock, carving potholes, canyons and various water channels. Interpretive signs explain the basics of the local geology.

JASPER'S ICEFIELDS

An icefield is a large area of interconnecting glaciers situated within a contained physical zone of high precipitation such as a mountain plateau. A large proportion of the world's icefields are located in Canada and Alaska, and the most famous – and one of the largest outside the Arctic Circle – is the Columbia Icefield splayed between Jasper and Banff National Parks. The Columbia's fame stems largely from its accessibility; it is only 1.6km (1 mile) from a major road (Hwy 93) and is consequently visited by in excess of one million people a year. Situated atop the triple Continental Divide on the border of Alberta and British Columbia, it counts eight major glaciers and covers an area of 325 sq km (125 sq miles), larger than the metropolitan district of Vancouver.

Yet the Columbia is just the start of a necklace of ecologically important icefields that ring Jasper and its surrounding wilderness areas. Invisible to the Icefields Parkway's car-driving hordes are the Chaba and Clemenceau Icefields; the former of which measures nearly 300 sq km (186 sq miles) and is only marginally smaller than the Columbia to which it is joined by a sinuous glacier. Equally imposing and inaccessible are the Hooker Icefield abutting Hamber Provincial Park and the Brazeau Icefield that surrounds the eponymous peak at the head of Maligne Lake on the eastern side of the Icefields Parkway. The massive meltwaters of these numerous icefields act as giant water storage tanks and empty into three separate oceans, the Pacific, Arctic and North Atlantic. Combined, they provide vital water supplies for millions of people across western Canada.

Jasper Town

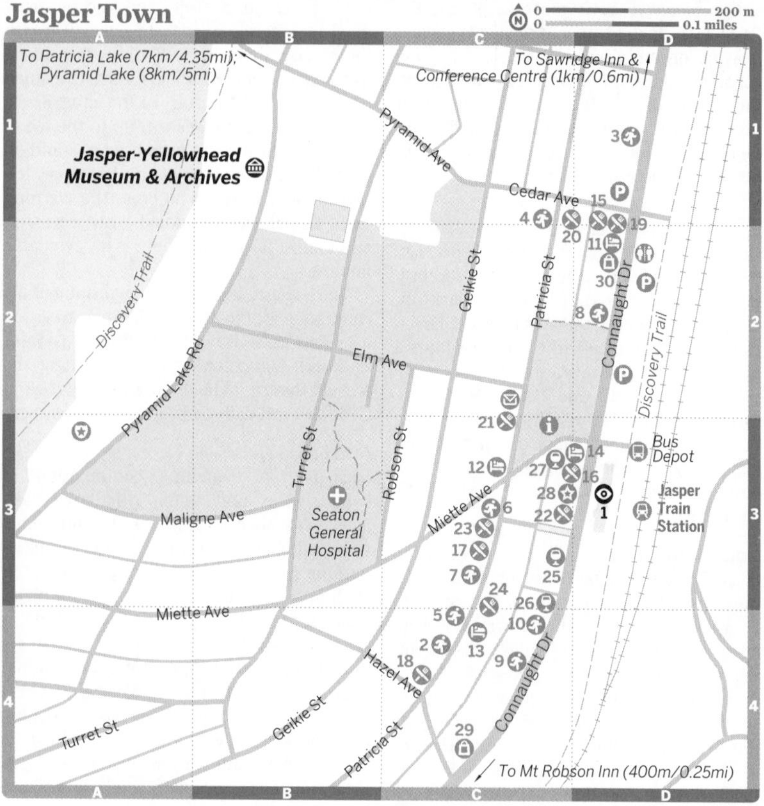

Sunwapta Falls WATERFALL

(Map p150) Meaning 'turbulent water' in the native tongue, 18m (60ft) Sunwapta Falls formed when the glacial meltwaters of the Sunwapta River began falling from a hanging valley into the deeper U-shaped Athabasca Valley. Close to the Icefields Parkway and the Sunwapta Falls resort and restaurant, the falls are a popular stop for travelers plying this scenic highway. They're also the start of a 25km (15.5-mile) biking and hiking trail to remote Fortress Lake in Hamber Provincial Park (p175).

Horseshoe Lake LAKE

(Map p150) This idyllic blue-green, horseshoe-shaped lake, just off the Icefields Parkway, is missed by many visitors, making a stopover here all the more alluring. A choice spot for a bracing summer swim or a short stroll around the perimeter, the lake is surrounded by steep cliffs and is hence occasionally frequented by ill-advised cliff divers. Don't be tempted to join them.

Mt Edith Cavell MOUNTAIN

(Map p150) Rising like a snowy sentinel over Jasper Town, 3363m (11,033ft) Mt Edith Cavell is one of the park's most distinctive and physically arresting peaks. What it lacks in height it makes up for in stark, ethereal beauty. Accessed via a winding, precipitous road that branches off the Icefields Parkway 6km (3.7 miles) south of Jasper, the mountain is famous for its flower meadows and its wing-shaped Angel Glacier.

First climbed in 1915, it was named the following year in honor of a humanitarian British nurse who was executed by a German firing squad during WWI, after helping to smuggle over 200 wounded allied soldiers into neutral Holland.

Jasper Town

Jasper Town & Around

Built in the early 1900s at the confluence of three river valleys, Jasper Town (originally known as Fitzhugh) is surrounded by mountains and blessed with one of the most easily accessible trail systems in North America. Characterized by a mishmash of low-rise shops and residential properties – not all of which are attractive – the town these days maintains strict development laws, meaning its tenure as an expanding urban hub is well and truly over. While the main sights lie outside the town, it makes a good evening base and, should the weather turn ugly, you can linger in an excellent museum, and ponder some interesting railway memorabilia.

Jasper Tramway CABLE CAR

(Map p154; www.jaspertramway.com; Whistlers Rd; adult/child C$30/15; ⏲9:30am-6:30pm late Apr-Jun & Sep, 9am-8pm Jul & Aug) Ascending 973m (3243ft) in a mere seven minutes, the Jasper Tramway carries you up a gondola (cable car) to an eagle's-eye lookout over the eastern Rockies, complete with café and boardwalk. From here you can hike a steep 1.5km (0.9 miles) to the summit of Whistlers Mountain or enjoy the views from the café. Dusk sees fewer crowds and is arguably the most beautiful time for the trip. Trams depart every 10 minutes. To reach the tramway, follow Hwy 93 south and turn right into Whistlers Rd after 3km (1.9 miles). Alternatively, you can catch the Jasper Tramway Shuttle (p173).

Discovery Trail HERITAGE TRAIL

(Map p144) An interesting mix of interpretive walk, heritage trail and outdoor museum, the Jasper Discovery Trail completely circumnavigates the town via an 8km (5-mile) part-paved, part-unpaved pathway. Split into three sections highlighting the town's natural, historical and railroad legacies, the trail makes a worthwhile evening stroll or bracing early morning jog. Interpretive boards en route provide an educational introduction to both town and park and, on the northwestern side, the trail dips in and out of montane forest, offering excellent views over the surrounding mountains. The train station is a good place to start.

TOP CHOICE **Patricia & Pyramid Lakes** LAKE

(Map p140) Of the patchwork of small lakes that lie to the north and northeast of Jasper Town these two are the most striking and oft-visited. Lying in the imposing shadow of rust-colored **Pyramid Mountain**, these two bejeweled bodies of water sit on the higher expanses of Pyramid Lake Rd and offer ideal opportunities for recreation and escape. In 1943 Patricia Lake was the site of a bizarre WWII project known as Operation Habbakuk, which attempted – unsuccessfully – to build a prototype aircraft carrier out of ice and sawdust. The plan was abandoned when the ship, unsurprisingly, melted and the wooden supports sank to the bottom of the lake, where they remain a favorite haunt for visiting scuba divers.

The slightly larger Pyramid Lake is popular for picnicking and boating, with rental available from a jetty opposite the upscale Pyramid Lake Resort. Further up the road, the pinprick-sized **Pyramid Island** is joined to the shore by a quaint wooden footbridge. This gorgeous island has picnic tables, a shelter and a wheelchair-accessible path with stunning views of Mt Edith Cavell across the calm water.

Lake Annette LAKE

(Map p160) Jasper's most popular swimming lakes lie to the northeast of the town and are easily accessible by car and bike, or on foot. Sporting a small beach, Lake Annette can be circumnavigated by a 2.4km (1.5-mile) partly wheelchair-accessible trail (no bikes) with peek-a-boo mountain views. If you're brave, try dipping your toe in the water, or alternatively run in up to your waist (summer only) for a quick glacial-fed bath. Come back in winter and you'll more likely be skating across the lake than jumping in it, after the water turns to ice.

The lake is a few kilometers (approximately 2 miles) to the northeast of Jasper Town. To get to it, head east on Hwy 16, turn right onto Maligne Rd and right again onto Lodge Rd. Take the left turn for Lake Annette; the parking lot is on the right.

Lakeside views include the rocky summit of Roche Bonhomme to the northeast, the rust-colored Pyramid Mountain to the northwest and snowcapped Mt Edith Cavell to the southwest.

Lac Beauvert LAKE

(Map p160) Dominated by the Fairmont Jasper Park Lodge and golf course, crystal-clear Lac Beauvert (literally 'beautiful green' in French) is another Athabasca Valley glacier-fed lake. It's a popular place for boating during summer and ice-skating in winter and has a more pastoral feel than other local bodies of water.

Fairmont Jasper Park Lodge HISTORIC BUILDING

(Map p160) Part of a select chain of historic national-park lodges built in the early 20th century, the Jasper Park Lodge started life as a tent city set up by two pioneering railway workers, the Brewster brothers, on the shores of Lac Beauvert in 1915. Opened as a proper hotel in 1921, the property was taken over by the newly inaugurated Canadian National Railway (CNR), which marketed it as the largest single-level log building in the world. The current lodge dates from 1953 and was built to replace the original structure, which burned down in a fire the previous year. Illustrious former guests include Marilyn Monroe and Bing Crosby, who is pictured inside practicing his putting on the adjoining 18-hole golf course with a black bear as his caddy. For hotel information, see p169.

Jasper-Yellowhead Museum & Archives MUSEUM

(Map p144; www.jaspermuseum.org; Pyramid Lake Rd; adult/reduced C$6/5; ⏲10am-5pm daily summer, 10am-5pm Thu-Sun winter) Furnished with a well-laid-out chronology of Jasper's brief but compelling history, Jasper's main museum brings to life the nomad hunters, fur traders, travelers, explorers, artists, mountaineers, gold prospectors and pioneers who shaped both the town and park of Jasper. It's very well put together and definitely worth an hour or two's contemplation, even on a sunny day.

Old Fort Point HISTORIC SITE

(Map p140) One of Jasper Town's most accessible and instantly rewarding trails is the short, steep climb up to a nearby *roche mountonnée* (a bedrock knob shaped by glaciers) known as Old Fort Point. Unfortunately, you won't find any old abandoned fort here. Instead, the name refers to the likely site of a one-time fur trading post known as Henry House that was built near here in 1811 by William Henry, a colleague of Canadian-British explorer David Thompson.

The best way to reach the trailhead is by foot; simply follow Hwy 93A out of town to Hwy 16, cross the road and then pick up trail No 1b on the other side. This will bring you out by a bridge across the Athabasca River with the Old Fort trailhead situated on the other side.

The quickest way up to Old Fort Point is to take the wooden steps from the small parking lot to a lookout with panoramic views over Jasper Town and the Athabasca Valley.

Jasper Train Station LANDMARK

(Map p144; 607 Connaught Dr) Jasper grew up as a railway town and the train station, constructed by the CNR, is one of its oldest and most attractive buildings. Designed in an unusual arts and crafts-meets-national park architectural style it was completed in 1925 to blend into its rustic surroundings. The interior has been upgraded, but remains sympathetic to the golden railroad era with heavy wooden benches and art deco travel posters from the 1940s and '50s.

Maligne Lake Area

Maligne Canyon CANYON

(Map p149) As dramatic as Maligne Lake is placid, Maligne Canyon is one of the deepest canyons in the Canadian Rockies. Formed when the Maligne River cut back through the ancient limestone in its effort to reach the Athabasca Valley at the end of the last ice age, the gorge is over 15m (50ft) deep at its deepest point and, measuring only 2m (6.5ft) across in places, is extraordinarily narrow. Other interesting features include eroded potholes, fossils, frost-affected rock, mossy canyon walls and evidence of resourceful rock-dwelling wildlife. Crossed by six different bridges, various trails lead out from the parking lot on Maligne Lake Rd. You'll also find a standard café and gift shop here.

The canyon is best appreciated with a hike along the meandering riverside trail that traverses five narrow bridges. Starting from the parking lot 7km (4.3 miles) along Maligne Rd from Hwy 16, the trail heads directly down to **Second Bridge**, where the narrow 51m (170ft) deep canyon falls away like a rocky crevasse into eerie darkness. From here, the paved Upper Canyon Trail takes you back to **First Bridge** and the park's highest waterfall at 23m (75ft), an angry torrent that is reduced to a mere trickle during winter. The canyon decreases in depth above First Bridge, revealing a water-eroded web of potholes, channels and lichen-covered rocks. You'll also spy fossils on the ground and sunken gardens where the water's spray has brought to life small pockets of ferns deep within the gorge.

THE WORLD'S GREATEST TRAIN RIDE?

Most come to Jasper for the outdoor action, but weaving its way through the park like an iron artery (and surprisingly invisible to all but a savvy few) is one of the greatest engineering feats of the industrial era – Canada's cross-continental railway. The second of two railroads laid across the nation in the late 19th and early 20th centuries, the Canadian Northern Railway reached Jasper in 1911, linking it with Vancouver to the west and Edmonton, Winnipeg and Toronto to the east. Its construction was a technological triumph, but came at a great financial and human cost – though no official figures exist, it has been estimated that approximately one in 30 of the Chinese 'coolies' who worked on Canada's trans-continental railways died from accidents or disease.

In 1918 the Canadian Northern was nationalized to save it from bankruptcy and renamed the Canadian National Railway (CNR) and in 1978 its passenger services were placed under the auspices of a new government corporation known as VIA. Since 1990 VIA has operated *The Canadian*, Canada's only cross-continental train, running three times a week between Toronto and Vancouver. The journey from Toronto to Jasper takes 63 hours (from Vancouver 19½ hours) and passengers are accommodated luxuriously in Economy Class (with huge reclining seats) or Sleeper Touring Class (with roomettes including all meals). All trains are equipped with restaurant cars, cafés and a dome observation car, where you can relax with ever-changing Rocky Mountain views. In a fortuitous money-saving scheme in the 1990s, the train reutilized its 1955 streamliner cars, providing a nostalgic throwback to the days when railroads – not cars – were king.

Jasper is also the eastern terminus to another historic railway, the Jasper–Prince George–Prince Rupert line that was originally laid by the Grand Trunk Pacific Railway (GTPR). The two-day trip leaves Jasper three times weekly.

TOP CHOICE **Maligne Lake** LAKE

(Map p149) Though it was first spotted as early as 1875 by Canadian Pacific Railway surveyor Henry McLeod, Maligne Lake will forever be synonymous with feisty Pennsylvania-born explorer Mary Schäffer, who was a female ahead of her time and the park's first real tourist. Schäffer originally arrived here in 1908, guided by a map drawn from memory by Assiniboine Aboriginal Sampson Beaver, who had himself visited the area 16 years previously.

In the years since, the lake has enjoyed a place of pride on most tourists' itineraries. Stretching 22km (14 miles) north to south and surrounded by a craning circle of rocky, photogenic peaks, the lake is a stunner, and has caused many an enraptured visitor to take a step back in amazement. The real draw is **Spirit Island**, a speck of tree-covered land with spiritual significance for First Nations people and a regular feature on every postcard and photo-calendar this side of Calgary.

Unless you feel up to some long-distance kayaking (perfectly doable given that there are two lakeside campgrounds), the only way to catch sight of the island is by **tour boat** (p165). Summer schedules run 10am to 5pm in peak season, but the boats get busy and reservations are recommended. Maligne Lake also has some fantastic trailheads and is a wonderful spot for oar-powered forays around the shimmering shoreline.

Medicine Lake LAKE

(Map p149) A geological rarity, Medicine Lake is perhaps best described as a sinking lake that has holes in the bottom and functions rather like a plugless bathtub. In summer, when the run-off is high, the lake fills more quickly than it can drain away and the body of water appears deep and expansive. In winter, as the run-off slows, the water empties, causing the lake to shrink to the size of a small stream. What bewildered Aboriginals and other early visitors was the apparent lack of any water outlet. In fact, the water actually flows out of the lake via a series of small holes on its floor, before passing into a complex underground cave system. The river then re-emerges 16km (10 miles) downstream near Maligne Canyon. In the 1950s a ferry service across the lake was briefly attempted, but efforts to plug the holes with sandbags, mattresses and bundles of magazines all proved futile.

North of Jasper Town

Pocahontas HISTORIC SITE

(Map p140) A one-time mining community that produced heaps of poor quality, smokeless coal for the allied war effort during WWI (1914–18), Pocahontas was once the largest settlement in Jasper National Park and home to hundreds of miners. When the market price for coal fell in 1921 the town fell into a rapid decline, becoming a veritable ghost town nine years later when the 1930 National Parks Act banned mining in the park for good. All that remains of Pocahontas today are some overgrown ruins, an antiquated superintendent's home and a set of rather plush tourist facilities, otherwise known as the Pocahontas Cabins. Visitors can amuse themselves on a 1km (0.6-mile) wheelchair-accessible interpretive trail that meanders around the old mining site, recreating the days when the government encouraged resource extraction from the park in return for handsome royalties. To get here take the Miette Hot Springs Rd off Hwy 16 and turn first right into the parking lot.

Miette Hot Springs SPA

(Map p140; Miette Hot Springs Rd; adult/child C$6.05/5.15; ⌚8:30am-10:30pm Jun 24-Sep 5, 10:30am-9pm May, Jun, Sep, Oct; 👪) While the discovery of healing waters at Banff triggered the development of Canada's first national park, the founding of Miette Hot Springs was slightly less dramatic. A rough trail to the Rockies' hottest natural mineral springs, long known to First Nations people, was first bushwhacked in 1909. A log bathhouse was slung together four years later and from 1934 to 1938 Depression-era workers constructed a hugely popular aquacenter at the end of Jasper's first paved road. Bursting from the earth at a scalding 54°C (129°F), the modern-day springs are cooled to 39°C (103°F), with a cold pool to plunge yourself into afterward – if you're brave enough. The latest bathing facility, built in 1986, is situated outdoors and surrounded by tree-covered mountains. Visitors can rent lockers, swimsuits and towels, and have lunch in the adjoining café.

Situated 17km (10.5 miles) down a winding road from Pocahontas, a couple of trails lead out from the Miette Hot Springs parking lot. One takes you up to the top of Sulphur Mountain, while the other leads 1km (0.6 miles) to the **source** of the underground springs, now overlooked by the ruins of the original aquacenter. If you have time en route, be sure to take in the giant, vertical **Ashlar Ridge** from the viewpoint at 8.9km (5.5 miles) from Hwy 16.

DRIVING

Driving along Jasper's well-maintained and uncrowded roads, amid rugged mountains and seemingly endless forests, is one of life's simple pleasures. Keep your eyes peeled for wildlife foraging by the roadside.

The Maligne Wildlife Show

Duration 45 minutes one way

Distance 46km (28.5 miles)

Speed Limit 60km/h (37mph)

Start Maligne Lake Rd turnoff on Hwy 16

Finish Maligne Lake

Nearest Town Jasper (p145)

Summary A necessarily slow drive through some of the Rocky Mountains' prime wildlife habitat to the region's largest natural lake.

The Maligne Lake Rd is as scenic as the destination. Wildlife is rife and with luck you'll spot a wolf, a bear or a moose. Be sure to obey speed restrictions and watch for animals bounding across the road.

Begin the tour 2km (1.2 miles) north of Jasper Town; follow Hwy 16 to the turnoff for Maligne Lake Rd, crossing the **Athabasca River** and following the road left. Ahead are views of Roche Bonhomme, with its Old Man summit, and to the west lies the rust-colored Pyramid Mountain. At 3km (1.9 miles), the **Fifth Bridge** crosses the powerful **Maligne River**; if you're feeling ambitious, you can head over this suspension bridge and climb the trail into **Maligne Canyon**, one of the deepest in the Rockies. An easier way to see this dramatic canyon is via the **Upper Canyon Trail**; the trailhead is 7km (4.3 miles) along the route.

The road continues east between the Colin Range to the north and the Maligne Range to the south. At 22km (13.6 miles) there's a pull-off to Maligne River, though it only carries water here if Medicine Lake floods. Instead, the water flows downstream in an underground waterway. Aboriginals in the area believed the water was whisked away by magic (or bad medicine) and feared it.

The next turnoff, on the northwest corner of **Medicine Lake**, offers superb views across the water. Along the north side of the lake, the craggy Colin Range leans flat-faced

The Maligne Wildlife Show Driving Tour

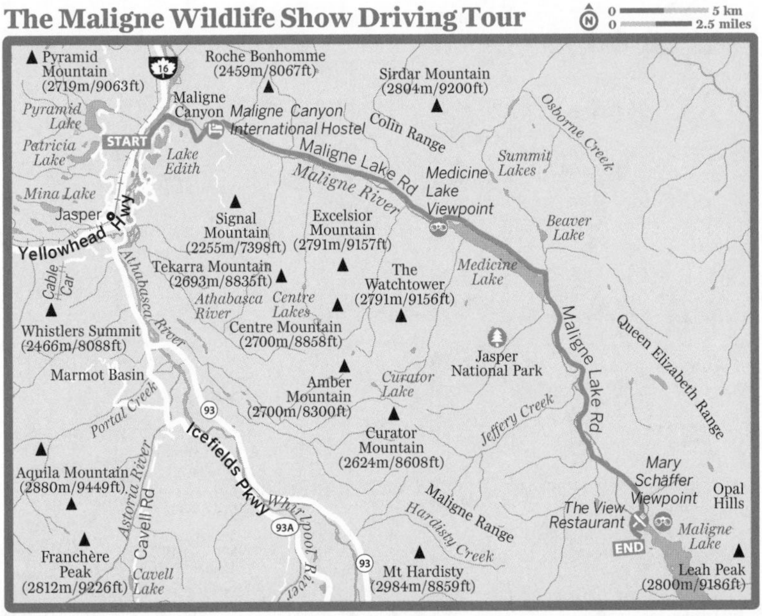

toward the road, and a delta on the far eastern side of the lake often hosts caribou in early spring and late fall.

At 32km (19.8 miles), look up. Above, you'll see limestone arches cut into the summit of the Queen Elizabeth Range, caused by water that's freezing in the crevices, expanding and shattering the rock. If you've brought a picnic and are hoping for a little peace, try the rest stop at 40km (24.8 miles), where you can relax beside the river before reaching the more hectic **Maligne Lake**, 6km (3.7 miles) up the road.

Icefields Parkway

Duration 2 hours

Distance 103km (64 miles)

Speed Limit 90km/h (56mph)

Start Jasper

Finish Columbia Icefield Centre

Nearest Town Jasper (p145)

Summary Frequently described, but rarely done justice, the Parkway is the drive of a lifetime that has to be seen to be believed.

Icefields Parkway Driving Tour

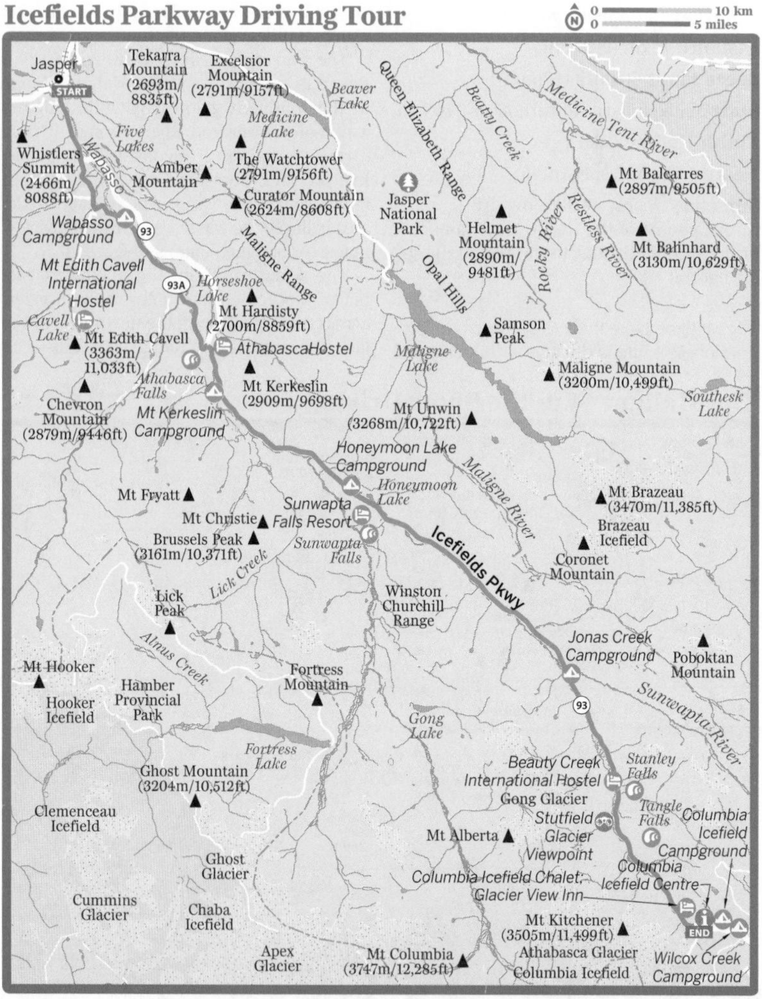

Considered one of the most scenic drives in North America, the Icefields Parkway – or the 'road through the clouds' – is a kaleidoscopic mélange of cascading waterfalls and spectacularly carved peaks, whose crowning glory is the glistening Columbia Icefield on the park's southern limits. Measuring 230km (144 miles) from Jasper Town down to Lake Louise, a bejeweled 108km (67-mile) segment of the route traverses Jasper National Park, incorporating some of the region's star attractions.

Driving south out of Jasper, the first highlight is **Mt Edith Cavell**, the town's snowcapped guardian, accessible via a winding spur road off Hwy 93A. Stop here to stroll through flower-filled meadows and catch a glimpse of the peak's wing-shaped **Angel Glacier**. Rejoin the main parkway for 20km (12.4 miles) and you'll pass **Horseshoe Lake**, with its steep-sided cliffs and clear, bracing waters, followed quickly by the **Athabasca Falls**, the park's most voluminous waterfall, which throws its frigid glacial meltwater over a 21m (70ft) limestone cliff.

Look out for wildlife on the next section of the route as you head south through a wide corridor of mountains that runs parallel to the Continental Divide. At **Honeymoon Lake** there's a good viewpoint over the Athabasca River, while 2km (1.2 miles) further on, at **Sunwapta Falls**, you can refuel at the homey restaurant or stretch your legs on the short hike to the waterfall. This is also the start of an excellent hiking and biking trail to Fortress Lake at 25km (15.5 miles).

As the tree cover thins and the river becomes a confusing maze of different channels you'll start to notice the glaciers. Stop at the **Stutfield Glacier viewpoint** just past Beauty Creek to admire this outlying tentacle of the Columbia Icefield; 2km (1.2 miles) further on you'll pass **Tangle Falls** and the start of the scenic Wilcox Pass Trail. The drive's apex is the green-roofed Columbia Icefield Centre and the world-famous **Athabasca Glacier**, which slides like an icy river down toward the road. Stop here for interpretive displays, a walk around the Forefield Trail and an excursion on one of the unique Snocoaches.

DAY HIKES

Even when judged against other Canadian national parks, Jasper's trail network is mighty and, with comparatively fewer people than its sister park, Banff to the south, you've a better chance of seeing more wildlife and less humans.

The park claims to have 1200km (660 miles) of hiking trails, many of which are shared with horseback riders and off-road cyclists. It is rightly famous for the abundance of trails leaving directly from its urban hub, Jasper Town, meaning shuttles or time-consuming drives to trailheads are not always necessary. Many of these trails crisscross the tree-covered plateau situated immediately behind the townsite known as the Pyramid Bench. Others track the Athabasca River Valley and its numerous small lakes. To help you pick the perfect hike, see our handy chart on p34.

Icefields Parkway

Geraldine Lakes

Duration 3-4 hours round-trip

Distance 10km (6.3 miles)

Difficulty Moderate-difficult

Start/Finish End of Geraldine Fire Rd

Elevation Change 407m (1335ft)

Nearest Town Jasper (p145)

Transportation Private

Summary A rocky scramble through a staircaselike valley replete with lakes and waterfalls.

Geraldine Lakes is a hike of two different halves. The first part to Lake No 1 is easy; beyond that you'd better have strong ankles, a head for heights and a penchant for scrambling over bare, sometimes slippery rock.

The hike starts at a parking lot at the end of Geraldine Fire Rd, an unpaved track which branches off Hwy 93A. Take the obvious trail through the trees and ascend moderately to Geraldine Creek at 1.5km (0.9 miles). In another 300m (328yd) you'll spy the first **Geraldine Lake** through the trees – so far, so easy.

The going gets tougher as you skirt the north shore of the lake on a rougher trail and come up against your first obstacle, a large waterfall at the lake's far end. The trail (no longer obvious) climbs steeply up to the right of the waterfall for 100m (328ft), requiring scrambling skills and a firm footing. The path reappears briefly at the top and then disappears again in another rock field. Watch carefully for small cairns and a yellow marker here that will direct you across the small valley (over the now underground creek), and into some trees on the other side where the trail materializes once again. Coming out of the trees, you'll approach a photogenic second waterfall and another rocky climb and scramble up to lake number two, which lies a good 400m (0.25-mile) rock-hop from the summit. By now you'll have ascertained the unique staircase design of the valley. There are actually two more Geraldine Lakes above Lake No 2, but the trail to reach them is practically nonexistent. Most hikers are satisfied with turning round at the second lake, though a 1.2km (0.7-mile) trail that tracks its southern shore leads to a backcountry campground at the far end.

Path of the Glacier & Cavell Meadows Trails

Duration 3 hours round-trip

Distance 9.1km (5.6 miles)

Difficulty Moderate-difficult

Start/Finish Cavell Meadows parking lot

Elevation Change 400m (1300ft)

Nearest Facilities Icefields Parkway (p142)

Transportation Private

Summary Angelic glaciers and heavenly scenery give this recently restored mountain trail a distinctly ethereal quality.

With its wings spread celestially between Mt Edith Cavell and Sorrow Peak, Angel Glacier gives the appearance of hovering over a small sapphire lake that is afloat with icebergs. The lake's ice-blue sheen is made all the more dramatic for the barren, stony surroundings that were created by the glacier's not-so-long-ago flight across the valley.

The Path of the Glacier Loop is the most popular hike in the area but, for greater solitude and a brilliant wildflower display (in July), head further up the peak to Cavell Meadows.

To reach the trailhead from Jasper, follow Hwy 93A south to Cavell Rd and then drive 12km (7.4 miles) to a parking lot. Interpretive signs along the route tell the story of both Edith Cavell and the glacier.

Beginning with a climb through rocky moraine you'll pass the Cavell Meadows Trail turnoff after 0.5km (0.3 miles). The Path of the Glacier Trail continues ascending another 1km (0.6 miles) to a fantastic viewpoint of Angel Glacier, reflected in tiny

Path of the Glacier & Cavell Meadows Trails

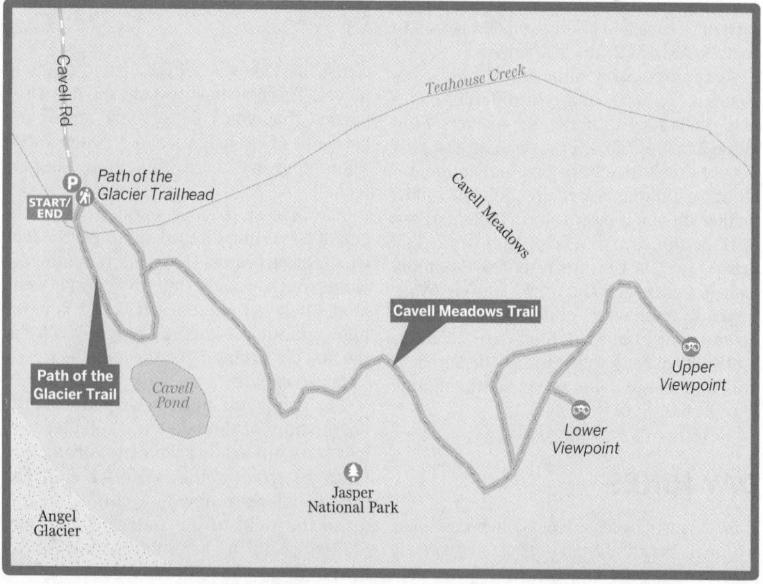

Cavell Pond. Although the trail descends to the water, approaching the famous ice caves here is extremely hazardous. Keep your distance from the caves and beware of falling ice.

From the lake, the path levels out and loops back to the parking lot. This area was covered by the glacier until the 1950s, and small trees and plants are only just beginning to reappear.

A loop around **Cavell Meadows** will treat you to fantastic views and an even better workout. Take the left turn off the Path of the Glacier Trail at 0.5km (0.3 miles) and begin a steep ascent north. The trail soon levels off with clear views of the glacier to the right. This area is strewn with boulders up to 4m (13ft) high, left behind by the glacier. After crossing a stream, switchbacks take you north into the forest; keep right at the junction – 2.2km (1.4 miles) – crossing two more streams before entering an open, flowery meadow. At 3km (1.9 miles) a side trail branches right to the **Lower Viewpoint**.

Returning to the main trail, a brief climb brings you to another junction. If you've had enough, head left to meet up with the Path of the Glacier Trail; if you've still got some energy and a penchant for climbs, turn right for the Upper Viewpoint.

The way is steep, and the rock-strewn trail becomes fainter and slippery. Continuing uphill to the right brings you to a high subalpine **meadow** with an explosion of flowers. The path runs along a bank of loose shale with a steep drop on the left; then it turns right, where it becomes incredibly steep and rather treacherous.

You'll know you've reached the **Upper Viewpoint** by the yellow marker; the views are also something of a giveaway. Southwest is Mt Edith Cavell; Pyramid Mountain lies to the north and Roche Bonhomme to the northeast. Angel Glacier is suspended to the west; from this height you have an impressive view of its wings and upper half.

Heading back, the descent along the loose shale is tricky. At the junction, turn right to return through lush meadows to the Path of the Glacier Trail.

Beauty Creek & Stanley Falls

Duration 1 hour round-trip

Distance 3.2km (2 miles)

Difficulty Easy

Start/Finish Icefields Parkway

Elevation Change Negligible

Nearest Facilities Columbia Icefield Centre (p143)

Transportation Sundog Tours

Summary This once popular waterfall half-hidden from the Icefields Parkway since the 1960s can be reached on a surprisingly straightforward and rewarding hike.

Simple, but effective, this short easy trail gets you to a revered beauty spot with minimal effort. The object of your yearnings is Stanley Falls, a series of eight waterfalls that carry Beauty Creek through a narrow canyon to its confluence with the Sunwapta River.

The hardest part of the hike is finding the trailhead on the Icefields Parkway, 2km (1.2 miles) south of the Beauty Creek Youth Hostel at a spot where two water diversion dykes go underneath the main highway. The tiny parking area on the Beauty Flats aside the Sunwapta River is on the edge of the caribou range and is thus heavily protected. Follow the dyke east from the road through a clump of trees to the old Icefields Parkway, abandoned after it was modernized and redirected in the 1960s. Turn right on the road and after 600m (0.4 miles) you'll reach an old bridge over Beauty Creek. Turn left here onto a hiking trail and you'll quickly find yourself heading toward to a series of eight waterfalls that cut through a sinuous canyon. The last waterfall – the 'proper' **Stanley Falls** – is 800m (0.5 miles) upriver from the old road. You can actually continue for another 2km (1.2 miles) up the creek bed to three more waterfalls, although the path is practically nonexistent. Return by retracing your steps.

Jasper Town & Around

Mina & Riley Lakes Loop

Duration 3 hours round-trip

Distance 9km (5.6 miles)

Difficulty Easy-moderate

Start/Finish Jasper-Yellowhead Museum

Elevation Change 160m (525ft)

Nearest Town Jasper (p145)

Transportation Bus/train

Summary A straightforward tramp to a trio of peaceful lakes that will give you a tantalizing taste of the scope of Jasper's surrounding wilderness.

A whole network of trails heads west from Jasper Town into the forest-covered foothills of the Athabasca Valley. Venture less than 1km (0.6 miles) into this lake-speckled mini-wilderness and you'll quickly leave the hustle and bustle of the townsite behind.

Considered a good first-day orientation hike, the Mina & Riley Lakes Loop leaves from the northwest corner of the Jasper-Yellowhead Museum parking lot. Following trail No 8, climb gently up behind the town before turning rather abruptly into the forest. Keep to the right at the next three junctions, heading west through a mixture of pine, fir and spruce trees until the path widens out into a man-made meadow and fire break.

After crossing the gravel Cabin Creek Rd, the route plunges quickly back into a thick forest sprinkled with stands of closely packed birch trees. Swampy **Lower Mina Lake** will appear within minutes on your left-hand side, a large pond guarded by ptarmigan and Barrow's goldeneye ducks. Just beyond is the larger **Upper Mina Lake**, where you'll often spot loons gliding across the green surface.

At the western edge of the lake, turn right and climb up and down some gentle hills to a second junction. Foot-sore first-timers can short-cut back to town here via trail No 8c. Old stalwarts, meanwhile, can descend the long hill down to **Riley Lake**, which glimmers ethereally with Pyramid Mountain framed behind it. The trail briefly skirts the moss-green edge of the lake before tracking back into the forest. Take a right at the next junction and ascend to Cottonwood Slough, which has open views over to the Roche Bonhomme. Continue east to the road, from where trail No 2 returns south to the museum parking lot.

Whistlers Summit

Duration 3½ hours one way

Distance 7.9km (4.9 miles)

Difficulty Difficult

Start Trailhead on Whistlers Rd

Finish Summit of Whistlers Mountain

Elevation Change 1280m (4125ft)

Nearest Town Jasper (p145)

Transportation Jasper Tramway Shuttle

Summary A long walk up a steep hill – with a wicked 360-degree view at the top.

If you're a peak bagger, this arduous climb through three different life zones to the top of Jasper's most visited summit – and a handy energy-refueling café – could be the lung-bursting wake-up call you've been waiting for. While most sane people get the tramway, there are always one or two masochistic maniacs punishing themselves on this 7.9km (4.9-mile) uphill slog.

To get to the trailhead, proceed 2.8km (1.7 miles) down Whistlers Rd to a short, unpaved spur road on the left, which dead-ends in a small parking lot. The hike begins in what is known as the montane life zone of the mountain, consisting of thick forest and healthy aspen growth but, within 2km (1.2 miles), your uphill endeavors will be rewarded with a rich display of colorful wildflowers. Progressing up toward the tree line, the crippling switchbacks ease momentarily as you pass underneath the midpoint tower of the **Jasper Tramway** at approximately 1640m (5380ft) of elevation.

Above the tree line the landscape becomes ever more stony and barren, with eagle-eye views of the Athabasca Valley and Jasper Town unfolding like a satellite map beneath you. For the final 1.5km (0.9 miles), from the tramway's upper terminal to the top, you should have plenty of company as annoyingly fresh tramway riders join in for the relatively undemanding dash for the 2466m (8088ft) **summit**. The stupendous

Whistlers Summit

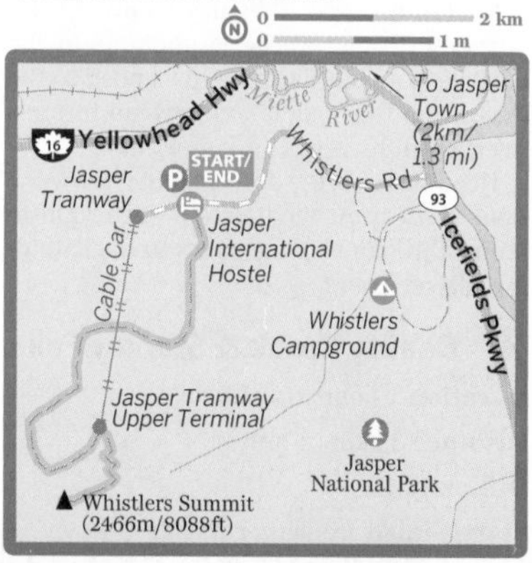

views of lake-speckled valleys and row after row of endless snow-coated peaks are spellbinding.

Maligne Lake Area

Mary Schäffer Loop

Duration 45 minutes round-trip

Distance 3.2km (2 miles)

Difficulty Easy

Start/Finish Maligne Lake parking lot

Elevation Change Negligible

Nearest Facilities Maligne Lake area (p147)

Transportation Maligne Lake Shuttle

Summary View the lake through the eyes of one of Jasper's earliest 'tourists' on this easy waterside ramble.

Following the eastern shoreline of Maligne Lake before dipping into the surrounding forest, this trail gives you a chance to take in the view seen by the first European explorer to cross this body of water. When Mary Schäffer stepped off her raft in 1908, she wrote, 'There burst upon us…the finest view any of us had ever beheld in the Rockies.'

To reach the **Mary Schäffer viewpoint**, follow a paved, wheelchair-accessible path past **Curly's historic boathouse** for about 800m (0.5 miles) to where a quartet of informative signs tell the story of the lake's early-20th-century 'discovery.' Beyond the lookout, the trail continues inland through a spruce, pine and fir forest, with copious roots underfoot barring any further access to wheelchairs and strollers. After passing through a meadow, stay left at two junctions.

Along this path you'll see **kettles**, which are giant depressions left by glacial ice trapped beneath sand and silt. At the third junction, head right to return to the boathouse.

Moose Lake Loop

Duration 45 minutes round-trip

Distance 2.6km (1.6 miles)

Difficulty Easy

Start/Finish Maligne Lake parking lot

Elevation Change Negligible

Nearest Facilities Maligne Lake area (p147)

Transportation Maligne Lake Shuttle

Summary Escape from the crowds on this short, but surprisingly untrampled, path, which leads to a tranquil lake renowned for its moose sightings.

Offering a quick escape from the Maligne Lake hordes, this short, easy loop delivers you to a gorgeously placid lake framed by craning trees and embellished by the glacier-chiseled summit of Samson Peak. A moose sighting along the trail is another distinct possibility.

The trail starts in the parking lot at the end of the Maligne Lake Rd and follows the Bald Hills fire road for the first few hundred meters (approximately 300yd). Turn left at the first signpost and you'll quickly enter dense forest, with the lake and its attendant boat cruisers a distant memory.

This new path is the Maligne Pass Trail, but a left at the second junction will divert you in the direction of **Moose Lake** and, if you're extremely lucky, a glimpse of one of those giant Eeyores of the forest swimming, foraging or hanging out near the shoreline. Moose or no moose, the scenery here is lovely.

With your curiosity satisfied, head north through the woods to the western shore of Maligne Lake and back to the trailhead parking lot.

Opal Hills Loop

Duration 3 hours

Distance 8.2km (5.1 miles)

Difficulty Difficult

Start/Finish Maligne Lake parking lot

Elevation Change 500m (1640ft)

Nearest Facilities Maligne Lake area (p147)

Transportation Maligne Lake Shuttle

Summary A super-steep grunt up to the flower-filled meadows above Maligne Lake where you can lie amid a grassy wilderness admiring both flora and views.

The Opal Hills were named by explorer Mary Schäffer in the early 20th century for the gemlike brilliance of their extensive flower meadows, and the sight of them still billowing above Maligne Lake makes this steep hike (it gains 500m/1640ft of elevation over just 3km/1.9 miles) worth the dramatic energy expenditure. Note: the Opal Hills lie in an important woodland caribou habitat, meaning pets are banned from this trail.

From the parking lot at the northern end of Maligne Lake the hike starts by traversing a pleasant meadow. Turn left at two early path junctions (both exits for the easier Mary Schäffer Loop) and within no time at all you will be gasping your way up a steep, almost switchback-free ascent to a junction at 1.6km (1 mile), which is the start of the official loop. Most people turn right here and undertake the loop counterclockwise. The ascent continues a little less savagely through forest for another 1km (0.6 miles), depositing you serendipitously in a mountain meadow where the trail levels off and views open out over the lake (below) and the Bald Hills (opposite). Fork right along a short spur trail for the best lookout. Going back to the main trail, follow it round some grassy knolls and through wildflower meadows for 2km (1.2 miles) before dropping down relatively steeply through forest to the end of the loop. From here, retrace your steps down the steep 1.6km (1-mile) descent to the finish.

Beaver, Summit & Jacques Lakes

Duration 6-7 hours

Distance 24km (15 miles) round-trip

Difficulty Easy-moderate

Start/Finish Beaver Lake Picnic Area

Elevation Change 90m (300ft)

Nearest Facilities Maligne Lake area (p147)

Transportation Maligne Lake Shuttle

Summary This is one of the simplest 'long' hikes in the park thanks to its wide paths and minimal elevation gain, but the peek-a-boo views of nearby mountains are immense.

Three lakes and three turnaround options; this popular trail is flat (the elevation gain is negligible) but scenic with decent views of the Colin and Queen Elizabeth mountain ranges opening out around the lakes. The hike is also notable for its accessibility year-round; in winter it becomes a cross-country ski trail and in autumn, thanks to its lower altitude, it remains doable long after other paths have been snowed under.

From the start point at the southern end of Medicine Lake the trail progresses along a wide dirt track (an old fire road), past some horse stables, to **Beaver Lake** at the 1.6km (1-mile) mark, a small body of water popular with fishermen and birdwatchers. Hike along the lake's west shore with views of the craggy limestone cliffs of the Queen Elizabeth Range to your right. The foot traffic drops off noticeably as you approach the **First Summit Lake** at 4.8km (3 miles). Follow the eastern shore and in 1.2km (0.8 miles) you'll reach **Second Summit Lake**, where the trail can be muddy after rain thanks to heavy horse traffic. The valley swings due east at this point and the path enters denser forest on its journey to **Jacques Lake**, 5.2km (3.3 miles) away. This lake is the turnaround point for most day hikers, although there is a campground at its eastern end. Fishing is not permitted. Beyond here, the path continues along the epic Southern Boundary Trail, 164 more kilometers (102 miles) of eerie isolation.

North of Jasper Town

Sulphur Skyline

Duration 3 hours round-trip

Distance 8km (5 miles) round-trip

Difficulty Moderate-difficult

Start/Finish Miette Hot Springs parking lot

Elevation Change 700m (2297ft)

Nearest Facilities Miette Hot Springs (p148)

Transportation private

Summary A short, rarely dull hike that delivers spectacular views from a ridge high over one of Jasper's more remote corners.

Two hikes lead out from Miette Hot Springs: a pleasant ramble along the Sulphur River to Sulphur Pass at the start of the backcountry Fiddle River Trail, or this energetic scramble up to the 2050m (6724ft) Sulphur Skyline.

The fickle weather is notorious on this hike and hot sun and thunderstorms can hit in the same afternoon; travel prepared for either eventuality. The hike starts innocuously enough at Miette Hot Springs on a wide, paved, sometimes crowded, path, which is also the start of a longer hike to Mystery Lake. Ascend gradually and watch as the path narrows to a single track within 1km (0.6 miles). At the 2.2km (1.4-mile) mark at the Shuey Pass Junction, turn right and begin the real climb. Over the next 1.8km (1.1 miles) you'll gain 400m (1312ft) of elevation as the trail switchbacks through scattered forest and grassy slopes. Miraculously, the earlier crowds drop off to just a handful. At the tree line look out for a giant white boulder left over from an erstwhile glacier. From here it's not far to the **summit** (4km/2.4 miles from the start), where a sea of mountaintops awaits. Look out for Utopia Mountain due west and the distinctive shape of Pyramid Mountain to the northwest. To the south lies the Fiddle River, gradually disappearing off into remote backcountry.

OVERNIGHT HIKES

Jasper has a huge backcountry, most of it pretty lightly trodden even in peak season, and the most popular multiday hike – the Skyline Trail – is considered one of the best in the nation. If the park has a weakness, it's the lack of overnight trips starting and finishing at the same point. The Saturday Night Lake Loop (described here as a bike trip) is one of the better options on this score and can easily be hiked over two days overnighting at one of three backcountry campgrounds.

The hiking chart on p34 provides a quick overview of all the backcountry hikes covered in this section.

Skyline Trail

Duration 2 days one way

Distance 45.8km (28.7 miles)

Difficulty Moderate-difficult

Start Maligne Lake

Finish Maligne Canyon

Nearest Facilities Maligne Lake area (p147)

Transportation Maligne Lake Shuttle

Summary Enjoy challenging terrain and splendiferous views on what is, quite simply, one of the most rewarding backcountry hikes in Canada.

The crème de la crème of backcountry hiking in the Canadian Rockies, the Skyline Trail is a North American classic that hovers on or above the tree line for nearly 46 serendipitous kilometers (28.5 miles). Some hikers spread the expedition over three days, others tackle it in two, while the odd gung-ho trail runner has been known to knock it out in just one. But don't get too ambitious. With a notable lack of trees and little natural shelter en route, the Skyline is notoriously open to the elements and fickle weather has taken the wind out of many an experienced hiker's sails.

A good, comfortable overnight option for two-day hikes is to reserve a room at the historic Shovel Pass Lodge (see the boxed text, p159) at the halfway point. Alternatively, there are half-a-dozen backcountry campgrounds en route (campfires are prohibited, though), and for a comfortable three-day outing you could camp at Snowbowl and Tekarra Campground, leaving the final descent for the third morning. Transportation to both trailheads is easy via the Maligne Lake Shuttle (p173).

DAY 1: MALIGNE LAKE TRAILHEAD TO SHOVEL PASS LODGE

7 HOURS, 20.4KM (12.6 MILES)

For this walk most hikers start at the Maligne Lake trailhead and follow the Lorraine and Mona Lakes Trail through the woods for the first 5km (3.1 miles). Beyond the turnoff for Mona Lake, switchbacks leave the trees behind, passing Evelyn Creek Campground – keep right at the junction – and bringing you into meadows. Upon the slopes of Maligne Range, **Little Shovel Pass**, at 10.2km (6.3 miles), gives you views back over Maligne Lake and to the gray Queen Elizabeth Range, to the east.

From here the trail dips down into the **Snowbowl**, a lush if somewhat boggy meadow crisscrossed with streams and stretching 7.3km (4.5 miles) along the Maligne Range. Snowbowl Campground is at 11.8km (7.3 miles).

At the end of the Snowbowl, a short climb brings you up to **Big Shovel Pass**, which has more great views. Keep left at the junction, continuing northwest for 2.1km (1.3 miles) and taking the trail left to Curator Campground and **Shovel Pass Lodge**.

DAY 2: SHOVEL PASS LODGE TO MALIGNE CANYON HOSTEL

8 HOURS, 25.2KM (15.6 MILES)

Begin the day with a brisk climb up to the tiny **Curator Lake**, which is surrounded by vast, windswept terrain. The trail becomes steep as it climbs to **The Notch**. At 2510m (8733ft), this is the high point of the trail,

Jasper Skyline Trail

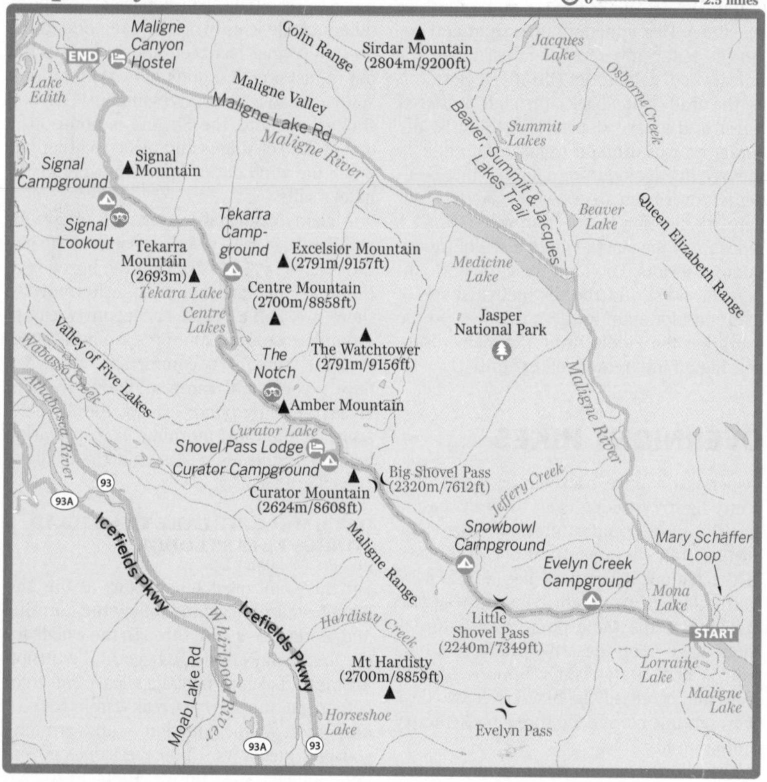

with breathtaking views along the Athabasca Valley and, if you're lucky, all the way to Mt Robson in the northeast. Continue on to the summit of **Amber Mountain**, below which the trail switchbacks down to **Centre Lakes**, with the sentinel Centre Mountain to the northeast. The trail heads through a small valley to **Tekarra Lake** and then follows around the north side of Tekarra Mountain, amid the first trees you'll have seen all day. Tekarra Campground lies at 11.3km (7 miles), between the peaks of its namesake and Excelsior Mountain.

Coming back out of the trees, you'll have views of Pyramid Mountain to the northwest and the Roche Bonhomme to the north. It's worth taking the short detour left at 16.9km (10.5 miles) to **Signal Lookout** for even better views. Signal Campground is just beyond this junction, and from here the old fire road descends through the forest to Maligne Canyon Hostel.

Tonquin Valley

Duration 2-3 days round-trip

Distance 53.2km (33 miles)

Difficulty Difficult

Start/Finish Marmot Basin Rd

Nearest Facilities Icefields Parkway (p142)

Transportation Private

Summary A true wilderness experience, hiking through archetypal Jasper terrain with the crenellated Ramparts glowering in the background.

Wildlife, lush meadows, sparkling lakes and gorgeous views make the roadless Tonquin Valley a mecca for hikers and horseback riders alike. The valley's crowning glory is the Ramparts, a collection of 10 peaks that tower like giant Gothic fortresses over the network of backcountry trails. According to

BACKCOUNTRY HUTS & LODGES

Jasper offers half-dozen-or-so huts and lodges modeled on the European alpine tradition. All situated a good day's hike from the nearest road, these venerable backcountry retreats offer a unique wilderness experience without the hassle of tent erection or listening to strange noises go 'bump' in the night.

Huts

The Alpine Club of Canada maintains three rustic backcountry huts in Jasper National Park. For each hut, you must bring your own bedding, food, matches, toilet paper and dishcloth, and must pack out all of your garbage. Reservations (C$36) are required and can be made through the **Alpine Clubhouse** (☎403-678-3200; www.alpineclubofcanada.ca) in Canmore. You are also required to have a Parks Canada wilderness pass.

Wates-Gibson Hut (Map p140; Tonquin Valley) This hut is a beautiful log cabin built in 1959 with a wood-burning stove, sleeping mattresses (C$30/24 in summer/winter) and a propane-powered cooking system (utensils available). In summer you can hike here via the 18km (11.2-mile) Astoria River Trail from the Mt Edith Cavell International Hostel (p167). Add on another 12km (7.5 miles) in winter when the Mt Edith Cavell Rd is closed.

Mt Colin Centennial Hut (Map p140; Colin Range) Used mainly by climbers, this six-bed hut is accessed by a demanding six- to eight-hour hike off the Overlander Trail. It has a Coleman stove, mattresses and cooking utensils, and is closed in winter.

Sydney Vallance (Fryatt) Hut (Map p140) This 12-bed hut, situated 24km (15 miles) up the Fryatt Valley from the Icefields Parkway, is perhaps the most isolated hut and was given a complete renovation in 1999. It's open year-round and facilities include propane cooking and lighting and a wood-heating stove.

Lodges

In Tonquin Valley, **Tonquin Amethyst Lake Lodge** (Map p140; ☎780-852-1188; www.tonquinadventures.com) and **Tonquin Valley Backcountry Lodge** (Map p140; ☎780-852-3909; www.tonquinvalley.com; r C$160, incl meals) provide rustic accommodations in historic cabins with views of the lake and Ramparts, approximately 24km (15 miles) from the nearest road. Both lodges run multiday horseback riding treks in summer; in winter you can cross-country ski to the lodges.

Built in 1921 and rebuilt in 1991, the **Shovel Pass Lodge** (Map p158; ☎780-852-4215; www.skylinetrail.com; r C$170), situated halfway along the emblematic Skyline Trail (p157), is the oldest lodge in the park. Boasting seven guest cabins plus a main chalet and dining room, the lodge can accommodate up to 18 people. Meals, bed linen and propane lights and heating are provided, though you'll have to bring your own towel. The price includes accommodations, three meals and transportation of up to 6.8kg (15lb) of gear (by horse). Three-day horseback riding treks are also available. It's open June to September; reserve well in advance.

First Nations people, they harbor supernatural spirits.

The trail begins from Marmot Basin Rd, off Hwy 93A and about 16km (10 miles) south of Jasper Town. While there is a shorter, less-grueling approach to Amethyst Lakes from the south, this route is far more scenic.

The hike to Amethyst Campground is a full day's hike; you can break the journey by staying at one of the two campgrounds en route, or stretch it to a three- or four-day trip by continuing along one of the trails from Amethyst Lakes. Campfires are not permitted at any of the campgrounds.

From Marmot Basin Rd, the trail follows **Portal Creek** southwest and climbs into the **Portal**, a narrow canyon amid the Trident Range. The path crosses large rockslides beneath Peveril Peak and then descends into a forested valley. A gradual climb takes you past Portal Campground and up toward **Maccarib Pass** at 11.7km (7.3 miles). As you ascend above the tree line, you can't help but notice Oldhorn Mountain to the south.

Beyond the pass, you begin your descent into the meadowland of **Tonquin Valley** with ever-impressive views of the Ramparts to the west. Maccarib Campground is next to a small creek at 17.8km (11 miles). The trail heads southwest for 6km (3.7 miles) to the northern shore of the glistening **Amethyst Lake**. At the junction, head right if you've reserved a bed at **Tonquin Valley Backcountry Lodge** (see the boxed text, p159), or continue along the shoreline to Amethyst Campground at 26.6km (16.5 miles). On still days, the water reflects the snow-cloaked Ramparts like a mirror.

Either pack up camp the following day and make the return journey along the same route or, if you have the time, spend a day exploring around Amethyst Lakes before heading back to the trailhead on the third day.

BIKING

Jasper is well known for its extensive network of multipurpose trails fanning out from the central hub of Jasper Town, including some fantastic singletrack. Cyclists experience few limitations here – in contrast to more rule-ridden US national parks – resulting in some of the most scenic, varied and technically challenging rides in North America. An excellent trail map highlighting cycling routes is available from the Jasper Information Centre and most hotels. Bears are prevalent in the park, so ride with caution. The season runs from May to October.

Rentals

If you didn't bring your own bike, you can easily rent a top-notch machine from a number of different outlets. Prices start at C$12/24/32 per hour/three hours/day for front-suspension mountain bikes.

Jasper Source for Sports (Map p144; www.jaspersports.com; 406 Patricia St) and **Vicious Cycle** (Map p144; www.viciouscyclecanada.com; 630 Connaught Dr; ⏲9am-6pm) are recommended options.

Freewheel Cycle BIKE SHOP
(Map p144; www.freewheeljasper.com; 618 Patricia St; ⏲9am-10pm) Freewheel also rents chariots to pull young children (C$24 per day).

Athabasca River Valley Loop

Duration 3 hours round-trip

Distance 18km (11.2 miles)

Athabasca River Valley Loop

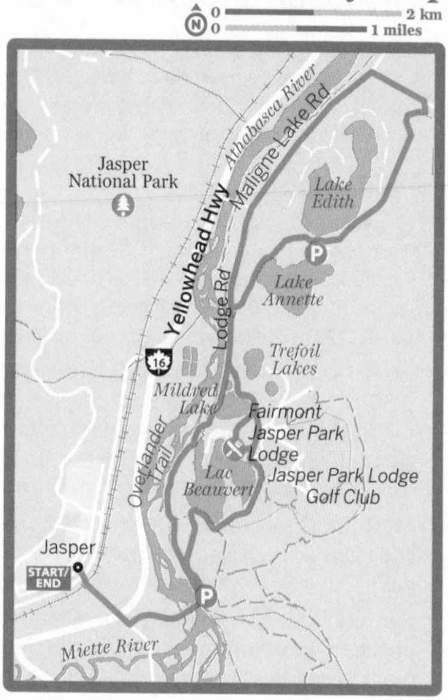

Difficulty Easy

Start/Finish Jasper

Nearest Town Jasper (p145)

Summary A paved but traffic-light sojourn around the verdant Athabasca River Valley that should whet your appetite for further biking adventures elsewhere.

If you're looking for a safe, flat family bike ride, or just prefer the certainty of a paved road to singletrack, this 18km (11.2-mile) spin around three luminous lakes on the southeast side of the Athabasca River Valley is an ideal option.

Start by tracking south from Jasper Town on Hwy 93A, crossing both the railway line and busy Hwy 16 before turning left into Old Fort Rd. Follow the road east down to a narrow bridge across the Athabasca River and past the Old Fort trailhead. Another 1km (0.6 miles) further on you'll come to the shores of beautiful **Lac Beauvert** with the **Fairmont Jasper Park Lodge** perched on its opposite shoreline. Circumnavigate the lake via the scenic golf course – listening out for shouts of 'fore!' – to the lodge itself, which is well worth closer inspection, before proceeding past the entrance gate and branching off onto the **Lake Annette**

Rd. With its picnic tables, small beach and paved **lake loop**, this is a great place for lunch. Almost adjacent to Lake Annette is **Lake Edith**, and an old road, now closed to cars, leads along its south shore. Ultimately this will bring you out onto the busier Maligne Lake Rd. Turn left here and speed back to the Jasper Park Lodge Rd at 3.2km (2 miles), where you can either retrace your route or tack onto trail No 7 (the Overlander Trail) back to Old Fort Point and – ultimately – Jasper Town.

Saturday Night Lake Loop

Duration 3-4 hours

Distance 27.4km (17 miles)

Difficulty Moderate-difficult

Start/Finish Jasper

Nearest Town Jasper (p145)

Summary An interesting technical ride through a root-ridden and sometimes swampy forest with plenty of nature-watching opportunities and half a dozen quiet unspoiled lakes.

If Jasper lacks one thing, it is long-distance loop trails, which makes this rollercoaster jaunt all the more satisfying. Even better, it begins and ends in the townsite, yet never feels particularly close to civilization. Sometimes erroneously called the 20-mile loop (it's nearer 27km/17 miles), the trail is numbered 3, gains 540m (1771ft) in elevation and never rises above the timberline. There are some tough technical stretches in the middle part of the ride involving mud, roots and short steep descents.

From the center of Jasper follow Patricia St southwest to Patricia Cres. Turn right at the T-junction and the trailhead is on your left. Proceeding counterclockwise around the loop means you save the best descents till last, so take the right-hand No 3 option and follow the switchbacks out of town up onto the Pyramid Bench. A little over 1km (0.6 miles) of climbing brings you to the end of the dirt Cabin Lake Rd at the eastern end of **Cabin Lake**. From here take the single track along the lake's northeast shore and begin a gradual wooded ascent to smaller **Saturday Night Lake**, 4.3km (2.7 miles) distant (a 400m/437yd spur trail leads off the main trail to the lake and its campground). The going gets tougher for the next 9km to 10km (5 to 6 miles) with muddy, swampy sections along the base of the Victoria Cross Range interspersed with some narrow creek crossings and plenty of tree roots. The trail begins to loop back east at the 11.5km (7.2-mile) mark at a log bridge at the bottom of

WORTH A TRIP

THE DESOLATE NORTH

Steal a glance at a map of Jasper National Park and you'll see that the whole area to the north of east–west Hwy 16 is almost blank. Although this extensive zone comprises over one-third of the park's total area, it contains no roads, no facilities and warrants virtually no mention at all in any of the standard park literature. So, what's the story?

Covered in a dense mountainscape, Jasper's north is a rugged pastiche of bugs, bogs and roaming caribou where the infrastructure begins and ends in a handful of primitive campgrounds. For the curious and brave, this is backcountry of the highest order, where you're often three or four days' walk from civilization, and a week or more can pass without seeing another hiker. The only serviceable path through the region is the mythical **North Boundary Trail**, 192km (120 miles) of brooding backcountry speckled with 20 primitive campgrounds. Long stretches of shadowy forests and mosquito-infested marshes are juxtaposed with reaffirming highlights, such as misty **Snake Indian Falls**, the glacial intensity of **Berg Lake** and the meadowed magnificence of **Snake Indian Pass**. If you hike east–west starting at Celestine Lake, 53km (33 miles) northeast of Jasper Town, you'll save the best part until last: the dramatic north face of **Mt Robson** rising like an impregnable wall above Berg Lake.

Although lightly trafficked, the North Boundary trail is well-maintained and all river crossings have rudimentary bridges. The hike is unusual in that it runs east–west rather than tracking the Continental Divide. It is generally tackled over eight to 12 days ending near Mt Robson on Hwy 16, 88km (55 miles) west of Jasper Town. Call in at the Jasper Information Centre for trail conditions and maps.

a waterfall. Just beyond here is High Lakes and the second campground (the trail is also a popular two- to three-day hike). You'll be descending now over roots and rocks past Minnow Lake, whereupon things settle down to a smoother pace to **Caledonia Lake**, a peaceful pond amid the trees. Fork left at the trail junction just past the lake and continue for 4km (2.4 miles; passing Marjorie Lake) back to the start point in Jasper Town.

Valley of the Five Lakes

Duration 3 hours round-trip

Distance 27km (17 miles)

Difficulty Difficult

Start/Finish Jasper

Nearest Town Jasper (p145)

Summary The holy grail for Jasper cyclists, riders travel from far and wide to test their mettle on this tough but scenic two-wheeled odyssey.

A hair-raising but gloriously scenic spin through the attractive Athabasca Valley to five turquoise mountain lakes, this trail has it *all,* including sweeping singletrack, bone-rattling rocks and roots, sudden downhills and tough, technical inclines. No wonder serious cycling junkies rate it as one of the best off-road rides in North America.

Accessible via trail No 1, which cuts around the back of Old Fort Point, Valley of the Five Lakes is popularly tackled as an out-and-back trip from Jasper Town. Linking up with trail No 9 after 2km (1.2 miles), the ride gathers pace with a narrow but nontechnical path meandering seamlessly through quiet tracts of sun-dappled forest to the lakes themselves, approximately 10km (6.2 miles) to the south. With **Lake 1** in sight things start to get hairy and, if you can make it around all five of these bejeweled watery havens without getting off to push (at least once), consider yourself an aficionado.

After looping around **Lake 4** with its resident loons and shimmering emerald coloration, the trail winds up at a crossroads that offers bikers three distinct options. The first is to double back on the opposite side of the lakes and link up again with trail No 9 for a return ride to Jasper. The second is to cross the plank bridge over the **Wabasso Creek Wetlands** and make for the trailhead and parking lot on Hwy 93. The third is to head south toward **Wabasso Lake** and a second Hwy 93 trailhead 9km (5.6 miles) away. Look out for wildlife if you elect to follow this last trail, and be particularly aware of bears and deer.

OTHER ACTIVITIES

Got any energy left tired hiker/biker/driver? Thought so! Read on...

White-Water Rafting & Float Trips

Charging rivers course their way through Jasper National Park. The Athabasca and Sunwapta Rivers are the two most utilized by rafters, who travel mainly on organized trips. The Athabasca has class II rapids meaning it's considered family-friendly and will give you more enjoyment than stress. The word 'Sunwapta' means 'turbulent river' in the Stony First Nations language, hinting at tougher challenges. The rapids are rated III here (on a scale of I to VI), meaning some previous experience is recommended. The rafting season is from mid-May to the end of September. Prices are pretty generic, costing C$59/89 for the Athabasca/Sunwapta Rivers for three- to four-hour trips with transportation.

Maligne Rafting Adventures Ltd RAFTING
(Map p144; ☎780-852-3370; www.raftjasper.com; 616 Patricia St, Jasper Town) Lots of options including paddle rafting, overnight trips and float trips.

Raven Adventures RAFTING
(Map p144; ☎780-852-4292; www.ravenadventure.com; 610 Patricia St, Jasper Town) Run out of a popular equipment store in Jasper Town.

Jasper Raft Tours RAFTING
(Map p144; ☎780-852-2665; www.jasperrafttours.com; 604 Connaught Dr, Jasper Town; adult/child C$55/15) Specializes in family-orientated trips on the milder Athabasca River with favorable rates for kids.

Boating

The Athabasca Valley is speckled with hidden lakes and misty ponds, most of which allow rowboats, kayaks and canoes. Of the bodies of water around Jasper Town, Pyramid Lake is the most popular spot, an oasis of tranquility caught in the distinctive shadow of Pyramid Mountain. As the largest lake in the Canadian Rockies, Maligne Lake offers visitors the archetypal Jasper experience.

Pyramid Lake Boat Rentals BOATING
(Map p140; www.pyramidlakeresort.com; Pyramid Lake Rd) Pyramid Lake Boat Rentals has canoes, rowboats, kayaks and paddleboats for hire.

Maligne Lake Boathouse CANOEING, KAYAKING
(www.malignelake.com; canoes & rowboats per hr/day C$30/90, kayaks C$35/100) To escape the crowds and get a bit of arm-powered exercise, head to the vintage Maligne Lake Boathouse, first opened in 1928 by the charismatic Donald 'Curly' Phillips, for canoe or kayak rental. For longer backcountry kayaking trips on the lake, it is possible to overnight in the lakeside Fisherman's Bay (four-hour trip) and Coronet Creek (six-hour trip) campgrounds. Camping passes and reservations are necessary for both.

Fishing

Fishing is popular throughout the park, with both locals and visitors. Waters frequented by anglers include Celestine, Princess, Maligne and Pyramid Lakes – though there are many smaller nooks.

Fishing is permitted in these lakes as well as many of the park's other lakes and rivers, including parts of the Athabasca, Maligne and Miette Rivers, as long as you are in possession of a valid permit (day/year C$9.80/C$34.30). Most of these waters are only open for short seasons, and many others are closed throughout the year. Visit the Parks Canada website or drop into one of its offices for opening dates and fishing restrictions.

Maligne Tours FISHING
(Map p144; www.malignelake.com; 616 Patricia St, Jasper Town; half-/full day per person from C$199/249; ⏲May-Sep) Maligne Tours will guide you around Maligne Lake in search of rainbow and eastern brook trout.

On-Line Sport & Tackle FISHING
(Map p144; 600 Patricia St, Jasper Town) Rents gear, teaches fly-fishing and runs lots of fishing trips, including 10-hour marathons.

Climbing

Because of its preponderance of sedimentary rock, Jasper doesn't draw as many ambitious rock climbers as other Rockies hotspots, such as Canmore. The advantage of this is relative solitude. Located up the trail from Fifth Bridge, off Maligne Lake Rd, Rock Gardens is the most popular crag and has the easiest approach. A more recent addition is Lost Boys, 'discovered' in 1994 and situated 25km (15.5 miles) south on Hwy 93A from the junction with Hwy 93. From the parking spot it's a 20-minute hike in to the quartzite crag. For climbers with experience (and preferably a guide), Mt Edith Cavell offers incredible vistas for climbers, while Ashlar Ridge and Morro Ridge are strictly the terrain of the experts.

Peter Amann ROCK CLIMBING
(☎780-852-3237; www.incentre.net/pamann) Peter Amann can introduce you to the art of rock climbing with two-day beginner courses (C$250) and he also offers personal guiding courses. He also offers a very useful one-day course on mountain navigation, which costs C$120.

Gravity Gear ROCK CLIMBING
(Map p144; www.gravitygearjasper.com; 618 Patricia St, Jasper Town) If you already know what you're doing, Gravity Gear has all the equipment to get you to the summit.

Horseback Riding

With horseback riders sharing trails with hikers and bikers, Jasper trumps most other parks when it comes to equestrian adventures. Rival stables on either side of the Athabasca Valley ply routes around Lake Patricia and Lake Annette, while further afield stunning backcountry trips can be organized in the Tonquin Valley, Maligne Pass, Jacques Lake and Bald Hills. Permits and regulations apply.

Skyline Trail Rides HORSEBACK RIDING
(www.skylinetrail.com; rides per 2/4.5hr C$68/125) Leads daily scheduled rides, as well as overnight trips that include meals and accommodations.

Tonquin Valley Adventures HORSEBACK RIDING
(www.tonquinvalley.com) Specializes in rustic five-day jaunts around the Tonquin Valley, staying at the backcountry Tonquin Amethyst Lake Lodge; prices start at C$1250 per person, including meals and accommodations.

Watching Wildlife

With 69 different mammals, 277 species of bird and 16 amphibians and reptiles, your chances of spotting wildlife in Jasper National Park are pretty high. A trip down

Maligne Rd or Miette Hot Springs Rd may score you a bear, wolf or mountain-goat sighting, and elk tend to linger just south of Jasper Town, at the end of Hwy 93. About 0.5km (0.3 miles) north of Jasper Town, on the eastern side of the road, a salt lick is frequented by goats and sheep in summer.

Alpine Art-Eco Tours WILDLIFE WATCHING
(Map p144; ☎780-852-3709; www.alpineart.ca; Rocky Mountain Unlimited, 414 Connaught Dr, Jasper Town; half-day per person C$69) Runs year-round safaris in search of elk, grizzlies, moose and the like. In summer it takes in the wildflowers, and in winter you can hike along on snowshoes.

Jasper Adventure Centre WILDLIFE WATCHING
(Map p144; ☎780-852-5650; www.jasperadventurecentre.com; 604 Connaught Dr, Jasper Town; 3hr per adult/child C$55/27.50) Runs wildlife searches, with a chance to see animals up close through a spotting scope.

Walks & Talks Jasper WILDLIFE WATCHING
(Map p144; ☎780-852-4945; www.walksntalks.com; 626 Connaught Dr, Jasper Town; adult/child C$70/30) These guides will take you on a morning Birding & Wildlife Watch.

Ranger Programs

Whistlers Outdoor Theatre INTERPRETIVE PROGRAM
(Map p140; Whistlers Campground) Each summer, Parks Canada sponsors live theater and free family-geared interpretive programs at 9pm nightly at Whistlers Outdoor Theatre, 3km (1.8 miles) south of Jasper Town. Non-campers are welcome. Topics vary from bear tips to park history.

Friends of Jasper INTERPRETIVE PROGRAM
(Map p144; www.friendsofjasper.com; 415 Connaught Dr, Jasper Town) Friends of Jasper hosts a nightly historical walking tour at 7:30pm throughout the summer, leaving from the Jasper Information Centre. Groups are limited to 30 and tickets are available in advance from the information center. Other interpretive walks include a Saturday stroll in Pocahontas, departing at 2pm, and a Junior Naturalist program (5pm Wednesday to Sunday) for six to 10 year olds at the Whistlers Campground.

Occasional theatrical events take place during the evenings on the lawn outside the Jasper Information Centre.

Golf

Fairmont Jasper Park Lodge Golf Club GOLF COURSE
(Map p140; www.fairmontgolf.com/jasper; green fees C$115-180; ⏲mid-May–mid-Oct) Overlooking the shores of shimmering Lac Beauvert is one of the most prestigious courses on the continent. Designed in 1925 by Stanley Thompson, the 18-hole course is as stunning as it is challenging. There's also a driving range, and you can rent shoes and clubs.

Skiing & Snowboarding

Marmot Basin SKIING, SNOWBOARDING
(Map p140; www.skimarmot.com; Marmot Basin Rd; full-day pass adult/child C$72/58) Jasper National Park's only downhill ski area is Marmot Basin, which lies 19km (11.8 miles) southwest of town off Hwy 93A. Though not legendary, the presence of 86 runs and the longest high-speed quad chair lift in the Rockies mean Marmot is no pushover, and its relative isolation compared to the trio of ski areas in Banff means shorter lift lines.

On-site are some cross-country trails and a predictably expensive day lodge, but no overnight accommodations. Seriously cold weather can drift in suddenly off the mountains so dress with this is mind.

Cross-Country Skiing & Snowshoeing

True to its ethos of 'multipurpose trails for all,' many of Jasper's hiking and biking paths are given over to cross-country skiing and snowshoeing in winter. Trails track-set for classic and skate skiing are centered on three main areas. Close to Jasper Town you can try the 4.5km (2.8-mile) Whistlers Campground Loop or the 10km (6.2-mile) there-and-back Pipeline Trail sandwiched between Hwy 16 and the Miette River. Near Maligne Lake is the 10km (6.2-mile) round-trip Beaver and Summit Lakes Trail following a popular and scenic summer hiking route with little gradient; and the easy 2.3km (1.4-mile) Moose Lake Loop.

The third and most comprehensive track-set skiing area can be found on and around Hwy 93A, which is left unplowed in winter for 10.5km (6.5 miles) between the Meeting of the Waters picnic area and Athabasca Falls. Branching off this road is a trail to Moab Lake, or further north you can tackle the steep 11km (6.8-mile) unplowed Edith Cavell Rd skiable as far as Cavell Meadows.

For the more adventurous, there's cross-country skiing to the remote Tonquin Valley.

Other Winter Activities

Half of Jasper shuts down in winter; the other half just adapts and metamorphoses into something just as good (if not better) than its summertime equivalent. Lakes become skating rinks, hiking and biking routes become cross-country skiing trails, waterfalls become ice climbs, wildlife migrates to lower climes, and – last but by no means least – prices become far more reasonable.

There are two hotspots for outdoor skating. The Fairmont Jasper Park Lodge clears an area on Lac Beauvert in front of the hotel that is floodlit after dark. Another far better Zamboni-cleared oval is maintained on Mildred Lake on the other side of the hotel. Benches are set out here, spontaneous hockey games often erupt and free hot chocolate reinvigorates shivering bystanders. For a quieter more romantic skate under a full moon head up to Pyramid Lake, 6km (3.7 miles) northeast of the townsite. You can rent skates at **Jasper Source for Sports** (Map p144; 406 Patricia St, Jasper Town).

BACKCOUNTRY SKIING THE TONQUIN

Want a white-knuckle backcountry adventure without face-whitening risks? Look no further than the Tonquin Valley in winter when you can ski up frozen Portal Creek to Maccarib Pass before descending into a rampart-guarded wilderness for a couple of nights at the cozy backcountry Tonquin Amethyst Lake Lodge (see the boxed text, p159). By February, the Tonquin trail has been 'broken in' by other skiers, yet it remains inspiringly remote. Pushing the stress down further is the low avalanche risk (though *always* check ahead) and minimal bear paranoia. It's 22km (13.8 miles) from the Portal Creek trailhead to the lodge and then another 29km (18.1 miles) out again via the gorgeous Astoria River/Cavell Rd route. You can go it alone, or join a guided group with **Tonquin Valley Adventures** (www.tonquinadventures.com). The lodge has a two-night minimum stay in the winter – ideal for less frenetic side trips.

The area around Pyramid Bench is maintained for **winter hiking** (weather permitting). Along these trails you'll be sheltered by the woods and have a good chance of spotting wildlife. The Mina and Riley Lakes Loop (p153) is well-trodden most of the year by enterprising locals who include it in their early morning jogs.

Slightly less athletic is the iconic three-hour Maligne Canyon Ice-walk offered by **Jasper Adventure Centre** (www.jasperadventurecentre.com; adult/child C$55/25), a walk through a series of frozen waterfalls viewable from December to April. Extremists tackle these slippery behemoths with rappels and ice axes. **Gravity Gear** (Map p144; 618 Patricia St, Jasper Town) can rent equipment.

TOURS

Jasper Motorcycle Tours MOTORCYCLE TOURS
(www.jaspermotorcycletours.com) Runs chauffeured Harley Davidson sidecar tours around the park's main sights; they'll even dress you up in the full Canadian leather garb. Three-hour trips start at C$179 per person.

Maligne Tours BOAT TOURS
(Map p144; www.malignelake.com; 616 Patricia St, Jasper Town; ⌚high season 10am-5pm, operates May-Oct) Maligne Tours runs a lake cruise (adult/child C$55/27.50) that is the holy grail for most visitors intent on witnessing the much-photographed sight of Spirit Island with the craning Rockies stacked up in the background. Boats cruise down the lake up to eight times daily in the height of summer, but be warned – they're popular.

Snocoach GUIDED TOURS
(www.columbiaicefield.com; ⌚10am-5pm Apr-Oct) Operated by Brewster, Jasper's famous Ice Explorers enable visitors to get up close and personal with the massive Columbia Icefield (you can even walk on it, under supervision). Ninety-minute tours (adult/child C$49.95/24.95) leave from the Columbia Icefield Centre every 15 to 30 minutes in peak season. You are first taken a short distance by standard coach before transferring onto specialized Snocoaches that drive out across the ice. Dress warmly and wear good shoes. Tickets can be procured in the Icefield Centre or purchased online.

Sundog Tours SIGHTSEEING TOURS
(Map p144; ☎888-786-3641; www.sundogtours.com; 414 Connaught Dr, Jasper Town; ⏱8am-8pm) Offers sightseeing tours of the Maligne Valley (adult/child C$60/35) and a guided hike around Mt Edith Cavell (C$59/40). Other tours include Columbia Icefield (C$75/45) and half-day trips by train (C$95/55).

SLEEPING

Aside from its one historic lodge, Jasper has a pretty varied stash of hotels, motels, hostels, cabins, B&Bs and campgrounds. Notwithstanding, in July and August you'd be wise to make reservations a long way in advance. Jasper Town is the operations center for the park's various accommodation establishments, with a handful of economical hotels and a good smattering of privately run B&Bs. The park's biggest campground, Whistlers, is a veritable giant situated 3km (1.8 miles) to the south of town, while the region's rustic quintet of HI youth hostels provides cheap beds for travelers on a budget.

Reservations (☎877-737-3783; www.pccamping.ca) are taken for three Jasper campgrounds: Whistlers, Pocahontas and Wapiti. All other campgrounds operate on a first-come, first-served basis.

Icefields Parkway

Camping

Wabasso CAMPGROUND $
(Map p150; Hwy 93A; campsites C$21.50; ⏱Jun-Sep) Peaceful and remote, this campground is nevertheless located relatively near to sights and Jasper Town on quiet Hwy 93A. Despite having 228 sites (51 of these have electricity), the grounds are spread out and fairly private. Walk-in tent sites along the river are wooded and lovely. Amenities include hot water, flush toilets as well as wheelchair accessible sites. Wabasso is a good staging post for forays into the Tonquin Valley.

Honeymoon Lake CAMPGROUND $
(Map p150; Icefields Parkway; campsites C$15.70; ⏱Jun-Sep) With lake access, these rustic sites are fairly popular. Sites 26 to 28 are right next to the water, and the rest of the 35 sites are wooded and fairly large. Dry toilets and a water pump are the only home comforts, but the Sunwapta Fall restaurant is only 4km (2.4 miles) to the south.

Wilcox Creek CAMPGROUND $
(Map p150; Icefields Parkway; campsites C$15.70) At the park's southern tip on the Icefields Parkway at the trailhead to the Wilcox Pass hike, this 46-site campground has trees and privacy. Facilities are minimal with dry toilet, a water pump and payphones, but it is one of only two park campgrounds that are open year-round.

Columbia Icefield CAMPGROUND $
(Map p150; Icefields Parkway; tent sites C$15.70; ⏱mid-May–mid-Oct) While somewhat exposed to the elements, its 33 sites are relatively secluded from the parkway yet afford excellent glacier views. Facilities are limited to dry toilets and a water pump.

Jonas Creek CAMPGROUND $
(Map p150; Icefields Parkway; campsites C$15.70; ⏱mid-May–early Sep) The park's smallest campground has 25 sites. Unserviced and with no electricity or dump station, the place has a real backcountry feel, despite its location just off the Icefields Parkway.

Mt Kerkeslin CAMPGROUND $
(Map p150; Icefields Parkway; campsites C$15.70; ⏱late Jun-early Sep) Across from its towering namesake, this campground has 42 sheltered sites and is routinely overlooked. Facilities are limited to dry toilets and a water pump.

WHEN THERE'S NO ROOM AT THE INN

Jasper gets seriously busy in July and August, and finding a room on the spur of the moment can be extremely difficult. Fortunately, aside from the standard clutch of hotels, motels and campgrounds, Jasper Town – which has a permanent population of 4500 – has over 100 B&Bs in private houses. The **Jasper Home Accommodation Association** (www.stayinjasper.com) maintains an excellent website of inspected B&Bs inside the park, complete with descriptions, contact details and web links. Prices range from C$60 to C$150 in high season and facilities often include kitchenettes, private entrances and cable TV. Reserve ahead.

Lodging

Sunwapta Falls Resort RESORT $$$
(Map p150; ☎780-852-4852; www.sunwapta.com; Icefields Parkway; r C$229-239; ⊙May-Oct; 🐾) This handy pit-stop on the Icefields Parkway has recently upped the bar by refurbishing its comfortable wooden lodge rooms, suites and hideaways with classy modern appliances befitting of a townsite hotel. The resort is cocooned in pleasant natural surroundings near the eponymous falls and also has a small shop and restaurant that's popular with the tour-bus crowd. You'll need wheels (two or four) if you're staying here.

Glacier View Inn HOTEL $$$
(Map p150; ☎877-423-7433; Columbia Icefield Centre, Icefields Parkway; r mountain view C$115-209, glacier view C$130-229; ⊙May-Oct) Forget the chalet tag, this rather businesslike hotel is on the 3rd floor of the Columbia Icefield Centre and offers exceptional views over the surrounding glaciers. But despite the rather plush and modern interior, the 32 rooms in the center lack character and, as a result, feel a little antiseptic. Your dinner options are also limited to the mediocre on-site restaurant (the next-nearest facilities are 108km/67 miles to the north). It's worth a sleepover if you're tired of driving, but two nights would be pushing it.

Athabasca Falls International Hostel HOSTEL $
(Map p150; ☎780-852-3215; www.hihostels.ca; Icefields Parkway; dm C$23-27; ⊙closed Tue Oct-Apr) A super-friendly hostel in the woods with an ingenious watering-can shower (summer only), a big, alpine-style kitchen-sitting area, table tennis and heated dorms in separate wooden cabins. There's no running water (just an outdoor pump) and the toilets are in outhouses, earning the place a 'rustic' tag.

Mt Edith Cavell International Hostel HOSTEL $
(Map p150; ☎780-852-3215; www.hihostels.ca; Icefields Parkway; dm C$23-27; ⊙mid-Jun–mid-Oct) Rustic with a capital R - don't expect basic luxuries such as flush toilets, running water or electricity here. However, you can draw strength from the knowledge that your small but congenial dorm sits pretty in the foothills of one of the Rockies' most sublime mountain peaks. Enjoy the scenery from the deck or the outdoor firepit, before retiring for the night to a communal cabin - and your snoring companions.

Beauty Creek International Hostel HOSTEL $
(Map p150; ☎780-852-3215; www.hihostels.ca; Icefields Parkway; dm C$23-27; ⊙Apr-Oct) Located only 87km (54 miles) south of Jasper and 17km (10.5 miles) north of the Columbia Icefield, Beauty Creek is a wilderness hostel that has no electricity or running water. Lights, stoves and heating are powered by propane, toilets are outside and water is from a well. If none of this whets your appetite, then the C$5 all-you-can-eat pancake breakfast with real Quebec maple syrup undoubtedly will. The hostel makes a great stopover for cyclists laboring along the Icefields Parkway.

Jasper Town & Around

Camping

TOP CHOICE **Wapiti** CAMPGROUND $
(Map p140; Hwy 93; campsites/RV sites C$27.40/32.30; ⊙year-round) In summer this campground has full facilities and fills up very quickly. All of its 362 sites are wooded; the ones that back onto the river are the most private. In winter only 93 sites remain open and facilities are limited to flush toilets. A 3km (1.8-mile) trail links this campground with Jasper Town.

Whistlers CAMPGROUND $
(Map p140; Whistlers Rd; campsites/RV sites C$22.50/32.30; ⊙early May–mid-Oct) Verging on a camping city, this huge campground supports an astounding 781 sites. A full list of amenities, including showers, wheelchair access and an interpretive program, keeps it packed throughout summer. Sites are wooded but not particularly private. The latest addition is a stash of canvas-walled 'cottage tents' (C$70) equipped with kitchen facilities, wooden beds and electricity, sleeping up to six people.

Lodging

TOP CHOICE **Park Place Inn** BOUTIQUE HOTEL $$$
(Map p144; ☎780-852-9770; www.parkplaceinn.com; 623 Patricia St; d C$229; ❄📶) Giving nothing away behind its rather ordinary exterior above a parade of downtown shops, the Park Place isn't really what you expect from a national park lodge. Exhibiting 14 luxurious rooms decked out in marble, fine art and fluffy bathrobes, the inn's self-proclaimed heritage tag is well earned, with an

JASPER NATIONAL PARK CAMPGROUNDS

CAMPGROUND	LOCATION	DESCRIPTION	NO OF SITES
Columbia Icefield	Icefields Parkway	Tents only and basic facilities, but campground is secluded and views are tremendous	33
Honeymoon Lake	Icefields Parkway	Small and quiet with some sites on lakeshore	35
Jonas Creek	Icefields Parkway	Close to highway with some seclusion if you choose the right site	25
Mt Kerkeslin	Icefields Parkway	Basic campground with sheltered sites close to Athabasca Falls	42
Wabasso	Icefields Parkway	Well-serviced but relatively remote campground off main highway and close to Mt Edith Cavell hikes	228
Wilcox Creek	Icefields Parkway	Close to Columbia Icefield Centre and Wilcox Pass trailhead	46
Wapiti	Jasper Town & Around	Offers 40 serviced sites and showers; numbers limited in winter	362
Whistlers	Jasper Town & Around	A mini-town with every facility imaginable; great for families	781
Pocahontas	North of Jasper Town	Quiet and wooded; close to eastern park entrance	140
Snaring River	North of Jasper Town	Rustic with no RVs; situated off highway 15km (9.5 miles) north of Jasper Town	66

Drinking Water *Flush Toilets* *Great for Families* *Grocery Store Nearby*

intimate atmosphere and professional yet friendly staff welcoming you as soon as you cross the threshold. The heftier price tag is worth every penny.

Patricia Lake Bungalows BUNGALOWS **$$$**
(Map p140; ☎780-852-3560; www.patricialakebungalows.com; Pyramid Lake Rd; ste/cabin C$155/214; ⏰May–mid-Oct; ❄@) Hidden in trees 400m (0.25 miles) off the Pyramid Lake Rd, and often overlooked, these choice bungalows could have been plucked innocently out of a quiet, upscale city suburb. Melting imperceptibly into the surrounding forest and located right next to the shores of placid Patricia Lake, the comfy abodes sleep up to six people and are equipped with kitchens, bathrooms, fireplaces and TVs. With a hot tub, playground, bike and boat rental and on-site laundry, the atmosphere is relaxed and family-oriented.

Athabasca Hotel HOTEL **$**
(Map p144; ☎780-852-3386; www.athabascahotel.com; 510 Patricia St; d C$159, without bathroom C$89; ❄@📶) Built in 1929, the Athabasca has a rather traditional English-pub feel downstairs, though stuffed animal heads quickly remind you that you're still definitely in Canada. Upstairs, small rooms are comfortable and well-equipped with sinks and TVs. Some of the rooms have (clean) shared bathrooms. Others are perched above a rather noisy nightclub. At the height of summer, this is one of the few places that might still be able to offer rooms at short notice.

Mt Robson Inn HOTEL **$$$**
(off Map p144; ☎780-852-3327; www.mountrobsoninn.com; 902 Connaught Dr; d C$229; ❄@📶) This hybrid Jasper motel-lodge on the west side of town spins no tricks with its facilities and service. Service is professional and the ambience congenial, upping the ratings of

ELEVATION	OPEN	RESERVATIONS NEEDED?	DAILY FEE	FACILITIES	PAGE
2012m (6600ft)	May-Oct	no	C$15.70		p166
1310m (4300ft)	Jun-Sep	no	C$15.70		p166
1500m (4920ft)	May-Sep	no	C$15.70		p166
1200m (3936ft)	Jun-Sep	no	C$15.70		p166
1125m (3690ft)	Jun-Sep	advisable Jul-Aug	C$21.50		p166
2012m (6600ft)	year-round	no	C$15.70		p166
1070m (3510ft)	year-round	advisable Jul-Aug	C$27.40		p167
1070m (3510ft)	May-Oct	advisable Jul-Aug	C$22.50		p167
1200m (3936ft)	May-Oct	advisable Jul-Aug	C$21.50		p170
1050m (3445ft)	May-Sep	no	C$15.70		p170

Restaurant Nearby *Payphone* *Summertime Campfire Program* *RV Dump Station*

its myriad rooms ranging from standards to suites. Communal facilities include two outdoor whirlpools and an on-site steakhouse.

Tekarra Lodge CABINS **$$$**
(Map p140; ☎780-852-3058; www.tekarralodge.com; Hwy 93A; 1/2 bedroom cabins C$249/279; ⊙mid-May–early Sep) The most atmospheric cabins in the park are set next to the Athabasca River, amid tall trees and splendid tranquility. Hardwood floors, wood-paneled walls, a fireplace and kitchenette inspire a warm, cozy feeling. You might only be a kilometer or two (1 mile) outside town but you'll feel as if you're far away.

Fairmont Jasper Park Lodge HOTEL **$$$**
(Map p140; ☎780-852-3301; www.fairmont.com; Old Lodge Rd; r C$449;) Jasper's 'parkitecture' classic is not as grand as its Banff and Lake Louise equivalents with much of the accommodation spread over outlying buildings, but the location on the quiet shores of Lac Beauvert still lends it a definable regal quality. Once the haunt of royalty, artists and members of the international jet set, the original lodge burned down in 1952 and was replaced by the current building, with its rather utilitarian underground shopping mall, the following year. Rambling across several hectares (7 acres), the outlying log cabins and cedar chalets offer wonderful views across the small lake and golf course, but tired furnishings and slightly wooden service don't always justify the astronomical price tag.

Pyramid Lake Resort RESORT **$$$**
(Map p140; ☎780-852-4900; www.pyramidlakeresort.com; Pyramid Lake Rd; r C$239-388; ⊙Apr-Oct;) Jasper's second-grandest lodge, after the Fairmont, is this tastefully renovated mini-resort perched on a knoll above placid Pyramid Lake. Despite the on-site bustle and

attendant pub, the amenity-packed rooms are quiet and have pleasant views of the lake. The top-end loft rooms come with kitchenettes and can sleep four. Overall, the resort is relatively deluxe, and value is added by its prime location and surprise extras (20% of boat rental, outdoor hot tub and gym).

Whistlers Inn HOTEL **$$**
(Map p144; ☎780-852-9919; www.whistlersinn.com; cnr Connaught Dr & Miette Ave; r C$195; @🛜≋) A central location and above-standard rooms give Whistlers an edge over many of its rivals. The rooftop hot tub alone is worth spending the night for – watch the sun dip behind the hills as the recuperative waters soak away the stress of the day. What more could you ask for?

Astoria Hotel HOTEL **$$$**
(Map p144; ☎780-852-3351; www.astoriahotel.com; 404 Connaught Dr; d from C$207; 🛜) With its gabled Bavarian roof, the Astoria is one of the town's most distinctive pieces of architecture and one of an original trio of Jasper hotels that has been owned by the same family since the 1920s. Journeyman rooms are functional and comfortable, and are bolstered by the presence of a downstairs bar (De'd Dog) and restaurant (Papa George's).

Sawridge Inn & Conference Centre HOTEL **$$$**
(Map p140; ☎780-852-6590; www.sawridgejasper.com; 76 Connaught Dr; d from C$269; ❄@🛜≋🐾) Yes, it's large and a little bit corporate but, on the face of it, Jasper (and the Sawridge) isn't such a bad place to organize a business conference – and many do. For all its slickness, the hotel has plenty of nooks to escape into plus an impressive plant-filled central atrium for more social animals. If you want smooth Edmonton-standard facilities to offset the ruggedness of the terrain outside, this could be your bag.

Jasper International Hostel HOSTEL **$**
(Map p140; ☎780-852-3215; www.hihostels.ca; Whistlers Rd; dm C$23-27) Jasper's most 'luxurious' hostel has hot showers, plenty of lounging space and a big kitchen. Large male/female dorms sleep up to 40 and there are private rooms for those looking for more privacy.

Jasper House Bungalows BUNGALOWS **$$**
(Map p140; ☎780-852-4535; www.jasperhouse.com; Hwy 98; d/ste C$160/195; @🛜) A quiet escape 3.5km (2.1 miles) south of Jasper Town on the Athabasca River, these alpine bungalows with all-wood interiors come in a variety of sizes, some with Jacuzzis and river-view balconies.

Maligne Lake Area

Maligne Canyon International Hostel HOSTEL **$**
(Map p140; ☎780-852-3215; www.hihostels.ca; Maligne Lake Rd; dm C$23-27) Well positioned for cross-country skiing and summer sorties along the Skyline Trail, this very basic hostel is poised a little too close to the road to merit a proper 'rustic' tag. Die-hards can get back to nature with six-bed dorms, outhouse toilets and regular visits to the water pump.

North of Jasper Town

Camping

Pocahontas CAMPGROUND **$**
(Map p140; Miette Hot Springs Rd; campsites C$21.50; ⊙mid-May–mid-Oct) Spacious and densely wooded, you'd never know this place has 140 sites. Facilities are minimal with flush toilets and wheelchair-accessible sites, though they're very well maintained.

Snaring River CAMPGROUND **$**
(Map p140; off Hwy 16; tent sites C$15.70; ⊙May-Sep) The park's most isolated and primitive campground is located 16km (9.9 miles) north of Jasper Town. There are 66 unserviced sites beside a river, along with a water pump and pit toilets.

Lodging

Miette Hot Springs Resort MOTEL, CABINS **$$**
(Map p140; ☎780-866-3750; www.mhresort.com; Miette Hot Springs Rd; motel/bungalows/cabins C$87/120/150) Right next to the bathhouse, wood is the binding theme at this low-key 'resort' that is situated in a collection of old-fashioned but charming cabins, bungalows and motel rooms dating from 1938 to the 1970s. Bungalows and cabins sleep up to six and some of the 17 motel rooms have kitchenettes. The adjoining restaurant has reasonably priced standard meals.

Pocahontas Cabins RESORT **$$**
(Map p140; ☎780-866-3732; www.mpljasper.com; cnr Hwy 16 & Miette Hot Springs Rd; cabins C$159-

245;) Once a thriving mining community, the settlement of Pocahontas now consists of this single cabin resort, equipped with a small restaurant, hot tub, outdoor swimming pool and small grocery store. The one- and two-bedroom cabins are relatively plush by park standards with hanging flower baskets and a clean refurbished feel. You can go up a notch by nabbing the luxury Cedar Lodge with private balcony and gas fireplace.

EATING

While Jasper's culinary scene is a long way from the bright lights of Calgary and Edmonton, budding gastronomes needn't starve. Outside of the small cluster of sterile fast-food franchises and the usual cache of post-hike refueling joints, fine diners can travel the world in cosmopolitan Patricia St, touching down in such exotic locales as Spain, Korea, Italy and Greece.

Icefields Parkway

Sunwapta Falls Resort AMERICAN $$

(Map p150; Icefields Parkway; lunch/dinner C$12/25; deli 11am-6pm, dining room 6-9pm May-Nov) One of the better tourist-orientated restaurant–gift shop combos on the Icefields Parkway, the Sunwapta does familiar ranch-style breakfasts and tasty salads, sandwiches and soups. Arrive early for lunch before the daily tour-bus invasion.

Columbia Icefield Centre Dining Room CAFETERIA $

(Columbia Icefield Centre, Icefields Parkway; snacks C$8-10, mains C$20; 8-10am & 6-9pm May-Oct) Fantastic views of Athabasca Glacier will likely keep you from noticing the lack of atmosphere in the Icefields Parkway eateries. The 2nd-floor dining room does breakfast, dinner and a buffet lunch. Handier is the hectic canteen (open 9am to 6pm April to October), good for hot dogs, noodles and other quickies.

Jasper Town & Around

TOP CHOICE **Bear's Paw Bakery** CAKES, PASTRIES $

(Map p144; www.bearspawbakery.com; 4 Cedar Ave; pastries C$3-5; 6am-6pm) The Bear's Paw is one of the best bakery-café combos west of Winnipeg, so thank your lucky stars it's situated here, just where you need it most at the end of an energy-sapping hike/bike/ski. Try any in a list of insanely addictive scones, cookies, muffins and foccacia-like breads. The coffee's equally gratifying. There's a second better positioned branch called **Other Paw Bakery** (610 Connaught Dr; 7am-6pm) opposite the train station.

Patricia Street Deli DELI $

(Map p144; 606 Patricia St; sandwiches C$5-9) The rule of thumb in a national park is simple no-nonsense North American food with minimal embellishment. After all, who comes on a hiking/fishing/rafting trip to hobnob with gastronomes over foie gras and champagne? All this accounts for the continuing success of the Patricia Street deli, where homemade bread is made into generously filled sandwiches by people who are just as generous with their hiking tips. Join the queue and satiate your ravenous backcountry appetite.

Co-Co's Café CAFÉ, BREAKFAST $

(Map p144; 608 Patricia St; breakfast C$4-7) Organic fair-trade coffee, vegan options, delicious breakfast wraps and fresh scones to write home about, Co-Co's is another popular Jasper wake-up call. Small, relaxed and trendy, it would get more recognition if it wasn't living in the shadow of the Bear's Paw.

Evil Dave's INTERNATIONAL $$$

(Map p144; 780-852-3323; www.evildavesgrill.com; 622 Patricia St; meals C$19-39; 4-11pm) One of two Jasper restaurants with claims on gastronomic status, Evil Dave's succeeds because it never strays too far from the well-worn basics – meatloaf, AAA Alberta steak and cheesecake – bolstered with some tasty creative twists.

Jasper Pizza Place PIZZERIA $$

(Map p144; www.jasperpizza.ca; 402 Connaught Dr; pizza from C$11; 11am-11pm) Loud, boisterous and seemingly disorganized, there's a method to the madness here if you're prepared to stick around long enough to fight for a table. While queuing for pizza might not be everyone's idea of an authentic wilderness experience, the food is surprisingly good when it finally arrives, and you can diversify with ribs, burgers and salad if your taste buds can't take any more cheese and tomato. Love it or hate it, it's a Jasper institution.

La Fiesta TAPAS $$

(Map p144; www.lafiestajasper.com; 504 Patricia St; tapas C$11-15; 11.30am-11pm) A tapas restaurant with a Mexican slant, this Mediterranean-styled place behind the Jasper Information Centre offers tasty tapatizers and tempting mains – if you ever get that far. Have fun mixing up a variety of tapas plates, including baked calamari, artichoke dip, grilled lamb and rosemary sausage, and tortilla-crusted chorizo and goat's cheese cakes. It's not particularly Spanish, but who cares?

Something Else GREEK, STEAKHOUSE **$$**
(Map p144; 621 Patricia St; mains C$13-24;) Essentially a Greek restaurant, Something Else wears many hats (American, Italian, Cajun etc) and doesn't always succeed. What it *is* good for is space (even on a Saturday night), decent beer, menu variety, copious options for kids and the good old homemade Greek stuff. Try the lamb or chicken souvlaki.

Cassio's Trattoria ITALIAN **$$**
(Map p144; 602 Connaught Dr; meals C$14-30; 7:30am-11pm) In the long-standing Whistlers Inn, the Cassio family concentrates on presenting *real* Italian fare – gnocchi, meatballs, veal masala, pasta marinara and a well-stuffed antipasto plate.

Papa George's AMERICAN **$$**
(Map p144; www.papageorgesrestaurant.com; 404 Connaught Dr; meals C$12-30; 7am-2pm & 5-10pm) Almost as old as the park, this stalwart has been in business since 1925 and something about the original rock fireplace, salt-of-the-earth service and know-what-you're-getting food still rings true.

Kimchi House KOREAN **$$**
(Map p144; 407 Patricia St; mains C$13-20; 11am-9.30pm) There aren't many opportunities to go Asian in Jasper, so jump on this one where sautéed seafood, deep-fried dumplings and seaweed arrive quickly amid minimalist decor.

Maligne Lake Area

The View Restaurant CAFETERIA **$**
(Map p149; Maligne Lake Lodge; snacks C$5-10; 9am-7pm May-Oct) A pricey cafeteria-style restaurant perched on the north shore of Maligne Lake offering the usual sandwich/soup combo plus above-average pastries, Nanaimo bars and cinnamon buns.

DRINKING & ENTERTAINMENT

Jasper Brewing Company BREWERY, PUB
(Map p144; www.jasperbrewingco.ca; 624 Connaught Dr; 11:30am-1am) The font of Jasper's après-hike scene is this unpretentious welcome-all brewpub with a good range of made-on-site Europhile beers, from Irish-style stout to English-inspired IPA. The food menu has a spicy Southern twist and is restaurant standard.

Atha-B Pub BAR, NIGHTCLUB
(Map p144; Athabasca Hotel, 510 Patricia St) Nightclubbing in a national park is about as congruous as wildlife viewing in West Edmonton Mall. Bear this in mind before you hit the Atha-B, a pub-slash-nightclub off the lobby of the Athabasca Hotel where mullets are still high fashion and the carpet's probably radioactive.

Downstream Bar BAR
(Map p144; 620 Connaught Dr; 4pm-late) A comfy pub that hosts open-mic sessions, jazz, blues or reggae.

Whistle Stop Pub PUB
(Map p144; cnr Connaught Dr & Miette Ave) Shock horror! You may actually meet a local as opposed to a tourist in this salt-of-the-earth pub attached to the Whistlers Inn.

Chaba Cinema CINEMA
(Map p144; 604 Connaught Dr) A cinema is a rarity in a Canadian national park, so make the most of the popcorn, pop and dating potential at this quaint two-screen affair.

SHOPPING

Stuffed bears, scented candles, flimsy trinkets and slogan-bearing T-shirts; shopping in Jasper is invariably of the incidental variety. If you're addicted to the ritual, Canada's largest mall lies four hours east in Edmonton. Sundog Tours runs daily bus shuttles.

Tangle Creek Gifts BOOKS, SOUVENIRS
(Map p144; 640 Connaught Dr) Sift through the tourist kitsch for books on local history and wildlife.

Totem Ski Shop OUTDOOR EQUIPMENT
(Map p144; 408 Connaught Dr) An outdoor outfitter selling everything from camping gear to topographical maps; it also rents ski gear and other supplies.

INFORMATION

Internet Access

Internet access is available in the park, primarily in Jasper Town. A growing number of hotels and cafés also offer free wi-fi. Try the following:

More Than Mail (Connaught Sq, Connaught Dr; per min C$0.10; ⏲9am-10pm)

Laundry

The best place to get your clothes washed is at **Coin-op Laundry** (607 Patricia St; ⏲9am-9pm Mon-Fri, 10am-9pm Sat & Sun), where you can also buy coffee and pastries.

Medical Services & Emergency

For emergencies dial ☎911. The 24-hour park warden can be contacted on ☎780-852-6155. For local hospitals, see p267.

Money

Most of your monetary needs can be dealt with by **CIBC** (416 Connaught Dr), next to Jasper Information Centre.

Post

Jasper maintains one bona fide **post office** (Map p144; 502 Patricia St).

Telephone

All park hotels, lodges and nonprimitive campgrounds have public phones. Courtesy phones (local calls only) are located in Jasper Information Centre. Cell (mobile) phone reception is patchy.

Tourist Information

Built in 1913, the attractive **Jasper Information Centre** (Map p144; ☎780-852-6176; www.parkscanada.ca; 500 Connaught Dr; ⏲9am-7pm summer, 9am-4pm winter) has maps, brochures and up-to-date trail information. Parks Canada is represented here and also has a desk at the **Columbia Icefield Centre** (⏲9am-6pm May-Oct), 103km (64 miles) south of Jasper Town on the Icefields Parkway.

Also in the Jasper Information Centre, **Jasper Tourism & Commerce** (www.jaspercanadianrockies.com) carries lots of brochures on accommodations and services within the park. **Friends of Jasper** (☎780-852-4767; www.friendsofjasper.com) also has a shop here with maps and specialist guides to the park. Proceeds from sales are reinvested via grants and volunteer services back into the park.

Websites

Head to **Lonely Planet** (www.lonelyplanet.com/canada/alberta/banff-and-jasper-national-parks) for planning advice, author recommendations, traveler reviews and insider tips.

GETTING THERE & AWAY

Most people arrive in Jasper by car, utilizing its three main roads that connect the park to Lake Louise (south), Edmonton (east) and British Columbia (west), but there also some good public transport options. **Greyhound** (www.greyhound.ca) buses connect daily from Vancouver via British Columbia, and Edmonton, while more comfortable Sundog Tours/Brewster buses serve Banff/Calgary and Edmonton daily year-round.

Bus

Sundog Tours (www.sundogtours.com; 414 Connaught Dr) runs a daily bus between Jasper and Edmonton International Airport (C$95/59). This service operates year-round. From October to May, Sundog runs another daily shuttle south along the Icefields Parkway to Calgary airport (adult/child C$129.95/64.95). The southbound bus departs Jasper at 1:15pm and arrives at Calgary airport at 9pm. The northbound bus leaves Calgary airport at 11:30am and arrives in Jasper at 6:25pm. Buses also stop in Lake Louise and Banff, where passengers must transfer to a Brewster bus for the final leg of the journey (price included in your ticket).

In the summer months (May to October), the entire Jasper–Calgary airport bus route is operated by **Brewster** (www.brewster.ca). This bus can stop at the Columbia Icefield Centre by prior arrangement. Check the website for schedules.

Train

The luxurious if pricey **VIA** (www.viarail.ca) train connects Jasper with Toronto to the east, and Vancouver to the west, stopping at numerous stations en route.

GETTING AROUND

Although most people get around the park by private vehicle, with a bit of patience and flexibility, carless travel is also possible.

Bicycle

With numerous bike outlets in Jasper, it's easy to rent a bike to get you around the town and its main sights (see p160). Alternatively, you can bring your own.

Fortuitously, the park also has one of the most extensive bike-trail networks in Canada. Wide highways with ample shoulders and strict speed limits make road biking easy. The truck-free Icefields Parkway south to Lake Louise and Banff is a particularly popular ride.

Bus

Brewster (www.brewster.ca) buses stop at the Columbia Icefield Centre daily in summer (May to October) on their Jasper–Banff run. **Sundog**

Tours (www.sundogtours.com) shuttles visit many areas of the park during summer, but to use them you'll have to sign up and pay for one of their sightseeing tours. See the website for details.

Maligne Lake Shuttle (www.malignelake.com; 616 Patricia St) runs a daily shuttle bus from Jasper Town to Maligne Lake (Maligne Lake/Maligne Canyon C$20/15, May to late September), stopping en route at the Fairmont Jasper Park Lodge, Maligne Canyon, the Skyline trailhead (north and south) and the Jacques Lake trailhead. The service runs four times daily in peak season.

The **Jasper Tramway Shuttle** (780-852-4056) runs a bus from the train station to the Jasper Tramway (C$36 including tramway ticket).

Car & Motorcycle

Jasper Town has a number of gas stations. Car rental is available at the VIA railway station with **Thrifty** (607 Connaught Dr; per day from C$49).

AROUND JASPER NATIONAL PARK

Jasper National Park is buffered by additional protected zones to the north and west (Banff National Park borders it to the south). To the west – and in British Columbia – is Mt Robson Provincial Park, home of the Canadian Rockies' highest summit and the headwaters of the mighty Fraser River, along with the roadless Hamber Provincial Park (accessible via the 35km/22-mile Fortress Lake Trail starting on Hwy 93). To the north and lying wholly within Alberta, the Willmore Wilderness Park lures travelers with a penchant for utter solitude.

Mt Robson Provincial Park

Bordering Jasper National Park in the west and flanked by the Selwyn Range, the drive through Mt Robson Provincial Park follows a historic pathway of fur traders. Rejected by the Canadian Pacific Railway as a route through the Rockies, it was later adopted by Grand Trunk Pacific and Canadian Northern Pacific Railways and is today a major railway route. The views of snowy mountains and glacial lakes are magnificent.

Bisected by Hwy 16 on its way between Jasper and Prince George, Mt Robson Provincial Park abuts Jasper National Park at the **Yellowhead Pass**, 24km (15 miles) west of Jasper Town. Covering 224,866 hectares (555,420 acres), the park's main hub is an excellent **information center** (250-566-4325; www.elp.gov.bc.ca/bcparks; 8am-5pm Jun & Sep, to 8pm Jul & Aug) near the western border. Here you can pick up trail information, register for hikes with BC Parks staff and take in exhibits on local geography and history – including a short interpretive trail. You'll also find a gas station and café situated next door. On clear days the neck-craning views of ice-glazed Mt Robson, glowering like a fiery beacon overhead, are truly amazing.

Sights & Activities

The tallest mountain in the Canadian Rockies, **Mt Robson** in British Columbia towers like a misplaced Everest over the surrounding peaks and valleys, dwarfing other rugged giants in its 3954m (12,969ft) shadow. Approaching from the east, no words can prepare you for the sight of its craggy southern face, which rises like a vertical wall over 2439m (8000ft) above Berg Lake. Visible for less than 14 days a year, the mountain has left onlookers awestruck for centuries; Aboriginals called it 'Mountain of the Spiral Road' and trappers and explorers revered it as unconquerable. It wasn't until 1913 that the mountain was first officially climbed, and, even today, only approximately 10% of summit attempts are successful.

Hiking is what draws most visitors to the park. The famous 22km (13.6-mile) **Berg Lake Trail** takes you through the Valley of a Thousand Falls, next to Mt Robson and past the stunning, glacier-fed lake itself, filled with shorn-off chunks of ice. You must register to undertake the hike, which takes two to three days, and while the majority of spaces are filled on a first-come, first-served basis, **reservations** (800-689-9025) are accepted for particularly busy periods. Seven backcountry campgrounds are located en route (C$5 per person per night). Trail information, permits and maps can all be found at the information center.

For those with less time, the first segment of the Berg Lake Trail (bikes allowed) can be taken as far as the **Kinney Lake** picnic site and viewpoint at 9km (5.6 miles). Look out for mountain goats, black bears, caribou and porcupine. Alternatively, you can heli-hike, ie take a helicopter into the Berg Lake area and hike out. For details enquire with **Robson Helimagic Inc** (www.robsonhelimagic.com; Hwy 5N, Valemount, British Columbia; per person from C$179).

Boating is popular within the park, although fishing isn't particularly good. Launch your boat in the green waters of Moose or Yellowhead Lakes. Rearguard Falls, just west of the information center, is known for its salmon viewing (mid-August to early September).

Sleeping & Eating

Lucerne Campground CAMPGROUND $
(☎800-689-9025; Hwy 16, Yellowhead Lake; campsites C$16) With large, wooded sites, the spacious Lucerne is a great place to set up home for the night. A number of the 36 sites are level and have pull-through for RVs; others are built up for tents. There are two walk-in, lakeside tent sites and a water pump.

Mt Robson Mountain River Lodge HOTEL, CABINS $$
(☎250-566-9899; www.mtrobson.com; cnr Hwy 16 & Swift Current Creek Rd; lodge/cabins incl breakfast C$135/179) On the western border of the park, this friendly lodge commands stunning views of the giant peak – when it's visible. There's a main lodge and a couple of cabins that share a cozy, away-from-it-all atmosphere.

Hamber Provincial Park

Tiny Hamber Provincial Park is cocooned in an alcove on the western border of Jasper National Park. It is the domain of black and grizzly bears, but recent years have seen an influx of backpackers. While there is no road access into the park, an improved 22km (13.6-mile) trail from Sunwapta Falls along the Icefields Parkway leads to **Fortress Lake**, on the park's eastern border. Fishing for brook trout is popular here, and an air-accessed commercial fishing camp is located on the southern shore.

Along the lake's northeast shore are three basic campgrounds, each with a pit toilet and bear pole. You do not need a permit to camp, but you must register your vehicle with Parks Canada if you plan to leave it at Sunwapta Falls.

For more information about the park and current trail conditions, contact **BC Parks** (☎250-566-4325; www.env.gov.bc.ca/bcparks).

Willmore Wilderness Park

Spreading across the foothills and mountain ranges north of Jasper National Park, Willmore Wilderness Park has more wildlife passing through it than people. If you really want to get off the beaten track, consider the 750km (465 miles) of trails crossing this park. Access is by foot only from Rock Lake, Big Berland or Grande Cache. At 95km (59 miles), **Mountain Trail** is the longest and most continuous route through the park, from Rock Lake to Grande Cache. The scenic 33km (20.5-mile) **Indian Trail** is popular for hunting and wildlife watching and is in better condition than many of the other trails.

Very little trail maintenance is done here, and while there are designated camping areas, you'll find nothing at them. Water is from lakes and rivers only and must be treated before you consume it. Permits to hike or camp in the park are not required. Be sure to tell someone where you're going and when to expect you back, and be prepared to deal with any emergencies or wildlife you meet on the trail.

For more information on Willmore Wilderness Park, see **Travel Alberta** (www.travelalberta.com). From Jasper Town, the closest source of information is at the **Hinton Visitor Information Centre** (☎780-865-2777; Hwy 16, Hinton), 77km (28 miles) north.

Glacier National Park

Includes »

Best Hikes

- Carthew-Alderson Trail (p213)
- Highline Trail (p189)
- Iceberg Lake Trail (p191)
- Crypt Lake Trail (p214)
- Dawson-Pitamakin Loop (p191)

Best Places to Stay

- Many Glacier Hotel (p204)
- Glacier Park Lodge (p222)
- Sperry Chalet (p193)
- Izaak Walton Inn (p222)
- Prince of Wales Hotel (p217)

Why Go?

Few of the world's great natural wonders can compete with the US national park system, and few national parks are as magnificent and pristine as Glacier. Created in 1910 during the first flowering of the American conservationist movement, Glacier ranks among other national park classics such as Yellowstone and Yosemite. Perennial highlights include its quartet of historic 'parkitecture' lodges, the spectacular Going-to-the-Sun Rd and a rare fully intact pre-Columbian ecosystem. This is the only place in the lower 48 states where grizzly bears still roam in abundance and smart park management has kept the place accessible yet, at the same time, authentically wild. Among a slew of other outdoor attractions, the park is particularly noted for its hiking, wildlife spotting, and fishing and boating lakes.

Although Glacier is popular, few people stray far from the Going-to-the-Sun Rd and almost all visit between June and September. Choose your moment and splendid isolation is yours.

When to Go

West Glacier, MT (USA)

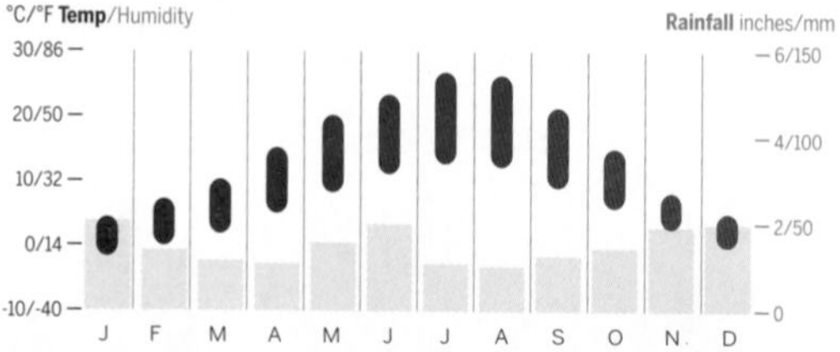

May-June The thaw begins and lower altitude destinations attract the intrepid and hardy.

July-August Peak summer when most trails and all park facilities are open.

September Less crowds, quieter campgrounds and a reliable weather window before the first snows.

Entrances

Glacier National Park has six official entrance gates. The two busiest are the West Entrance, just north of West Glacier, and the East Entrance, near St Mary at the opposite end of the iconic Going-to-the-Sun Rd. The other entrances are the Camas Creek Entrance and the Polebridge Ranger Station, both off the Outside North Fork Rd on the park's western side, and the Two Medicine Entrance (on Two Medicine Rd, west of Hwy 49) and the Many Glacier Entrance (on Many Glacier Rd, west of US 89) over on the eastern side.

Boards at entrances indicate which park campgrounds are open or full.

INTERNATIONAL PEACE PARK HIKE

A unique opportunity to visit two parks – and two different countries – in one day, the International Peace Park Hike leads participants on a free guided 13.7km (8.5-mile) walk alongside twinkling Upper Waterton Lake, from Waterton Townsite in Canada to Goat Haunt in Glacier National Park in the US. Led by a duo of rangers from both nations, hikers follow a gently undulating path south through sun-dappled forest and scenic shoreline, to the unguarded border. Arriving at Goat Haunt late afternoon, you are first required to show your passport to special customs rangers. After that you are free to soak up the impressive mountainscape and examine exhibits in a small 'peace pavilion' at the boat dock. When making your reservation you will have assured passage on the 5:25pm boat back to Waterton (adult/child C$24/12).

The International Peace Park Hike departs Waterton at 10am every Saturday from early June to late August. Places are available for up to 30 people, but reserve beforehand at the Waterton Visitor Centre (p220) as the hike is perennially popular.

When You Arrive

- Glacier National Park is open year-round. Entry per car, or RV, costs US$25. People arriving on foot, bicycle or motorcycle pay US$12 per person. Both tickets are valid for seven days. Entrance fees are reduced in winter. Fees for Glacier do not include entrance to Waterton Lakes National Park.
- Staff at the entrance stations hand out free detailed Glacier-Waterton maps, a quarterly newspaper and the *Glacier Explorer*, a schedule of events and activities, including ranger-led day trips.

PLANNING TIP

Backcountry camping permits (US$5 per adult per night) can be purchased from the **Apgar Backcountry Office** (⏲7am-5pm May-late Oct) in Apgar Village. The office can also make reservations.

Fast Facts

- Area: 4046 sq km (1562 sq miles)
- Highest elevation: 3190m (10,466ft)
- Lowest elevation: 980m (3215ft)

Reservations

Glacier National Park operates 13 campgrounds. Sites at Fish Creek and St Mary Campgrounds can be **reserved** (☎800-365-2267; www.recreation.gov) up to six months in advance; and at Apgar up to a year in advance. All other campgrounds are first-come, first-served.

Resources

- Glacier National Park: www.nps.gov/glac/index.htm
- Glacier Park Inc: www.glacierparkinc.com
- Parks Canada: www.pc.gc.ca/pn-np/ab/waterton/index.aspx

Orientation

Cocooned in northwest Montana and abutting the border with the Canadian provinces of Alberta and British Columbia, Glacier is bisected by the Continental Divide and contained within the 'Crown of the Continent' natural ecosystem. The 4046-sq-km (1562-sq-mile) park's natural delineators are the North Fork of the Flathead River (west), Marias Pass on US 2 (south), US 89 and the Blackfeet Indian Reservation (east) and the Canadian border (north).

The park's main areas, clockwise roughly northeast to northwest, are Goat Haunt, at

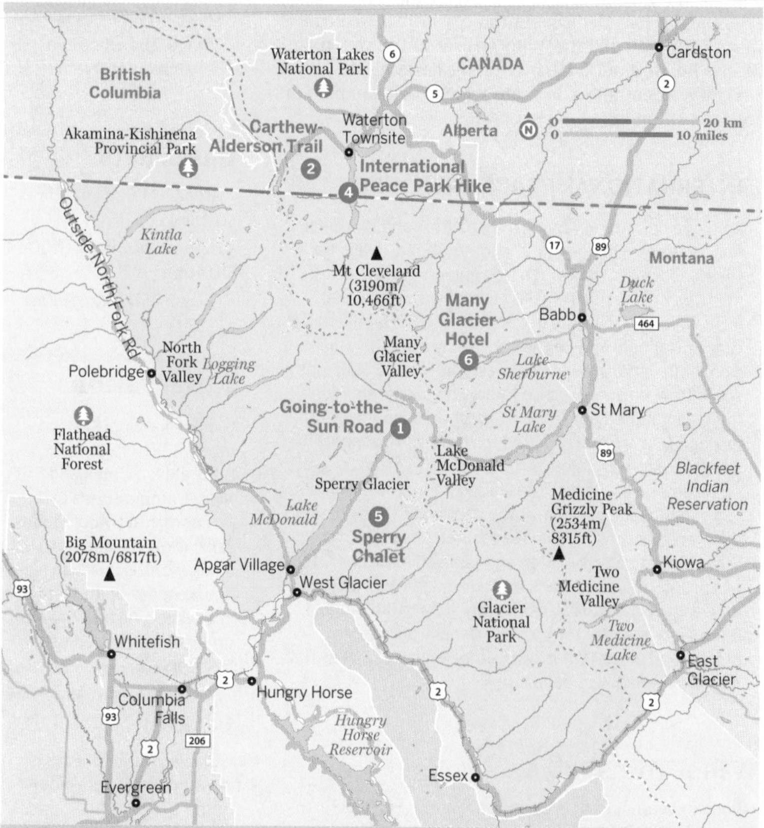

Glacier Highlights

❶ Park the car and take a free shuttle across the spectacular **Going-to-the-Sun Road** (p179)

❷ Absorb pretty lakes, subalpine meadows and dramatic cross-park views on the **Carthew-Alderson Trail** (p213)

❸ Step aboard a historic boat launch for a guided **boat-hike excursion** (see boxed text, p197) on one of a quintet of park lakes

❹ Visit two countries in one multifarious walk on the cross-border **International Peace Park Hike** (see boxed text, p177)

❺ Ride a horse up one of the park's oldest paths to the historic backcountry **Sperry Chalet** (see boxed text, p193)

❻ Watch wildlife roaming around Swiftcurrent Lake while listening to the resident pianist in the lobby of the **Many Glacier Hotel** (p204)

❼ Learn about the spirituality and traditions of the Blackfeet tribe at a **Native American Speak** (p205)

the base of Upper Waterton Lake; Many Glacier, a popular hiking valley; St Mary, best known for its photogenic namesake lake; Two Medicine, a rugged but secluded valley replete with wildlife; Logan Pass, at the apex of the Going-to-the-Sun Rd; the Lake McDonald Valley, home to Apgar Village; and the North Fork Valley, the most remote and least visited corner of the park.

Park Policies & Regulations

Glacier supports a delicate natural ecosystem and various rules and regulations have been formulated to keep it that way. No fireworks or firearms are allowed in the park, and all litter and garbage must be packed out, or disposed of in bear-proof bins. It is illegal to collect environmental souvenirs such as rocks, flowers and plants.

Pets are prohibited from all park trails and backcountry campgrounds. Elsewhere, they must be leashed at all times to prevent them from provoking wildlife.

Hikers should always keep to designated trails and refrain from taking shortcuts across fragile soils and vegetation.

Park regulations allow visitors to collect up to a pint of berries per person per day, but think twice before going on a picking binge. Bears and other creatures depend on this food for sustenance.

BIKING

Bikes are prohibited from all park trails. From June 15 through Labor Day cyclists are restricted from using the Going-to-the-Sun Rd between Apgar Village and Sprague Creek Campground, and Logan Creek to Logan Pass, between 11am and 4pm.

CAMPING

Campgrounds generally open mid-May to the end of September. Only Apgar Picnic Area and St Mary Campground offer primitive winter camping.

RVs are allowed at all campgrounds except Sprague Creek, though footage regulations vary. Large units are not recommended at those accessed via dirt road, ie Bowman Lake, Cut Bank, Kintla Lake, Logging Creek and Quartz Creek.

Drive-in campers should store their edibles in a hard-sided vehicle or in a bear-proof food locker. Stoves, coolers, containers and utensils (even if they're clean) and scented toiletries should never be left out unattended. Garbage should be disposed of in the bear-proof bins available in all frontcountry campgrounds.

Most stores within and around the park sell wood for campfires.

DRIVING

The speed limit is 64km/h (40mph) on all park roads, dropping to 40km/h (25mph) at the upper part of the Going-to-the-Sun Rd and 16km/h (10mph) in campgrounds. Vehicle restrictions are imposed on Going-to-the-Sun Rd only. Vehicles or combinations wider than 2.4m (8ft) or longer than 6.4m (21ft) are prohibited between Avalanche Creek to just east of Sun Point. State law requires motorcycle operators and passengers under 18 years old to wear helmets. Limited parking is available at most trailheads.

BOATING

Motorboats are permitted on Sherburne, St Mary, McDonald and Lower Two Medicine Lakes. On Bowman and Two Medicine Lakes, motorcraft must be 10HP or less. Read Glacier's *Boating Regulations* pamphlet. Jet skis are not allowed on Glacier's waters. Water-skiing is permitted only on St Mary Lake and Lake McDonald, and only during daylight hours.

Dangers & Annoyances

Glacier is prime grizzly bear country and, although you're more likely to be involved in a car accident than be maimed by a bear, attacks have happened. Bear spray costs US$50 and is available in all outdoor stores in and around the park.

The Going-to-the-Sun Rd is crowded and vertiginous with a steep drop-off. Since it is a historic monument there are no modern guard rails. Drive with care.

SIGHTS

Going-to-the-Sun Road

If it were possible to mathematically measure 'magnificence,' the Going-to-the-Sun Rd would surely hit the top end of the scale. Chiseled out of raw mountainside and punctuated by some of the sheerest and most vertiginous drop-offs in the USA, this vista-laden artery of asphalt that bisects the park west to east is an engineering marvel without equal. In the circumstances, it is hardly surprising that it's considered by many motorists to be the best drive in the country.

Glacier National Park

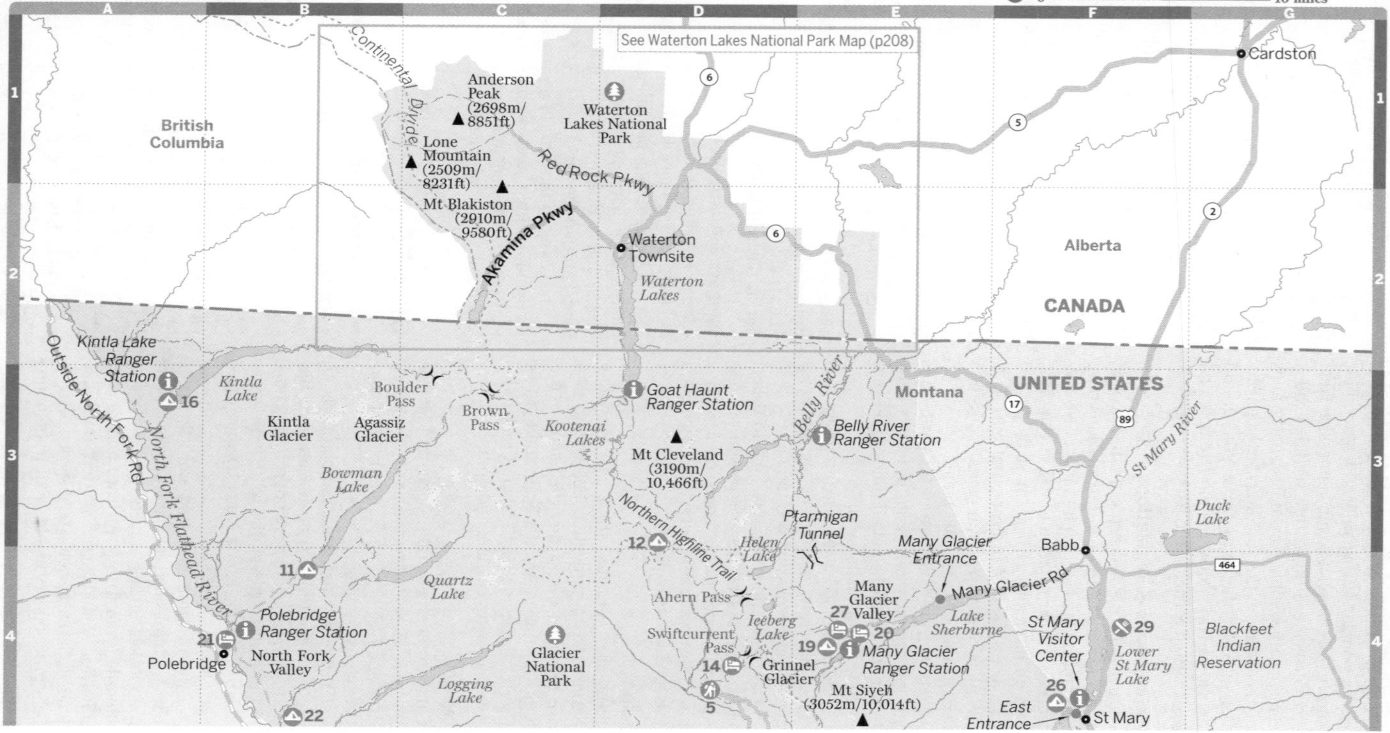

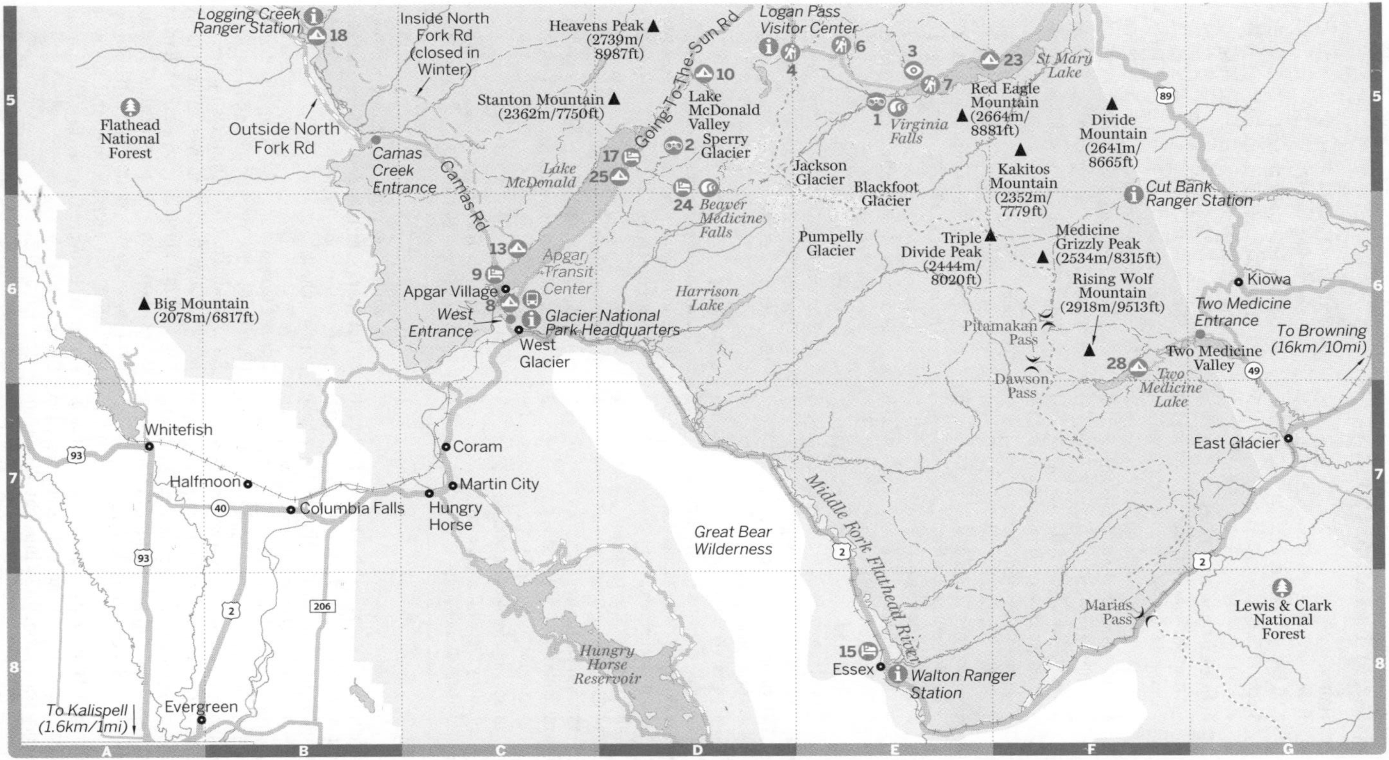
Logging Creek
Ranger Station
18
Inside North
Fork Rd
(closed in
Winter)
Heavens Peak
(2739m/
8987ft)
Going-To-The-Sun Rd
Logan Pass
Visitor Center
4
6
3
23
St Mary
Lake
7
Flathead
National
Forest
Outside North
Fork Rd
Stanton Mountain
(2362m/7750ft)
10
Lake
McDonald
Valley
2
Sperry
Glacier
1
Virginia
Falls
Red Eagle
Mountain
(2664m/
8881ft)
Divide
Mountain
(2641m/
8665ft)
89
Camas
Creek
Entrance
Camas Rd
Lake
McDonald
17
25
24
Beaver
Medicine
Falls
Jackson
Glacier
Blackfoot
Glacier
Kakitos
Mountain
(2352m/
7779ft)
Cut Bank
Ranger Station
13
9
Apgar
Transit
Center
Apgar Village
8
Pumpelly
Glacier
Triple
Divide Peak
(2444m/
8020ft)
Medicine
Grizzly Peak
(2534m/8315ft)
Rising Wolf
Mountain
(2918m/9513ft)
Kiowa
Big Mountain
(2078m/6817ft)
West
Entrance
Glacier National
Park Headquarters
West
Glacier
Harrison
Lake
Pitamakan
Pass
Two Medicine
Entrance
To Browning
(16km/10mi)
28
Two Medicine
Valley
49
Dawson
Pass
Two
Medicine
Lake
Whitefish
93
Coram
East Glacier
Halfmoon
Martin City
40
Columbia Falls
Hungry
Horse
Middle Fork Flathead River
Great Bear
Wilderness
93
2
2
206
2
Marias
Pass
Lewis & Clark
National
Forest
Hungry
Horse
Reservoir
15
Essex
Walton Ranger
Station
To Kalispell
(1.6km/1mi)
Evergreen
A
B
C
D
E
F
G
5
6
7
8

Glacier National Park

Sights

1 Jackson Glacier Overlook E5
2 Mt Brown Lookout...................D5
3 Sunrift Gorge...................E5

Activities, Courses & Tours

Avalanche Lake Trailhead...........(see 10)
Dawson-Pitamakin Trailhead ......(see 28)
Gunsight Pass Trailhead............... (see 1)
4 Hidden Lake Overlook Trailhead D5
Highline Trailhead ....(see 4)
Iceberg Lake Trailhead ....(see 27)
Mt Brown Lookout Trailhead .... (see 17)
5 Northern Highline-Waterton Valley Trailhead...................D4
6 Piegan Pass Trailhead...................E5
Quartz Lakes Loop Trailhead........(see 11)
7 Sun Point to Virginia Falls Trailhead...................E5
Swiftcurrent Lake Nature Trailhead.................. (see 20)
Swiftcurrent Pass Trailhead ....(see 27)

Sleeping

8 Apgar Campground C6
9 Apgar Village Lodge C6
10 Avalanche Creek Campground............D5
11 Bowman Lake Campground...................B4
12 Fifty Mountain Campground...................D3
13 Fish Creek Campground C6
14 Granite Park Chalet...................D4
15 Izaak Walton Inn...................E8
16 Kintla Lake Campground A3
17 Lake McDonald Lodge D5
18 Logging Creek Campground...................B5
19 Many Glacier Campground...................E4
20 Many Glacier Hotel...................E4
21 North Fork Hostel & Square Peg Ranch B4
22 Quartz Creek Campground...................B4
23 Rising Sun Campground F5
Rising Sun Motor Inn ....(see 23)
24 Sperry Chalet...................D5
25 Sprague Creek Campground...................D5
26 St Mary Campground...................F4
27 Swiftcurrent Motor Inn...................E4
28 Two Medicine Campground...................F6
Village Inn...................(see 9)

Eating

Eddie's Cafe ....(see 9)
Italian Garden Ristorante .... (see 27)
Jammer Joe's Grill & Pizzeria.......(see 17)
Polebridge Mercantile ....(see 21)
Ptarmigan Dining Room ....(see 20)
Russells Fireside Dining Room ....(see 17)
Two Dog Flats Grill...................(see 23)
Two Medicine Campstore ....(see 28)
29 Two Sisters Cafe...................F4

Drinking

Lake McDonald Lodge ....(see 17)
Many Glacier Hotel ....(see 20)
Northern Lights Saloon ....(see 21)

Entertainment

Lake McDonald Lodge ....(see 17)
Many Glacier Hotel ....(see 20)

Shopping

Lake McDonald Lodge ....(see 17)
Many Glacier Hotel ....(see 20)

St Mary Lake LAKE

(Map p186) Located on the park's dryer eastern side, where the mountains melt imperceptibly into the Great Plains, St Mary Lake lies in a deep, glacier-carved valley famous for its astounding views and ferocious winds. Overlooked by the tall, chiseled peaks of the Rockies and scarred by the landscape-altering effects of the 2006 Red Eagle Fire, the valley is spectacularly traversed by the Going-to-the-Sun Rd and punctuated by numerous trailheads and viewpoints.

Jackson Glacier Overlook LOOKOUT

(Map p180) A popular pull-over located a short walk from the Gunsight Pass trailhead, where you can steal telescopic views of the park's fifth-largest glacier that sits close to the eponymous peak – one of the park's highest.

Sunrift Gorge CANYON

(Map p186) Just off the Going-to-the-Sun Rd and adjacent to a shuttle stop lies this narrow canyon carved over millennia by the gushing glacial meltwaters of Baring Creek. Look out for picturesque **Baring Bridge**, a classic example of rustic Going-to-the-Sun Rd architecture, and follow a short, tree-covered trail down to misty **Baring Falls**.

Sun Point LOOKOUT
(Map p186) This rocky, often windy promontory overlooks St Mary Lake and was the site of some of the park's earliest and most luxurious chalets (now demolished). Trails link to Baring Falls and **St Mary Falls**.

Wild Goose Island ISLAND
(Map p186) A tiny stub of an island with a handful of lopsided trees that perches precariously in the middle of St Mary Lake, providing a perfect photo op for incurable camera-clickers.

Rising Sun LANDMARK
(Map p186) You'll welcome this handy pit stop on the Going-to-the-Sun Rd, with useful tourist facilities including a motel, restaurant and boat launch. At peculiarly named **Two Dog Flats** nearby, thick trees give way to grassy meadows making it much easier to spot bears, coyotes and elk.

TOP CHOICE **Logan Pass** LANDMARK
(Map p186) Perched above the tree line, atop the wind-lashed Continental Divide, and blocked by snow for most of the year, 2026m (6646ft) Logan Pass – named for William R Logan, Glacier's first superintendent – is the park's highest navigable point by road. Two trails, Hidden Lake Overlook and Highline, lead out from here.

Garden Wall LANDMARK
(Map p186) The sharp steep-sided arête that parallels the Going-to-the-Sun Rd as it ascends to Logan Pass from the west was carved by powerful glaciers millions of years ago. Its western slopes, bisected by the emblematic Highline Trail, are covered by a quintessential Glacier Park feature: steep velvety meadows embellished by an abundance of summer wildflowers.

Weeping Wall WATERFALL
(Map p186) Located 610m (2000ft) below the Garden Wall, the glistening Weeping Wall creates a seasonal waterfall that was formed when Going-to-the-Sun Rd construction workers drilled their way across a network of mountain springs. The water has subsequently been diverted over the lip of a 9m (30ft) man-made cliff, and frequently gives unwary cars and motorbikes a good soaking.

Bird Woman Falls WATERFALL
(Map p186) For a more natural waterfall, look across the valley from the Weeping Wall at these distant falls, a spectacular speck of spray that drops 152m (500ft) from one of Glacier's many hanging valleys.

The Loop LANDMARK
(Map p186) This sharp hairpin bend acts as a popular trailhead for hikers descending from the Granite Park Chalet and the Highline Trail; consequently it's normally chock-a-block with cars. The slopes nearby were badly scarred by the 2003 Trapper Fire, but nature and small shrubs have begun to reappear.

Lake McDonald Valley LAKE, FOREST
(Map p186) Greener and wetter than the St Mary Valley, the Lake McDonald Valley harbors the park's largest lake and some of its densest and oldest temperate rainforest. Crisscrossed by a number of popular trails, including the wheelchair-accessible, 1.3km (0.8-mile) **Trail of the Cedars**, the area is popular with drive-in campers, who frequent the Sprague Creek and Avalanche Creek campgrounds, as well as winter cross-country skiers who use McDonald Creek and the Going-to-the-Sun Rd as seasonal skiing trails.

Lake McDonald Lodge HISTORIC BUILDING
(Map p186) On the south shores of the lake, this rustic lodge first built in 1895 as the Glacier Hotel is the park's oldest hotel. Replaced by a newer Swiss-style structure in 1913, before any roads had penetrated the region, the current lodge's imposing entrance was built facing the lake, meaning modern-day road travelers must enter via the back door.

Apgar Village LANDMARK
(Map p186) In contrast to the sizeable townsites in Banff, Jasper and Waterton National Parks, Apgar Village is miniscule, supporting little more than a couple of lodges, a gift shop and a restaurant, all of which sit quietly on the western shores of Lake McDonald. Dimon Apgar, for whom the settlement is named, built the first road from Belton to the lake in 1895, allowing a handful of early homesteaders to make this choice spot their dream home.

A fire destroyed much of the early settlement in 1930, but it spared the original **schoolhouse**, dating from 1915, which is now a gift shop. Nearby, the tiny **Discovery Cabin** (1929) acts as an activity center for children. Junior ranger programs start here at 9am and 1pm in July and August.

South of Going-to-the-Sun Road

With no hotels, no restaurants and only one dead-end road, the Two Medicine Valley is a favorite haunt for ambitious hikers intent on reaching one of a trio of high-altitude passes that guard the gusty Continental Divide. The more intrepid forge further west, beyond Cut Bank Pass, where faintly marked trails descend into the barely visited Nyack Creek Wilderness, a rough mélange of fordable rivers and primitive campsites that surround the isolated hulk of Mt Stimson, the park's second-highest peak at 3091m (10,142ft).

TWO MEDICINE VALLEY

Before the building of the Going-to-the-Sun Rd in the 1930s, the Two Medicine Valley was one of the park's most accessible hubs, situated a mere 19.2km (12 miles) by horseback from the Great Northern Railway and the newly inaugurated Glacier Park Lodge. Famous for its healthy bear population and deeply imbued with Native American legends, the region is less visited these days, though it has lost none of its haunting beauty. Hikers can grab a picnic at the historic **Two Medicine Campstore**, once the dining hall for the now defunct Two Medicine Chalets and the venue for one of President FD Roosevelt's famous 'fireside chats.' Towering authoritatively over sublime **Two Medicine Lake** (Map p180) is the distinctive hulk of **Rising Wolf Mountain** (Map p180), named for Canadian-turned-Piegan Native American, Hugh Monroe, who was the first white person to explore the region in the mid-19th century.

Located 5km (3.1 miles) to the northwest, 2444m (8020ft) **Triple Divide Peak** (Map p180) marks the hydrologic apex of the North American continent. Empty a bucket of water on its summit and it will run into three separate oceans: the Pacific, the Atlantic and the Arctic.

North of Going-to-the-Sun Road

You can penetrate the park's rugged north from both east and west sides. The northeast is accessible through the popular Many Glacier nexus and is crowned by an historic lodge. The northwest is more remote and requires a good car, self-sufficiency and an adventurous spirit.

NORTH FORK VALLEY

Glacier's most isolated nook is a riot of grassy meadows and regenerated forest that protects the park's only pack of wolves and hides some of its best backcountry trails and campgrounds. North and east of Polebridge, bone-rattling roads lead to a couple of secluded lakes. Due east, **Bowman Lake** (Map p180) is Lake McDonald without the tourists, an ideal spot to enjoy a picnic, launch a canoe or scan the horizon for wildlife. Meanwhile, 22.5km (14 miles) further north, **Kintla Lake** (Map p180) is a secret haven for solitude-seeking fishermen. Stalwart hikers venture out from here along the backcountry Boulder Pass Trail.

MANY GLACIER VALLEY

Dubbed the 'heart and soul' of Glacier by park purists, Many Glacier Valley is a magical mélange of lush meadows and shimmering lakes, where the pièce de résistance is the strategically positioned **Many Glacier Hotel** (Map p180), constructed by the Great Northern Railway in 1915. Known traditionally for its 'rivers of ice' – though there aren't quite so *many* of them these days – the valley nurtures some of the park's most accessible glaciers, including the rapidly shrinking Grinnell Glacier, first spotted by conservationist and naturalist George Bird Grinnell in 1885, and the Salamander Glacier that sits tucked beneath the saw-toothed Ptarmigan Ridge, so-named for its distinctive amphibian-like shape. Other 'unmissables' include **Iceberg Lake** (Map p180), where turquoise waters are fed from a surrounding snowfield, and the **Ptarmigan Tunnel** (Map p180), a 56m (183ft) corridor through the rock, blasted out of the mountain in the 1930s to cut some distance off the hike to Belly River Valley (an environmental anomaly that would win few backers today).

Many Glacier is probably the best place in the park to spot wildlife. Avalanche chutes around the lakes attract bears, and mountain goats are easy to pick out on the steep scree slopes above Swiftcurrent Lake.

DRIVING

Blessed with one of America's most spectacular roads, Glacier promises steely nerved motorists the drive of their life. Those less enthusiastic about crawling in second gear up gravity-defying chicanes can find solace in the park's less demanding back routes.

Going-to-the-Sun Road

Duration 3 hours one way (with stops)

Distance 85km (53 miles)

Speed Limit 40km/h (25mph) on upper sections; 64km/h (40mph) on lower sections

Start West Glacier

Finish St Mary

Nearest Town Apgar Village (p183)

Summary Quite literally, one of the greatest and most spectacular drives in the US.

Giving few hints of the coming splendor, the Going-to-the-Sun Rd starts inauspiciously at the park's western entrance near Apgar Village before tracking east alongside translucent **Lake McDonald**. Encased in dense rainforest and characterized by the famous Lake McDonald Lodge, the valley here is lush and verdant, though a quick glance through the trees will highlight the graphic evidence of the destruction wreaked by the 2003 Robert Fire on the opposite side of the water.

After tracking alongside McDonald Creek for approximately 16km (10 miles), the road begins its long, slow ascent to Logan Pass with a sharp turn to the southeast at the **Loop**, a famous hiking trailhead and the start of an increasingly precipitous climb toward the summit. Views here vary from amazing to even more amazing as the road cuts precariously into the **Garden Wall**, a 2743m (8999ft) granite arête that delineates the west and east regions of the park along the Continental Divide. Look out for **Bird Woman Falls** at 43km (27 miles), stunning even from a distance, and the more in-your-face (literally, if you've got the roof down) **Weeping Wall** at 46km (29 miles), as the gaping chasm to your right grows ever deeper.

Nearly everybody stops at 2026m (6646ft) **Logan Pass**, at 52km (32 miles), to browse the visitor center or stretch their legs amid alpine meadows on the popular Hidden Lake Overlook Trail. Be forewarned: the Logan Pass parking lot can resemble a shopping mall parking lot in July and August, particularly between 11am and 3pm.

Descending to the east the scenery almost grows in grandeur. At 58km (36 miles), you can pull over to spy one of only 25 remaining park glaciers at the **Jackson Glacier Overlook**, while a few clicks further on, you can sample narrow **Sunrift Gorge** near the shores of St Mary Lake. With an elevation of 2939m (9642ft), majestic **Going-to-the-Sun Mountain** – for which the road is named – is omnipresent to the north. **Wild Goose Island** is a tiny stub of land with a handful of lopsided trees that perches precariously in the middle of St Mary Lake, providing a perfect photo op for incurable camera-clickers. If you're in need of gifts or a bite to eat, **Rising Sun** has a store and the no-nonsense restaurant.

The St Mary Visitor Center, at 85km (53 miles), on the lake's east end, is journey's end. The plains on this side of the park stretch east from St Mary to Minneapolis.

No vehicles over 6m (21ft) are allowed from east of Sun Point to Avalanche Creek.

Looking Glass Hill Road & Highway 89

Duration 1 hour with stops

Distance 43km (27 miles)

Speed Limit 112km/h (70mph)

Start East Glacier

Finish St Mary

Nearest Town East Glacier (p222)

Summary A short, vista-laden drive across the Blackfeet Indian Reservation where steep mountains meet flat plains.

Part of the drama of Glacier National Park is how its sharp, razor-ridged mountains contrast with the flat, grassy prairies to the east; and there's no better place to see this geological melding than on this rugged, twisting road named for a former Nez Perce chief that runs just outside the park's southeastern boundary.

The drive starts in East Glacier, famous for the formidable **Glacier Park Lodge**, aka 'the Big Tree Lodge,' where you can enjoy a relaxing pre-drive drink (nonalcoholic, of course!) in the hotel's magnificent rustic lobby. Heading north, thin clumps of aspen quickly turn to grassland as you round sentinel-like **Looking Glass Hill**, once used by the Blackfeet Native Americans to spot enemies advancing from across the plains.

Distracting views of **Two Medicine** soon appear on your left-hand side, urging you to stop at one of a handful of rough pullovers. Though incorporated into Glacier National

Going-to-the-Sun Road Driving Tour

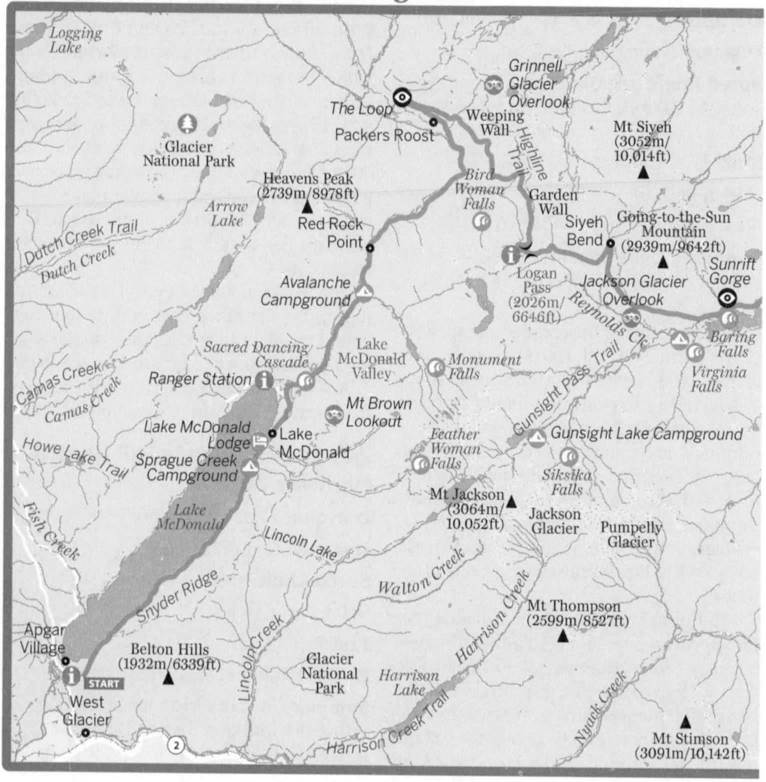

Park in 1910, Two Medicine is central to the Blackfeet creation story and was the starting point for many a warrior *vision quest* (tribal initiation). Its three instantly striking mountains are **Rising Wolf** (2918m/9513ft), named for a Canadian trapper called Hugh Monroe who lived with – and was later initiated into – the Blackfoot Nation in the early 1800s; pyramid-like **Sinopah**, named for his native wife; and **Lone Walker**, a tribal chief and Monroe's father-in-law.

As you continue north, watch out for blind bends, steep drop-offs (with no guard-rails) and iffy road quality thanks to winter freeze and thaws. Look out also for wildlife; elk, moose, deer, bears, wolves, coyotes, bighorn sheep and mountain goats have all been spotted here.

Veering away from Two Medicine, Looking Glass Hill Rd (Hwy 49) swings briefly east to join US 89. Turn left here and drive north past the Cut Bank Creek turnoff, an unpaved road that leads to a campground and some choice backcountry trails. The imposing hulk of 2641m (8665ft) **Divide Mountain** looms large to the west as you approach St Mary and become encased in the burnt carnage caused by the 2006 Red Eagle Fire. Meanwhile, over to the east, big skies and pancake-flat prairies melt away into a barely perceptible horizon.

DAY HIKES

You don't have to be an aspiring Everest climber to enjoy the well-tramped trails and scenic byways of Glacier National Park. Indeed, two of the park's most popular hikes are wheelchair accessible, while countless more can be easily tackled by parents with children, vacationing couch potatoes or nervous novices. To help you pick the perfect hike, see our handy chart on p36.

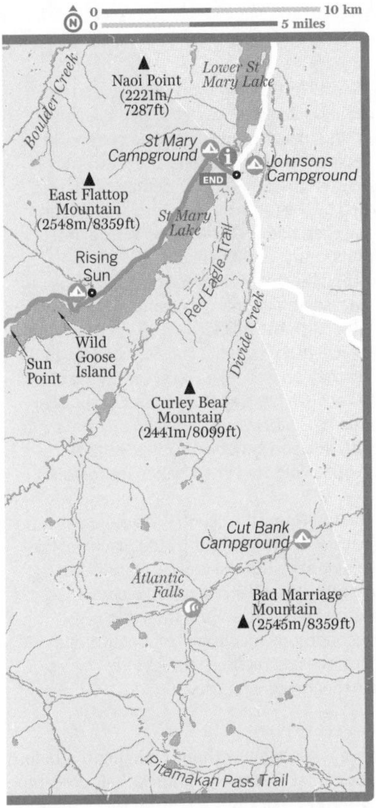

Going-to-the-Sun Road

Avalanche Lake Trail

Duration 2½ hours round-trip

Distance 6.4km (4 miles)

Difficulty Easy-moderate

Start/Finish Avalanche Creek shuttle stop

Elevation Change 145m (475ft)

Nearest Town Apgar Village (p183)

Transportation Going-to-the-Sun Rd shuttle

Summary A pleasant, family-friendly stroll through shady forest to the park's most accessible alpine lake, replete with glacier-strewn boulders and cascading waterfalls.

A handy stop on the new shuttle route, the Avalanche Lake Trail provides quick and easy access to one of Glacier National Park's most gorgeous alpine lakes – and you don't have to bust a gut to get there. As a result, the trail is invariably heaving in peak season with everyone from flip flop–wearing families to stick-wielding seniors making boldly for the tree line. But don't be deceived; while the walk itself might be relatively easy, it's highly recommended you come prepared with bottled water, layered clothing and the appropriate footwear.

Starting from the Going-to-the-Sun Rd, the path meanders for 800m (0.5 miles) along the paved Trail of the Cedars to a signposted three-way junction. Bear right here, diverting into thick rainforest, and follow the path along a scenic section of narrow **Avalanche Creek**. Shaded from the summer sun by mature, old-growth cedar and western hemlock trees, the forest floor is strewn with huge moss-covered boulders, the remnants of a once-powerful glacier.

After half an hour of hopping over tree roots and fording trickling creeks, you'll emerge, as if by magic, at luminous **Avalanche Lake**, a circle of water fed by cascading waterfalls and overlooked by the steep, rocky escarpments of Bearhat Mountain. The surrounding scenery is sublime and well worth the moderate 3.2km (2-mile) march to get here. Relax on the lakeshore with a pair of binoculars, keeping a lookout for birds and other wildlife (there's a pit toilet nearby) before heading back down.

Hidden Lake Overlook Trail

Duration 2 hours round-trip

Distance 5km (3.2 miles)

Difficulty Easy-moderate

Start/Finish Logan Pass Visitor Center

Elevation Change 150m (494ft)

Nearest Facilities Logan Pass (p183)

Transportation Going-to-the-Sun Rd shuttle

Summary An über-popular hike that's part boardwalk and part path, bisecting lush meadows and melting snowfields before descending to a translucent glacial lake.

For many Glacier visitors this relatively straightforward hike is the one occasion in which they step out of their cars and take a sniff of the sweet-scented alpine air for which the area is famous. Starting at the

DON'T MISS

RIDING THE RAILS

Glacier National Park owes its existence to the Great Northern Railway constructed by Canadian-born entrepreneur James J Hill in the 1890s and later used to carry the park's first pioneering visitors into some of America's most uncompromising backcountry. Still running daily between West Glacier and East Glacier Park train stations, the line remains one of the best ways to view the park's impressive southern perimeter demarcated by the Middle Fork of the Flathead River and guarded by the rampart-like mountains of the Lewis Range. On the south side of the line lies the even wilder **Great Bear Wilderness Area**, a roadless landscape, uninhabited bar for its bears, beavers et al.

The journey of one hour and 40 minutes between the two stations costs a giveaway US$14 for reclining business-class seats and access to an onboard café and observation car on the legendary *Empire Builder*. Board the train in West Glacier 1km (0.6 miles) from the park's western entrance and let the geographical drama unfold. The Flathead River is your constant companion as the train labors its way up to Marias Pass, the mythical mountain crossing that once eluded Lewis and Clark. On the way you'll pass **Essex Station**, the only 'flagstop' (request stop) on the *Empire Builder* route between Seattle and Chicago. Clearly visible from the train is the **Izaak Walton Inn**, built by the Great Northern in 1939 and now a favored stopover for train buffs who stay in old cabooses restored as luxury accommodation.

Soon after Essex you reach 1590m (5213ft) **Marias Pass**, the country's lowest pass over the Continental Divide, once hailed as the 'backbone of the world' by the Blackfeet Native Americans. An obelisk stands next to an imposing statue of the green-before-his-time US president, Theodore Roosevelt, darling of the early US conservationist movement.

The vegetation quickly thins out as you approach East Glacier Park train depot, a historic station that marks the sudden almost incongruous meeting of mountains and prairie. Disembark here and walk 365m (400yd) across manicured lawns to the classic 'parkitecture' East Glacier Lodge, an apt end to a magnificent journey.

busy Logan Pass Visitor Center, the hike ascends gradually along a raised boardwalk (with steps) through expansive alpine meadows replete with monkey-flower and pink laurel. Melting snowfields add a mild challenge for those who decided, misguidedly, to wear flip flops but, rain or shine, this trail is a hit with everyone – from tiny babies to spry septuagenarians – and the people-watching is almost as interesting as the wildlife.

After about 1km (0.6 miles), the boardwalk gives way to a gravelly dirt path. If the snow has melted, the diversity of grasses and wildflowers in the meadows around you is breathtaking. Resident trees include old Engelmann spruce, subalpine fir and whitebark pine. Hoary marmots, ground squirrels and mountain goats are not shy along this trail. The elusive ptarmigan, whose brown feathers turn white in winter, also lives nearby. Up-close mountain views include Clement Mountain north of the trail and Reynolds Mountain in the southeast.

A few hundred meters (328yd) before the **overlook**, you will cross the Continental Divide – probably without realizing it – before your first stunning glimpse of deep-blue **Hidden Lake** (and a realization of what all the fuss is about), bordered by mountain peaks and rocky cliffs; look out for glistening Sperry Glacier visible to the south.

Hearty souls continue on to Hidden Lake via a 2.4km (1.5-mile) trail from the overlook, steeply descending 233m (765ft).

Sun Point to Virginia Falls

Duration 4 hours round-trip

Distance 11.5km (7 miles)

Difficulty Easy

Start/Finish Sun Point shuttle stop

Elevation Change 90m (300ft)

Nearest Town St Mary (p220)

Transportation Going-to-the-Sun Rd shuttle

Summary Shelter from the famous St Mary Lake winds on this shady but sun-dappled trail that takes you to a tempestuous trio of waterfalls.

Handily served by the free park shuttle, the myriad of trailheads along the eastern side of the Going-to-the-Sun Rd offers plenty of short interlinking hikes, a number of which can be pooled together to make up a decent morning or afternoon ramble.

This particular variation starts at the Sun Point shuttle stop, where you can track down a 400m (0.25-mile) trail to a rocky (and often windy) **overlook** perched above sparkling St Mary Lake. In the 1910s the Great Northern Railway built some of Glacier's earliest and showiest chalets here in an accommodation chain that stretched from Many Glacier to the Sperry and Granite Park Chalets. Falling into neglect after WWII, the Sun Point chalets were demolished in 1949, though the view remains timeless.

Take the path west through sun-flecked forest along the lake toward shady **Baring Falls**, at 1km (0.6 miles), for a respite from the sun and/or wind. After admiring the gushing cascades, cross the river and continue on the opposite bank to link up with the busy **St Mary Falls Trail** that joins from the right. Undemanding switchbacks lead up through the trees to the valley's most picturesque falls, set amid colorful foliage on St Mary River. Beyond here, the trail branches along Virginia Creek, past a narrow gorge, to mist-shrouded (and quieter) **Virginia Falls** at the foot of a hanging valley.

Retrace your steps to Sun Point for the full-length hike or, if your legs start to tire, shortcut to the St Mary Falls or Sunrift Gorge shuttle stops (follow the signs) and hop onto a bus.

Highline Trail

Duration 7½ hours one way

Distance 18.7km (11.6 miles)

Difficulty Moderate

Start Logan Pass Visitor Center

Finish The Loop

Elevation Change 255m (830ft)

Nearest Facilities Logan Pass (p183)

Transportation Going-to-the-Sun Rd shuttle

Summary A vista-laden extravaganza that cuts underneath the Garden Wall ridge just below the Continental Divide to the famous Granite Park Chalet.

A Glacier classic, the Highline Trail cuts like an elongated scar across the famous Garden Wall, a sharp, glacier-carved ridge that forms part of the Continental Divide and the summer slopes of which are covered with an abundance of alpine plants and wildflowers. The stupendous views here are some of the best in the park and, with little elevation gain throughout its 12km (7.6-mile) course, the treats come with minimal sweat.

Cutting immediately into the side of the mountain (there are handrails for those with vertigo), the trail presents stunning early views of the Going-to-the-Sun Rd and snowcapped Heaven's Peak. Look out for the toy-sized red 'jammer' buses motoring up the valley below you and marvel as the sun catches the white foaming waters of 152m (500ft) Bird Woman Falls opposite.

After its vertiginous start, the trail is flat for 3km (1.8 miles) before gently ascending to a ridge that connects Haystack Butte with Mt Gould at the 5.6km (3.5-mile) mark. From here on it's fairly flat as you bisect the mountainside on your way toward the Granite Park Chalet. At approximately 10.9km (6.8 miles), with the chalet in sight, a spur path (on your right) offers gluttons for punishment the option of climbing up less than 1.6km (1 mile) to the **Grinnell Glacier Overlook** for a peek over the Continental Divide.

The **Granite Park Chalet** (see boxed text, p193) appears at around 12km (7.6 miles), providing a welcome haven for parched throats and tired feet (stock up at the chalet on chocolate bars and soda or water).

From here you have three options: you can retrace your steps back to Logan Pass; head for Swiftcurrent Pass and the Many

Highline Trail

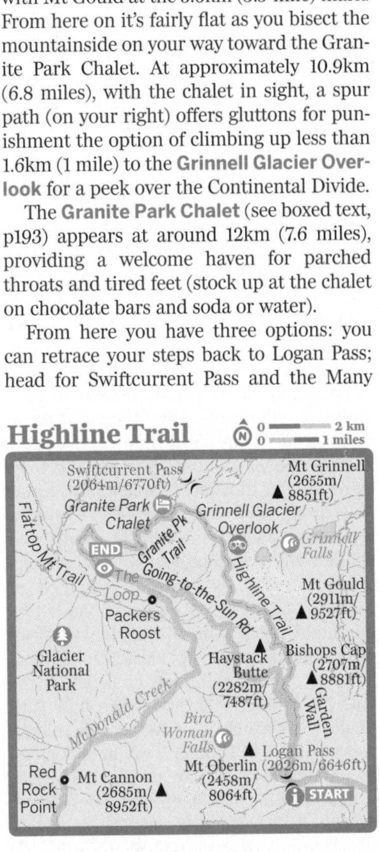

Glacier Valley; or descend 6.4km (4 miles) to the Loop, where you can pick up a shuttle bus to all points on the Going-to-the-Sun Rd.

Mt Brown Lookout

Duration 6 hours round-trip

Distance 17.3km (10.8 miles)

Difficulty Difficult

Start/Finish Lake McDonald Lodge

Elevation Change 1318m (4325ft)

Nearest Facilities Apgar Village (p183)

Transportation Going-to-the-Sun Rd shuttle

Summary Glacier's steepest day hike involves no technical skills, but a good level of fitness to reach a lofty historic lookout on Mt Brown.

This hike is a means to an end; a steep 8.6km (5.4-mile) grunt up through thick forest to a historic 1929 lookout last manned in 1971 (and refurbished in 1999) on the southwest ridge of 2610m (8565ft) Mt Brown, located about 457m (1500ft) below the summit. The views from here are outstanding but no mountaineering skills are required - just a strong pair of lungs.

The hike starts on the Going-to-the-Sun Rd opposite the Lake McDonald Lodge on the heavily used Sperry Chalet trail. Pass the horse corral and head up alongside Snyder Creek, which soon drops away to your right. The Mt Brown Lookout trail is the first of three trails to branch off, swinging left after 2.9km (1.8 miles) and starting a climb that makes your ascent so far seem like a Sunday afternoon stroll. The first five switchbacks are the toughest; after that the 20 or so remaining curves are a little more manageable and occasional glimpses through the trees en route offer hints of the splendor to come. As you approach the lookout you'll emerge into meadows swaying with beargrass and wildflowers. The **Lookout**, with its distinctive pyramid-shaped roof, is perched at 2263m (7425ft) and is often frequented by mountain goats. The 270-degree view includes the full spread of Lake McDonald and its surrounding mountains. Look out for the Lake McDonald Lodge and the Granite Park Chalet. The summit of **Mt Brown** blocks views northeast. Though it might look close, mountaineering skills are needed to reach it.

Take care on the steep and (sometimes) slippery trail as you descend.

Piegan Pass

Duration 6 hours

Distance 20.5km (12.8 miles)

Difficulty Moderate-difficult

Start Siyeh Bend shuttle stop

Finish Many Glacier

Elevation Change 509m (1670ft)

Nearest Facilities Many Glacier (p184)

Transportation Going-to-the-Sun Rd shuttle

Summary A forest, an alpine meadow, a glacier, a pass and a long descent through Glacier's premier wildlife corridor; Piegan Pass isn't lacking in variety.

A popular hike among Glacier stalwarts, this trail starts on the Going-to-the-Sun Rd at a handy shuttle stop on Siyeh Bend just east of Logan Pass and deposits you in Glacier's mystic heart, Many Glacier, with transport connections back to St Mary. It also bisects colorful Preston Park, one of the region's prettiest and most jubilant alpine meadows.

The initial climb is through forest from the Siyeh Bend starting point heading directly for the flower-adorned oasis of **Preston Park**. Turn left and head north at the first trail junction at 1.9km (1.2 miles), and left again at the 4.3km (2.7 miles) mark, where the Siyeh Pass Trail veers off to the right. The trail crosses a creek and begins to traverse more barren terrain across the base of Mt Siyeh and Cataract Mountain. At the 7.2km (4.5 mile) mark you'll reach **Piegan Pass** on a saddle between Mt Piegan and Mt Pollock. The ruined foundations of a building provide some shelter from the whistling winds. Some people turn around and retrace their steps here, but the savvy descend on the pass's north side to Cataract Creek in the Many Glacier Valley. **Morning Eagle Falls** is reached at the 12.3km (7.7 mile) mark and at 14km (8.8 miles) you'll enter the Grinnell Lake trail system, popular with boat-hike groups from the Many Glacier Hotel. Stay right at the Grinnell Lake Trail junction and right again at the Josephine Lake link trail and you'll find yourself roaming through classic subalpine scenery with turquoise glimpses of the lakes through the trees. The well-signposted trail will ultimately deposit you in the upper parking lot of the Many Glacier Hotel.

South of Going-to-the-Sun Road

Dawson-Pitamakin Loop

Duration 8 hours round-trip

Distance 30km (18.8 miles)

Difficulty Difficult

Start/Finish North Shore trailhead, Two Medicine Lake

Elevation Change 910m (2935ft)

Nearest Facilities Two Medicine Valley (p184)

Transportation East Side Shuttle

Summary Cross the Continental Divide twice on this strenuous but spectacular hike along exposed mountain ridges that provide prime habitat for grizzly bears.

This lengthy hike can be squeezed into a one-day itinerary, if you're fit and up for it. Alternatively, it can be tackled over two or three days with sleepovers at the No Name Lake and Oldman Lake backcountry campgrounds (permit required). Blessed with two spectacular mountain passes and teeming with myriad plant and animal life, it is often touted by park rangers as being one of Glacier's hiking highlights.

As the hike is a loop, departing from the North Shore trailhead on **Two Medicine Lake**, you must first decide which direction you want to go. Progressing clockwise and tackling Dawson Pass first packs the 915m (3000ft) elevation gain into one sharp segment. Head anticlockwise and the same ascent is more drawn out. Walking clockwise, you'll be entering prime grizzly bear country (rangers have actually used it as a study area), so be on guard and make plenty of noise. Around 8km (5 miles) in you'll reach **No Name Lake**, a prime fishing spot. The trail ascends steeply from here, gaining 366m (1200ft) in 3.2km (2 miles) during a pulse-racing climb to **Dawson Pass**, an exposed col notorious for its high winds – 160km/h (100mph) has been recorded. Follow the narrow, sheer-sided path north along the Continental Divide, taking care with your footing amid stunning high-country views. You'll cross the divide again at **Cut Bank** before descending to **Pitamakin Pass** and **Oldman Lake**, a gorgeous blue body of water encased in a cirque and framed by jagged peaks.

From the lake the hike descends into the **Dry Fork Drainage**, through fields of huckleberries interspersed with clumps of dense forest. Look out for diggings, scat and other evidence of bear activity as you make for Two Medicine Lake and your starting point.

North of Going-to-the-Sun Road

Swiftcurrent Lake Nature Trail

Duration 1 hour

Distance 4km (2.5miles)

Difficulty Easy

Start/Finish Many Glacier Lodge

Elevation Change Negligible

Nearest Facilities Many Glacier (p184)

Transportation East Side Shuttle

Summary From civilization to bear-infested wilderness in less than 60 seconds; natural juxtapositions don't get much more dramatic than this.

Anchoring the trail system that connects Many Glacier's three navigable lakes – Swiftcurrent, Josephine and Grinnell – this easy flat nature trail offers a potent taste of the valley's rugged essence. Take note: despite heavy usage and its proximity to the hotel, the trail often posts bear warnings.

Heading south from the Many Glacier Hotel along the shoreline of deceptively shallow Swiftcurrent Lake (9m/30ft at its deepest point), you'll pass an old boathouse and ranger station now used as accommodation for summer guides. At a junction for the Grinnell Lake Trail at the southern end of the lake stay right and take a wooden footbridge across the channel between Swiftcurrent and Josephine Lakes. Very soon after you'll pass a small dock used by boat trip groups organized out of the hotel. Continue to the right and finish your lake circumnavigation amid widening mountain views, peeks of the distinctive **Salamander Glacier**, and possible moose sightings along the willowy shoreline. After skirting close to the Many Glacier campground the trail turns east and deposits you back in a picnic area adjacent to the handsome hotel.

Iceberg Lake Trail

Duration 5½ hours round-trip

Distance 14.5km (9 miles)

Difficulty Easy-moderate

Start/Finish Swiftcurrent Motor Inn

Elevation Change 370m (1190ft)

Nearest Facilities Many Glacier (p184)

Transportation East Side Shuttle

Summary A well-trodden, wildlife-studded trail through relatively open terrain to the unique and otherworldly Iceberg Lake.

Famed for the bobbing bergs that float like miniature ice cubes in its still waters all summer long, the Iceberg Lake hike has long been a classic Glacier National Park pilgrimage. The popularity of the hike is understandable. Enclosed in a deep glacial cirque and surrounded on three sides by stunning 914m (3000ft) vertical walls, the lake is one of the most impressive sights anywhere in the Rockies. The 366m (1200ft) ascent to get there is gentle, and the approach is mostly at or above the tree line, affording awesome views.

Wildflowers fans will go ga-ga in the meadows near the lake. The Iceberg and Ptarmigan Trailhead is just past the Swiftcurrent Motor Inn. Bears are often sighted on this trail, so check at the ranger station before setting out and take all of the usual precautions.

Starting steeply, the trail packs most of its elevation gain into the first few kilometers (2 miles). But once you emerge onto the scrubby slopes above Many Glacier the gradient is barely perceptible. After 3.2km (2 miles) the path enters a small section of mature forest and arrives at Ptarmigan Creek, crossed by a footbridge, just upstream from **Ptarmigan Falls**. Here you climb gently through pine to the Ptarmigan Tunnel Trail junction, which heads right.

Continuing toward Iceberg Lake, you'll fall upon the first of several beautiful meadows under **Ptarmigan Wall**. Descend for a short distance to cross Iceberg Creek via a footbridge, and then climb up past **Little Iceberg Lake** before dropping down to the shores of your hallowed destination, the icy-blue cirque lake.

Iceberg Lake is 45.7m (150ft) deep and about 1.2km (0.75 miles) across; the granite walls average 914m (3000ft) in height, easily on a par with the big walls of Yosemite. The glacier is now inactive but, as the lake lies in the shadows on the north side of Mt Wilbur, the area remains cool all through summer.

Swiftcurrent Pass Trail

Duration 6 hours one way

Distance 12km (7.6 miles)

Difficulty Moderate-difficult

Start/Finish Swiftcurrent Motor Inn

Elevation Change 650m (2100ft)

Nearest Facilities Many Glacier (p184)

Transportation East Side Shuttle

Summary A pleasant meander through the Many Glacier Valley, followed by a steep climb up to the Continental Divide.

This popular trail departs from the west side of the Swiftcurrent Motor Inn parking lot and can be linked up with the Loop or Highline Trails (p189) to make an arduous one-day, or slightly less arduous two-day, hike.

Easing in slowly, the first 6.4km (4 miles) of the trail are relatively easy, bisecting low lodgepole forest sprinkled with aspen, the result of dynamic regrowth following the 1936 Heaven's Peak Fire. Looking around, you'll see the highest visible summit, Mt Wilbur, to the northwest, jagged Grinnell Mountain to the south, and Swiftcurrent Mountain, which this path eventually ascends, to the southwest.

Hiking through the potentially hot open terrain, you will soon find relief amid the foliage, including Englemann spruce, subalpine fir, fireweed, maple and the shade-giving quaking aspen. Wildflower spotters will enjoy colorful landscapes dotted with forget-me-nots, paintbrush, harebell, yellow columbine and Siberian chive. Watch for stinging nettle along the way and make plenty of noise to ward off Many Glacier's many bears.

Less than 2.4km (1.5 miles) into the trail, the path brushes the northern tip of **Red Rock Lake**, and the waterfalls become visible in the distance. Beavers are active along streams in this valley; look out for beaver lodges on the other side of the lake. At 5.3km (3.3 miles) you'll hit **Bullhead Lake** and from here you'll begin a 4.8km (3-mile) climb up to Swiftcurrent Pass, with an elevation of 2064m (6770ft), gaining 610m (2000ft) in the process. The switchbacks on the ascent are numerous and the path, which cuts sharply into the mountainside, becomes ever more vertiginous as you climb (if you suffer badly from vertigo, give this part a miss). The Continental Divide at **Swiftcurrent Pass** is marked by an unruly pile of rocks surrounded by dwarf trees. For a far better view, take the spur trail up a further set of switchbacks to the **Swiftcurrent Lookout** for one of the park's most tower-topping views. Returning to the pass, either retrace your steps, or head 1.5km (0.9 miles) down to the Granite Park Chalet to link up with other trails.

Quartz Lakes Loop

Duration 7 hours round-trip

Distance 20.5km (12.8 miles)

Difficulty Moderate

Start/Finish Bowman Lake Campground

Elevation Change 765m (2470ft)

Nearest Facilities Polebridge (p224)

Transportation Private

Summary Lakes, solitude and scenery are three of the North Fork Valley's primary draws, and all are on display during this multifarious hike.

Remote and hard to get to without a car, the wild North Fork Valley is a solitude seeker's utopia. The Quartz Lakes Loop is one of the area's only loop trails, a hiking staple renowned for its wonderful scenery and close-up views of a forest still regenerating after recent (natural) fires.

From the trailhead, cross Bowman Creek before beginning a gradual ascent along the shores of **Bowman Lake**. After 1.6km (1 mile) or so you'll start a more precipitous climb up to **Cerulean Ridge**, with an elevation of 1676m (5500ft), where you'll be afforded fantastic views of a triumvirate of beautiful lakes – Quartz Lake, tiny Middle Quartz Lake and Lower Quartz Lake – shimmering like tinfoil below. The path drops down to the west side of **Quartz Lake**, passing in and out of forest and providing graphic evidence of the effects of the 1988 Red Bench Fire.

Once in the valley, skirt the edges of all three lakes via a clearly marked path ending up, after 5km (3 miles), in a backcountry campground at the south end of Lower Quartz Lake. From here it's a 2.4km (1.5-mile) ascent to the crest of Cerulean Ridge – for the second time – before you drop back down to Bowman Creek.

OVERNIGHT HIKES

Backcountry hiking is what Glacier's all about and hitting the high trails will quickly introduce intrepid travelers to a side of the park that few other visitors see. Aside from the two options listed here you can also split the Dawson-Pitamakin Loop into a two-day hike. Another option is to join the Swiftcurrent Pass Trail with the Highline Trail, overnighting in the Granite Park Chalet or campground.

The hiking chart on p36 provides a quick overview of all the backcountry hikes covered in this section.

BACKCOUNTRY ACCOMMODATIONS

Sperry Chalet (Map p180; ☎406-387-5654; www.sperrychalet.com; r US$125-180, incl meals) Built by the Great Northern Railway in 1914, this 17-room historic chalet (which is a notch up from the Granite Park Chalet) is part of an old accommodations network that once spanned the park before the construction of the Going-to-the-Sun Rd. Still a good three-hour hike from the nearest road, guests must either walk or horseback ride here via an ascending 10.5km (6.5-mile) trail that begins at Lake McDonald Lodge. With no lights, heat or water, staying at the Sperry rates alongside a night in the African bush. But don't fret. Rooms are private and rates include three meals. There's just the small matter of the shared restrooms, which are outside. Bring a flashlight for midnight trips to the toilet!

Granite Park Chalet (Map p180; ☎406-387-5555; www.graniteparkchalet.com; r US$73-85) Another historic chalet from the park's early-20th-century heyday, the Granite is even more basic than the Sperry, though its off-road setting is no less magnificent. A popular stopping point for hikers on the Swiftcurrent Pass and Highline Trails, a rustic kitchen and dining room are available for use (with propane-powered stoves), though you must bring and prepare your own meals. You can also purchase snacks, freeze-dried meals and sodas. Twelve guest rooms sleep two to six people each. Book in advance as it gets busy.

Gunsight Pass Trail

Duration 2 days one way

Distance 32km (20 miles)

Difficulty Moderate-difficult

Start Jackson Glacier Overlook

Finish Lake McDonald Lodge

Elevation Change 930m (3000ft)

Nearest Facilities Logan Pass (p183)

Transportation Going-to-the-Sun Rd shuttle

Summary A great introduction to Glacier's backcountry, with tremendous views and abundant wildlife, plus the opportunity to stay in the park's historic Sperry Chalet.

Truly bionic hikers knock out this spectacular trail in one day but, with copious snowfields, glaciers and lakes sprinkled along the 32km (20-mile) route that straddles the lofty Continental Divide, two days is a more appropriate time span. The trail is doable in either direction, but most hikers kick off at the Jackson Glacier Overlook on the Going-to-the-Sun Rd (a designated free shuttle stop) and head west toward the Lake McDonald Lodge. If you are planning to spend the night at the historic Sperry Chalet (see boxed text, p193) en route, you'll need to book your space well in advance (a move that will save you carrying camping equipment).

DAY 1: JACKSON GLACIER OVERLOOK TO SPERRY CHALET/CAMPGROUND

6 TO 9 HOURS, 21.7KM (13.6 MILES)

On the first day follow the trail southeast through fir and spruce forest until it stumbles upon Reynolds Creek. The path follows the creek past Deadwood Falls to a junction with the Gunsight Pass Trail at 2km (1.3 miles); take the trail on the right. It crosses a bridge past Reynolds Creek Campground and then heads alongside the St Mary River. At 6.4km (4 miles), a junction offers a 1km (0.6-mile) trail to Florence Falls.

Carry on up the valley below Citadel and Fusilade Mountains (east and west respectively), taking in views of glaciers clinging to a high ridge between Blackfoot Mountain and Mt Jackson. Soon after the Gunsight Lake Campground, 9.6km (6 miles) in, a suspension bridge traverses St Mary River and leads up numerous switchbacks through cow parsnip and alder shrub.

In all, it's a two- to three-hour hike from the campground to **Gunsight Pass**, with an elevation of 2117m (6946ft) on the Continental Divide. Reaching the pass involves walking over cliff ledges high above the

Gunsight Pass Trail

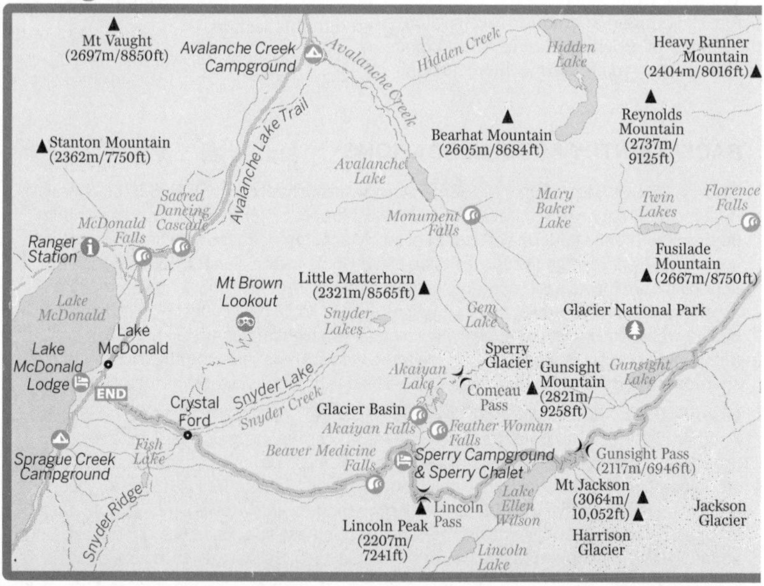

lake, but the trail is broad. A basic emergency shelter (day-use only) stands on this narrow saddle.

Steeply descending switchbacks lead to the north shore of **Lake Ellen Wilson**, a spectacular alpine lake lying in a deep trough ringed by sheer, glaciated rock walls. The trail continues around the lake's western shore, passing above Lake Ellen Wilson Campground.

Go up the slope to a high shelf overlooking Lincoln Lake. The trail turns gradually to cross the apex of the hike, **Lincoln Pass**, with an elevation of 2149m (7050ft), just north of Lincoln Peak, then winds its way down past Sperry Campground. Four scenic sites here overlook Lake McDonald far below. Mountain goats regularly visit the camp, so always use the pit toilet.

Close by is the historic **Sperry Chalet**.

DAY 2: SPERRY CHALET/ CAMPGROUND TO LAKE MCDONALD LODGE

2½ TO 3 HOURS, 10.3KM (6.4 MILES)

On this day drop past Sperry Glacier Trail and across small Sprague Creek. The trail leads down into fir-spruce forest, past **Beaver Medicine Falls**. It continues 4km (2.5 miles) downvalley to cross Snyder Creek on a footbridge. You'll pass turnoffs to Fish Lake, Snyder Lakes and Mt Brown Lookout as the trail descends through a mossy forest of cedar, hemlock, grand fir, larch and yew to Going-to-the-Sun Rd. Watch out for horse droppings covering the trail; it's a favorite with riders from the Lake McDonald Corral.

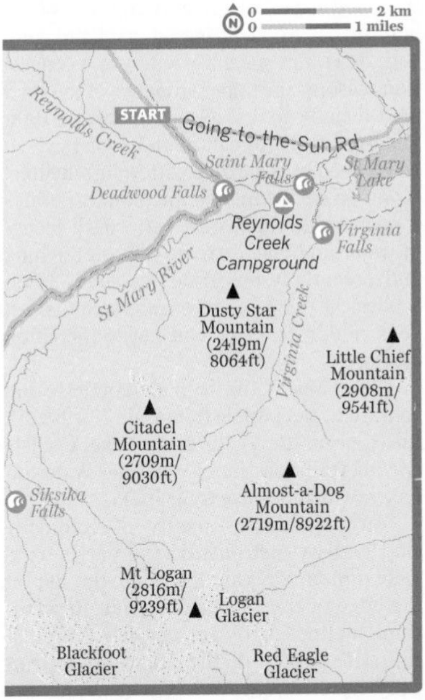

Northern Highline-Waterton Valley

Duration 2-3 days

Distance 46km (28.8 miles)

Difficulty Moderate-difficult

Start Going-to-the-Sun Rd

Finish Goat Haunt

Elevation Change 1280m (4200ft)

Nearest Facilities Logan Pass (p183)

Transportation Going-to-the-Sun Rd shuttle

Summary Follow the splendiferous Highline Trail beyond the Granite Park Chalet to Waterton, Canada, end-point of the 5000km (3100-mile) Continental Divide Trail.

An extension of the popular 'Garden Wall' section of the Highline Trail, this trail, often known as the Northern Highline, forges deeper into the backcountry across open subalpine terrain toward the Goat Haunt region and the border with Canada. It is also the end point of the 5000km (3100-mile) Continental Divide Trail (CDT) that runs from Mexico up to Canada (Glacier National Park guards the final 176km/110-mile segment of the route).

DAY 1: GOING-TO-THE-SUN ROAD TO FIFTY MOUNTAIN CAMPGROUND

8 TO 9 HOURS, 24.9KM (15.6 MILES)

Start this hike from the Loop, a tightly angled switchback on the Going-to-the-Sun Rd, 12.8km (8 miles) west of Logan Pass that also serves as a free shuttle stop. An alternative starting point is the trailhead for the Highline Trail at Logan Pass, an option that will add a scenic 5.8km (3.6 miles) to your overall trip.

From the Loop, the climb begins almost immediately through landscape scarred by the 2003 Trapper Fire. Burnt tree trunks characterize a mountainside slowly coming back to life after the inferno. The views are superb. After 1km (0.6 miles) the Packers Roost trail joins in from the left. Continue walking uphill gaining 701m (2300ft) of elevation within 6.4km (4 miles) to reach the historic **Granite Park Chalet** (see boxed text, p193), built in 1915 as the last link in a chain of backcountry chalets constructed by the Great Northern Railway (only two remain). The chalet offers hostel accommodation (reserve ahead), a campground, drinks and snacks. There is no running water.

You may want to spend the night at the chalet and incorporate a short side trip up to Swiftcurrent Pass and Lookout. If you're pressing on, get moving quickly as it's 18.5km (11.6 miles) to the next campground – Fifty Mountain.

Take the trail to Swiftcurrent Pass and fork almost immediately left to follow the far less crowded Northern Highline Trail as it parallels the Continental Divide through high subalpine terrain with tremendous vistas of peaks, meadows and safe-from-a-distance wildlife (grizzlies, moose and wolves have all been spotted here). After about 8km (5 miles) an overlook trail to **Ahern Pass** and a view of Helen Lake forks off to the right. If you're not up for the detour, continue straight ahead climbing up toward the Continental Divide, which you will cross after a short sharp climb 17km (10.5 miles) from the Granite Park Chalet.

The **Fifty Mountain Campground** is just over the other side situated in an alpine bowl below a meadow. It is named for the number of mountains you can see from its stunning viewpoint (count them!) and is arguably the finest backcountry campsite in the park.

DAY 2: FIFTY MOUNTAIN CAMPGROUND TO GOAT HAUNT

5 TO 6 HOURS, 21.1KM (13.2 MILES)

Wake up amid the moody magnificence of Fifty Mountain and try to tear yourself way from the view and the braver-than-usual deer. Day 2 (or 3 depending on your schedule) involves a 732m (2400ft) descent down into the Waterton Valley and Goat Haunt on Upper Waterton Lake. Most of the descending is in the first 8km (5 miles) as you drop from the Fifty Mountain plateau to the intersection with the Stoney Indian Trail at 4.2km (2.7 miles). Soon after, you'll come across the Pass Creek ranger hut and footbridge. Back beneath the timberline is the epiphanic sight of **Kootenai Lakes** (reached via a short trail on the left) often frequented by day-hikers from Goat Haunt. The lake is renowned for its moose sightings. Continue along the valley for a further 4km (2.5 miles) to the Goat Haunt ranger station where you will need to show your passport in order to board a boat (or alternatively hike 11.2km/7 miles) to Waterton Townsite in Canada.

BIKING

Glacier National Park diverges from Banff, Waterton and Jasper in that none of its trails are open to cyclists. An alternative for two-wheeled travelers is to make use of the park's only allocated bike path (a flat 4km/2.5-mile ramble from West Glacier to Apgar Village), or ply the limited road network – essentially the Going-to-the-Sun Rd – which has further restrictions on when you can and can't use it. A third deterrent for aspiring cyclists is the lack of any bike rental facilities in the park. You can choose from a limited stash of basic machines in the **St Mary KOA Campground** (106 West Shore Rd, St Mary; per hr/day US$2.50/20). Better bicycles are available at **Glacier Cyclery** (www.glaciercyclery.com; 326 2nd St, Whitefish; hybrid bike per day/week from US$25/125) in Whitefish 72km (45 miles) southwest, a fine establishment staffed by experts.

Nevertheless, committed cyclists can be spied daily throughout the summer attempting Glacier's blue riband ride, the 85km (53-mile) Going-to-the-Sun Rd, where the spectacular vistas and copious twists and turns are befitting of a challenging Tour de France stage. For safety and congestion reasons, the upper stretches of the road are officially shut to cyclists between 11am and 4pm daily (mid-June to Labor Day), so you'll need to be flexible with your schedule. If you do decide to take the plunge (and it's a memorable ride), start early, pack plenty of water and take extreme care on the long and potentially precarious descents. From a physical point of view, it's easier to start your ride in St Mary and tackle the climb east–west.

The closest thing to a mountain-biking venture in the park is the Inside North Fork Rd (Glacier Rte 7) to Kintla Lake. Cyclists craving trail rides should consider Waterton Lakes, which has five trails (p215).

You'll encounter plenty of colorfully clad cyclists just outside the park's eastern boundary, plying Hwys 49 and 89, on the edge of the Blackfeet Indian Reservation. Inclines here are gentler, although the stiff winds off the adjacent prairies can be punishing.

Hiker-biker campgrounds are available at Apgar, Avalanche, Fish Creek, Many Glacier, Rising Sun, Sprague Creek, St Mary and Two Medicine Campgrounds.

OTHER ACTIVITIES

Boating

McDonald, Bowman, Swiftcurrent, Two Medicine and St Mary Lakes have launching ramps available for boats. Sailors might find St Mary Lake's winds to their liking. If bringing your own watercraft to Glacier, see p179.

Glacier Park Boat Co KAYAKING, CANOEING
(www.glacierparkboats.com) Rents out small boats (kayaks, canoes and rowboats) in summer at Apgar, Lake McDonald, Two Medicine and Many Glacier for US$15 per hour. Rowing boats go for US$18 per hour.

White-Water Rafting & Float Trips

The North and Middle Forks of the Flathead River are very popular with rafters, though all rafting tours take place on or outside the park's boundaries. The best water flow is from May to September with the rapids ranking an unterrifying class I to III.

Glacier Raft Co RAFTING
(www.glacierraftco.com; 6 Going-to-the-Sun Rd) Glacier Raft Co, in West Glacier Village behind the Alberta Visitor Center, is arguably the most reputable raft company in the area. Prices for trips down the North Fork and Middle Fork of the Flathead River start at US$49/84 for a half-/full day.

Wild River Adventures RAFTING
(www.riverwild.com) Offers similarly priced trips to Glacier Raft Co, including a scenic family float for adult/child US$51/41.

Fishing

The fishing season in streams and rivers is late May to late November, though lakes are open for fishing year-round. While anglers explore easily accessible waters like Lake McDonald and St Mary Lake, it is some of the hike-in destinations that can prove the most tranquil getaways; try Hidden Lake, Oldman Lake or Red Eagle Lake. Most of Glacier's fish were introduced to provide 'sport' for visitors up until the 1960s. Species include cutthroat trout, northern pike, whitefish, burbot, kokanee salmon, brook trout, rainbow trout, mackinaw and grayling.

A Montana state fishing license is not required within Glacier National Park, though anglers should familiarize themselves with the general park regulations available at any visitor center. Anglers are generally limited to possession of five fish daily, with caps varying by species. Some waters, including Hidden Lake and the North and Middle Forks of the Flathead River, are purely catch-and-release zones. Read the park's *Fishing Regulations* pamphlet. Portions of the North Fork and Middle Fork of the Flathead River outside the

BOAT & HIKE COMBOS

Six historic boats – some dating back to the 1920s – ply five of Glacier's attractive mountain lakes and some of them have the added bonus of combining the watery ride with a short guided hike led by interpretive, often witty guides. One of the best excursions leaves from the Many Glacier Hotel twice daily (July to September) and chugs slowly across shallow Swiftcurrent Lake to a landing point on the opposite (southern) side. From here groups disembark and stroll 400m (0.25 miles) to the shores of Josephine Lake where another boat whisks you ever closer to the Continental Divide. Upon landing, your guide will lead you a further 2.4km (1.5 miles) overland to Grinnell Lake for wondrous glacial views. This is prime grizzly bear country and the safety-in-numbers groups put many nervous hikers at greater ease.

A similar boat-hike combo can be undertaken on Two Medicine Lake, which marries a 45-minute cruise with a 3.2km (2-mile) walk to double-flumed Twin Falls. On St Mary Lake boats departing from Rising Sun incorporate a 1½-hour cruise with a longer 4.8km (3-mile) hike to St Mary Falls.

All boat trips are run by the **Glacier Park Boat Co** (www.glacierparkboats.com) and can be booked in person at boat docks in Many Glacier, Lake McDonald Lodge, Two Medicine and Rising Sun (St Mary Lake). The cost is a generic adult/child US$25/12.

park are subject to Montana state fishing regulations. Part of Lower Two Medicine Lake is on reservation land and subject to Blackfeet Indian Reservation regulations.

Glacier Guides Inc FISHING
(www.glacierguides.com) This company runs half-day (US$358) and full-day (US$465) fishing trips to the Middle and North Forks of the Flathead River. It also runs a part-classroom, part-practical fly-fishing school (US$465).

Glacier Outdoor Center FISHING
(www.glacierraftco.com) From the Glacier Outdoor Center you can organize longer two- to seven-day trips from US$399 per day.

Rock Climbing

While Glacier's sharp ridges and steeply stacked cliff faces might look like a rock-climber's paradise, the opposite is often the case. Due to the nature of the Rocky Mountains' loose sedimentary rock – much of it metamorphosed mudstone and limestone – technical climbing in the park is not the sport of choice. *A Climber's Guide to Glacier National Park* by J Gordon Edwards, available at visitor-center bookstores, runs through the area's basics. Climbers and adrenaline junkies can find solace in the tough, but nontechnical, ascent of the park's highest peak, Mt Cleveland, which is 3190m (10,466ft), or some more demanding high ridgeline walking or glacier traveling. Interested parties should enquire at visitor centers and ranger stations, and sign a register before setting out.

Horseback Riding

Glacier may be stingy toward cyclists, but there are far fewer restrictions toward horseback riders – this, after all, is Cowboy-land Montana.

Swan Mountain Outfitters HORSEBACK RIDING
(www.swanmountainoutfitters.com; early May-early Sep) Back in the 'old' days, before the Going-to-the-Sun Rd was built, getting around by horse between the various tourist chalets was the primary means of transport and horses still run a regular supply line up to the Sperry Chalet, a route that can be incorporated into an excellent day ride with Swan Mountain Outfitters, the park's *only* horseback riding guides. The company offers a variety of other trips lasting from a one-hour circumnavigation of Josephine Lake (US$40) to an all-day foray to Cracker Lake (US$160). Its three corrals are maintained at Lake McDonald, Many Glacier Corral and Apgar Village. It also staffs a small **ticket booth** (406-888-5557) in Apgar Village, next to the visitor center. All trips are led by experienced wranglers who'll furnish you with plenty of entertaining tales.

Ranger Programs

Throughout summer there are a whole host of free evening ranger talks, slide shows and guided walks available in Glacier National Park's hotels, campgrounds and visitor centers. Topics vary from culture and history to ecology and Native American Speaks. You'll find a printed schedule posted at all park visitor centers, or listed in the *Activity Schedule* newspaper. Alternatively, you can scan the official park website at www.nps.gov/glac. Popular spots are Many Glacier Hotel, St Mary Visitor Center and the Apgar Campground outdoor amphitheater.

The nonprofit **Glacier Association** (www.glacierassociation.org) works in cooperation with the National Park Service to raise money for park educational and scientific projects through the sale of park-related publications at bookshops and visitor centers. You can become a member; see the website for details.

Glacier Institute WORKSHOPS, CAMPS
(www.glacierinstitute.org) The Glacier Institute, founded in 1983, offers one-/two-/three-day workshops, youth camps and courses year-round from US$65 to US$270.

Glacier Guides Inc HIKING TRIPS
(www.glacierguides.com) Leads guided day hikes and backpacking trips from mid-May through September.

Golf

Two golf courses lie just outside the park limits.

Glacier Park Lodge Golf Course GOLF COURSE
(www.glacierparkinc.com) Located in East Glacier, this is the oldest golf course in Montana, and the most picturesque.

Glacier View Golf Club GOLF COURSE
(www.glacierviewgolf.com) Overlooking the Middle Fork of the Flathead River, this golf club, in West Glacier, is another scenic gem. Green fees are US$20/29 for nine/18 holes. Club rental starts at US$14.

Cross-Country Skiing & Snowshoeing

Jasper and Banff this is not. From October to May, when the Going-to-the-Sun Rd is snowed under, most services in Glacier close, leaving the park to wildlife and intrepid, self-sufficient cross-country skiers and snowshoers, most of whom base themselves out of Whitefish or Kalispell.

The one exception is the **Izaak Walton Inn** (www.izaakwaltoninn.com) in Essex, a handy Amtrak train stop on the park's southern boundary that maintains its own small network of groomed and partly floodlit cross-country skiing and snowshoe trails (33km/20.5 miles worth) from November to April. Instructors based here can organize private ski lessons (US$45) or take you on customized backcountry skiing or snowshoeing trips (US$115 to US$200) into the almost deserted winter park. The inn rents out skis/snowshoes for US$30/15 per day.

Self-sufficient cross-country skiers can choose from a number of popular marked but ungroomed trails in the park itself, the bulk of them emanating from Apgar Village and Lake McDonald. A well-used favorite is to ski along an unplowed section of the Going-to-the-Sun Rd from the (closed) Lake McDonald Lodge to Avalanche Creek. The road is always plowed as far as the lodge, allowing easy access by car. Another regularly tackled trail is the 18.5km (11.5-mile) **McGee Meadow Loop** heading up the unplowed Camas Rd and back down the Inside Fork Rd to Apgar Village. Far more difficult is the steep 8.3km (5.2-mile) ascent to the **Apgar Lookout**.

Other lesser used park penetration points are St Mary for the Red Eagle Lake Trail, Polebridge for the Bowman Lake trail, and Two Medicine for the unplowed Two Medicine Rd as far as Running Eagle Falls.

Although all hotels and restaurants stay closed and the park registers only a handful of visitors, Glacier's mountains and valleys remain gloriously open all winter to those intrepid enough to breach them. For ultimate safety organize a guided backcountry ski tour with **Glacier Park Ski Tours** (☎406-892-2173; www.glacierparkskitours.com), which operates out of Whitefish. Day rates hover at around US$200 per person. Add on US$40+ a day for longer trips, where you'll be taught to build and sleep in your own igloos.

TOURS

Red Jammer Buses BUS TOURS

Run by **Glacier Park Inc** (www.glacierparkinc.com), Glacier's stylish red 'jammer' buses (a legacy of when drivers had to 'jam' hard on the gears) are synonymous with the park and a nostalgic reminder of the pioneering days of early motorized transportation. Introduced on the Going-to-the-Sun Rd between 1936 and 1939, the buses have been serving the park loyally for over 70 years, save for a two-year sabbatical in 1999 when the fleet was briefly taken out of service to be reconfigured by the Ford Motor Company. Sparkling afresh after an extensive makeover that has made the buses safer, sturdier and 93% more environmentally friendly (they now run off propane gas), jammers are once again transporting visitors along a dozen memorable routes interspersed with plenty of scenic stops. As much a part of the scenery as the glaciers themselves, it is difficult to imagine the park without them.

Jammer tours range from the Western Alpine Tour (adult/child US$50/25), a 3½-hour trip between Lake McDonald Lodge and Logan Pass, to the Big Sky Circle Tour (adult/child US$80/40), an 8½-hour journey that circles the park via US 2. The International Peace Park Tour departs Many Glacier (adult/child US$55/27.50) and St Mary Lodge (adult/child US$65/32.50) daily, rumbling through the east side of the park before heading to Waterton Lakes National Park in Canada in time for an optional high tea at the Prince of Wales Hotel.

Sun Tours BUS TOURS

(☎406-226-9220; www.glaciersuntours.com) Blackfeet tribal members lead these interpretive tours (adult/child US$40/20) of the Going-to-the-Sun Rd. Air-conditioned buses leave from various points in East Glacier, St Mary and Browning; tours last for approximately four hours.

Glacier Park Boat Co BOAT TOURS

(www.glacierparkboats.com) Offers boat tours (adult/child US$25/12.50) departing at least five times daily from the docks at Lake McDonald Lodge, Two Medicine, Many Glacier Hotel (for Swiftcurrent and Josephine Lakes) and Rising Sun (for St Mary Lake). All trips are on boats dating from the 1920s and '30s and are narrated

NATIVE AMERICAN NEXUS

Where the grassy plains of the prairies meet the saw-toothed mountains of Glacier National Park three legendary Native American tribes once intermingled – and the results weren't always peaceful.

One of the most populous tribes in the Montana region was the Blackfeet (Niitsítapi), a westward-dwelling subset of the Algonquian-speaking Plains Native Americans, a linguistic group that included the Crow, Cheyenne and Sioux. Warlike and highly mobile, the Blackfeet acquired horses in the 1730s from the Shoshoni people, and they used their new bounty to hunt buffalo and assert territorial rights over the mountains east of the Continental Divide where numerous sacred sites (including Two Medicine and Chief Mountain) were integral to the tribe's creation story.

Glacier's western slopes, meanwhile, were the domain of the more peaceful Plateau Native Americans, most notably the Flathead and Kootenai tribes. The former were Salish people, related through language to a much larger family of tribes that spread west as far as the Pacific coast. The latter were a cultural anomaly whose anthropological roots remain sketchy, and whose language is a linguistic isotope unrelated to any other Native American tongue.

The Salish and Kootenai were skilled fishermen and canoeists who subsisted on a diet of salmon plucked from the region's teeming rivers, but who sometimes crossed the Rockies to hunt buffalo. It was on these eastern forays that they came into contact and – inevitably – conflict with the more numerous Blackfeet. Though the Flatheads, over time, adopted some Plains Native American characteristics (horses and teepees for instance), the superior firepower of the Blackfeet meant that they slowly pushed the Plateau tribes back west.

In 1805–06 all three tribes had their first contact with white settlers when the Lewis and Clark expedition passed through the region on an abortive attempt to find a northern route over the Rockies. Relations were initially cordial, particularly among the Salish and Kootenai with whom the explorers traded horses, but events took a turn for the worse on the expedition's return leg when a small party led by Lewis got into a skirmish with a group of Blackfeet and two braves were killed. Tellingly, they were the only fatalities of the group's two-year adventure.

All three tribes suffered during the westward expansion of white settlers in the early 19th century and the near extinction of the buffalo that ensued. Relying increasingly on government money Native Americans had little choice but to agree to one-sided treaties in 1855. The Salish and Kootenai were signatories to the ambiguous Hellgate Treaty, which merged them into the Confederated Salish and Kootenai tribes of the Flathead Nation on the Flathead Indian Reservation in northwest Montana. The Blackfeet, meanwhile, signed the Lame Bull Treaty the same year, creating a sprawling reservation a little larger than Delaware. The reservation originally included all of the Glacier National Park region east of the Continental Divide; however, in 1896, due to continuing economic difficulties, the Blackfeet sold a further 3200 sq km (2000 sq miles) of this land for US$1.5 million to the US government, intent on prospecting for copper and gold. When no minerals were found the government, recognizing the area's potential as a tourist destination, formed Glacier National Park in 1910.

Today approximately 8500 Blackfeet live on a 6100-sq-km (3812-sq-mile) reservation immediately to the east of the park that includes important park nexuses such as St Mary, East Glacier and Lower Two Medicine Lake. To the southwest approximately 6800 Flathead and Kootenai Native Americans inhabit a 5000-sq-km (1938-sq-mile) reservation between Kalispell and Missoula.

by an interpretive guide; some include an optional short hike (see the boxed text, p197). Cocktail cruises depart the Rising Sun (6:30pm) and Lake McDonald (7pm) docks.

Kruger Helicop-Tours HELICOPTER TOURS
(☎406-387-4565; www.krugerhelicopters.com) To get a view from above the eagles' nests, consider a helicopter tour run by this outfit, which has offices on US 2, 1.6km (1 mile) west of West Glacier. Hourly rates start at US$230 per person.

SLEEPING

In the early 1910s James Hill's Great Northern Railway built a series of grand hotels to lure rich tourists to Glacier National Park. Two of these so-called parkitecture structures, Many Glacier Lodge and Lake McDonald Lodge, still stand within the park boundaries, conjuring up nostalgic memories of times gone by.

In keeping with the park's back-to-nature ethos, the lodges have been kept religiously 'rustic,' ie they are bereft of distracting modern appliances such as TVs, room phones and wi-fi. All are also nonsmoking and offer at least one wheelchair-accessible room. Operated by **Glacier Park, Inc** (406-892-2525; www.glacierparkinc.com), the lodges can be booked through a central reservations system.

Going-to-the-Sun Road

Camping

All of the Going-to-the-Sun Rd campgrounds act as bus stops on the free summer shuttle route, making link-ups with trailheads and visitor centers refreshingly easy.

Two campgrounds – St Mary and Apgar – are open in winter. St Mary takes advance **reservations** (406-888-7800).

Avalanche Creek Campground CAMPGROUND $
(Map p180; campsites US$20; mid-Jun–early Sep) This lush campground abutting the park's old-growth cedar forest gets more rainfall than most. Some sites are overshadowed by old stands of hemlock, cedar and Douglas fir, but you're close to Lake McDonald and right in the path of a couple of popular trailheads.

Rising Sun Campground CAMPGROUND $
(Map p180; campsites US$20; early Jun-early Sep) Situated on Glacier's more unprotected eastern side, 8km (5 miles) west of St Mary entrance station, sites here vary, with lush and diverse vegetation providing some shade. A host of facilities, including the Rising Sun Motor Inn, a store, a restaurant and a boat launch, are nearby.

Sprague Creek Campground CAMPGROUND $
(Map p180; campsites US$20; mid-May–mid-Sep) Off Going-to-the-Sun Rd on the upper shores of Lake McDonald, the park's smallest campground draws mostly tents – no vehicles over 6.4m (21ft) are allowed – and feels more intimate than many of the park's other options, at least at night when the passing traffic goes to bed. Arrive early to claim a site overlooking the lake.

Apgar Campground CAMPGROUND $
(Map p180; campsites US$15-20; early May-Oct, Dec-late Mar) This large wooded campground is a good choice for its proximity to Apgar Village. A handy cycle path connects it to a store and restaurant, and the brand-new transit center.

St Mary Campground CAMPGROUND $
(Map p180; 406-888-7800; campsites US$23; late May-late Sep, Dec-late Mar) Cottonwood and aspen trees predominate in the most shaded sites at this campground just west of St Mary entrance station, though sites in the B loop are less protected.

Lodging

TOP CHOICE **Village Inn** MOTEL $$
(Map p180; 406-888-5632; www.villageinnatapgar.com; s/d US$130/185; late May-late Sep) Occupying a serene setting at the southern end of Lake McDonald in Apgar Village, this well-placed accommodation option is far posher than its motel billing implies. The rooms are the usual rustic, gadget-free zones, but lean out on your sunrise-facing balcony and you are, quite literally, within cherry-stone spitting distance of the park's largest and most tranquil lake.

Lake McDonald Lodge HOTEL, CABINS $$
(Map p180; 406-888-5431; www.lakemcdonaldlodge.com; r cabin/motel/lodge US$122/134/153; late May–mid-Sep;) Built on the site of an earlier lodge commissioned by park pioneer George Snyder in the 1890s, the present building was constructed in 1913 in classic US parkitecture style. Fronting luminous Lake McDonald, the establishment originally welcomed its guests by boat, meaning that present-day visitors must enter the lodge through the back door. Once inside, a huge fireplace ignites a cozy ambience and colorfully painted paper lamps add an attractive Native American touch. Small, old-fashioned lodge rooms (sans TV and air-con) are complemented by cottages and a 1950s motel. The location, next to boat docks and hiking trails, is perfect.

GLACIER NATIONAL PARK CAMPGROUNDS

CAMPGROUND	LOCATION	DESCRIPTION	NO OF SITES
Apgar	Going-to-the-Sun Rd	The park's largest campground is near trails, a lake and Apgar Village	196
Avalanche Creek	Going-to-the-Sun Rd	In old growth forest and close to hikes; also has an outdoor amphitheater for evening programs	87
Rising Sun	Going-to-the-Sun Rd	Part-open, part-covered sites close to camp store, restaurant and boat launch	83
Sprague Creek	Going-to-the-Sun Rd	No RVs allowed, but tranquil lake views are hindered by proximity to Going-to-the-Sun Rd	25
St Mary	Going-to-the-Sun Rd	Large and fairly open, with cracking views; visitor center nearby	148
Bowman Lake	North of Going-to-the-Sun Rd	Remote and basic, but great for tent campers; pit toilets available; bring mosquito repellent	48
Fish Creek	North of Going-to-the-Sun Rd	Large, wooded campground that offers plenty of privacy	180
Kintla Lake	North of Going-to-the-Sun Rd	The park's most remote campground; listen to the howls of wolves at night	13
Logging Creek	North of Going-to-the-Sun Rd	Small and primitive with no services; there are pit toilets	8
Many Glacier	North of Going-to-the-Sun Rd	One of the park's most popular campgrounds, set in a beautiful valley with facilities nearby	110
Quartz Creek	North of Going-to-the-Sun Rd	Smallest campground in the park, this place is primitive; RVs not recommended	7
Two Medicine	South of Going-to-the-Sun Rd	Secluded campground with space for larger RVs, and an evening ranger program	99

Drinking Water · *Flush Toilets* · *Grocery Store Nearby* · *Summertime Campfire Program*

Rising Sun Motor Inn MOTEL **$$**
(Map p180; ☎406-732-5523; www.risingsunmotorinn.com; r motel/cabin US$118/122; ⌚mid-Jun–early Sep) One of two classic 1940s-era motor inns in the park, Rising Sun lies on the upper north shore of St Mary Lake, in a small complex that includes a store, campground, restaurant and boat launch. Rustic motel and cabin rooms with wooden floors offer everything an exhausted hiker could hope for, although TV addicts and obsessive Blackberry users might find the dearth of technical gadgets a shock to the system.

Apgar Village Lodge MOTEL, CABINS **$$**
(Map p180; ☎406-888-5484; r US$95-135, cabins US$125-200; ⌚May–mid-Oct) The only privately owned accommodations within the park; this lodge (one of two in Apgar Village) offers well-maintained motel-style rooms and cabins. The cabins are spacious and most come with kitchenettes, while the smaller rooms are more rustic.

South of Going-to-the-Sun Road

Camping

Two Medicine Campground CAMPGROUND **$**
(Map p180; Two Medicine Valley; campsites US$15; ⌚late Jun-late Oct) This campground below Rising Wolf Mountain, 4.8km (3 miles) southwest of Two Medicine entrance station, is your only accommodation in the park's rudely ignored southwest corner. There are good sites near the lake and some nice wooded spots.

ELEVATION	OPEN	RESERVATIONS NEEDED?	DAILY FEE	FACILITIES	PAGE
960m (3153ft)	May-Oct, Dec-Mar	no	US$15-20		p201
1067m (3500ft)	Jun-Sep	no	US$20		p201
1463m (4800ft)	Jun-Sep	no	US$20		p201
1067m (3500ft)	May-Sep	no	US$20		p201
1372m (4500ft)	May-Sep, Dec-Mar	available	US$23		p201
1372m (4500ft)	May-Nov	no	US$12		p203
1067m (3500ft)	Jun-Sep	available	US$23		p204
1372m (4500ft)	May-Nov	no	US$15		p203
1372m (4500ft)	Jul-Sep	no	US$10		p203
1372m (4500ft)	Jun-Oct	no	US$15		p203
884m (2900ft)	Jul-Nov	no	US$10		p204
1585m (5200ft)	Jun-Oct	no	US$15		p202

RV Dump Station

North of Going-to-the-Sun Road

Camping

All campgrounds are first-come, first-served except Fish Creek.

TOP CHOICE **Many Glacier Campground** CAMPGROUND $
(Map p180; Many Glacier; campsites US$15; ⏲mid-Jun–late Oct) Its access to phenomenal trails makes this campground, next to Swiftcurrent Motor Inn, one of the park's most popular with the hiking set. It's also strolling distance from a restaurant, hot showers, a laundry, camp store and the sublime Many Glacier Hotel with its relaxing lobby.

Bowman Lake Campground CAMPGROUND $
(Map p180; North Fork; campsites US$12; ⏲mid-May–mid-Nov) Rarely full, this campground, 9.7km (6 miles) up Inside North Fork Rd from Polebridge, offers spacious sites in forested grounds. It has a visitor's information tent with reference books and local hiking information.

Kintla Lake Campground CAMPGROUND $
(Map p180; North Fork; campsites US$15; ⏲late May–mid-Nov) If you've come to Glacier to dip your nose into *Ulysses* and *War and Peace*, you'll find little to disturb you at this primitive campground, at the top of Inside North Fork Rd.

Logging Creek Campground CAMPGROUND $
(Map p180; North Fork; campsites US$10; ⏲early Jul-late Sep) It takes some determination to reach this primitive campground, on Inside

North Fork Rd, 27.4km (17 miles) north of Fish Creek Campground, but it is worth it if you're looking for tranquility amid the trees. The atmosphere is very still here but for the sound of a flowing creek.

Quartz Creek Campground CAMPGROUND $
(Map p180; North Fork; campsites US$10; ⏲early Jul-late Nov) The campground here, on Inside North Fork Rd, is similar to the one at Logging Creek, though its thicker vegetation lends a more private air.

Fish Creek Campground CAMPGROUND $
(Map p180; ☎406-888-7800; campsites US$23; ⏲early Jun-Sep) Cocooned inside a dense cedar-hemlock forest, around 5.6km (3.5 miles) northwest of the main park entrance, this campground offers sites that are tucked among the trees.

Lodging

TOP CHOICE **Many Glacier Hotel** HISTORIC HOTEL $$
(Map p180; ☎406-732-4411; www.manyglacierhotel.com; Many Glacier Valley; r US$145-180; ⏲mid-Jun–early Sep) Enjoying the most wondrous setting in the park, this fine old parkitecture-style lodge sits pretty on the northern shore of aquamarine Swiftcurrent Lake, within binocular-viewing distance of shimmering glaciers and foraging bears. Built in the style of a huge Swiss chalet by the Great Northern Railway in 1915, the hotel sprawls over five floors with an imposing open-plan lobby, complete with a huge fireplace and a resident pianist tinkling on the ivories. Large bar windows frame a postcard-perfect view, while upstairs rustic rooms offer comfortable beds, but no TVs or phones.

Swiftcurrent Motor Inn MOTEL $$
(Map p180; ☎406-732-5531; www.swiftcurrentmotorinn.com; Many Glacier Valley; cabin US$90, without bathroom US$70, motel US$134; ⏲mid-Jun–early Sep) A relic from the early days of the motor car, the Swiftcurrent, conveniently located next to numerous Many Glacier trailheads, purposefully replicates the austerity of the 1940s with basic but cozy facilities. A mixture of cabins and motel-style rooms come with or without showers and are bereft of modern luxuries such as TV and air-con. Directly outside the front door is a handy store, a restaurant and a laundry facility. If the lack of modernity becomes too much, you can always borrow an ironing board or hair dryer from the front desk.

EATING

Going-to-the-Sun Road

Jammer Joe's Grill & Pizzeria PIZZERIA, AMERICAN $
(Map p180; Lake McDonald Lodge; mains US$7-10; ⏲late May–mid-Sep; 👪) In downtown New York or Chicago you wouldn't give this wannabe pizzeria-family diner a second glance, but in Glacier it can be a pleasant apparition for exhausted hikers who have just returned from a protracted wind up Sperry Chalet/Mt Brown Lookout Trails. Kids are equally enamored by the simple no-frills menu.

Russells Fireside Dining Room INTERNATIONAL $$$
(Map p180; Lake McDonald Lodge; lunch & dinner US$12-30; ⏲late May–mid-Sep) Lake views and stuffed animal heads characterize the interior of this handsome restaurant at the Lake McDonald Lodge, where you can enjoy hash browns for breakfast, substantial sandwiches for lunch, and crab cakes and Caesar salad for dinner.

Two Dog Flats Grill AMERICAN, TEX-MEX $$
(Map p180; Rising Sun Motor Inn; mains US$15-20; ⏲mid-Jun–early Sep) With zilch competition, and a clientele made up primarily of tired, famished hikers, the Two Dog doesn't have to try too hard, embellishing its standard Montana fare with a faintly discernable Tex-Mex twist.

Eddie's Cafe AMERICAN $$
(Map p180; Apgar Village; mains US$12-22; ⏲late May–mid-Sep; 👪) If they were ever to invent a gastronomic genre called 'national park cuisine,' Eddie's would be a major exponent. Summer jobbers man the tables inside Apgar Village's only eating joint serving up meatloaf, fish and chips and buffalo burgers from a kitchen where quantity rules over quality. A couple of side windows rebalance the equation, knocking out decent smoothies, muffins as well as bucket-sized cups of coffee.

South of Going-to-the-Sun Road

Two Medicine Campstore SANDWICHES $
(Map p180; ☎406-892-2525; Two Medicine Valley; ⏲7am-9pm) While Two Medicine Valley has no standard restaurants, you can pur-

chase coffee, ice cream and enough ingredients to make up a decent picnic at this historic building-cum-grocery store that once served as a dining hall for the erstwhile Two Medicine Chalets. It was from here that President FD Roosevelt, accompanied by John D Rockefeller Jr, chose to give one of his famous 'fireside chats' in the 1930s.

North of Going-to-the-Sun Road

Ptarmigan Dining Room INTERNATIONAL **$$$**
(Map p180; Many Glacier Hotel; mains US$15-30; ⏲mid-Jun–early Sep) Stay safe at the top of the food chain inside this refined Many Glacier Hotel restaurant where you can enjoy steak, seafood and pasta as bears munch on berries in the bushes outside. Magnificent lake views make the average food seem a lot more appealing.

Italian Garden Ristorante PIZZERIA, ITALIAN **$**
(Map p180; Swiftcurrent Motor Inn; breakfast US$6-13; ⏲mid-Jun–early Sep) Take the Italian moniker with a pinch of salt. *Molto bene* this isn't, though the pizzas and soup/sandwich combos should tide you over until you re-enter the more refined gastronomic climes of Whitefish or Missoula. Breakfast is the best bet – standard American pancakes and eggs. A well-stocked camp store next door sells soda and sandwiches, and the restaurant can prepare a hiker's lunch with one day's notice.

DRINKING & ENTERTAINMENT

Both the Many Glacier Hotel and Lake McDonald Lodge have cozy bars, good for a post-hike alcoholic beverage. Many Glacier also has a pianist and occasional live music in its lobby.

The park visitor centers give out a free newspaper listing evening programs, including ranger talks, educational slide shows, exhibits on the park's geography and geology, and Native American Speaks. Summer events kick off nightly between 7:30pm and 8pm, rotating between the Lake McDonald Lodge, St Mary Visitor Center and the Apgar, Many Glacier and Two Medicine Campgrounds.

SHOPPING

All three of the park's main visitor centers, at Apgar, Logan Pass and St Mary, stock an excellent selection of park-related books and literature, including maps and guidebooks. A more limited selection can be found in the lobbies of the Many Glacier Hotel and Lake McDonald Lodge. The latter two places also have gift shops selling Native American artifacts and some reasonable art.

You can buy bear spray and stock up on basic camping supplies at general stores at Lake McDonald Lodge, Rising Sun and Apgar Village. Apgar has a couple of specialist gift shops including one in the old village schoolhouse.

INFORMATION

Internet Access

Internet service in the park is almost nonexistent. Laptop users may be able to plug in and dial up their own service long-distance from the Lake McDonald Lodge. If you're desperate, head to internet points in St Mary or West Glacier.

Laundry & Showers

The camp stores at Rising Sun and Many Glacier have **showers** (per 8min US$1.25; ☎6:30am-10pm). The latter also has laundry facilities.

Medical Services & Emergency

Basic first aid is available at visitor centers and ranger stations in the park. For the nearest hospitals, see p267. For emergencies dial ☎911.

Money

Canadian currency is not widely accepted in Glacier. The nearest banks are in Columbia Falls and Browning. Many Glacier Hotel and Lake McDonald Lodge have 24-hour ATMs. There's an ATM at the camp store at Eddie's Cafe (p204) in Apgar Village.

Post

All Glacier hotel sites have mail boxes. There's a summer-only postal substation at Lake McDonald Lodge where you can post mail and buy stamps.

Telephone

All park lodges and nonprimitive campgrounds have public phones. Cell (mobile) phone reception in the park is sporadic and unreliable.

Tourist Information

The park has three informative visitor centers and three fully staffed ranger stations scattered within its midst. All are overseen by knowledgeable and helpful rangers during peak season. Visitor centers usually offer other amenities such as restrooms, drinking water, bookstores, maps and interpretive displays. Call in at any of the following:

Apgar Visitor Center (Map p180; ☎406-888-7939; ⏲daily early May-late Oct, Sat & Sun only in winter) A small information center in Apgar Village, close to all amenities.

Logan Pass Visitor Center (Map p180; ⏲usually early Jun–mid-Oct) Opens when the Going-to-the-Sun Rd is fully functional. Books, toilets, water and interpretive displays, but no food.

Many Glacier Ranger Station (☎406-732-7740; ⏲late May–mid-Sep) Call here for local hiking information and details of recent bear activity.

Polebridge Ranger Station (Map p180; ☎406-888-7842; ⏲late May–mid-Sep) A small historic station with North Fork information.

St Mary Visitor Center (Map p180; ☎406-732-7750; ⏲early May–mid-Oct) Holds interesting geological exhibits and an auditorium featuring slide shows, ranger talks and Native American Speaks.

Two Medicine Ranger Station (☎406-226-4484; ⏲late May–mid-Sep) A good source for Two Medicine area hikes.

Infrequently staffed ranger stations are also situated at Goat Haunt, Cut Bank, Walton, Belly River, Logging Creek and Kintla Lake.

For information on the Glacier National Park Headquarters, see p224.

Websites

Head to **Lonely Planet** (www.lonelyplanet.com/usa/rocky-mountains/glacier-national-park) for planning advice, author recommendations, traveler reviews and insider tips.

GETTING AROUND

Bicycle

Getting around by bike is feasible on the Going-to-the-Sun Rd at certain times of day – although the ride is tough. With all trails out of bounds, cyclists are confined to plying the park's scant road network. A 4km (2.5-mile) paved bike path runs between Apgar Village and West Glacier.

Bus

Public transportation has improved exponentially in the park since the introduction of free park shuttle buses on the Going-to-the-Sun Rd in 2007. As a result, all of the park's major trailheads (bar those in the remote North Fork area) are well served by public transportation. Smaller 12-seater shuttles on the western side of the park ferry passengers from the Apgar Transit Center (via Apgar Village) up to Logan Pass. Here you must change to a larger 24-seater shuttle to continue on down to the St Mary Visitor Center. Shuttle services run every 15 to 30 minutes between 7am and 8:30pm from July 1 to Labor Day. The buses are wheelchair accessible and run on biodiesel. The larger buses can also accommodate bicycles. Clear route maps are provided at every shuttle stop or can be viewed on the park website at www.nps.gov/glac.

On the park's eastern side, the East Side Shuttle runs a less comprehensive paying service between East Glacier and Waterton (Canada), calling at Two Medicine, Cut Throat Creek, St Mary, Many Glacier and Chief Mountain. Journeys cost US$10 per trip segment and are rarely full; contact **Glacier Park, Inc** (www.glacierparkinc.com) for more details. These shuttle buses generally run from July 1 to Labor Day.

Car & Motorcycle

The only paved road to completely bisect the park is the 85km (53-mile) Going-to-the-Sun Rd. The unpaved Inside North Fork Rd links Apgar with Polebridge. To connect with any other roads, vehicles must briefly leave the park and re-enter via another entrance.

Cars can be rented from **Kruger Helicop-Tours** (☎406-387-4565; www.krugerhelicopters.com), 1.6km (1 mile) west of West Glacier on US 2. Other outlets can be found at Glacier Park International Airport and in the nearby town of Whitefish.

Train

Largely responsible for opening up the region in the 1890s, the train has been a popular method of transport to Glacier since the park's inception in 1910. Amtrak's *Empire Builder* continues to ply the Great Northern Railway's historic east–west route from Chicago to Seattle once daily (in either direction) stopping in both East Glacier (6:45pm westbound, 9:54am eastbound) and West Glacier (8:23pm westbound, 8:16am eastbound). The same train also connects with Whitefish and (by request only) Essex.

AROUND GLACIER NATIONAL PARK

Waterton Lakes National Park

Who? What? Where? The name Waterton Lakes National Park is usually prefixed with a vexed question rather than a contented sigh of recognition. While its northern cousins Banff and Jasper brim with tourists, and southern neighbor Glacier is lauded as one

THE LONELIEST BORDER CROSSING IN THE US

Welcome to what must be the most low-key and pleasant border crossing in the US; and with not a car in sight! Goat Haunt is a rare foot-traffic only land border between the US and Canada located at the southern end of Upper Waterton Lake, 9.6km (6 miles) below the 49th parallel international boundary. The nearest US road to this lonely outpost is the Going-to-the-Sun Rd, 46km (28.8 miles) to the south via a steep but visually stunning trail. Consequently most people arrive here from Canada on the *MV International*, a historic boat that sails south from Waterton Townsite four times daily (summer only). The boat has a 30-minute scheduled stopover that allows visitors to check out the 'haunt's' very basic facilities: a boat dock, restrooms, a hiker shelter, drinking water, the peace pavilion interpretive exhibit (chronicling the history of the park and exploring the meaning of the word 'peace' worldwide) and a tiny **ranger station** (⌚11am-5pm) that doubles up as one of North America's smallest border posts. Anyone staying longer must clear customs, show valid photo ID and – should they be non-Canadian/Americans – have their passport stamped with a unique print of a goat! Long- and short-term hiking options abound. You can walk 11.2km (7 miles) back to Waterton along the lakeshore, undertake a wild backcountry adventure up Waterton Valley beneath the shadow of 3190m (10,466ft) Mt Cleveland (the highest peak in the peace park), or indulge in one of half a dozen shorter hikes before catching a later boat back to Waterton.

of the US's great gilded-age parks, Waterton exhibits more hush than rush. Inaugurated in 1895 and part of a Unesco World Heritage site, Unesco Biosphere Reserve and International Peace Park, 525-sq-km (328-sq-mile) Waterton is geographically almost identical to Glacier but, with a compact townsite, less strict trail regulations, a golf course and a stash of rather modern TV-sporting hotels, they clearly do things a little differently in this neck of the woods. Despite the less rustic infrastructure, Waterton's diminutive size has ensured that its trail network remains both multifarious and accessible. Indeed, the park is unrivaled in North America for offering almost instant access to rugged stretches of high alpine terrain located well above the tree line. It also equals Glacier for flora and fauna: the park is a sanctuary for numerous iconic animals - grizzlies, elk, deer and cougar - along with 800-odd wildflower species.

Sitting right on the 49th parallel wholly to the east of the Continental Divide, Waterton is a good spot to forge neighborly relations with the Glacierites to the south (you can even flash your passport and do a poly-country backcountry adventure). Together the two parks comprise Waterton-Glacier International Peace Park formed in 1932. Although the name evokes images of maple leaves mingling enthusiastically with stars and stripes, in reality each park is operated separately, and entry to one does not entitle you to entry to the other.

History

Englishman Peter Fidler, of the Hudson Bay Company, is thought to be the first European to have explored this southern portion of the Canadian Rockies, setting out in 1792. Explorer Thomas Blakiston first came upon Waterton Lakes in 1858, naming them after famous British naturalist Charles Waterton.

The seed to designate the area a reserve was sown by Fredrick William Godsal, a rancher and conservationist in southern Alberta who had the prescience to see that, if the beautiful lakes region was not hastily set aside as protected land, private interests would soon take hold. In 1893 he wrote a letter to William Pearce, the superintendent of mines who, in turn, urged government officials in Ottawa to consider the issue and, in 1895, what is now known as Waterton Lakes was given protective status by the Canadian federal government as a forest park.

In the days before the 1930 National Parks Act, Cameron Valley had a brief stint as an 'Oil City,' beginning in 1902, when copious barrels of the liquid gold poured out from western Canada's first oil well. The oil discovery also led to the foundation of a townsite, whose first structures included a cookhouse, stable and blacksmith's shop. In 1910, 150 town lots were offered for leasehold at C$15 per annum and the settlement opened up its first hotel but, when the oil dried up prematurely a few years later, local businesses quickly turned their attention to tourism.

Waterton Lakes National Park

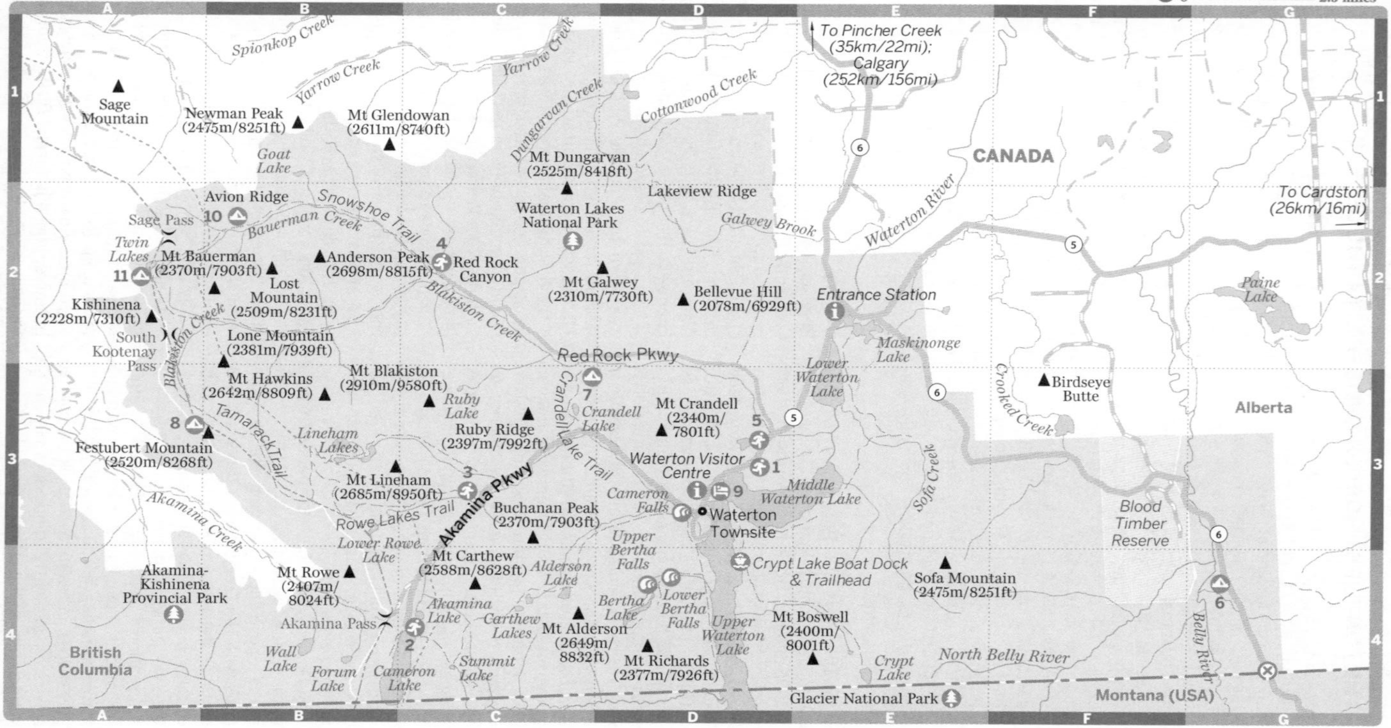
0 5 km
0 2.5 miles
To Pincher Creek (35km/22mi); Calgary (252km/156mi)
To Cardston (26km/16mi)
CANADA
Alberta
British Columbia
Montana (USA)
Sage Mountain
Newman Peak (2475m/8251ft)
Mt Glendowan (2611m/8740ft)
Spionkop Creek
Yarrow Creek
Dungarvan Creek
Cottonwood Creek
Goat Lake
Mt Dungarvan (2525m/8418ft)
Lakeview Ridge
Avion Ridge
Sage Pass
10
Snowshoe Trail
Bauerman Creek
Waterton Lakes National Park
Galwey Brook
Waterton River
Twin Lakes
11
Mt Bauerman (2370m/7903ft)
Anderson Peak (2698m/8815ft)
4
Red Rock Canyon
Lost Mountain (2509m/8231ft)
Mt Galwey (2310m/7730ft)
Bellevue Hill (2078m/6929ft)
Entrance Station
Paine Lake
Kishinena (2228m/7310ft)
Blakiston Creek
South Kootenay Pass
Lone Mountain (2381m/7939ft)
Maskinonge Lake
Red Rock Pkwy
Mt Blakiston (2910m/9580ft)
Mt Hawkins (2642m/8809ft)
Ruby Lake
7
Crandell Lake
Lower Waterton Lake
Birdseye Butte
Crooked Creek
Mt Crandell (2340m/7801ft)
5
8
Tamarack Trail
Lineham Lakes
Ruby Ridge (2397m/7992ft)
Crandell Lake Trail
Festubert Mountain (2520m/8268ft)
Waterton Visitor Centre
1
Mt Lineham (2685m/8950ft)
3
Akamina Pkwy
9
Middle Waterton Lake
Sofa Creek
Cameron Falls
Waterton Townsite
Akamina Creek
Rowe Lakes Trail
Buchanan Peak (2370m/7903ft)
Upper Bertha Falls
Blood Timber Reserve
Lower Rowe Lake
Crypt Lake Boat Dock & Trailhead
Mt Carthew (2588m/8628ft)
Alderson Lake
Sofa Mountain (2475m/8251ft)
Akamina-Kishinena Provincial Park
Mt Rowe (2407m/8024ft)
Akamina Lake
Bertha Lake
Lower Bertha Falls
6
Akamina Pass
Carthew Lakes
Mt Alderson (2649m/8832ft)
Upper Waterton Lake
Mt Boswell (2400m/8001ft)
Belly River
2
Wall Lake
Mt Richards (2377m/7926ft)
North Belly River
Forum Lake
Cameron Lake
Summit Lake
Crypt Lake
Glacier National Park
A
B
C
D
E
F
G
1
2
3
4

Waterton Lakes National Park

Fortunately, the changes occurred just as Louis W Hill, son of Great Northern Railway magnate and 'Empire Builder' James J Hill, was formulating a plan to link Waterton to his great chain of railway-inspired hotels as a means of circumventing prohibition in the USA. A Swiss-style hotel, occupying a prime perch overlooking windy Upper Waterton Lake, opened in 1927 and was named for the then Prince of Wales (later Edward VIII).

Linked with Glacier in the world's first International Peace Park in 1932, Waterton had the distinction of becoming the first Canadian national park to be designated a Unesco Biosphere Reserve in 1979. In 1995 it was declared, along with Glacier, a Unesco World Heritage site.

When You Arrive

The park is open 24 hours a day, 365 days a year, although many amenities and a couple of park roads close in winter. Entry costs C$7.80/3.90 per adult/child aged six and up per day. Passes, to be displayed on your vehicle's windshield, are valid until 4pm on the date of expiration. If you enter the park when the booth is shut, get a pass early the next morning at the Waterton Visitor Centre (p220) or the Parks Canada Administration office (p220). An annual Waterton pass costs C$39.20.

Free park admission is de rigueur on Canada Day (July 1) and Parks Day (third Saturday in July).

Upon entering, you'll receive a map of Waterton Lakes and Glacier National Parks, and the quarterly information-packed newspaper *Waterton-Glacier Guide*.

Orientation

Waterton Lakes National Park lies in Alberta's southwestern corner, 130km (81 miles) from Lethbridge. From the British Columbia border to Chief Mountain Hwy, it covers 525 sq km (203 sq miles). That border is traced by the Continental Divide, which separates the provinces of Alberta and British Columbia.

Waterton Townsite sits prettily on the west side of Upper Waterton Lake, which stretches south across the US border. The lake is a major centerpiece of the park, with boat tours, shuttles and limited motorboats. Waterton Ave (Main St) and its surroundings are full of lodgings, restaurants and other services, such as bicycle rentals, a post office, ATMs, internet and phones.

The closest town with full services is Pincher Creek (population 3665), 55km (34 miles) north via Hwy 6. To the east, Cardston (population 3475) is 56km (36 miles) from the park on Hwy 5. En route to Cardston, the small hamlet of Mountain View, 20km (12.6 miles) from the park, has limited amenities.

ENTRANCES

The one road entrance into the park is in its northeast corner along Hwy 5. Most visitors coming from Glacier and the USA reach the junction with Hwy 5 via Hwy 6 (Chief Mountain International Hwy) from the southeast. From Calgary and Pincher Creek to the north, Hwy 6 shoots south toward Hwy 5 into the park. From the east, Hwy 5 through Cardston heads west and then south into the park.

Park Policies & Regulations

As part of the International Peace Park, Waterton's policies are similar to Glacier's. Don't stray off trails, keep pets on a leash and refrain from taking even the smallest rock home as a souvenir. Other prohibited activities include hunting, paragliding, snowmobiling and jet-skiing.

CAMPING

Rules for food storage at campgrounds are similar to those in Glacier. Waterton's informative *Bare Campsite Program* brochure is handed out in park campgrounds.

Waterton Townsite

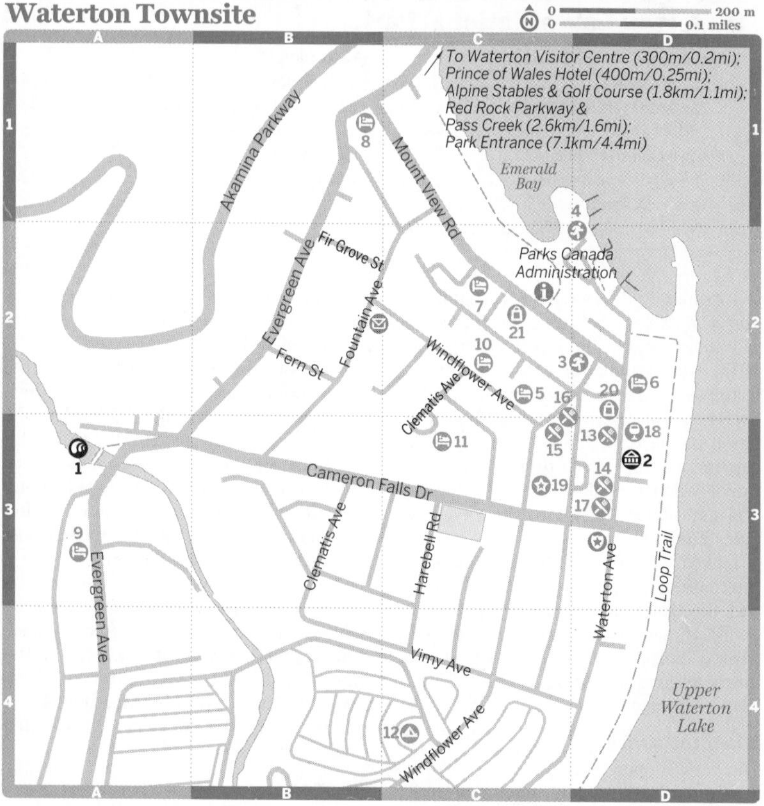

Campgrounds hold central steel bear-proof lockers and have designated areas for wastewater.

Campfires are OK in designated areas, but be particularly cautious when it is windy, which is often.

WILDERNESS PERMITS & REGULATIONS

Permits are not required for day hikes, but overnight trips do require them. Up to 24 hours before the start of your journey, make arrangements at the visitor center. The nightly fee is C$9.80 per adult. Kids 16 years and under get free permits. All of the backcountry sites are reservable, and advance **reservations** (☎406-859-5133) can be made up to 90 days ahead; an extra fee of C$11.70 is charged. You can also put in your request by mail to **Parks Canada Administration** (Waterton Lakes National Park, Box 50, Alberta TOK 2MO).

BOATING

Motorboats and water skis are permissible only on Upper and Middle Waterton Lakes. Wear a wetsuit as the water is cold. **Waterton Shoreline Cruises** (Map p210; www.watertoncruise.com) manages the docking facilities at the townsite's marina; see the website for more details.

TRASH & RECYCLING

Waterton's recycling efforts are commendable. Park brochures can be deposited in boxes in the townsite and at the visitor center for reuse. Brown bear-proof trash bins are all over the townsite and campgrounds, as are blue recycling bins for glass, plastic and aluminum containers. Green bins for cardboard can be found in the townsite.

A green trailer in the marina parking lot accepts all of the aforementioned recyclables, as well as office paper, tin cans, newspapers and magazines.

Waterton Townsite

Sights

With its own mini town, two national historic sites and plenty of 21st-century services, Waterton Lakes is less daunting and a little more user-friendly than adjoining Glacier.

WATERTON TOWNSITE

Waterton's diminutive yet attractive townsite exudes the peaceful ambience of a small village, though its wintertime population shrinks to around 30 permanent residents. Finding your way around the townsite is not difficult, with a number of short walking trails making the most of the lakeside vistas. A 3.2km (2-mile) **loop trail** along Upper Waterton Lake and around the townsite provides a good introduction to the area. There's also a shorter 2km (1.2-mile) **Emerald Bay Loop**.

FREE Waterton Heritage Centre MUSEUM

(Map p210; Waterton Ave; ⌚10am-6pm mid-May–late Sep) A museum of sorts run by the nonprofit Waterton Natural History Association. Inside you'll find exhibits of park flora, fauna and history, a small bookstore and a large mural of homesteader and oil prospector John 'Kootenai' Brown's arrival in Waterton in the 1870s by Albertan artist Donald Frache.

Cameron Falls WATERFALL

(Map p210) Located at the west end of Cameron Falls Dr, a short hop from the central townsite, is a dramatically poised torrent of foaming water that is notable among geologists for harboring the oldest exposed Precambrian rocks in the Canadian Rockies. Estimates suggest they are 1.5 billion years old, give or take the odd millennium. The lookout here is paved for wheelchair access and the falls are rather fetchingly lit up at night.

Upper Waterton Lake LAKE

(Map p210) Visible all over town, this is the deepest lake in the Canadian Rockies, sinking to a murky 120m (394ft). One of the best vantage points is from the Prince of Wales Hotel, where a classic view is framed by an ethereal collection of Gothic mountains, including Mt Cleveland, Glacier National Park's highest rampart. A more placid spot is Emerald Bay, around by the marina, famous for its turquoise waters and ever popular with scuba divers.

CAMERON LAKE

Backed by the sheer-sided slopes of Mt Custer, placid Cameron Lake (Map p208), with an elevation of 1660m (5445ft), is tucked tantalizingly beneath the Continental Divide at the three-way meeting point of Montana, Alberta and British Columbia.

The climax of the 16km (10-mile) Akamina Parkway, the lake is a popular destination with day-trippers who come here to picnic, hike and rent boats. From foamflowers to fireweed, copious wildflower species thrive here, while grizzly bears are known to frequent the lake's isolated southern shores.

There are some interesting interpretive displays outlining the area's flora and fauna under a shelter adjacent to the parking lot, along with restrooms and a hut that sells small snacks and soda. A number of trails start from here, including the short Cameron Lakeshore and the ever-popular Carthew-Alderson (p213).

Driving

With only three paved roads, none of which measure more than 24km (15 miles) in length, opportunities for lengthy road trips in Waterton are limited. If you arrive by car, you'll probably end up plying at least one of the following two routes.

Akamina Parkway

Duration 20 minutes one way

Distance 16km (10 miles)

Speed Limit 50km/h (30mph)

Start Waterton Townsite

Finish Cameron Lake

Nearest Town Waterton Townsite (p211)

Summary Winter cross-country skiing trail and summer wildlife corridor, the Akamina makes for a dreamy afternoon motoring trip.

The road begins 500m (0.3 miles) from the townsite center. After you've climbed the first 500m (0.3 miles), you'll get a sideways glance at the town and lake below. Rocky cliff faces on your right and tree-packed slopes on your left predominate during the first few kilometers (2 miles), and soon you'll glimpse **Cameron Creek**.

The curious structure 7.6km (4.7 miles) from the start of your journey is the **Lineham Discovery Well National Historic Site**, the first oil well in western Canada. It was struck in 1902, along with premature optimism that led to dubbing the area 'Oil City.' After two years the flow was poor, and the well dripped her last in 1936.

The parkway ends at the stellar **Cameron Lake**.

Red Rock Parkway

Duration 20 minutes one way

Distance 15km (9 miles)

Speed Limit 50km/h (30mph)

Start Waterton Townsite

Finish Red Rock Canyon

Nearest Town Waterton Townsite (p211)

Summary A short but sweet sojourn to Red Rock Canyon, driving past over 500 million years of geological history.

Red Rock Parkway originates at a junction with Hwy 5, about 8km (5 miles) south of the park entrance. This road, running alongside Blakiston Creek for much of its route, is full of wildflower-speckled prairie spilling onto incredible mountains. South of the parkway, the awe-inspiring Mt Blakiston is Waterton's tallest peak at 2910m (9580ft). A few picnic spots are along the way, and 4.8km (3 miles) in, a small **native history exhibit** is worth a stop.

Most visitors persevere to the end of the road, 15km (9 miles) in, where **Red Rock Canyon** sits colorfully aglow. A 700m (0.4-mile) self-guided loop trail circuits the edge of the canyon. Consisting of ancient Grinnell argillite, the canyon is a fantastic introduction to one of the geologically wondrous aspects of Waterton.

Day Hikes

There are around 200km (125 miles) of trails in Waterton, and a number of them are multipurpose routes, accommodating hikers, horseback riders, cross-country skiers and cyclists. Short, easy hikes lie in the vicinity of the townsite, while further afield, day hikes such as the much-lauded Carthew-Alderson Trail can rival anything in Glacier or Banff National Parks for variety of scenery. To help you pick the perfect hike, see our handy chart on p36.

Rowe Lakes

Duration 3 hours round-trip (Lower Lake), 5 hours (Upper Lake), 4 hours (Rowe Meadow)

Distance 8km/5 miles round-trip (Lower Lake), 12.6km/7.9 miles (Upper Lake), 10.4km/6.5 miles (Rowe Meadow)

Difficulty Easy-moderate

Start/Finish Akamina Parkway

Elevation Change 250m (820ft)

Nearest Town Waterton Townsite (p211)

Transportation Tamarack hiker shuttle

Summary A tempting foray to the cusp of Waterton's easily accessible backcountry that may have you coming back for more.

This fine hike starts innocuously enough on the Akamina Parkway approximately halfway between Waterton Townsite and Cameron Lake. The first section to Lower Rowe Lake is moderately easy. Beyond this, you can hike further up to Rowe Meadow and Upper Rowe Lake. For backcountry hikers this is the start/end point of the multiday Tamarack Trail.

From the Akamina Parkway, follow a sinuous but well-defined trail through a mix of larch and evergreen trees alongside Rowe Creek. The path can be muddy after rain, but with only 250m (820ft) of elevation gain spread over the first 4km (2.5 miles) to Lower Rowe Lake, the ascent is only gradual.

After 3.8km (2.4 miles) a trail branches off to the left. Take this to reach **Lower Rowe Lake** (200m/60ft), a small, beautifully clear body of water laid out in a natural amphitheater. A 150m (492ft) waterfall links it with Upper Rowe Lake that sits in a hanging valley above.

Back at the main trail you have a choice. Turn right and retrace your steps to the parkway or turn left toward **Rowe Meadow**, a wonderful array of wildflowers situated on the edge of the timberline. After crossing a creek at the far end of the meadow, you'll encounter another junction. The Tamarack Trail goes right here up to Lineham Ridge. A left turn offers a last steep climb to **Upper Rowe Lake**, actually two alpine lakes backed by the vertiginous cliffs of the Continental Divide. Look out for marmots and bighorn sheep along the way.

Retrace your steps to the parkway. Strong, speedy hikers might want to climb a further 3.4km (2.1 miles) from the trail junction below Upper Rowe Lake to **Lineham Ridge**, one of the highest paths in the park with views stretching for 50km (31 miles).

Carthew-Alderson Trail

Duration 6 hours one way

Distance 19km (11.8 miles)

Difficulty Moderate

Start Cameron Lake

Finish Cameron Falls

Elevation Change 610m (1968ft)

Nearest Town Waterton Townsite (p211)

Transportation Tamarack hiker shuttle

Summary A panoramic parade through myriad forests, lush meadows and rough scree, showcasing the best of Waterton Lakes National Park.

Carthew-Alderson Trail

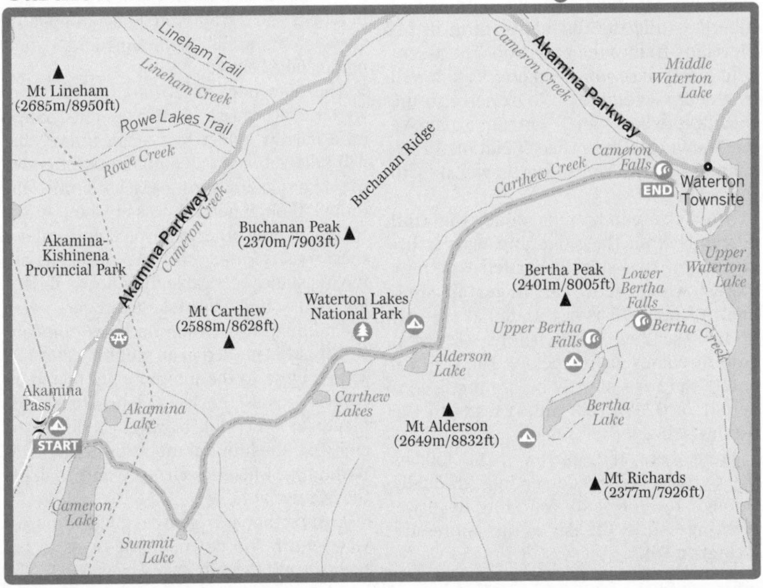

When one of America's leading outdoor magazines lists a hike as 'one of the best high alpine day hikes anywhere' (as it did with this one), you know you're in for something special. It perhaps comes as no surprise to find that many seasoned visitors rate this scenic sojourn as the best in the park (and the subject of many repeat visits). As a result, the trail is well trafficked, though none of this takes away from its multifarious beauty and incredible sweeping views.

Most hikers embark from **Cameron Lake** in the west (at Akamina Parkway's end) and tramp east back to Waterton Townsite (thus incorporating a gentler elevation gain). This scenario is made possible courtesy of the Tamarack hiker shuttle (p220) that runs from Waterton to Cameron Lake daily at 8am and 9am in summer (trail conditions permitting).

The trail heads southeast from the Cameron Lake boat ramp (and tiny store) and enters a pine-encased slope alongside the lake's eastern shore, before ascending through a series of switchbacks to the smaller **Summit Lake**. This pool, surrounded by meadow and pine, incorporates the bulk of the hike's 612m (2000ft) elevation gain.

Turn left (northeast) here for the Carthew Lakes Trail, a more gradual ascent through scrub, grass and then just open mountainside, with stupendous views over Montana, British Columbia and Alberta, while the distinctive form of Mt Cleveland frames the backdrop. The ascent culminates in several switchbacks followed by a sharp scramble up loose scree to the ridgeline, where you'll get an expansive panorama: northern Glacier National Park summits to the south, Carthew Lakes to the north.

After the climbing is done, the trail descends from the ridge and weaves between the two starkly located **Carthew Lakes**, where snow can linger all summer. A steep cliff is negotiated at the exit of the Carthew basin before **Alderson Lake** becomes visible below. The trail reenters the trees shortly before the lake; a detour of 0.5km (0.3 miles) leads to the water itself.

From here the narrow path follows the Carthew Valley, descending gradually through the forest to Waterton Townsite. A fitting end to the day is the impressive **Cameron Falls**.

Crypt Lake Trail

Duration 6 hours round-trip

Distance 17.2km (10.3 miles)

Difficulty Difficult

Start/Finish Crypt Landing

Elevation Change 710m (2329ft)

Nearest Town Waterton Townsite (p211)

Transportation Water taxi

Summary A veritable obstacle course that incorporates a ride in a water taxi, a climb up a ladder and a crawl through a narrow rocky tunnel to gorgeous Crypt Lake.

Crypt Lake or Carthew-Alderson? The choice is a toss up. Indeed, both hikes have gained kudos from leading outdoor writers for their interesting nooks and delightful scenery. Throw the dice and take your pick.

Once an overnight jaunt, Crypt Lake Trail is now tackled in a single day thanks to a new water taxi (for details, see p220) that transports hikers to the trailhead from the townsite marina twice daily, at 9am and 10am. The return taxi is in the afternoon, allowing hikers time for a relaxed lunch break at Crypt Lake.

From the trailhead, the ascent begins quickly, forging through thick green vegetation and copious clumps of wildflowers. Make plenty of noise here as this trail has been known to attract the odd bear. Once in more open terrain, you'll take in up-close views of waterfalls, mountains and an unnamed lake below.

The hike now turns into something of an obstacle course. First, you must climb up a narrow ladder to a small tunnel that will take you – via a combination of crawling or crouching – to a glacial cirque (the tunnel, though natural, was enlarged in the 1960s). On the other side you'll encounter a sheer rock face that must be negotiated with the assistance of a cable. It is not as terrifying as it sounds, but take extra care when it's raining. The cirque encloses gorgeous **Crypt Lake**, nestled in an amphitheater-like setting close to the international boundary (which crosses the lake's southern shore). Plenty of other hikers will, no doubt, be enjoying lunch in the exquisite natural surroundings. Choose your spot and soak up the beauty.

Ensure that you allow enough time for your return trip down, as the boats to the townsite are the only easy way back!

Overnight Hikes

Slip on the backpack for a true adventure in the wilds of Waterton.

Tamarack Trail

Duration 2 days one way

Distance 31.6km (19.6 miles)

Difficulty Moderate-difficult

Start Rowe Lakes trailhead

Finish Lone Lake trailhead

Elevation Change 1460m (4700ft)

Nearest Town Waterton Townsite (p211)

Transportation Tamarack hiker shuttle

Summary A tough meander along Waterton's northern fringes through landscapes tinged yellow by the deciduous-coniferous Tamarack tree.

Waterton's only real backcountry adventure is this moderately difficult hiking trail, which is usually tackled over two days overnighting at the Lone Lake, Upper Twin Lakes or Snowshoe Campgrounds. Choose between two starting points: the Rowe Lakes Trail off Cameron Lake Rd for a clockwise loop, or the Lone Lake Trail from Red Rock Canyon for a counterclockwise alternative.

From the Rowe Lakes trailhead, the hike junctions with the main Tamarack Trail at 5.1km (3.2 miles) before ascending Lineham Ridge. Offering breathtaking panoramic views, this ridge is a true highlight of the trip. Tricky descents over scree, extreme winds at high altitude and long stretches without treatable water sources are potential difficulties that must be considered before heading out. The recompense is immersion in the scenic beauty of northwestern Waterton, with views sweeping over the mountainous grandeur of Waterton and Akamina-Kishinena Provincial Park. Glacial moraines and wildflowered meadows, lakes and larch, and perhaps even an animal or two, are viewed along the way.

Early autumn is the best time to make this journey, when the namesake Tamarack tree or alpine larch (a deciduous conifer) sheds its needles in a riot of rustic yellows. The reservation-only Tamarack hiker shuttle (p220) can deliver you to the trailhead.

Biking

In contrast to Glacier, Waterton has five trails open for cycling. On top of the two we've described you'll also find the **Akamina Pass Trail**, which is 1.3km (0.8 miles) one way; the **Wishbone Trail**, which is 21km (33.8 miles) round-trip; and the new 6.9km (4.3-mile) **Kootenai Brown Trail** that parallels the entrance road from the park gate to the townsite.

Cyclists on park trails should adhere to a few basic rules. Ride single file to prevent trail damage or erosion; alert hikers ahead of you when passing; and when encountering a horse, get off your bike and stand aside until it passes. Always stay on the trail and be careful not to surprise wildlife.

Mountain bikes can be rented in Waterton at **Pat's** (Map p210; 224 Mount View Rd; per hr/day C$8/34). Helmets are included.

Crandell Lake Loop

Duration 3 hours round-trip

Distance 20.6km (12.8 miles)

Difficulty Moderate

Start/Finish Waterton Townsite

Nearest Town Waterton Townsite (p211)

Summary Mix road biking with singletrack on a multifarious romp around Waterton's classic parkways.

Incorporating the hikeable Crandell Lake Trail with the paved Akamina and Red Rock Parkways, this popular loop can be tackled from one of three starting points: Waterton Townsite; the Crandell Mountain Campground (off the Red Rock Parkway); or a trailhead 6.4km (4 miles) along the Akamina Parkway.

All three approaches make for a varied and pleasant half-day ride that mixes 6.4km (4 miles) of rocky off-road with 10km (6.2 miles) of smooth asphalt. The only technicalities come with the ascent to the lake (less steep if you travel anticlockwise), which involves a 100m (328ft) elevation gain from the respective parkways. The clear **Crandell Lake**, with Mt Crandell visible to its southeast, is a serene setting with sandy areas and rocks perfect for a picnic perch. Cyclists should beware of hikers on the Crandell Lake Trail and wildlife (including bears) on both parkways.

Snowshoe Trail

Duration 1½ hours round-trip

Distance 16.4km (10.2 miles)

Difficulty Moderate

Start/Finish Red Rock Canyon parking lot

Nearest Town Waterton Townsite (p211)

Summary Tackle part of the Tamarack Trail on this short but steep sojourn into Waterton's northwestern corner.

One in a quartet of fine Waterton cycle rides, the Snowshoe Trail follows Bauerman Creek on an abandoned fire road from the Red Rock Canyon parking lot. The turnaround point is a Snowshoe Warden Cabin, 8.2km (5.1 miles) further on.

Don't be deceived by the initial wideness of the track; the gradient gets noticeably steeper beyond the Goat Lake turnoff, and there are also a couple of rocky streams that will need to be forded in late spring and early summer.

Wedged into the park's northwestern corner, mountain views are excellent throughout this ride and vibrant wildflowers add color during summer. Although bikes aren't allowed on any of the connecting trails (including Castle Divide and Twin Lakes), the ride makes for a popular bike-hike excursion, with cyclists locking their bikes close to the trail junctions, before continuing along spur paths to destinations such as **Goat Lake** and **Avion Ridge**.

Other Activities

Waterton offers all the activities available in Glacier with a couple of hidden extras thrown in for good measure. Golf is possible inside the park perimeter, there's scuba diving to an old wreck in Emerald Bay and aficionados rave about the park's ice-climbing potential.

Boating & Kayaking

Cameron Lake Boat Rentals KAYAKING, CANOEING
(Map p208; www.cameronlakeboatrentals.com; kayak per hr C$25; ⌚8am-6:30pm Jun-Sep) Rents boats for kayaking, canoeing or rowing on the exquisite Cameron Lake.

Diving

Committed scuba divers brave the frigid waters of Upper Waterton Lake. The most popular spot to get down under is Emerald Bay, where a 1900 paddle wheeler named *Gertrude* sits 20m (66ft) below the surface.

Awesome Adventures DIVING
(☎403-328-5040; www.awesomeadventure.ca; 314 11th St S, Lethbridge) With no in-park dive specialists your closest equipment rental and guide service is with this company located in Lethbridge.

Fishing

Fishing is popular in Waterton Lakes National Park, with the waters swimming with 24 species of fish, including northern pike, whitefish and various types of trout.

A Parks Canada permit is required to fish in Waterton. Permits cost C$9.80 for the day or C$34.30 for the season and can be purchased at the visitor center, park headquarters or at campground entry booths. Not all lakes are open to fishing and there are some seasonal regulations; check at the visitor center. There has been a general move toward more catch-and-release fishing among anglers in recent years.

Popular hike-in destinations for anglers include Bertha Lake and Carthew Lakes.

Rock Climbing

Because its sedimentary rock is soft and crumbly, Waterton is not hugely popular for rock climbing, but the upper and lower bands of Bear's Hump offer 10 approaches ranging from grades 5.4 to 5.8.

Horseback Riding

Alpine Stables HORSEBACK RIDING
(Map p208; www.alpinestables.com; guided rides per hr from C$35) Visitors interested in horseback riding should hook up with Alpine Stables, off Hwy 5 and across the road from the golf course. It has handsome horses suited for all levels, from never-ridden-before to advanced.

Golf

Waterton Lakes Golf Course GOLF COURSE
(Map p208; www.golfwaterton.com; green fees 9/18 holes C$32/48) Sterling scenery is part of the game at Waterton Lakes Golf Course.

Winter Activities

In winter Akamina Parkway is the most popular access point for **cross-country skiing**, while the Cameron Lake area is a favorite for **snowshoeing**. Waterton, along with Kootenay, Jasper and Banff, is considered to be one of the world's premier waterfall **ice-climbing** destinations. Since the sport comes loaded with a number of inherent risks, aspiring climbers are encouraged to check **avalanche bulletins** (☎1-800-667-1105; www.avalanche.ca). *Waterfall Ice, Climbs in the Canadian Rockies* is the definitive text on the topic.

Tours

Waterton Shoreline Cruises BOAT TOURS

(Map p210; www.watertoncruise.com) Waterton Shoreline Cruises operates boats (adult/child C$24/12) holding up to 200 passengers on Upper Waterton Lake. The service operates from early May to early October and leaves four times daily (10am, 1pm, 4pm, 7pm) during July and August. Boat guides are knowledgeable and amusing and the laughter and chatter of the passengers often drifts across the lake to the shoreline. The 2¼-hour cruises, which are conducted on the vintage *MV International* boat, made in 1927, stop at Goat Haunt, Montana, for 30 minutes. Round-trip boat passengers to Goat Haunt do not have to go through customs before heading toward the Canadian sector again, though if you take the boat one way, hiking to or from Goat Haunt, you'll need a passport. The company also provides the return boat for walkers on the guided weekly International Peace Hike (see the boxed text, p177).

Sleeping

Compared to Glacier, Waterton – with its busy townsite – is loaded with accommodation options, although they're generally more expensive than their US counterparts. Unlike its southern neighbor, the park also offers 21st-century gadgets such as TVs, wi-fi, air-con and phones. July and August are insanely busy; book ahead.

Camping

In high season Waterton Townsite Campground can fill by late morning. If staying at Crandell Mountain or Belly River Campgrounds, you can use the showers at Waterton Townsite Campground free of charge.

Waterton Townsite Campground CAMPGROUND $

(Map p210; Hwy 5; campsites C$27.40-38.20; mid-May–mid-Oct) The park's largest campground, on Hwy 5 at the southern end of town, has full facilities on grassy grounds. Though largely unshaded, it is near the waterfront and the townsite center. Due to gusty winds, RVs are usually placed near the lake, and tents get more shelter near the creek.

Crandell Mountain Campground CAMPGROUND $

(Map p208; Red Rock Parkway; campsites C$21.50; mid-May–Sep) Much of this tranquil campground is wooded with lodgepole pines and there are five 'luxury' teepees (maximum occupancy six people) with Astroturf floors that can also be hired for C$55. Fortunately mosquitoes are not too rampant here.

Belly River Campground CAMPGROUND $

(Map p208; Chief Mountain Hwy; primitive/group campsites C$15.70/4.90; mid-May–early Sep) Outside of the pay area of the park, this primitive campground sits in placid parkland terrain with aspen trees and far-off views of the mountains. No reservations are available.

Lodging

All of the lodging is based in and around the townsite. Only three lodges stay open year-round.

TOP CHOICE **Prince of Wales Hotel** HOTEL $$$

(Map p208; in season 403-859-2231, other times 406-756-2444; www.princeofwaleswaterton.com; Prince of Wales Rd; r C$234-299; mid-May–Sep;) With a Hogwarts-like setting on a bluff overlooking Upper Waterton Lake, the grand Prince of Wales is something of an ambiguity: a regal hotel built by the US-owned Great Northern Railway as the only Canadian link in its chain of historic accommodations. Blending Swiss-style architecture with the atmosphere of a Scottish castle (Balmoral perhaps), the hotel is more Old Empire than New World, exhibiting such inherent British-isms as waitresses in kilts and high tea in the main lounge. Not far outside the large lake-facing windows, a rawer wilderness awaits.

Waterton Lakes Resort RESORT $$$

(Map p210; 403-859-2150; www.watertonlakeslodge.com; 101 Clematis Ave; lodge C$185-205, ste C$215-275; year-round;) A family-orientated sprawler with the kind of ample facilities that will make you feel a million miles from rustic Glacier, this place has a gym, indoor pool, hot tub, and snazzy on-site lounge and grill (Vimy's). Large lodge rooms (up to four people) come in standard or deluxe – the latter have fireplaces and Jacuzzis. Suites have kitchenettes.

Aspen Village Inn HOTEL $$$

(Map p210; 403-859-2255; www.aspenvillageinn.com; Windflower Ave; r C$185-250; May-Oct;) Another sprawler, consisting of two main buildings and several cottage units, the Aspen is a family favorite with an on-site

WATERTON LAKES NATIONAL PARK CAMPGROUNDS

CAMPGROUND	LOCATION	DESCRIPTION	NO OF SITES
Belly River	Chief Mountain Hwy	Primitive campground in placid parkland terrain	24
Crandell Mountain	Red Rock Parkway	Tranquil place away from the urban hub of Waterton	129
Waterton Townsite	Waterton Townsite	Huge campground close to lakeside, town and trailhead; immensely popular	238

Drinking Water *Flush Toilets* *Restaurant Nearby* *RV Dump Station*

kids' playground and resident deer-finding shade in the grounds. Barbecues and picnic tables invite a warm summer-night ambience while satellite TV can take the chill out of a damp autumn evening.

Northland Lodge B&B **$$**
(Map p210; 403-859-2353; www.northlandlodgecanada.com; 408 Evergreen Ave; r C$130-215; mid-May–mid-Oct;) Can't afford the Prince of Wales? For a small drop in price and a comparable rise in privacy you can enjoy this cozy B&B, built in 1927 by none other than Louis Hill, the genius behind most of the peace park's venerable lodges. The difference with the Northland is that Hill built it for *himself*. Located on the edge of the townsite, within hearing of gushing Cameron Falls, the nine rooms in this Swiss-style establishment are suitably deluxe, all with private baths.

Waterton Glacier Suites HOTEL **$$$**
(Map p210; 403-859-2004; www.watertonsuites.com; Windflower Ave; r C$199-279; year-round;) A slightly more upmarket version of the Aspen Village Inn next door, this polished year-round lodge counts 26 rooms, all fully equipped with whirlpool bath, satellite TV, gas fireplace, fridge, microwave and air-con. If it's the wilderness you're after, stick to the backcountry campgrounds. If you prefer a little frontcountry luxury, this could be your bag.

Bayshore Inn RESORT **$$**
(Map p210; 403-859-2211; www.bayshoreinn.com; 111 Waterton Ave; r C$174-225; @) A large, spread-out place with rooms with balconies facing the lakefront, the Bayshore offers amenities that you won't find over in rustic Glacier, such as satellite TV, heart-shaped bath tubs, coffee machines and honeymoon suites. There are also four on-site eating and drinking options from the dignified Kootenai Brown dining room to the rocking-and-rolling Thirsty Bear Saloon.

Bear Mountain Motel MOTEL **$$**
(Map p210; 403-859-2221; www.bearmountainmotel.com; 208 Mount View Rd; s/d C$95/120; mid-May–late Oct;) A bog-standard motel with none of the nostalgic value of the Swiftcurrent or Rising Sun in Glacier, the Bear Mountain offers serviceable, clean rooms at an affordable (for Waterton) rate.

Crandell Mountain Lodge HOTEL **$$**
(Map p210; 403-859-2288; www.crandellmountainlodge.com; 102 Mount View Rd; r C$140-220;) Doing a good impersonation of a Tudor cottage plucked from a quiet English village, the Crandell has stood alone since its historic neighbor, the Kilmorey Lodge, burnt down in 2009.

Eating

Bel Lago Ristorante ITALIAN **$$$**
(Map p210; www.bellagoristorante.com; 110 Waterton Ave; mains C$19-32; noon-10pm) Homemade pasta in North American National Park shock! While the decor's relatively simple, the chef studied in Italy and this is probably Waterton's most ambitious eatery with tasty (but not gigantic) mains sticking to that old Italian ethos of 'grow local where possible.' The wine list's international with an Italian bias (Amarone anyone?).

Wieners of Waterton HOT DOGS **$**
(Map p210; www.wienersofwaterton.com; 301 Windflower Ave; hot dogs C$10) Gourmet hot dogs have been tried elsewhere in Alberta (Calgary springs to mind), so why not Waterton where appetites are more ravenous than most? In operation since 2009, Wieners has

ELEVATION	OPEN	RESERVATIONS NEEDED?	DAILY FEE	FACILITIES	PAGE
1200m (3936ft)	May-Sep	no	C$15.70		p217
1300m (4264ft)	May-Sep	no	C$21.50		p217
1280m (4200ft)	May-Oct	available	C$27.40		p217

reaffirmed that not all wieners are junk and even serves much-sought-after vegetarian varieties. It's ridiculously popular.

Zum's Eatery AMERICAN **$$**

(Map p210; 116b Waterton Ave; mains C$16-20) Car license plates from all over North America decorate this friendly eatery in Waterton Townsite staffed by keen students on their summer break. While sophisticated flavors might be in short supply, the menu is peppered with good home-style cooking of the burger, pizza and fish-and-chips variety.

Pearl's CAFÉ **$**

(Map p210; www.pearlscafe.ca; 305 Windflower Ave; wraps C$10; wi-fi) You can flirt with urbanity in this modern coffee bar that attracts more hikers than computer geeks, especially on the sunny front patio. The wraps and French toast are recommended.

Big Scoop Ice Cream Parlor ICE CREAM **$**

(Map p210; 114 Waterton Ave; 12:30-10pm) Celebrate completing the Carthew-Alderson Trail with a large dollop of ice cream in a homemade waffle cone in any one of 32 different flavors.

Drinking & Entertainment

Waterton Townsite has more of a laid-back buzz than Glacier, with a larger concentration of people in one place inspiring more spontaneous forms of entertainment. Hang around the lakefront of an evening and chances are somebody will be tuning up a guitar or cracking open a few beers.

Thirsty Bear Saloon PUB

(Map p210; Waterton Ave; 7pm-2am) The townsite's drinking nexus is a large open pub and performance space that puts on weekly live music and karaoke (not every national park visitor's cup of tea!). Expect mildly inebriated young ladies in cowboy hats cavorting with cool dudes over by the foosball machine.

Waterton Lakes Opera House Cinema CINEMA

(Map p210; cnr Cameron Falls Dr & Windflower Ave) Waterton even has its own historic cinema. Expect Hollywood movies rather than polished performances of *Madame Butterfly*.

Shopping

Akamina Gifts & Book Nook SOUVENIRS, BOOKS

(Map p210; 108 Waterton Ave) Akamina Gifts & Book Nook can satisfy any desires for maple syrup, kitschy gifts and replacement T-shirts, along with park-related literature.

Tamarack Outdoor Outfitters OUTDOOR EQUIPMENT

(Map p210; www.watertonvisitorservices.com; Mount View Rd; 8am-8pm) The most comprehensive equipment store, which stocks everything from backpacks to bear spray.

Information

Internet

Internet terminals are available at Zum's Eatery and there is wi-fi at Pearl's (see p218).

Medical Services & Emergency

Fire (403-859-2113)

Medical emergencies (403-859-2636) For full medical assistance, see p267.

Royal Canadian Mounted Police (403-859-2244)

Money

Most businesses in Waterton Townsite will accept US dollars. The following have ATMs:

Pat's (Map p210; 224 Mount View Rd)

Prince of Wales Hotel (Map p210; Prince of Wales Rd; ⌚mid-May–Sep)

Tamarack Outdoor Outfitters (Map p210; Mount View Rd; ⌚8am-8pm) Can also exchange money.

Post

The **post office** (Map p210; 102a Windflower Ave) is open weekdays.

Showers & Laundry

The **Waterton Health Club & Recreation Centre** (101 Clematis Ave) has public showers (C$3) and a laundry; you can use the whole facility (pool, spa, sauna and gym) for C$6 per day.

Tourist Information

Waterton Visitor Centre (off Map p210; ☎403-859-5133; www.parkscanada.gc.ca/waterton; ⌚8am-7pm early May-early Oct), across the road from the Prince of Wales Hotel, has a wealth of front and backcountry information. The park has no separate ranger stations, though staff at Waterton Townsite and Crandell Mountain Campgrounds can provide area information.

From early October to early May, **Parks Canada Administration** (Map p210; ☎403-859-2224; Mount View Rd; ⌚8am-4pm Mon-Fri) serves as the visitor center.

Getting There & Away

Waterton is a weak link in Alberta's already scant public transportation network. If you're carless, it's actually easier to enter via the US using Glacier National Park's East Side Shuttle (see p220). From the north the nearest public transport that will get you to the park is from the town of Pincher Creek on a daily **Greyhound** (www.greyhound.ca) bus from Calgary. From here you'll need to book a taxi with **Crystal Cabs** (☎403-627-4262) to ply the last 45km (30 miles; 45 minutes) to Waterton Townsite. The journey costs approximately C$70 for up to four people. Reserve ahead.

Getting Around

Bicycle

In marked contrast to Glacier, biking in Waterton is both popular and encouraged. Indeed, you can rent out everything from mountain bikes to large two-person rickshaws from **Pat's** (224 Mount View Rd; per hr/day C$8/34) in the townsite. The new multipurpose Kootenai Brown Trail links the park gate with the townsite and there are four further designated trails open to bicycles.

Car & Motorcycle

The speed limit in the townsite is 30km/h (19mph) unless otherwise posted; campgrounds post 20km/h (12mph) limits. Akamina Parkway has a limit of 50km/h (31mph) unless otherwise posted.

The town's two gas stations are at Pat's and Tamarack Outdoor Outfitters, both on Mount View Rd and open May to October; to fuel up in winter, head to Mountain View. Parking is simple around town. There are no meters or any unusual restrictions, and the town has a few free parking lots (no parking between 11pm and 6am).

Public Transportation

BOAT **Waterton Shoreline Cruises** (www.watertoncruise.com) operates a water shuttle service to the east shore of Upper Waterton Lake for the Crypt Lake trailhead. The boat leaves Waterton marina at 9am and 10am and picks up at the trailhead at 4pm and 5:30pm during July and August. Throughout May, June and September the service is reduced to one boat daily (10am depart and 5:30pm pickup). The round-trip fare is C$15/7.50 per adult/child.

BUS **Tamarack Outdoor Outfitters** (☎403-859-2378; www.watertonvisitorservices.com; Mount View Rd) runs hiker shuttles that depart daily from the store in season. The Cameron Express (C$10) to Cameron Lake – handy for Carthew-Alderson Trail hikers – leaves daily at 8am and 9am; reserve your seat at least a day in advance (reservations can be made in person or by phone). Another shuttle buses hikers returning by boat from Goat Haunt back to the Canadian–US border and the Belly River parking area (C$20). The shuttle is coordinated to link up with the East Side Shuttle (see following). This service must be reserved.

Glacier Park, Inc (www.glacierparkinc.com) runs the daily East Side Shuttle leaving from the Prince of Wales Hotel at 3pm to the following points in Glacier National Park: Chief Mountain (US$10), Many Glacier (US$20), St Mary (US$30) and Glacier Park Lodge (US$50). This is a round-trip only service; ie you will have had to have entered Canada using the same bus from the USA.

St Mary

Sitting on the Blackfeet Indian Reservation just outside the park's east entrance, St Mary makes a handy base for exploring Glacier's dryer eastern side. Though less salubrious than its western counterpart, West Glacier, the views of the mountains are better here and it's a shorter walk (1km/0.6 miles) to the first free shuttle stop on the Going-to-the-Sun Rd (outside the St Mary visitor and transit center). A cluster of handy services not found inside the park crowd around the junction of Hwy 89 and the Going-to-the-Sun Rd, including campgrounds, a motel, a supermarket, a gas station and the region's swankiest modern hotel. The East Side Shuttle provides easy access to East Glacier, Two Medicine, Many Glacier and Waterton.

Sleeping

St Mary Lodge & Resort RESORT **$$**
(☎406-732-4431; www.glacierparkinc.com; cnr Hwy 89 & Going-to-the-Sun Rd; r US$139-179, cabins US$279; ⏱mid-May–early Oct; ❄📶) This large resort and its affiliates, situated just outside the park boundary, were recently added to the Glacier Park, Inc stable. Comfort-wise it takes the Montana rustic theme to a whole new level, though for setting and gilded-age ambience it can't compete with the Many Glacier and Lake McDonald lodges. Myriad facilities include a gift shop, coffee bar, the Snowgoose Grill and a grand stash of rooms, from motel-style to luxury teepees to plush rooms in the main Great Bear Lodge. Eschewing rustic park tradition most rooms have TVs, coffee machines as well as other gadgets.

Johnson's of St Mary CAMPGROUND, CABINS **$**
(☎406-732-4207; www.johnsonsofstmary.com; off US 89; tent/RV sites US$25/35, cabins US$149; 👪) Set on a knoll overlooking the village, RV sites here get gorgeous views of St Mary Lake with the crenellated peaks of the Continental Divide glimmering in the background. Tents sites are shaded peacefully by some alder trees. Also available are cabins, a cottage and Johnson's World Famous Historic Restaurant.

St Mary KOA Campground CAMPGROUND, CABINS **$**
(☎406-732-4122; www.koa.com/campgrounds/st-mary; 106 West Shore Rd; campsites/4-person cabins US$32.95/175; 📶👪) Encased in a meadow 1.6km (1 mile) down a paved road, beside St Mary's eponymous river, this unshaded campground can accommodate tents and RVs and also offers some cottages and cabins. A plethora of other services include bike rental (per hour/day US$2.50/20), canoe rental (per hour US$10), a grocery store, coffee counter, laundry, hot tub, playground and the A-OK Grille.

Red Eagle Motel MOTEL **$**
(☎406-732-4453; US 89; r US$75; ⏱late May-late Sep; @) Perched on a small hill above St Mary Village, this basic motel is an agreeable crash pad for visitors intending to spend most of their waking time outdoors. Enjoy tranquility away from the gadgetry of TVs, microwaves or fridges (although there's internet access in reception). Various restaurants are a short stroll down the hill and the views of the park from the front balcony are to die for.

Eating

TOP CHOICE **Park Café** BREAKFAST, AMERICAN **$**
(www.parkcafe.us; US 89; breakfast $7-12; ⏱7am-10pm) Almost as celebrated as the historic Going-to-the-Sun Rd, the Park Café is lauded, less for its astounding views, and more for its astoundingly delicious huckleberry pie. Playing a strong supporting role are the fortifying breakfasts best enjoyed at the diner counter while discussing the merits of bear spray over playing dead. Only in Montana!

Snowgoose Grill STEAKHOUSE **$$$**
(US 89; breakfast & lunch US$5-9, dinner US$12-28; ⏱May-Oct) If you're craving an opportunity to break away from the hikers' breakfast/picnic lunch monotony, try this wheelchair-accessible restaurant in the St Mary Lodge & Resort, where the steaks are succulent and the footwear is more heels than hiking boots.

Two Sisters Cafe AMERICAN **$$**
(Map p180; www.twosistersofmontana.com; US 89; mains US$7-15; ⏱11am-10pm Jun-Sep) 'Aliens welcome,' blasts the colorful sign on the roof of this bohemian-looking joint that is situated halfway between Babb and St Mary. But, while the bright purple café run by (guess what) two sisters of the Blackfeet Tribe might look like a vegan-only enclave plucked straight out of San Francisco, the Cajun chicken and eclectic fish dishes here are actually rather good.

ℹ Information

St Mary lies less than 1km (0.6 miles) from the park's eastern entrance where the Going-to-the-Sun Rd meets US 89. Most facilities can be found at the convenience store, gift shop and gas station that adjoin the Park Café (p221). The store also offers **internet access** (per 15min US$2).

ℹ Getting There & Around

The free Going-to-the-Sun Rd shuttles terminate at the St Mary Visitor Center (Map p180), a five-minute stroll from St Mary's diminutive core. They run every 30 minutes July to September. The three-times-daily East Side Shuttle links St Mary with Waterton, Many Glacier, Cut Throat Creek, Two Medicine and East Glacier.

East Glacier

A summer-only stop on Amtrak's *Empire Builder* route, East Glacier grew up around the train station (which splits the small slightly scruffy settlement in half) and the adjacent Glacier Park Lodge. While its eating and sleeping options offer more variety than West Glacier, its location away from the Going-to-the-Sun Rd makes quick forays into the park less convenient.

Sleeping

TOP CHOICE **Glacier Park Lodge** HISTORIC HOTEL **$$**
(406-226-5600; www.bigtreehotel.com; r US$140-180, ste US$359; mid-May–late Sep;) Set in attractive flower-filled grounds and overlooking Montana's oldest golf course, this historic 1914 lodge was built in the classic national park tradition with a splendid open-plan lobby supported by lofty 900-year-old Douglas fir timbers (imported from Washington State). Eye-catching Native American artwork adorns the communal areas and a full-sized teepee is wedged incongruously onto a 2nd-floor balcony. Other quirks include an outdoor swimming pool, rocking chairs on the porch and a singing janitor who'll bellow out erstwhile show tunes as he industriously removes yesterday's mud from the plush reception carpet. In keeping with national park tradition the rooms here are 'rustic' with no TVs, telephones or air-con.

Brownie's HOSTEL **$**
(406-226-4426; www.brownieshostel.com; 1020 Hwy 49; dm US$20, r US$55) Above Brownie's Grocery & Deli, this casual HI hostel is packed with travelers staying in the eight-person single-sex dorms or private doubles. It has a common room and kitchen, and lockout is roughly 10am to 4pm. Sheets, blankets and pillows are provided free of charge.

Firebrand Pass Campground CAMPGROUND **$**
(406-226-5573; campsites US$23) This small campground, 4.8km (3 miles) west of East Glacier and off US 2, has 26 sites for both tent and full RV hookup. The grassy, shady grounds have an air of seclusion; the bathroom and laundry facilities are clean.

Circle R Motel MOTEL **$**
(406-226-4432; 402 US 2; r $54-108) On East Glacier's little mall strip just east of the train station, Circle R has both old and new sections. The latter's rooms have TVs, large bathrooms, fridges and microwaves, a rare treat in and around Glacier.

WORTH A TRIP

IZAAK WALTON INN

Situated like a misplaced fragment of Shakespearean England within snowball-throwing distance of Glacier National Park's southern boundary, the mock-Tudor **Izaak Walton Inn** (Map p180; 406-888-5700; www.izaakwaltoninn.com; 290 Izaak Walton Inn Rd; r US$117-168, cabooses US$230;) was originally built in 1939 to accommodate local railway personnel. Located close to the Park Creek area, the lodge became something of an incongruity after WWII, when a plan to build a new southern park entrance in the vicinity never materialized. Dubbed the 'Inn between' in the years since, the Izaak has recently enjoyed a modern renaissance with cozy rooms, a sauna and easy access to skiing trails. Caboose cottages with kitchenettes are available along with a historic GN441 locomotive refurbished as a luxury four-person suite (US$299). The inn remains a daily flag-stop (request stop) on Amtrak's *Empire Builder* train route.

Eating

Serrano's Mexican Restaurant MEXICAN **$$**
(www.serranosmexican.com; 29 Dawson Ave; mains US$11-16; 5-10pm) This Mexican place, just across the road from the train station, is East Glacier's most talked about restaurant. Renowned for its excellent iced margaritas, it also serves economical burritos, enchiladas and quesadillas in the vintage Dawson house log cabin, originally built in 1909. There's a small backpackers hostel out the back.

Brownie's Grocery & Deli DELI, CAFÉ **$**
(1020 Hwy 49; sandwiches US$5-8; 7am-10pm) A true Montana salt-of-the-earth mercantile, Brownie's is an enterprising culinary one-man band selling pastries, strong coffee, sandwiches, internet time and even the odd brownie or three. As if that wasn't enough, it also doubles up as the popular and affordable hostel, Brownie's.

Great Northern Steak & Rib House INTERNATIONAL $$$
(Glacier Park Lodge; mains US$17-24; ⏲mid-May–late Sep) This big restaurant in the Glacier Park Lodge is a smooth operation, serving steak, seafood and chicken. If you're burgered-out, try the salmon Niçoise or the chicken masala.

Two Medicine Grill BREAKFAST, BURGERS $
(314 US 2; breakfast US$5-9; ⏲6.30am-9pm) This tiny dive-diner by the railway tracks is best enjoyed in the space upfront in view of the short-order chefs as they whip up sourdough pancakes and huckleberry smoothies.

Information

East Glacier lies just outside the park's southeastern corner at the junction of Hwy 49 and US 2. The famous Great Northern Railway bisects the settlement, which is dominated by the historic Glacier Park Lodge. Other facilities include a **post office** (15 Blackfoot Ave; ⏲8:30am-noon & 1:30-5pm Mon-Fri), ATMs, internet at Brownie's and a couple of gas stations.

Getting There & Around

The three-times-daily East Side Shuttle links East Glacier with Two Medicine (US$10), Cut Throat Creek (US$20), St Mary (US$30), Many Glacier (US$40) and Waterton (US$50). The **Amtrak** (www.amtrak.com) *Empire Builder* stops at the train station once daily traveling in either direction.

West Glacier

Lying less than 1km (0.6 miles) from the park's busiest entrance gate and equipped with an Amtrak train station, West Glacier is the park's most pleasant gateway town with its attractive cluster of serviceable facilities befitting of Glacier's rustic parkitecture image. Known as Belton until 1949, the settlement was the site of the park's oldest hotel, the Belton Chalet, built in 1910 and still hosting guests.

Sleeping

Belton Chalet HISTORIC HOTEL $$
(☎406-888-5000; www.beltonchalet.com; r US$155-170) Built and opened the same year as the national park (1910), this affectionate Swiss chalet overlooking the railroad tracks in West Glacier was Glacier's first tourist hotel and has a plusher feel than many of the park's other vintage lodges – a result, perhaps, of an extensive 1998 restoration. A one-time café, pizza parlor and Civilian Conservation Corps accommodation, the family-run chalet lay rotting until its 1990s refurb, which dusted off 25 traditional yet elegant rooms, arts and crafts-style furnishings, a spa (with massage and foot rubs) and a celebrated Mediterranean-influenced taproom (see p224).

West Glacier Motel & Cabins MOTEL, CABINS $
(☎406-888-5662; www.westglacier.com/motel.html; d/cabins US$90/170) A bed and a bible are the only two guarantees at the closest motel to the park entrance located on the north side of the railroad tracks in West Glacier Village. Motel-style rooms are situated in the village while cabins are perched on a bluff overlooking Flathead River. There are no TVs, fridges, coffee machines or wi-fi. It's the wilderness, don't you know?

Vista Motel MOTEL $
(☎406-888-5311; www.glaciervistamotel.com; US 2; r US$95-125; wifi, pool) A cheap and relatively cheerful motel, the no-nonsense Vista does at least have a vista, along with comfortable beds, powerful showers and a rather spatially challenged swimming pool. Located a 0.8km (0.5-mile) hike along US 2 (there's a wide shoulder) from the West Glacier train station, it's a viable crash pad if you're arriving by train and plying the park by public transport.

Glacier Guides Lodge B&B $$
(☎406-387-5555; www.glacierguides.com; Highline Blvd; r US$171; air-con, wifi) Newly refurbished to meet environmental LEED standard, this wooden B&B-style lodge run by a local guide company is a good option for people who want rustic authenticity without forsaking wi-fi or TV. It's just off US 2 opposite the West Glacier train station. All rooms have private baths and continental breakfast is included.

Glacier Highland Resort Motel MOTEL $
(☎406-888-5427; www.glacierhighland.com; US 2; r US$70-100) A perennially popular place across from the West Glacier train station, next to a restaurant of the same name. There are 33 units and an indoor hot tub.

Glacier Campground CAMPGROUND $
(☎406-387-5689; campsites US$19-24) This campground, located 1.6km (1 mile) west of West Glacier and off US 2, sits on 16 hectares (40 acres) of lovely wooded grounds. It also offers basic wooden cabins.

Eating

TOP CHOICE West Glacier Restaurant & Bar AMERICAN $$
(200 Going-to-the-Sun Rd; mains US$11-17; ⊙7am-10pm May-Sep) Boy the food here is fantastic – and such large portions! Perched invitingly on the cusp of the park, this ultrafriendly restaurant is a sure bet for filling, calorie-packed Montana cooking. The breakfast classic is a stack of buttery pancakes while dinner veers toward spaghetti and meatballs. Casual diners can sit diner style at the counter and enjoy the state's most generous portions of ice cream, milkshakes and dessert pies. The adjoining bar is where West Glacier's nightlife begins and ends.

Belton Chalet Grill Dining Room & Taproom INTERNATIONAL $$$
(www.beltonchalet.com; mains US$25-34; ⊙3-10pm) For a step up from unadorned meatloaf, hit West Glacier's historic chalet for some equally historic food. The sit-down restaurant sports tablecloths, wine glasses and menu items that have been 'sugar-cured' and baked with 'yuzu passion fruit reduction drizzle.' The adjoining taproom is a more casual, economical affair that offers an excellent antipasto plate and some inventive sandwiches and microbrews.

Shopping

Glacier Outdoor Center OUTDOOR EQUIPMENT
(www.glacierraftco.com; 11957 US 2E; ⊙7:30am-9pm) Just outside the park, in West Glacier about 800m (0.5 miles) from the train station on US 2, this is the best one-stop shop for outdoor gear. It rents and sells gear for rafting, fishing, mountain biking, camping and backpacking.

Information

Most basic facilities can be found here, including a gas station, a grocery-gift store, a post office and an ATM.

Alberta Information Centre (☎406-888-5743; off US 2; ⊙8am-7pm) A potent advertisement for wilderness junkies keen on heading north to Waterton Lakes, Banff and Jasper National Parks.

Glacier National Park Headquarters (☎406-888-7800; www.nps.gov/glac; West Glacier, MT 59936; ⊙8am-4:30pm Mon-Fri) Inhabits a small complex just south of the west entrance station. This location is the focus for visitor information from November to April.

Glacier Natural History Association (www.glacierassociation.org; US 2; ⊙8am-4:30pm Mon-Fri) The nonprofit association, in West Glacier's train station, is an excellent resource for books, maps and information.

Glacier Photo (Going-to-the-Sun Rd; per 15min US$5; ⊙8am-8pm) Internet is available here.

Getting There & Around

A 4km (2.5-mile) paved cycle path links West Glacier with Apgar Village and transit center inside the park, from where you can catch free Going-to-the-Sun Rd shuttles. Amtrak's *Empire Builder* stops at the West Glacier train station once a day traveling in either direction.

Polebridge

Glacier's most isolated outpost spins on two hubs: the Northern Lights Saloon and the historic Polebridge Mercantile, a combination store, post office and gas station. Sandwiched between the towering Livingstone and Whitefish mountain ranges, the 'town' is a low-key place with more wildlife than people. Expect no electricity, few facilities and even fewer worries.

Sleeping & Eating

North Fork Hostel & Square Peg Ranch HOSTEL $
(Map p180; ☎406-888-5241; www.nfhostel.com; 80 Beaver Dr; tents US$14, teepees US$45, dm US$20, cabins US$50; wi-fi) Glacier's quirkiest hostel requires a bit of legwork to get to and lacks the basic comforts of other park lodges (there's no electricity), but in many ways that's part of the attraction. There are 13 dorm spaces, a couple of cabins, some teepees and vintage homesteads (US$80 for up to six people) at the Square Peg Ranch up the road. Facilities include wi-fi and a phone powered by an independent power source. There's also a fully equipped kitchen with a propane stove, hot showers and outhouse toilets. The Polebridge Mercantile is 800m (0.5 miles) away; phone ahead to arrange a lift from West Glacier train station.

Northern Lights Saloon AMERICAN, BAR $$
(Map p180; Polebridge Loop Rd; mains US$9-14; ⊙4pm-midnight May-Sep) Most visitors to isolated Polebridge arrive with pretty low culinary expectations, meaning they walk away more than satisfied after a trip to this Old West–style park institution. Cool and very, very casual, the Northern Lights' standard

GLACIER'S GLACIERS

Unless you've been living on the moon for the last decade, you'll know all about melting glaciers and the global preoccupation with climate change. Glacier National Park currently lists 25 glaciers, significantly less than other American national parks such as the North Cascades (with 300) and Mt Rainier (with 26 on one mountain). But, thanks to a Glacier Research Monitoring program carried out by the US Geological Survey, the Montana park's icy monoliths have been more studied than any of their counterparts.

Current figures procured by high-tech sensing equipment and repeat photography suggest that, if current trends continue, the park could be glacier-free by 2030. These tentative estimates are based on studies undertaken on the Sperry, Agassiz, Jackson and Grinnell Glaciers, all of which have lost approximately 35% of their volume since the mid-1960s. However, whatever scenario ultimately transpires, the park – contrary to popular opinion – will not have to change its name. The 'glacier' label refers as much to the dramatic ice-sculpted scenery as it does to its fast-melting rivers of ice, and these remarkable geographical features ought to be dropping jaws for a good few millennia to come.

beer-and-burgers menu is supplemented by some surprising vegetarian dishes and potent glasses of organic ale washed down amid tales of intrepid backcountry hikes and close encounters of the furry (read, bear) kind.

Polebridge Mercantile PASTRIES, SUPERMARKET **$**
(Map p180; Polebridge Loop Rd) Next door to the saloon and dubbed 'the Merc' by those in the know, the Polebridge creates sweet and savory pastries that are talked about all over the park – nay state. The small shop also stocks other foodstuffs.

Information

Polebridge is located on the Outside North Fork Rd, 42km (26 miles) northwest of the park's western entrance. The **Polebridge Ranger Station** (Map p180; ☎406-888-7842; ⊙late May–mid-Sep) lies 1.6km (1 mile) to the east, next to the park entrance.

Getting There & Around

Driving a car is the only reliable way of getting to Polebridge, although you'll need good snow tires in the winter. The North Fork Hostel (p224) sometimes runs a shuttle service from West Glacier; phone for more details.

Blackfeet Indian Reservation

The short-grass prairie east of Glacier is home to the Blackfeet Nation, which includes the Northern Piegan (Blackfeet), Southern Piegan and Blood tribes that came south from the Alberta area in the 1700s. Originally an agrarian people, the Blackfeet took quickly to horses and guns, eventually developing a reputation as the fiercest warriors in the West. Today approximately 7000 tribal members reside on or around the **reservation** (www.blackfeetnation.com), where the major industries are ranching, farming and pencil manufacturing. Browning, 29km (18 miles) east of Glacier National Park, is where most of the reservation's amenities lie.

Welcome to one of Montana's better Native American museums, **Museum of the Plains Indians** (cnr Hwys 2 & 89, Browning; adult/child US$4/1; ⊙9am-4:30pm), which honors the culture of the Crow, Cree, Sioux, Cheyenne and above all the Blackfeet. Extensive descriptions accompany exhibits of costumes, art and craftwork. In summer skilfully adorned teepees are set up outside.

Rising Wolf Wilderness Adventures (☎406-338-3016) runs guided hikes and fishing trips in and around Blackfeet Indian Reservation. The activities are run by Blackfeet women, and geared toward women.

Sleep in a teepee looking onto the plains at the **Lodgepole Gallery & Tipi Village** (☎406-338-2787; www.blackfeetculturecamp.com; US 89; 1/2/3 person teepees US$60/75/90), 3.2km (2 miles) west of Browning.

Browning is a seasonal stop on Amtrak's *Empire Builder* operating from October to April with daily trains to Seattle and Chicago.

Whitefish

To be both 'rustic' and 'hip' within the same square kilometer is a hard act to pull off, but tiny Whitefish (population 8000) makes a good stab at it. Once sold as the main gateway to Glacier National Park, this charismatic New West town has earned enough kudos to merit a long-distance trip in its own right. Aside from grandiose Glacier (which is within an easy day's cycling distance), Whitefish is home to an attractive stash of restaurants, a historic train station and an underrated ski resort.

Sights & Activities

Whitefish Mountain Resort SKI RESORT
(www.bigmtn.com; lift ticket adult/child US$56/27) Whitefish's star attraction, formerly known as Big Mountain, is situated 11.2km (7 miles) north of downtown. It has a whopping 1214 hectares (3000 acres) of skiable terrain along with a snowboard-hopping terrain park. The winter season runs late November to mid-April. From June to September, 32.2km (20 miles) of trails host hiking and mountain-biking aficionados. The gondola to the mountaintop offers great views of Flathead Valley; you can ride or hike down.

FREE **Stumptown Historical Society Museum** MUSEUM
(www.stumptownhistoricalsociety.org; 500 Depot St; ⏲10am-4pm Mon-Sat) Whitefish's fine old Tudor Revival Great Northern Railway Depot built in the 1920s doubles up as a history museum displaying train memorabilia and fascinating photos of early Whitefish.

City Beach Park BEACH, PARK
Glued to the southern shore of Whitefish Lake, this is where the whole town comes to date and debate in the summer months. The swimming area is roped off. Parking is free.

Glacier Cyclery CYCLING
(www.glaciercyclery.com; 326 2nd St E; per day/week rental US$30/155) A super-friendly and knowledgeable bike store (with rentals available) located in the center of Whitefish that extols the virtues and benefits of cycling in and around Whitefish and Glacier.

Sleeping

A string of chain motels lines US 93 south of Whitefish, but the savvy dock in town at one of the following.

Downtowner MOTEL $
(☎406-862-2535; www.downtownermotel.cc; 224 Spokane Ave; r US$67-117; ❄📶) Whitefish's reliable, slap-bang-in-the-middle-of-town option is a 17-room motel with an extra dorm available for groups. Comfortable rooms are large and packed with an excellent range of amenities. All guests get free use of the motel's outdoor Jacuzzi, sauna and adjacent gym. Downstairs, the tasty Wrap and Roll house (open 11am to 9pm Monday to Saturday) sells burritos and gyros.

Garden Wall B&B $$
(☎406-862-3440; www.gardenwallinn.com; 504 Spokane Ave; r US$155-195, ste US$275; 📶) Take one of the most elegant homes in affluent Whitefish, make it into a sharply run B&B, and you've got a national park adventure that promises to be as refined as it is rustic. Shoehorned into a shady spot on Spokane Ave, the Garden Wall's five guest rooms are stuffed with art deco artifacts. A real log fire blazes in the living room, and the welcoming owner – a qualified chef – is known to rustle up gourmet breakfasts preceded by a wake-up coffee tray delivered to your room. The suite can sleep four.

Pine Lodge HOTEL $$
(☎406-862-7600; www.thepinelodge.com; 920 Spokane Ave; r US$79-142; ❄📶🏊) A more upmarket abode with a plush modern wood-themed Montana look that would have made Hemingway feel jealous. There's a handy free airport pickup, along with a swimming pool and gym.

Whitefish Lake State Park Campground CAMPGROUND $
(☎406-862-3991; State Park Rd; campsites US$20; ⏲late May-early Oct) On the southwest edge of Whitefish Lake, shady forested grounds hold 25 first-come, first-served sites, including one that is wheelchair-friendly.

Eating

Buffalo Café BREAKFAST, AMERICAN $
(www.buffalocafewhitefish.com; 514 3rd St E; breakfast US$7-10) Take heed of the local taxi driver's advice and you'll probably end up here along with everyone else who passes for local in Whitefish. The Buffalo's longtime specialty is breakfast, which involves lashings of huevos rancheros, mountains of hash browns and slow but engagingly friendly service. As a special bonus, the Buffalo has recently started offering dinner, meaning it's a café in name only.

Tupelo Grille SOUTHERN $$$
(☎406-862-6136; www.tupelogrille.com; 17 Central Ave; mains US$19-29; ⏲5-11pm) Named after Elvis' Mississippi hometown, this locally famous fine-dining establishment has

food with a strident Southern tinge. Clever Cajun and Creole dishes come without the pretensions of other posh eateries and are interspersed with the odd Thai and stir-fry favorites. Viticulture aficionados will enjoy the wine list.

Wasabi Sushi Bar & the Ginger Grill JAPANESE **$$**
(☎406-863-9283; www.wasabimt.com; 419 2nd St E; meals US$12-21; ⊙5-11pm Tue-Sat) Yes, you're in Montana and, yes, this is exceptionally good sushi. Confirming Whitefish's cosmopolitan credentials, this place delivers the fish in both traditional and fusion styles. For those who don't crave it raw, you can choose from an array of cooked pan-Asian main dishes. Reservations are recommended.

Third Street Market SUPERMARKET **$**
(☎406-862-5054; cnr 3rd St & Spokane Ave; ⊙9am-6pm Mon-Sat) Middle America goes organic at this alternative local grocery that wouldn't look out of place on New York's Upper East Side. Choose from a range of natural foods, bulk-bin items, vitamins, organic produce and even healthy grub for your pet.

Drinking

TOP CHOICE **Montana Coffee Traders** CAFÉ
(www.coffeetraders.com; 845 Wisconsin Ave; ⊙7am-6pm Mon-Sat, 9am-5pm Sun;) Get ready for another 'I must be in the Pacific Northwest' moment. Whitefish's homegrown microroasters run this always busy café, cum gift shop, cum computer geek hangout situated in the old Skyles building in the center of town. The organic, fair-trade beans are roasted in an old farmhouse on Hwy 93; the formidable paninis are prepared in-house.

Great Northern Brewing BREWPUB
(www.greatnorthernbrewing.com; cnr Central Ave & Railway St; ⊙11am-11pm) Encased in an impressive glass 'gravity flow' building with giant windows revealing a Willy Wonka-like array of beer-making equipment, this renowned microbrewery is one of the most celebrated in the state and has become a jubilant part of Whitefish's après-ski scene. The showcase Black Star Double Hopped Golden Lager can be tasted in the on-site Black Star Draught House and free tours of the brewery at 1pm and 3pm Monday to Friday in summer.

Information

Check with the **Whitefish Visitor Center** (www.whitefishvisit.com; 307 Spokane Ave; ⊙9am-5:30pm Mon-Fri) for more info on activities.

Getting There & Around

Glacier Park International Airport (FCA; www.iflyglacier.com) located between Whitefish and Kalispell has direct flights to and from Seattle, the Twin Cities, Las Vegas, Salt Lake City and Denver. **Flathead Transportation** (☎406-892-0133) runs taxi shuttles to Whitefish (US$25) and West Glacier (US$50). Reserve ahead.

Rimrock Trailways (www.rimrocktrailways.com) runs daily buses from Whitefish train station to Kalispell (US$13) and Missoula (US$39.50).

The **Amtrak** (www.amtrak.com) *Empire Builder* train leaves the **Whitefish train station** (500 Depot St) daily at 7:46am eastbound to West Glacier (US$7), East Glacier Park (US$14) and Chicago (US$204), and westbound to Portland and Seattle at 9:16pm.

Kalispell

Kalispell, 21km (13 miles) south of Whitefish, is a nothing-to-write-home-about commercial hub 5km (3.1 miles) north of the humungous Flathead Lake. Though hardly as charming as Whitefish, it's a handy place to refuel and resupply. Its concentration of budget lodging makes it a frequented gateway to Glacier, less than an hour's drive northeast. It's also used by visitors to the popular Flathead Lake, the largest natural lake west of the Mississippi, 15 to 20 minutes' drive south by way of US 93.

Kalispell Chamber of Commerce (☎406-758-2800; 15 Depot Park; ⊙8am-5pm Mon-Fri) has maps and information.

The completely restored 1895 Norman-style **Conrad Mansion** (www.conradmansion.com; cnr Woodland Ave & 3rd St E; adult/child US$8/3; ⊙10am-5pm mid-May–mid-Oct), built in 1895, is worth touring. Contemporary work by Montanan artists is displayed at **Hockaday Museum of Art** (www.hockadaymuseum.org; 302 2nd Ave E; admission US$5; ⊙10am-5pm Tue-Sat).

Kalispell has a good range of lodgings and eateries. **Rocky Mountain 'Hi' Campground** (☎406-755-9573; www.glaciercamping.com; 825 Helena Flats Rd; tent sites US$20, RV sites US$26-29;), off US 2 east of Kalispell, has a huge playground and is great for families. Aside from the camping and RV sites there are six- and eight-person cabins (US$60 to US$105).

The town and its surroundings are awash with most of the familiar chain hotels from pricey to cheap. By far the most original downtown pick is the independent and refreshingly historic **Kalispell Grand Hotel** (406-755-8100; www.kalispellgrand.com; 100 Main St; r US$102-111;).

The menu at **Capers** (www.capersmontana.com; 121 Main St; mains US$17-24; 5-9pm Tue-Sat) is known for its brick-oven pizza (US$10 to US$14). There are also more adventurous dishes such as pan-seared duck breast, Mediterranean chicken, local rainbow trout and Hawaiian mahi-mahi.

Rimrock Trailways (www.rimrocktrailways.com) runs daily buses from Kalispell to Whitefish and Missoula. Glacier Park International Airport is 16km (10 miles) to the north of the town center.

Understand Banff, Jasper & Glacier

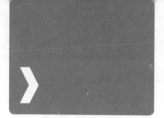

population per sq mile

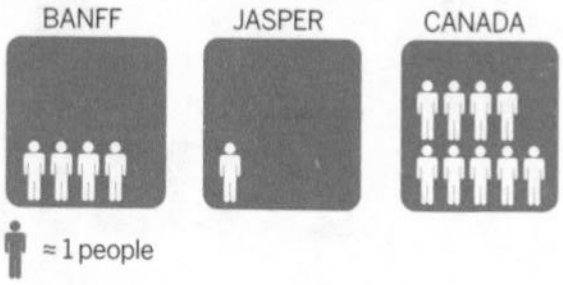

The Parks Today

Visitor Experience v Ecological Integrity

As four of the world's oldest and most symbolic national parks, Banff, Jasper, Glacier and Waterton face a difficult modern quandary. On one hand they proudly represent what – in the words of a 2009 Emmy award-winning documentary – was 'America's best idea.' On the other, they remain litmus tests for the planet's ongoing battle to protect its wild but delicate ecosystems from multiple human threats.

Set up in the late 19th and early 20th century as 'parks for the people,' the underlying philosophies that guide how these protected areas are managed have shifted significantly in the last decade with the focus moving away from the 'visitor experience' mantra of the early conservationist movement toward the more pressing question of 'ecological integrity.' This debate has grown more heated since the 1960s when the damage wreaked by millions of annual visitors first became worryingly apparent.

» Population of Banff Townsite: 8721

» Average number of hours spent by a visitor in Glacier National Park: 11.9

» Mammals killed by cars in Jasper 2010: 132

Banff at the Crossroads

These days an estimated five million people pass through Banff annually and, due to the environmental pressure caused by such large numbers, many feel that the town has been stretched to its limit. Actions to tackle this problem began in the early 1990s and in 1996, after two exhaustive years of research, the Banff-Bow Valley study compiled a 75-page document called *At the Crossroads*. Echoing the fears of many, the report stressed that if Banff's development plans and burgeoning visitor numbers were allowed to continue unchecked, the park's ecological integrity would be irrevocably harmed.

In the years since, the park management has become more coordinated and less visitor-centric, placing caps on townsite development and employing seasonal hiking restrictions in sensitive areas to reduce

Top Films

» **Brokeback Mountain** (2005) Lean dialogue and stupendous acting characterize this unorthodox cowboy tale partly filmed in Kananaskis Country.

» **The Shining** (1980) The opening scene tracks a car plying its way along the Going-to-the-Sun Rd in Glacier National Park.

» **River of No Return** (1954) The peroxide beauty of Marilyn Monroe is pitted against the natural beauty of Banff and Jasper.

» **Days of Heaven** (1978) Terrence Malick's Magnus opus utilized Waterton and Banff for its stunning cinematography.

Top Books

» **The National Parks: America's Best Idea** (2009) by Dayton Duncan and Ken Burns

» **Indian Trails of the Canadian Rockies** (1911) by Mary Schäffer

» **Night of the Grizzlies** (1969) by Jack Olsen

ecoregions of Banff
(% of national park)

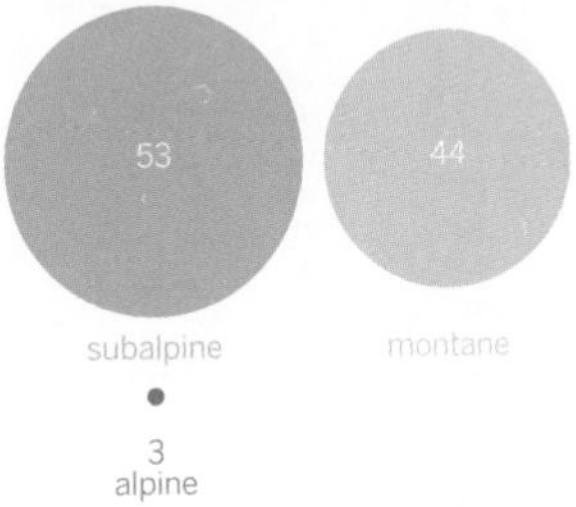

if 100 people come to the parks

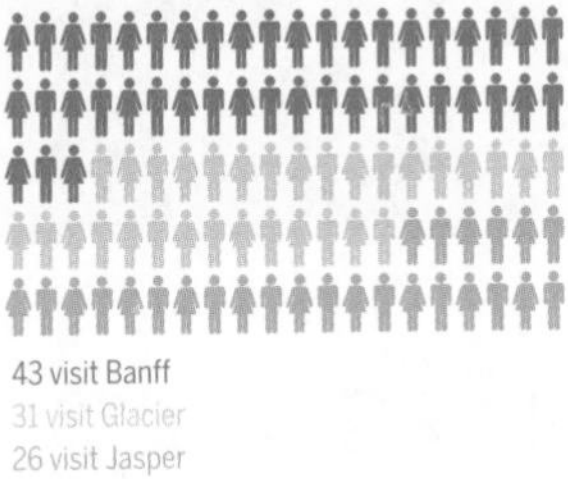

human–wildlife encounters. Additionally both short- and long-term plans are now formulated and reviewed regularly in consultation with tourism, environmental, community and aboriginal groups to push innovations – including wildlife 'bridges' across the Trans-Canada Hwy – designed to redirect the park toward a more sustainable future.

» Banff: 3,132,086 (2010 visitors)

» Jasper: 1,868,797 (2010 visitors)

» Glacier: 2,200,948 (2010 visitors)

» Waterton: 382,861 (2010 visitors)

Turning up the Heat

South of the 49th parallel, Glacier National Park juggles issues of both the hot (forest fires) and cold (melting glaciers) variety. Ongoing studies by the US Geological survey on Glacier's 'rivers of ice' have revealed that many of these frozen behemoths have shrunk by over a third since the 1960s, evidence enough, suggest some scientists, of potentially damaging climate change. Meanwhile, at a microlevel, the park authorities have attempted to chip away at the causes with innovative pilot schemes. In 2007 a free shuttle bus was introduced to help ease traffic congestion on the Going-to-the-Sun Rd and, by 2010, the service was successful in persuading 170,000 of Glacier's annual summer drivers to leave their cars at specially built transit centers.

Glacier has always faced an annual battle with summer fires, but the summer of 2003 was the hottest on record, blazing over 10% of the park's total tree cover. Unfortunately, the fires also burned a large hole in the area's tourist-dependent economy. The heat was turned up again in 2006 when over 12,950 hectares (32,000 acres) was razed in the Red Eagle Fire on the south side of St Mary Lake. While contemporary thinking acknowledges forest fires as important natural processes, they become problematic when they are human-ignited (as in Glacier's 2003 Robert's Fire) and/or threaten property and livelihoods. How park authorities react to them has thus become a delicate balancing act.

Top Wildlife

» **Nonthreatened** Mountain goat, bighorn sheep, elk, moose, deer, hoary marmot, white-tailed deer, beaver, pika, black bear, mountain lion

» **Endangered** Grizzly bear, Canadian lynx, wolverine, gray wolf, woodland caribou, Banff Springs snail

Best Maps

» **Gem Trek Publishing** (www.gemtrek.com) Excellent 1:100,000 maps covering the Canadian Rockies

» **National Geographic Trails Illustrated** (www.natgeomaps.com) Useful 1:100,000 map of Glacier/Waterton Lakes

Do & Don'ts

» **Do** deposit your garbage in bear-proof containers

» **Do** carry bear spray

» **Do** pack out everything you pack in

» **Don't** stray off the trails

» **Don't** remove rocks or flowers from the parks

History

It is only since the mid-19th century that the international border separating Glacier National Park with its three Canadian counterparts – Waterton, Banff and Jasper – has borne any significance. In the preceding millennia First Nations people such as the Blackfeet, Kootenay, Piegan and Stoney lived in scattered nomadic tribes observing only the vaguest of territorial boundaries. Details of the Rockies' prehistoric people remain sketchy. Uncovered at Vermilion Lakes near Banff in the 1980s, the region's oldest remains date back nearly 11,000 years and are thought to belong to descendents of primitive Stone Age people who ventured over a frozen land bridge across the Bering Strait during the last ice age.

For a comprehensive history of the Rocky Mountain parks go to the website of Parks Canada (www.pc.gc.ca) or the US National Park Service (www.nps.gov).

The Rockies' human history became infinitely more complex in the late 18th century when European exploration edged unstoppably west, stoked by the thriving fur trade and sponsored by powerful commercial corporations such as the Hudson Bay Company and its bitter rival, the Northwest Company. In a bid to establish new trading routes nearer the Pacific, Scotsman Alexander Mackenzie became the first European to cross the Rockies in 1793, when he navigated along the course of the Peace River to the headwaters of the Fraser and, with the help of Aboriginals, bush-whacked his way through to Bella Coola in British Columbia. Other explorers soon followed, most notably Lewis and Clark, who passed within 80km (50 miles) of Marias Pass near Glacier in 1805–06.

Exploration quickly led to exploitation. Some of the pristine land now diligently protected in Jasper, Banff and Glacier was (briefly) mined for minerals while other parts were earmarked by profit-hungry cross-continental railroad companies anxious to repay their huge construction costs. The real genesis of the parks came through an unconventional alliance between foresighted conservationists eager to safeguard North America's increasingly threatened wilderness areas, and large railway entrepreneurs who, recognizing the business potential of tourism, started to market the region as America's very own Swiss Alps.

TIMELINE

10,000 BC

First Nations tribes begin to settle and hunt throughout the Rockies. Groupings include the Kootenai and Stoney from the high plateaus; and the bison-hunting Piegan (North Blackfeet) from the plains.

1750

European explorers and traders arrive in the area via the fur trade. The introduction of modern weapons, European diseases and horses filters down to First Nations tribes, causing disruption.

1793

British explorer Alexander Mackenzie becomes the first European to cross the Rocky Mountains via the Peace and Fraser River systems on his journey to the Pacific coast in British Columbia.

All four parks in this book were inaugurated between 1885 and 1910 during the first flowering of the conservationist movement in North America led by pioneering figures such as Teddy Roosevelt, John Muir and George Bird Grinnell. Remaining true to their original philosophy, the parks have changed little in the years since. For truly current events in the parks, see p230. For the history of Waterton Lakes National Park, see p207.

Banff National Park

The history of Banff National Park begins in 1875 with the selection of Kicking Horse Pass, just west of the present-day park, over the more northerly Yellowhead Pass (in present-day Jasper), as the route for the nascent Canadian Pacific Railway (CPR). It was during the building of this railway in 1882 that two railroad laborers, William McCardell and Frank McCabe, stumbled upon the Cave and Basin hot springs at the base of Sulphur Mountain.

While Stoney Aboriginals had known about the springs and their supposed healing powers for centuries, it took the entrepreneurship of McCardell and McCabe to bring the waters to national attention. But, caught up in an acrimonious battle over ownership rights, the workers' tentative proposal to develop the springs as a lucrative tourist destination was rudely quashed by a Canadian government that had already, surreptitiously, made similar plans of its own.

In 1885, as the last spike was driven into the transcontinental railway at Craigellachie in British Columbia, a 26-sq-km (10-sq-mile) federal reserve was established around Banff Springs by the Conservative government of John A MacDonald. Sensing a tourist bonanza, not just from the recuperative springs, but from the astounding mountainscapes that surrounded them, the fledgling CPR was quick to jump on the bandwagon. 'If we can't export the scenery, we'll import the tourists,' announced CPR president William Van Horne portentously in 1886. His idea was to build a luxurious chain of grand hotels across the railway network that would lure in wealthy tourists and repay the railway's outstanding loans. The plan clearly worked. Opened in 1888 as the grandest and most expansive hotel in the chain, the chateau-style Banff Springs Hotel was a runaway success and quickly established itself as an icon of Canadian architecture.

By 1888 over 5000 tourists had been ferried into the embryonic park to be rejuvenated in the magic spring water, and Banff Town listed 300 permanent residents, as well as churches, hotels, saloons and shops. The national park, which had been Canada's first – and the world's third – when it was created in 1885, was expanded in 1892 to include the area

In 1885 Banff became the world's third national park (and the first in Canada), after Yellowstone in the US, inaugurated in 1872, and Royal National Park in Australia, founded in 1879.

History & Culture Museums

- Whyte Museum of the Canadian Rockies
- Museum of the Plains Indians
- Jasper-Yellowhead Museum & Archives
- Waterton Heritage Centre

1800s

Dislocated First Nations tribes begin to settle in their hunting grounds along the Athabasca Valley using the area's various passes and valleys as migratory routes.

1805–06

The Lewis and Clark expedition passes close to the Glacier area, but misses Marias Pass. On their return journey Lewis gets into a skirmish with the Blackfeet tribe.

1811

Heading west from a post near present-day Jasper Town, David Thompson becomes the first European to cross the Athabasca Pass on his way to the Columbia River and the Pacific.

1813

The Northwest Company opens up a permanent trading post on Brulé Lake near present-day Pocahontas; by 1817 it was known as 'Jasper's House' after the presiding clerk Jasper Hawse.

surrounding Lake Louise and, before long, Banff had spawned another of Van Horne's fairy-tale hotels, the beguiling Chateau Lake Louise.

Welcoming the Masses

A coach road was opened to Banff in 1911, and the following year public traffic was allowed into the park. Suddenly the wilderness was accessible to all kinds of visitors, rather than just wealthy Victorians, and the opportunities for outdoor recreation multiplied. Campsites were set up on Tunnel Mountain and at Two Jacks Lake, and affordable lodging began to appear in the Bow Valley. Pursuits diversified; skiing, the arts and short-lived sports like ice boating all drew participants and spectators. A road was built to Norquay ski slopes, and Lake Louise soon began to welcome skiers as well. The year 1917 saw the initiation of the Banff Winter Carnival, a week of everything from dances to dogsled races.

Throughout WWI, immigrants from enemy countries were detained in camps below Castle Mountain and near Cave and Basin hot springs. Forced to labor, they established much of the infrastructure throughout the park, including making horse trails car-friendly. In the 1930s similar work was taken up by relief workers during the Depression, when the Icefields Parkway was first initiated. Relief workers also built gardens in Banff Town and an airfield for private planes.

The National Parks Act, passed in 1930, established the boundaries of the park much as they are today, along with many of the conservation laws that are still in place. While the number of tourists to the park diminished during WWII, Banff became a popular honeymoon destination in the 1940s and 1950s, attracting returning war veterans and their brides. By 1962, when the Trans-Canada Hwy officially opened, the park had begun to market itself as an international holiday destination.

Historic Lodges & Hotels

- Chateau Lake Louise, 1913
- Lake McDonald Lodge, 1913
- Banff Springs Hotel, 1914
- Many Glacier Hotel, 1915
- Prince of Wales Hotel, 1927

Banff unsuccessfully bid for the Winter Olympics three times in 1964, 1968 and 1972. The 1972 bid was controversial when environmental groups lobbied the government. The bid was ultimately withdrawn.

Balancing Act

Banff gained further global recognition as a summer and winter resort with the 1988 Winter Olympics in nearby Calgary. Although events were actually held at Nakiska ski resort in Kananaskis Country and the Nordic Centre in neighboring Canmore, the Olympics drew tourists and publicity to the park. Banff Town's economy boomed, further strengthening the tourism infrastructure. In 1990, after more than a century of being governed federally, Banff Town was granted the right to become a self-governing community. That year, the CPR train service, which had played such an important role in the town's late-19th-century take-off, was discontinued.

Banff has boomed in recent years, but greater numbers of tourists have led to worries about ecological imbalance. As a result, the public

1862

The pioneering 'Overlanders' pass through on their epic trek west from Ontario to BC in search of gold. Short on supplies, they barely survive their journey through the Yellowhead Pass.

1882

Two railway workers, William McCardell and Frank McCabe, discover the Cave and Basin hot springs near present-day Banff and unwittingly usher in the age of tourism.

1885

The Trans-Canada Railway is completed, and a federal reserve is established around Cave and Basin hot springs in response to a dispute about who had the right to develop them commercially.

1885

Naturalist George Bird Grinnell visits the Glacier area and discovers the Grinnell Glacier in the Many Glacier Valley. He coins the term 'Crown of the Continent' and lobbies for protective status.

zeitgeist has changed and the park today energetically promotes environmental as well as economic concerns.

Jasper National Park

First Nations peoples traditionally used the land that is now Jasper National Park as seasonal hunting and gathering grounds. It wasn't until the 1800s, when fur traders began to push west across the continent, dislocating various indigenous groups, that some First Nations tribes began utilizing the Athabasca Valley as a more permanent base.

Soon after, a dispute with Piegan people, over access to Howse Pass near present-day Banff, led British-Canadian explorer David Thompson to look for a new route across the Rockies to link up with lucrative trading centers on the west coast. Veering north during the winter of 1810, he trudged with his party through deep snow to the top of Athabasca Pass, crossing the Continental Divide in January 1811.

Before departing for Athabasca Pass, Thompson left fellow explorer William Henry in the Athabasca Valley, where he established Henry House, the region's first staging post, situated close to Old Fort Point, near present-day Jasper Town. In 1813 the Northwest Company established a more permanent post, 40km (25 miles) to the east, at Jasper House on Brulé Lake, which remained in operation until 1884.

In an effort to build good trade relations, the traders were encouraged to take Aboriginal wives. In doing so, a distinct Métis (French for 'mixed blood') culture was formed, and the unique language of Michif arose. Descendents of the Métis continued to farm in the Athabasca Valley well into the 20th century, greatly influencing the area's development. In 1910 they were given compensation payments and forced to leave their land, which by then had become a federal reserve.

Named After

» **Banff** Banffshire in Scotland

» **Jasper** Jasper Hawse, Northwest Company clerk

» **Waterton** Charles Waterton, English naturalist

» **Yoho** Cree word for 'awe'

» **Kootenay** Kootenay River

Waterton Lakes was originally known as the Kootenay Lakes Forest Reserve, Banff was once called Rocky Mountains Park, and Jasper formerly went under the name of Jasper Forest Park.

Adventurers & Mountaineers

In the early 1860s, around 200 pioneers set out from Ontario with their sights on the gold rush in British Columbia. The Overlanders, as they would come to be known, passed through Jasper and struggled over Yellowhead Pass, the park's present-day boundary with Mt Robson Provincial Park. The planned two-month journey turned into six months of near starvation. Poorly equipped and inexperienced, a number of men died en route, either swept away by turbulent rivers or from hypothermia. The only woman to accompany the group managed to survive, giving birth upon reaching Kamloops.

With the fur trade in decline and a new national park in Banff prospering to the south, mountaineers and adventurers began heading into Jasper's rugged wilderness in search of unnamed peaks and fabled glacial lakes. In 1906 Irish-born mountaineer and surveyor AO Wheeler founded

1888

Banff Springs Hotel opens as an original 'log cabin' hotel constructed by the Canadian Pacific Railway. The hotel is rebuilt in its more grandiose stone palace style in 1914.

STEPHEN SAKS/LONELY PLANET IMAGES ©

» Banff Springs Hotel (p65)

1891

James J Hill's Great Northern Railway arrives in the region, crossing Marias Pass and establishing stations in East Glacier Park, Essex and West Glacier.

the Alpine Club of Canada and began organizing periodic assaults on Mt Robson. Three years later he was instrumental in helping two colorful local characters, Reverend Kinney and Donald 'Curly' Philips, in their brave but ultimately abortive attempt on the summit. The mountain was eventually conquered by Austrian Conrad Kain in 1913.

The Emergence of a Park

Jasper's founding, rather like Banff's, is closely entwined with the development of the railway. Passed over in the 1880s by the CPR in favor of Kicking Horse Pass in Banff, Jasper got its revenge in 1903 when Wilfred Laurier's government gave the go-ahead for the Grand Trunk Pacific Company to build a line from the west coast through Yellowhead Pass. All too aware of how the railway had significantly boosted the fortunes of Banff, the Ministry of the Interior opportunistically created Jasper Forest Park in 1907, the Rocky Mountains' fifth – and Canada's sixth – national park.

Built between 1910 and 1913, construction of the railway reached the tiny settlement of Fitzhugh at mile marker 113 in 1911, bringing an immediate influx of adventurers, mountaineers and railway workers. Almost overnight the burgeoning town jumped from a population of 125 to around 800 and was promptly renamed Jasper after Jasper Hawse, a fur trading manager who had been based at the Jasper House trading post in the 1820s.

Before the passage of the National Parks Act in 1930, the park faced far fewer limitations on its industrial and commercial development. Consequently, in the 1910s, local outfitters and guides, eyeing a potential business bonanza, sprang up all over the Athabasca Valley intent on bringing the wilderness to the masses. Plans for an enlarged town were laid out, a school was built, and clearing began for roads and climbing trails. The first grocery store opened in 1914, meaning that residents no longer had to wait for a month's supply by train from Edmonton. The following year, 10 crudely constructed tents were set up for visitors on the shores of Lac Beauvert, an encampment that would soon metamorphose into the Jasper Park Lodge.

In 1910 a coal mine was established at Pocahontas, near the eastern boundary of the park. A small mining town grew up in the vicinity, but was short-lived. The coal that was mined from the area burned at a high heat and was virtually smokeless, making it useful for warships during WWI. But, with the war over by 1918, and competition heating up with larger operations in the industrial east, the mine was shut down and the town dismantled by 1921.

Historic Sites

- » Old Fort Point (Jasper)
- » Many Glacier Hotel (Glacier)
- » Prince of Wales Hotel (Waterton)
- » Cave & Basin National Historic Site (Banff)

1892

The Banff reserve, which originally measured only 26 sq km (10 sq miles), is enlarged to include Lake Louise as alpinists drafted over from Europe begin scaling the area's peaks.

1896

The Blackfeet reluctantly accept the US government's offer to purchase all of the land east of the Continental Divide in what is now Glacier National Park for US$1.5 million.

1907

Jasper Forest Park is established as Canada's sixth national park, although it doesn't acquire its present-day boundaries until the passing of the National Parks Act in 1930.

1908

Mary Schäffer discovers Maligne Lake with her Stoney Aboriginal guide and opens up what is to become one of Jasper's most alluring sights and tourist attractions.

MARY SCHÄFFER

Breaking the mould in an era when most women didn't even have the right to vote, Mary Schäffer was a rather unlikely park pioneer who, according to some, was Jasper's and the Rocky Mountains' first real tourist. A spirited Philadelphia widow, Schäffer first ventured to Jasper in the early 20th century to – in her own words – 'turn the unthumbed pages of an unread book.' Her quest was an elusive mountain lake known to the Stoney people as Chaba Imne. Guided by a map sketched from memory by Stoney Aboriginal Sampson Beaver 14 years earlier, she became the first non-Aboriginal to set eyes on Maligne Lake in July 1908. Her subsequent book about her brave and sometimes turbulent adventures, *Old Indian Trails of the Canadian Rockies*, was republished on its 100th anniversary in 2011 and still resounds with poignant, poetic aphorisms.

Sharing the Limelight

The road from Jasper to Edmonton was opened in 1928, and by the onset of WWII legions of Depression-era workers had completed the legendary Icefields Parkway linking Jasper to Lake Louise. In 1930 the National Parks Act was passed, fully protecting Jasper as the largest park in the nation and tourists began visiting in their droves; famous guests included King George VI, Marilyn Monroe and Bing Crosby. By 1948 the Athabasca Glacier had become a major sight, and the Banff-based Brewster brothers manufactured a ski-equipped Model A Ford truck to cart tourists out over the ice.

Since the 1950s Jasper's tourism infrastructure has been gradually strengthened. Major highways into the park have been paved and roads to sights like Maligne Lake and Miette Hot Springs have been cleared or upgraded. In 1961 the Marmot Basin ski area got its first rope tow while, three years later, the Jasper Tramway took its first trip to the top of Whistlers Mountain.

Since 2001 Jasper Town has been governed jointly by the Specialized Municipality of Jasper and Parks Canada. These days there are strict development laws in place (eg no second homes are allowed) and, in 2010, the two bodies drafted the town's first Community Sustainability Plan.

Winter sports were first ignited in the Rockies at the Banff Winter Carnival in 1917. Skiing began at Mt Norquay in the 1920s and at Sunshine Village in the 1930s. Norquay installed Canada's first chairlift in 1948 and, in 1961, Jasper added its own ski resort, Marmot Basin.

Glacier National Park

The ancestors of Montana's present-day Native Americans have inhabited the Glacier region for over 10,000 years. At the time of the first European contact, two main indigenous groups occupied the Rocky Mountains region. The prairies in the east were controlled by the Blackfeet, a fiercely independent warrior tribe whose territory straddled the border with

1910

US President Taft signs a bill creating Glacier as the nation's ninth national park. William Logan is named as the park's first superintendent.

1911

Grand Trunk Pacific's railway reaches the shantytown of Fitzhugh, which is renamed Jasper two years later. Almost simultaneously the Canadian Northern Railway builds a second line through the park.

1912

The Great Northern Railway begins building grand hotels and chalets within Glacier National Park (and later, Waterton Lakes) to promote its railway line and open up the region to tourism.

1914–18

Prisoners of war – most notably from Germany, Austria and the Ukraine – are detained in camps within Banff National Park; their labor is used to improve the park's infrastructure.

DAVID THOMPSON

The history of Jasper National Park will always be synonymous with indefatigable British-Canadian explorer David Thompson, born in London in 1770, but resident in Canada from 1784 where he was nicknamed 'Stargazer' by First Nations people and 'the greatest mapmaker who ever lived' by those who had the good fortune to follow in his footsteps.

Thompson developed his prodigious navigational skills working as a fur trader, first for the Hudson Bay Company and later for their bitter rivals the Northwest Company, with whom he was mandated the task of establishing fur trading posts along the hotly contested US–Canadian border. In 1806, in response to the American-sponsored Lewis and Clark expedition, Thompson was sent west to establish new Northwest Company posts closer to the Pacific, a journey that soon turned into a race over which group would reach the mouth of the Columbia River first. The explorer's biggest challenge was crossing the Rocky Mountains through precipitous terrain still largely controlled by Native American tribes. Thompson found his preferred southern route over Howse Pass near Banff blocked by the hostile Piegan tribe, forcing him to tack north toward the uncharted lands of what is now Jasper National Park. Enlisting the help of a local aboriginal, Thomas the Iroquois, he forged a route across Athabasca Pass in January 1811, becoming the first white person to cross the Rockies via a northerly route. For the next 50 years until the advent of the railway era, Athabasca Pass became the preferred route of fur traders making for the Pacific.

Canada, while the valleys in the west were the hunting grounds of the Salish and Kootenay.

In the mid-18th century, when trappers and explorers began to arrive out west, the Blackfeet controlled most of the northern plains and adjacent mountain passes. Although they resisted the European invaders at first, a catastrophic smallpox epidemic in 1837 dealt them a deadly blow, wiping out 6000 of their 30,000 population. Linked spiritually to the land, the Blackfeet knew Glacier as the 'Backbone of the World' and within the area of the park, many sites – such as oddly shaped Chief Mountain – were considered sacred to the people.

A romantic wanderer, James Willard Shultz spent many years living among the Blackfeet people, whom he considered his relatives and closest friends. As a result, he became one of the first European American men to lay eyes on much of Glacier's interior. In the 1880s he introduced the area to Dr George Bird Grinnell, a leading conservationist who lobbied Congress vociferously for a decade until, in 1910, President Taft signed the bill that created Glacier National Park.

1920s

Automobile organizations lobby for a road through Jasper and in 1922 the first car breaches the Yellowhead Pass. The road to Edmonton opens in 1928 and the Yellowhead Hwy in 1970.

1932

The Going-to-the-Sun Rd is completed east–west across Glacier National Park. Two new motels are constructed at Rising Sun and Swiftcurrent Lake to cater for the new influx of auto traffic.

1940

The Icefields Parkway opens linking Lake Louise with Jasper Town to the north; a remarkable feat of engineering, it is named for the copious icy behemoths visible from the roadside.

ORIEN HARVEY/LONELY PLANET IMAGES ©

» Icefields Parkway (p68)

From Gilded Age Railroads to Modern Age Cars

Visitors began coming regularly to the park around 1912, when James J Hill of the Great Northern Railway instigated an intense building program to promote his newly inaugurated line. Railway employees built grand hotels and a network of tent camps and mountain chalets, each a day's horseback ride from the next. Visitors would come for several weeks at a time, touring by horse or foot, and stay in these elegant but rustic accommodations.

But the halcyon days of trains and horse travel weren't to last. In response to the growing popularity of motorized transportation, federal funds were appropriated in 1921 to connect the east and west sides of Glacier National Park by a new road. Over a decade in the making, the legendary Going-to-the-Sun Rd was finally opened in 1932, crossing the Continental Divide at 2026m (6646ft) Logan Pass and opening up the park to millions.

That same year, thanks to efforts from Rotary International members in Alberta and Montana, Glacier joined with Waterton Lakes in the world's first International Peace Park, a lasting symbol of peace and friendship between the USA and Canada.

WWII forced the closure of almost all hotel services in the park, and many of Glacier's rustic chalets fell into disrepair and had to be demolished. Fortunately, nine of the original 13 'parkitecture' structures survived and – complemented by two wood-paneled motor inns that were added in the 1940s – they form the basis of the park's accommodations today.

Over the years, the Going-to-the-Sun Rd has been the primary travel artery in the national park and, for many, its scenic highlight. Still sporting its original stone guardrail and embellished with myriad tunnels, bridges and arches, the road has been designated a national historic landmark. In the 1930s a fleet of bright red 'jammer' buses was introduced onto the road to enable tourists to gain easy access to the park's jaw-dropping scenery; the same buses still operate today.

Of the four national parks in this book, Glacier remains the most timeless and the truest to its original conception. Recent landscape-altering changes have been the result of natural rather than man-made causes, most notably forest fires and melting glaciers.

The term 'parkitecture' was used to describe the type of rustic architecture used in national parks in the early 20th century. Employing local materials in order to blend in with the forests from whence they sprang, the buildings took root in numerous national parks including Glacier and Waterton Lakes.

Founded in 1906 by Irish-born surveyor and mountaineer AO Wheeler, the Alpine Club of Canada still stands at the sharp end of mountaineering in the Canadian Rockies. Check out its excellent website, www.alpineclubofcanada.ca.

1960s

New developments in Jasper National Park include an ambitious ski resort, the Marmot Basin opened in 1961, and the Jasper Tramway, a lofty gondola on Whistlers Mountain which opens in 1964.

1984

Banff, along with Jasper, Yoho and Kootenay, is declared a Unesco World Heritage site, adding an extra layer of protection but invoking more environmental commitments.

1990

Banff Town becomes self-governing, though it is still subject to national park planning and development laws. The Canadian Pacific Railway passenger service is discontinued after 105 years.

2010

Jasper's Marmot Basin ski area moves with the times by installing the Canadian Rockies' longest high-speed quad chair, with a capacity of 2400 people an hour.

Geology

Majestic, indomitable and bursting with life, the Canadian Rockies are environmentally unique. Formed over 170 million years ago when a massive collision in the earth's crust caused a giant lateral displacement known as the Lewis Overthrust, the mountains today are the product of several millions of years of glaciation.

Anointed rather regally with the title 'Crown of the Continent,' national parks from Glacier up to Jasper support diverse and sizable populations of animals as well as myriad trees, shrubs, wildflowers and lichens. The region also exhibits a plethora of powerful glaciers, relics of a colder and mightier age, although their numbers are rapidly dwindling.

The Rocky Mountain Trench is a large valley up to 25km (15.6 miles) wide that runs from Montana up to the Yukon/BC border separating the Rocky Mountains from the Columbia/Cassiar Mountains to the west. Although partially glaciated, it was caused primarily by faulting.

The Land

Geologically speaking, the Canadian Rockies are a rock-lover's paradise, a caustic mix of towering mountain chains and multicolored terrain that is considered to be one of the most important fossil localities in the world. Everywhere you look you'll see graphic evidence of 1.5 billion years of the earth's history laid out like hieroglyphics in well-preserved sedimentary strata. Even more dramatic are the region's crenellated peaks and U-shaped valleys, a lasting testimony to the formidable power of ancient glaciers and ice fields.

The First Supercontinent

In the beginning there was nothing much at all. And then, approximately 1.5 billion years ago, sediments began to be laid down in an inland sea within a supercontinent known as Rodinia (a combination of landmasses that later broke apart into the continents we recognize today). Consisting of sands, silts and cobbles, these ancient sedimentary layers are now so deeply buried that they appear on the earth's surface in only a few places, two of which are Waterton and Glacier National Parks.

Situated on the western side of the continental divide, Yoho National Park receives over 884mm (35in) of rain annually; meanwhile dryer Banff National Park on the eastern side gets 472mm (19in).

On the west side of the parks, the oldest layer is known as the Pritchard Formation and preserves evidence of a deep sea that can be seen in thin layers of fine green rock along MacDonald Creek. Other strata such as the Altyn, Appekunny and Snowslip formations are also evident in places such as St Mary Lake and Logan Pass. Perhaps the most eye-catching and easy-to-recognize layer of rock is the brick-red coloration of the Grinnell Formation that is spectacularly exposed in Red Rock Canyon, in Waterton Lakes National Park.

The Big Breakup

About 750 million years ago, the supercontinent Rodinia began to break up along a giant rift, creating a new shoreline where North America split off from the future continents of Australia and Antarctica. Various sediments accumulated in an ancient sea during this epoch and, over time, these deposits hardened to form limestone, mudstone and sandstone.

A significant transition occurred around 570 million years ago, with the onset of the Cambrian period, a transitional era that sparked an incredible proliferation of complex new fauna in what became known as the 'Cambrian explosion.' Embedded in the region's rock, many well-preserved fossils of multicellular organisms remain from this period, and have taught scientists much about evolution and the development of species diversity worldwide. Some of the planet's best Cambrian fossils were uncovered at the Burgess Shale site in Yoho National Park in 1909.

The Cambrian era was followed by a long period of relative stability as desert landmasses eroded and sedimentary layers accumulated along the continental coastline. For a period of over 350 million years the dozens of different rock layers that comprise the bulk of the peaks in today's Canadian Rockies were laid down in contrasting bands, documenting an encyclopedia of geological history, a record that shows how seas advanced and retreated numerous times across the region.

Highest Peaks

- Jasper: Mt Columbia 3747m (12,293ft)
- Banff: Mt Forbes 3612m (11,850ft)
- Yoho: Mt Goodsir 3567m (11,703ft)
- Kootenay: Deltaform Mountain 3424m (11,234ft)
- Glacier: Mt Cleveland 3190m (10,466ft)

Collision Course

This period of stability came to a close around 200 million years ago when the continental plate began a steady march westward, pushing against the part of the earth's crust that lies under the Pacific Ocean. Like a slow-motion collision, the leading edge of the continental plate buckled against the impact. At first, the buckled edge may have simply created folds in the earth's crust, but over time these folds became steeper and started to fracture under the stress.

Extending progressively eastward, the fractures reached the region of the Canadian Rockies about 100 million years ago where dynamic tectonic movement pushed up a huge wedge of rock and displaced it over 80km (50 miles) to the east, forming the basis of the mountains we see today.

The main period of compression reached its apex 60 to 80 million years ago, then subsided slowly, leaving behind layers of deep old Paleozoic rock wedged up on top of younger Mesozoic rock. This compressing process is known as thrust faulting and it geologically sets the northern Rockies apart from their smoother southern cousins, which were formed by broader tectonic uplifting.

Glaciers

For the past 60 million years, the primary force in the Canadian Rockies has been erosion, not deposition. The most dramatic erosive process has been that of glaciation, precipitated by the great glaciers and ice fields of

GETTING UP CLOSE & PERSONAL WITH THE ROCKY MOUNTAINS GLACIERS

Four of the park's glaciers are easily accessible to day hikers.

- **Victoria Glacier** (Banff) The crystal crown of Banff is visible from the Chateau Lake Louise at the far end of the eponymous lake or in close up on the Plain of Six Glaciers trail.
- **Sperry Glacier** (Glacier) Perched above the backcountry Sperry Chalet on Gunsight Mountain, this dwindling glacier is accessible by a steep but rewarding hike across high-alpine terrain.
- **Grinnell Glacier** (Glacier) Named for the famous US naturalist, this river of ice is Glacier National Park's most photographed and precarious. A 8.8km (5.5-mile) trail leads out from the Many Glacier Hotel.
- **Athabasca Glacier** (Jasper) The Rockies' most famous glacier dips its toe close to the Icefields Parkway from where you can arrange excursions to walk or drive (yes, drive!) on it with a Snocoach tour.

THE GLACIAL LANDSCAPE OF THE ROCKIES

The Rocky Mountains national parks provide a perfect outdoor classroom for wannabe students trying to digest the geological features of glacial erosion. Here are some of the best examples. There are plenty more.

FEATURE	DEFINITION	BEST EXAMPLE
Hanging Valley	Small side valleys left 'hanging' above a deeper U-shaped glacier-carved valley	Maligne Valley (Jasper)
Moraine	An accumulation of glacial rock and soil	Moraine Lake (Banff)
Arête	A thin sharp ridge that forms between two parallel glaciers	The Garden Wall (Glacier)
U-shaped Valley	A steep-sided, flat-bottomed valley formed by a glacier moving downhill	St Mary Valley (Glacier)
Glacial Cirque	A bowl-shaped amphitheater formed at the head of a valley glacier	Iceberg Cirque (Glacier)
Rouche Moutonnée	Tear-shaped hills formed when a glacier erodes down to the bedrock	Old Fort Point (Jasper)
Glacial Horn	A pyramidal peak formed when three glacial cirques form together	Mt Assiniboine (Mt Assiniboine Provincial Park)
Glacial Lake	A lake left behind when glaciers retreat	Lake Louise (Banff)

the Ice Age that have sculpted rugged peaks and gouged out deep valleys from Pocahontas to Marias Pass. Two million years ago, huge sheets of ice covered much of the Canadian Rockies. These giant sheets produced incredible amounts of weight and pressure, and as tongues of ice crept across the landscape they tore apart rocks and transformed narrow V-shaped ravines into broad open valleys. Trillions of tons of debris were left behind when the ice finally retreated 10,000 years ago, much of it forming distinctive ridges called moraines, such as the one that the chateau at Lake Louise is perched on.

Nearly every feature seen in the Canadian Rockies today is a legacy of the Ice Age. Peaks that were simultaneously carved on multiple sides left behind sharp spires called horns, as can be seen at Mt Assiniboine. Mountains that had glaciers cutting along two sides ended up as sharp ridges known as arêtes. Side streams flowing into valleys that were deepened by glaciers were often left hanging in midair, creating hanging valleys, with the streams pouring out as waterfalls down sheer cliffs.

A common feature of a hanging valley is a waterfall caused when a river drops from the higher side valley down to the U-shaped valley below. Visible from Glacier National Park's Going-to-the-Sun Rd, 152m (500ft) Bird Woman Falls near Mt Oberlin is a classic example of this.

Glaciers Today

Even though the Ice Age ended 10,000 years ago when the great ice fields gradually retreated, the story of ice and glaciers in the Canadian Rockies is far from over. Mini ice ages have regularly altered the climate in the years since, the most recent of which peaked in the 1840s when the frozen tip of the Athabasca Glacier reached as far as the present-day Icefield Center – it has retreated 1.6km (1 mile) since 1844. Even today, along the spine of the Continental Divide, smaller ice fields continue to craft and shape the landscape, although recent concerns about climate change suggest that the glaciers in Glacier National Park (which now number only 25) will be all but extinct by the year 2030. The much larger ice fields in Banff and Jasper are probably safe for a good couple of centuries whatever the warming effects. Waterton Lakes National Park is already a glacier-free zone.

Wildlife

Rising like snow-coated sentinels above the plains and prairies of Alberta and Montana, the Rockies protect a narrow, wildlife-rich corridor that stretches across the continent from northern Canada to Mexico. With the adjacent lowlands taken over by roads, farms and cities, the mountains have provided a final refuge for wolves, mountain lions, bears, elk, deer and many other large mammals. While populations of these animals are only a fraction of their former numbers, they are still impressive enough to lure wildlife enthusiasts to the region by the truckload.

There have been 10 human fatalities from bear attacks in Glacier National Park's 101-year history. By remarkable coincidence two of them occurred on the same night 13 August 1967, 10 miles apart in separate attacks by different bears. Both victims were 19-year-old females.

Animals

While the prospect of seeing 'charismatic mega-fauna' is one the region's biggest draws, the Canadian Rockies support nearly 70 species of mammals, including eight species of ungulate (hoofed mammal). In the fall and winter, many large mammals move down into valleys for protection against the weather; high concentrations can be seen along the Icefields Parkway during these seasons.

Very few amphibians and even fewer reptiles do well in the relative cold of these northern latitudes.

Bears

The black bear roams montane and subalpine forests throughout the Canadian Rockies in search of its favorite food: grasses, roots, berries and the occasional meal of carrion. Frequently, they can be seen along roadsides feeding on dandelions. While most black bears are black in color, they can also be light reddish brown (cinnamon). Black bears are somewhat smaller than grizzlies and have more tapered muzzles, larger ears and smaller claws. Small claws help them climb trees and avoid their main predator, grizzly bears, which are known to drag black bears out of their dens to kill them. Although they are generally more tolerant of humans and less aggressive than grizzlies, black bears should always be treated as dangerous.

The endangered grizzly bear once roamed widely in North America, but most were killed by European settlers, who feared this mighty carnivore. Today a few hundred or so inhabit the parks covered in this book, but with males roaming 3885 sq km (1500 sq miles) in their lifetimes, they aren't particularly easy to see or count. Male grizzlies reach up to 2.4m (8ft) in length (from nose to tail) and 1.05m (3.5ft) high at the shoulder (when on all fours) and can weigh more than 315kg (700lb) at maturity. Although some grizzlies are almost black, their coats are typically pale brown to cinnamon, with 'grizzled,' white-tipped guard hairs (the long, coarse hairs that protect the shorter, fine underfur). They can be distinguished from black bears by their concave (dish-shaped) facial profile, smaller and more rounded ears, prominent shoulder hump and long, nonretractable claws.

Both bears are omnivorous opportunists and notorious berry eaters with an amazing sense of smell that's acute enough to detect food miles away. Their choice of food varies seasonally, ranging from roots and winter-killed carrion in early spring to berries and salmon in the fall. Before hibernation, bears become voracious. Black bears will eat for 20 hours straight and gain an incredible 1.8kg (4lb) each day before retiring to their dens, and grizzly bears are known to eat 200,000 buffalo berries a day.

2010 figures for grizzly bear numbers in Alberta Province, Canada (Jasper, Banff and Waterton National Parks) are cited as approximately 691, down from 841 in 2000.

Some time in October, bears wander upslope to where snows will be deep and provide a thick insulating layer over their winter dens. There the bears scrape out a simple shelter among shrubs, against a bank or under a log and sink into deep sleep (not true hibernation, since their body temperatures remain high and they are easily roused). Winters are particularly hard, since bears live entirely off their fat and lose up to 40% of their body weight. Females who have been able to gain enough weight give birth to several cubs during the depths of winter, rearing the cubs on milk while she sleeps.

Coyotes

The cagey coyote is actually a small opportunistic wolf that devours anything from carrion to berries and insects. Its slender, reddish-gray form is frequently seen in open meadows, along roads and around towns and campgrounds. Coyotes form small packs to hunt larger prey such as elk calves or adults mired in deep snow. Frequently mistaken for a wolf, the coyote is much smaller – 11.3kg to 15.8kg (25lb to 35lb), versus 20.3kg to 65.3kg (45 to 145lb) for a wolf – and runs with its tail carried down (a wolf carries its tail straight out).

Wolves

The gray wolf, once the Rocky Mountains' main predator, was nearly exterminated in the 1930s, then again in the 1950s. It took until the mid-1980s for them to reestablish themselves in Banff, and today they are common only from Jasper National Park north; in Glacier National Park, wolves can be found in North Fork Valley. Wolves look rather like large, blackish German shepherds. Colors range from white to black, with gray-brown being the most common color. They roam in close-knit packs of five to eight animals ruled by a dominant (alpha) pair. The alpha pair is the only members of a pack to breed, though the entire pack cares for the pups. Four to six pups are born in April or May, and they remain around the den until August. Packs of wolves are a formidable presence, and they aren't afraid of using their group strength to harass grizzly bears or kill coyotes, but more often they keep themselves busy chasing down deer, elk or moose for supper.

The Canadian Rockies is home to 69 naturally occurring species of mammals, including elk, coyote, wolves and grizzly and black bears, and the only fully protected caribou herd in North America.

Bighorn Sheep

Living on high slopes near rocky ridges and cliffs, bighorn sheep are generally shy creatures of remote areas. Unlike other parts of their range, however, bighorn sheep in the Canadian Rockies come down to roadsides in search of salts, invariably causing traffic jams of excited visitors. Males, with their flamboyant curled horns, spend summer in bachelor flocks waiting for the fall rut, when they face off and duel by ramming into each other at 96km/h (60mph). Their horns and foreheads are specially modified for this brutal but necessary task. When not hanging around roadsides looking for salt and handouts (strictly forbidden), bighorn sheep use their extraordinary vision and smell to detect humans up to 300m (1000ft) away and keep their distance, making them extremely difficult to approach.

Mountain Goats

Occupying even steeper cliffs and hillsides, pure white mountain goats are a favorite with visitors. Finding one is another matter altogether, because goats live high on remote cliffs and are seldom observed close up. These cliffs provide excellent protection from predators, and both adults and kids are amazingly nimble on impossibly sheer faces. Occasionally they descend to salt licks near roads. In Jasper they occur in high densities on Mt Kerkeslin; around Banff try scanning the slopes of Cascade Mountain; and in Glacier National Park you might see goats at Logan Pass.

Deer

Two species of deer are common in valleys and around human dwellings throughout the region. More common by far are the mule deer of dry, open areas. Smaller, and with a large, prominent white tail, are the white-tailed deer of heavily forested valley bottoms. Both species graze extensively on grasses in summer and on twigs in winter. Delicate, white-spotted fawns are born in June and are soon observed following their mothers. Adult males develop magnificent racks of antlers in time for their mating season in early December.

Elk & Moose

Weighing up to 450kg (1000lb) and bearing gigantic racks of antlers, male elk are the largest mammals that most visitors will encounter in these parks. Come September, valleys resound with the hoarse bugling of battle-ready elk, a sound that is both exciting for its wildness and terrifying, because hormone-crazed elk are one of the area's most dangerous animals. Battles between males, harem gathering and mating are best observed from a safe distance or from your car. While numbers increase dramatically in winter, quite a few elk now spend their entire year around towns like Banff and Jasper, where they can be dependably observed grazing in yards and on golf courses.

At 495kg (1100lb), the ungainly moose is the largest North American deer. Visitors eagerly seek this odd-looking animal with lanky legs and periscope ears, but they are uncommon and not easily found. Moose spend their summers foraging on aquatic vegetation in marshy meadows and shallow lakes, where they readily swim and dive up to 6m (20ft). Visitors can look for moose in the Miette Valley of Jasper, around Upper Waterfowl Lake of Banff, in the McDonald Valley of Glacier and in similar areas. The male's broadly tined antlers and flappy throat dewlap are unique, but like their close relative the elk, moose can be extremely dangerous when provoked. Moose are no longer as common as they were in the days when they freely wandered the streets of Banff; numbers have been reduced due to vehicle traffic (roadkills), a liver parasite and the suppression of the wildfires that rejuvenate their favorite foods.

Pikas, Marmots & Beavers

Hikers into the realm of rock and open meadow will quickly become familiar with two abundant mammals. When you encounter a pika, you are likely to hear its loud bleating call long before you spot the tiny, guinea pig–like creature staring back at you with dark beady eyes. Pikas live among jumbles of rocks and boulders, where they are safe from predators, but they still have to dart out into nearby meadows to harvest grasses that they dry in the sun to make hay for their winter food supply.

Another rock dweller is even more of a tempting morsel for predators. Hoary marmots are plump and tasty, but they have a system for protecting themselves. First, they stay near their burrows and dart in quickly when alarmed. Second, all the marmots on a hillside cooperate in watching out

Estimated Species Numbers in Banff

- Grizzly Bears: 60
- Black Bears: 40
- Wolves: 35-40
- Mountain Lions: 7-10
- Woodland Caribou: 5

Estimated Species Numbers in Jasper

- Bighorn Sheep: 3000
- Woodland Caribou: 300-400
- Moose: 150
- Grizzly Bears: 100-120

Estimated Species Numbers in Glacier

- Black Bears: 800
- Bighorn Sheep: 800
- Grizzly Bears: 300
- Wolves: 60

for predators and giving shrill cries whenever danger approaches. Marmots may shriek fiercely when humans come near, warning everyone in the neighborhood about the approach of two-legged primates. The Whistlers, a mountain outside Jasper, is named after these common rodents.

The aquatic beaver has a long history of relations with humans. Reviled for its relentless efforts to block creeks and praised for its valuable fur, the Canadian Rockies' largest rodent is now widely recognized as a 'keystone species,' an animal whose activities have a tremendous influence on the lives of many other species. Dozens of animals, like ducks, frogs, fish, moose and mink, depend on beavers for their livelihood. Although their numbers have declined as much as 90% in recent decades, beavers are still fairly common around marshes and ponds in valley bottoms. Here, each beaver cuts down as many as 200 aspens and willows per year, feeding on the sweet inner bark and using the trunks and branches to construct dams.

Three members of the cat family are found in the parks: the mountain lion (cougar), the Canadian lynx, and the bobcat. All are elusive and rarely seen by humans, moving mainly at night. The Canadian lynx has been listed as threatened since 2000. Lynx hunt hares, mountain lions prefer deer.

Birds

Although more than 300 species have been found in the Canadian Rockies, birds are readily overshadowed by the presence of so many eye-catching large mammals. It takes a real bird nut to turn their attention to a diminutive mountain chickadee when they could be watching male elk battle over harems of females or bighorn sheep scale rocky cliffs. However, casual observers will notice some of the more conspicuous species without even trying.

You'd be hard pressed to find a campsite or picnic table where you aren't quickly approached by gray jays hoping for a handout. They stash most of their food away in small caches for winter. The stash master, however, is the larger Clark's nutcracker. Each nutcracker buries up to 98,000 seeds in thousands of small caches across miles of landscape then returns to dig them up over the course of several years – an unbelievable test of memory.

Two large raptors (birds of prey) are worth mentioning because they are so frequently encountered. Working their way along rivers and lakes are white and brown fish hawks, better known as ospreys. Fairly common from May to September, when the ice is melted, ospreys specialize in diving into water to catch fish. Ospreys are most often seen soaring over lakes, scanning the water for fish. Plunging feet first into the water, ospreys grab fish up to 90cm (3ft) deep then fly off to eat their scaly meal on a high perch. Osprey nests are enormous mounds of sticks piled on top of dead trees or man-made towers.

In recent years the Canadian Rockies has gained some fame for its spectacular golden eagle migration. Each year 6000 to 8000 golden eagles migrate both north and south along a narrow corridor on the east side of the main mountain divide (the official count site is near Mt Lo-

GONE TO THE DOGS?

Dog-sledding with a team of huskies through the parks and valleys of Jasper or Banff has long held a primeval attraction for visitors searching for the purist type of winter wilderness. But, in early 2011, following a high-profile incident in the host Winter Olympic resort village of Whistler, BC, that involved the large-scale culling of dogs used for dog-sledding, the ethics and code regarding this winter activity was brought into question. While most outdoor operators undoubtedly still follow perfectly ethical practices, it would be pertinent to do some homework before you embark on your next dog-sledding adventure.

Start your search by checking through the outfitters listed in this book. The Jasper Adventure Centre (p164) offers decent, if pricey, dog-sledding excursions on its busy winter activities schedule.

FISH TALES

That dreamy image of a philosophical fisherman sitting with rod and line enjoying 'the contemplative man's recreation' beside a high country lake might seem like a typical Rocky Mountains idyll, but the reality is a little less pure. In truth, high mountain lakes do not naturally support native fish. Instead, countless non-native species were introduced to the national parks over a period of 50 years in a bid by wildlife and park agencies to 'improve' the visitor experience and attract more fishing tourists. Today Banff counts at least 119 lakes stocked with non-native fish (when only 26 contained fish historically). As a consequence, native fish populations and aquatic ecosystems in lower lakes have suffered, while several species of non-native fish have thrived. Though the fish stocking policies have been phased out (in 1971 in Glacier and 1988 in Banff and Jasper) millions of non-native species remain.

Surviving native fish include the threatened bull trout, whose dwindling populations are protected by law. Once the most widespread native fish in the Canadian Rockies, bull trout are now seen at only a few sites. Your best bet is Peter Lougheed Provincial Park, south of Canmore, where they migrate up creeks out of Lower Kananaskis Lake from late August to mid-October. They are distinguished from other trout by their lack of black lines or spots. Return them to the water if you accidentally catch one.

Representative of the nine non-native fish that have become most common, brook trout are found in most low-elevation streams and lakes. Brook trout can be recognized by their olive-green color, reddish belly and yellow squiggly lines along their back.

Aquatic habitats in the Canadian Rockies support many more kinds of fish than just trout – 40 species in all. One of the healthiest populations is mountain whitefish, a bottom-feeder that preys on small invertebrates in the major watercourses and lakes.

rette, in Kananaskis Country, just east of Banff). Spring migration peaks at the end of March, and fall migration peaks in October. Over 1000 golden eagles have been counted in a single day, so bring your binoculars. While migrating, golden eagles do little feeding, though some pairs stay for the summer and nest on high, remote cliffs.

Of the region's eight species of owl, only the great horned owl is familiar to most visitors. Fearless around humans, highly vocal and sometimes active in the daytime, these large birds are a perennial sight around towns and campgrounds at lower elevations.

Plants

The Canadian Rockies are home to over 1000 species of plants, comprising a fairly diverse mix for such a relatively cold, northern climate. One of the main reasons for this mix is that the Continental Divide not only creates a strong elevational gradient but also splits the region into westside and eastside habitats. With a wet, ocean-influenced climate on the west side and a dry, interior climate on the east side, this geographic split is a very significant division. Adding to the region's botanical diversity are alpine plants from the arctic, grassland plants of the eastern prairies and forest plants from the Pacific Northwest.

Because the parks cover such a span of habitats and elevations, it's possible to find flowers from March until the end of August, and taking time out to smell the flowers will definitely enrich your park visit.

Trees

Except for areas of rock, ice or water, landscapes of the Canadian Rockies are mostly covered with coniferous forest. Only a handful of species are present, and these are easy to identify – learning to recognize these species is a lot of fun, plus it makes it easier to understand the layout of life zones and to predict where you might find specific animals.

Montane and subalpine forests are dominated by two spruces, white spruce and Engelmann spruce. Both have sharp-tipped needles that prick your hand if you grasp a branch. White spruce occurs mainly on valley bottoms, and Engelmann spruce takes over on higher slopes, but the two frequently overlap and hybridize. Cones on white spruces have smooth, rounded tips on their scales, but Engelmann spruces have narrow, jagged tips on theirs. Many animals feed on spruce seeds or rely on spruce forests for their livelihood in some way.

Sharing the higher slopes with the Engelmann spruce is the subalpine fir, the namesake tree of the subalpine zone in the Canadian Rockies. Recognized by their flattened, blunt-tipped needles, subalpine firs have narrow, conical profiles. This shape allows the trees to shed heavy winter snows so their branches don't break off under the weight.

Synonymous with the expansive evergreen forests of Alberta and British Columbia, the Douglas fir tree is named after Scottish botanist David Douglas (1799–1834), who first visited Jasper in 1827, when he wrongly declared Mt Brown and Mt Hooker to be the highest peaks in North America.

At the uppermost edges of the subalpine forest, mainly growing by themselves on high, windswept slopes, are whitebark pines. Intense wind and cold at these elevations can cause these trees to grow in low, stunted mats. Their squat, egg-shaped cones produce highly nutritious seeds favored by Clark's nutcrackers and grizzly bears, but an introduced disease is threatening this important tree and the animals that depend on it.

One of the oddest trees of the Canadian Rockies is the subalpine larch, a rare tree found most easily in Larch Valley, just south of Lake Louise. Although it's a conifer, this remarkable tree has needles that turn golden in September then drop off for the winter in October. This makes places like Larch Valley a photographers' paradise during the peak display.

After fires or other disturbances, lodgepole pines quickly spring up and form dense 'doghair' thickets. In some areas, lodgepoles cover many square kilometers so thickly that the forests are nearly impossible to walk through. These conditions eventually promote hot fires that create seedbeds for more lodgepoles; in fact, lodgepole cones are sealed in resin that only melts and releases seeds after a fire.

A beautiful tree of dry, open areas, the quaking aspen has radiant, silver-white bark and rounded leaves that quiver in mountain breezes. Aspen foliage turns a striking orange-gold for just a few weeks in fall.

Shrubs

With berries that are delicious and sweet instead of bitter, blueberries provide an immensely popular treat for humans and bears alike. Half a dozen species of this shrub occur in the Canadian Rockies, with common names like huckleberry, grouseberry, bilberry and cranberry. Often these plants grow in patches large enough that berries for a batch of pancakes or muffins can be harvested within minutes.

The mountain pine beetle is an insect that attacks and kills mature trees (turning their needles a distinctive red color). Rather like wildfires, this process is a natural part of the Rocky Mountain ecosystem and park management bodies have tried to let it continue with minimal interference.

Closely related and similar in appearance to blueberry plants is the kinnikinnik, also known as bearberry. This ground-hugging shrub has thick glossy leaves and reddish woody stems. Its leaves were once mixed with tobacco to make a smoking mixture, and the berries have been a staple food for many First Nations peoples.

It's something of a surprise to encounter wild roses growing deep in these woods, but at least five types grow here. All look like slender, somewhat scraggly versions of what you'd see in a domestic garden, but otherwise, there's no mistaking them. Their fruits are pear-shaped and turn red-orange during fall; popularly known as rose hips, these fruits are rich in vitamins A, B, C and E and are used to make tasty jams or teas.

Wildflowers

The flowering season in the Canadian Rockies begins as soon as the snows start to melt. Though delicate in structure, the early rising glacier lily pushes up so eagerly that the stems often unfurl right through the snow crust. Abundant in montane and subalpine forests or meadows,

BEST PLACES TO SEE WILDLIFE

WHAT	WHERE	WHEN
Grizzly Bear	Many Glacier (Glacier), Carthew-Alderson Trail (Waterton)	May-Oct
Black Bear	Bow Valley Parkway (Banff), Maligne Lake Rd (Jasper)	May-Oct
Bighorn Sheep	Lake Minnewanka (Banff), Highline Trail (Glacier)	Nov-Apr
Mountain Goat	Logan Pass (Glacier)	year-round
Marmot	Skyline Trail (Jasper), Highline Trail (Glacier)	May-Sep
Elk	Vermillion Lakes (Banff), Maligne Lake Rd (Jasper)	Mar-May
Moose	Moose Lake (Jasper), Kootenai Lake (Glacier)	May-Aug
Caribou	Tonquin Valley (Jasper)	Nov-May
Wolf	North Fork Valley (Glacier), Lake Minnewanka (Banff)	Nov-Apr

each lily produces several yellow flowers, with six upward-curled petals. Wherever lilies occur in great numbers, grizzlies paw eagerly through the soil in search of the edible bulbs.

Within days of snowmelt, pretty purple pasqueflowers (aka prairie crocuses) cover montane slopes. Growing close to the ground on short, fuzzy stems, these brilliant flowers stand out because of their yellow centers. Later in the summer, 'shaggy mane' seed heads replace the flowers. All parts of this plant are poisonous and may raise blisters if handled.

One of the most photographed flowers of Glacier National Park is the striking beargrass. From tufts of grasslike leaves, the plant sends up 1.5m-high (5ft) stalks of white, star-shaped flowers that may fill entire subalpine meadows. Grizzlies favor the tender spring leaves, hence the plant's common name.

Hike almost anywhere in these mountains and you're bound to encounter the easy-to-recognize bluebell, with its large, bell-like flowers held up on a long, skinny stem. This plant's other common name, harebell, comes from Scotland, but its meaning is not certain. After flowering, seeds are produced in capsules that close in wet weather then open in dry winds to scatter the seeds far and wide.

The Rockies feature three different life zones: the montane (warm, dry tree-filled valley bottoms), the subalpine (wetter forests of smaller stunted trees) and alpine (high windy slopes of flower meadows and barren rock).

Many visitors know the familiar Indian paintbrush for its tightly packed red flowers, but fewer know that the plant is a semiparasite that taps into neighbors' roots for nourishment. By stealing some energy from other plants, paintbrushes are able to grow luxuriantly in desolate places like roadsides or dry meadows, where they are often the most conspicuous wildflower. Of the dozen species in the Canadian Rockies, a great number attract hummingbirds, making paintbrush patches one of the best sites for finding the beautiful birds.

The big, showy cow parsnip, with its huge, celerylike stalks and umbrella-shaped flower clusters, is a familiar sight along streams and in moist aspen groves throughout the region. This plant can grow over 1.8m (6ft) high, and walking among them can make you feel small. The stems are eaten by many animals and favored by grizzlies, so caution is urged when approaching a large cow parsnip patch. Humans are advised against eating these plants because of their similarity to several deadly species.

More localized in its distribution, but sometimes confused with cow parsnip because it has the same large leaves, is the devil's club. This stout, 2.7m-high (9ft) plant practically bristles with armor. Completely covered in poisonous spikes (even the leaves are ribbed with rows of spines) that break off in the skin when contacted and cause infections, this plant further announces itself with its strong odor and large clusters of brilliant red berries. Despite these features, devil's club has a rich and important history of medicinal use among First Nations tribes of the area.

Conservation

Despite their remoteness and relatively late colonization, the Rocky Mountains parks have long been pioneers in the field of wilderness protection. Banff was Canada's first – and the world's third – national park when it was inaugurated in 1885, while Jasper, Waterton and Glacier (all given protective status by 1910) were three more early beneficiaries of the nascent North American conservation movement. But, with conflicting commercial interests and an inordinate influence wielded by the all-powerful cross-continental railway companies, early park rules were sketchy and haphazard. Waterton once supported an oil well, Jasper and Banff flirted briefly with coal mining, while all three Canadian parks developed – and still retain – significant and relatively prosperous town sites.

When Lewis and Clark traversed America in the early 1800s, there were approximately 100,000 grizzly bears roaming the Lower 48 states of the US. Now there are no more than 1000 occupying an area that is less than 1% of their traditional range.

As the public perception of wilderness areas changed, so did the parks. In 1911 the Canadian government formed the Dominion Parks Branch (an early incarnation of Parks Canada) as the world's first national park coordinating body, and in 1930 the National Parks Act laid down the first firm set of ground rules for conservation and preservation. While the parks today still promote recreation and education as a crucial part of the overall wilderness experience, the concept of ecological integrity has taken center stage since a shift toward a more populist strand of environmentalism in the 1980s.

The Early Conservationists

The American environmental movement was born during the progressive era in the late 19th and early 20th centuries at a time when early eco-thinkers were separating into two philosophical camps: the conservationists led by US president Teddy Roosevelt and his chief environmental advisor Gifford Pinchot; and the more radical preservationists epitomized by John Muir, founder of the Sierra Club. The former professed federal intervention in order to manage and conserve natural resources; the latter considered nature to be sacred and tourism sustainable only under strict limits.

While Muir remains an icon to modern environmentalists, it was the conservationists who had the biggest impact on the public zeitgeist during the early flowering of the North American national park network in the 1890s. In the Rocky Mountains, their chief exponent was George Bird Grinnell, an anthropologist and naturalist from New York City who was more at home mingling with the Blackfeet Native Americans and leading sorties into the mountains of northwest Montana than he was tramping the streets of Manhattan. It was Grinnell who christened the Glacier/Waterton region 'the crown of the continent' and, using his influential position as editor of *Field and Stream* magazine, he badgered the US Congress relentlessly for protective status. His entreaties were rewarded in 1910 when Glacier became the US's seventh national park. The huge debt owed to him and his contemporaries by our current generation is immeasurable.

Contemporary Environmental Issues

Fatefully, the work of Grinnell et al was just the beginning of an elongated process. Tourism and the ongoing impact of millions of visitors trampling through important wildlife corridors is one of the parks' most ticklish issues in modern times and nowhere is this problem more apparent than in Banff. Hosting an incorporated town with a permanent population of over 8000 people, along with main roads, a ski resort and over three million annual visitors, Banff's environmental credentials have long been a subject for hot debate. Comparisons with Glacier (governed by the US parks system) further south are particularly telling.

Long lauded as one of the continent's most pristine parks, Banff's smaller American cousin is a veritable wilderness with no population center, no fast-food franchises and no water-sapping golf courses. Furthermore, Glacier bans bikes from all park trails, runs an environmentally friendly free shuttle service to minimize car pollution, and has barred its historic lodges from installing supposed modern 'luxuries' such as TVs and room phones. Not surprisingly, the park's unique ecosystem is frequently acclaimed for its rich biodiversity, and its grizzly bear population is said to be one of the healthiest in the whole of North America.

Of all the Rocky Mountains parks, Glacier-Waterton Lakes is the best protected, listing four different layers: National Park (1895 Waterton, 1910 Glacier), International Peace Park (1932), Unesco Biosphere Reserve (1979) and Unesco World Heritage site (1995).

Jasper sits somewhere between the two extremes. While it is closer to Banff in infrastructure and park policies (it hosts a townsite, golf course, pubs and restaurants), its superior size and smaller annual visitor count (less than half of Banff's) means environmental pressures are less corrosive. Its most symbolic conservation issue is the preservation of the woodland caribou, a species no longer present in Banff, but still surviving precariously further north.

SUSTAINABILITY TIPS

The behavior of individual visitors in the parks can play a vital part in ensuring their long-term health and sustainability. Here are a few green recommendations:

» Glacier National Park runs a free shuttle bus designed to ease congestion on the increasingly traffic-choked Going-to-the-Sun Rd. The Canadian parks have a number of paying shuttles.

» Stay on friendly terms with bears by using bear-proof containers and recycling bins, making noise on the trails, and giving bears a wide and respectful berth.

» Look into local volunteer organizations. Many people work tirelessly to protect fragile park wildernesses from degradation and neglect, and it's easy to join them.

» By staying in a Glacier National Park–run hotel you are lodging with a profoundly 'green' organization whose policies include large-scale garbage recycling, use of low-energy light fixtures and donation of old furniture to charity.

» Jasper and Glacier National Parks can still be reached by using that classic gilded-age method of transport – the train. The VIA/Amtrak services are economical, scenic, 'green' and far more comfortable than an airplane.

» You can gain more in-park knowledge by talking to rangers, reading the local literature and swapping ideas with other hikers on the trail.

» Glacier's Red Jammer Buses use buses that run on propane and emit 93% less pollutants than their gas-powered equivalents.

» Stay on the trail – wandering 'off-piste' or bushwhacking your own path damages flora and causes erosion.

Solutions

In 1996 a two-year investigation by the Banff-Bow Valley study group provided a crucial turning point in Banff's modern evolution. Putting forward 500 urgent recommendations – a list that included everything from population capping to quotas on hiking trails – the study prompted the implementation of a 15-year development plan designed to redress the park's ecological balance and save its priceless wilderness from almost-certain long-term damage. More than 13 years on and progress has certainly been made, though recent concerns about climate change have given the issue fresh urgency.

Meanwhile, further north, Jasper Town was made a Specialized Municipality in 2001 and began drafting a similarly comprehensive Community Sustainablity Plan in the late 2000s.

South of the border, the US Geological Survey's ongoing studies at the Northern Rocky Mountain Science Center on Glacier's eroding glaciers, ecosystems and fire management policies have been equally pertinent. The future is still anyone's guess.

Unhindered by manmade forces, wildfires are perfectly natural events that open up new habitats, promote the growth of fresh seedlings and replenish soil nutrients with decomposed organic matter. Understanding this, park authorities today carefully monitor annual blazes and let them run their natural course, unless they have been human-ignited or are directly threatening property and livelihoods.

Survival Guide

Directory A–Z

This chapter provides useful practical information that applies to all the parks covered in this book. For more specific details on each park, consult the relevant chapter.

Accommodations

There is an enormous choice of accommodations both inside and around the national parks, ranging from campsites and hostels through to B&Bs, country cabins and top-end hotels. Rates are a lot more expensive compared to many other areas of Canada and the US, however, and it can be extremely hard to find a room if you leave things to the last minute.

» Prices increase considerably during the peak summer months of July and August, and during the main ski season from December to March. Book well ahead if you want to stay during either period.

» In Banff and Jasper, most of the accommodations are concentrated around the main townsites.

» Staying beyond the park boundaries can be a good way to find cheaper hotel rates: for example, consider staying in Canmore for visiting Banff, Field for Lake Louise, or St Mary, Babb and Polebridge for East and West Glacier.

» Skiing as part of an organized package (including lift passes and accommodations) is usually much cheaper than booking both separately – but not always. Many hotels offer good deals during ski season to compete with package tours.

ACCOMMODATION PRICE RANGES

Throughout this guidebook, we have used the following price ranges in all our accommodation reviews. Prices are all based on a double room with private bathroom in high season; cheaper rates may often be available in shoulder and low seasons.

CATEGORY	SYMBOL	CANADA	US
Budget	$	<C$100	<US$100
Midrange	$$	C$100-200	US$100-200
Top end	$$$	>C$200	>US$200

B&Bs & Guesthouses

Staying with locals can be a great way to immerse yourself in the park and get some insiders' tips on the best things to see and do during your stay. Many residents offer B&B (bed and breakfast) rooms in their own homes to travelers, but standards vary widely. Some places are fairly basic, while others will give many top-end hotels a run for their money. B&Bs are less common in Glacier than the Canadian parks.

» Breakfast is nearly always included in room rates, but if you have special requirements (eg vegetarian, vegan, gluten-free) let the owners know in advance.

» Not all B&B rooms have private bathrooms, so check before booking if that's important to you.

» Remember to check the B&B's policies on pets, kids and credit cards. Some will accept all three, while others won't accept any.

Camping

FRONTCOUNTRY CAMPING

Camping is a wonderful (and popular) way of experiencing the national parks. All of the Canadian and US parks offer a good range of frontcountry campgrounds that are accessible from the main roads.

Facilities vary widely: large campgrounds might have flush toilets, drinking water, public phones, fire pits and RV hookups, while others might only have pit toilets and a standpipe for drinking water. In general, the more popular campgrounds (especially those near to tourist centers) are better equipped than those further afield.

» In the Canadian parks, the only campgrounds that currently accept reservations are Tunnel Mountain and Lake Louise (in Banff); Pocahontas, Whistlers, Wapiti and Wabasso (Jasper); and the townsite campground in Waterton. Contact the **Parks Canada Reservation Service** (☎1-877-737-3783; www.pccamping.ca). Reservations can be made up to three months ahead for a C$10.80 fee.

» In Glacier National Park, reservations are available up to six months in advance at Fish Creek and St Mary campgrounds through the **National Park Reservation Service** (☎1-800-365-2267; www.recreation.gov).

» All other sites operate on a first-come, first-served basis. Arrive before checkout time at 11am for the best chance of securing a site. Campground availability bulletins are published regularly and are available at visitor centers and on park radio.

» Most campgrounds are suitable for tents, campervans and RVs, although not all have pull-throughs or paved sites.

» At more remote campgrounds, facilities are generally limited to pit toilets and drinking water, although some also have recycling bins and bear-proof storage lockers.

» Some campgrounds operate on a self-registration basis. Find an available site first, then fill in your details (name, site number, length of stay, registration number) on the payment envelope and drop it in the box near the entrance.

» The maximum stay at any campground is usually 14 days.

» Fires are usually allowed in designated fire pits (provided no fire restrictions are currently in force), although you'll need to buy a fire permit.

BACKCOUNTRY CAMPING

Backcountry campgrounds are mainly geared for hikers exploring the trails, so facilities are extremely rudimentary. Most only offer cleared tent pads and a pit privy; some also have food storage cables where you should suspend toiletries, garbage and food items to avoid attracting bears to the campground.

» Overnight backcountry stays require a special permit, known in Canadian parks as a **wilderness pass** (C$9.80 per night) and in US Parks as a **backcountry permit** (Glacier, US$5 per night).

» Visitor numbers on backcountry trails are limited, so you'll usually need to specify your campgrounds when you purchase your wilderness pass. The maximum stay at one campground is generally three nights.

» In some very remote areas of the parks, wild camping is allowed – choose a site at least 50m from the trail, 70m from water sources and 5km (3 miles) or more from the trailhead.

» See the useful **Leave No Trace** (www.leavenotrace.ca) website for tips on how to travel responsibly in the backcountry.

Hostels

Another cheap way of visiting the parks is to stay in a hostel. They're not just for backpackers and hikers these days: most are happy to rent out whole dorms and private rooms, making them ideal for families or couples on a budget. The best hostels in Banff and Jasper are run by **Hostelling International** (HI; www.hihostels.ca), which has flagship hostels in Banff Town, Lake Louise and Jasper Town. Dorm rooms cost between C$25 and C$40 depending on the season.

» Accommodations are usually in dorms with four to 10 beds, with a communal kitchen and lounge. Some also have cafés, games rooms and TV rooms.

» Dorms are often (but not always) organized along gender lines. Bathrooms and showers are shared. Some hostels have en suite bathrooms for each dorm, while others have communal bathrooms in the corridor.

» HI members qualify for discounts on nightly rates. Annual membership costs C$35 and is free for people under the age of 17.

» The HI also runs several basic wilderness hostels (eg at Mosquito Creek and Rampart Creek), which are essentially wood cabins with a kitchen, dining area and communal lounge (often with a cozy wood-burning stove).

» The **Alpine Club of Canada** (☎403-678-3200; www.alpineclubofcanada.ca) operates simple hut hostels in the backcountry, mostly used by climbers and hikers. Reservations are essential.

Hotels

There's no shortage of hotels in Banff, Jasper and Glacier, but they're generally not cheap. Room rates, especially in Banff, are notoriously expensive, and always shoot upward in the peak season between May and September. Things are a bit more affordable in Jasper, as well as in the neighboring provincial parks.

BOOK YOUR STAY ONLINE

For more accommodations reviews by Lonely Planet authors, check out hotels.lonelyplanet.com. You'll find independent reviews, as well as recommendations on the best places to stay. Best of all, you can book online.

Except at the top end of the price ladder, the standard of accommodations is often pretty mediocre for the price you'll pay.

» Nearly all hotel rooms come with en suite bathroom, telephone and cable TV, and most places offer free wi-fi for guests. Breakfast is often charged as an extra.

» Some hotels (such as Num-Ti-Jah Lodge on Peyto Lake and Jasper's heritage hotels) make a deliberate point of not providing TVs and telephones.

» Room rates are nearly always quoted per room, but without sales tax.

» There's usually a string of cheap motels on the edge of the larger towns.

Condos & Vacation Apartments

Local by-laws prohibit the rental of vacation homes or apartments in Banff, Lake Louise and Jasper, but many hotels offer suites or chalets that are specifically intended for families, often including a full kitchen, bathroom and two or three bedrooms.

Vacation apartments and condos are available outside the park borders, however (eg in Canmore, Kootenay or Golden), but only certain properties are licensed to be used for the purpose. Make sure you use a legitimate operator, avoid arranging anything directly with the owner or paying anything up front, and always check the terms and conditions carefully before booking.

Some useful websites:

Rentals in the Rockies (www.rentalsintherockies.com) Agency based in Canmore.

Canmore Holiday Accommodation (www.canmoreholidayaccommodation.com) Canmore condos and apartments.

Tourism Golden (www.tourismgolden.com/accommodations/vacation-homes) Listings of self-catering apartments around Golden.

Field (www.field.ca/accommodations) Options for Field.

Business Hours

Unless we've specified otherwise in the guide, you can assume the place in question has opening hours that are pretty close to the following ranges.

» Standard opening hours for retailers and services are from 9am to 5:30pm, although grocery and convenience stores, tourist services, gift shops, cafés and chain stores often open later.

» Banks open 9am to 5:30pm Monday to Friday.

» Standard restaurant hours are from around 7am to 10:30am for breakfast, 11am to 3pm for lunch and 5pm to 10pm for dinner.

» Bars open any time from 4pm onwards to around midnight or later.

Customs Regulations

» Visitors entering either Canada or the US can bring 200 cigarettes (one carton), 50 cigars and 14 ounces of tobacco; 1.1L or 40 imperial ounces (one bottle) of liquor or wine, or 24 cans of beer; and gifts up to the value of C$60 (US$100) per item.

» There are strict restrictions on the import of plants, seeds and animal products to prevent the spread of pests and diseases.

» Importing firearms, explosives and other weapons (including pressurized canisters of bear spray) is illegal unless you're carrying an appropriate permit.

Food

Restaurants, diners and cafés are plentiful around the park townsites, but choice is a lot more limited once you get out into the rest of the national parks. If you're eating out, remember that service is usually not added to your bill – a tip of 15% to 20% is the expected norm.

Throughout this book, we've arranged our reviews by order of preference, and included price indicators based on the cost of a main meal.

Budget ($) Less than C$10 (US$10)

Midrange ($$) Between C$10 and C$20 (US$10 and US$20)

Top end ($$$) C$20 (US$20) or more

Insurance

Travel insurance is always a worthwhile investment if you're visiting another country. Worldwide travel insurance is available at www.lonelyplanet.com/travel_services. You can buy, extend and claim online any time – even if you're already on the road.

» Choose your policy carefully, especially for coverage against flight delays, 'acts of God' or *force majeure* events, and baggage loss.

» If you're undertaking outdoor activities such as hiking, biking, climbing or water sports, and especially if you're skiing or snowboarding, make sure your travel insurance policy covers you against medical treatment and emergency repatriation (many off-the-shelf policies don't).

» Most standard US health plans aren't valid for treatment in Canada, so you'll need to ensure you're covered under a separate travel-insurance policy.

» Non-US and Canadian travelers should make extra sure the policy has good coverage against medical costs, as hospital bills are cripplingly expensive.

» Check the excess to be paid in the event of a claim.

» Auto insurance purchased in Canada and the US is usually applicable to either country, but confirm this with your provider before you leave home.

» Many auto insurance policies extend to rental cars, and some credit-card providers provide coverage if you pay for the car with your card.

Internet Access

Net access is widespread around both of the Canadian parks, but it's still patchy in Glacier.

» Most hotels offer free wireless access to customers with their own laptops, and wi-fi hot spots are becoming increasingly common in cafés and restaurants.

» Where we've used this icon (📶), it denotes wireless access is available.

» Where we've used this icon (@), it denotes that there is a computer available for public use.

» Most public libraries offer internet access, usually for a small fee.

Legal Matters

It's illegal to remove any flora or fauna from the national parks, including rocks, minerals and fossils, as well as birds' eggs, plants and wildflowers.

» Tree bark and pine cones harbor destructive parasites such as pine beetle, so don't collect them.

» Hunting and firearms are not permitted in the national parks.

Maps

The best topographical maps are produced by **Gem Trek Publishing** (www.gemtrek.com), which has several excellent 1:100,000 maps covering Banff, Jasper and Waterton Lakes, as well as Lake Louise and Yoho, Bow Lake and The Crossing, Columbia Icefield, Canmore, Kananaskis and several other areas.

INTERNATIONAL VISITORS

Entering the US & Canada by Air

Visitors from many countries, including the US, most European Union nations, the UK, Australia and New Zealand do not require a visa to enter Canada. You are usually permitted to remain in the country for six months, after which you will have to apply for an extension to your visa.

If you're arriving in the US from one of these countries, you should qualify for entry under the Visa Waiver Program. This will qualify you to remain in the US for a stay of up to 90 days. As of January 2009, citizens of the 27 countries in the US Visa Waiver Program will need to register with the government online (https://esta.cbp.dhs.gov/) three days before their visit. The registration is valid for two years.

Citizens of other countries will need to apply for a visitor's visa from either the **Citizenship and Immigration Service Canada** (☎1-888-576-8502; www.cic.gc.ca) or the **US Citizenship and Immigration Services** (☎1-800-375-5283; www.uscis.gov.uk), or apply directly to the embassy or consulate in their own country.

There's a comprehensive list of Canadian consular offices at www.cic.gc.ca/english/information/offices/apply-where.asp and of US embassies at www.usembassy.state.gov.

Entering the US & Canada via the Land Border

Most US-based visitors heading for Canada cross via the land border, either by train, bus or more likely by car. With thousands of people crossing the border on a daily basis it's one of the busiest land borders in the world and, unsurprisingly, the wait times can be horrendously long. You can get the heads-up on the likely delays at specific checkpoints via the **Canada Border Services Agency website** (www.cbsa-asfc.gc.ca/general/times/menu-e.html).

At the checkpoint, you'll need to present your passport, plus driver's license, insurance and registration if you're arriving by car. Note that if you're bringing a rental car across the border, you will have to have cleared this with the rental company beforehand, and you might have to present your rental agreement to border officials for inspection. If you're on public transportation, you may have to disembark and carry your own luggage across the border.

Be prepared to answer standard questions from border guards about the purpose of your visit, length of stay and any items you're intending to bring across the border. Unless you fancy prolonging the experience, answer sensibly and politely; this is definitely not a time for wisecracking. It's also probably best if you leave those CND and Che Guevara T-shirts at home.

For rules on items that are legally allowed to cross the US border, see the Customs Regulations section (p256).

All major trails and points of interest are clearly marked on the maps, which are supposedly waterproof and tear-proof (although in practice they'll only take so much punishment). They're available everywhere, including from retail stores, bookstores, grocery stores and many gas stations.

National Geographic's *Trails Illustrated* series offers topographical, waterproof, tear-proof maps of Glacier and Waterton Lakes, while the United States Geological Survey (USGS) publishes a 1:100,000 topographical map for Glacier National Park.

Map Art Publishing (www.mapart.com) produces a range of road maps covering the Canadian Rockies.

Money

Canada

Banks and ATMs are fairly widespread in the main townsites, and you'll find branches of at least one major bank (CIBC, ATB, Scotiabank or Bank of Montreal) in Jasper, Banff and Canmore as well as in several other gateway towns. Many gas stations, supermarkets and malls also have ATMs, and there are handy ATMs at Samson Mall in Lake Louise Village and Saskatchewan Crossing on the Icefields Parkway.

» Banks generally offer better exchange rates than currency bureaus.

» If your bank is a member of the Cirrus or Maestro networks, you should be able to withdraw cash from overseas ATMs, but fees for using the facility can be high.

» Visa, MasterCard and American Express are accepted practically everywhere.

» Prices for almost everything in Canada are quoted without GST.

» Traveler's checks are becoming increasingly difficult to cash; consider bringing a pre-paid currency instead.

USA

In Glacier, the nearest banks are in Columbia Falls and Browning. The lodges at Lake McDonald, Glacier Park and Many Glacier have ATMs, as does Eddie's Camp Store in Apgar and the St Mary supermarket.

» For exchange services in Waterton, head for Waterton Visitor Services at **Tamarack Outdoor Outfitters** (Map p210; ☎403-859-2378; Mount View Rd; ⏲8am-8pm). The closest banks are in Cardston and Pincher Creek.

» Credit cards and traveler's checks are widely accepted.

» There's no sales tax in Montana.

Post

Mail services are much the same in the national parks as in the rest of the US and Canada, although it can take longer for letters to arrive in winter, when heavy snow sometimes causes delays. Banff, Jasper and Glacier all have large, efficient post offices, while you'll find smaller branches in most gateway towns.

Public Holidays

Both Canada and the USA observe a number of national holidays, when most shops, visitor attractions and services shut or operate on limited hours, and banks, schools and post offices are all closed. Accommodations, transportation and main highways are usually very busy around major holidays, especially Easter, Labor Day, Thanksgiving and Christmas.

Canada

New Year's Day January 1
Good Friday March/April
Easter Monday First Monday after Good Friday
Victoria Day Monday preceding May 25
Canada Day July 1
Labor Day First Monday of September
Thanksgiving Day Second Monday of October
Remembrance Day November 11
Christmas Day December 25
Boxing Day December 26

USA

New Year's Day January 1
Martin Luther King Day Third Monday in January
President's Day Third Monday in February
Memorial Day Last Monday in May
Independence Day July 4
Labor Day First Monday in September
Columbus Day Second Monday in October
Veterans' Day November 11
Thanksgiving Day Fourth Thursday in November
Christmas Day December 25

Telephone

Cell Phones

Cell phone coverage outside the main towns can be extremely erratic, especially in the backcountry.

» It's always worth taking a cell with you if you're on a wilderness trip, but don't automatically assume it'll have reception.

» Canadian and US cellphone networks are generally compatible. If you're bringing a phone from abroad, check that it works with the cell phone systems in the US and Canada.

» A temporary pay-as-you-go SIM card is a good way to avoid expensive roaming charges.

Payphones

You'll find plenty of payphones in the main towns, as well as major campgrounds and visitor attractions. In Canada, it costs 50¢ to make a call from a payphone, or 35¢ in the US.

PRACTICALITIES

» Distances in Canada are quoted in kilometers, with elevations in meters. In the US it's miles and feet. Both countries quote weights in imperial pounds.

» In Canada, power plugs have two flat angled pins, while in the US there are two round pins. Note that these plugs are different to European two-pin power plugs. The power supply in both countries is 120V/60Hz. Adaptors to convert power plugs are easily available from electrical outlets and travel shops.

» The NTSC TV system is used in both Canada and the US. DVDs are encoded in the Region 1 standard.

» The most widely read daily newspapers in Alberta are the *Calgary Herald* and *Edmonton Journal*, plus the *Calgary Sun* and *Edmonton Sun* tabloids.

» There are many regional newspapers; look out for the historic *Crag & Canyon*, the *Canmore Leader* and the *Rocky Mountain Outlook*. In Montana look for the *Whitefish Pilot* and *Daily Inter Lake*.

» The nationwide Canadian Broadcasting Company (CBC) is the main radio service in Canada, although reception is patchy across the parks; try 96.3FM for CBC Radio One in Banff and 98.1FM in Jasper. The volunteer-run Banff Park Radio is on 101.1FM. In Montana KJJR (880AM) has news and talk.

» GST (Goods and Services Tax) of 5% is added to most goods in Alberta, but across the border in British Columbia the new HST (Harmonized Sales Tax) is charged at 12%. Montana has no sales tax.

Phone Codes

Area codes are denoted by the first three digits of phone numbers (eg ☎403 or ☎780 in Alberta, ☎406 in Montana). If you're outside the area code, you'll need to dial it along with the relevant phone number.

Other commonly used dialing codes:

☎1 International prefix, used for calling the US and Canada from abroad

☎1-800 Toll-free

☎1-888 Toll-free

Time

Alberta and Montana are both in the 'Mountain Timezone,' one hour ahead of Pacific Time (used by the US west coast and western parts of British Columbia), one hour behind Central Time, two hours behind Eastern Time (the US east coast) and seven hours behind Greenwich Mean Time (London).

Like most Canadian provinces, Alberta observes daylight saving time between the second Sunday in March and the first Sunday in November. The clocks are put forward one hour during this period so mornings are shorter and evenings are longer.

Toilets

Public toilets are common in the major townsites as well as visitor attractions. If you're out and about in the national parks, you'll find pit toilet cabins at most of the trailheads.

Tourist Information

For general information on the national parks, your first port of call should be the comprehensive websites for either **Parks Canada** (www.pc.gc.ca) or the **US National Park Service** (www.nps.gov). For more specific information, the staff at the main park visitor centers are hugely knowledgeable and very helpful, and can provide leaflets, brochures and guide booklets on practically every imaginable activity in the park. All the provincial parks have their own visitor centers – see the relevant chapters for details.

Banff

Banff Information Center (☎403-762-1550; http://www.pc.gc.ca/pn-np/ab/banff/index.aspx)

Banff Tourism Bureau (☎403-762-8421; www.banfflakelouise.com)

Lake Louise Visitor Center (☎403-522-3833; ll.info@pc.gc.ca)

Glacier

Apgar Visitor Center (☎406-888-7939)

Glacier National Park (☎406-888-7800/6; www.nps.gov/glac)

St Mary Visitor Center (☎406-732-7750)

Jasper

Icefield Center Parks Information (☎780-852-6288)

Jasper Information Centre (☎780-852-6176; www.pc.gc.ca/pn-np/ab/Jasper/index.aspx)

Jasper Tourism & Commerce (☎780-852-3858; www.jaspercanadianrockies.com)

Waterton Lakes

Waterton Lakes National Park (☎403-859-2224; http://www.pc.gc.ca/eng/pn-np/ab/waterton/index.aspx)

Waterton Visitor Centre (☎403-859-5133)

Travelers with Disabilities

Visiting Banff, Jasper and Glacier still presents quite a challenge for people with auditory, visual or physical disabilities and people with restricted mobility.

Your best bet is to contact parks visitor centers directly with questions on specific activities. In the US, the National Parks Service publishes the *Accessibility Guide*, with lots of helpful information and details for Glacier.

» Most hotels have at least some wheelchair-accessible rooms.

» The larger campgrounds at Tunnel Mountain, Johnston Canyon and Lake Louise (plus Waterfowl Lakes) in Banff, as well as Whistlers, Wabasso and Wapiti in Jasper, have limited facilities for disabled users, including wheelchair-friendly campsites and washrooms.

Banff

Most of the main sights in Banff, including Lake Louise, Banff's museums, Upper Hot Springs Pool and Peyto Lake along the Icefields Parkway are all wheelchair-accessible, as is the main visitor center.

» Paved trails ideal for wheelchair users include the lower section of Johnston Canyon, the paved section of the Lake Minnewanka Shoreline Trail, the Lake Louise Shoreline Trail and the mixed-use Sundance Trail in Banff.

» Most restaurants in Banff are on the ground floor, so should be accessible to wheelchair users.

» In Kananaskis Country, William Watson Lodge has been designed specifically to give people with disabilities access to the area, with 22 fully accessible cottages and over 18km of accessible trails.

Glacier & Waterton Lakes

» In Glacier, two short, scenic trails are paved for wheelchair use: Trail of the Cedars, off Going-to-the-Sun Rd, and the Running Eagle Falls Trail in Two Medicine.

» Hearing-impaired visitors can get information at ☎406-888-7806.

» Park visitor centers have audio guides for visually impaired visitors.

» At least one or two ground-floor, wheelchair-friendly rooms are available at all in-park lodges.

» The Waterton townsite campground has wheelchair-accessible bathroom facilities. The hostel can accommodate travelers using a wheelchair, as can a few of the lodges in the townsite.

Jasper

Jasper's museum, Miette Hot Springs, Maligne Lake, Medicine Lake, Jasper Tramway and the visitor center are all wheelchair-accessible, as is Athabasca Falls and the Icefield Center along the Icefields Parkway.

» Several trails are good for wheelchair users, including the initial paved section of the Mary Schäffer Loop, Maligne Lake, the Clifford E Lee Trail at Lake Annette and Pyramid Isle in Pyramid Lake.

» Few accommodations in Jasper have dedicated rooms for wheelchair users, although most have elevators, and there are usually ground-floor rooms that can accommodate disabled visitors.

» Many of Jasper's restaurants are on ground floors and have accessible toilets.

Volunteering

There are many organizations that volunteer their efforts for free to ensure the continuing welfare of the parks.

Among the best-known are the **Friends** organizations (Friends of Banff, Friends of Jasper, Friends of Kootenay), which undertake everything from administrative work and fundraising to trail maintenance. They're often looking for volunteers to help with current programs: visit **Friends of Banff** (www.friendsofbanff.com) and **Friends of Jasper** (www.friendsofjasper.com) for more information and links to the other local Friends organizations.

Banff Volunteer Program (http://www.pc.gc.ca/pn-np/ab/banff/edu/edu5v.aspx) Park-wide volunteer opportunities, ranging from trail ambassadors to citizen scientists. There are regular 'drop-in' days if you have limited time.

Banff Volunteer Centre (www.volunteerbanff.ab.ca) Organizes community volunteer programs in and around Banff.

Alberta Institute for Wildlife Conservation (www.aiwc.ca) Wildlife charity that helps protect native species through animal rehabilitation, habitat protection and volunteer training.

Glacier National Park Associates (www.glaciernationalparkassociates.org) Volunteer group that tackles projects such as trail maintenance, building preservation and habitat regeneration.

Glacier Institute (www.glacierinsitute.org) Educational courses promoting understanding of the national park.

Women Travelers

The national parks don't present many unusual dangers for women traveling alone. Both the parks and the main townsites are generally friendly and safe places to visit, although obviously it pays to take the usual precautions – avoid unlit or unpopulated areas after dark, join up with other people if you're walking home late at night, and don't hitchhike.

Transportation

GETTING THERE & AWAY

Air

Airports & Airlines

BANFF & JASPER NATIONAL PARKS

Calgary (YYC; www.calgaryairport.com) and **Edmonton** (YEG; www.edmontonairports.com) are the closest international airports to Banff and Jasper respectively.

» It's feasible to fly into **Vancouver** (YVR; www.yvr.ca), but you'll have a long drive – it's 845km (523 miles) to Banff and 795km (492 miles) to Jasper.

» Air Canada and Westjet cover the majority of Canadian routes, and connect through Montreal and Toronto to many European destinations.

» US-based airlines, including Continental and United, connect through major American cities.

» British Airways mainly serves London Heathrow.

» Cheaper fares are often available through Air Transat and Thomas Cook, who both fly into London Gatwick.

GLACIER NATIONAL PARK

Glacier's nearest airport is **Glacier Park International Airport** (FCA; www.iflyglacier.com), halfway between Whitefish and Kalispell. It's currently served by Delta, Alaska Airlines and United. Year-round destinations include Salt Lake City, Minneapolis, Denver and Seattle, plus seasonal flights to Chicago and Atlanta.

The only other options are both a long drive from Glacier:

Great Falls International Airport (GTF; www.gtfairport.com) Located 249km (155 miles) away.

Missoula International Airport (MSO; www.msoairport.org) Located 241km (150 miles) away.

WATERTON LAKES NATIONAL PARK

Lethbridge County Airport (YQL; ☎403-329-4466) is the closest to Waterton Lakes, 129km (80 miles) to the northeast. It's served by Air Canada and Integra Air, but the limited flight schedule usually means it's more convenient (and cheaper) to fly into Calgary, 266km (165 miles) north of Waterton.

Bus

Banff & Jasper National Parks

AIRPORT SHUTTLES

There are a number of shuttle services from Calgary to Jasper and Banff.

Airporter Shuttle Express (☎403-509-1570; www.airportshuttleexpress.com) Charter minibuses costing from C$257/300 for five/10 people between Calgary airport and any Banff hotel. Buses can also be chartered to Jasper. Also runs a half-hourly shuttle bus from the

CLIMATE CHANGE & TRAVEL

Every form of transport that relies on carbon-based fuel generates CO_2, the main cause of human-induced climate change. Modern travel is dependent on aeroplanes, which might use less fuel per kilometer per person than most cars but travel much greater distances. The altitude at which aircraft emit gases (including CO_2) and particles also contributes to their climate change impact. Many websites offer 'carbon calculators' that allow people to estimate the carbon emissions generated by their journey and, for those who wish to do so, to offset the impact of the greenhouse gases emitted with contributions to portfolios of climate-friendly initiatives throughout the world. Lonely Planet offsets the carbon footprint of all staff and author travel.

airport to downtown Calgary (including the Greyhound depot) for C$15.

Banff Airporter (☎1-888-449-2901; www.banffairporter.com) Scheduled shuttle service that runs 12 times daily between Calgary airport, Canmore and Banff. In Banff there's a door-to-door service; in Canmore the bus stops at the Radisson Hotel (511 Bow Valley Trail). Rates from the airport to Banff are one way adult/child C$53/26.50, return C$106/53.

Banff Airport Taxi (☎403-678-2776; www.banffairporttaxi.com) Private shuttle bus to Banff hotels plus Lake Louise on request. Ski shuttle service available in season. Monitors incoming flights, so if you're delayed it'll adjust pickup time accordingly. One to three passengers is C$225 one way, C$425 return.

Brewster (☎1-800-760-6934; www.brewster.ca) Scheduled bus that links Calgary airport with Banff (one way adult/child C$49.95/24.95) and Lake Louise (C$69.95/34.95) six times daily, with an early morning bus to Jasper (one way C$129.95/64.95). Free wi-fi on board.

Sundog Tours (☎780-852-4056; www.sundogtours.com) One daily bus between Jasper and Edmonton airport for C$95/59. Services from Calgary airport to Banff are run by Brewster but can be booked through Sundog.

PUBLIC BUSES

Greyhound (☎1-800-661-8747; www.greyhound.ca) runs five daily buses that run north-south along Hwy 1, stopping at Calgary, Canmore (C$23.60 one way, 1¼ hours) and Banff (C$27.30 one way, 1¾ hours). Note that this bus does *not* currently stop at Calgary airport, so you'll either have to catch a taxi into the city (C$30 to C$45), or take the half-hourly shuttle bus provided by **Airporter Shuttle Express** (see above), then take the Greyhound from there.

There are also four daily Greyhounds between Jasper and Edmonton International Airport (one way/return C$64.70/129.40), and four daily from Vancouver to Golden, Field, Lake Louise and Banff.

The following are sample fares and fastest journey times from Vancouver:

DESTINATION	ONE WAY (C$)	DURATION (HRS)
Golden	122.20	11
Field	128.20	12¼
Lake Louise	128.30	12¾
Banff	128.30	13½

» Cheaper advance fares are available by booking online, but these are nonrefundable and you won't be able to change your dates without incurring a fee.

» Banff and Jasper's Greyhound depots are both inside the townsite train stations.

Glacier & Waterton Lakes National Parks

AIRPORT SHUTTLES

Public transport from Glacier airport is limited. The only regular shuttle bus is provided by **Flathead-Glacier Transportation Co** (☎toll-free 1-800-829-7039, 406-892-3390).

If you're flying into Calgary, you can charter minibuses to Glacier and Waterton with **Airport Shuttle Express** (☎403-509-1570; www.airportshuttleexpress.com) for C$360 for one to five people.

PUBLIC BUSES

Greyhound (www.greyhound.ca) stops in Pincher Creek, 53km (33 miles) from the Waterton townsite.

Crystal Cabs (☎403-627-4262) offers transfers from Glacier airport to Whitefish (US$25) and West Glacier (US$50), and from Pincher Creek to Waterton (around C$70 for up to four people).

Car & Motorcycle

Major Routes

BANFF & JASPER NATIONAL PARKS

There are various road routes into the parks.

» Trans-Canada Hwy (Hwy 1) runs from Calgary to Canmore, Banff and Lake Louise before continuing into Yoho National Park.

» Hwy 93 (aka the Icefields Parkway) travels from Jasper to Lake Louise and Castle Junction, then south into Kootenay National Park and Radium Hot Springs.

» Hwy 11 heads west from Red Deer and enters Banff on the Icefields Parkway, just south of the border with Jasper.

» To reach Jasper from Edmonton, take Hwy 16 west.

GLACIER & WATERTON LAKES NATIONAL PARKS

The west side of Glacier is most easily reached from Whitefish, Kalispell and Flathead Lake; the east side is closer to Great Falls and Helena. West Glacier and East Glacier are connected by US 2, below the southern boundary of the park.

If you're traveling north into Waterton Lakes, you'll have to pass through customs en route. You'll need two forms of ID; driver's license and passport are standard.

Port of Peigan/Carway (☎in Canada 403-653-3009, in US 406-732-5572; ⊙7am-11pm) On Trans-Canada Hwy 2 (US Hwy 89); open year-round.

Port of Chief Mountain (☎in Canada 403-653-3535, in US 406-732-5572; ⊙7am-10pm Jun-Aug, 9am-6pm Sep) On US 17; closed in winter.

Car Rentals

The vast majority of people visiting the parks rent a car. It's the most convenient way to travel, allowing you to explore at your own pace and visit even the most remote sights, though you have to factor in fuel costs, traffic and breakdown.

All the major car-rental agencies have branches at the main airports and townsites. Airport branches generally stay open from around 6am to midnight; town branches keep regular business hours.

» Booking online will get the best rates, but check carefully for hidden extras such as high excess, mileage caps, limits on interstate travel and GST. If you're doing a lot of driving, get an all-inclusive mileage deal.

» One-way rentals will incur a 'drop fee,' usually between C$50 and C$100 depending on the vehicle and how far you're taking it.

» Airport rentals charge a different tax rate, so it's worth checking equivalent rates with town branches (eg in Banff and Canmore): it can work out cheaper for long rentals, even with the one-way drop fee.

» Think about whether you need Collision Damage Waiver (CDW); you may be covered by your own auto or travel insurance, or by your credit card company if you use the card to pay for the rental.

Recreational Vehicles & Campervan Rentals

Cruising the parks in a recreational vehicle (RV) has many advantages – you won't incur hotel bills, you can cook your own meals and experience a taste of the outdoors without having to rough it too much.

There are drawbacks, though: they're big, unwieldy, heavy on fuel and slow, and can be difficult to maneuver if you're not used to driving a big vehicle.

» Make sure you get a full rundown on the vehicle before you leave the rental agency.

» Check that the campground you're staying at has spaces suitable for RVs.

» Rates spike in peak season. Deals are often available at other times.

» Popular van sizes are often booked out in summer, so reserve well ahead.

» Mileage is nearly always extra to the quoted rental rates.

Key companies:

CanaDream (☎800-461-7368; www.canadream.com) Rents truck campers, campervans and motor homes from locations in Calgary, Edmonton and various other locations. Prices start from around C$140 per day for a mid-sized motor home.

Cruise Canada (☎800-671-8042; www.cruisecanada.com) Rents three sizes of RV from locations in Calgary and Vancouver. Rates start at around C$650 to C$750 per week plus mileage. Three-night minimum rental.

Cruise America (☎480-464-7300; www.cruiseamerica.com) The same company rents RVs in the US, although there are no dealerships in Montana.

Hitchhiking

Hitching is never entirely safe in any country, and we don't recommend it. Travelers who decide to hitch should understand that they are taking a small but potentially serious risk. That said, thumbing a lift is an option in the mountain parks, although you might find you're waiting on the highway for quite a while before anyone stops.

As always, take the usual precautions: hitch in groups, avoid hitching in remote areas and after dark, and make sure you keep an eye on your pack.

On the trail you can often hook up with hikers who have their own transport by hanging around at the trailhead. Many people will give you a lift if you smile sweetly and they've got space in the car.

Train

Banff National Park

The only passenger trains which stop in Banff are run by:

Rocky Mountaineer Rail Tours (www.rockymountaineer.com) Scenic train trips through the Rockies, Banff and Jasper. Most of the travel is done during daylight hours, and prices include park passes, hotel accommodations and day trips. Cheapest packages start from around C$899.

Royal Canadian Pacific (www.royalcanadianpacific.com) Luxury train trips through the Rockies in a heritage train carriage with full silver service, starting at C$5800. You need to book at least a year ahead.

Jasper National Park

Jasper is served by mainline intercity trains provided by **Via Rail** (☎1-888-842-7245; www.viarail.com), which stop in Jasper on their route between Vancouver and Edmonton at least three times per week. You can connect onto this route from most other US and Canadian cities. Sample fares from Jasper:

DESTINATION	ONE WAY (C$)	DURATION (HRS)
Edmonton	126	5½
Vancouver	175.35	20
Saskatoon	168	14½
Winnipeg	256.20	26¼

Glacier & Waterton Lakes National Parks

Amtrak (☎1-800-872-7245; www.amtrak.com) operates the cross-country *Empire Builder* line from Seattle all the way to Chicago, serving stations in East Glacier, West Glacier and Whitefish.

Eastbound trains run in the early morning; westbound trains travel through in the early evening. There are ticket offices at East Glacier and Whitefish, but you'll have to pre-book or buy on board from West Glacier. Sample one-way fares:

Whitefish to West Glacier (US$9 to US$15, 30 minutes)

Whitefish to East Glacier (US$18 to US$31, 2 hours 8 minutes)

West Glacier to East Glacier (US$18, 1 hour 38 minutes)

GETTING AROUND

Practically all the main sights in the national parks are accessible by road. Jasper and Glacier have a growing number of public transport options, but Banff still leaves a lot to be desired.

Bicycle

Cycling is a popular and ecofriendly way of getting around the parks, but the distances between sights are long, so bikes are mainly useful for commuting around the townsites.

» Bikes are readily available for rent in Banff, Jasper, Glacier as well as Waterton. Expect to pay C$12 to C$15 per hour or C$35 to C$45 per day.

» Bikes are banned on all trails (but not roads) in Glacier.

» Relatively few trailheads have bike racks.

Bus

Getting around by bus in the parks is just about possible, but takes some planning.

BANFF TO JASPER

Officially, there's no public bus service between Banff and Jasper, but you can easily hop on board one of the scheduled services offered by Greyhound, Brewster and Sundog Tours, as long as there's space. See p114 for further details.

BANFF NATIONAL PARK

Banff's public buses are known as **Roam** (☎403-762-1215; www.banff.ca/locals-residents/public-transit-buses/roam.htm). There are three color-coded routes serving the townsite: all routes travel via Banff Ave, and serve destinations including the Banff Gondola, Tunnel Mountain Campgrounds, the Banff Centre and Sulphur Mountain.

White Mountain Adventures (☎403-760-4403; www.whitemountainadventures.com; adult/child C$55/30; ⏲mid-Jun–Oct) runs a summer shuttle bus from Banff townsite to Sunshine Meadows.

To get to other trailheads, you'll have to drive or organize your own transport with one of the private hike-and-bike shuttles. See p94.

JASPER NATIONAL PARK

Jasper's bus system is fairly limited, but there are a couple of useful services to a couple of the most popular sights.

» **Maligne Lake Shuttle Service** (www.malignelake.com; 616 Patricia St) travels from Jasper townsite to Maligne Lake and Canyon (C$20/15, four daily).

» **Jasper Tramway Shuttle** (☎780-852-4056; C$35) runs from the train station and includes a tramway ticket.

GLACIER NATIONAL PARK

Glacier is the easiest park to get around by bus thanks to the free **biodiesel shuttle buses** along the Going-to-the-Sun Rd, which run every 15 to 30 minutes throughout the summer. All are wheelchair-accessible, and the larger ones can carry bikes. See p199 for full details.

The **East Side Shuttle Bus** travels between East Glacier and Waterton (Canada), calling at Two Medicine, Cut Throat Creek, St Mary, Many Glacier and Chief Mountain. Journeys cost US$10 per trip segment and run from July 1 to Labor Day.

Car & Motorcycle

For road distance information, see the boxed text, p265.

Automobile Associations

Alberta Motor Association (☎in Calgary 403-240-5300; www.ama.ab.ca) is the province's main motoring organization and is affiliated with the Canadian Automobile Association (CAA). It can help with queries on driving in Alberta, as well as arrange breakdown cover and insurance for members; you'll also sometimes qualify for special rates on hotels and other services.

The **American Automobile Association** (☎406-758-6980; www.aaa.com; 135 Hutton Ranch Rd, Ste 106, Kalispell) is the US equivalent, and offers a similar range of services. There are other branches in Missoula, Great Falls and Bozeman.

Driver's License

» Foreign driver's licenses can be used in Alberta for up to three months. International driver's licenses can be used for up to 12 months.

» It's required that you carry your license and vehicle registration at all times.

Fuel & Spare Parts

» Gas is readily available in the main townsites, but make sure you fill your tank before setting out on a driving tour.

» There are gas stations at Castle Mountain and Saskatchewan Crossing in Banff, but prices are much more expensive here.

» Most car-rental companies provide breakdown cover as part of the rental package.

» If you're driving your own vehicle, it is probably worth joining one of the major breakdown agencies to avoid getting stranded.

Road Conditions

Most of the main roads are well-maintained, although minor roads to trailheads and mountains are often steep, narrow and winding, making them nasty driving for RVs.

» Some roads (such as the Smith-Dorrien Hwy from Canmore into Kananaskis) are unsealed, so take extra care when driving on them.

» Ice and snow are frequent hazards in winter, so be prepared if you're driving during the colder months.

» Accidents involving trains and automobiles are one of the major causes of animal fatalities in the mountain parks. Wildlife can appear suddenly, and bolt across the road when scared, so slow down and be alert.

» Some road passes (such as the Highwood Pass in Kananaskis) are closed in winter due to snow.

ROAD DISTANCES (KM)

	Banff	Calgary	Canmore	Edmonton	Field	Golden	Lake Louise	Jasper
Calgary	129							
Canmore	25	106						
Edmonton	420	296	396					
Field	83	207	106	501				
Golden	139	264	162	557	58			
Lake Louise	61	183	82	476	29	85		
Jasper	289	417	316	364	258	314	238	
Vancouver	845	971	870	1159	766	712	793	795

Driving in Winter

Driving around in winter in any of the parks can be dangerous, but especially so in the Canadian parks, which are blanketed by snow and ice for well over six months of the year. Whiteouts are not uncommon and several roads (including the Icefields Parkway) are closed during midwinter or periods of heavy snow – check ahead with the parks offices and keep abreast of local news and traffic bulletins.

In Banff and Jasper, it's legally required that you carry snow tires or chains on all roads in winter except the main Trans-Canada Hwy 1 (obviously it's also worth knowing how to fit them). Car-rental agencies should provide these if you're renting from them in winter, although you might be charged extra.

It's also worth carrying a small emergency supply kit, including antifreeze, blankets, water, flashlight, snow shovel, matches and emergency food supplies – a cell phone will also come in handy in case you need to phone for an emergency tow. Top up antifreeze, transmission, brake and windshield-washer fluids.

Be especially careful of invisible patches of ice on the road, especially once the temperature drops at night. Slow down, take extra care and use your gears rather than your brakes to slow down (look for the 'L' or 'Low' gear if you're driving an automatic). Slamming on your brakes will only increase your chances of skidding.

Road Rules

In Canada and the US, driving is on the right. You are legally required to wear a seatbelt at all times, and headlights must be turned on when visibility is restricted to 150m (500ft) or less. Motorcyclists are required to wear helmets and drive with headlights on.

One rule which often confuses overseas drivers is that it's legal to turn right on a stoplight (as long as there is no traffic coming from the left). At four-way stop junctions, drivers should pause and allow the first vehicle that stopped to pull away first.

Speed limits in Alberta are as follows:

100km/h (62mph) on major highways

90km/h (56mph) on main routes within the park limits

70km/h (43.5mph) on minor roads unless otherwise indicated

50km/h (31mph) or less in townsites

Health & Safety

Keeping healthy while on vacation in the national parks depends on your pre-departure preparations, your daily health care while traveling and how you handle any medical problems that develop. While the potential problems can seem quite daunting, in reality few travelers experience anything more than an upset stomach.

If you have an emergency while staying in the national parks dial ☎911. Major centers like Banff, Jasper and Waterton have medical facilities; see p267. If you're traveling out of your home country, be sure to purchase medical insurance before you leave. It is also important to read the policy's small print and ascertain exactly what you are being covered for. Medical services in Canada and the US are not reciprocal.

BEFORE YOU GO

If you require medications bring them in their original, labeled, containers. A signed and dated letter from your physician describing your medical conditions and medications, including generic names, is a good idea. If carrying syringes or needles, be sure to have a physician's letter documenting their necessity.

Some of the walks in this book are physically demanding and most require a reasonable level of fitness. Even if you're tackling the easy or easy-moderate walks, it pays to be relatively fit, rather than launch straight into them after months of fairly sedentary living. If you're aiming for the demanding walks, fitness is essential.

Unless you're a regular walker, start your get-fit campaign at least a month before your visit. Take a vigorous walk of about an hour, two or three times per week, and gradually extend the duration of your outings as the departure date nears. If you plan to carry a full backpack on any walk, carry a loaded pack on some of your training jaunts.

If you have any medical problems, or are concerned about your health in any way, it's a good idea to have a full check up before you start walking.

Medical Checklist

- acetaminophen (paracetamol) or aspirin
- adhesive or paper tape
- antibacterial ointment for cuts and abrasions
- antibiotics
- antidiarrheal drugs (eg loperamide)
- antihistamines (for hay fever and allergic reactions)
- anti-inflammatory drugs (eg ibuprofen)
- bandages, gauze swabs, gauze rolls
- DEET-containing insect repellent for the skin
- elasticized support bandage
- iodine tablets or water filter (for water purification)
- nonadhesive dressing
- oral rehydration salts
- paper stitches
- permethrin-containing insect spray for clothing, tents and bed nets
- pocket knife
- scissors, safety pins, tweezers
- sterile alcohol wipes
- steroid cream or cortisone (for allergic rashes)
- sticking plasters (Band-Aids, blister plasters)
- sun block
- sutures
- syringes and needles – ask your doctor for a note explaining why you have them
- thermometer

Further Reading

International Travel Health Guide by Stuart R Rose MD (Travel Medicine Inc) is the only traveler's health book that is updated annually.

Medicine for Mountaineering & Other Wilderness Activities by James A Wilkerson is an outstanding reference book for the layperson. It describes many of the medical problems typically encountered while trekking.

Hypothermia, Frostbite and Other Cold Injuries by James A Wilkerson is good background reading on the subject of cold and high-altitude problems.

Backcountry Bear Basics: The Definitive Guide to Avoiding Unpleasant Encounters by Dave Smith is good on the basics of bear behavior and biology.

Mountaineering: The Freedom of the Hills, edited by Don Graydon and Kurt Hanson, discusses outdoor fundamentals from beginners to advanced.

IN THE PARKS

National parks are pristine wilderness areas that are enjoyed annually by millions of people. But, due to the natural hostilities present in regions replete with mountains, glaciers, wild animals and fickle weather, visiting city dwellers will need to keep their wits about them in order to minimize the chances of suffering an avoidable accident or tragedy. Dress appropriately; tell people where you are going; don't bite off more than you can chew; and, above all, *respect* the wilderness and the inherent dangers that it conceals.

Crime is far more common in big cities than in sparsely populated national parks. Nevertheless, use your common sense: lock valuables in the trunk of your vehicle, especially if you're parking it at a trailhead overnight, and never leave anything worth stealing in your tent.

Medical Assistance

Banff National Park

For medical emergencies, head to the modern **Mineral Springs Hospital** (Map p62; ☎403-762-2222; Bow Ave). For all other emergencies, dial ☎911.

Jasper National Park

The two local hospitals are **Seaton General Hospital** (☎780-852-3344; 518 Robson St) and **Cottage Medical Clinic** (☎780-852-4885; 505 Turret St).

Glacier National Park

Basic first aid is available at visitor centers and ranger stations in the park. The closest hospitals to the west side are **Kalispell Regional Medical Center** (☎406-752-5111; 310 Sunnyview Lane) and **North Valley Hospital** (☎406-863-3500; 6575 Hwy 93 S) in Whitefish. If you're in the northeast, you may find that **Cardston Municipal Hospital** (☎403-653-4411; 144 2nd St W, Cardston), in Alberta, Canada, is the closest bet, though customs could consume time en route.

Waterton Lakes National Park

The summer-only number for ambulance service and other medical emergencies in Waterton is ☎403-859-2636. Full medical help is available at **Cardston Municipal Hospital** (☎403-653-4411; 144 2nd St W) and **Pincher Creek Municipal Hospital** (☎403-627-1234).

Infectious Diseases

Giardiasis

While water running through the mountains may look crystal-clear, much of it carries *Giardia lamblia*, a microscopic parasite that causes intestinal disorders. To avoid getting sick, boil all water for at least 10 minutes, treat it with water tablets or filter at 0.5 microns or smaller. Iodine doesn't destroy giardiasis.

Symptoms include stomach cramps, nausea, a bloated stomach, watery, foul-smelling diarrhea and frequent gas. Giardiasis can appear several weeks after you have been exposed to the parasite. The symptoms may disappear for a few days and then return; this can go on for several weeks.

Seek medical advice if you think you have giardiasis, but where this is not possible, tinidazole or metronidazole are the recommended drugs. Treatment is a 2g single dose of tinidazole or 250mg of metronidazole three times daily for five to 10 days.

> **EMERGENCY NUMBERS**
>
> The following are the emergency 24-hour park warden numbers for each park:
>
> **Banff** (☎403-762-4506)
>
> **Glacier** (☎406-888-7800)
>
> **Jasper** (☎780-852-6155)
>
> **Waterton Lakes** (☎403-859-2224)

Environmental Hazards

Altitude

Altitude sickness can strike anyone heading up into the mountains, whether it's your first visit or your 100th. Thinner air means less oxygen is reaching your muscles and brain, requiring the heart and lungs to work harder. Many trailheads begin at high elevations (particularly along the Icefields Parkway), meaning that you don't have to go very far before feeling the effects.

Symptoms of acute mountain sickness (AMS) include headache, lethargy, dizziness, difficulty sleeping and loss of appetite. AMS may become more severe without warning and can be fatal. Severe symptoms include breathlessness, a dry, irritating cough (which may progress to the production of pink, frothy sputum), severe headache, lack of coordination and balance, confusion, irrational behavior, vomiting, drowsiness and unconsciousness. There is no hard-and-fast rule as to what is too high – AMS has been fatal at 3000m – although

3500m to 4500m is the usual range.

Treat mild symptoms by resting at the same altitude until recovery, usually a day or two. Paracetamol or aspirin can be taken for headaches. If symptoms persist or become worse, however, *immediate descent is necessary;* even 500m can help. Drug treatments should never be used to avoid descent or to enable further ascent.

The drugs acetazolamide and dexamethasone are recommended by some doctors for the prevention of AMS; however, their use is controversial. They can reduce the symptoms, but they may also mask warning signs; severe and fatal AMS has occurred in people taking these drugs. In general we do not recommend them for travelers.

To prevent acute mountain sickness:

» Ascend slowly – have frequent rest days, spending two to three nights at each rise of 1000m. If you reach a high altitude by trekking, acclimatization takes place gradually and you are less likely to be affected than if you fly directly to high altitude.

» It is always wise to sleep at a lower altitude than the greatest height reached during the day if possible. Also, once above 3000m, care should be taken not to increase the sleeping altitude by more than 300m per day.

» Drink extra fluids. The mountain air is dry and cold and moisture is lost as you breathe; evaporation of sweat may occur unnoticed and result in dehydration.

» Eat light, high-carbohydrate meals for more energy.

» Avoid alcohol and sedatives.

Bites & Stings

MOSQUITOES

Mosquitoes can be rampant in all parks, particularly on summer evenings. In Banff and Jasper, you'll notice them around lakes and on wooded hikes; they are particularly prevalent along parts of the remote North Boundary Trail. In Glacier and Waterton Lakes, mosquitoes tend to be more annoying on the west side of the park than in the windier east. Use repellent, wear light-colored clothing and cover yourself in the evening.

TICKS

Ticks are most active from spring to autumn, especially where there are plenty of sheep or deer. They usually lurk in overhanging vegetation, so avoid pushing through tall bushes.

If a tick is found attached to the skin, press down around its head with tweezers, grab the head and gently pull upward. Avoid pulling the rear of the body as this may squeeze the tick's gut contents through its mouth into your skin, increasing the risk of infection and disease. Smearing chemicals on the tick will not make it let go and is not recommended.

Lyme's disease is a tick-borne illness that manifests itself in skin lesions and, later on, intermittent or persistent arthritis. To avoid contracting it, use all normal mosquito preventative measures, including wearing long-sleeved shirts and trousers, checking clothing for ticks after outdoor activity, and using an effective brand of DEET or insect repellent.

Rocky Mountain Spotted Fever is another tick-borne disease that is potentially lethal but usually curable if diagnosed early. Symptoms include fever and muscle pain followed by the development of a rash. Treatment is with antibiotics, but to prevent it take the usual anti-tick measures especially when walking in areas of tall grass or brush.

Cold

HYPOTHERMIA

This occurs when the body loses heat faster than it can produce it and the core temperature of the body falls.

It is frighteningly easy to progress from very cold to dangerously cold due to a combination of wind, wet clothing, fatigue and hunger, even if the air temperature is above freezing. If the weather

WATER PURIFICATION

To ensure you are getting safe, clean drinking water in the backcountry you have three basic options:

Boiling

Water is considered safe to drink if it has been boiled at 100°C for at least a minute. This is best done when you set up your camp and stove in the evening.

Chemical Purification

There are two types of chemical additives that will purify water: chlorine or iodine. You can choose from various products on the market. Read the instructions carefully first, be aware of expiration dates and check you are not allergic to either chemical.

Filtration

Mobile devices can pump water through microscopic filters and take out potentially harmful organisms. If carrying a filter, take care it doesn't get damaged in transit, read the instructions carefully and always filter the cleanest water you can find.

WALK SAFETY – BASIC RULES

» Allow plenty of time to accomplish a walk before dark, particularly when daylight hours are shorter.

» Study the route carefully before setting out, noting the possible escape routes and the point of no return (where it's quicker to continue than to turn back). Monitor your progress during the day against the time estimated for the walk, and keep an eye on the weather.

» It's wise not to walk alone. Always leave details of your intended route, number of people in your group and expected return time with someone responsible before you set off; let that person know when you return.

» Before setting off, make sure you have a relevant map, compass and whistle, and that you know the weather forecast for the area for the next 24 hours. In the Rockies always carry extra warm, dry layers of clothing and plenty of emergency high energy food.

deteriorates, put on extra layers of warm clothing: a wind and/or waterproof jacket, plus wool or fleece hat and gloves are all essential. Have something energy-giving to eat and ensure that everyone in your group is fit, feeling well and alert.

Symptoms of hypothermia are exhaustion, numb skin (particularly toes and fingers), shivering, slurred speech, irrational or violent behavior, lethargy, stumbling, dizzy spells, muscle cramps and violent bursts of energy. Irrationality may take the form of sufferers claiming they are warm and trying to take off their clothes.

To treat mild hypothermia, first get the person out of the wind and/or rain, remove their clothing if it's wet and replace it with dry, warm clothing. Give them hot liquids – not alcohol – and some high-energy, easily digestible food. Do not rub victims: instead, allow them to slowly warm themselves.

FROSTBITE

This refers to the freezing of extremities, including fingers, toes and nose. Signs and symptoms of frostbite include a whitish or waxy cast to the skin, or even crystals on the surface, plus itching, numbness and pain. Warm the affected areas by immersion in warm (not hot) water, or with blankets or clothes, only until the skin becomes flushed. Frostbitten parts should not be rubbed. Pain and swelling are inevitable. Blisters should not be broken. Get medical attention right away.

Heat

DEHYDRATION & HEAT EXHAUSTION

Dehydration is a potentially dangerous and generally preventable condition caused by excessive fluid loss. Sweating combined with inadequate fluid intake are one of the common causes in trekkers, but other causes are diarrhea, vomiting and high fever.

The first symptoms are weakness, thirst and passing small amounts of very concentrated urine. This may lead to drowsiness, dizziness or fainting on standing up, and finally, coma.

It's easy to forget how much fluid you are losing via perspiration while you are trekking, particularly if a strong breeze is drying your skin quickly. You should always maintain a good fluid intake – a minimum of 3L a day is recommended.

Dehydration and salt deficiency can cause heat exhaustion. Salt deficiency is characterized by fatigue, lethargy, headaches, giddiness and muscle cramps. Salt tablets are overkill; just adding extra salt to your food is probably sufficient.

HEATSTROKE

This is a serious, occasionally fatal, condition that occurs if the body's heat-regulating mechanism breaks down and the body temperature rises to dangerous levels. Long, continuous periods of exposure to high temperatures and insufficient fluids can leave you vulnerable to heatstroke.

The symptoms are feeling unwell, not sweating very much (or at all) and a high body temperature of around 39°C to 41°C (102°F to 106°F). Where sweating has ceased, the skin becomes flushed and red. Severe, throbbing headaches and lack of coordination will also occur, and the sufferer may be confused or aggressive. Eventually the victim will become delirious or convulse. Hospitalization is essential but, in the interim, get victims out of the sun, remove their clothing, cover them with a wet sheet or towel, and then fan continually. Give fluids if they are conscious.

Snow Blindness

This is a temporary painful condition resulting from sunburn of the surface of the eye (cornea). It usually occurs when someone walks on snow or in bright sunshine without sunglasses. Treatment is to relieve the pain – cold cloths on closed eyelids may help. Antibiotic and anesthetic eye drops are not necessary. The condition usually resolves itself within a few days and there are no long-term consequences.

Sun

Protection against the sun should always be taken seriously. Particularly in the rarified air and deceptive coolness of the mountains, sunburn occurs rapidly. Slap on the sunscreen and a barrier cream for your nose and lips, wear a broad-brimmed hat and protect your eyes with good-quality sunglasses with UV lenses, particularly when walking near water, sand or snow. If, despite these precautions, you get yourself burnt, calamine lotion, aloe vera or other commercial sunburn-relief preparations will soothe.

SAFE HIKING

Avalanches

Avalanches are a threat during and following storms, in high winds and during temperature changes, particularly when it warms in spring. Educate yourself about the dangers of avalanches before setting out into the backcountry. Signs of avalanche activity include felled trees and slides. For up-to-date information on avalanche hazards, contact ☎403-762-1460 in Banff, Kootenay and Yoho, ☎780-852-6176 in Jasper and ☎250-837-6867 at Roger's Pass. For other areas, contact the **Canadian Avalanche Association** (☎800-667-1105) or local park information centers.

Before adventuring in Waterton, check with the **park warden** (☎403-859-5140) for avalanche updates, as winter trails are not maintained. In Glacier, call ☎406-257-8402 or ☎800-526-5329 for information. Local radio stations broadcast reports on area

BEAR ISSUES

Although people have an inordinate fear of being hurt by bears, the Canadian Rockies are a far more dangerous place for the bears themselves. In Banff National Park alone, 90% of known grizzly bear deaths have occurred within 400m (0.25 miles) of roads and buildings, with most bears either being killed by cars or by wardens when bears and people got mixed up. Cross-continental trains traveling through the parks have also killed many of these magnificent beasts.

Bears are intelligent opportunists that quickly learn that humans come with food and tasty garbage. Unfortunately, once this association is learned, a bear nearly always has to be shot. Remember: 'A fed bear is a dead bear,' so never feed a bear, never improperly store food or garbage, and always clean up after yourself.

Bears are also dangerous creatures that can sprint the length of a football field in six seconds. Although such encounters are rare, bears will readily attack if their cubs are around, if they're defending food or if they feel surprised and threatened. Your best defenses against surprising a bear are to remain alert, avoid hiking at night (when bears feed) and be careful when traveling upwind near streams or where visibility is obscured.

To avoid an encounter altogether, hike in groups (bears almost never attack hiking groups of more than four people) and make noise on the trail, preferably by talking or singing. Jangling bear bells aren't really loud enough to be effective.

If you do encounter a bear, there are several defensive strategies to employ, but no guarantees. If the bear doesn't see you, move a safe distance downwind and make noise to alert it to your presence. If the bear sees you, slowly back out of its path, avoid eye contact, speak softly and wave your hands above your head slowly. Never turn your back to the bear and never kneel down.

Sows with cubs are particularly dangerous, and you should make every effort to avoid coming between a sow and her cubs. A sow may clack her jaws, lower her head and shake it as a warning before she charges.

If a bear does charge, do not run and do not scream (which may frighten the bear and make it more aggressive), because the bear may only be charging as a bluff. Drop to the ground, crouch face down in a ball and play dead, covering the back of your neck with your hands and your chest and stomach with your knees. Do not resist the bear's inquisitive pawing – it may get bored and go away.

If the bear continues to attack you, it may be a (rare) predatory bear in which case you should fight back aggressively. Most park authorities recommend hikers carry bear spray, which can be used as a last resort. It has proved to be effective if aimed into the face of a charging bear from a range of about 10m (33ft). For more bear advice, check http://usparks.about.com/od/backcountry/a/Bear-Safety.htm.

avalanche conditions studied by the Northwest Montana Avalanche Warning System.

If you are caught in an avalanche, your chance of survival depends on your ability to keep yourself above the flowing snow and your companions' ability to rescue you. The probability of survival decreases rapidly after half an hour, so the party must be self-equipped, with each member carrying an avalanche beacon, a sectional probe and a collapsible shovel.

Crossing Streams

Sudden downpours are common in the mountains and can speedily turn a gentle stream into a raging torrent. If you're in any doubt about the safety of a crossing, look for a safer passage upstream or wait. If the rain is short-lived, it should subside quickly.

If you decide it's essential to cross (late in the day, for example), look for a wide, relatively shallow stretch of the stream rather than a bend. Take off your trousers and socks, but keep your boots on to prevent injury. Put dry, warm clothes and a towel in a plastic bag near the top of your pack. Use a walking pole, grasped in both hands, on the upstream side as a third leg, or go arm in arm with a companion, clasping at the wrist, and cross side-on to the flow, taking short steps.

Lightning

If a storm brews, avoid exposed areas. Lightning has a penchant for crests, lone trees, small depressions, gullies, caves and cabin entrances, as well as wet ground. If you are caught out in the open, try to curl up as tightly as possible with your feet together and keep a layer of insulation between you and the ground. Place metal objects such as metal-frame backpacks and walking poles away from you.

Rescue & Evacuation

If someone in your group is injured or falls ill and can't move, leave somebody with them while another one or more goes for help. They should take clear written details of the location and condition of the victim, and of helicopter landing conditions. If there are only two of you, leave the injured person with as much warm clothing, food and water as it's sensible to spare, plus the whistle and torch. Mark the position with something conspicuous – an orange bivvy bag, or perhaps a large stone cross on the ground.

SAFE BIKING

One of the most common problems cyclists will encounter is unobservant motorists busy gawping at the scenery. This issue is particularly prevalent in areas frequented by wildlife, such as the Bow Valley Parkway in Banff and the Maligne Lake Rd in Jasper. While most of Banff and Jasper's roads are wide and spacious, the arterial Going-to-the-Sun Rd in Glacier, built in the early days of the motor car, is notoriously precipitous and narrow, with no shoulders for cyclists. Jammed with dawdling people-carriers and oversized SUVs, the highway is a cycling obstacle course and, as a result, cyclists are prevented from using it between 11am and 4pm (June to September), largely for their own safety.

Wildlife is another problem, particularly for off-roaders who run the risk of surprising large animals such as moose or bears when progressing rapidly along twisting forested trails. To avoid potentially dangerous encounters with foraging megafauna, cyclists are encouraged to take heed of posted trail warnings and make plenty of noise on concealed corners and rises (remember, a bear can easily outsprint a cyclist).

Helmets are mandatory in all North American national parks. Off-roaders may also want to invest in elbow and knee pads.

Clothing & Equipment

Just as you can judge a man by his shoes, you can usually judge a hiker by his or her boots. But successful hiking is about more than just footwear. Take the time to get kitted out correctly and you're near guaranteed to have a safer, surer and more comfortable trip.

Visitors to the Rocky Mountains should prepare themselves for fickle weather, whatever the season. Jasper can be chilly in July while in Glacier, in 1992, 30cm (1ft) of snow fell in August, flushing hundreds of hikers out of the backcountry. On top of all the equipment listed here, you may want to consider carrying pepper spray to use as a last resort against aggressive wild animals, especially bears.

Clothing

Layering

A secret of comfortable walking is to wear several layers of light clothing, which you can easily take off or put on as you warm up or cool down. Most walkers use three main layers: a base layer next to the skin; an insulating layer; and an outer, shell layer for protection from wind, rain and snow.

For the upper body, the base layer is typically a shirt of synthetic material that wicks moisture away from the body and reduces chilling. The insulating layer retains heat next to your body, and is usually a (windproof) fleece jacket or sweater. The outer shell consists of a waterproof jacket that also protects against cold wind.

For the lower body, the layers generally consist of either shorts or loose-fitting trousers, thermal underwear ('long johns') and waterproof overtrousers.

When purchasing outdoor clothing, one of the most practical fabrics is merino wool. Though a little pricier than other materials, natural wool absorbs sweat, retains heat even when wet, and is soft and comfortable to wear. Even better, it doesn't store odors like other sports garments, ie you can wear it for several days in a row without inflicting antisocial smells on your tent mates.

Waterproof Shells

Jackets should be made of a breathable, waterproof fabric, with a hood that is roomy enough to cover headwear but still allow peripheral vision. Other handy accessories include a capacious map pocket and a heavy-gauge zip protected by a storm flap.

Overtrousers are best with slits for pocket access and long leg zips so that you can

ROUTE FINDING

While accurate, our maps are not perfect. Inaccuracies in altitudes are commonly caused by air-temperature anomalies. Natural features such as river confluences and mountain peaks are in their true position, but sometimes the location of villages and trails is not always so. This may be because a village is spread over a hillside, or the size of the map does not allow for detail of the trail's twists and turns. However, by using several basic route-finding techniques, you will have few problems following our descriptions:

» Be aware of whether the trail should be climbing or descending.

» Check the north-point arrow on the map and determine the general direction of the trail.

» Time your progress over a known distance and calculate the speed at which you travel in the given terrain. From then on, you can determine with reasonable accuracy how far you have traveled.

» Watch the path – look for boot prints and other signs of previous passage.

pull them on and off over your boots.

Footwear, Socks & Gaiters

Running shoes are OK for walks that are graded easy or moderate in this book. However, you'll probably appreciate, if not need, the support and protection provided by boots for the more demanding walks. Nonslip soles (such as Vibram) provide the best grip.

Buy boots in warm conditions or go for a walk before trying them on, so that your feet can expand slightly, as they would on a hike. Most walkers carry a pair of sandals to wear at night or at rest stops. Sandals are also useful when fording waterways.

Gaiters help to keep your feet dry in wet weather and on boggy ground; they can also deflect small stones or sand and maintain leg warmth. The best are made of strong fabric, with a robust zip protected by a flap, and secure easily around the foot.

Walking socks should be free of ridged seams in the toes and heels.

Equipment

Backpack & Daypacks

For day walks, a day pack (30L to 40L) will usually suffice, but for multiday walks you will need a backpack of between 45L and 90L capacity. Even if the manufacturer claims your pack is waterproof, use heavy-duty liners.

Bear Spray

Most of the hikes/activities described in this book are in bear country. As a last resort bear spray (pepper spray) has been used effectively to deter aggressive bears and park authorities often recommend that you equip yourself with a canister when venturing into backcountry. Be sure to familiarize yourself with the manufacturer's instructions before use, and only use as a last resort (ie on a charging bear approximately 9m to 15m/30ft to 50ft away from you). Most shops in or around the parks stock bear

EQUIPMENT CHECKLIST

This list is a general guide to the things you might take on a walk. Your list will vary depending on the kind of walking you want to do, whether you're camping or planning to stay in hostels or B&Bs, and on the terrain, weather conditions and time of year.

Clothing

» boots and spare laces

» gaiters

» hat (warm), scarf and gloves

» overtrousers (waterproof)

» rain jacket

» runners (training shoes) or sandals

» shorts and trousers

» socks and underwear

» sunhat

» sweater or fleece jacket

» thermal underwear

» T-shirt and long-sleeved shirt with collar

Equipment

» backpack with waterproof liner

» bear spray

» first-aid kit*

» flashlight (torch) or headlamp, spare batteries and bulb (globe)

» food and snacks (high energy) and one day's emergency supplies

» insect repellent

» map, compass and guidebook

» map case or clip-seal plastic bags

» plastic bags (for carrying rubbish)

» pocket knife

» sunglasses

» sunscreen and lip balm

» survival bag or blanket

» toilet paper and trowel

» water container

» whistle

Overnight Walks

» cooking, eating and drinking utensils

» dishwashing items

» matches and lighter

» sewing/repair kit

» sleeping bag and bag liner/inner sheet

» sleeping mat

» spare cord

» stove and fuel

» tent, pegs, poles and guy ropes

» toiletries

» towel

» water purification tablets, iodine or filter

Optional Items

» backpack cover (waterproof, slip-on)

» binoculars

» camera, film and batteries

» candle

» cell (mobile) phone

» emergency distress beacon

» GPS receiver

» groundsheet

» mosquito net

» notebook and pen

» swimming costume

» walking poles

» watch

* see the Medical Checklist (p266)

NAVIGATION EQUIPMENT

Maps & Compass

You should always carry a good map of the area in which you are walking, and know how to read it. Before setting off on your walk, ensure that you are aware of the contour interval, the map symbols, the magnetic declination (difference between true and grid north), plus the main ridge and river systems in the area and the general direction in which you are heading. On the trail, try to identify major landforms such as mountain ranges and valleys, and locate them on your map to familiarize yourself with the geography.

Buy a compass and learn how to use it. The attraction of magnetic north varies in different parts of the world, so compasses need to be balanced accordingly. Compass manufacturers have divided the world into five zones. Make sure your compass is balanced for your destination zone. There are also 'universal' compasses on the market that can be used anywhere in the world.

How to Use a Compass

This is a very basic introduction to using a compass and will only be of assistance if you are proficient in map reading. For simplicity, it doesn't take magnetic variation into account. Before using a compass we recommend you obtain further instruction.

READING A COMPASS

Hold the compass flat in the palm of your hand. Rotate the bezel so the red end of the needle points to the N (north point) on the bezel. The bearing is read from the dash under the bezel.

ORIENTING THE MAP

To orient the map so that it aligns with the ground, place the compass flat on the map. Rotate the map until the needle is parallel with the map's north-south grid lines and the red end is pointing to north on the map. You can now identify features around you by aligning them with labelled features on the map.

TAKING A BEARING FROM THE MAP

Draw a line on the map between your starting point and your destination. Place the edge of the compass on this line with the direction of travel arrow pointing toward your destination.

spray which sells for approximately US$50. It is best kept close at hand on a belt around your waist.

Tent

A three-season tent will fulfil most walkers' requirements. The floor and the outer shell, or fly, should have taped or sealed seams and covered zips to stop leaks. The weight can be as low as 1kg for a stripped-down, low-profile tent, and up to 3kg for a roomy, luxury, four-season model.

Dome- and tunnel-shaped tents handle windy conditions better than flat-sided tents.

Sleeping Bag & Mat

Down fillings are warmer than synthetic for the same weight and bulk but, unlike synthetic fillings, do not retain warmth when wet. Mummy-shaped bags are best for weight and warmth. The given figure (-5°C, for instance) is the coldest temperature at which a person should feel comfortable in the bag (although the ratings are notoriously unreliable).

An inner sheet helps keep your sleeping bag clean, as well as adding an insulating layer; silk 'inners' are lightest but they also come in cotton or synthetic fabric.

Self-inflating sleeping mats work like a thin air cushion between you and the ground; they also insulate from the cold. Foam mats are a low-cost, but less comfortable, alternative.

Stoves & Fuel

The easiest type of fuel to use is butane gas in disposable containers; true, it doesn't win many environmental points but it's much easier to come by than liquid fuels. The most widely used brands are Coleman and Camping Gaz, available from outdoor gear shops and, in some remote areas, from small supermarkets.

Liquid fuel includes Coleman fuel, methylated spirits and paraffin. Again, outdoor gear shops, possibly hardware stores or even small supermarkets are the best places to look for it. You may be able to obtain small quantities of unleaded petrol from service stations.

Airlines prohibit the carriage of any flammable materials and may well reject

Rotate the bezel until the meridian lines are parallel with the north-south grid lines on the map and the N points to north on the map. Read the bearing from the dash.

FOLLOWING A BEARING

Rotate the bezel so that the intended bearing is in line with the dash. Place the compass flat in the palm of your hand and rotate the base plate until the red end points to N on the bezel. The direction of travel arrow will now point in the direction you need to walk.

DETERMINING YOUR BEARING

Rotate the bezel so the red end points to the N. Place the compass flat in the palm of your hand and rotate the base plate until the direction of travel arrow points in the direction in which you have been walking. Read your bearing from the dash.

Global Positioning System

Originally developed by the US Department of Defense, the Global Positioning System (GPS) is a network of more than 20 earth-orbiting satellites that continually beam encoded signals back to earth. Small, computer-driven devices (GPS receivers) can decode these signals to give users an extremely accurate reading of their location – to within 30m, anywhere on the planet, at any time of day, in almost any weather. The cheapest hand-held GPS receivers now cost less than US$100 (although these may not have a built-in averaging system that minimises signal errors). Other important factors to consider when buying a GPS receiver are its weight and battery life.

Remember that a GPS receiver is of little use unless used with an accurate topographical map. The receiver simply gives your position, which you must then locate on the local map. GPS receivers will only work properly in the open. The signals from a crucial satellite may be blocked (or bounce off rock or water) directly below high cliffs, near large bodies of water or in dense tree cover and give inaccurate readings. GPS receivers are more vulnerable to breakdowns (including dead batteries) than the humble magnetic compass – a low-tech device that has served navigators faithfully for centuries – so don't rely on them entirely.

empty liquid-fuel bottles or even the stoves themselves.

Buying & Renting Locally

Specializing in the great outdoors, the national park towns offer some stellar options for buying and renting gear. Check out the individual park chapters for stores in Banff (p113), Jasper (p172, Waterton (p219) and Glacier (p205).

More specialized gear such as bikes (rental per day C$30), snowshoes (C$15), hiking poles (C$5) and climbing harnesses (C$5) can usually be rented either in the parks or in one of the surrounding settlements.

behind the scenes

SEND US YOUR FEEDBACK

We love to hear from travelers – your comments keep us on our toes and help make our books better. Our well-traveled team reads every word on what you loved or loathed about this book. Although we cannot reply individually to postal submissions, we always guarantee that your feedback goes straight to the appropriate authors, in time for the next edition. Each person who sends us information is thanked in the next edition – and the most useful submissions are rewarded with a free book.

Visit **lonelyplanet.com/contact** to submit your updates and suggestions or to ask for help. Our award-winning website also features inspirational travel stories, news and discussions.

Note: We may edit, reproduce and incorporate your comments in Lonely Planet products such as guidebooks, websites and digital products, so let us know if you don't want your comments reproduced or your name acknowledged. For a copy of our privacy policy visit lonelyplanet.com/privacy.

OUR READERS

Many thanks to the travelers who used the last edition and wrote to us with helpful hints, useful advice and interesting anecdotes:

Trees Dechaene, Ronald Fonteijn, Lucy Franklin, Anne Grey-Davies, Joel Hagen, Gillian Kennedy, Dominik Kriegner, Karla Martinez, Brian Miller, Emily Nicholl, Seth Parker, Gene Sullivan, Jeremy Torr, Johan Van Vrijaldenhoven, Helen Waters, Tom White

AUTHOR THANKS

Oliver Berry

A big thanks to all the people I met on my Banff journey, including Jim Jones, Frank Kamenka, Jeannie Cook and Avi Taiar. Thanks also to Susie Berry, Mo and Gracie for keeping the home fires burning. Massive thanks to Kathleen Munnelly and Kirsten Rawlings for steering the Lonely Planet ship, and of course to my co-author Brendan for all his work up in Jasper and down in Glacier (next beer in Vancouver is on me). A special thanks to Parks Canada staff for all the work they do to keep the parks pristine.

Brendan Sainsbury

Thanks to all the untold bus drivers, tourist info volunteers, restaurateurs, national park rangers, weather forecasters, ice-cream sellers and innocent bystanders who helped me during my research, and particularly to Kathleen Munnelly for offering me the gig in the first place and Olly Berry for being a supportive coordinating author. Special thanks to Andy McKee for his fast-paced hiking in Glacier National Park. Thanks also to my wife, Liz, and five-year-old son, Kieran, for their company on the road.

ACKNOWLEDGMENTS

Climate map data adapted from Peel MC, Finlayson BL & McMahon TA (2007) 'Updated World Map of the Köppen-Geiger Climate Classification', *Hydrology and Earth System Sciences*, 11, 163344.

Cover photograph: Wenkchemna Peaks and Moraine Lake, Banff National Park, Gavin Hellier/JAI/Corbis.

Many of the images in this guide are available for licensing from Lonely Planet Images: www.lonelyplanetimages.com.

THIS BOOK

This 3rd edition of Lonely Planet's *Banff, Jasper & Glacier National Parks* guidebook was researched and written by Oliver Berry and Brendan Sainsbury, who both also authored the second edition along with David Lukas. The first edition was written by Korina Miller, Susan Derby and David Lukas.

This guidebook was commissioned in Lonely Planet's Oakland office, and produced by the following:

Commissioning Editor Kathleen Munnelly
Coordinating Editors Carolyn Boicos, Kristin Odijk
Coordinating Cartographer Andy Rojas
Coordinating Layout Designer Adrian Blackburn
Managing Editor Kirsten Rawlings
Senior Editors Susan Paterson, Angela Tinson
Managing Cartographer Alison Lyall
Managing Layout Designer Jane Hart
Assisting Editors Anne Mulvaney, Saralinda Turner, Helen Yeates
Assisting Cartographers Valeska Cañas, Hunor Csutoros, Mark Griffiths, Alex Leung, Marc Milinkovic
Cover & Image Research Sabrina Dalbesio
Thanks to Sasha Baskett, Helen Christinis, Ryan Evans, Chris Girdler, Liz Heynes, Heather Howard, Yvonne Kirk, Trent Paton, Anthony Phelan, Gerard Walker

index

000 Map pages
000 Photo pages

D

E

F

G

H

I

000 Map pages
000 Photo pages

Q

R

S

000 Map pages
000 Photo pages

how to use this book

These symbols will help you find the listings you want:

- Driving
- Hiking
- Biking

These symbols give you the vital information for each listing:

- Telephone Numbers
- Opening Hours
- Parking
- Nonsmoking
- Air-Conditioning
- Internet Access
- Wi-Fi Access
- Swimming Pool
- Vegetarian Selection
- English-Language Menu
- Family-Friendly
- Pet-Friendly
- Bus
- Ferry
- Metro
- Subway
- London Tube
- Tram
- Train

Reviews are organised by author preference

Look out for these icons:

- TOP CHOICE — Our author's recommendation
- FREE — No payment required
- A green or sustainable option

Our authors have nominated these places as demonstrating a strong commitment to sustainability – for example by supporting local communities and producers, operating in an environmentally friendly way, or supporting conservation projects.

Map Legend

Sights
- Beach
- Buddhist
- Castle
- Christian
- Hindu
- Islamic
- Jewish
- Monument
- Museum/Gallery
- Ruin
- Winery/Vineyard
- Zoo
- Other Sight

Activities, Courses & Tours
- Diving/Snorkelling
- Canoeing/Kayaking
- Skiing
- Surfing
- Swimming/Pool
- Walking
- Windsurfing
- Other Activity/Course/Tour

Sleeping
- Sleeping
- Camping

Eating
- Eating

Drinking
- Drinking
- Cafe

Entertainment
- Entertainment

Shopping
- Shopping

Information
- Post Office
- Tourist Information

Transport
- Airport
- Border Crossing
- Bus
- Cable Car/Funicular
- Cycling
- Ferry
- Metro
- Monorail
- Parking
- S-Bahn
- Taxi
- Train/Railway
- Tram
- Tube Station
- U-Bahn
- Other Transport

Routes
- Tollway
- Freeway
- Primary
- Secondary
- Tertiary
- Lane
- Unsealed Road
- Plaza/Mall
- Steps
- Tunnel
- Pedestrian Overpass
- Walking Tour
- Walking Tour Detour
- Path

Boundaries
- International
- State/Province
- Disputed
- Regional/Suburb
- Marine Park
- Cliff
- Wall

Population
- Capital (National)
- Capital (State/Province)
- City/Large Town
- Town/Village

Geographic
- Hut/Shelter
- Lighthouse
- Lookout
- Mountain/Volcano
- Oasis
- Park
- Pass
- Picnic Area
- Waterfall

Hydrography
- River/Creek
- Intermittent River
- Swamp/Mangrove
- Reef
- Canal
- Water
- Dry/Salt/Intermittent Lake
- Glacier

Areas
- Beach/Desert
- Cemetery (Christian)
- Cemetery (Other)
- Park/Forest
- Sportsground
- Sight (Building)
- Top Sight (Building)

OUR STORY

A beat-up old car, a few dollars in the pocket and a sense of adventure. In 1972 that's all Tony and Maureen Wheeler needed for the trip of a lifetime – across Europe and Asia overland to Australia. It took several months, and at the end – broke but inspired – they sat at their kitchen table writing and stapling together their first travel guide, *Across Asia on the Cheap*. Within a week they'd sold 1500 copies. Lonely Planet was born.

Today, Lonely Planet has offices in Melbourne, London and Oakland, with more than 600 staff and writers. We share Tony's belief that 'a great guidebook should do three things: inform, educate and amuse.'

OUR WRITERS

Oliver Berry

Coordinating Author, Banff National Park Oliver has trekked through many of the world's mountain ranges, but he has never found anywhere that compares to the Canadian Rockies. He has hiked pretty much every trail in Banff and the surrounding national parks over the years, so he jumped at the chance to do them all again while writing this guidebook. He's written regularly for Lonely Planet on many guidebooks, including *France*, *Great Britain* and *The Lake District*, and also writes regularly for film, music and travel publications, including *Lonely Planet Magazine*. When he's not out on the road or up a mountain, he can probably be found on the beaches of his home county in Cornwall, UK. You can see some of his latest work at www.oliverberry.com.

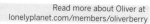

Read more about Oliver at lonelyplanet.com/members/oliverberry

Brendan Sainsbury

Jasper National Park, Glacier National Park UK-born Brendan once ran 100 miles across the Cascade Mountains in an ultra-distance marathon, so researching the hikes for this book seemed like a dream job. He currently lives near Vancouver, Canada, with his wife and young son, but makes regular sorties for Lonely Planet to Cuba, Italy, Spain and the US in order to research. He co-authored the previous edition of this guide and also covered Jasper and Banff National Parks in Lonely Planet's current edition of *Canada*. When not writing, he likes playing piano and guitar, and visiting his favorite cities – London, Havana and Granada in Spain.

Read more about Brendan at lonelyplanet.com/members/brendansainsbury

Published by Lonely Planet Publications Pty Ltd
ABN 36 005 607 983
3rd edition – February 2012
ISBN 978 1 74179 405 2

10 9 8 7 6 5 4 3 2 1
Printed in China